# REVOLUTION
# SONG

*East Haddam, Connecticut, where Venture Smith*
*chose to settle as a free man.*

# REVOLUTION SONG

*A Story of*

AMERICAN FREEDOM

## Russell Shorto

W. W. NORTON & COMPANY

*Independent Publishers Since 1923*

New York • London

IMAGE CREDITS: Page xvi: F. Bartoli, Ki On Twog Ky (also known
as Cornplanter), 1786, oil on canvas, unframed: 30 × 25 in.; framed:
44¾ in. × 391⁵⁄₁₆ in. × 5 in.; object #1867.314, New-York Historical Society.
Page 12: © National Portrait Gallery, London. Page 74: Washington-Custis-
Lee Collection, Washington and Lee University, Lexington, Virginia.
Page 394: The Miriam and Ira D. Wallach Division of Art, Prints and
Photographs: Print Collection, Rosenthal, Max (1833–1918), New York Public
Library. Page 504: Letter from Margaret (Moncrieffe) Coghlan, December 28,
1803. The Robert R. Livingston Papers, New-York Historical Society.
Pages iv, xvi, 12, 74, 394, 504 (background image): Abzee / iStockphoto.com.

For information about permission to reproduce selections from this book, write to
Permissions, W. W. Norton & Company, Inc., 500 Fifth Avenue, New York, NY 10110

For information about special discounts for bulk purchases, please contact
W. W. Norton Special Sales at specialsales@wwnorton.com or 800-233-4830

Manufacturing by QUAD Graphics, Fairfield
Book design by Michelle McMillian
Production manager: Beth Steidle

ISBN 978-0-393-24554-7

W. W. Norton & Company, Inc.
500 Fifth Avenue, New York, N.Y. 10110
www.wwnorton.com

W. W. Norton & Company Ltd.
15 Carlisle Street, London  W1D 3BS

1 2 3 4 5 6 7 8 9 0

*For Pamela*

# CONTENTS

## PART THREE

# PREFACE

This is a nonfiction story. By that I mean two things: that it is true, and that it is about people, the intimate texture of their lives, the aches and sweetnesses, the things that propelled them forward in the period in which the American nation was forged.

In a sense, the American Revolution never ended. Many later events that we tend to think of on their own—the Civil War, to give one prominent example—can be seen as extensions of it. That is because the American Revolution was fundamentally a promise of freedom, and that promise was only partially fulfilled with the end of hostilities in 1783.

The fighting has erupted anew in our era, with such passion and intensity it is sending people back to America's founding documents in search of answers and context. What do freedom of speech and of the press mean when disinformation can be so easily spread? What are the checks on presidential power? Have the quaint phrasings of the eighteenth century lost all relevance? If so, then who are we?

I am not offering here answers to those questions, but I am offering a change of focus. Politics is, after all, about people. The idea behind this book is that there might be insight to be gained from following the people who experienced America's founding firsthand.

But which people? Traditional accounts of the Revolution assume that there were two sides: the British and the breakaway American colonists. That simple packaging was useful once, but it doesn't fit who we are today, and frankly it didn't fit the people of the time. There were many "sides" involved in the conflict, many different people writhing and clamoring and clawing over freedom. While the region of North America that broke with England was English in a sense, it was also Iroquois, Cherokee and Shawnee. It was African. It was Irish, Dutch and German. It was male and female. It was rich and poor, powerful and powerless.

This book, then, weaves six very different lives into one story. Most of its protagonists are unknown or little known today, but their very obscurity may afford a fresh way of seeing their era. I have tried not to preach or even teach in its pages. Instead, using primary source material, drawing on letters, diary entries and account books, pathetic handwritten pleas and scribbled battlefield directives, I have tried to create a kind of narrative song. The six voices sing different parts, revealing, perhaps, that we are still connected to them, that the issues that animated the people who took part in the founding of the American nation are alive in us, that we are still fighting the Revolution.

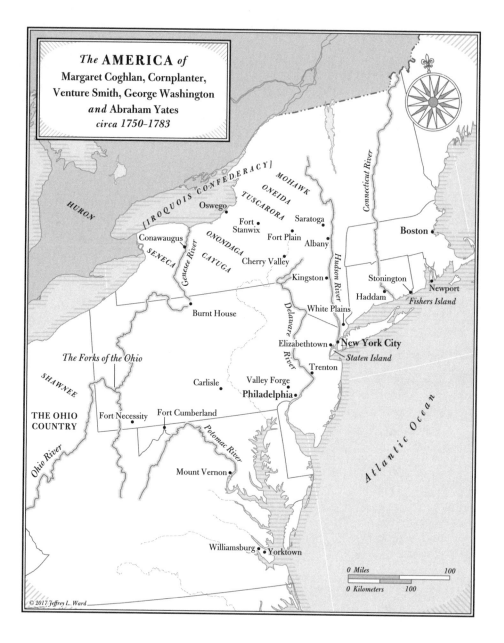

The **AMERICA** of
Margaret Coghlan, Cornplanter,
Venture Smith, George Washington
*and* Abraham Yates
*circa 1750–1783*

HURON

[IROQUOIS CONFEDERACY]

MOHAWK
ONEIDA
TUSCARORA
ONONDAGA
CAYUGA
SENECA

Connecticut River

Oswego
Conawaugus
Genesee River
Fort Stanwix
Saratoga
Fort Plain
Albany
Cherry Valley
Kingston
Hudson River
Delaware River
White Plains
Burnt House

Boston
Stonington
Haddam
Newport
Fishers Island

The Forks of the Ohio

SHAWNEE

THE OHIO
COUNTRY

Ohio River

Fort Necessity
Carlisle
Fort Cumberland
Potomac River

Valley Forge
Philadelphia
Trenton
Elizabethtown • New York City
Staten Island

Atlantic Ocean

Mount Vernon

Williamsburg • Yorktown

0 Miles                    100
0 Kilometers          100

© 2017 Jeffrey L. Ward

# REVOLUTION
# SONG

# PROLOGUE

He was a wise man, a family man, with a kind face and soulful eyes, and he was about to kill. The people he was going to kill called themselves Americans. That word had nothing to do with him, though it would be foisted onto his identity and that of his people. He was a Seneca, a leader of the Haudenosaunee, the confederacy that the whites called the Iroquois. His name was Kayéthwahkeh. Its meaning in the Seneca language had within it the idea of planting. That, coupled with the fact that corn was the most visible crop around Seneca villages, led Americans to call him Cornplanter.

Cornplanter was a young man, in the prime of life, tall, broad-shouldered, built for action. On this night, July 27, 1779, under cover of darkness, he led 120 men, armed with muskets and tomahawks, along a stream that fed into the Susquehanna River in central Pennsylvania. They surrounded a rough stockade. Inside were 21 American militiamen and about 50 women and children. At dawn one of the men in the makeshift fort appeared at the gate; the gunshot hit him with a force that knocked him back inside. Rather than accept the warning, the militiamen started shooting back. They were outnumbered and inexperienced;

*Cornplanter in 1786, painted by Frederick Bartoli.*

they had no idea what was to come. The puff and crack of musketfire filled the morning air.

Cornplanter had not wanted to be in this position: he hadn't wanted to kill Americans. But there were others who had a say, and as a political leader he understood compromise and majority rule. Earlier, at the British fort in Oswego, on the shore of Lake Ontario in Seneca country, representatives of the king of England—alien creatures in their red-and-white dress, smelling of beef and vinegar—had organized a formal council with leaders of the Iroquois confederacy, including Cornplanter. They brought out a wampum belt whose rows of colored beads signified the age-old alliance between Great Britain and the Iroquois nation. They talked about the war that was going on between their country and the American colonists, told of the majesty and might of Britain and her king, and of the inferiority of the Americans. They wanted the Iroquois to join the fight on their side. They gave presents: brass kettles, muskets with their beautifully long and cold barrels, gunpowder, sharp knives of the kind the Iroquois preferred for scalping.

The Iroquois leaders then conferred among themselves. Over the years their people had had frank business dealings and even friendships with American settlers, but settlers had also burned Iroquois villages, murdered their families and taken over their lands. The Mohawk Thayendanegea, a worldly and domineering war chief who also went by the English name Joseph Brant, argued forcefully that if the Americans defeated the British the land-grabs would continue, therefore the Iroquois should fight alongside the British. Besides, the British were stronger; it would be better to back the likely winner.

Then Cornplanter rose to speak. There must have been some fidgeting, for he was an unusual man and the others knew it. While he was a trained fighter—something of a killing machine, in fact—he had the temperament of a philosopher. He was a ponderer, a quiet, slow thinker given to aphoristic pronouncements, whose words, belying his relative youth, often reflected the pain and sadness of life. He had not been swayed by the arguments or the gifts of the British. Cornplanter called the war between the British and the Americans a "family quarrel." He suggested that it was wiser to stand back and let the white tribes fight it out. "War is war, death is death, a fight is a hard business," he said.

Joseph Brant had evidently been expecting this sort of thing from Cornplanter. He leaped to his feet, commanded Cornplanter to "stop speaking" and referred to him as "nephew"—a term of subordination, even though they were equals. He branded Cornplanter a "coward," and urged the others to vote to fight alongside the British.

The vote went against Cornplanter. The Iroquois became part of the American Revolutionary War, launching a murderous string of assaults on American villages and forts. Cornplanter, the philosopher, led the way, leaving horror in his wake.

Three thousand miles away, across the vast buffer of the Atlantic Ocean, sat the man who had forced Cornplanter's hand. As Secretary of State for the American Department, Lord George Germain was England's de facto secretary of war, the man whose job it was to devise a strategy for quelling the rebellion.

Where Cornplanter's world comprised forest trails and longhouse villages, Germain's was one of London gentlemen's clubs and country estates, of diamond broaches for the ladies and bumpers of claret for the men, of such novel distractions as Samuel Johnson's dictionary and symphonies by Herr Mozart. He was a tall man, "rather womanly" in the way his body expanded in the middle, as an acquaintance put it, yet with the bearing of the war-hardened soldier he had once been. He was a convivial socializer, but so charged with aggression that even friends tended to hold him at arm's length.

Germain had thought it would be quick, this business of corralling the Americans. The original plan he put in motion was, as he said, "decisive, direct, and firm." British armies would take command of the Hudson River and drive a wedge between New England and the rest of the colonies. Split in two, America would end its rebellion. But in December 1777 news reached London that General John Burgoyne had been beaten so decisively at Saratoga that he had had to surrender his entire 6,000-man army to American forces on the banks of the Hudson. The outcry in Parliament was immediate, and the blame was showered on George Germain. The word his enemies unfurled was precisely the one the Mohawk chief had flung at Cornplanter: *coward*. It was a strange term to use for a plan that had involved full and direct military engagement. But Germain's many enemies weren't referring so much to his strategy on the Hudson River; they were looking into his past, to a spectacular battlefield error he had made as a younger man. They were raking open an old wound. Indeed, Germain's conduct in running the war against the American revolutionaries had a deeply personal bent to it. He was, in a real sense, using the vast, world-historic conflict to exorcise a personal demon.

Stung by his political enemies' attacks, Germain devised a new strategy for defeating the Americans. From now on the English offensive would be more complex, carried out on a grander scale and with fewer scruples. Among other things, he issued precise instructions for bringing the Iroquois into the conflict on the British side.

If George Germain forced Cornplanter's hand, then the attacks that Cornplanter and his fellow Iroquois unleashed—a reign of terror across Pennsylvania and New York that left dismembered bodies and traumatized survivors—likewise forced the hand of the colonial army leader. From his military camp in Middlebrook, New Jersey, General George Washington made the hard decision to pull 4,000 men—nearly a quarter of his entire army—out of the fight against the British and direct this force at the Iroquois.

At this point, three years into the war, Washington was beset with difficulties. The British had taken two forts on the Hudson River, and it seemed they might yet achieve the goal of splitting the colonies in half. The American soldiers were practically barefoot: the army was desperately in need of shoes. And now Washington had to divide his army to fight Indians. The news from his home, Mount Vernon, meanwhile, was also bleak: crops hadn't been planted, and there was no money for upkeep.

Washington was forty-seven years old, a Virginia planter who, with his ascendance to lead the American army, had achieved what he had craved all his life: attention, honor, status. He was fastidious in dress and took great care in public appearances—making sure, for instance, that he always showed himself to his men, even when all was mud and slop, wearing the most resplendent uniform and atop the finest horse. Like George Germain, he was deeply ambitious, but where Germain's drive seemed to blare from his being, Washington kept his hunger for success hidden behind a frosty reserve.

Also like Germain, Washington had personal motivations as he led his army. Throughout his teens and twenties he had strived for a place in Britain's military. Time after time he had been rejected by the British system as a mere colonial, and he became progressively more bitter. The Revolution slowly brought about a transformation in him. He had grown up with a fawning admiration for all things British, yet he was now the leader of the greatest-ever rebellion against Britain. He was an Anglo-American who, increasingly, saw himself simply as an American.

As the war ground on, the Seneca warrior Cornplanter, the British aristocrat George Germain (whose name at birth was George

Sackville), and the American general George Washington were propelled by a common drive. Each was a leader of his people. The concept of political freedom, which swept through the eighteenth century with unprecedented urgency, thrust them together in conflict.

But political freedom and representative government, the ideas that we most associate with the American Revolution, earthshaking though they were, were part of an even larger force that was in the air at the time. This broader change in how humans saw themselves had been building for more than a century by the time Washington, Germain and Cornplanter were active. I was first struck by it while researching my 2004 book *The Island at the Center of the World*, about the Dutch founding of New York in the 1600s. In that century people began to distrust old ways of knowing and developed a new appreciation for the human mind and what it could discover. In the mid-1600s, René Descartes, the so-called father of modern philosophy, proposed the radical notion that knowledge ought not to be grounded in "received wisdom"—that whatever the church or the king said was true—but on the human mind and its "good sense." Every single person had within himself or herself a tool called reason, which connected to the world and the universe in a mysterious and profound way.

From this came an elevation of the individual, a newfound fascination with the individual—or, better said, a new meaning of "individual." Before, your definition of yourself was inextricably bound up with your relationships and networks: your family, guild, village, manor, parish. "You" were a thread in a web. Then, suddenly, you were . . . *you*. And *you* were uniquely special and important.

As the eighteenth century progressed, the focus on the individual led people to new insights, new proclamations and assertions of rights. Across Europe, a particular word was suddenly bandied about in every conceivable context. Vrijheid. Liberdade. Liberté. Svoboda. Saoirse. *Freedom*. Kings, armies and churches, whether you sided with them or not, all exerted power over individuals; all, in their very existence, constrained these newly assertive individuals. In country after country, people began agitating for freedom of one kind or another. The furor built through the decades until the leaders in America had the brilliant idea to package this force. They gave it a sharp political frame and turned it against the English, who had themselves been at the forefront of the freedom movement. The Americans declared that it was "self-evident" that all are created equal, and that all are entitled to "liberty."

The people featured in this book were part of this sweeping change. They were, like us, vibrantly aware of themselves as individuals, alive to promise and possibility in a way that previous generations had not been. But the new valuing of the individual went only so far. "Liberty" had strict limits in the early American republic.

Yet people who were left out of the "all men are created equal" struggle in the period of America's founding pushed forward in their own ways. The three other protagonists of this book, whose lives weave through and around those of Washington, Germain and Cornplanter, didn't lead armies, but they personified "revolution" as fully as did the man who became the first president.

Venture Smith, who was born in Africa (his original name was Broteer Furro) and brought to America as a slave, embodied the complications of the struggle for freedom better than any patriot soldier. While America's leaders packaged the power of individual freedom and wove it into grand, idealistic language, it did not inspire them to end slavery. That failure led to what has probably been the greatest source of strife in American society. For many, it continues to make the project of American history feel hollow. But Venture Smith cut his own path: buying himself and his family out of slavery, acquiring land and, against all odds, fostering a community of free blacks.

The emancipation of slaves at least was a topic of debate in the eighteenth century. Women's freedom—the idea of women being independent actors, able to make their own way in life—was mostly unimagined. Margaret Moncrieffe was the daughter of a military officer who chose to fight on the British side, and the whole trajectory of her life was shaped by his decision. A young woman couldn't express herself with anything like the independence that men could assert, but she clutched at one hopeful change that women were advancing just as she came of age: the rejection of forced marriage. Defying both her father and her abusive husband, however, came with a heavy price. Most of her life unfolded in London and Paris as she cycled back and forth between high society and the depths of poverty. From today's vantage point we can see that she was trying to make it on her own. That was virtually impossible for a woman of the time, but she had tools at her disposal, including her femininity and a remarkably modern flair for self-promotion, which she employed with great skill.

We are used to seeing the American Revolution through the eyes of the elites of the period: men in powdered wigs who scratched out words of wisdom on rag paper. Like many of the founding fathers, Abraham Yates Jr., of Albany, New York, made freedom his life's work, but he stayed resolutely at street level. He was the son of a blacksmith who was relegated to the humblest of careers, that of shoemaker. He seems to have been born with a keen sense of injustice, however, a feeling that the "better classes" were trampling the commoners. So he taught himself the law and rose through a succession of local political offices. He was among the first Americans to grow impatient with British rule, one of the first to bring the writings of John Locke to bear on the American situation, and among the first to join the patriot cause. But his voluminous writings have little of the loftiness of the founding fathers' documents. Instead, they are pragmatic and suspicious, always reflecting his tradesman's perspective and distrust of elites, British and American alike.

In one sense, these three people of the eighteenth century stand for others, people whose freedom was limited. But to define them in terms of issues—slavery, women's liberty, the struggle of commoners versus elites—feels too cramped. They were not representatives of groups. They were gorgeously themselves. As I researched their lives, they seemed to reject categorization; like each of us, they demanded uniqueness.

This book, then, tries to avoid abstract labels and stays close to the lives of its six protagonists. It follows the whole sweep of those lives, from birth to death. My objective is to offer not just an account of the era in which the American nation was founded, but a sense of what it felt like. Philosophers say that human subjectivity is the one wall science can never break down: we will never know scientifically what it is like to experience life from someone else's perspective. But art can do this, and I believe that history has an element of art in it.

Chronologically, the book opens in the early 1700s and ends in the 1830s, when steam engines accelerated the pace of the nation's growth. And while it mostly takes place in America, the story begins in England: pastoral, green England, the land of both Empire and Enlightenment, which was in so many ways the cradle of America.

# PART ONE

## Chapter 1

SONS OF FATHERS

In the summer of 1716, a carriage made its rumbling way southeast from London, following the turnpike road toward a tiny village called Sevenoaks. Entering the county of Kent, it traversed luxuriantly green hills and meadows stippled with color. Inside, braced against the turbulence of the ride, and maybe the only thing to disrupt the peace of the journey, was the reason for it: a newborn baby.

As the trip neared its end, the travelers tending to the infant could see ahead of them what to the unknowing eye looked like a cityscape rising up from the countryside. Gabled brick houses, built of mottled Kentish ragstone, formed the outline of a medieval English town. But as one drew nearer, the optical illusion faded. It wasn't a town at all but a single house.

The house was called Knole. It had been owned by a succession of luminaries that included the Archbishop of Canterbury, King Henry VIII and Queen Elizabeth, but for some generations now it had been the estate of the Sackvilles, one of England's most deeply aristocratic families. Knole was a supreme manifestation of an architectural fetish that developed among European nobility in the sixteenth and seventeenth centuries: the calendar house. It had 12 separate

*George Germain (aka George Sackville), painted in 1760 by Nathaniel Hone.*

entrances, to represent each month of the year, 52 staircases, one for every week, 7 interior courtyards, which corresponded to the days of the week, and no fewer than 365 rooms. In total, it comprised four acres of interior space, all of it gilded, tapestried and hung with stately art—"spendidly sombre and sumptuous," as a later inhabitant would say. It was the most famous private house in England and one of the grandest houses in the world. For the baby boy who was carried through its front door for the first time that summer, past rows of dutifully arrayed servants (there were forty-two for the interior alone), it would simply be home.

His name was George. He was the third son of Lionel Sackville, the Duke of Dorset. Despite his low place in the birth order, he became his father's favorite. His childhood unfolded against a backdrop of extreme privilege, starting with his baptism, at which George I, the king of England, served as his godfather. The boy grew up playing in the endless corridors (he was well into his teens before he was able to venture through the whole house without fear of getting lost), amid the beech, chestnut, pear and cherry trees of the garden, and in the deer park, which flowed so seamlessly toward the paneled interior of the house that a Sackville once stepped into the central hall to find himself standing face-to-face with a live stag.

Much of that garden—10,000 beech trees, to be exact—had been installed by Knole's only boarder. Elizabeth Germain, familiarly known as Lady Betty, was a wealthy widow whose three children had died young. Her late husband, Sir John Germain, had been a friend of the Sackville family, and upon his death George's parents had offered her a wing of the house. She spent her time and money in improving Knole and in supporting various charities. Her husband had left her one thing besides a fortune: a request that she eventually bequeath her wealth to one of the Duke of Dorset's sons. Like the duke, Lady Betty favored young George—who, if and when he inherited the Germain fortune, would take the family name as well. So, all in all, the boy's prospects could not have been brighter.

Lord George Sackville had the best tutors and teachers, and while literature did not move him—"I have not genius sufficient for works of mere imagination," he once said—when it came to English history he was in his element. History books of the time told the story of England as a grand pageant, starting with the colonization of the island by the Romans, bringers of literature and government. Then the Germanic tribes swept in: the Saxons and the Jutes and the Angles, from the latter of which the island would get its name. The Norman invaders from France introduced a new overlay of language and civilization. King John's concessions to the barons at Runnymede in 1215 were recognized in the eighteenth century as the beginning of a constitutional form of government. Then came the age of the explorers, and the period in which the English broke their inward focus, sent ships into distant waters, and began to comprehend a new, seemingly unlimited horizon. They battled with the wily Dutch in the far-off East Indies over control of sea lanes and access to spices. They defied malaria and sunstroke to install sugar plantations on Caribbean islands.

Young George was particularly drawn to political history. Beginning in the decades before he was born, a revolution in ideas swept over England, which would transform the political landscape. Focusing on the human mind as the arbiter of knowledge led certain men to argue that the most just society was one in which power was in the hands not of a monarch or an elite but of individuals. The concepts of "natural law" and "toleration" became the foundation of a political party, the Whigs, which favored Parliament over the monarchy. A simultaneous revolution was taking place in science. All of this led some to the optimistic belief that, thanks to English ideas and inventions, a new, more modern and civilized world was coming into being. England, by this thinking, was the land of expanding freedom, the land of the future.

This did not preclude England also becoming a major colonizing power. After the restoration of the monarchy in 1660, a grand scheme coalesced in the minds of a handful of leaders: to extend "the boundaries of Empire," as the charter of the Royal Society declared. (The Society—of which George Sackville's grandfather was a member—was founded to advance not only English science but English dominion.) In particular, those boundaries would encompass two continents, Africa and America, tying them inextricably to England and to one another. The Stuarts, England's ruling family, together with several other aristocratic families and members of the Royal Society, formed a company, the Royal Adventurers Trading to Africa, which would have a monopoly to exploit the continent and a mission to "set to sea ships &c with ordnance &c" in order to secure "mines of gold and silver," which would be used "for the buying and selling bartering and exchanging of for or with any negroes slaves good wares merchandises whatsoever." The scheme, in short, was to expand outposts in West Africa for obtaining slaves and gold, and to use these to develop the Caribbean sugar fields and the colonies in North America. A vast, rambling system came into being in which sugar, tobacco, guns and other products, not the least of which were human beings, got cycled around the Atlantic Ocean. Over the decades from the 1660s to the 1720s, profits streamed into the home country, in particular into the purses of the shareholders of the Royal African Company (as it became known), which encouraged more ships to set sail for the West African coast and more English settlers to make their homes in America.

This was the backdrop to George Sackville's upbringing and education: a sense of England rising inexorably, thanks in large part to its management of a network of trade and exploitation that ran from the west coast of Africa to the east coast of North America. British youths learned about this network with pride; they saw it as the capstone of a saga that stretched all the way back to the founding by the Romans of a city they called Londinium. Punctuating this saga, for a history student such as George Sackville, was the toll of the kings and queens of England and details of their reigns. And for every monarch associated with the pageantry and sweat that had steered England toward greatness there was a corresponding Sackville: this one Chancellor of the Exchequer for Queen Elizabeth, that one Lord Chamberlain to Charles I.

Through his childhood young George thoroughly absorbed the lesson of Knole and its illustrious family. The feudal truths mortared into its walls—of the greatness and inexorability of England, its rise and its noble families—became part of his being. He listened reverently to the war stories of his grandfather, who had fought on the Continent. He grew big and strong. He became an accomplished horseman. His personality developed: combative, coltish. He yearned to test himself in battle, to fight for England's ever-widening empire.

B roteer Furro opened his eyes for the first time—this would have been when Lord George Sackville was about ten years old and racing about the endless corridors of Knole—onto the blue sky yawning above the West African savanna. His village, called Dukandarra, was located in the interior of what was generally referred to as Guinea. It was a place of low shrubs, fiery sun and kaleidoscopic birdlife. Cows, goats and donkeys milled thickly: his family had wealth. His father, Saungm Furro, was a local prince, the head of the village. Broteer had two younger brothers.

Broteer's people may have been Fulani, herders who had slowly spread out from their original homeland in the Senegal River valley, in westernmost Africa, eastward as far as Lake Chad, near the center of the continent. Their basic communal unit was the ruga, or cattle camp. Cows were the center of life. As a very small child, Broteer would have developed a close bond with the animals. He may have learned the Fulani creation myth, according to which the Fulani and their cows were kindred beings. In one variation, a girl named Bajemongo was bathing in a river when the spirit of the river rose up and took her, impregnating her with two sons. When the boys were old enough, the spirit provided for each of them by bringing forth from the river twenty-two cattle: ten cows and one bull for each boy to tend. Slaveholding was a fixture of Fulani life from ancient times, and in the creation story the spirit also produced from the river a pair of slaves for each boy, one male and one female.

Years passed, and Broteer learned the rhythm of the seasons. When rain fell, it was like a curtain. The grassland carried onward like an ocean, the grass so high a boy could be swallowed up in it. At dry times it was perishingly hot, and animals needed to be moved in search of water.

Along with the other boys of Dukandarra, Broteer would have developed strength and self-reliance by practicing a ritualized form of stick-fighting. He also apparently received ritual scarring on his face. Girls hoisted dried calabashes filled with sour milk onto their heads and walked with them to nearby villages to sell. Everyone drank milk and ate a gruel of sour milk and millet. They also ate meat, but if they were indeed Fulani, they would not have eaten pork, for they were one of the earliest African peoples to convert to Islam.

One day when Broteer was about ten, there was a terrible argument between his mother and his father. Broteer was old enough to comprehend its complexity. As his father's first wife, his mother was, by tradition, entitled to be consulted on the subject of subsequent wives. Presumably, his father had asked for her blessing when he chose a second wife, but he picked a third without telling Broteer's mother. For her this was a matter of honor and pride. The fight ended with her hoisting up Broteer's two younger siblings, one on her back, the other in her arms, and marching off, out of the village, with Broteer running to keep up.

Broteer was also old enough to notice and be concerned about the fact that his mother, in her haste and anger, brought nothing else: no cloth to use for a bed, and no food. She stopped periodically and foraged for fruit for herself and the children. After two days, they came to the edge of a desert, and she headed straight into it. At night they curled up next to each other and listened in terror to the howls of wolves and lions.

After five days of travel, the desert ended and they entered a countryside such as the boy had never seen before. There was a wide and sparkling river surrounded by flat land lush with vegetation, with mountains brooding in the distance. They had arrived at his mother's destination: the house of a farmer whom she knew.

And here, abruptly, his mother left him. He was to stay with this man and help him tend his sheep. So his life started anew. Every morning Broteer and another boy drove a herd of sheep out to pasture on the plains, and as the sun set they returned. The farmer had no children of his own, and he treated Broteer with kindness. When one day Broteer was attacked by dogs and bitten so severely that the scars would stay for the rest of his life, the man carried him home and cared for him, tenderly nursing him back to health.

Life, for all its strangeness, was good. Broteer was big-boned, strong, and growing fast. He witnessed the changing of the seasons in his new home. In June, the rains came, and the river flooded the plains. As the flood waters rose to seven feet and more, people retreated to the hills. When the water receded Broteer saw that it left a fresh coating of black mud behind, and with it fertility. People came back to the plains, and the planting of crops began.

George Washington entered the world about four years after Broteer Furro. It was a winter's morning, February 1732, in tidewater Virginia, the heartland of British North America. As the season changed, nature slowly began to reveal itself. In spring, the baby could squint up toward the bright sun through red cedars and towering loblolly pines. The family's simple brick house sat on a gentle slope just above Popes Creek, which flowed into the Potomac River. There were fish in the creek; turtles lurked around the marsh just behind. But the boy would have few memories of playing or fishing here, for when he was three years old the family moved to another, even wilder and more fertile portion of Virginia.

The new home was a place the Washingtons called Little Hunting Creek Plantation: 2,500 soaringly panoramic acres of forested hills and valleys stretched out along the Potomac River, much of which had been owned by the family since George's great-grandfather's time. The English had been in North America for more than a century, and the infant George was the fourth generation of Washingtons to call it home. He was the third son of Augustine Washington, whose grandfather had emigrated from Oxfordshire in 1656.

Gus Washington, as people called him, was the kind of father a young boy could admire. He was tall, gentle and famed for his strength. Someone said he could "raise up and place in a wagon a mass of iron that two ordinary men could barely raise from the ground." He was also restless, endlessly striving. He served in the local militia and local government. He was the county sheriff. He ran an ironworks. Like his forebears, he had bought up Virginia acreage, but in even greater quantities than they had. The transcontinental economic system that fostered the rise of England's empire was now in full swing, so that his ambitions exceeded his father's. And where in Gus Washington's grandfather's time much of the work had been done by white indentured servants, Gus himself came of age along with a new system, in which Africans, supervised by whites, did the work in teams. When Gus was born, there had been about 5,000 slaves in the whole region. By the time he himself started having children, the number was above 40,000; slaves made up 20 percent of the population, and the numbers were growing. As Europeans fell in love with tobacco—partly for what they took to be its medicinal properties—more slaves were needed, to plant, prime, top, cure and prize tobacco that would be smoked in London cafés.

Gus Washington was on the rise, but he was also of the earth. He was rugged, pink-complected: very much an Englishman, but born and bred to the woods and farmland of Virginia.

As George grew, he became aware of the complexities of his family. His father had had another wife, who had died before he was born; thanks to their marriage, George had two older half-brothers whom he didn't know—they were at school in England—and there had also been a half-sister, Jane, who died when he was a toddler. As much as George must have idolized his father, the man was away much of the time. Though the family moved yet again in order to be near the ironworks that Gus Washington managed—to a new farm on the banks of the Rappahannock River, a place they called the Home Farm—he also traveled to England on business, and on horseback up and down the coastal plain and west toward the wild hinterland of the Blue Ridge Mountains, between his farms and on behalf of the British administration of the colony.

That meant that George's mother was the dominant presence in his life. Mary Ball, as she was known before she married Gus Washington, was a backwoods woman: hard-nosed, domineering, illiterate. She didn't fancy dressing up or trying to fit into society. She had bad teeth. She may have smoked a pipe. She was miserly and hectoring. A plausible impetus for Gus Washington to have offered marriage to a woman who seemed to inhabit a different realm of the social universe was the fact that she had inherited 600 acres of land, which adjoined his.

There was a pattern to life in George's early years. His father was continually under stress—tobacco prices were down in Europe, and the greedy plants quickly exhausted the soil, requiring him to keep moving his family further into virgin lands—yet he was determined to succeed, to move up in society. When he was home, there was the clatter of hooves outside: visitors, dinners, tea served in Wedgwood cups and saucers. When his father was away, the social hubbub vanished. In its place were chores, dull responsibilities. George's sister, Betty, had been born a year after him; then in rapid succession came Samuel, John, Charles and Mildred. With his father gone and his mother a needy and demanding presence, George had work to do.

Then, when he was eleven years old, and visiting his cousin, he was ordered to go back home at once. His father had caught a fever while traveling in a storm, and was dying.

As challenging as George's life was before Gus Washington's death, it had had considerable promise. His father had been outgoing, open. He had built up a small fortune. But his will directed most of it to his sons from his first marriage. (George would inherit ten slaves, though these were to remain his mother's "property" until he turned twenty-one.) There wasn't even money for George to attend a proper school. Before, he had had the prospect of formal education in England, of becoming a businessman and a member of the local gentry. Now his future occupation looked more likely that of a harassed nanny. He was up at dawn every morning, saddled with the responsibility of helping to feed and care for his younger siblings and with the challenge of handling his mother, who seems to have berated him as much as she leaned on him, and of whom one of his cousins later declared, "I was more afraid than of my own parents."

The American colonies constituted a significant portion of Britain's empire by the 1730s, but not all of England's holdings were an ocean away from London. Ireland, a few dozen miles across the Irish Sea, had been subject to English will, in one form or another, as far back

as the twelfth century. England ruled the Irish through an official called
the Lord Lieutenant of Ireland. When George Sackville was fourteen,
his father was named to that position. The boy went to Dublin with
him, leaving behind the great estate of Knole, where he had been raised,
and wading for the first time into the wider world.

Dublin, circa 1730, was a city on the move—in two directions at
once. Grand medieval houses were being given clean modern facades,
and a new Parliament House—the world's first purpose-built bicamer-
cal legislature—was under construction. But it was also a city of fam-
ines and riots. Gentlemen and ladies who went walking in the streets
complained of being swarmed by beggars. Outside its urbane heart, the
streets and alleys seethed with crowds of poor people. "If they happen
to hear of the death of a horse, they run to it as to a feast," a pamphleteer
lamented. If George Sackville had had a sublimely sheltered upbringing, Dublin was a sharp introduction to reality.

As it happened, the boy received a world-class chaperone in Dublin.
His father was preoccupied by politics during his time as Lord Lieutenant, but Lady Betty Germain, his in-house benefactor at Knole, had
written a friend—a sixty-seven-year-old scholar, a man with a round face,
a penetrating gaze and a tendency to sport a resplendently flowing wig—
asking him to look after the boy. The friend was Jonathan Swift, the
dean of St. Patrick's Cathedral and one of the most celebrated writers
of his or any other age. His masterpiece, *Gulliver's Travels*, had been
published six years earlier, and it had made him internationally famous.
Swift wrote to the new Lord Lieutenant, accepting the commission to
watch over the boy in the most fawning terms: "I must here by the way
take notice that not only the University but even the whole kingdom are
full of acknowledgments for the honor your Grace hath done them in
trusting the care of educating one of your sons to Dublin College. . . ."

Swift knew where the power lay, and was skilled at manipulating
it. He was a dynamo of a man, whose daily life mixed academics, pol-

itics and church affairs, and he blended all of it into his writing with a combination of intellect and lacerating wit. George Sackville's association with the great man gave the boy an excellent opportunity to study how power worked in the British system. All of the places in which the British Empire held sway shared certain features, having to do with accommodation to the distant power, yet each colony, dominion, outpost and protectorate had its own manner of accommodation. The system that had developed in Ireland involved three interest groups. One was the Irish people. Then there was England. The third group was the so-called Protestant Ascendancy, which was the ruling class of Ireland. Beginning more than a century earlier, England had kept the Irish subordinate by passing laws that discriminated against the Roman Catholic majority, decreeing that only members of the Protestant Church of England could own land or serve in government. England had confiscated tracts of land and installed English and Scottish colonizers, who then took control of Irish society and government. Swift was not only part of this Protestant ruling class, but, as the dean of St. Patrick's, the seat of Protestant Irish faith, he was at the very center of the web of Anglo-Irish life.

Young George Sackville must have absorbed a good deal of the complexity of imperial politics in his first two years in Dublin. Then, when he turned sixteen, he enrolled at Trinity College, the great Irish university, which was serious enough educationally to rival Cambridge and Oxford. Even here he was in the middle of politics. The university stood just across College Green from parliament, and a few minutes' stroll away was Dublin Castle, the seat of British power in Ireland and the base from which his father carried out his duties.

When George finished his studies, he began his apprenticeship in the mechanism of the empire in the most direct manner, by working as his father's secretary. At eighteen, sitting in the Lord Lieutenant's office in Dublin Castle, handling quill and ink, he suddenly found himself involved in the great issue of the day between England and Ireland: finance. In order to raise an army and expand its empire, England had, over the previous four decades, pioneered the concepts of a paper currency and a national debt. Dutifully following suit, Ireland's parliament had begun its own debt, which was financed by taxes on ordinary people. Ireland's debt was intended to serve its own interests, but the needs of Britain's overseas empire were so pressing that the Irish people—without a say in the matter—saw their tax money get rechanneled to fund other British concerns, as far away as the American colonies.

George Sackville's aged but still wily mentor, Jonathan Swift, played a part in this taxation-without-representation debate. As a member of the Protestant leadership, his inclination was to support England, and as an Anglican he was a fierce opponent of Irish Catholic nationalists, both politically and religiously. Yet he was still Irish and was appalled that England should use the Irish debt for other purposes. Not only that, he found the new ideas coming out of England to be morally reprehensible. Along with the economic innovations came a new way of thinking about poverty. Whereas in Elizabethan times "the poor" were seen as a class that society was obliged to aid, the new mercantilist economists tended to see "the impotent poor"—those too young, old or sick to work—as a burden that had to be lightened. To that end, some argued that poor children could go to work as early as age four or five.

It may have been as much due to his delicate political situation as to his temperament that Swift became a master of the use of satire. He published *A Modest Proposal* in the midst of this economic debate. The small pamphlet exploded on society. Those unfamiliar with the genre of satire must have been gobsmacked to read his argument "for Preventing the Children of Poor People From Being a Burthen to Their Parents or Country, and for Making Them Beneficial to the Publick."

Claiming to have heard that "a young healthy child well nursed, is, at a year old, a most delicious nourishing and wholesome food, whether stewed, roasted, baked, or boiled," he proposed, in elaborate terms, that the children of the poor be sold for meat. Such a scheme, he said, would greatly lessen the number of "Papists" and, overall, turn an economic problem into an advantage.

Swift's pamphlet skewered the new economic theorists by carrying their scientific detachment to its logical extreme. At the same time, it went at the British policies that kept the Irish mired in poverty even as they were forced to pay taxes for the upkeep of the empire. And the indirectness of his expression allowed him to evade official censure. He managed to remain on very good terms with the Lord Lieutenant.

By the time George Sackville was installed as his father's secretary, the boy had had several years' experience of both the complexities of Irish politics and the cleverness of Dean Swift. And by this time he had developed an understanding of his father. The Duke of Dorset was known, as one contemporary said, for his "good breeding" and "decency of manners," and for the fact that "He never had an opinion about public matters." He was, in other words, a diplomat to a fault: courtly, genial, inoffensive, always exquisitely attired in full wig and flowing silk. Swift and other Irish leaders liked him. If England's rule was harsh, Lionel Sackville, as representative of the foreign power, avoided confrontation.

Maybe what drew him to his third son was an opposite temperament. Unlike him, the boy had a fire in his belly. Young George Sackville was not an intellectual, but he was smart and he had galloping ambition. He believed in England and in himself; he wanted to earn glory in service to the crown. It wouldn't have been long before the young man, as he scraped his quill across sheets of paper, taking down his father's dictated letters, recognized the man's mildness. He opened beseeching letters from Swift, meanwhile, and saw the Irishman dancing with witty verbiage and extravagant praise ("I cannot but think that your Grace, to whom God hath given every amiable as well as usefull talent, and in so great a measure, is bound when you have satisfyed all the expectations of those who have the most power in your club, to do something at the request of others who love you better . . ."), and in public injecting mawkish praise with shots of satire.

Somewhere along the way the son formed his own opinions about governing an empire. And he developed a directness that would stay with him for the rest of his life. "He studied no choice phrases, no superfluous words," a contemporary said of him, but rather always employed "the simplest and most unequivocal" language. As for the Irish, young George decided, they were too clever for their own good. They needed a firm hand.

In 1737, Lionel Sackville's term as Lord Lieutenant ended, and he returned to Knole. George, however, stayed on in Dublin and became secretary to the new Lord Lieutenant. He updated his father on events, expressing his own increasingly clear and not especially diplomatic opinions. Regarding his new boss, for whom he had little respect, he wrote, "My Lord Lieutenant's speech is very well lik'd; he spoke it so low that few people could hear it." And despite the help he had gotten from Swift, he exhibited more contempt than fondness for his old mentor. "The Dean has shown himself more mad and absurd than ever," he wrote his father.

George Sackville was twenty-one. He had concluded that running an empire required not finesse but firmness, not affection but efficiency.

A year after Broteer Furro's mother left him to tend the sheep of a farmer in a distant province, a man on horseback arrived. He gave the farmer some money, then took the boy onto his horse and they rode off—back to Broteer's home of Dukandarra. When the boy got to his village, he saw that his parents had made up their quarrel. They greeted him joyfully. His old life could begin again.

Six weeks later, however, a messenger came into the village from the very province where Broteer had been living, with a message for Broteer's father. The news was ominous. Although Broteer may not have been aware of it until now, all of Guinea had been churning with violence for decades. Much of the region, especially the rainforested lands to the south, was controlled by one or another of the Akan kingdoms. These states—the main ones were Akyem, Asante, Akwamu, Fante and Denkyira—allied with each other, and at times fought with each other, over control of the region's major products: ivory, kola nuts (which contain caffeine and were chewed by many West Africans), slaves and gold, which was mined in the inland forests. The Akan were a distinct culture, decidedly unlike Broteer's people. The Akan language, Twi, would have been alien to the boy. The Akan peoples lived in rooted communities, in clay houses, sometimes with columns decorated with swirling relief images. Their cultures were built around their kings, who had elaborate courts and the symbol of whose authority was a throne, called a stool. Gold, goldsmithing and jewelry were important to the Akan. So were weaving, pottery and crafting products from iron. Unlike the herders of Dukandarra, they lived in fixed societies.

Europeans had first reached the coast and begun trading for gold and slaves as far back as the 1450s. By the 1480s, Portuguese ships were sailing away from West African ports with as many as 3,500 slaves a year. Europeans had not introduced slavery. The practice of capturing and enslaving other Africans had long been a feature of many cultures in the region—in some places the slave population outnumbered the native—but as more European nations sent ships, their trade played a part in reshaping the native economies, politics and even diet. Prior to European contact, the Akan and others in the region had a lack of carbohydrates in their diet. The Europeans brought corn, which the

Akan took to growing, and it helped spark a population surge, especially among the Fante on the coast. The agricultural revolution in turn gave the Akan kingdoms a greater need for slave labor.

The Danes, the Dutch, the English and the Portuguese established themselves at "castles" along the Gold Coast, which were essentially trading bases. They were not fortresses from which they controlled the Africans; the Europeans were very much subordinate. They paid rent and forged alliances with the local kingdoms. By the early decades of the 1700s, as slavery became a truly massive industry, the alliances—among Akan states and between Akans and Europeans—shifted often as parties jockeyed for advantage.

In 1737 and 1738, a complex situation unfolded, with the Dutch and the Danes exerting pressure on different Akan factions, while the Akyem kingdom, in an attempt to gain dominance over other Akan states, sent armies into Fante territory along the coast. The governor of the Danish-controlled territory reported to his bosses in October 1738 that the Akyem "have for the last month been at war with the Fantes and have defeated them, just as they have destroyed the market place that was in Agona. . . ."

The Akyem power grab seems to have set off a chain reaction in which other states, eager to get guns from the Europeans with which to defend themselves, roamed northward, out of the forest and into the savanna, in search of slaves they could trade.

The news from the messenger to Saungm Furro was that the territory astride the wide river where Broteer had lived with the farmer had been invaded. Unlike the invaders, Broteer's people had no guns. The locals weren't equipped to fight. The messenger asked Broteer's father if the people from his village could take refuge in his lands. Saungm Furro agreed. But a few days after the refugees arrived came word that the invading army was headed toward Dukandarra. The newcomers fled, but Saungm Furro and his people remained in their homes.

When the advance party appeared, soldiers gave Broteer's father their demands. The army would leave him and his people alone provided he paid them. They wanted three hundred cattle, equally large numbers of other animals, and money. Cattle were precious, but Broteer's father paid what was demanded. After he paid, however, he learned that the foreign soldiers were preparing to attack anyway, so he ordered his people to flee in small groups. At dawn, Broteer sneaked away from the village with his mother and two brothers. His father left together with his other two wives.

The little party met up on a plain some distance from the village, where they crouched in the brush and hid. Eventually, figuring that the coast was clear, they decided to cook some food. But a scouting party spotted the smoke from the fire and charged at them. Saungm Furro had his bow and arrows for defense; he started shooting at the soldiers. Broteer, the other children and the women hid themselves in tall grass, but eventually they were captured.

Then the world stopped: the forend of a rifle, used as a club, smashed into Broteer's head. He felt a hand at his throat. Then there was a rope around his neck; he was tied to the women. His father had likewise been captured and bound. They were marched to the soldiers' camp.

The soldiers knew who Saungm Furro was, knew that he was the head of the village and that he had wealth. Much of that wealth was in animals, which they already had. But they knew he had gold. They wanted it.

When it had been a matter of turning over his animals in order to save the village, he had willingly done so. But something else was at stake now. This perhaps had to do with a Fulfulde word, *pulaaku*, which translates as "the Fulani way." It related to a code of conduct, the chief tenets of which were personal reserve, aloofness, strength, fortitude. Implicit in the code, which was instilled in Fulani during childhood, was a sense of shame that comes if a person violates behavioral standards. *Pulaaku* was a code of honor.

Saungm Furro refused to say where his treasure was hidden. The torture began. The son looked on. His father was a large and powerful man, six and a half feet tall according to the son's memory, but he had no power now—none but what came from maintaining his honor. The soldiers cut the man's body, pummeled him, demanded that he reveal his hiding place. In answer, he taunted them. The torture intensified. He refused to talk. As Broteer watched, transfixed, he may have thought of the Gumbala, the Fulani epic poem of courage, which was typically sung to the accompaniment of a single stringed instrument and women beating gourds on the ground:

> *Allah, for the sake of my mother's prayers*
> *Allah, for the sake of my father's fasts*
> *Do not slay me with a small and shameful death*
> *That of dying in bed.*

More than sixty years later, this moment in time was still with Broteer Furro. "The shocking scene is to this day fresh in my mind, and I have often been overcome while thinking on it," he said as an old man recounting the story in peaceful, smalltown Connecticut. Long after his father's death, in a place fantastically removed from the African savanna, after having lived a life he could not have imagined, he was able to distill what he took to be the central good about his father:

"He thus died without informing his enemies of the place where his money lay."

As he watched his father die, watched him be tortured, cut and stabbed and beaten to death rather than give up his wealth, Broteer absorbed the last and most vital lesson he would take from him. Your monetary worth, your honor, your identity as a man: the three things were all bound up together. They were, perhaps, one and the same.

For a boy growing up in Virginia planter country, there was also an honor code to be learned and followed. Curiously, the code that George Washington grew up with was much like that of Broteer Furro's people. A planter was the elite of Virginia society. The planter's code of honor had two components. The inward element was one's conscience: a confidence in the ability to choose right over wrong, not only for oneself but for others. Beyond that, a planter—a *gentleman*, serene and austere, literally high on his horse—had to exhibit the manners and skills that would win the approval of others and distinguish him as worthy of respect and status.

A proper education was elemental to becoming a planter. In his overall temperament, young George Washington, like George Sackville, was more doer than thinker. He was a big, sturdy boy, and when he could get away from nannying and from overseeing the family's ten slaves in farm chores—the sticky stripping and prizing of tobacco leaves, working wheat and corn fields—he liked to ride, to hunt, to fish, to revel in, as he said, "the trees and richness of the land," to wander from the hilltop homestead down to the languid banks of the Rappahannock for a swim. But at the same time he longed for the education he believed was his due. After his father's death, it became clear that George wouldn't be going to England as his half-brothers had.

But he was unusually determined, and at some point he decided he would piece together an education for himself. Though throughout his life he would feel keenly the lack of subjects that were considered the mark of true breeding, such as Latin and Greek, and he never learned French, the language of cultivated discourse, he threw himself, probably with the aid of a local teacher, into the study of mathematics, astronomy and geography, and began a lifelong fascination with maps and charting the world. And if he couldn't have the full substance of a gentleman's education, he was determined to get the form right. He got his hands on an abridgement of a book called *Youths Behaviour, or Decency in Conversations Amongst Men,* which was itself a translation of a French work published by the Jesuit order in about 1595. It became his bible, his guide to becoming a gentleman. In ten neat pages of flowing ink, he copied out 110 "rules of civility," which he would subsequently live by. They started with basic bodily manners that would set a gentleman apart from a commoner. "Spit not in the Fire." "If You Cough, Sneeze, Sigh, or Yawn, do it not Loud but Privately."

The contrast that had existed between his parents was sharp in his mind, and while his mother's behavior could be ill mannered to the point of embarrassment, he had learned from the gatherings his father had hosted that social dining was an arena in which gentlemen set themselves apart from others. Thus in his slightly wobbly hand the boy carefully recorded precepts such as: "Put not your meat to your Mouth with your Knife in your hand, neither Spit forth the Stones of any fruit Pye upon a Dish, nor Cast anything under the table."

A boy bent on following such rules would not only copy them but practice them, like an actor rehearsing for a role he intended to play for the rest of his life, traipsing, along with an imaginary "person of quality," from hall to parlor to back room. "In walking up and down in a house," he copied, "only with One in company, if he be Greater than yourself, at the first give him the Right hand, and Stop not till he does, and be not the first that turns, and when you do turn let it be with your face towards him. If he be a Man of Great Quality, walk not with him Cheek by Joul but somewhat behind him; but yet in Such a Manner that he may easily Speak to you."

The rules of civility helped the boy to mold a public persona, one guided by dignity, decorum and restraint: "Let your Countenance be pleasant but in Serious Matters Somewhat grave." "Shew not yourself glad at the Misfortune of another though he were your enemy."

He didn't have to go far to start strutting in society. From his house he could hear the horn blast signaling that the ferry across the Rappahannock River was about to depart. He boarded often. The Rappahannock crawled with boat traffic—from canoes to oceangoing vessels—and a mile north, on the opposite shore, sat the fast-growing town of Fredericksburg. Though the site of the town had been explored as far back as 1608—by Captain John Smith, a founder of Jamestown, the original English settlement in Virginia—it had only been incorporated in 1727. The streets George Washington frequented were rough, but they had regal associations: the planters were so eager to express their English identity that they had named all the main thoroughfares after members of the royal family.

Because of its location as a trading center and tobacco depot, Fredericksburg quickly burst its original boundaries. It was a shaggy place, and the government had to pass ordinances against erecting haphazard and highly dangerous structures such as wooden chimneys. Shipments were constantly being offloaded from the dock—from London, from Philadelphia, from Antigua and Barbados—and hauled noisily through the dusty roads: bushels of Indian corn, casks of beer, barrels of flour, firkins of butter, pipes of wine. Tobacco—sweet-smelling hogsheads—was everywhere. Farmers came rolling into town via horse- and oxen-drawn carts laden with it. Tobacco was currency: for every 1,000-pound hogshead, a planter received from one of the English merchants in town a tobacco note, which was used for credit against which he could buy whatever he needed. The rector of St. George's Church had his salary paid in tobacco.

The big event in Fredericksburg was the twice-yearly fair, where major buying and selling took place. But there were lots of other occasions for people to congregate: lesser fairs, balls, bonfires, election days, horse races. Many featured sideshow entertainment: puppet shows, cockfights, "roape dancings." George was often on the scene. He danced: jigs, cotillions, reels, minuets. Some events were refined, others raucous. There was music in the air, sung by locals but much of it imported from England. There were songs of love:

> *Phillis, lay aside your Thinking,*
> *Youth and Beauty should be Gay,*
> *Laugh and talk, and mind your Drinking:*
> *Whilst we pass the Time away....*

And songs of lewdness to make the farmers and backwoodsmen howl:

> *There is a Thing which in the light*
> *Is seldom used, but in the Night*
> *It serves the Maiden Female crew,*
> *The ladies and the good Wives too:*
> *They used to take it in their Hand,*
> *And then it will uprightly stand;*
> *And to a Hole they it apply,*
> *Where by it's good will it could Dye:*
> *It wastes, goes out, and still within,*
> *It leaves it's Moisture thick and thin....*

And there were romping songs in praise of England and her imperial army:

*The Britains through the Woods pursued*
*The nimble French to take;*
*And with their Cries the Hills and Dales*
*And every Tree did shake.*

George was keen for diversion, but he was also interested in observing, hoping eventually to climb the social ladder, to audition for a substantial role in society. Yet all the while, whether he was playing or studying, he seemed to have a hollowness inside him. Virginia planter society considered the father the ground of all things. George Washington lost his father at virtually the same age that Broteer Furro did. In both cases, the death left the son without a foundation. It was the kind of void one could spend a lifetime trying to fill.

⎯⟨∝⟩⎯

## Chapter 2

# A TIDE IN THE
# AFFAIRS OF MEN

It was June 1743, late in the millennium, but the sight that greeted George Sackville as he brought his horse to a halt was seemingly out of the Middle Ages. Tens of thousands of soldiers, packed into tidy regiments, with ensigns fluttering, ranged and outfitted by nationality—Hanoverian, Austrian, British—stretched for two miles along the northern bank of the Main River in Bavaria. Sixty yards away, on the opposite shore, and dressed all in glorious white, stood their enemy, the French. A rolling, gathering cheer sounded as the news spread through the allied columns that George II, king of England, had arrived. For the first time in generations, and for the last time in history, an English monarch would lead troops in battle.

Sackville was the king's personal attendant. Officially, he was a lieutenant colonel in the 28th Regiment of Foot, but he owed his special position not to rank and regiment but to family connections. From earliest childhood he had longed for a military career. When he was still in Dublin, acting as his father's secretary, he had signed on as a junior officer in the Irish establishment and was fitted for an officer's uniform. The War of Austrian Succession was on, an arcane European conflict, involving several subwars, at the center of which was a difference of

opinion about the succession to the Habsburg throne. More particularly it was an excuse for France and England to square off against
each other in their seemingly eternal struggle for dominance. The war
engulfed nearly all of Europe, and whatever it may have meant to ordinary Englishmen, for a young aristocrat eager to win personal glory, it
provided an array of possibilities.

He celebrated when his call to arms came. And it was no ordinary
call. He presented himself to a sixty-year-old man whose flaccid red
face was familiar to him not just from its likeness on shillings and half-
guineas but from long family association. The monarch's father, the first
King George, had been a family friend and George Sackville's godfather.

George II was not a bookish man, and not much interested in courtly
regalia. He preferred to be in the saddle, leading troops. Until now he
hadn't had the chance; thus the monarch and the young aristocrat were
both eager to prove themselves. The two of them, and hundreds of other
soldiers, as well as a long retinue of horses, carriages and hangers-on,
had made their ponderous way to the coast, boarded ships, and endured
the pitching waves of the English Channel.

On reaching the banks of the Main, King George took stock. Even
as he did, the French made their first move, cutting off the supply lines
of the allied English and German soldiers. The king was forced to
order a retreat. The long snake of the allied army made its way along the
north bank of the river. As it approached the village of Dettingen, word
came that the French had taken positions there. The king ordered his
army into position and prepared for a standoff. Then, to his surprise
and against military logic, the French line advanced out of the village
and toward the allies. There was confusion in the wake of this unorth-
odox move, but the king seized on what he saw as a tactical error and
ordered an attack. In the end, the allies won a victory so decisive, and
so special for it being led by a monarch, it was celebrated throughout
England. Georg Friedrich Handel, the court composer, wrote an ode

in honor of the battle. George Sackville distinguished himself amid the gore and mayhem. As a reward for his valor, he was made aide-de-camp to the king.

Throughout the following year Sackville was on the move with the army—Worms, Ostend, Bruges—gaining confidence and writing letters to his father filled with careful observations about the maneuvers being undertaken by both sides.

By now France was pushing into Dutch territory. In May 1745 more than 100,000 troops faced off on the Flemish plain near the city of Tournai. Serving under the king's son, the Duke of Cumberland, Sackville led a regiment on a murderous charge. They burst through the enemy line. At the height of the encounter, Sackville found himself flying into a curtain of enemy bullets.

And then he was done: physically thrust backward by an unseen force. Eventually, he realized that he had been shot in the chest. For him the battle was over. He was loaded onto a wagon with the rest of the wounded. The surgeon rooted around inside his body but couldn't pull the musket ball out; it would stay in him.

Back at the family townhouse in London, he rested. He had carried his uniform with him. He regarded the crisp hole in it as much an emblem of his service as the bullet that had caused it; he would treasure the possession for the rest of his life.

He was exhausted but not cowed—something like the opposite of it. His spirit had been energized by the vital act of sanctioned bloodshed, of war in service to king and country.

While Britain was allied with German states in opposing France on battlefields in Europe, throughout most of the 1740s it was simultaneously fighting Spain over control of parts of the Caribbean and South America. In 1743, as George Sackville was riding across the war-torn Low Countries in the retinue of the king, England's conflict with Spain reached George Washington's bucolic Virginia doorstep in the form of another resplendently outfitted officer: his brother. Lawrence and Augustine, his two older half-brothers, whom he hardly knew, had returned from overseas adventures around the time of Gus Washington's death. George, in his search for a substitute father, was particularly drawn to Lawrence.

Lawrence had seen action in the Caribbean and South America and was full of tales of war. The Battle of Cartagena, in which the British failed miserably but for which they mustered 186 ships and 12,000 soldiers, gave material enough—blasting cannons, heroic sallies, agonizing deaths—for Lawrence to fill the imagination of the boy. Lawrence Washington had a round face and a soft, bland expression, but to George he no doubt seemed fiercely impressive, fully grown and full of life and the world.

And then he was gone. He had inherited the rambling estate where George's family had previously lived, which they had called Little Hunting Creek Plantation, and was intent on making it his own. He renamed it in honor of his commanding officer at Cartagena, Admiral Edward Vernon. Henceforth, it would be known as Mount Vernon.

More or less from that moment, George's attention and interest shifted to Mount Vernon. As often as he could get away, he made the 40-mile trip north to his brother's house overlooking the Potomac River. Lawrence too was determined to move up in planter society, and he took a decisive step in that direction when, three months after their father's death, he married Ann Fairfax, daughter of one of the richest men in Virginia. The Fairfax family controlled 5.2 million acres of land, an area larger than the entire colony of Massachusetts. They were the drivers of Virginia society, and in marrying into their clan Lawrence Washington instantly fulfilled for himself the dream his father had worked toward his whole life.

George, on his visits to Mount Vernon, became a regular at Belvoir, the estate occupied by Colonel William Fairfax. It was laid out along the lines of a true English country manor. Here before him was all that he aspired to: pomp, dances, powdered wigs, embroidered waistcoats, silk shoes with silver buckles, low bows, the decorous scraping of bow on violin strings, painted cherubs on high. Not only were fine manners on display, he would have encountered at Belvoir a new room that was just coming into vogue, which was intended expressly and exclusively for eating meals. At home there was a room simply called the "hall," which could be used for eating, preparing meals, socializing or even sleeping. In the new "dining room," members of the social elite gathered at a long table to enjoy each other's company.

George became friends with the colonel's son, George William, an edgy, nervous, somewhat pompous young man who was eight years older. At the same time, he became positively smitten by George William's girlfriend, Sarah Cary, who went by Sally. He kept up a frankly flirtatious relationship with her even after she had become Mrs. Sally Fairfax. But his closest relationship was with the colonel himself. William Fairfax, fifty-two, was a capable man with broad experience of the world—he had served the British Empire as governor of the Bahamas then as tax collector in the port of Salem, Massachusetts—but he had a gentle spirit. His softness may have been due to the fact that, while his family had great power and influence going back more than a century, he himself was of a minor branch, and he lived in the shadow of his illustrious cousin, Lord Thomas Fairfax, the actual owner of the Fairfax patent. Colonel William Fairfax, for all his seeming power, was merely an agent administering his cousin's vast holdings in Virginia.

The colonel was charmed by the earnest, eager brother of his new son-in-law. He may have seen something of his young self in the boy. As a youth, he too had been trapped by circumstances: he had had powerful family ties but no promise of income, and his aristocratic titles meant he couldn't train for an ordinary job. He solved the problem by getting a commission in the Royal Navy. Now he proposed the same for his fourteen-year-old protégé. The colonel wrote the necessary letters, and George later said that he had his "baggage prepared for embarkation" onto a vessel, with a career as a British naval officer before him, but at the last minute his mother—who regularly blocked him from pursuing any activity that would keep him from helping her at home—scotched the plan.

Whereupon the colonel changed his strategy and focused on making up for the boy's lack of formal education. He gave him a history of England to read, so that George was able to develop some context: to comprehend the rise of the island nation, its growing dominion over much of the world and the role the American colonies played in the empire. Colonel Fairfax believed that a man of distinction should have ambition but not show it: he prided himself on his ability to wear a mask of inscrutability. His personal models were the ancient Romans, and he advised young George to read ancient writers, notably Julius Caesar's *Commentaries*, in which the ruler detailed nine years of waging war against the Gauls. Manliness, directness, steadfastness, boundless ambition hidden behind an emotionless visage: these were the virtues it extolled. During this time George also read novels, including Henry Fielding's *Tom Jones*—its theme of a boy trying to make his way in the world probably struck a nerve—but he seemed to take the Roman writers most closely to heart.

With Colonel Fairfax and Lawrence as his guides and models, George entered into a training regimen. Horse riding and dancing were among the chief means by which a man showed himself to be worthy of the status of a Virginia planter. He had always been a good rider, but now he undertook a serious study of the art of horsemanship and developed a true "planter's pace"—a regal, stiff-backed trot that would earn him lifelong admiration. Working under a dancing master, he also became expert at both formal dances and country jigs. He was growing into an excellent physical specimen—tall, muscular, long-limbed—and he learned to use his body to social advantage.

Outward appearance was also vital to achieving status, and George turned himself into a fastidious dresser. At age seventeen, he scribbled a note for a tailor that revealed a meticulousness and attention to detail—not to mention a self-regard—that was elemental to his nature:

Memorandum to have my Coat made by the following Directions. To be made: a Frock with a Lapel Breast, the Lapel to Contain on each side six Button Holes and to be about 5 or 6 Inches wide all the way equal and to turn as the Breast on the Coat does. To have it made very Long Waisted and in Length to come down to or below the Bent of the knee. The Waist from the armpit to the Fold to be exactly as long or Longer than from thence to the Bottom. Not to have more than one fold in the Skirt and the top to be made just to turn in, and three Button Holes. The Lapel at the top to turn as the Cape of the Coat and Bottom to Come Parrallel with the Button Holes. The Last Button hole in the Breast to be right opposite to the Button on the Hip.

There was, however, a serious impediment to his progress up the social ladder. He was, relatively speaking, painfully poor. For all his father's ambition, he had left behind little in terms of money or tangible goods. (The farm was a ramshackle place, and the inventory following his death showed that the pride of his estate, his "plate," amounted to a soup spoon, eighteen small spoons, seven teaspoons, a watch and a sword, together valued at a little over 21 pounds.)

Once again the Fairfax family provided a solution. Lord Fairfax wanted to sell off portions of his vast patent. In order for that to happen it first had to be divided into lots. That meant work for teams of surveyors.

With so much wild land in North America, surveying was a desirable and prestigious occupation, and one that would complement the ambitions of a planter. George's father had left a set of surveying equipment among his effects. George trained, practiced a bit at home, then set off with a small party into the wilderness of the Fairfax lands.

It was a month of fording icy streams, shooting at turkeys, roasting bits of meat on forked sticks over a campfire, sleeping on a "Thread Bear blanket with double its Weight of Vermin such as Lice Fleas &c.," and marching through heavy rains. For some the experience would have been misery. For him, it was a transformational adventure that simultaneously confirmed him for a life of ruggedness and bonded him with the American wilderness. At one point the group encountered thirty Indians who were themselves exhausted, having returned from a battle. George's party offered them liquor, which cheered them so much that they set to dancing. George took notes, which mixed anthropological observation with teenaged bemusement:

> They clear a Large Circle & make a great Fire in the Middle then seats themselves around it the Speaker makes a grand Speech telling them in what Manner they are to Daunce after he has finish'd the best Dauncer Jumps up as one awaked out of a Sleep & Runs & Jumps about the Ring in a most comicle Manner. He is followd by the Rest then begins there Musicians to Play. . . .

More surveying work followed. He was constantly traveling now: canoeing through seething currents, tramping up snowy mountainsides. The next year he was named the official surveyor of Culpeper County (the entirety of which fell within the Fairfax patent). His mother couldn't complain about his being away so much, for surveying was lucrative. And along the way he engaged in a profitable sideline: scoping out choice land and using his earnings to buy it for himself. In two years' time he purchased more than 2,000 acres.

He was not alone in seeking land. Owning acreage of the raw wilderness that stretched limitlessly westward amounted to a passion among Virginia's planter class. In 1748 his brothers and George Fairfax, the colonel's son, put themselves down as charter members of a new venture, the Ohio Company of Virginia, whose aim was to buy westward land, parcel it and begin to settle it. Lawrence Washington was named the company's president.

The Ohio Company promised unparalleled adventures, but before George was able to take part in any, Lawrence fell ill. After a period of violent coughing fits, his worst fears were realized when blood showed up in his handkerchief. People associated the symptoms of tuberculosis with imminent death. Prevailing medical wisdom held that tropical air was a possible cure. George desperately wanted to help, and he offered to accompany his brother on a trip to Barbados. After more than a month of violently pitching seas, they arrived on the Caribbean island. Despite the grave purpose of the trip, he couldn't help but feel "enraptured," as he wrote, at the bright, blistering sun and tropical vegetation. He ate wondrous new things—an "avagado pair" and a "Pine Apple"—and went to the theater for probably the first time in his life.

Soon after, however, he himself fell ill, with smallpox. He slowly recovered—the pox left scars on his nose that would stay for the rest of his life—but Lawrence did not. He managed to survive a return voyage to Mount Vernon, and died there, at age thirty-four.

George Washington had lost a second father figure. But overcome as he was with grief, his propulsive ambition compelled him to begin planning the next phase of his life even while tending to his brother in his last days. Lawrence had served as adjutant general in the Virginia militia: the highest military post in the colony and also a social office. He himself may have been the one to propose, from his deathbed, that George apply to take over the job.

George needed little persuading, and he does not seem to have been bothered that he had absolutely no military experience. He was soon logging miles on horseback, paying visits to influential men, lobbying for their support. He ended up being named adjutant of the Northern Neck district. It was mostly a ceremonial title, but he craved titles and recognition. Like his brother before him, like the Romans he had studied, he was now a military man.

While he was riding high on his success, he figured he would follow in Lawrence's footsteps in another way as well. He asked William Fauntleroy, a militia officer, member of Virginia's House of Burgesses and one of the colony's wealthiest and most aristocratic planters, if he could call on his sixteen-year-old daughter, Betsy. George was now twenty years old; simultaneously marrying and moving himself up another rank in society seemed a grand idea.

Mr. Fauntleroy—who traced his aristocratic lineage back to the time of William the Conquerer and who was wealthy enough to order a carriage in London made to his specifications and sporting his family's coat of arms—gave the young man a dose of reality when he rejected him as not being good enough for his daughter. George Washington may have been full of ambition, but, as all Virginia's better class knew, he was still a backwoods boy with a crazy mother.

Dukandarra was no more.

Turning away from the sight of his father's tortured corpse on the most fateful day of his life, Broteer Furro had to face the larger disaster that had befallen his people. The slave-hunting army had destroyed his village. Then, immediately after killing Broteer's father, the leader, a man named Baukurre, ordered his soldiers to move on. Their destination lay hundreds of miles away.

Broteer found himself attached to the advance party, which was to scout ahead of the main army. His captors must have noted that he was strong and smart, for he was given the job of assisting the party's leader, and was even tasked with carrying the man's gun. While still in the savanna—undulating grasslands and scrubby desert-like regions, punctuated by the occasional fat-trunked baobab tree—the scouts came upon a small settlement of herders. Broteer watched how efficiently they operated: sweeping in, corralling the inhabitants, cowing them into submission, then butchering the thirty or so cattle they found and processing them into food.

Later, Broteer's job changed. The army brought with it a millstone, which weighed upward of 25 pounds. The boy was made to carry it, along with other cooking supplies, as they hiked mile after mile in the heat and dust. Sixty-odd years later, he was still burdened with the pain caused by damage to his developing body.

On they went. The army denuded villages, capturing men, women and children and taking everything that could be eaten or sold.

Then the nature of the march changed. There came a long, grueling stretch, perhaps hundreds of miles of merciless plodding. They had presumably miscalculated the distance, or else assumed there would be more villages to plunder on the last stretch of the journey. The soldiers as well as their captured slaves were ground down. At last, weakened and thinned in numbers, the army staggered into their destination: the town of Anomabo, and the coast.

Immediately on entering Anomabo they found themselves under sudden, sustained attack. Rather than let the inland warriors bring their prisoners into the town and trade them, the locals had an army of their own ready to strike. What Broteer evidently became caught up in was the West African practice of panyarring—"man-stealing." It meant taking something or someone by force as repayment of a debt. The people of Anomabo, which was part of an alliance of Fante tribes along the coast, apparently believed that the interior tribe that had come to sell slaves had done them wrong in the past.

The depleted army that had taken Broteer from his home collapsed under the attack. The slaves, now in the hands of new captors, were marched down from the main coastal road. For Broteer, who had been raised on the sparsely populated savanna, the hike through town must have been a wonder, even amid the confusion. Anomabo was a center of the slaving industry on the coast, with a polyglot population from a jumble of tribes—Mossi, Grunshi, Mamprusi, Asante—as well as white men of different nations, dressed in all manner of garb, haggling or being haggled over under the relentless sun. It was a wild place, like port towns all around the Atlantic Rim, alive with whoring, drinking and gambling, but it had its own order. A religious shrine set in a sacred grove in the neighboring town of Mankessim, the spiritual center of the coast, provided a social foundation. Besides priests, farmers, fishermen and traders, Anomabo had specialized workers who serviced the slave industry: canoemen, haulers, interpreters, cooks, middlemen and brokers. And the town had its own slaves.

At the bottom of the hill lay the ramshackle cluster of the fishing village, stinking of rotting fish, huddled around the shallow scallop of the bay, with dugout canoes fanned out along the beach. Here too was the most surreal and alien of sights for a boy from the interior: the sea.

On the beach and jutting from the shallow water were the clusters of rock from which the place got its name: Anomabo meant "bird rocks." It had been a tiny fishing village until the 1500s. As Europeans began their age of exploration, Portuguese traders showed up looking for gold. The town and others like it along the water rose not on the slave trade, but as a trading post for gold that was mined in the interior, thus earning the name the Gold Coast. In time, the Dutch broke down the Portuguese monopoly; then Swedish, Danish, French and English ships muscled in. The Europeans built their forts along the coast, for which they paid rent to the regional kingdom. At Anomabo the leaders became especially sophisticated at managing the trade. They let the English build a fort, but refused to allow them a monopoly. Instead they encouraged ships of different nations to anchor and do business in the harbor—"boat trade," it was called—so that the town's leaders could play the Europeans off against one another.

Then in the late 1600s the gold trade fell off at the same time that Europeans were expanding their colonies and looking for slaves to work them. In the early 1700s the Akan kingdoms in the interior began their series of wars, resulting in masses of displaced people who could be turned into slaves. The Fante coastal trading towns retooled to meet the new need. But slavery was a dangerous business, so they merged into a coalition, united by the opportunity and by their common ethnic identity.

As he was being marched down to Anomabo's waterfront, Broteer was seeing the slave trade at nearly its height. He was part of a humming, seething industry, employing thousands, processing millions.

Since the leaders of the town had not given the English a monopoly on slaving, the English had let their fort fall into decay. But it still dominated the waterfront, and was probably the largest structure Broteer had ever seen, with man-made walls as high as cliffs. Derelict though it was, it was good enough to house slaves.

Slaves were packed together in small cave-like cells, with a small hole in the roof through which captors poured food and water. Inside it was dank and terrifyingly dark. Once a day the slaves were marched outside to be aired. On such occasions Broteer may have been able to see, in the harbor, a newly-arrived ship. She had sailed more than 4,300 nautical miles from her home port of Newport, Rhode Island.

Her captain, James Collingwood, after having been rowed ashore and making his way past the fort, had a ten-minute walk from the fishing village to the upper town, where the important people lived. He was probably drunk: European slavers usually were. It was a way to deal with the constant fear and anxiety, for they knew it was only a matter of time before yellow fever, malaria, tuberculosis or dysentery struck, and there was the perpetual danger of negotiations turning violent. They wanted to make their deal and get out.

When the town had shifted its trade from gold to the more dangerous business of dealing in slaves, its traditional rulers had been pushed aside by a new breed of strongmen. The leader of the town now, the man to whom ships' captains headed, was Eno Baisie Kurentsi, known to European traders as John Currantee. He was about fifty years old, and was feared by locals and Europeans alike. In time he would become exalted enough that his son would be a presence in London, where he would meet King George II and be dubbed the "Royal African." Collingwood likely found him in his bathtub, the perch from which he preferred to handle affairs, sipping rum and smoking a pipe so long its head sat on the ground. Bargaining took place in a hybrid language that contained elements of Portuguese—"black Portuguese," traders called it.

Kurentsi wasn't alone in representing Anomabo. Selling slaves was a complicated business, which involved priests from the local shrine, town elders, and prominent traders. The leaders of Anomabo sometimes wanted payment in guns and gunpowder, but their demands and desires changed frequently, and since they were the ones in charge, the Europeans were constantly at pains to please them. A leader like Kurentsi might suddenly insist on tallow, or brandy, or copper rods, in exchange for slaves. A European slave ship thus left its home port with its hold stocked like a warehouse, with cases of Turkish rugs, Dutch cotton sheets, chintz, brass kettles, fish hooks, bells, locks, pots, pans, boxes of scales and weights, quart tankards, slope-pointed knives, as well as hundreds of gallons of liquor and chests of cutlasses and firearms. The captain had to hope that the leaders of the port city wanted at least some of the items in his floating department store. A trader named John Atkins expressed exasperation that at none of the Gold Coast ports where he put in were the "many considerable Articles of my Invoyce ever asked for," and he ended his voyage with a net loss. James Collingwood had better luck. He ended his negotiations by purchasing 87 slaves.

Broteer remained in the pen with the other slaves until Collingwood arranged for provisioning. Eventually, he was hustled down to the beach and into a dugout canoe. Then came a flash of fright on experiencing for the first time in his life the imponderable force of the pitching waves. As the canoe reached the side of the ship, if he heard its name pronounced by one of the crew the incongruity of its meaning would have been lost on him; it would have sounded as forbidding as any cluster of incomprehensible syllables could: the *Charming Susanna*. Up the side the slaves went, then down onto the hard planks of the deck, the nostril-sting of pine tar cutting through the salty tang of the air.

Then came some new confusion: shouts and laughter. Something was going on—whatever was happening to Broteer, he was being treated differently from the other slaves that were herded onboard. Later he was able to piece it together. The young man who was suddenly at his side—the ship's steward; Robinson Mumford was his name—had struck a deal with Captain Collingwood. He liked the look of this boy, and bought him for his own use. He didn't pay cash but instead handed over the trade goods he had brought on board: four gallons of rum and a piece of calico fabric. Then a thought struck him. An old term for personal cargo was still in use in the eighteenth century; Shakespeare had employed it in *Julius Caesar*, in a nautically themed passage as weighted with despair as the boy must have now felt:

*There is a tide in the affairs of men,*
*Which, taken at the flood, leads on to fortune . . .*
*On such a full sea are we now afloat,*
*And we must take the current when it serves,*
*Or lose our ventures.*

Venture: that's what Robinson Mumford had given up for the boy. On the spot he decided that that was what he would call him.

## Chapter 3

# THE TURTLE'S BACK

B efore there was the world, there was the Sky World. It was a place of trees and flowers and animals and people, but the source of light and energy was not the sun but rather a Tree of Light, whose flowers glowed. In one of the houses of the Sky World, together with their families, there lived a boy and girl. One day the girl combed the boy's hair, and as a result she became pregnant. Shortly after, the boy died. It was decided that the girl, Mature Blossom, would marry Standing Tree, the chief of the Sky World, who was the keeper of the Tree of Light. After the marriage, Standing Tree became suspicious about her pregnancy and had a dark dream. The dream's message was that the Tree of Light was to be uprooted. With sadness, the people of Sky World followed the dream's command and pulled up the Tree of Light. Standing Tree and his wife then sat at the edge of the hole where the tree had been. As Mature Blossom peered down to see what was below, her jealous husband suddenly pushed her into the hole.

Sky Woman—as she was known henceforth—fell through space toward the primal sea. Birds swooped in, grasped her, and guided her down onto a turtle's back. Ducks and other creatures helped her by getting mud from the bottom and plastering it to the turtle's shell, creating land. As Sky Woman walked on the land, plants and trees sprang up around her. Eventually, Sky Woman gave birth to a girl. One day when her daughter was grown, the west wind blew into the girl and she became pregnant. She gave birth to twin boys. Sky Holder was a child of order; his brother, Flint, of chaos. The mother died while giving birth to Flint, so Sky Woman, their grandmother, raised the twins. Sky Woman favored Flint and cast Sky Holder out to fend for himself. Sky Holder set off to walk the earth in search of his father. Along the way he learned to hunt, to grow crops, to make fire. Sky Holder and Flint engaged in ongoing conflict. More people appeared; moral complexity—duplicity, revenge—crept into the world.

Over the course of centuries, the story of Sky Woman and her creation was woven and rewoven. Variations and digressions blossomed. Each nation of the Iroquois league—the Mohawk, Onondaga, Oneida, Cayuga, Seneca and Tuscarora—favored its own version. Children sat by firelight in their smoky longhouses and listened to it unfold over many nights. Elements of the world they knew—the turtle, the wolf, medicine from forest herbs, techniques for growing corn, centuries of accumulated wisdom and tradition—appeared in the story and had their significance ratified.

The Senecas were the westernmost of the six Iroquois nations. The wooded landscape they lived in rolled on and on, demarcated by rivers, by gorges—stratified rock walls, plunging waterfalls—and by long, deep, cold lakes. The whole terrain baked in the summer heat and in winter filled up high as a man's head with snow. Home for some was Gen-nis'-hee-yo: Genesee, "this beautiful valley," with its river running through it, the river mirroring the world, holding on its surface the clouds, the limbs of fallen trees, the visiting moon.

A boy was born here, sometime in the 1740s, in a longhouse framed by log posts and covered in elm bark. The longhouses had sleeping platforms built against the posts and hearths spaced at regular intervals down the center aisle. A group of such houses constituted the village, named Conawaugus. There was a sulfur spring nearby, and that's what the name meant: stinking water.

His mother was called Gah-hon-no-neh. Mothers are always vital to their children, but in the case of the Iroquois a mother was something more. They were a matrilineal society, so Gah-hon-no-neh's group, the Wolf Clan, would become central to her son's identity. A clan was divided into "lineages," extended family groups, and Gah-hon-no-neh was a "lineage matron." It was a title of authority, for among the Iroquois these women made decisions that affected the whole community. Among other things, they chose the men who would lead. Unless there was a reason not to, a lineage matron often chose her son.

We don't know what Gah-hon-no-neh called her son at birth. Senecas typically had two names: the childhood one was exchanged for another in adulthood. As an adult, he was called Kayéthwahkeh. Iroquois names did not necessarily have referents in the physical world, but as the Iroquois came to realize that Europeans expected a translation, they did their best to connect elements in a name to the physical world. "Kayéthwahkeh" had to do with planting; in adulthood, he would become known among the English as Cornplanter.

The child didn't look quite like other people in the village. Boys, he later said, "took notice of my skin being a different color from theirs, and spoke about it." His father was a white man named John Abeel, who was largely absent from his upbringing but was well known in Seneca villages. He was an itinerant trader who roamed far from his home base near Albany, New York, to service Indians, typically trading rum for furs. He wasn't much liked. Some Senecas accused him of cheating them. Alcohol abuse was a perennial problem, and the Iroquois associated him with it even as many of them traded with him for it. Among his own people in Albany, meanwhile, John Abeel's reputation was, if anything, worse. Sir William Johnson, England's Superintendent of Indian

Affairs, referred to him as "that incorrigible villian [*sic*]," complained that he "constantly carried great quantitys of Rum to the Senecas Country Contrary to Law, & in open defiance of all authority," and repeatedly tried to rein him in.

Abeel's ancestor had come to America two centuries earlier from Amsterdam to be part of the Dutch colony of New Netherland. Its capital, New Amsterdam, was on Manhattan Island, but the Abeels had settled to the north, in the city that, after the English took over, became Albany. They prospered; one became a city magistrate, another became mayor. John Abeel, however, was the black sheep: he would show up repeatedly in city records for violent, drunken behavior, not only toward Indians, but also toward members of his own family.

Still, Abeel had features that might have made him appealing to a Seneca woman. He knew the woods as well as an Indian, spoke their language, knew how to talk and listen and work angles. Gah-hon-no-neh would not have been ostracized by her people for taking up for a time with the white trader. Among the Iroquois the sexes had an equality that was unfathomable to Europeans. Men and women each had their prescribed duties; beyond these, both were largely able to do what they wanted. And because they were a matrilineal society, who the boy's father was mattered less than who his mother was. Culturally, Cornplanter was one of them.

As Cornplanter grew, the world of the Senecas came into focus for him. Generations before, they had grouped themselves in cities whose inhabitants numbered in the thousands, built on high, defensible ground, but in recent times they had changed their settlement patterns. Now there were many small villages like his, with populations numbering only in the dozens, scattered up and down the Genesee River, ending at Lake Ontario to the north, as well as others farther east. Typically, these were a day's walk apart. Some of the clusters of multifamily longhouses and smaller two-family cabins were on hilltops, others close to the river. In some the houses were grouped around a central green. All had cornfields on the outskirts, as well as plots for beans and squash. There were dogs underfoot. The Senecas kept pigs and chickens, and some kept cattle and horses, and grew hay to feed the animals. The feel of a Seneca village was domestic, settled, agricultural.

Beyond the village, children learned the tribal territory and customs by seasonally exploring with their families. In March, family groups fanned out and spent weeks in the forest, covering sometimes dozens of miles by foot to reach clusters of maple trees to which they had traditional rights, which they tapped for sap. Back home, while the women boiled the sap into sugar, the boys learned the river, spearfishing with the men. Later in the spring, passenger pigeons descended on the forests. The birds, which would later be hunted into extinction, were at the time of Cornplanter's childhood so numerous that a European observer witnessed a single flock that "extended 3 or 4 English miles in length, and more than one such mile in breadth, and they flew so closely together that the sky and the sun were obscured by them." The pigeons roosted in their favorite trees, which became so laden that the sound of branches snapping under their weight echoed through the forest. Hunting passenger pigeons was an activity that occupied the whole family.

Summer was a time to be at home: women tended crops, children played. Then came fall, and the main hunting season. A family traveled as a group in a canoe to a favored spot, where they erected a makeshift cabin. From here, the man marched off in search of game. When he killed a deer, he would skin it on the spot, hang the carcass from a tree and mark the place. It was the woman's job to come after and haul the meat back.

All of these activities revolved around the father. But Cornplanter's father might as well have been dead, as Broteer Furro's and George Washington's were. It is likely, though, that his mother married after she was done with John Abeel, for she had a daughter who was born after Cornplanter, and then another son.

Seneca children also learned about their world through stories. Winter evenings especially were times for storytelling. Besides the tale of creation, the other elemental story that unfolded on special occasions was that of the forming of the Iroquois league. In the distant past, it held, the Mohawk, Onondaga, Oneida, Cayuga and Seneca nations, all of which spoke interrelated languages, warred with each other until three leaders brought them together. Two chiefs, Deganawidah, the Peacemaker, and Hiawatha, his disciple, devised a plan for unity, called the Great Law of Peace. Hiawatha preached this gospel of unity to members of the five tribes, convinced them of its wisdom, offered a name for the confederacy—Haudenosaunee, "People of the Long-house" (though Europeans would refer to them by the French-coined name "Iroquois")—then sailed off in a mystical "white stone" canoe. The third leader, Jikonsaseh, the Peace Mother, provided the hearth where the peace was made, and insured that the new league recognized the rights of women. Not long before the time of Cornplanter's birth, a sixth nation, the Tuscarora, became part of the league.

By the time of Cornplanter's childhood, the league had developed an ornate system for settling disputes and making important decisions, which involved a great deal of travel by extended family groups and highly ritualized meetings headed by the fifty chiefs who formed its hereditary council, with lengthy speeches and replies and the giving of wampum belts to symbolize what had been agreed.

The territories of the six nations were ranged between the Hudson River and the Great Lakes. The Mohawks were the easternmost nation, and thus the one closest to European settlement. Because of this, they had long since altered their way of life. Their traditional hunting-and-gathering routines were constrained by English and Dutch settlers having claimed much of the territory. They had taken to living in log cabins and were pushed to make other changes by England's agents for Indian affairs and by American missionaries. But the Senecas, at the far western edge of Iroquois territory, still lived according to their own rhythms. The Senecas also had the largest territory of the six nations and were the most populous. The populations of all the Iroquois had fallen dramatically in the previous century as a result of war and of diseases brought by Europeans for which they had no immunity, but by Cornplanter's time the numbers were back up to where they had once been. The overall population was small, though: about 4,000 Senecas lived spread out over several thousand square miles. They were a people in flux—and yet this was a relatively stable time.

In many ways, the individual villages were more important than the tribe or the league. A village was self-sustaining; each did its own trading with Europeans, making deals with the English or French depending on circumstances and on who had a better offer. In the balance of power with the Europeans, the Senecas had the upper hand. They got what they wanted out of the relationship: clothing and textiles, nails, copper, pots, guns, bullets, rum. Sometimes, as a bonus or incentive to trade, the English or French would send a small party of blacksmiths to set up a forge and live near a Seneca village to make and repair metal tools. The villages communicated with each other over an intricate series of paths that they kept cleared, and sometimes via canoe. Iroquois communication was a source of amazement to white settlers, who noted that a trained messenger could cover 100 miles a day on foot. And the pathways seemingly went on forever. The Iroquois interacted with far-flung tribes—Ojibwas, Miamis, Wyandots, Illinois, Catawbas, Cherokees, Chickasaws—and traveled, traded and made war deep into Canada, as far south as the Carolinas and as far west as the Mississippi River. The Senecas knew where they were in the world.

As the boy Cornplanter grew up in the Seneca world, a particular trait emerged in him. He was not only smart but unusually sensitive to nuance, appreciative of complexity, such as was found in the labyrinth of the Seneca creation story. He was deliberative and measured, able to hold conflicting ideas in his head. And he had a frankness of expression that went with these qualities: a square, solid face, and deep eyes that seemed both penetrating and pondering.

At the same time, he was not only an excellent fighter but a ferocious one. As in European civilization, war was a means to personal glory and power, but Iroquois warfare had an additional element: it was an antidote to suffering, a way of maintaining psychological balance. When someone in the village died and the loved ones were plunged into grief, a woman from the aggrieved family would order the men to attack an enemy tribe. It was not necessarily a matter of retribution. The idea was to redress the imbalance the death had caused, to deal with the loss either by killing an outsider or by taking one prisoner and forcing the outsider to take the place of the loved one. If the victim was to be killed, his ordeal began with torture—and everyone took part, with the oldest women leading the way by pulling out the victim's fingernails. If the victim was to be adopted into the tribe, the ritualistic adoption likewise involved initiation by torture. The torture was considered to be for the captive's benefit: one who survived it with bravery won esteem. After the ordeal, the former enemy was "dead," and the new person was welcomed into the tribe with soothing words and the dressing of wounds.

Violence, therefore, was a sacred act. Particularly for a boy such as Cornplanter, who as the son of a powerful mother was destined for leadership, becoming adept at it was a part of growing up.

Two hundred and forty miles east of Cornplanter's village, on the banks of the Hudson River in the town of Albany, New York, another family was making its way in the world, following its own traditions and rhythms. Theirs was a humble home, for Christoffel Yates, the father and provider, was a blacksmith, a man of modest means. But the household was boisterous, for Christoffel and his wife Catalina had no fewer than eight children. The routine uproar was interrupted one summer day in 1724 by a period of hushed expectancy followed by the cries of a newborn as Catalina gave birth to her ninth child. They called him Abraham.

Abraham Yates grew up without frills or advantages, but he was ferociously inquisitive and quickly learned his world. The river, broad and ever-changing in its moods, dominated the town. Near his home was a wide common pasture where everyone's cows ranged in one large herd. Most of Albany's three hundred houses had a garden, a well and a tree in front; they spread along the western shore of the river and up the hillside that sloped away from it. Technically it was an English town, of course, part of the British province of New York. It was also in a sense an Iroquois town; the boy got used to seeing Mohawk Indians coming and going, for Albany was the center for trade with the Iroquois and, as a service to keep the Indians happy, blacksmiths like his father repaired their tools and guns free of charge.

Most of all, though, Albany was Dutch: its roots in the Dutch colony of New Netherland were apparent everywhere. Houses had gables; fireplaces were surrounded by blue-and-white Delft tiles. Many households were bilingual. Yates's was one of these, for, like Cornplanter, he had Dutch ancestry. Dutch women of the region like his mother kept up traditions passed down from their mothers and grandmothers. They served butter chicken, pickled herring and cole slaw, and made "koekjes" (the origin of the American "cookies") for their children. The Dutch festival of St. Nicholas, when children received presents on December 6, was a more substantial holiday than Christmas.

Being the ninth child of a blacksmith did not exactly position one for greatness. Abraham couldn't even take up his father's trade; his four older brothers filled the available spots at the Yates forge at the southern edge of town. So he was shunted into an even humbler trade: shoe-maker. The apprenticeship was long—typically four to seven years—but Abraham was industrious by nature, so he did his time and eventually went into business for himself.

Yates kept his account books in English and Dutch, depending on the customer's preferred language. It was his practice to go over an entry with the client. So to the family of Jacob Gerritse van Schaick, who lived in the farming community of Half Moon farther along the Hudson River, he wrote that he sold "Een paar schoenen voor je kind" ("one pair of shoes for your child") and a pair of men's shoes. He did good work, and his clients came back to him repeatedly.

But it was a plodding, low-profit business, and as time went by, Abraham Yates chafed. He was in his twenties now. He was smart and he knew it. He wanted more out of life.

He was a keen follower of local affairs, and early in life he developed a chip on his shoulder, a sharp sensitivity to injustice. He itched to get into politics. But that was almost impossible. Throughout the American colonies politics was a gentleman's business: you were supposed to be of a certain class to run for office. The roots of the local political structure went all the way back to the city's beginnings as the Dutch town of Beverwijck. In the New Netherland period, New Amsterdam, on Manhattan Island, was the polyglot, relatively urbane capital, while in Beverwijck—150 miles north in the brooding wilderness—life was more basic and society was more uniformly Dutch. Everything revolved around the fur trade, which came to be dominated by a few families.

Those same families still ran things in Yates's time. The power monopoly was graphically arrayed for him every Sunday. When he walked through the doors of the Dutch Reformed Church at the intersection of State Street and Broadway he was not free to choose a seat in front but had to walk up into the balcony, where the slaves also sat. Below, the town's rulers—the Schuylers, De Peysters, Van Rensselaers,

Cuylers and Livingstons—spread themselves before him like the powerful pieces on a chess board. Seating was segregated by sex as well as power. In winter, the women of these families had braziers at their feet, fed with coals by their slaves from the church's stove. The men occupied the important church offices and sat in high benches along the walls near the front; their seats were passed down from one generation to the next.

Political offices in Albany were divided up among the same families. At the age of twenty-two, Yates made his first effort at wedging himself into this political monopoly, taking a step that was considered appropriate to his class. His father had served as constable for the second ward; Abraham ran for the same office, and won. It was the smallest of political jobs, and unpaid, but it was a start.

His next upward step involved making repeated rides on horseback 15 miles north, following the course of the Hudson River. At meadow breaks he had views across to the line of mountains, tawny or gray depending on the sunlight, that signaled what any enterprising young man knew was the future: the west. Cutting eastward then, he entered deep forest. This wilderness was different from the one that George Washington knew. That was a lusher, more southerly forest, of buckeyes and sweetbays and water tupelos. Here, 400 miles to the north, the woods had a harsher aspect; it was a landscape that cracked with cold in winter. Young Abraham Yates traveled past Dutch farms and settlements, past the falls at Cohoes, where the Mohawk River spilled down into the Hudson.

His destination was a little agricultural crossroads called Schaghticoke. A wealthy farmer named Cornelis de Ridder lived here with his second wife, Gerritje. Abraham had his eye on the farmer's daughter, Anna, who was also called by the Dutch diminutive Antje. He would have presented the idea of marriage to the girl's father as a quasi business proposition. What he brought was intelligence and ambition.

De Ridder offered as dowry a parcel of land he owned in Albany, together with a house. Abraham and Anna were married in the little log structure of the Dutch Reformed Church in Schaghticoke. Then Abraham brought her back to Albany.

Now that he was set up with a wife and a home, he prepared to make a bolder move into politics. Things were changing. The fur trade, the power base of the town's mighty families, was diminishing; at the same time, the wider region was growing and the city was becoming a center for tradesmen and craftsmen like him: coopers, tanners, masons and tinsmiths, who came from New York City and as far away as Europe.

Yates expanded his client base, selling shoes to the families of these newcomers. At the same time he saw an opportunity to take advantage of the growing consumer base by diversifying; he began selling products from the Caribbean islands—rum, sugar, molasses—and later added others, such as tea, wine and writing paper.

But the more rooted he became in his city's economic life, the more Yates came to resent its leading families, who had written laws to favor their own business. Slowly, however, it dawned on him that the influx of newcomers gave him the opening he had been looking for. They weren't bound by the old ways of the city. They had no inbred awe or special regard for the elite families of Albany. In September 1753 he made his break with convention: he decided to run for an office that had power. Assistant alderman for the third ward was a low post on the city council, but it would involve him in the governing of the city. His novel strategy was to appeal directly to voters (free white property-owning males over the age of twenty-one), and to focus on those at the lower end: a sawmaker named John Price; Thomas Sharp, who was a barber; the tailor, Jellis Winne; tavernkeeper Edward Williams; Indian trader Samuel Pruyn. He tramped into homes and workshops, stirring people up by telling them it was time they took charge of their affairs, time they elected one of their own. He liked to say he stood for "the rights of the people," which sounded vaguely dangerous but also exciting. He also liked to say he represented not the elites but the "middle sort." Abraham Yates—the shoemaker, the blacksmith's son—had by now spent years cultivating such people, building their trust. He won.

For the sick, life consisted of fever, vomiting, blisters, lethargy and eventual death. For the well, a steady diet of "slauber sauce," which tasted as it sounded. For everyone there was misery, violence and the ceaseless undulation of the waves.

Abraham Yates was still a teenager learning the shoemaker's craft when Venture, who was about three years younger than Yates, left Africa and crossed the Atlantic Ocean. As an old man looking back, he described his experience on a slave ship with grim economy: "An ordinary passage, except great mortality by the small pox." If Captain Collingwood followed the procedure used aboard other slave ships, he would have begun the ordeal by having the male slaves stand in shackles on the deck as they weighed anchor at Anomabo, keeping them bound securely while giving them a chance to absorb the reality that they were leaving all they had ever known, on the theory that the shock and despair would render them pliable. Then they would be taken down to the hold, where they spent much of the voyage shackled in suffocating darkness.

Which is not to say that the European captors had no care for the welfare of the Africans. The financial success of the voyage depended on keeping them alive and reasonably healthy. But of course people sickened and died anyway. The menu of available diseases contained many options: dysentery ("the flux"), tuberculosis ("consumption"), yellow fever, yaws and, in the case of the *Charming Susanna*, smallpox. Of the 87 slaves Captain Collingwood bought at Anomabo, 13 died on the crossing.

Disease was one regular feature of a slave voyage. Violence and confusion were others. The mix of people from different tribes meant communication among the captives was difficult. They separated by language. One or more groups typically tried to launch an insurrection. Slaves would surreptitiously break out of their manacles and pass chisels or marlin spikes to one another to use as weapons. Crews employed violence and intimidation strategies, such as mounted guns aimed into the slave quarters. An experienced officer—such as Thomas Mumford, the first mate of the *Charming Susanna,* who was the cousin of the man who had bought Venture—would select a few slaves to be "guardians," who were assigned to watch the other captives.

Somehow the boy negotiated the intricacies of the floating system of violence and control as it made its way across the ocean. The ship reached its first port of call, the Caribbean island of Barbados, two months after leaving Anomabo. George Washington, on his own arrival at the same island in his effort to find treatment for his brother's tuberculosis, would note drinking tea with the local gentry, riding "in the cool of the evening," and being "perfectly enraptured with the beautiful prospects, which every side presented to our view,—the fields of cane, corn, fruit-trees, &c. in a delightful green." He did not mention the presence of 40,000 slaves who worked those fields. Barbados was a main port of call for slavers, for it was a center of the British sugar industry, the source not only of the "white gold" to which Europeans were by now happily addicted but also rum, the principal hard liquor of the time, and molasses—a true staple, which was used in everything from beer to medicine to Boston baked beans.

The attractive landscape was in perfect contrast to the work conditions, for sugar cane was brutally hard to plant, tend, harvest and process, and the slave code gave the English overlords who owned the island's individual estates near-absolute control over their slaves. The industry was as lucrative as it was brutal—Britain's Caribbean plantations brought in far more income than did North America, and over the century Barbados alone had almost as many slaves working its fields as were shipped to the thirteen colonies. Of the 74 slaves aboard the *Charming Susanna* that survived the voyage, 70 disembarked to spend the rest of their lives working the Barbados sugar fields.

But Venture was spared that nightmare. Because he was already the property of the steward of the *Charming Susanna*, he watched the cane fields slip from view as the ship sailed back out of the harbor. When it entered its home port of Newport, Rhode Island, on August 23, 1739, 321 days after it had departed, a new life began.

Robinson Mumford delivered him first into the keeping of his sister Mercy, in Newport, so that the boy could learn some English and begin to comprehend the alien entity that was American society. The Mumford family had wealth, and so did the town. Newport was one of the four or five busiest ports in North America, with more than a hundred wharves and a harbor thick with sailing vessels. Much of the industry was due, directly or not, to slavery. Newport outfitted more slaving ships than any other city in the thirteen mainland colonies.

Fashions on the street reflected the city's mixed society, which had heavy concentrations of sailors, Quakers (dourly dressed moralists, already calling for the abolition of slavery, to no avail), Portuguese Jews, and an African slave presence that totaled about 10 percent of the city's population. Venture took in the cityscape and processed the functioning of a well-to-do New England family's house and all that went with it: porcelain teacups, silk handkerchiefs, paintings and mirrors on walls, and the noisy and beguiling wooden box that governed life, the hall clock. Learning English was synonymous with learning the nouns and verbs of service. Water, pot, hearth, boil. Wood, ax, chop, haul. Privy, night soil, shovel. Autumn was coming on; a chilly and unfamiliar wind was whipping the sails in the harbor. Venture noted everything, but kept his head down and worked.

Eventually, Robinson Mumford came to collect the boy to bring him to his father's estate, on Fishers Island, between the Connecticut coast and the tip of Long Island. Mercy would have confirmed things he had already surmised from the ocean voyage. Venture was smart. He learned fast. He worked hard. He seemed trustworthy. Robinson was himself a young man, barely twenty-one, and had some innocence, at least compared to the other men in his family, who were veteran slavers. He seems to have developed a fondness for Venture, a desire to trust him.

Trustworthiness was indeed a part of the code of honor that Venture had inherited, and at this point an incident occurred that the boy saw as a test of his character. He traveled with Mumford by ship westward from Newport and put in at Narragansett. Here, Mumford, apparently having an appointment on the mainland, decided that he would go by road westward and Venture would continue on to Fishers Island with the ship. Also onboard was Mumford's father, George, who was himself a ship's captain. Before he left, Robinson Mumford handed the boy a set of keys, telling him they were to his private trunks and that he was to keep the keys in his possession at all times and not let anyone open the trunks. He made a point of mentioning his father in particular.

The ship put in at Fishers Island. Venture unloaded his master's belongings, and Mumford's father promptly ordered him to hand over the keys to the trunks. Venture said that his master had told him to give the keys to no one until he returned. "I had given him my word to be faithful to the trust," he said later. The father got aggressive, threatened to punish him. But the boy refused, with enough conviction that the man went away. Still, Venture felt uneasy, and fashioned the keys on a chain around his neck. At night he took the precaution of sleeping with them under his body.

Robinson Mumford's first act on arriving home was to ask for Venture. The boy heard, appeared in the room, and said, in his newly minted English, "Here, sir, at your service." Mumford asked for the keys. Venture took them off his neck and handed them over. Mumford petted the boy's hair as he took the keys, and, as if guessing what had transpired, opined to his father that young Venture was "so faithful" that no one could have gotten the keys from him except by superior strength. During the ocean voyage Venture must have told his owner something of his life in Dukandarra, for Mumford went on to say that he believed he could trust the boy with his whole fortune, since "he had been in his native place so habituated to keeping his word, that he would sacrifice even his life to maintain it."

Venture settled into life on Fishers Island. The island was seven miles long, skinny, craggy and covey, wooded sections alternating with pastureland. Especially in winter, it was an isolated, windswept place to come of age. But he made one friend. His owner's youngest sister, Rebecca, was fifteen years old. There were no other white families on the island, no one for her to play with. Venture, who was about five years younger, bonded with her. She improved his English and became the closest thing he had to family.

In time, Venture came to realize that he was closer to his home-land than he had thought. Fishers Island lay two miles from the New England shore, but its recent history, like that of the Mumford family and the entire surrounding region, was intimately tied to West Africa, slavery, the Caribbean, sugar and rum. Rich soil and a seafaring tradi-tion resulted in the development of plantations in southern Connecticut and Rhode Island, as well as the nearby islands, which provided pro-duce to sustain Caribbean slaves. The plantations were much smaller than those in George Washington's Virginia, but they also relied on slave labor, so that while in New England as a whole black slaves were only 3 percent of the population, here, along the coast, about 13 percent of the inhabitants were slaves.

Venture apparently lived in the Mumford house. Southern

plantations of the type that George Washington knew had separate slave quarters, but farm slaves in southern New England typically slept in the main house, either in the kitchen or the attic, so he was able to observe carefully the life of his owners. He noticed that some of the people who came and went at the house were treated with great respect. Among other things, the finest bedroom was reserved for their use. These were members of the Winthrop family. The island had been owned by the Winthrops since John Winthrop Jr., the governor of the Connecticut colony in the mid-1600s, had obtained it. The Mumfords leased the island from the Winthrops.

Going back some generations, Mumfords had insinuated themselves in every facet of the trade between New England, the Caribbean and West Africa, working as ship's captains, slave peddlers, rum runners and produce suppliers.

Venture learned that the Mumford business on Fishers Island was raising sheep and cattle that would become food for slaves in the Caribbean. His job, in effect, was to help feed the very people who had been sold into slavery in Africa along with him, who were now working the cane fields in Barbados to support Britain's colonial empire. He wasn't just a victim of the slave trade, but an active part of it.

Initially, because of his youth, Venture worked in the house, doing jobs such as carding wool. Robinson Mumford, who regularly went off to sea, gave him steadily more responsibilities and put continued trust in him, and Venture repaid it. As he grew, his horizon expanded. He learned the area in which he lived: people on the island made regular visits to the coastal Connecticut towns of New London, Groton and Stonington, for work, to socialize, to buy products. He heard about other places further afield: Providence, New Haven, Cape Cod, Boston.

One day momentous news arrived: Robinson Mumford had died at sea. Robinson's father, George Mumford, became the boy's owner. Venture's life changed from that moment. He was sent outdoors and given progressively more strenuous tasks, such as pounding four bushels of corn every night as chickenfeed. As his teen years went by, he grew uncommonly big and strong, and so did the burdens. The main work—helping tend more than 1,000 sheep and 300-odd cattle—was, ironically, precisely what he had grown up doing in his village of Dukandarra. But that was just the beginning. A farm had land to be tilled, oats to be stacked, apples to be gathered, cider to be pressed, brush fence to be made and mended, meat to be salted, cellars to be plastered, wood to be chopped—all in quantity, no matter what the weather. Fishing was a regular part of life as well, and Venture became skilled at handling boats and negotiating the tricky currents of Fishers Island Sound.

All of this Venture could manage, toiling alongside other slaves. He prided himself on his strength, and performed feats to impress others. Once he carried a tierce of salt—weighing 350 pounds—a distance of about forty feet. He was showing off, but might also have been developing his reputation, trying to increase his value. He enjoyed learning new skills, each of which he seemed to feel might be of value to him in the future. But then came the hardest task: as he said, "to serve two masters." George Mumford's son James, brother of Robinson, took a special interest in him. He seemed to sense a latent willfulness in this particular slave, this giant of a young man whose tests of strength seemed a kind of challenge. He had a coiled energy that needed to be tamed. James began taking it upon himself to give Venture orders.

One day, when George Mumford was away, James issued a long list of chores for Venture to perform. Venture informed him that he had no time to carry them out because his master's orders took precedence. Whereupon, Venture said, James Mumford "broke out into a great rage, snatched a pitchfork and went to lay me over the head therewith." Venture acted fast, grabbed a pitchfork of his own, and used it to defend himself. James Mumford called three other men to come to his aid. They got a rope and tried to tie him up, but the young man had grown strong enough that, fueled by sudden rage, he was able to hold them off. Mumford gave up; he informed his mother that Venture had become too unruly to deal with. At this, Venture—angry at himself for letting his temper flare—changed tactics. He became meek, let the men tie him up. James had him dragged to a hook used for hanging up dead cows that were to be butchered and the men hoisted him onto it. He told them to go to the peach orchard and cut whips—he intended to teach the slave a lesson. But then, perhaps figuring that when his father returned he would not like to find Venture scarred, he thought better of it. He let the slave hang on the meat hook for an hour, then hauled him down.

The incident colored the ensuing years of Venture's life on Fishers Island. He determined not to lose his self-control again. Thereafter, he was a loyal slave. In addition to his customary work, he was eventually allowed to look about for ways to earn money on the side. He caught muskrats and minks and sold them. He farmed a little patch where he grew potatoes and carrots, which he also sold. When gentlemen came to visit, or when he sailed to New London or Stonington, he offered to clean their shoes. He saved everything he earned.

When he was about twenty-five years old, Venture was rewarded for his faithful service. He had fallen in love with another of Mumford's slaves, a woman of about the same age. Her name was Marget; she went by Meg. Venture asked George Mumford for permission to marry her. Physically, they were a mismatched couple: Meg was a tiny woman, and Venture was enormously tall and broad. But in truth they were made for each other. Their union was, Venture said, "for love." Beyond that, they had some elemental things in common. Both were Africans living in forced servitude on a continent far from their homeland. And whether or not the man who claimed ownership of them would have thought so, both were also, like him, Americans. Mumford allowed the marriage. In one way, at least, Venture could consider himself a man.

# PART TWO

*Chapter 4*

## THE CHARMING SOUND
## OF BULLETS

The horse thundered south through the Virginia countryside, expertly coaxed by its rider, who would have been all but oblivious to the glory of the fall foliage through which he sped. When he reached his destination—the building in Williamsburg serving as the temporary capitol of the colony while a new one was being erected—he made his way straight to the corpulent and fastidious older man presiding there, and placed himself, sweaty and ramrod-straight, at his service.

Lieutenant Governor Robert Dinwiddie may have been somewhat bewildered. The job he needed performed involved a difficult, delicate, and quite possibly dangerous piece of international diplomacy in the Ohio Country. The man before him, George Washington, acknowledged that he had no military or diplomatic experience. For that matter he barely had whiskers: he was only twenty-one years old. Beyond that, how had Washington learned of this secret mission and traveled 150 miles to offer himself for it so soon after Dinwiddie himself realized it needed doing?

The answer, probably, was William Fairfax, Washington's mentor, who also happened to be one of Dinwiddie's advisors. Fairfax had recognized something special in Washington from early on; he knew of

*George Washington in 1772, at age forty, painted by Charles Willson Peale.*

the young man's grit and guile, knew that thanks to his surveying trips he had gained an understanding of much of the Ohio Country, which few others had. Fairfax must have sent a letter to Washington informing him of an opportunity to advance himself and simultaneously advised Dinwiddie to consider him.

George Washington's rigorous study of the outward manifestations of good breeding served him well as he stood before the acting governor of the colony. The newly appointed major in the Virginia militia came off as serious, poised, intelligent. He exuded ambition, and was clearly the ardent English patriot that he proclaimed himself to be, ready to fight for king and country. Dinwiddie may have sighed, he may have mulled, but something had to be done quickly. He chose Washington.

Dinwiddie's problem—England's problem in North America, which was suddenly unavoidable—was France. Throughout the seventeenth century and into the eighteenth, while England was developing its thirteen colonies along the eastern seaboard, its bitterest rival in the quest for colonial expansion had established bases at Quebec and New Orleans and had planted settlements at many places in between, around the Great Lakes and along the length of the Mississippi River, including Detroit, St. Louis and Baton Rouge. As English settlers began moving westward into the Ohio country in search of new land, the French were moving eastward from the Mississippi. When George Washington's brother Lawrence, his patron William Fairfax and other prominent Virginians established the Ohio Company, with an object to settle the region, the French saw it as a direct threat.

They countered first by sending a flotilla of canoes carrying more than 200 soldiers down the Ohio River, stopping at intervals to bury a series of lead plates, on each of which was inscribed a notice that the king of France claimed possession of the river and "all the territories on both sides."

Buried lead plates could be ignored, but in 1753 the French strengthened their position by constructing a series of primitive forts along the Ohio. Among those who were most alarmed at this development was Dinwiddie, a merchant from Scotland who had first been assigned as customs collector in Bermuda before being given the post in Virginia. Not long after his arrival, Dinwiddie had irritated Virginia's planters by enforcing British tax laws that colonists had previously ignored. But when it came to westward expansion, he not only backed the colonists politically but joined forces with them financially, becoming a major shareholder in the Ohio Company. Meanwhile, in his official capacity he was responsible for maintaining British interest in the Ohio territory. The French forts were a threat to both his job and his investment.

Dinwiddie dashed off a letter to London alerting Britain's rulers that the French had made a move of global significance. The response was signed by King George II himself: Dinwiddie was to send a messenger to the French, to "require of them peaceably to depart." And if they refused, Dinwiddie was to "drive them off by force of arms." What Washington was to deliver was nothing less than a threat of war.

Washington headed off from Williamsburg the very day he got his commission. There was no time to lose: it was late October, and bad weather was coming. As he rode north toward the wilderness, he stopped to engage a small party of woodsmen as guides. Also, he had the idea to ask his former fencing instructor in Fredericksburg, a Dutchman named Jacob van Braam, to come along. Washington knew he would need someone who could speak French; he remembered Van Braam said he could.

Winter came early and with unusual ferocity that year. After weeks of "excessive Rains and a vast Quantity of Snow," as Washington recorded, of ice-swollen rivers and treacherous mountain passes, he and his party made it to the place where the Allegheny and Monongahela rivers meet to form the Ohio. Since the Ohio was the highway westward, the forks of the Ohio, English leaders had guessed, would be the perfect place to plant a fort that would be both a defense against the French and a base from which English settlements would grow. Washington wrote to Dinwiddie that indeed "the Land in the Fork" was "extremely well situated for a Fort, as it has the absolute Command of both Rivers." The boy who only months earlier had been making youthful surveying forays was now advising on the future of American expansion.

Washington wanted to have Indian allies with him as he approached the French. He found his way to an Indian settlement called Logstown, and there announced that he desired to meet with the most noted Indian in the Ohio Country, the Seneca leader Tanacharison, known among the English as the Half King. This was hundreds of miles from the Seneca homeland, but as the beaver population had diminished, many Iroquois had made their way west and south into the Ohio Country, where they had formed new villages and, exerting their collective might, cowed Delaware, Shawnee and other tribes in the region into accepting their dominance. Over the years, they had struck deals with the French, and more recently with the English, to allow the Europeans access to the Ohio Country, but as far as the Senecas were concerned, they were the stewards of this region. Now that the two European powers were both making serious moves on the land at the same time, the Ohio Country Senecas—known to the English as Mingos—felt a new kind of threat. The Half King was their leader, though, as his title indicated, he had a lesser status than a chief in the Iroquois homelands. It was up to him to deliver the Iroquois response to this new development.

Tanacharison was away when Washington arrived, so Washington had to wait for a time. When the Indian finally appeared—in his mid-fifties, hardened, confident, formidable—he impressed the young officer. He also astonished Washington by greeting him as "Conotocarious," or Town Destroyer. Washington had apparently grown up knowing this word. It had been applied by Algonquians to his great-grandfather in the 1670s, after John Washington participated in massacres of Indians in Virginia. The memory of the name had been passed down by the Washington family. It had also been passed down in Algonquian oral history. Presumably, Algonquian Indians at Logstown, on learning the name of the young colonial messenger who was waiting to speak with the Seneca leader, told Tanacharison of it, so that he could now put his inexperienced guest off-balance by bequeathing the name to him, letting him know that the Iroquois were far from simple savages but in fact a people whose intelligence extended even to the young man's ancestral past.

Tanacharison had earlier made a treaty with the English, which Washington believed was done in the name of the Iroquois Confederacy, granting the English the right to settle in the Ohio Country. Tanacharison now informed Washington that he had several reasons for loathing the French (one very good reason: he said the French had not only killed his father but cooked and eaten him), and he repeated to him what he had told the French commander. But his recap caused Washington as much bewilderment as the ancient nickname had. What he objected to, Tanacharison said, was for *any outsider* to build "houses upon our land." The Half King declared, regarding the land in question, that "the Great Being above allowed it to be a place of residence to us," and therefore it could not be settled by the French or the English. Surely the Iroquois leader realized that the treaty he had signed gave the English rights to live in the Ohio Country. Washington was learning on the fly that diplomacy between Europeans and natives was never straightforward.

Washington managed to hold his peace about this issue and focus on the matter at hand, and felt that he had scored a victory when he got the Half King to agree to accompany him. Tanacharison brought three other Senecas with him; one of them, Guyasuta, whom Washington called "The Hunter," was the uncle of the boy named Cornplanter who was presumably at this moment 250 miles to the northeast in his village of Conawaugus, taking part in the late fall hunt. After ten more days of difficult travel "through many mires and swamps," they reached the French headquarters of Fort Le Boeuf, 15 miles from the shores of Lake Erie. The fort was home to more than 100 soldiers and bristled with weaponry; Washington was taut with nerves at entering the domain of England's long-standing enemy. He did his best to clear off the muck of hard travel, and presented himself to the commander, Jacques Legardeur de Saint-Pierre, an elderly aristocrat who, while bemused at Washington's youth and inexperience, treated him with "Distinction." There was an exchange of pleasantries, then Washington handed over the letter from Dinwiddie, which informed the French commander that as "The Lands upon the River Ohio, in the Western Parts of the Colony of Virginia" were "notoriously known to be the Property of the Crown of Great-Britain," he was forced to demand the "peaceable Departure" of the French troops.

Legardeur gave Washington a letter in return to be delivered to Dinwiddie. If Washington expected that his mission, and the threat of war implicit in it, would make the French back off, he was disappointed. The Frenchman's letter referred to the "incontestable rights of the King, my master, to the lands situated along the Ohio." And it noted: "As to the summons you send me to retire, I do not think myself obliged to obey it."

There were maybe two or three dozen forced laborers on George Mumford's plantation on Fishers Island, and not all of them were African. Over the course of the seventeenth and eighteenth centuries, thousands of poor whites from the British Isles were taken from orphanages and prisons and shipped to the colonies. Some were called indentured servants, since they had a contract that granted them freedom after a number of years of service to a master. But contract or no, most were treated as slaves. One of Mumford's "slaves" was an Irishman named Joseph Heday. Heday was a talker, an instigator, a dreamer. While feeding the cattle and tending the sheep alongside Venture, he began whispering to the African about a plan of escape.

At first Venture was having none of it. Loyalty was part of his honor code; besides, he had recently gotten married. He said later that it was the brashness of youth that caused him to start listening to Heday's ideas. And it wasn't like it was unheard of: the newspapers were full of ads taken out by slave owners, giving physical details of runaways and promising rewards to whoever found them. Slaves who lived on large plantations were often kept in ignorance of the world beyond it; to them, the idea of running away probably came with a clench of terror. Those who knew something of the world, however—latitude and longitude, tidal currents, how to follow the course of a river, how to dress and act like a free man—for such slaves the idea of freedom came with something more: the flavor of possibility. In March, after repeatedly dismissing the idea, Venture suddenly changed his mind and told Heday he was in.

Heday lined up two more of Mumford's slaves to join them. One, a man named Fortune, was African; the other, Isaac, was what Mumford called a "mustee," aka an octoroon, a mixed-breed. They made an ungainly group: Heday short, stocky and red-faced, wearing a bold red overcoat; Venture, six feet two inches and broad-shouldered, towering over the little Irishman; Fortune also tall but quite thin; and Isaac a small, sour man with bushy hair and an awkward, creaky way of walking. They made their move by night, hauling 60 pounds of Mumford's butter, 64 pounds of cheese, baskets of bread and as much clothing as they could carry—most of which they intended to sell to fund their onward journey—down to the dock. The Mumfords had the lease to the whole island, so once the runaways cleared the house they could be pretty sure of going undetected until morning. At midnight they loaded up Mumford's two-masted boat and slipped away into the blackness of the water.

As they headed south in the icy darkness, breathing in the salt tang of the open ocean and the wild scent of freedom, they swore an oath: "not to betray or desert one another on pain of death." They made first for Montauk Point, the easternmost tip of Long Island, 15 miles away. Venture was an experienced sailor, and it didn't take him long to realize that Fortune and Isaac were inept. When they put ashore, they divided tasks. Fortune and Isaac got to work making a fire and preparing food; Venture and Heday went in search of fresh water. After a while, Heday announced that he was heading back to check on the other two.

When Venture returned to camp sometime later, he got blank stares from Fortune and Isaac. All the clothes were missing from the boat. As Heday was missing too, Venture could only conclude that he had betrayed them, and taken what they would need to sell in order to continue. Time passed, Heday stayed gone, and his suspicion was confirmed.

Venture had by now determined that Fortune and Isaac were hopeless as companions on such a dangerous mission. On a whim, he had risked everything—even in captivity, a chance for happiness with a wife was something precious, he was probably now realizing—on one mad throw of the die, a slash at freedom, a life fully his own. And one day into it the plan was already in ruins. What had he been thinking, anyway? What, truly, could a hunted slave do on his own in eighteenth-century America, a place gridded by social networks: by congregation, village, farm? Even slavery involved a community. He was alone, with a desolation of heath and moorland at his back and, ahead, the pounding surf and a sea the forbidding color of dull steel. Alone, for the first time since he had been taken from his family more than a dozen years before. Standing on that easternmost point of land, he may have been gripped by the mordant realization that 4,000 miles across that same ocean lay the shores of Africa.

A few months later, as the summer of 1754 was making its way into the streets of London, many of that city's most important men, particularly those who occupied governmental posts, hastily opened copies of a newly published pamphlet entitled *The Journal of Major George Washington*. These British leaders were well aware of America's importance to the empire. Half of all British shipping involved the colonies across the Atlantic; they generated £7.5 million in revenue per year for Britain while consuming a quarter of British goods annually. But until now the focus of these gentlemen was, as it had always been, on the British Isles in relation to the European continent. Regarding America, they bothered themselves with a few sketchy details: the names of distant ports—Boston, Philadelphia, Norfolk—and some knowledge of products, such as slaves, tobacco, lumber and cattle. The recent news of ominous French maneuvers in America, however, had them suddenly aware of the sizable gaps in their knowledge of their overseas possessions. What was it, exactly, that the French were threatening to take from them?

After slogging his way back from Fort Le Boeuf to Virginia, completing a death-defying, 900-mile, three-month journey in order to deliver a letter, Washington had presented Governor Dinwiddie with an unexpected trove of information. He had kept a journal of the experience, including detailed notes of the geography and of the French fort and troops. Dinwiddie had it printed in Williamsburg, then his superiors in London ordered another edition, by Thomas Jefferys of St. Martin's Lane, London. Jefferys, who was the royal cartographer, had included a map in his edition, for the benefit of those members of the British public who were not so well acquainted with American geography. It did not bother with the thirteen mainland colonies but showed the area immediately to the west, from the Great Lakes to the Ohio River to the Mississippi, in considerable detail. If the thirteen colonies were the present, *this* was the future, or it could be, provided the French didn't steal it.

The journal was a vivid travelogue, part wilderness adventure but above all a graphic display of backwoods diplomacy conducted on their behalf by a greenhorn colonial militiaman. Crossing an ice-swollen Allegheny River on horseback, getting spun by native diplomacy, injecting himself directly into the palisaded heart of the enemy: Washington came off as an impossibly eager emissary, personally pushing forward the next chapter in the story of Britain's vast North American holdings.

Many important figures in the British government read the pamphlet. And now counted among those leaders was George Sackville. After recovering from his battle injury, Sackville had gone right back into the fight against France on the European continent in 1747, once again serving under the Duke of Cumberland, son of George II. He was as ferocious and single-minded as before; the Duke praised him for his "gallantry," and gave him the honor of proceeding across the battlefield (with "a French trumpet and an English drum") to the opposing French officer and negotiating terms by which the French would surrender.

Afterward, in 1751, Sackville headed back to Ireland, accompanying his father on his second stint as Lord Lieutenant. But this time, the personalities of the two men fully asserted themselves: the mild-mannered Duke of Dorset took a back seat and allowed his unstoppable thirty-five-year-old son to run the government in all but name.

Bringing his battle-honed decisiveness to bear, George Sackville made a quick decision to completely upend the recent course of affairs. Over the previous two decades, under the leadership of the hugely popular politician Henry Boyle, the Irish had taken several steps toward self-government, which successive English viceroys in Ireland had allowed. Sackville committed himself to aggressively reversing the trend—against the better judgment of his father, who knew that tact was needed in handling the Irish. He focused on the issue of Irish tax revenues. There was a surplus, which the Irish parliament intended to use; Sackville insisted instead that it be turned over to England. Sackville recalled vividly how the same issue was spun by Irishmen, including his mentor Jonathan Swift, during his first years in Dublin. He would now put his foot down and make the Irish remember that they were subjects of the British crown.

Boyle, the longtime Speaker of the Irish House and as skillful and wily a politician as Sackville was headstrong, protested the move in a way that would be copied by American subjects a decade later, as an unjust instance of taxation without representation. It was Irish money, raised by taxing the Irish people; it should be theirs to do with as they saw fit. Under Boyle's leadership, virtually all political factions in Ireland united in outrage against the English overlords. Sackville tried to maneuver by quietly offering Boyle a massive bribe: a pension of 1,500 pounds a year plus a peerage, if he would back down. Boyle was seventy years old; after a lifetime in politics, he knew exactly how to play this. "If I had a peerage, I should not think myself greater than now that I am Mr. Boyle," the Speaker declared, making the matter public and receiving cheers from the masses. As for the bribe, he said, "I despise it as much as the person who offers it."

Satiric poems were pasted on the streets of Dublin, lampooning Sackville and his father. Ballads sprouted. Angry crowds denounced father and son, and there was near-rioting in the Irish parliament. Meanwhile, a commemorative medal featuring a bust of Henry Boyle appeared. Decades later the affair was still talked of as the true beginning of Irish unrest over English rule. The matter brought such an avalanche of scorn on Sackville's father, in whose name it had all been done, that he quietly ended his public career.

Whatever he may have felt for the suffering he caused his father,

George Sackville returned to London and found that the Irish commotion he had stirred had had something like the opposite effect on his own reputation. England was building an empire; empires did not grow of their own accord and they didn't rise to greatness by coddling the people they conquered. Many in England thought it was dangerous to grant a colonized people the kind of freedom the Irish had been allowed. What an empire needed was men of grit: men like Sackville. He received a military promotion, to the rank of major-general. He stood for, and won, a seat in Parliament, where he gave a series of forceful speeches. "Nobody stands higher," the politician and gossip Horace Walpole wrote of him. "Nobody has more ambition and common sense."

By 1754, when George Washington's journal was published in London, George Sackville was a rising star in politics and the military. In both arenas, his great and special hatred was for France. Whenever the subject of French machinations on the world stage came up, his great gibbous eyes gleamed. French politics, as far as he was concerned, consisted of years of duplicity followed by sudden pushes for territory at the expense of Britain. If he ever needed a reminder, there was the French bullet still lodged in his chest. With this colonial militiaman, George Washington, reporting that 1,500 French soldiers were massing in the wilds of the Ohio Country, at the back door of the thirteen colonies, threatening British expansion in America, George Sackville understood better than anyone what was coming.

Throughout the spring of 1754 newspapers all over the colonies picked up the story of Washington's winter mission into the Ohio Country. While Americans began to acquaint themselves with the name of Washington, and with the increasingly threatening actions of the French, those in New York also had the chance to read an advertisement:

Run Away from George Mumford of Fisher's Island, the
27th Instant, four Men Servants, a white Man and Three
Negroes, who hath taken a large two-mast Boat, with a
square Stern. . . . The White Man named Joseph Heday . . .
The Negroes are named Fortune, Venture and Isaac;
Fortune is a tall, slim comely well spoken fellow. . . . Venture
had a Kersey dark colour'd Great Coat . . . he is a very tall
Fellow, 6 feet 2 inches high, thick square shoulders, large
bon'd, mark'd in the Face, or scar'd with a knife in his own
country. Isaac is a Mustee, a short Fellow, seemingly clumsy
and stiff in his Gate. . . .

Whoever takes up and secures said Run-aways, so that
their Master may have them again, shall have *TWENTY*
*POUNDS*, New-York Currency, Reward and all reasonable
charges paid, or equivalent for either of them; or secure the
Boat, that the Owner may have her again, shall be rewarded
by GEORGE MUMFORD.

Venture gave no one the chance to claim the reward. Instead, after
several days of hiding out, and after long and careful consideration of his
situation, he took action himself. Reasoning that Heday would have made
for the village of Southampton, he hired two local men to track him down.
They did what was asked of them, and returned with the Irishman.

Heday came back cowed and sheepish, an altogether different man
from the one on Fishers Island who had bragged about the great adventure of escape. Venture was in command now. He ordered Heday, Fortune and Isaac into the boat, and steered a course for Fishers Island.
The other three put up no fuss. At the plantation, George Mumford
was greeted by the curious sight of the giant African whom his son
had brought into their lives as a boy, and who had run off from him,
returning of his own free will and bringing his compatriots with him, as

though he had been sent out to capture them. But Venture didn't try to put such a spin on things. He confessed to Mumford that they had all made a break for it, that Heday had been "the ringleader of our revolt," and that after Heday had in turn betrayed the rest of them he, Venture, had come to his senses and decided the most practical course was for him to bring them all back and put them at their master's mercy.

George Mumford was sixty-five years old, hardened by years as a slave ship captain and driver of slaves on his plantation. He had seen a lot, yet he had never encountered such a thing as this. Dealing with Joseph Heday was easy: Mumford was sick of him, but also wasn't about to let him go. He turned him in to the authorities in New London, Connecticut, and he wound up in prison there. Venture was another matter. Mumford would have to ponder what course to take with him.


Some newspaper accounts of Washington's Ohio Country journey highlighted the French menace. Other writers did a bit of home-work and discovered that Washington's name was tied to the Ohio Company, and suggested that in his journal he overstated the threat from the French in order to get military support for a financial scheme from which he and his friends would benefit. It enraged Washington to have his honor besmirched, though he could not deny that the publica-tion of the journal of his trip could only support the cause of the Ohio Company and its backers.

In Williamsburg, meanwhile, he found the atmosphere chaotic. The government had voted to muster an army of volunteers to defend Virginia's borders, and farmers were scrambling to sign up after being promised land in exchange for their service. And he found that he was now something of a celebrity. The attention pleased him, but he expected it to yield tangible results. He wanted a raise and a promotion.

As had happened with Sackville, while some prominent people in

Virginia were critical of Washington's aggressiveness, this same quality did indeed earn him a promotion—to lieutenant colonel. But his most ardently held wish, to become a regular officer in the British army, was thwarted again. The commission was still only in Virginia's militia. And when the Virginia General Assembly voted to grant him a very modest reward of 50 pounds for his work, he responded with indignation. "I was employed to go on a journey in the winter (when I believe few or none would have undertaken it)," he wrote to his brother Augustine, "and what did I get by it? My expenses borne!" The prominent qualities of his youthful self—seething ambition and an acute sense of being slighted—were on full display.

But he had little time to stew, for Dinwiddie asked him to lead the new "army" back into the wilderness to assess the movements of the French. It was a mission that required caution, cunning and restraint: he had 160 untrained recruits, and the latest report said the French were already at the Forks of the Ohio, building a redoubt they were calling Fort Duquesne, with a force of 1,000 seasoned soldiers. Washington's best move would be to make his presence known and otherwise await reinforcements. He was, in any event, not to provoke but "to act on the Difensive." But the prime motivation of a Virginia planter—the pursuit of honor—was a fire raging in Washington's psyche. He allowed himself to believe that impossible odds could be translated into great glory. He marched his men through the gnarled and mountainous wilds of Maryland and western Pennsylvania, retracing the route he had just followed. He had sent word to Tanacharison, and the Half King and a contingent of Indian warriors met up with him. Almost at once the two men fell to arguing about tactics and goals. Washington couldn't figure out what game the Indians were playing, whose side they were truly on, English or French. It seems not to have occurred to him that they were on their own side. But he needed them now, so he settled for whatever help they would provide.

Indian scouts informed him that a party of French soldiers had left the Forks and were headed toward them. Fifty miles south of the Forks, they learned the French party—35 men—was on the other side of a heavily wooded hill. Rather than try to evade them, Washington headed up the hill with 40 of his men and a group of Indians; they marched all night, and at dawn reached the top of a ravine. The French soldiers were camped just below, nestled in a deep cleft in the rocks. The Indians slipped around to block the path out of the ravine, and the Americans took positions on top.

What happened next would be the subject of intense dispute. A shot sounded in the early morning air; it was followed by fifteen minutes of musket fire. Washington's men easily routed the enemy, killing ten of them and losing only one of their own. For a moment, Washington must have thought that he had won a great victory, surprising a war party that was attempting to surprise him.

Then chaos erupted again. According to one of the French soldiers, as the leader of the French, Joseph Coulon de Villiers, Sieur de Jumonville, stepped forward, Tanacharison cried out to the man in French and with familiarity—"Tu n'es pas encore mort, mon père" (You aren't dead yet, father)—split his head open with a tomahawk and rinsed his hands with the man's brains. The rest of the Indians took this as a signal to scalp the other French victims.

Washington was stunned—whatever knowledge he had of the Iroquois and the role they perceived for themselves vis-à-vis the two European powers, he was certainly not used to seeing Iroquois justice graphically meted out; if there was a message in this action, Washington was unable to fathom its meaning. When he got control of his nerves and of the situation, he learned that a letter Jumonville had been carrying, which was to be delivered to English authorities, was a declaration that the Ohio Country was French territory. The French contingent, in other words, had not been an attack party, but had been a mirror image of the diplomatic mission he had led a few months earlier.

Washington couldn't accept that his men had killed a diplomatic messenger. He was convinced the letter was a cover for warlike intentions. He believed he had taken part not in a massacre but in a battle—his first battle—between Europe's two colonizing empires. And he had frankly enjoyed the experience. He later wrote to his brother, "I heard the Bullets whistle, and believe me, there was something charming in the sound."

Nevertheless, he realized that when word got back to the main French contingent at the Forks they would come for him. He decided to retreat to a wide meadow and have his men build a palisade fort in the center of it. From here, they would hold off the attackers.

Tanacharison—who later described Washington as "good-natured" but inexperienced, and complained that he treated the Indians not as allies but like "slaves"—thought this an idiotic plan, and said so. Some reinforcements arrived—Washington's army now totaled 400 men—but they were still drastically outnumbered. "Fort Necessity," as Washington named it—as if to buttress his argument with Tanacharison that he had no choice but to fight here—was primitive, and horribly exposed. Before the French arrived, Tanacharison and the rest of the Indians disappeared into the forest.

The French, when they came, were strong and well disciplined. As if they needed more impetus to attack, their leader was the brother of Jumonville; on the way to meet the Americans, they had passed the site of the massacre and looked with horror on the man's desecrated body. When they attacked the pathetic little fort, however, it was not with fury but with precision. The French soldiers took positions behind trees and rocks and picked off the horses that were corralled outside, then aimed for the men inside. When more than a hundred of his men lay dead or wounded, Washington agreed to a surrender.

*Chapter 5*

❈

# WORLD ON FIRE

Protocol required that George Washington's surrender be in writing. The French wrote the capitulation document. Washington signed it.

Later, in an attempt to avoid disgrace, Washington tried to transfer blame for the diplomatic storm that followed onto his old fencing coach, Jacob van Braam, the Dutchman whom he had once again brought along to translate. In the hours after the battle, as a steady rain fell and the night deepened, he sent Van Braam to the French and the man brought their terms back to Washington, first shouting them over the wind and rain, then, after another parley, on paper. Washington later insisted that he thought the description of the battle that he put his name to said that his men had caused the "death" of the French leader Jumonville. In fact, the French word was "assassination," which made Washington's conduct seem considerably more reprehensible. Van Braam's French was probably not entirely fluent; still, Washington took no blame himself as leader, but declared that he was "deceived by our interpreter."

It mattered because of the tumble of events that ensued. Washington's capitulation—his admission, the French said, that an English colonial officer had opened fire and killed a party of messengers in a time of peace, "assassinating" its leader—was the excuse that France had been waiting for, an excuse to go to war with Britain over territory. It could have been another event, in America or Europe, since both countries were moving headlong in that direction. But as it happened, the series of missteps by an inexperienced provincial officer, whose signature carried the official weight of the British Empire, meant that, for the first time, an event in North America would trigger a war in Europe.

Once again, important men in London took note of the doings of George Washington. They may have been preparing for war anyway, but this time they were not impressed by the amateurism he had exhibited in their name. A British pamphleteer wrote that the articles of capitulation that Washington signed "were the most infamous a British Subject ever put his Hand to." Lord Albemarle, a general and England's ambassador to France, spoke for many in the British hierarchy when he wrote that "Washington and many such may have courage and resolution, but they have no knowledge or experience in our profession. Consequently, there can be no dependence on them." Someone got hold of a copy of Washington's letter to his brother, in which he bragged about finding the whistle of bullets to be a "charming sound," and it was published in *London Magazine*, to snide reactions. (King George remarked, "He would not say so if he had been used to hear many.") Horace Walpole, who had heaped praise on George Sackville, portrayed Washington's actions as foolishness with global consequences: "The volley fired by a young Virginian in the backwoods of America set the world on fire."

England prepared for war. Politicans gave speeches. Among the most vigorous were those of George Sackville, who, despite the inelegance with which Washington had conducted himself, exulted at the chance to go at the French once again. The king appeared before Parliament and declared that for "the Protection of Our Possessions in America" he was sending troops there, as well as encouraging "the several Colonies there, to exert themselves in their own Defense."

Who would lead the British troops in America? The heads of both parties were just now fawning over Sackville. He was widely seen as a hero of two great battles in Europe, and both sides looked to him as a man of wisdom and strength, particularly in military affairs. He was a logical choice to cross the ocean to America and tackle the detested French in the wilds of Pennsylvania and the Ohio Country.

Sackville was now thirty-eight; he had just gotten married—to Diana Sambrooke, a twenty-three-year-old woman from a good family, who was utterly devoted to him—and his tall, fleshy person was often seen these days huddled together in and around the Palace of Westminster with William Pitt, the most brilliant member of the cabinet and the most vocal advocate of all-out war against France. With Pitt's help, Sackville extricated himself from the American assignment. It was not that he had become battle-shy. Surely not. But he was nothing if not savvy in his career calculations. If Ireland, with its messy politics and rambunctious populace, was a place to risk ruining one's reputation, then in the American colonies that risk was elevated to near-certainty. The king had made clear that the colonies were to participate in the war effort, which required careful orchestration. But the governments of the individual colonies were always at each other's throats, and separately and together they bickered with the home country even in peacetime. Then there were the dozens of Indian tribes, who signed and then broke treaties with individual colonies as well as with each other. It was a foolhardy situation for a man who wanted to distinguish himself.

Sackville was relieved when the American assignment went to another man.


As George Washington and George Sackville maneuvered for position in the coming war with France, Abraham Yates and his wife, Antje, were in a state of gathering melancholy. In eight years of marriage

Antje had been pregnant four times, and four times they made a solemn procession to the graveyard of Albany's Dutch Reformed Church to bury a small body. Abraham, meanwhile, continued his work for the city council, but the pay was not enough to support them, so he was still making shoes. As winter settled in on the shores of the Hudson River late in 1753, he sat at his workbench and crafted a fine pair of leather boots for Ephraim Bogardus, for which he took as payment three heifers and a half gallon of rum. Then he made two pairs of gloves for Wouter Groesbeek. And he continued to work as a merchant, selling a pound of tea here, two pounds of chocolate there, a pound of "wilde" (i.e., unrefined) sugar, nine ells of checkered cloth. In the evenings, he and Antje had time to contemplate their empty cradle and the pains of human existence.

Then, as spring gave way to early summer, a sparkle of novelty appeared in the grayness of their life. It was late June of 1754 and hot, and in the steamy, rainy weather the people of Albany watched as men who seemed as exotic as turbaned potentates from faraway lands stepped by twos and threes off the ferry at the Hudson River landing and processed up the hill into the streets of their bucolic town. At 150 miles north of Manhattan, 240 from Philadelphia, and a good 500 miles from Williamsburg (about two weeks' ride on horseback), Albany was remote. Its inhabitants knew it; they felt the snugness of its parochialisms. And so this influx felt like an exotic parade.

The influx into Albany was the doing of George Montagu Dunk, the Earl of Halifax, a contemporary of George Sackville in the British government. As the First Lord of Trade he oversaw the committee—commonly known as the Board of Trade—that was responsible for the American colonies. The forts that the French had been constructing in America concerned him intimately. He knew as well as Sackville that order was lacking in the colonies, that some kind of overall control was essential. So he had sent letters to the governors of each, requesting that they come together and hash out a common plan. The most pressing issue concerned the Iroquois Confederacy. The upheaval in the Ohio Country, plus repeated instances of land fraud in Iroquois territory—colonists concluding treaties with Indians for land and then creatively redrawing borders to make the purchased area vastly larger—had brought the Iroquois to the brink of open conflict with the English. If the Iroquois chose to side with France, it would be disastrous. The conference, then, was to include representatives of the Iroquois nations as well. Abraham Yates's city may have been remote compared to some places, but its location was precisely why it had been chosen to host the gathering. For Albany was the main link of British North America not only to Iroquois country but to the French in Canada.

Among the delegates from distant colonies whom Abraham and Antje Yates could get a close look at were such notables as Elisha Williams, the distinguished former rector of Yale College, and John Penn, scion of the family that owned the Province of Pennsylvania. But the "foreigner" who drew the most attention was John Penn's fellow Pennsylvanian, the portly and courtly, the alternately learned and bawdy, Mr. Benjamin Franklin. The forty-nine-year-old Franklin was by this point known far and wide for his experiments with and bewildering promotion of electricity (five years earlier he had hosted a party featuring "a Turky . . . killed for our dinners by the Electrical Shock; and roasted by the electrical jack, before a fire kindled by the electrified bottle"), as well as for his publication *Poor Richard's Almanac*, his work as a member of the Pennsylvania Assembly, and as proprietor and publisher of and regular contributor to the *Pennsylvania Gazette*, the most widely read newspaper in the thirteen colonies. Even here in distant Albany, people could quote Franklin's aphorisms about daily life ("time is money") and politics: "Republics and limited monarchies derive their strength and vigour from a popular examination into the actions of the magistrates."

As the delegates sat down to meetings in the Town Hall, and waited day after humid day for the Indians to arrive, a committee of delegates, led by Franklin, put their heads together and drafted a plan to unite the colonies by which, as they wrote, "one general government may be formed in America, within and under which government each colony may retain its present constitution." The new government would be led by a "President-General." Among the delegates and back home in Pennsylvania, Franklin enthusiastically promoted the plan; it would give the thirteen colonies a single voice in dealing with the Indians and, for that matter, in dealing with Britain. He went so far as to publish a political cartoon (the first in America, by some reckonings) in his *Pennsylvania Gazette* to illustrate the situation:

The delegates in Albany voted in favor of the plan of union. But when they brought it back to their respective provinces, the colonial governments failed to ratify it, and the British Board of Trade, which had asked them to come up with just such an arrangement, didn't approve it either. The united colonial government would have been loyal to Britain, but to certain officials in England the plan looked like a step toward some kind of independence.

At last, the Indians arrived. A procession of 200 Iroquois, ceremonially robed, beaded and feathered, was not especially remarkable to people of Albany such as Yates, but it was an impressive sight for some of the delegates, particularly those who had recently come from England, one of whom noted that delegates hiked "up the hill on the Back of the Town to View the Indians &ca."

Abraham Yates was a hanger-on at the so-called Albany Congress—too minor an official to play a serious role—but he managed to use the occasion to advance his career. The assistant alderman on the city council, now thirty years old, knew well that Albany's fortunes hinged on the Iroquois. He paid careful attention to what transpired at the grand conclave, which went on for four long weeks and was held in the open air, with the delegations seated by colony and tribe. As tribal chiefs stood and spoke, the newcomers from England followed via interpreters ("almost all the Albany people speak Indian," one noted) and marveled at the native sense of decorum. Seneca, Cayuga, Onondaga, Oneida, Tuscarora and Mohawk speeches were punctuated by shouts of support from allied Indians that sounded to English ears like "Yoheigh-igh!" and were accompanied by wampum belts of polished beads the size and elaborateness of which was related to the importance of the speech. Yates may have noted a particularly serious-looking youth among the Seneca delegation—for it is possible that Cornplanter, still a boy but a leader in training, was among them. The Indians recounted past agreements and failures to live up to them. They recounted, in ceremonial language, their disappointment, even their pain. They said frankly that they feared the French, but also that they distrusted the English.

As Yates knew would happen, the Iroquois presentations revolved around one man on the New York delegation. William Johnson, thirty-nine years old, had emigrated sixteen years earlier from his native Ireland. Recognizing that it was possible to outflank Albany's oligarchy of fur traders, he had bought land to the northwest, which he set up as a trading post. He would eventually take a renowned Mohawk woman, Molly Brant, as his consort, learn the language, and don native dress. He got himself named head of New York's Board of Commissioners for Indian Affairs, and earned the trust of the Iroquois—even while buying tens of thousands of acres of land from them and representing the English crown in dealings with them—and at the same time garnered the enmity of Albany's leading families. By 1751 he had become so ensnared in sparring between Albany's great families and politicians in New York's provincial government that he quit the Indian Affairs commission. Other men took over, and their handling of things was a main complaint of the Iroquois now. The Indians gestured toward Johnson as the man they trusted. They wanted him reinstated.

They didn't get that—Johnson had too many enemies in New York politics—but they got assurances that things would be different. And they got presents, wagonloads of them, including four hundred guns.

The Indians also succeeded in getting the Indian Affairs commission revamped. In its new incarnation, Abraham Yates won the job of deputy secretary to the commissioners. It was a meaty role, which put him smack in the middle of his city's complexities. He would have access to goings-on between rival factions in Albany, between them and others in New York's colonial politics, and with the Iroquois. He would be a nexus of information.

No sooner was he awarded the job than the stakes were raised. In the middle of the congress, word reached Albany of the skirmish that George Washington and Tanacharison had engaged in with the French, at which the Half King had murdered Jumonville. The gathering in remote Albany suddenly took on global significance.

After the delegates left town, and Albany got back to its normal life, Yates dived into his new work. Drawing on the accounting skills he had developed as a shoemaker, he reorganized the files of the Indian commission and developed a deeper understanding of what the Indians felt their interest to be, where the fault lines lay. But if he found a certain sympathy for the Iroquois, he remained steadfastly an advocate of his city. Against critics who said the Indian Affairs Commission abused the Indians for their own profit, he declared that the commissioners had "the Wel being of their Country at heart." They were, he said, fairminded toward the Indians, but he also noted that the commissioners "governed themselves according to the following maxim: that an Indian will either fight or trade and that the only way to keep them from fighting is by trading with them." It was, he seemed to think, a sturdy slogan for the times ahead.

As 1754 came to a close, Abraham Yates could feel a sense of accomplishment even as rumors of war grew. At home, meanwhile, there was reason to be cautiously optimistic. Antje came to him with news. She was pregnant again.

A ntje Yates's pregnancy coincided with that of Meg, Venture's wife. In November of 1754, the chill of approaching winter on Fishers Island was made more endurable by the warmth of new life. Meg and Venture now had a daughter, whom they named Hannah. Venture wasn't one for open displays of affection, but family bonds were sacred to him. Hannah's arrival gave him a chance to ponder the wild vagaries of life: how in the normal course of events he could have expected to raise a family in the cattle camp where he had been born, surrounded by the comforting sounds and smells and heat of the savanna, but instead it was happening here, on a lonely island plantation, with views across to the winking lights of the Connecticut shore. With so little that was truly theirs, Venture and Meg could count themselves fortunate at least in this.

Everyone in the household would have been involved in the birth in some way. But any feelings of human conviviality between masters and slaves were short-lived. Within a matter of weeks, George Mumford decided what he would do about Venture. A slave who had run off, even if he had returned and brought his coconspirators in tow, was, in the estimation of many owners, damaged goods. He could never again be trusted. Work on the island was multifaceted. Slave or free, a worker needed to be out in the pastures, up into the hilly woods, around the farmhouse. Running the Mumfords' operation required regular trips by boat across the sound to New London, Groton or Stonington. George Mumford was getting too old to oversee the island farm. Newspapers said troubled times lay ahead. He was contemplating ending the lease on the property with the Winthrop family. He didn't need to be saddled with worries about the big African with the scarred face, who had been dutiful enough when Mumford's son Robinson was alive but had now exhibited the ornery longing for freedom that all slave owners feared.

Mumford made an arrangement with a man he had known all his life, Thomas Stanton, who lived in the village of Stonington, directly opposite the island on the mainland. Stanton agreed to buy Venture. But Stanton had no need for a female slave with a newborn baby. Somewhere around Christmastime, Venture climbed into a boat and sailed away from the island, while his wife and his month-old daughter stayed behind. In case he might for a moment have forgotten, he was reminded of the inexorable harshness of human affairs. Affection, love, consideration: these were soft and uncertain and not to be counted on. The truth he had absorbed as he witnessed his father's torture and death—that money was the hard and cold measure of things, the only solid ground in human affairs—was reinforced in him. As he sailed across the sound, he had with him his life's savings, which he tolled with precision: "two johannes, three old Spanish dollars, and two thousand of coppers, besides five pounds of my wife's money." Whatever the currency, whether paper notes or chinking coins, money would be his anchor.

George Washington had his hands in the earth, his fingers testing its grainy structure. He paced off fields, studied the December sky. He was pondering a new life for himself, that of . . . tobacco farmer.

After the travesty at Fort Necessity, Washington had made his way back to Williamsburg, where he was delighted to discover that Virginians were putting a positive spin on the affair, lauding him for bravery against impossible odds. The authorities, however, took a different view of things. Governor Dinwiddie gave him a cold reception, and he was informed that, due to a reorganization of the colonial militia, the rank of colonel would no longer exist. He would in effect be demoted to captain. Others in the same situation went along with the change, but Washington refused to live with it. He was offered a new commission, which would allow him to keep his title of colonel, but only unofficially. This annoyed him even more, to the point of near illegibility. "You must entertain a very contemptible opinion of my weakness," he wrote to the officer who made the offer, "and believe me to be more empty than the Commission itself." Rather than tolerate what he took to be a slap in the face, he chose the young man's dramatic gesture of quitting altogether, citing "the call of Honour" as his reason for doing so.

And so he "retired" and began to refashion himself as a gentleman farmer. Following his brother's death, Lawrence Washington's wife had remarried. Her plans, and those of her new husband, did not include Lawrence's estate of Mount Vernon. But they knew that George had coveted it, so they leased the property to him, along with eighteen "Negroe slaves." In Virginia society farming was nearly as much of an arena for garnering honor as the military, so that Washington's second ambition in life was to learn to grow tobacco on a commercial scale. It was a treacherously tricky business, however, and competition was cutthroat among the planters. But there were rewards: those who produced the sweetest leaf that garnered the best prices sat at the top of the social hierarchy. Washington began a serious study of the business.

At the same time, he kept a close eye on events in the wider world. The man who got the job that George Sackville had dodged—to lead British forces against the French in North America—was named Edward

Braddock. William, the Duke of Cumberland, the rambunctious son of King George, had made the selection. Cumberland knew both Sackville and Braddock well, and in deciding on Braddock, he seems to have opted for a weaker copy of Sackville. Both were aggressive and detail-minded. Braddock had not had an especially distinguished military career, and at age sixty he was old for such an arduous assignment, but the hope was that he would make up for it with his tenacity and his organizational abilities.

Braddock's biggest hindrance was his utter lack of knowledge about America. He knew nothing of the landscape, and didn't have a real appreciation of the distances and the difficulties of moving an army through the thickly wooded wilderness. He had little understanding of the relationships between the various colonial governments, and none whatsoever of Indian affairs.

When his ship sailed into Hampton Roads, Virginia, in February 1755, however, he had no sooner stepped ashore than colonial officials began trying to make him aware of the scope of his ignorance. The plan he was to execute—which had been dreamed up in London, by men who like him had little knowledge of America—involved leading an army to the Forks of the Ohio, kicking out the French, then continuing on to other places the enemy had constructed forts. These were wild lands, familiar to almost no colonials. His army, he knew, would need a guide.

Washington was aware of Braddock's predicament. He asked friends to discreetly remind General Braddock's staff that he knew the way to the Forks.

Not long after came a letter from Robert Orme, Braddock's aide-de-camp. Orme informed Washington that the general had heard of Washington's disappointment at having lost his rank, that he wished him to join his expedition, and that he had found an honor-saving way to make that happen. The general "will be very glad of your Company in his Family," Orme wrote, meaning that Braddock was inviting Washington to join him not as a ranked officer but as a volunteer and personal aide.

This satisfied Washington's sense of honor; he needed virtually no time to think about it. He put his younger brother Jack in charge of the plantation. He was ready to ride.

Then a familiar impediment stepped forward. His mother arrived at Mount Vernon and positively forbade him to go on the grounds that she couldn't do without him. She took up so much of his time in hectoring and complaining that he wrote again to Orme apologizing for his delay, and actually blamed it on "my Mother," who was, he admitted, "alarmd" at his leaving for so dangerous a mission.

In the end, he did go. The procession of Braddock and his army was the biggest thing ever to happen to the region, and he hurried to be a part of it. At Alexandria, Braddock had brought together the governors of five different colonies; Indians of various tribes received invitations to take part in a great military adventure, and many showed up to assess the situation in order to see what they would get out of such an alliance.

Washington caught up with Braddock in Frederick, Maryland. First impressions were disappointing. The general was fat and squat, and where Washington had an innate fondness for elaborate English mannerisms and high style, Braddock was blunt, rude and imperious. He however, seemed to take to Washington from the start.

But little else pleased the general just now. Braddock had issued orders to the colonial governors: he wanted men, arms, money, wagons. He got almost nothing he demanded. He didn't seem to understand that he was dealing with representatives of several political entities rather than army officers who were duty-bound to carry out his orders. In order to accomplish such a mission, he would have to get each governor and each provincial assembly to want to work with him, so that each would work with still others to make the expedition happen. Instead it was a disaster in the making. There were no wagons or horses to cart the vast artillery train the general had insisted on assembling.

Washington arrived on the scene in time to witness some deft politicking. When all looked lost for Braddock, Pennsylvania's cleverest resident—Benjamin Franklin—appeared, fresh from his efforts to forge a union of colonies in Albany. Braddock's impending mission had set off a competition among the various colonies, each of which hoped to benefit from it. Franklin came determined to promote Pennsylvania's interests and saw opportunity in the general's predicament. He took out advertisements in his newspaper, the *Pennsylvania Gazette*, which promised financial rewards to those who could provide the needed supplies and at the same time suggested that if the supplies weren't forthcoming Braddock's army would just take them. In this way he rounded up 150 horses and dozens of wagons from Pennsylvania farmers. Braddock was delighted. He promised Franklin that, once he had kicked the French out, the road west would go through Pennsylvania.

When he heard of the coup that Franklin had pulled off, Washington was furious. Washington had considered his difficult missions through the wilderness as being not on behalf of America but of his Virginia homeland. He had expected the opening up of the Ohio Country to benefit Virginia. The work of Dinwiddie and the other investors in the Ohio Company was likewise meant to ensure that the territory eventually became part of Virginia. Now Pennsylvania, which had provided no assistance to Washington's Fort Necessity mission, was to be rewarded by the mother country with a prize that would benefit it far into the future.

But first the army had to get to the Forks. The Ohio Company had built a storehouse for supplies at Wills Creek, on the shores of the Potomac River in the mountains of western Maryland; the army turned this into a fort, which Braddock saw fit to name after the Duke of Cumberland, the man who had given him his assignment. Fort

Cumberland—the westernmost outpost of English civilization in North America—was to be the staging area for the march of Braddock's army. From here, Washington would guide the 2,400 men—the largest army ever assembled in North America—on a grueling summertime march 120 miles west to the Forks. They would hack their way through thick forest, clearing a 12-foot road as they went.

In the midst of this major event in George Washington's life—with soldiers, Indians and horses milling, with a massing army getting itself ready to be led by him on a mission of vital importance to all the colonies—an acquaintance named Charles Dick arrived in camp bearing a letter from his mother. As though he were still the eleven-year-old she had leaned on after his father had died, she wrote that she wanted him to drop what he was doing and send her some butter, and to find a "Dutch servant" for her. And she complained that he had not stopped to see her as he headed off to join the army. With some impatience, he sent a reply:

> *Honourd Madam: I was favourd with your letter by Mr. Dick, and am sorry it is not within my power to provide you with a Dutch servant or the Butter agreeably to your desire, We are quite out of that part of the country where either are to be had, there being few or no Inhabitants where we now lie Encampd, & butter can not be had here to supply the wants of the army.*
>
> *I am sorry it was not in my power to call upon you as I went to, or returned from Williamsburg. The business I went upon (viz.: money for the army) would not suffer an hour's delay.*
>
> *I hope you will spend the chief part of your time at Mount Vernon, as you have proposed to do, where I am certain everything will be ordered as much for your satisfaction as possible . . .*

*As nothing else remarkable occurs to me, I shall conclude, after*
*begging my love and Compliments to all Friends*
  *Dear Madam Yr most Affecte and Dutiful Son*
  *Go: Washing . . .*

Soon afterward, the army began its march, but Washington did not lead the way. Dysentery had swept through the camp, and as they were about to set off, Washington fell so ill he was carried in a cart at the rear, and finally had to be left behind. The army would have to find its way without its guide.

The march was staggeringly difficult. Washington had counseled Braddock to lighten the load of artillery; now Braddock, whose battlefield experience had been on the plains of Europe, understood what it meant to try to haul heavy equipment across forested mountains with no roads in the heat of summer with pro-French Indians harassing the men from the wooded darkness. (One night, as they slept, Indians stole into camp and killed and scalped five men.) And it was harder still for the road-building team that went ahead, blasting rock with gunpowder, leveling rises, building bridges across streams. The army fell silent as it slogged past the grim ruins of Fort Necessity, where one officer observed "many human bones" littering the site.

Two weeks after they had set out, Washington stirred himself at last, and, though still sick and weak, plunged into the forest, riding hard to catch up with the main body. When he did, they were just a few miles from their destination. He brought his horse up to Braddock's side as the general was surveying a twist in the Monongahela River. The plan was to cross the river, make camp for the night, then attack Fort Duquesne the following day. Braddock knew the French in the fort numbered only in the hundreds, while his army was well over 2,000. He was confident that his charge of Fort Duquesne would mark the beginning of the end of the French presence in British North America.

Before setting out, Braddock had asked his young American aide for his advice on several matters. He followed what Washington had to say on one or two points, but he chose to ignore Washington's main plea. Washington had learned at Fort Necessity that the Half King had been right and he had been disastrously wrong: The way to fight in this landscape was not in the sort of traditional battle formation that armies engaged in in Europe. Here you had to take advantage of the forest. Washington didn't like the measured way Braddock was proposing to lead his men in the assault on Fort Duquesne, which completely exposed them to attack. A small party of Iroquois was also on hand, and they too felt Braddock's tactic was spectacularly unsuited to the landscape.

Indeed, just as the army crossed the river, French guns began firing. The enemy, knowing it was undermanned, had not waited for the English to come at them in the fort but had moved forward to meet them. Bullets came seemingly from nowhere, as the French and their Indian allies had staked out positions in the woods on both sides of their column. The officers on horseback were easy targets. Washington was shouting at men to stand their ground when he felt his horse give way beneath him. Bullets tore through his coat as it flapped, and through his hat. He watched appalled as inexperienced soldiers dropped to one knee and fired—directly into the forward line of their own men.

Washington was shouting now at Braddock over the din of battle: he wanted permission to lead a contingent of provincials on a flanking run, to, as he said, "engage the enemy in their own way." That wasn't how battles were fought; Braddock refused. Washington found another horse; it too was shot out from under him. He saw fellow officers go down. He watched men break ranks, leaving the artillery and ammunition as they ran. They were being routed by an inferior force. Then Braddock fell.

The battle ended in a total victory for the French, with 500 English and colonial soldiers dead. Washington led the remnant of Braddock's army in an eastward retreat, back along the road they had built, hauling the grievously wounded general in a horse-drawn cart. Four days later, near the site of Fort Necessity, Braddock died. One of his last acts was to give Washington his pistols and his ceremonial sash. Despite his exasperation at the old warrior's tactics and personality, despite the disastrous results, the young man felt a rush of warmth for the first general under whom he had served. Honor, after all, was bound up with loyalty. He would treasure the possessions for the rest of his life.

They came staggering through the ramshackle stockade and into the city of Albany, dazed and wild-eyed: Dutch families from the settlement of Hoosick, 30 miles away, out beyond the falls at Cohoes. The stories Abraham Yates heard were chaotic, but they soon clarified into a simple image. As the farmers were in their fields bringing in the harvest, a party of French soldiers and Indian allies had swept in. Two residents were killed, all the buildings set ablaze. The settlement was destroyed in no time. The whole community stood here now among them, looking around abstractedly, needing refuge.

So this was it: war.

The immediate problem, as far as Albany was concerned, was that the city's stockade was in shambles. Yates joined others in hastily setting up logs to patch gaps in the perimeter. Other rural dwellers soon appeared, also looking for protection. Albany's population doubled. The city sat within Albany County, 500 square miles of pasture and forest, which somehow needed to be protected. And the chief law officer, Sheriff James Wilson, chose this moment to become caught up in a sex scandal involving a daughter of one of the area's prominent families. Wilson was the hand-picked man of William Johnson, the power broker to the Iroquois, and Johnson was pushing to keep him in office. But the governor was under pressure to replace him.

Sensing an opportunity amid the chaos, Abraham Yates paid a visit to Robert Livingston, the sixty-six-year-old paterfamilias of one of Albany's powerful old clans. The major landowners—like Livingston, like William Johnson—had a big say in who the sheriff would be; each had their own candidate, who, they expected, would take special care to protect their property.

With Livingston's backing, Yates got the job. He wasn't in the least bit qualified for it. The sheriff's duties were rough: spending long days and nights on horseback, corralling fugitives, smugglers and rogue Indian traders, serving legal writs, running the city jail, overseeing hangings. The one extant picture of Yates shows a man who seems slight of build, squinty and short-sighted. But the work as deputy to the Indian Affairs commission had given him some involvement in the complex affairs of the county. And while he was not a trained lawyer, he had been voraciously reading up in his spare time.

In becoming the sheriff of Albany County, Yates knew he was stepping with both feet into the middle of local politics. He was Livingston's man now, and William Johnson's enemy. After Johnson got himself named as Sole Superintendent of the Affairs of the Six United Nations he disbanded the commission that Yates had been working for. But Yates had no time for the Indian Affairs job now anyway: the war with the French soon dominated everything. Word came into Albany about Braddock's encounter at the Forks of the Ohio. "A victory," Yates recorded. Then the next day came the correction: in fact, a massive defeat. Meanwhile, the English government was determined to knock the French out of Canada. William Johnson, now given the rank of general, had taken 1,500 Englishmen and 200 Mohawks northward with a mission to attack the French fort at Crown Point. Before they reached the fort, though, they encountered a French and Indian army of equal size at what the French called Sacrament Lake (which Johnson renamed Lake George in honor of the king). News trickled into Albany: the outcome was uncertain, but people were appalled to hear of hundreds killed on each side.

Yates became consumed by the war—but it wasn't French troops who occupied him night and day. As the fighting escalated, Albany found itself transformed into the military staging ground for the northern theater. British soldiers streamed into the city by the hundreds. William Shirley, the governor of Massachusetts, whom Braddock had made a general, appeared in Albany in November of 1755 and demanded that his 48th regiment be billeted. Yates told him it was "next to impossible" for "a great part of our houses were doubled by the people from Saratoga, Schaghticoke, Halfmoon, Nistigeione and Hoosick that have been obliged to fly from their habitations for fear of the enemy." Nevertheless, troops were packed in.

The soldiers got rowdy. Yates complained to James Abercrombie, the British general in charge of the northern theater. Soldiers who were billeted in private houses were behaving "like Brutes in Human Shape," trashing their homes. Abercrombie—a hardened veteran, who had fought in Flanders a decade earlier in the same battle at which George Sackville had been wounded—was unmoved. More soldiers arrived. On top of that the general sent military prisoners and ordered that the city hold them. The Albany jail, which Yates oversaw, was a small building with only two cells. The prisoners filled it, and chaos ensued, caused not only by the prisoners but by the soldiers assigned to guard them, who got drunk and fought with Yates's jailer. On another occasion soldiers arrived with bayonets fixed and demanded that Yates take a prisoner of theirs in his jail. When he refused, they broke into the jail, deposited the man, and left.

Meanwhile, residents were shocked when soldiers began disman-
tling the town stockade and using it for firewood. With mounting fury,
Yates went to Abercrombie. The general told him it wasn't his responsibility to maintain the city's stockade, that in fact his only concern was
for his soldiers. If Albany were attacked by the French, Yates recorded
the general as saying, he would "let the City Burn and be Damd."

Yates hoped for better when, in 1756, John Campbell, the Earl of
Loudoun, who after Braddock's death became the Commander in Chief
of British forces in North America, took up residence in Albany, superceding Abercrombie. Loudoun had the power to fortify the city and
restore sanity. Nothing of the kind happened. Instead, Loudoun determined that the city needed to develop proper respect for the military.
He had a criminal hanged on one of its busiest streets and left the body
dangling there all day—"to impress an idea upon the inhabitants," Yates
surmised, "that he could dispossess, hang, burn and destroy when he
pleased." Yates had befriended a twenty-year-old man named Peter Silvester, who had recently been admitted to practice law. Silvester rented
a room from Yates and his wife, and Yates had begun doing legal work
for him, serving writs in cases that Silvester handled. At Yates's instiga-
tion, Silvester issued a writ against a British officer, accusing him of mis-
conduct. In response, a group of soldiers attacked Silvester on Market
Street, leaving him for dead. Yates quoted another officer as saying, "Let
him now again take out writs against officers of the army."

While to the north the British and French armies went at each other
in battles that would determine the fate of the continent, Abraham Yates
worked day and night trying to keep his city from collapsing under the
weight of what was supposed to be a friendly army. Townspeople came
to him to report one form of depredation after another committed by
British soldiers. Homes were broken into, furniture and family objects
taken, women subjected to sexual harassment. Yates complained to
Loudoun; Loudoun rebuffed him, belittled his civil authority. Yates

then did what he thought was his duty. He arrested certain offending British soldiers and locked them up in his jail. At this Loudoun erupted and told Yates that if he imprisoned one more of his soldiers he would tear down the prison. Yates, in turn, said he would not condone any further quartering of military officers in private homes. Loudoun countered this move by having soldiers put military prisoners in Yates's civilian jail.

Yates wrote to Governor James De Lancey, carefully detailing Loudoun's abuses. Loudoun came to Yates and the two had a remarkable public confrontation. Loudoun said he had seen the letter Yates sent to De Lancey and that it was filled with lies. Yates replied that every sentence could be proved and supported by witnesses. Loudoun warned Yates against discharging a military prisoner from his jail. "Sir," Yates replied, "I have already discharged him." "By whose order?" Loudoun demanded to know. "By the King's writ," Yates responded. Loudoun then ordered the sheriff to stay daily within his sight—"and if you do not do so I shall send for you with a file of muskets, with their bayonets fixed." The people of Albany who were witness to the exchange must have thought that would be the end of it. Instead, the inexperienced and not terribly threatening-looking sheriff replied, "My Lord, I have no time to wait upon you. I have other business to attend." Loudoun, barely containing his fury, vowed that for Yates's insolence he would turn his house into a hospital for wounded soldiers and the local church into an artillery storehouse. "I don't know what you will do, My Lord," Yates replied coolly, "but I know you have no right to do it." At that, Loudoun informed him that he did indeed have a right: that the Lord Chancellor in England had decreed that when the army was required to defend a place, "there the law ceased" and the army's rule prevailed.

Apparently in direct response to the insolence Yates exhibited during this encounter, one of Loudoun's officers arrived at Yates's house and announced that he would be staying there henceforth.

Yates told him the house was already filled with soldiers. The captain replied that if necessary he would "lay in the same bed" with Yates and his wife. Antje was pregnant again (having lost yet another baby the year before). Around this time, perhaps due to the stress of the situation, she miscarried.

Something seemed to snap inside Yates. As his confrontation with Loudoun became personal, the situation inflamed his innate mistrust of power and elites. Until now, as people in Albany and many other parts of the colonies saw it, England had been mostly a benevolent abstraction, if not an actual ideal. They thought of themselves as subjects of the Crown, and assumed they were more or less on a par with those who actually lived in the British Isles. Now, though, they saw British soldiers and officers treating Americans not as fellow Englishmen but as something altogether else, lesser.

Yates set about preparing a highly unusual legal memorandum, one that charged the Commander of British forces in North America with crimes against the civilian population. He knew that precedence—history—was the foundation of the law. Like George Washington, he had not had the benefit of a proper education, so he took matters into his own hands. His patron, Robert Livingston, had a younger brother named William, who was a year older than Yates. Superficially, the two men inhabited different worlds, William Livingston having been born into extreme wealth and privilege. But they were contemporaries, both from Albany, both brought up in the Dutch Reformed Church. Both young men developed into impassioned spokesmen for the common man. Yates seems to have gotten inspiration and mentoring from Livingston.

William Livingston had begun his career in New York City as an apprentice to one of the most famous lawyers in America, James Alexander. Twenty years before Abraham Yates locked horns with the head of the British Army in North America, Alexander had wrangled with

William Cosby, then the British governor of New York. From the time of Cosby's arrival, in 1731, he impressed New Yorkers with his penchant for combining arrogance and corruption. Alexander founded a newspaper, the *New York Weekly Journal*, whose principal aim was to skewer Cosby. Cosby responded by charging the printer of the paper, John Peter Zenger, with criminal libel. James Alexander served as one of Zenger's attorneys. When Zenger was acquitted, it was a watershed moment in relations between Britain and her American colonies, for the case changed the definition of libel in America. Where before it had been considered libelous to print anything critical of the government, Zenger's legal team argued that if the reports were true then a publication had a right and duty to print them. From that moment, Americans began speaking of a right to "freedom of the press."

Under such tutelage, William Livingston developed a passion for representing the rights of individuals and an aversion to abuses of power and what he called "the bewitching Charms of despotic Sovereignty." He rebelled against the privileged circumstances into which he had been born ("the Vanity of Birth and Titles"). He became a sworn enemy of religious elites and the control they exercised over ordinary people. Politically, he was a radical Whig: a proponent of the idea that the government's power derives from the people. In the early 1750s, Livingston's focus of attention was James De Lancey, New York's lieutenant governor. De Lancey had been a protégé of Cosby—Cosby had named him Chief Justice of New York's Supreme Court during the Zenger trial—and Livingston considered him little better than his predecessor, calling him a "monopolizer of power." In 1752, he and two other young lawyers produced a journal of radical ideas, called the *Independent Reflector*, which Livingston personally funded and mostly wrote. He was eloquent and passionate in attacking what he saw as abuses by both civil and religious authorities and in supporting what he called "the civil and religious RIGHTS of my Fellow-Creatures."

Livingston was based in New York City, but he came back to Albany regularly, riding with the circuit judges. He was an ideal mentor for Yates and was just the person to help make up for Yates's lack of legal education. One of Livingston's pet peeves was the colonial system for training lawyers, which he felt was arcane and stressed meaningless labors over knowledge. He had developed a "Directions relating to the Study of the Law" manual for his own clerks. In addition, Yates was a keen reader of the *Independent Reflector*.

With Livingston as his advisor and lawyer, Yates sat down to compose his first legal memorandum, one of extraordinary scope and import, detailing the abuses that the British troops, and Loudoun himself, had wrought on the people of his jurisdiction. He began with a foundational observation: that every person has "a fixed, fundamental right, born with him, as to freedom of his person and property in his estate, which he cannot be deprived of."

He asserted, further, that "The King of England can neither change laws without the consent of his subjects nor yet change them with impositions against their wills . . ." for "a King is made and ordained for the defence of the law of his subjects. . . ." Then, picking up on Loudoun's pronouncements that the actions of the army in Albany transcended civil law, he declared, "The pretended power of dispensing with laws or the execution as it hath been assumed and exercised of late is illegal."

He outlined abuses that the people of Albany had endured at the hands of the British troops: "the most iniquitous and tyrannical violations . . . robberies, assault, batteries, burglaries and other most abominable crimes have been committed, some of them under colour and sanction of advancing His Majesty's service." He detailed how "oppressive numbers" of soldiers were quartered in private homes while nearby barracks remained empty. He charged that "We have been threatened by the Earl of Loudoun [that] our houses should be burned," and that troops did indeed burn houses and furniture. He charged that violence of soldiers had been "the means of frequent abortions," that drunken soldiers "have kept their whores in the rooms in defiance of the people," that soldiers had "stripped women naked to their waste and banished them out of the city with halters about their necks."

Among the authorities Yates cited was John Locke, whose *Two Treatises of Government*, written the previous century, had been important for the development of Livingston's own thinking. In particular, Locke's concept of "natural law," according to which all people had certain basic rights that could not be taken away, inspired both men. Very few people in America had read Locke, but Yates found his ideas to be suddenly pertinent to the situation that Americans found themselves in vis-à-vis the British. He referred to Locke in saying that when a government takes advantage of extraordinary circumstances to override the basic rights of its people, that government becomes "the product of force and violence."

Yates was ready to send off his memorandum, but William Livingston stopped him. It was too hot even for Livingston. In claiming that Loudoun put the military above civil authority, Yates was in effect accusing Loudoun of high treason. It was too much, too strong, and he convinced Yates to pull back. Yates got his point across without filing a formal complaint. Loudoun reacted with outrage that a minor functionary from an obscure outpost would dare challenge his authority. Yates had taken the precaution of getting the mayor and councilmen of the city to sign a statement certifying that "Abm: Yates Jun Esq: Now High Sheriff of the city and county of Albany is a person of a good character & reputation" who "has behaved in his office as Sheriff with impartiality, honest and integrity, as far as we know or believe." Yates soon heard from De Lancey. The acting governor informed the sheriff that he had had "repeated complaints that you are on every occasion ready to throw obstacles in the way of his majesty's service." He commanded Yates to make up with Loudoun so that the army would "preserve us from a Popish and cruel enemy."

But Yates was too riled up. Under no circumstances would he give in to either the most important man in North America or the most powerful politician in the province of New York. He fired a letter right back at the governor. He understood perfectly the need for troops, he said, ". . . but I don't think they should subvert the regular course of justice." Regarding his being punished, he added that "as I acted up to the best dictates of my judgment I humbly conceive I deserve no rebuke for it."

*Chapter 6*

# THIS LAND I HAVE MADE FOR
# YOU AND NOT FOR OTHERS

Vast undulating meadows. A two-story clapboard farmhouse. A barn, and a family burial plot with hand-carved tombstones. Venture's new home, to which he had been forcibily relocated, was a sleepy, bucolic place, far removed from the turbulence that Abraham Yates and the residents of Albany were enduring. Then again, with the village of Stonington, Connecticut, just a mile away—two meetinghouses, a town center, and neat New England saltbox homes lining its main street, which followed the peninsula of Stonington Point to where it ended at the waters of Long Island Sound—it was also, compared to the windswept isolation of Fishers Island, a place that hummed with life and society. Thomas Stanton, his new owner, was a young man with a wife and small children. Stanton was the great-grandson and namesake of one of Stonington's founders, who had sailed from England to Virginia in 1635, twenty years before George Washington's ancestor. That Thomas Stanton then relocated to New England, bought a tract of six acres along the Pawcatuck River in Connecticut and set himself up as a trader. He had a remarkable facility with languages, and learned several of the Indian languages of the region. He served as an interpreter in the so-called Pequot War of the 1630s, which all but wiped out the

Pequot tribe. Afterward, he was granted 300 acres of what had been Pequot land along the same river and along the shore of Long Island Sound. Besides being a founder of the town, he became one of its progenitors. By the time Venture intersected with the family, there had been ninety-two Stantons baptized in the First Congregational Church.

The father of the Thomas Stanton who bought Venture had died a year before, without a will; he and his brother divided his large estate between them. It was while he was preparing to take over his portion of the farm that he heard that George Mumford wanted to let go of his slave. Venture, who knew virtually every aspect of running a farm, would be a valuable asset. He arrived at the start of winter, which meant getting to work threshing oats, mending fences and foddering cattle. That January, of 1755, was warmer than any January people could remember, so that farmhands in the area took to doing some plowing and digging out stones, work that would normally wait for spring.

Life was busy, and relatively peaceful, though everyone knew of the war with France. A man-of-war left the harbor in January with a great boom from its guns. In September the business manager for the Winthrop family—a man named Joshua Hempstead, whom Venture surely knew—arrived in Stonington with news of William Johnson's engagement with the French at Lake George. He commented with satisfaction that the British and American forces had "killed their lieutenant general and taken the general and killed about seventy of their army, with a loss of 100 or 150." And he noted that among the Americans killed were two local men. The war—ranging though it did from Canada to Virginia— was knitting far-flung colonists together.

The Stanton brothers' farms were new ventures for them, which required money to get off the ground. Robert Stanton, the brother of Venture's owner, needed a loan. Venture made it known that he had brought with him his savings, which totaled about 21 pounds in New York currency. Venture was astute at finance. He understood the capital, loans, interest, and how to make money from money. A slave couldn't go to a bank and deposit his savings. Loaning his savings to his master's brother, and earning interest on it, would be better than keeping it hidden. Robert Stanton gave him a promissory note in exchange.

Venture got along reasonably well with his new owner, within the confines of a master-slave relationship. Besides his farming know-how and his steadiness, he had brought with him his reputation for feats of strength. Stanton liked to show him off, having Venture, in one instance, hoist a barrel of molasses (which would have weighed about 370 pounds). Venture too took pleasure in repeating such stories. Honor was the bright and shining coin of the day. If George Washington was able to seek it in military exploits involving European powers, and Abraham Yates could quench the eighteenth-century male need for it in local politics, Venture had only his body: a barrel of molasses, sweat-soaked clothes, glistening muscles, an exchange of looks.

Pleasing Stanton with his feats of strength was also to a purpose. Venture worked hard at impressing him. When he judged the time was right, he asked a favor. By then the two men had formed enough of a bond that Stanton granted it. He bought Meg and Hannah, and so reunited Venture with his family.

The war, meanwhile, mostly passed the Stanton homestead by. In May of 1756 two sloops from Boston appeared off New London, transporting troops from Massachusetts to Albany. In June of 1757 a seaman who had turned privateer sailed into New London bringing a prize French schooner he had captured in the waters off Bermuda. Two months later came the news of the siege of Fort William Henry, which ended with French general Louis-Joseph de Montcalm forcing the surrender of the British fort, located 60 miles north of Albany, and with the subsequent massacre of English men, women and children.

There was one point, in early March of 1756, when Venture could have gotten a glimpse of a newly minted celebrity of the war. Colonel

George Washington, of the Virginia militia, suddenly showed up in New London, resplendent in blue uniform trimmed with scarlet and silver, sword at his side and with a retinue of attendants. He had been written about in the newspapers, and his passage through the area excited a good deal of attention. Joshua Hempstead, the man who had been George Mumford's agent during Venture's time on Fishers Island, recorded in his diary the news that "Coll. Washington" was in town, having come from Boston. Hempstead didn't know Washington's business; he could only speculate that "he hath been to advise or be directed by Governor Shirley" of Massachusetts.

Venture knew the area as well as Hempstead, and kept alert to what was happening, so in the midst of his happiness at having recently been reunited with his wife and daughter he could have made his way to the New London dock to see the Virginian, whose unusual height would have caused him to tower over virtually everyone in a crowd except Venture himself. In New London, Washington hired from a man named Powers a sloop and two boats and sailed off across the sound, past Venture's former home on Fishers Island, making for Long Island on the business of a war.

That, however, was truly no business of Venture's. His deepest interests were here, close by. A hard day in the pasture, harrowing soil, sowing seed, setting fence; falling asleep to the sound of rain; waking to fields of snow. The goings-on of local people, all of whom he knew, was the news that mattered. Much of it concerned untimely death. Gedion Comstock died, leaving two children parentless. Lydia Harris, an "old maid" of about forty, who people thought of as "weak in her understanding, almost an idiot," died. So did Abrah Herculas, the twenty-year-old slave of Samuel Lattimer. Not long afterward, Samuel Bills's son, not yet ten, caught a fever and died.

Then, in June, came news that Venture's former master, George Mumford, had died suddenly, just months after giving up the plantation at Fishers Island and settling into his retirement. The world was turning; Venture's past was being swept away and his future was coming into being. A few months after Mumford's death, and several months after Washington had passed through, Meg gave birth to a son, Solomon. The next year a second son came, whom she and Venture named Cuff. Out in the wider world, distant European empires were throwing their might at one another, and the outcome, including the fate of the English colonies in North America, was all uncertain. But here on the tranquil Connecticut coast Venture had forged a pocket of security. He had health, strength and savings. He had a family of five, and everyone was together.

Around the time that Venture's third child was born—in late 1758— George Washington's military career came to an end yet again. "I have quit a military life," he wrote to his brother. He was twenty-seven years old and looking ahead to retirement.

It had been a dizzying—and ultimately frustrating—three years since the battle at which he served under General Braddock. That defeat was so unexpected and profound that, when the dying Braddock learned of its dimensions, he seemingly coined a phrase: "Who would have thought?" Washington had days in which to ponder and to replay scenes from the battle in his mind. He still admired, as he had as a small child, all things English, still dreamed of becoming a regular British officer, yet he had witnessed how poorly the British soldiers performed in the battle, whereas Braddock himself had remarked on the bravery and efficiency of the colonial troops. And he had watched a British general completely and devastatingly miscalculate. As with Abraham Yates, Washington's image of Britain as an indomitable, noble, world-conquering force had taken a blow.

Returning home from the defeat, Washington made it as far as Fort

Cumberland, in the Maryland panhandle, when he had to stop and recuperate, for he was still weak from the dysentery that had struck him before the battle. Ten days later, when he got back to Mount Vernon, a letter arrived from Belvoir, the Fairfax residence down the river. William Fairfax, his mentor, wrote as effusively as if he were his own son of his feelings upon learning that Washington had survived: "Your safe Return gives an uncommon Joy to Us. . . ." Nice as it no doubt was to receive such affection, the rest of the sentence must have puzzled Washington, for Fairfax said his sentiments must be shared "by all true Lovers of Heroick Virtue." How could someone who had shared in such a defeat be seen as an embodiment of heroic virtue?

But it proved to be true: as horrified as people in the colonies were by the scope of Braddock's defeat, newspapers grasped at the reports of Washington's steadfastness under fire. Robert Orme, Braddock's aide, perhaps single-handedly sealed a reputation with a quote that was picked up in many publications: "Mr. Washington had two Horses shot under him and his Cloaths shot thro' in several Places, behaving the whole Time with the greatest Courage and Resolution." The French threat to the colonists was real, and palpable. People needed something to rally around. Letters, even more than newspapers, were the means by which information was conveyed. From South Carolina to Massachusetts, people wrote of "the merit of Washington," saying that he "ought to be distinguished and taken notice of." The man who had been reviled following the disaster at Fort Necessity was now, in the wake of yet another disaster, branded a hero.

Governor Dinwiddie offered Washington command of the entire Virginia Militia. His mother insisted that he reject it. Washington replied to her more sternly than he had in the past: "it would reflect eternal dishonor upon me to refuse." He accepted, with the idea in his mind that now, finally, he would receive what his inflamed sense of honor demanded: a royal commission.

He traveled to Fort Dinwiddie—a hastily assembled jumble of stockades in the town of Winchester—and assessed the situation of the region. It could scarcely have been more grim. Ohio Country Indians had taken Braddock's defeat as a signal that in the war between the French and English the English were the weaker party. As it appeared to the colonists, many tribes threw their lot with the French, or else determined that, with Braddock's army having fallen back, they could freely attack the hundreds of small farms scattered throughout the region, from Pennsylvania into Ohio and throughout Virginia, pushing back against the westward encroachment of colonists. Washington was particularly piqued by the irony that in carrying out their attacks the Indians were using the road that Braddock's army had created. Soon the same road was crowded with bloodied settlers—survivors of Indian raids—trudging east to safety.

The immediate problem regarding being given command of the Virginia Militia was that there was no Virginia Militia. It had been an ad hoc thing, pulled together as occasion demanded, with great difficulty. Washington had to create the army he was to lead. He himself had had no formal military training. So, as he had done in copying out the "Rules of Civility" at age sixteen, he educated himself, poring over a British military manual published a decade earlier called *A Treatise of Military Discipline*, which gave him details on "How the Companies are to draw up in Battalion," "How the Officers are to take their Posts in the Rear by Beat of Drum" and "Method of sending for the Colours," and outlining the different procedures for "Parapet Firing," "Street Firing" and "Running-Fire, or *Feu de Joye*."

Always a stickler for dress, he personally designed the uniforms for his army (officers would be in blue trimmed with scarlet and silver). He handpicked his officers from the best families, being a great believer in the natural leadership abilities of "persons of quality," and gave each one instructions on recruiting common soldiers to fill out the ranks.

These were mostly farmers and itinerants. They got drunk; they drifted off into the woods. With Indians continuing to rain terror down all around them, and with the threat of being inundated by the French army, Washington came to insist on severe discipline. He ordered vicious floggings as punishment. He had a gallows built as a deterrent to desertion. It didn't do the trick, so, with the rest of the army watching, he had two serial deserters hanged. He preferred the gallows to a firing squad, he told Dinwiddie, because it "conveyed much more terror." The soldiers also got to see friendly Indians coming into camp carrying enemy scalps, for which Colonel Washington paid them: a practice that simultaneously reduced the number of enemy combatants, reinforced ties with friends, and impressed the common soldiers with the seriousness of the situation.

While he was busy ordering construction of a series of defensive stockades in Maryland, western Virginia and Pennsylvania, Washington clashed with a Maryland officer named John Dagworthy over who outranked whom. Washington, a colonel, was clearly above Dagworthy, who had the rank of captain; but Dagworthy had a Royal commission, which, he held, made him the superior officer. This was the issue that had dogged Washington's career. Dagworthy was pushing precisely the button that would send Washington into a fit.

He was so furious that he temporarily removed himself from the war. Putting his personal quest for honor ahead of everything else, he decided now was the time to force the British to give him a royal commission. He got Governor Dinwiddie to allow him to travel to Boston, where he would appeal to Massachusetts governor William Shirley, who was at that moment acting as head of British armed forces.

It was Washington's first trip through the colonies. He was seeing America in something like its totality for the first time. He knew that his fame had preceded him, and he was determined to build on it. In his quest to win recognition as an officer of the British army, he would put on a proper show. He traveled in full military regalia, with a retinue of four officers and attendants, and had his men sport his colors and his family coat of arms. He arrived in Philadelphia, the largest city in the colonies, in style, parading through the streets on horseback, sword at his side. At six feet two inches, he towered over the men he traveled with, offering those he passed in the streets a physical presence that matched what they had heard about his courage at Braddock's side. He meanwhile marveled at the sights and sounds of a northern city, with its energy and industry. He was something of a shopaholic, and the experience here was unlike anything available in Virginia; he spent more money than he had, on new clothes, saddles and jewelry.

New York seemed even more exotic. The shops around the fashionable district of Hanover Square exuded French elegance; the same area was also home to the opulent city mansions of Albany's patricians and other wealthy families. Taverns along the waterfront looked out on a harbor alive with sailing vessels. The streets teemed: bonneted Dutch housewives jostled German Jews and African slaves. British soldiers were everywhere.

Washington danced at balls and conversed at parties. He would have noted that stylish young New York gentlemen affected London mannerisms, crying, "Split me, madam!" or "Damn me!" He gambled with urban card sharps—and lost money to them. He was the guest of the Robinsons, one of the province's great families; he became interested in his host's sister-in-law, Polly Phillipse. He took her to see a European wonder, the "Microcosm or the World in Miniature," a kind of planetarium that played music while the heavenly bodies swept by in their orbits and mechanical figures enacted grand and comic scenes. Washington must have felt like a bumpkin as he gazed at this example of what technical wizards on the Continent were capable of; he went back a second time to see its show.

Heading further north, he traveled through the tranquil, riverine landscape of Connecticut. He rode well east of Albany, where Abraham Yates was working furiously to try to contain the depredations of British soldiers, and eventually reached Boston. The newspaper announced his arrival, calling him "a gentleman who has deservedly a high reputation of military skill, integrity, and valor," while also noting that "success has not always attended his undertakings."

The trip succeeded in giving Washington a greater sense of the American colonies, and it gave the American colonies a greater sense of him. But it failed in its chief objective: Governor Shirley did not make him a British officer. Not only that, he decided to put Horatio Sharpe, the governor of Maryland, in command not only of that colony's militia but of Virginia's as well. Washington despised Sharpe.

He grumbled all the way home. Instead of going overland the whole way, he decided to take a water shortcut across Long Island Sound at New London. It was here, a few miles from the Stanton house, that he more or less crossed paths with Venture. He continued on to New York, where he paid another visit to Polly Philipse. Riding from there to Philadelphia, he could hardly sit in the saddle, for the dysentery struck again; he was forced to spend several days in the city, not taking in sights but recuperating.

When he got back to his post at Winchester, his anger at being snubbed and underappreciated vanished, for he encountered a town filled with refugees from the Indian raids, backwoods people with hollowed, stricken visages who harangued him with stories of children murdered and homes burned. The spectacle cracked open his customary "Roman" facade; he was so moved that he wished himself into a Christ-like role, writing to Dinwiddie, "If bleeding, dying! would glut [the Indians'] insatiate revenge—I would be a willing offering to Savage Fury, and die by inches to save a people!" There was no question now where his duty lay: he would throw himself anew into the defense of his homeland.

But he hadn't forgotten his rebuff in Boston. Shortly after his return he got the news that Governor Shirley had been replaced as head of the army by the Earl of Loudoun. Washington sat down and wrote a meandering, pouting letter to Loudoun, trying yet again to get the royal commission that he coveted nearly to the point of distraction. Certainly, he wanted to ensure that his region of the country, which he feared Loudoun would neglect in his focus on taking Canada, would be fully defended; but he also wanted the general to see that soldiers of the American colonial militias were the equal of British troops.

Loudoun gave Washington no more satisfaction than he gave to Abraham Yates. In fact, as with Yates, he riled him further. Far from promoting colonial officers into the ranks of the regular army, he planned to import British officers to command the provincial militias, essentially demoting men such as Washington.

Washington tried to rechannel his mounting frustration to a productive purpose when he learned that a new expedition to the Forks of the Ohio was being mounted; he hoped to play a significant role in it. A new British general—John Forbes—would lead the march. Washington dashed off a letter to an officer he had served with on Braddock's campaign, who he hoped would recommend him to Forbes.

Along with other Virginians, Washington was angered to learn that the new expedition to the Forks would proceed not via the road Braddock's army had hacked northward from Fort Cumberland but westward from central Pennsylvania. Benjamin Franklin and other Pennsylvania leaders, communicating directly with officials in England, had continued to push the cause of a military road through their colony, with the idea that it would make Pennsylvania a commercial corridor. The Pennsylvania route was a blow to the financial hopes of Virginia's Ohio Company.

Given the desperate situation of his homeland, though, and his own quest for honor, Washington still wanted to be part of the Forbes expedition. The army turned out to be much larger than Braddock's—larger than any operation ever mounted in North America—with nearly 7,000 troops. The summer of 1758 was a hot one, and progress through the wilderness was slow. Diseases swept through the army as the summer advanced. Forbes himself was struck ill and had to be hauled over miles of difficult terrain in a makeshift bed strung between two horses. The army built simple forts along the way, at Raystown and Ligonier, as defensive works and supply stations. Washington spent most of the summer to the south, at Fort Cumberland, organizing men and supplies and awaiting orders to proceed. In September, the advance party of the army approached Fort Duquesne and—just as had happened with Braddock's army—were ambushed by the French and Indian forces, who had not waited to be attacked but come forward to surprise them. The advance party was routed; Forbes paused to ponder the situation.

Finally, in late November, a plan was put into action. Washington was ordered north to Raystown. Forbes carved out three brigades to march on the fort; Washington was given command of one. They advanced by night—and were utterly bewildered at what they found. As Washington himself reported to Francis Fauquier, who had replaced Robert Dinwiddie as lieutenant governor of Virginia, "The enemy, after letting us get within a day's march of the place, burned the fort, and ran away (by the light of it) at night. . . ." The English troops, steeled for a hard battle, strolled into the undefended fort. The sudden, bloodless taking of it, Washington noted, "has been a matter of great surprise to the whole army."

The explanation for the French decision to abandon the Forks lay 400 miles to the northeast, where William Johnson, whom Braddock had named Superintendent of Indian Affairs, had been working with great diligence. Following a series of British successes in Canada, Johnson, in July, had gathered leaders of the Iroquois and other tribes at his estate northwest of Albany, and gotten them to agree to a shift of allegiance. The Iroquois would henceforth back the English, and they would instruct their allies in the Ohio Country to do the same. In October, following from this breakthrough, colonial and Indian officials gathered at Easton, Pennsylvania, and signed a treaty in which the English and colonials agreed to cede back to the Indians certain lands and promised not to establish new settlements or outposts west of the Allegheny Mountains, and in exchange ten nations of Indians agreed they would not fight alongside the French. The French, faced with an increasingly difficult fight in Canada as well as a formal shift in Indian allegiances, thus made a strategic decision to abandon Fort Duquesne.

As far as General Forbes was concerned, a victory was a victory. The English now had what they had long coveted: control of the Forks of the Ohio, and thus of the way west. He ordered a new structure built on the site, which would be called Fort Pitt, after William Pitt, the mentor of George Sackville, who, on becoming Secretary of State, had engineered a turnaround in the British conduct of the war. Forbes likewise decreed that the area between the rivers around the site of the new fort would be called Pittsburgh. Then Forbes, who had studied medicine, and who had diagnosed his own condition as "the bloody flux" (aka dysentery), promptly died.

Pacing amid the smoking ruins of Fort Duquesne, Washington pondered the swift change of events. The Easton treaty didn't just end the threat of Indian invasions; it meant, essentially, that the war in his part of America was over. Though he was surely relieved for the sake of the local population, Washington's sharpest concerns were for himself. His bitterness ran deep: there would be no Royal commission. Loudoun, who had given both him and Abraham Yates such cold treatment, had been recalled to London as part of Pitt's shakeup, but the affronts hadn't come from one individual. They came from a system, one that, Washington now realized, did not and never would consider him to be worthy of the degree of honor that he felt was his due. Four years earlier he had cast the war against the French in soaringly patriotic terms, as an occasion for "the heroick spirit of every free-born Englishman to assert the rights and privileges of our king," a chance to win honor and glory by saving "from the invasions of a usurping enemy, our majesty's property, his dignity, and lands."

That heartfelt patriotism was now all but dead in him. His anger at the British system had reached its peak. He resigned from military service. He was done with war, done with seeking honor in arms, which, for all his effort, had eluded him. He made his way to his home at Mount Vernon. He wrote his brother that he hoped to find "more happiness in retirement than I ever experienced amidst a wide and bustling World."

As George Washington retired from the fight against the French in North America, George Sackville found himself astride his horse on a forested hillside above the Prussian town of Minden, gazing down onto another classic scene of European warfare. Column upon column of English infantrymen and their German allies—vivid in their scarlet and gold uniforms topped with tricorne hats and armed with muskets and bayonets—maneuvered into positions against equally uniform lines of French adversaries. He was in command of the allied cavalry. With the grunts and whinnies of horses sounding around him in the morning fog, he awaited his orders. It was August 1, 1759; depending on the outcome of what promised to be a stupendous battle—involving nearly 100,000 men—the war of empire between Britain and France, which had been started five years earlier by the blunders of an inexperienced colonial officer in North America, might end here.

Sackville had worked assiduously for four years to reach this moment: he was now the highest-ranking man in the British army. After successfully dodging the effort to send him to America to head the troops there—and seeing General Braddock succumb to precisely the fate he had most feared—he had ducked yet again when, following Braddock's death, leaders tried to enlist him a second time for the American role. They eventually picked Loudoun, and Sackville then maneuvered for the post he really wanted: Secretary of War. He lined up the necessary political backing, only to have his bid rejected by the king. Sackville was angry, but he could not have been surprised. George II had two excellent reasons for denying him the office. For one, it would unnecessarily stir up Irish outrage to have Sackville—whose name in Ireland was now synonymous with English arrogance—added to the cabinet.

The second reason had to do with British politics. Technically, power was split between the two parties: the Whigs and the Tories. The Tory Party had emerged in the previous century in support of the Stuart monarchy; its members rallied to withstand attempts by Parliament to strip the monarchy of most of its powers. The Whigs, meanwhile, generally backed Parliament and the idea of a constitutional monarchy; they advanced liberal political thinking, and took the writings of John Locke on political philosophy as a touchstone. By the mid-eighteenth century, however, these distinctions between the parties had faded. Politicians now divided themselves in terms of loyalties: those who supported George II, the ailing septuagenarian monarch, and those who backed his grandson and heir apparent, the Prince of Wales, who was also named George. The two Georges were utterly different, and they detested one another. Where the king was aggressive, impulsive and famous for his string of mistresses, the younger George was cautious and moralistic. (He once chastely remarked that "the conduct of this old King makes me ashamed of being his grandson.") The Prince of Wales openly worked against his grandfather's policies, and a kind of shadow government formed around him; his London mansion, Leicester House, was known as the Young Court.

In 1757, the king, disgusted with the way the war in America was going, had dissolved the cabinet and tried to form a new one. In particular, he wanted to remove William Pitt as Secretary of State. He asked Sackville to support a new government he was forming. Sackville replied decorously but defiantly: he believed Pitt to be the ablest politician in the country, who had the clearest vision for managing the war, and who lacked only the authority to implement his ideas. He would support Pitt. Pitt, meanwhile, was firmly in the camp of the Prince of Wales. In aligning himself with Pitt, Sackville was turning his back on the monarch he had once fought alongside. There was no possibility of the king approving his bid to become Secretary of War.

The king's effort to rebuild the cabinet failed; Pitt returned with even more power—a greater mandate for running the war as he saw fit—and, as a reward for Sackville's loyalty, Pitt chose him to work alongside him as Lieutenant-General of the Ordnance. From an office in the Tower of London, Sackville oversaw the arming and equipping of the British military. He worked closely with Jean-Louis Ligonier, the commander in chief of the armed forces, whom he had known from his first sojourn in Ireland. Ligonier was a distinguished gentleman in his seventies. He enjoyed Sackville's personality, the bracing force of it. Sackville spent time at Ligonier's green and serene estate in Surrey, Cobham Park, where the younger man held forth on strategy, pushing for alliances with Prussia and several German states.

The tactical question facing Pitt, Ligonier, Sackville, and others in the British hierarchy was how extensive the war would be, and where to put resources. The conflict involved much more than Britain and France. Austria, Sweden, Russia and various German states were also ranged in a complex struggle for territory and power. Pitt's vision was to see beyond the traditional European theater; he recognized that Britain could best negotiate the complexity—could break out of the medieval power struggle and into a new era of empire—by striking hard at France's colonial outposts. Doing so would put to best use Britain's chief advantage: the world's largest navy. Under his guidance, over the next three years British forces defeated the French in India, winning control of the province of Bengal, and went on to overwhelm French outposts in Africa and on the Caribbean island of Guadaloupe.

Meanwhile, Sackville and others believed that the French would not commit huge numbers of troops to North America; they gambled forcefully, shipping 25,000 soldiers to America, and decided to push hard against French strongholds in Canada. One result of this was the buildup of forces in Albany, with which Abraham Yates contended. Another was the decision by the French to give up on the Forks of the Ohio. A third was the decision to recall Loudoun. Yet again, military leaders wanted Sackville to go to America. Yet again he was able to dodge; he preferred to deploy in Europe, and Pitt wanted him there as well.

The strategy of going at the colonies hinged on Pitt's gambit of simultaneously playing the traditional game of warfare in Europe, which would require the French to keep the bulk of their army on the continent. But if England reigned supreme at sea, France had the largest army in Europe, so England needed to rely heavily on alliances. Foremost among Britain's allies was Frederick II, king of Prussia, who, in 1756, faced with imminent invasion by French, Russian and Austrian forces, had launched the preventive strike that had begun the current phase of European war.

Under the alliance Frederick entered into with England, both sides agreed that the vigorous, thirty-eight-year-old German prince Ferdinand of Brunswick would lead the combined armies. George Sackville headed off into the German hinterland to attend Ferdinand's army. Initially, he was second-in-command of English forces, under the British aristocrat Charles Spencer, the Duke of Marlborough. When Marlborough died unexpectedly, Sackville was promoted to lead the British forces.

Thus he found himself looking down into the plain of Minden, with the village and the River Weser in the distance, as two massive armies prepared to throw themselves at one another. Ferdinand set things in motion by directing a maneuver that seemed to the French general, the Marquis de Contades, to indicate that he had divided his army, weakening it. Contade had boat bridges erected across the river and ordered his men over them and into battle. Three times the French charged; three times the British and German forces repulsed them. Then Ferdinand ordered the counterattack. The French lines fell back and began to collapse. A victory would be a great thing, but a rout, which seemed to be in the offing, would conceivably lead the French to negotiate an end to the war. It was time for the cavalry to come thundering down the slope, decimating the enemy.

Sackville, who did not have a view of the action from his hillside position, suddenly saw a rider approaching. Colonel Fitzroy, a twenty-two-year-old nobleman, shouted Prince Ferdinand's orders: Sackville was to lead the cavalry in a charge.

Sackville didn't order a charge.

Shortly after, another messenger appeared and delivered the order to charge.

Sackville didn't charge.

Eventually, after getting a third message, he did. By then the battle was nearly over. The English and Prussian forces had won a solid victory—enough that, when news of it reached England, bonfires were lit in every street in celebration. But the rout that could have forced France to beg for peace never happened.

The allied officers met for dinner the evening after the battle. When Sackville entered the room, with a relaxed demeanor, Prince Ferdinand said to the others (French being the common tongue among gentlemen), "Voilà cet homme autant à son aise comme s'il avoit fait des merveilles!"—(Look at this man completely at ease, as if he had done something wondrous!).

Over the course of the next month the failure of Sackville to carry out the order to charge became the most talked-about event in England. Every level of society became absorbed with the story of the high-born aristocrat, famed for his military prowess, his ambition and his aggression, who was recently being talked about as a possible future prime minister, who shrank back shockingly at the moment his country needed him, who failed to attack not once but two times, and whose failure meant that war would drag on. The combination of the irony and the high stakes involved, noted one contemporary account, "kindled up such a blaze of indignation in the minds of the people, as admitted of no temperament or control," so that "an abhorrence and detestation of Lord George Sackville as a coward and a traitor became the universal passion, which acted by contagion, infecting all degree of people from the cottage to the throne." Sackville effigies were burned. He was lampooned in the press and in drawing rooms, referred to as "a damned chicken-hearted soldier" and "a stinking coward." Seemingly overnight, George Sackville became the most hated man in England.

But why? What, people around the country wanted to know, could possibly have accounted for his behavior?

The day after the battle, Sackville gave Prince Ferdinand his explanation. He said the first two messengers had given slightly different orders—one telling him to advance with the British cavalry only, the other with all the allied cavalry—and in addition he was confused because, from where he stood, he could not see the battle and didn't comprehend the situation. He insisted that very little time was lost by his delay—no more than eight minutes.

Ferdinand—arrogant, dandified, ferret-faced—responded with disgust. He said he was "mortified," for "I gave you the opportunity to decide the fate of the day."

Sackville did as honor required and offered his resignation to his superiors in London. The gesture was a formality; he was shocked—

and began to realize the scope of the reaction in England—when his resignation was immediately accepted.

He wrote to Pitt, saying he hoped he could count on his backing. Pitt's reply was as frank as a politician's could be: "I find myself under the painful necessity of declaring my infinite concern, at not having been able to find . . . any room . . . for me to offer support."

Sackville's natural aggression immediately asserted itself. He told Pitt he wanted a court-martial, a forum in which he could lay out his defense, after which he would be seen to have acted honorably. Pitt replied that he should be careful in what he wished for, for "delusion might prove dangerous."

The court-martial dragged on for months and, as Pitt had predicted, served to keep the sport of Sackville-bashing alive among the populace. Newspapers continued to malign him, some accusing him of unsubstantiated and wildly unrelated crimes, including sodomy. The king stripped him of his military rank and office. His father, who had once before been humiliated by his son's actions, retreated deeper into the confines of Knole House, permanently retired now from public life.

The government called a parade of witnesses in the trial, including the officers who had brought Ferdinand's orders to Sackville. One commented that, after he delivered the orders, "Lord Sackville seemed not to understand them, and asked how it was to be done?" The officer repeated and elaborated; still Sackville seemed not to comprehend. The picture the witnesses painted was of a man who had willfully but inexplicably disobeyed an order.

Sackville served as his own attorney. He was vigorous, incisive, flamboyant. He cross-examined witnesses, skewered them over inconsistencies. He seemed to onlookers perfectly confident in his case and his method.

It was to no avail. The court found him "guilty of having disobeyed the orders of Prince Ferdinand of Brunswick," and declared him to be "unfit to serve his Majesty in any military Capacity whatever." In predicting the outcome, William Pitt was not only assessing the overall mood of the country; it was obvious to any practical-minded politician that had the court ruled in Sackville's favor it would have created a split between Britain and Prussia, with devastating consequences for the war effort.

Not only was he found guilty, Sackville narrowly escaped being executed for his crime. A nobleman with knowledge of the affair later said that Sackville's father had made personal appeals to some of the judges, thus saving his son's life.

George II was said to be furious that Sackville was not hanged. He therefore decreed his own additional punishment. Sackville was barred from attendance at the royal court, and the sentence against him was to be read aloud to every British soldier around the world, so that they might understand that offenses such as Sackville had committed "are Subject to Censures much worse than Death, to a Man who has any Sense of Honour."

Sackville gave a strong closing statement in his defense, but it did little to explain his behavior. Nothing he said seemed to jive with the man he had been throughout his whole career to that point. Indeed, the ferocious anger of the British people seemed partly tied to the inexplicability.

What, then, was the reason for his refusal to carry out the order? It could not have been cowardice. Those with deep knowledge of British politics speculated that his conduct may have had to do with the power struggle between the Prince of Wales and the king. Sackville went to the Continent as the special emissary of the Prince of Wales, and the prince distrusted Ferdinand. Sackville had spent weeks before the battle sending the prince critical reports of Ferdinand's military movements and decisions, making a case that he was maneuvering in a way that benefited Prussia over Britain. Although he would have been honor-bound to withold such an explanation from the public, his action at Minden may have been an attempt to carry out the wishes of the Prince of Wales and to thwart both Ferdinand and King George II.

As it turned out, it misfired. His failure to lead the cavalry charge on the retreating French army had disastrous consequences for England and for him. His life had been one long, steady ascent to the heights of power, honor and influence in the British Empire. And a single decision—or nondecision—had wiped it all away. The political gossip Horace Walpole was among those who had thought Sackville was on the verge of becoming prime minister, only to lose everything. He penned what he expected would serve as Sackville's political epitaph: "So finishes a career of a man who was within ten minutes of being the first man in the Profession in the Kingdom."

George Sackville's blunder extended the British war against France that had been started by George Washington's blunder. Both men were fighting on the same side, though as time went on Washington's regard for Britain waned. Abraham Yates, meanwhile, came to feel outright animosity for the British. And Venture, while fully aware that the war was going on—he could see the sails of privateers in the Sound and hear the talk of soldiers who stopped in New London as they were being shipped northward—did not find that it affected his life, or even that it mattered to him. Indeed, while the other three men used the war to maneuver for personal advantage and honor, there was no deep sense of patriotism in their involvement. That was because the Seven Years' War, as it would become known, or the French and Indian War, as its American theater would be called, was not a revolution or a civil war; it didn't spring from idealism or long-standing grudges, the sorts of things that would roil up into tavern brawls. It was a global chess game that they were all caught up in, cool and abstract. In such wars, the greatest scheming takes place not between adversaries but among those on the same side, as they use the conflict for their own advancement.

But Cornplanter, who was a young man by the time of the war's end, was the exception. For him—for the Senecas, for the Iroquois, for all the native tribes in the affected regions of North America—the power struggle between the two European nations was about their land, their way of life, their relations with one another. For them, it did ignite feelings of patriotism and even spirituality, the selfless impulse to protect their sacred homeland.

Cornplanter came of age during the war; it shaped him as a man and a fighter. Though he had not yet entered the historical record by the war's end, his uncle and mentor, Guyasuta, had, and it is likely that at some point the son of Gah-hon-no-neh, lineage matron of the Seneca Wolf Clan, was at his side. In this time of rapidly shifting political ground, Guyasuta was a warrior-diplomat, traveling widely to ensure that the Senecas kept what was theirs. Along with the Half King Tanacharison, Guyasuta had guided George Washington to the French at Fort Le Boeuf in 1753. Then, with other Senecas, he had taken the other side and fought with the French at the Forks of the Ohio, defeating Braddock's army.

From Cornplanter's perspective, what unfolded through the 1750s and into the 1760s was not a contest between the English and the French, but a vastly more complicated flow of events, involving many players across more than a thousand miles of territory, with the lush and ravined valley of the Genesee, his homeland, at the center. He learned early on of the array of tribes between the Atlantic Ocean and the Mississippi River, how they related to one another, and how those relationships were evolving. The Munsee, for one, had originally lived in small, scattered villages away to the east, in the Delaware River valley and north as far as the area around Manhattan Island; they were the people who had had the closest contact with the Dutch in New Amsterdam, and who had "sold" Manhattan, as later history would have it, though from their side the agreement would have meant something more like a defensive alliance. Since the Munsee lacked a cohesive structure, which made it difficult to deal as a group with European settlers, they had, long before Cornplanter's time, entered into a relationship with the Iroquois League. The Iroquois would act on their behalf as diplomats with the Europeans and, if necessary, would fight on their behalf. As a boy, Cornplanter learned the story of Deganawidah and Hiawatha bringing the Law of Peace, which bound the nations of the Iroquois together into their league. Bringing the Munsee under Iroquois protection was a way of extending the peace. Neither of the two Indian nations looked at the arrangement as an act of conquest, but it was certainly one of dominance. Under the terms of this agreement, the Munsee became, according to the logic and language of both groups, symbolically, "women." They agreed to give up the manly work of fighting. The pact between them even involved a ceremony in which Munsee put on women's things—"petticoats" and jewelry—as a sign of their acceptance of their subordinate role.

Over the course of the next century the Munsee were steadily pushed out of their traditional homelands by white settlement and moved westward across Pennsylvania. When they came to live in the Ohio Country, their subordination to the Iroquois was still in effect; along with the Shawnee who also inhabited the area, and were likewise subordinated to the Iroquois, they held to their agreement not to go to war. Since many Senecas now also lived in the Ohio Country, they were the Iroquois tribe responsible for the protection of the subordinate peoples. The more than two hundred miles of forest trails between the traditional Seneca homeland and the Ohio Country did not stop the Senecas from moving between the two areas. Cornplanter's uncle, Guyasuta, traversed it, and so presumably did Cornplanter.

As Cornplanter came of age, he would have shared in the growing concern to maintain Iroquois authority over the Munsee, for with the pact that gave the Iroquois their dominance came the pressure to maintain the strength to protect, whether through diplomacy or warfare. Cornplanter absorbed lessons of power management as he watched his uncle and the Half King, the leaders of the Senecas in the Ohio Country, demonstrate to the Munsee that they were in charge.

For decades the Iroquois had managed affairs with both the French and the English. Sometimes they played the two off against one another. They also used the looseness of their tribal structure to advantage. If one nation of the Iroquois—or even a single village—found it useful to side with the French, they did so, even if others backed the English. Thus the Mohawks, who lived closest to English settlement, tended to side with the English, while the Senecas, whose territory abutted the French, backed them. In this way individual villages were able to play for immediate practical advantage, but at the same time the Iroquois as a confederacy worked to ensure that neither of the two European powers became ascendant.

The balance was disrupted when the French began constructing forts along the Ohio River. In September 1753 the Half King issued a warning that the Senecas would not allow what they saw as a direct incursion into their lands. He traveled to Presque Isle, a long fish-hook-shaped peninsula on Lake Erie that the Senecas had valued ever since they had forcibly taken it from another native people a century earlier. He told the French commander that the fort there violated the agreement between their peoples. The commander rebuffed him. Tanacharison's answer to the rebuff came eight months later when, while taking part in George Washington's defeat of a small French party that was on a diplomatic mission, he split open the skull of the party's leader, the Sieur de Jumonville. The action that Washington found dumbfoundingly savage was, from the Seneca perspective, logical and deft right down to its particulars: the horrific act would tell the French in no uncertain terms that the Senecas objected to their forts, and would likewise show the subordinate Munsee and Shawnee that the Iroquois League knew how to manage the Europeans. At the same time, since the Half King was operating under Washington's leadership, his assault on the Frenchman could not be considered a violation of arrangements between the French and the Iroquois League. Where Washington saw himself as the agent of one European power defeating another, Tanacharison saw Washington as a tool for executing his own diplomacy.

Tanacharison continued to act with perfect Iroquois logic in the ensuing Battle of Fort Necessity. The French force that attacked Washington's makeshift structure had included a contingent of Iroquois warriors. By pulling his own warriors out before the violence began, the Half King not only avoided fighting in what he knew would be a lost cause but kept true to the Great Law of Peace, which forbade Iroquois from fighting one another.

The Munsee stayed mostly on the sidelines as the situation between the French, English and Iroquois escalated. Increasingly, however, they came to feel that the Senecas were not up to the task of acting as warrior/diplomats for the native tribes. It seemed apparent to them that the French were gaining the upper hand against the English, and the Iroquois were losing their ability to play the European powers against one another. The Munsee had expected the Albany Congress, the great convocation of tribes and English colonists that Abraham Yates attended, to result in a new union, which would strengthen the English side, maintaining the balance; but the colonies had failed to unite. Not only that, but the Iroquois representatives at the conference, after being "handsomely entertained"—i.e., plied with alcohol—actually signed away to Pennsylvania colonists a large chunk of Munsee land.

The last straw for the Munsee was the defeat of Braddock's army at the Forks of the Ohio. It signaled that the English and their American colonists were losing, and that the French would overrun their lands. Groups of Munsee and Shawnee met with Seneca leaders and demanded an end to their subordination. "We expect to be killed by the French," one Munsee spokesman announced. "We desire, therefore, that you will take off our Petticoat, that we may fight for ourselves, our Wives and Children." In the following months the Munsee renounced their status as "women," armed themselves, stole through the forests of western Pennsylvania, Maryland and Virginia, and unleashed the violence that so stunned Washington and other colonial leaders. They burned the farms of families that had settled in the westernmost parts of those colonies and mutilated the bodies of men, women and children. The colonial leaders fumbled to respond. Viewing the events as a struggle between European powers, they were unable to comprehend the meaning behind the attacks, so that George Washington saw only "savage fury" and "the murder of poor innocent Babes, and helpless families."

From Cornplanter's perspective, then, the French-English war brought about a swirling transformation in tribal loyalties. Meanwhile, once William Pitt's strategy for running the war took hold, the British began to pile up victories. Under William Johnson, they took Fort Niagara in July 1759. Two months later, the French lost Quebec. After the fall of Montreal in 1760, Canada was in British hands. French soldiers began to board ships for other parts of the world; the global contest would continue for a time in other arenas, but the war in North America was essentially over.

It became evident to Cornplanter that a British victory was no victory for his people. The newest commander of British forces in America, who arrived in 1758, made that clear even before the French soldiers left their forts. Jeffrey Amherst was a year younger than George Sackville. He had been born within a few miles of Knole House; the two had known each other since childhood. Indeed, Amherst had served as page to Sackville's father in Dublin when Lionel Sackville was the Lord

Lieutenant of Ireland. Amherst's military career paralleled Sackville's; both fought on the Continent at Dettingen and Fontenoy. Within a short time of his arrival in America, he stung tribal leaders with his open disdain for them, which went so deep that he didn't feel it necessary to have an interpreter in his dealings with them; he wasn't interested in parsing the meaning of their lengthy utterances, and he didn't care whether they understood him.

As the French withdrew, Amherst made a decision that enraged virtually every Indian tribe in the northeast. The Treaty of Easton, signed in 1758, had helped turn the war around; by its terms, ten Indian nations, including the Munsee and the Iroquois Confederacy, had promised not to side with the French. One promise the English made in return was that they would establish no new outposts west of the Allegheny Mountains. This was a great victory from the Indian perspective: if the English would permanently stay east of the line that ran from central New York to western Pennsylvania and all the way to Georgia, the Ohio Country—i.e., the west—would be forever theirs. Less than two years later, however, Amherst ordered British soldiers to occupy the recently abandoned French forts in the Ohio Country and beyond. He would use the victory over the French to extend British reach more than a thousand miles westward, blatantly stealing the lands of dozens of tribes. William Johnson's deputy, after visiting the Senecas, reported to his boss that in the wake of Amherst's moves the tribe "expect nothing but that the general intends to attempt enslaving them."

Cornplanter's uncle, Guyasuta, was quicker than anyone to see what was happening. He called for all-out war against the British. He had little success in convincing the Iroquois, so he traveled west. The French fort on the straits connecting Lake Huron and Lake Erie, which they called Pontchartrain du Détroit (détroit being the French word for "strait") dated to 1701. The Ottawa and Ojibwa Indians of the region had had relations with the French going back even further than that;

they had come to depend on the French for trade. In 1761, Guyasuta appeared among them carrying a red wampum belt, which the Iroquois called a war hatchet: a plea to join in a general attack. But Sir William Johnson arrived shortly after, parleyed with tribal leaders, and got them to stand down.

Guyasuta's call to war was aided, however, by a spiritual voice. The teachings of a holy man named Neolin began to circulate among the Munsee in the Ohio Country as well as tribes to the west and the Iroquois in the east. Neolin had communicated with the Master of Life, who told him that all the native peoples had hurt him and blocked their own path to heaven by allowing the Europeans to settle among them. "This land where ye dwell I have made for you and not for others," the Master of Life told Neolin, according to an account by a Frenchman. To atone, the Indians had to purify themselves. And they had to fight. "As to those who come to trouble your lands," the Master of Life told Neolin, "drive them out, make war upon them. I do not love them at all."

By 1763, the darkness of the situation was clear to Indians as far west as the Illinois Country. With the signing of the treaty in Paris that ended the Seven Years' War, the French formally ceded all of their North American holdings to the British. In a single flourish, the English had "won" the continent as far west as the Mississippi River. The language of the treaty made no mention of the native tribes who had inhabited the lands since time immemorial.

Together, the treaty and Amherst's takeover of French forts meant disaster for the native peoples of much of the continent. It was evident that English colonizing would not be restricted by natural barriers or treaties. The English intended to keep going. The end of the French and Indian War ignited a chain of Indian outrage that extended as far west as Michigan.

Neolin's prophecy instructed the Indians on what they must do. Two years before, the Ottawas had refused Guyasuta's plea to go to war;

now, under their chief, Pontiac, who had become a follower of Neolin, they laid siege to Fort Detroit.

The rebellion spread. Allied bands of Indians—Ottawas and Ojibwas, Potawatomis and Hurons, Kickapoos, Weas and Mascoutens, Munsees and Shawnees and western Senecas—attacked British forts and settlers across a large swath of the so-called frontier territory. In six weeks they took over eight forts from Pennsylvania to Michigan. Thousands of people were killed, captured or displaced, in a display of wanton violence that was unprecedented in its geographic extent and in its network of alliances.

Most Iroquois, including most of the Senecas, refrained from participating in the uprising, but the western Senecas—Cornplanter's people—joined in. In June, Guyasuta was in western Pennsylvania, among a group of Munsees, Shawnees and Senecas who laid siege to Fort Pitt. It was better manned than the other forts the Indians attacked, so the soldiers there were well positioned to hold out. Unfortunately for them, smallpox broke out among the garrison, and the commander had to erect a makeshift hospital for its victims. This, in turn, gave rise to a ghoulish thought. On June 23, the day after the siege began, two Munsee chiefs, Mamaltee and Turtle's Heart, entered the fort to parley. After the negotiations failed, the chiefs requested some provisions. An English trader who was trapped in the fort with the soldiers reported that the commanding officer gave them "two Blankets and an Hankerchief out of the Small Pox Hospital." And he added, "I hope it will have the desired effect."

This same idea occurred almost simultaneously to Amherst, who was in New York at the time. "Could it not be contrived to Send the *Small Pox* among those Disaffected Tribes of Indians?" he wrote to the commander of the fort, and in a follow-up clarified that the idea was to infect "the Indians by means of Blanketts, as well as to Try Every other Method that can serve to Extirpate this Execrable Race."

Amherst didn't know that his strategy had already been employed. A smallpox epidemic did break out among the Indians in western Pennsylvania, though it had already appeared prior to the "two Blankets and an Handkerchief" being given to the Munsee chiefs. Whether or not there was a direct link between Amherst's idea and the outbreak, the native peoples understood perfectly well the regard the man held for them.

Fort Pitt withstood the siege. Shortly after, Amherst was recalled to London—where officials considered that his heavy-handed approach had sparked the uprising—and replaced by Thomas Gage, an officer who had come to North America as part of Braddock's army. Through a combination of negotiation and force, Gage brought the uprisings to an end in July of 1766. Henceforth, the British, and their American colonists, could look westward and see limitless opportunity. The French had withdrawn, and the natives had been taught a lesson.

The struggle would become known as Pontiac's Rebellion or Pontiac's War, though Pontiac was not the prime instigator—Guyasuta might have been a likelier candidate—and it was less a war than a massive spasm of protest at what Indians knew would be an unprecedented new threat to their way of life. They had stopped fighting not because they had been offered sweet deals or expansive promises, but out of exhaustion. They needed to rest, to regroup, to think. They needed new leaders.

Cornplanter had learned a great deal in these years. He had broadened his sense of the geography of the continent. He knew new faces, new tribes and customs and languages. And he had learned the strengths and limitations of the two rival European powers that had forced themselves into his world. He had seen how the British conquered and had witnessed the inexorable march of their settlements. He had perfected his battle skills: the ability to load and fire a musket several times a minute, how to throw a tomahawk and hit a man square in the back.

He had also learned the art of scalping, which, like so much else, was perceived differently by natives and whites. To an Iroquois, the whorl, or pattern of hair at the top of the head, was the seat of consciousness. Decorating one's hair whorl for battle was an expression of spiritual power. To slice away the scalp and whorl of a foe—laying the victim facedown, putting a knee in the back, making a long clean cut from the neck around the top of the forehead to the other side of the neck, and pulling sharply on the hair, all within a matter of seconds—was to remove the enemy's spirit. That you and your enemy went into battle knowing that either might carry out this exchange of power on the other made warfare an occasion not only of bravery but of spiritual engagement.

When it came to the American colonists, meanwhile, Cornplanter had learned the scintillating effect that the act had on their communities— the frank horror it generated. He knew he would be scalping again.

———⟡——

## Chapter 7

# THE SPIRIT THAT RAGES

June 1762. The sun was shining, the air was warm with promise, and everywhere new life was erupting. George Washington, no longer a military man but a gentleman farmer, was overseeing the planting of two hundred hills of tobacco at Mount Vernon and noted with manly approval one day his roan mare accepting the mating advances of a neighbor's horse. In Stonington, Connecticut, Venture had corn to tend and an abundant field of hay to cut. George Sackville, in the aftermath of his battlefield disgrace, pottered about his blossoming English estate of Knole as he and his wife anticipated the imminent birth of their third child. Cornplanter's village observed the annual strawberry festival, when the Senecas thanked the spirits for making the forest rich and sweet. And Abraham Yates and his wife celebrated, as, following so many failed attempts, Anna at last gave birth to a healthy child: a daughter whom they named Susanna, after Anna's mother.

Also in this month of new life, another girl, a feisty, seemingly indomitable creature named Margaret Moncrieffe, burst into the world. From the beginning she had what all throughout her life people would remark on as astounding beauty: lustrous dark hair, milky skin, "eyes full of witchery." She was born in Nova Scotia, probably in Halifax.

Like her, the town was an infant, having sprung up a few years earlier amid murderous waves of fighting for control of Canada's Atlantic coast that involved the British and French armies, the native Mi'kmaq people and the Acadians, descendants of French settlers of the previous century. The British eventually won, scattering the Mi'kmaq, who had for centuries hunted moose and caribou on the peninsula, and sending some of the Acadians down the Mississippi River to Louisiana (eventually to have their name corrupted to "Cajun"). The port town where the little girl took her first steps was a rough-weather place, of ice floes and blue mist, a hard-won outpost of empire.

She was thoroughly a child of the British army in North America. Her father, Lieutenant Thomas Moncrieffe, was aide-de-camp to General Robert Monckton, who had directed major assaults on French Canada. Her mother, Margaret Heron Moncrieffe, was the daughter of an officer. The girl's parents had named her older brother Edward Cornwallis Moncrieffe after the head of British forces in Nova Scotia.

Her early years were a kaleidoscope of life changes. Her father's regiment was transferred to New York and the family went with him. There, while she was still a toddler, her mother died. It happened that her father—a ramrod-straight soldier, an engineer and a man of exacting standards—was a particular favorite of General Thomas Gage, then the commander of all British forces in North America, who previously had fought alongside George Washington in Braddock's expedition. General Gage proposed to take in the young officer's children. So Margaret and her brother lived for a time in the general's household on Manhattan. She was with a family, and more than that she was with the army. The British military—the uniforms, the orderliness, the booming of male voices—was the foundation to her young life.

When she was three, however, her father decided his children needed more structure, so he shipped them off to be educated in Ireland. Margaret spent the next five years at a Dublin boarding school called

Miss Beard's, cut off from all warmth and family, with the memory of her mother rapidly receding, and without even the comfort of her brother's company, since he had been sent to a different institution.

Then one day when she was eight years old, a ghost appeared. Her father, now Major Moncrieffe, who after the passage of so much time had become a phantom presence in her young mind, stood on the doorstep of the school. He introduced Margaret to the woman at his side: his new wife, Mary. The family re-formed, this time with a stepmother in charge of the home. This woman was a member of the powerful Livingston family—the same who were benefactors of Abraham Yates—and she had a frigid hauteur that suited her wealth and status. Margaret's feelings were quickly set: "I did not like my new mother," she later declared, and pegged the woman with a double epithet: "a stranger to every social virtue, and a rigid Presbyterian."

Then her father was gone again, back to New York with his wife. This time, however, he left Margaret with a promise that before long he would send for her and her brother. She clung to the promise like a talisman. She still had a lot of growing to do, but the core of her personality had been formed. By his long absences and his arbitrary manner of shunting her here and there, by his rigid sense of discipline coupled with the occasional torrent of tenderness he showered on her, her father had created a volatile frisson in her young mind, a conviction that her sense of worth derived from him: receiving his attention, following his orders. She became a kind of soldier herself, at the beck and call of her commanding officer. And, inevitably, her longing for him was tied to a sharp bitterness. As she waited for her father to come yet again, to take her finally and truly to be with him, she both adored the man and hated him.

On October 25, 1760, George II, the king of England, woke at six in the morning as usual, drank a cup of chocolate, as usual, then went to the toilet. A moment later his *valet de chambre* heard a strange noise, rushed into the "little closet" and found him on the floor. The king was dead. His twenty-two-year-old grandson ascended to the throne. Where the old king had been vain, loud and a vigorous woman-izer, the new George was soft-spoken and pious. Yet he was every bit as determined to wield power.

George Sackville's universal public humiliation had been tied to the fractious relationship between the king and the Prince of Wales. He had openly sided with the prince, to the extent that the ruin of his career—his battlefield inaction at Minden—may have been derived from that loyalty. As soon as the prince took the throne, Sackville, in his headstrong way, reasoned that the no-doubt-grateful monarch would be ready to reward his loyalty, that the time was ripe for his rehabilita-tion. On the occasion of George III's first public reception, there was an audible gasp as people recognized the "coward of Minden" in the room; George Sackville triumphantly and obliviously processed to the throne and kissed the king's hand.

It was classic Sackville, his innate tendency to charge ahead, ren-dering him oblivious to political niceties. The old king had been much loved, and Sackville's long and very public court-martial, the wide-spread belief that he had betrayed England, was still in people's minds. Association with him was the last thing the new monarch needed as he was trying to win the country over. Sackville was formally advised not to show himself at court again.

He retreated back to Knole. There, for a time, he was happy, with his wife and family, in the endless halls where he had grown up. He kept a leisurely but mathematically regular routine, starting with breakfast from nine-thirty to eleven, followed by a tour of his grounds on horse-back, chatting with his laborers, noting when their cottages needed repairs and seeing that they were done, allowing their children to open gates for him in exchange for sixpence. He had been born into the quasi-feudal manor system, and he believed wholeheartedly in its notions of hierarchy and obligation.

The household bustled, and he played his part. When his wife went into labor, he actually participated (in some fashion) in the birth of his third child, telling a friend afterward, "I pretend now to some knowledge of midwifery," and jokingly offering his services as consultant to the man's wife. He coddled his newborn daughter Elizabeth, listened to his wife prattle to her in French and was pleased with the "uproar" the baby brought to the house.

But he couldn't hold back forever. In 1763 he tried again to reenter public life, this time by appealing to John Stuart, aka Lord Bute, the prime minister and close confidant of the king. When Bute told him the time was not yet right for his return, Sackville again pushed back in his overly aggressive manner, threatening that if the king would not welcome him back he would consider joining the opposition. Sackville knew that Bute was hugely unpopular: he was in effect threatening to bring the government down. Bute was disgusted, but the risky gambit may have worked. At any rate, the king and his prime minister appreciated Sackville's blunt energy and firm intelligence and wanted him in the government. But they had to check the very aggression they valued. The king told Bute to make Sackville wait just a bit more, until the memory of his infamy had faded, at which time "offices might be open to him that would lead to higher ones, and then what appeared dangerous now would become easy and indeed palatable."

Later that year Sackville was quietly invited to pay his respects to the king. A few newspapers squawked, but the fuss was manageable. He took the next step: he began asserting himself in the House of Commons, where he still had his seat. Momentous issues were afoot, and he was keen to weigh in on them.

The matters went to the very heart of the British system of government. A debate that had simmered for decades was suddenly boiling over. The furor was caused by a fellow member of the House named John Wilkes. Wilkes was from London but had been educated at Leiden University in the Netherlands, where he had imbibed a philosophy of radical republicanism and religious tolerance. He thrived on controversy, was confoundingly ugly—with a skull shaped like an arrowhead, a severe squint and bad teeth—yet, thanks to a magnetic wit, managed to be a notorious ladies' man. (He liked to say that given half an hour he could "talk his face away.") Wilkes was now giving full-throated expression to things that many Britons would only speak of quietly. Eighty years earlier, in 1688, the so-called Glorious Revolution had supposedly ushered in a new era, in which Parliament would take precedence over the monarchy. In 1689, Parliament had enacted a bill of rights that limited the powers of the monarch and enshrined the rights and freedoms of individual English subjects. That was to be the beginning of a truly republican England, one that followed ideas developed by men like John Locke, Thomas Gordon and John Trenchard, all of whom charted the widening terrain of individual freedom.

But instead the clock had seemingly moved into reverse in the eighteenth century, as the Hanoverian kings (Georges I, II and III) manipulated the judicial system, raised taxes over the heads of members of Parliament, installed a standing army without parliamentary approval and in other ways assumed near-absolute power. Droves of ordinary people were frustrated by the royal overreach, but no prominent politician dared take up the matter, in part because the political leadership was dominated by aristocrats and the aristocracy's power was tied to that of the king. Now John Wilkes chose to voice that popular anger, in print and in the House of Commons. Understanding the nature of the problem, he attacked not only the king but the aristocracy. And he did it for what he called "the cause of freedom."

George Sackville reemerged on the political scene in 1763, just as Wilkes was bringing his attacks to a new level by publishing an article excoriating the government and declaring that George III had reduced the monarchy to "prostitution." People in the streets thrilled with nervous excitement; the king ordered Wilkes imprisoned in the Tower of London. He was arrested on a general warrant, a sweeping order that did not name him but applied to all those associated with the publication of the offending material.

Wilkes, a natural showman, turned his trial into a national spectacle. Speaking in his defense at Westminster Hall, the center of the English legal system since the time of the Magna Carta, he argued in favor of a right to free speech. He peppered his speech with appeals to "English liberty," and declaimed that the liberty "of all the middling and inferior class of people, who stand most in need of protection, is, in my case, this day to be finally decided." He argued that a general warrant was unconstitutional, declaring that "the liberty of an English subject is not to be sported away with impunity, in this cruel and despotic manner." He won his case, promptly countersued the government and won 1,000 pounds in damages. Other people who had been arrested as part of the general warrant also won their cases, and the victory was seen as a major shift toward individual liberty in the British system. Wilkes was lionized in newspapers and church pulpits.

The Wilkes affair carried across the Atlantic and hit the shores of the American colonies. In many ways, the concerns of Americans— that they were denied certain basic rights that the British Constitution guaranteed—were the same as those of ordinary English, Scottish and Irish subjects. The outcome of Wilkes' trial gave hope. If the system could be adjusted, so that Parliament was able to check the monarchy, that would translate into more freedom for ordinary British subjects, whether they were in Britain or America.

George Sackville's position on these matters was clear. He detested John Wilkes personally (and Wilkes returned the favor, bringing up Minden whenever he could), and as to Wilkes's victory in court and his championing of "liberty," Sackville thought it amounted to so much hot air, noting drily that "the Juries of London show their disposition to favour the name at the expense of real liberty."

But there was another issue beneath the gauzy talk of liberty that concerned Sackville more. What had gotten Wilkes riled up in the first place was the peace treaty that ended the Seven Years' War. Britain had won the war, and now British leaders had to deal with its consequences. Chief among these was a banking collapse in Amsterdam, where much of the debt to finance the war had been held. The financial crisis spread across Europe, causing credit to dry up and leaving British merchants in a panic.

One way out of the financial crisis was to make America more profitable. France had relinquished control of a huge portion of the continent, from the Appalachian Mountains to the Mississippi River. That land was waiting to be developed and made profitable. Sackville and his colleagues knew they couldn't entrust its settlement to the existing colonies. For years they had watched as the leaders of the various colonies fought each other like dogs over matters large and small. The British government had to come up with a plan. The disastrous series of attacks known collectively as Pontiac's War showed that the plan had to include establishing permanent boundaries with the Indian tribes. And there would have to be an extended British military presence to keep peace and to ensure that the French did not try to reassert themselves. But keeping a permanent army in North America would cost money. The treasury was spent from the war, and the home population was already heavily taxed. What was to be done?

As Sackville was busy politicking on his own behalf (dinner with the Duke of Bedford, having Lord Middlesex to Knole for a relaxing week in the country) in a calculated effort to lift himself back into a position of prominence, a possible solution to the American question arrived in the form of a letter to Prime Minister Bute. Robert Dinwiddie, the former royal governor of Virginia, wrote from his retirement in England with some advice. As an investor in the Ohio Company, Dinwiddie had had firsthand experience of Virginia's leaders and their keen ambition for westward expansion. He believed that desire could be channeled to serve the government's needs. It was true that the colonies had never before been taxed by the home country, and the Americans were clearly a feisty lot, but Dinwiddie was of the opinion that they could be made to see that a tax would be in their interest. The money would be used for their own defense, and they would be the first to benefit from organized westward expansion. He even suggested the method he thought would work best with the colonists: "a Stamp Duty . . . similar to that Duty in Great Britain."

Bute's government fell a short while later, and the new prime minister, George Grenville, asked other leaders their thoughts on the wisdom of taxing the Americans. There was a question of constitutionality. Parliament had the power to legislate affairs in the colonies, but since it did not contain representatives from the colonies, opinions were divided as to whether it could legally impose a tax on them. Americans had long believed that their own colonial assemblies had the sole right to tax them, and until now Parliament had not challenged that belief.

George Sackville's feelings on the matter were as firmly etched as his feelings about John Wilkes. The theory that the colonies could not be taxed without representation was, in his words, "a strange doctrine." England was the home country; Parliament was the master of the colonies; it made the decisions, and this was a matter of financial necessity and common sense. Besides which, the Americans were taxed much less heavily by their colonial legislatures than ordinary Englishmen were by Parliament. They had received the benefit of British military protection. They could now begin to share the cost.

Prime Minister Grenville was a man of similar temperament. He put forth legislation to impose the first-ever direct tax on the Americans.

Following Dinwiddie's suggestion, he proposed a stamp tax, which would require any printed matter, from newspapers to playing cards, to be produced on paper that had been stamped to show a duty had been paid on it. And no doubt Dinwiddie was right: if the wisdom of the tax was made clear to the Americans, they would go along with it. George Sackville—standing with his soldier's posture in the House of Commons, delivering speeches with what an observer called "nervous compactness"—supported the bill with all his heart.

The bride wore a yellow silk gown and purple silk shoes. At five feet tall, she was fourteen inches shorter than the strapping gent at her side. They had met ten months earlier, having sought each other out. She'd heard about George Washington: gallant soldier, fine dancer. He knew that Martha Dandridge Custis was an attractive widow, at twenty-seven only a year older than he was, and who, with the sudden death of her fabulously wealthy first husband, was the possesser of 17,500 acres of choice Virginia farmland and a matching fortune. They had probably arranged their first meeting with a potential marriage in mind; having discovered a mutual attraction, they found no reason to delay. Soon they loved each other and, social advancement aside, wanted each other, and wanted to keep wanting each other: Washington was excited enough after the wedding night that he put in an order with his London agent for four ounces of the aphrodisiac Spanish Fly.

With his marriage George Washington felt a newfound serenity. The restless striving to be noticed and approved of eased. He had won military fame, and, while his desire for a career in the British army had been thwarted, he was ready to excel in the equally honorable capacity of tobacco planter. Thanks to Martha, he had the resources to do it.

In fact, he had taken the first step toward that goal even before his marriage. A planter of distinction should also be invested in local politics, so Washington ran for a seat in the Virginia House of Burgesses. His notable friends and associates, including the Fairfaxes and officers from his regiment, made the rounds on his behalf, beseeching eligible voters (white men who owned at least 100 acres of unimproved or 25 acres of improved land) to support him. They believed they could count on the gentry, but weren't so sure about ordinary folk. One of Washington's backers warned him that "there is no relying on the promises of the common herd, the promise is too oft forgot when the Back is turned."

As it happened, the renowned militia leader won the election easily. As a burgess, who would take his seat in the oldest elective legislature in the colonies, he now had another badge of honor. When not engaged in political business in Williamsburg, he could devote himself to his tobacco. The goal was not merely to make money. It was to produce the finest, sweetest leaf, which would be the talk of the county, win the admiration of ladies and gentlemen and fetch the highest prices from London merchants. He tried with all his might. He rode the fields, observing and questioning and guiding his slaves and overseers. He toiled under the hot sun on his rolling hillsides, with the wide Potomac sprawling below. (Washington "strips off his coat and labors like a common man," a visitor remarked.) He spent lavishly. He copied what his neighbors were doing, and he also experimented with new varieties, with different conditions and fertilizers. He drove his slaves—300 who had come with Martha, plus others he bought—in the effort to succeed. Nothing worked. His leaf was acceptable but not top-grade. Time after time, his London business agent, Robert Cary, wrote to report a sale price far below what Washington had expected.

And yet his honor demanded that he succeed. If he couldn't do so from the start, he made the perilous decision that he must at least look like a prosperous planter. So he put in waves upon waves of orders to London for the finest accoutrements of highborn living. He bought coaches, linens, lace, crimson velvet breeches, silk hose, kid gloves, the "most fashionable cambric pocket handkerchiefs" by the dozen, hog-heads of porter, gallons of rhenish wine, punch bowls, china mugs and, to adorn the rooms of his manor, sculpted busts of Alexander the Great, Julius Caesar and the king of Prussia. He purchased it all on credit.

Then, in April 1763, four years after his marriage, he had to acknowl-edge failure. He confessed to a friend that all the outlays had "swal-lowed up . . . all the money I got by Marriage nay more" and "brought me into debt."

Washington's skill as a farmer, or lack thereof, surely contributed to his failure. But many other Virginia planters were finding it impossible to turn a profit. They too had built up mountains of debt. In fact, they were coming to the conclusion that the system was rigged. English mer-chants had the products that a colonial planter needed. English politi-cians made rules stipulating whose products Americans could buy, the price they had to pay and the terms of credit. And the terms had steadily become more onerous. The merchants and banks in England had not suddenly become greedy; rather, they were caught up in the financial crisis that was sweeping Europe, which was tied to the end of the Seven Years' War. In raising interest rates and demanding payment of debts, the English creditors were simply passing along some of the misery.

The Virginians were not inclined to explain away their suffering by looking at it through the prism of global economics. The fault, as they saw it, lay with England and its colonial policies. For the plant-ers, more than their livelihood was at stake. From the time of Washing-ton's grandfather the hallmark of a Virginia planter was his personal independence: the ability to carve acreage out of raw wilderness, tame it, make it productive, and so make oneself the master of a portion of the continent. This was why a successful planter was so admired and respected. Order and civilization came to Virginia not through decrees of the British government or by the establishment of cities but via such individuals, men of grit and will and power. The truth of this was stitched into George Washington's being. His goal was the achievement of personal independence, which came about through establishing economic independence. As he became mired in debt, he linked this ideal of personal independence to what he called "a free mind."

In the early 1760s "freedom" was suddenly a preoccupation for Washington and his fellow planters. One of his contemporaries complained openly to his English creditor that he feared that through the onerous economics the colony would "be condemned forever to a state of Vassalage & Dependence." Some began to think of Virginia's tobacco culture as a trap, a kind of slavery. The irony that the planters were themselves employing slave labor to further enslave themselves to overseas creditors wasn't lost on everyone. Some rued ever having gotten themselves into the position of slaveholders. Seeking to distance themselves from the causes of the growing misery, they lashed out at England for having brought Africans to America in the first place and begun the forced-labor system. Under the pressure from the economic squeeze, some discovered a newfound sense of morality, and railed against the institution as evil.

Washington, at this stage, showed little remorse over the institution of slavery. The only indication of any distaste he may have felt for the existential divide between him and his slaves was his avoidance of the term "slave"; he generally favored "servant." Indeed, he had become skilled at enforcing order among his "servants," and as the financial pressures on him increased, he worked them that much harder. He split Mount Vernon into five separate farms for ease of control; each of his slaves knew which farm he or she worked and had to stay put. He had no difficulty ordering disobedient slaves to be whipped, though he did not tolerate overseers who were overly fond of punishment.

When he was not at Mount Vernon, Washington was in Williamsburg, where the economic crisis was suddenly a top priority for the House of Burgesses. In May 1763 he wrote his old military comrade Robert

Stewart, sending him a loan of 302 pounds that Stewart had asked for, and signed off hurriedly because "Our Assembly is suddenly called in consequence of a Memorial of the British Merchants to the Board of Trade representing the evil consequences of our Paper emissions. . . ." The "Paper emissions" referred to paper currency, which the Virginia legislature had begun issuing because in the economic crisis there was a shortage of pounds sterling. The English merchants to whom the Virginia planters owed large sums of money had complained to Parliament, for no sooner had Virginia begun printing money than its value plummeted. Reports arrived that Parliament was debating whether to bar American colonies from issuing legal tender. That would put yet another financial squeeze on the colonists. The issue was so pressing that, before saddling up for Williamsburg, Washington worried that it would "set the whole Country in Flames."

Other problems were converging on Washington as well. As his tobacco venture was failing, he had lunged outward in an investment scheme. He joined with forty-nine other Virginia gentlemen in forming the Mississippi Land Company, with a monumentally ambitious and brazen plan to capitalize on the English victory over the French by claiming 2.5 million acres of former French territory—a swath that cut through the future Kentucky, Illinois and Tennessee all the way to the Mississippi River—in order to resell it to settlers. They wrote to the king humbly asking permission to develop the region, declaring that it would be for the "increase of the people, the extension of Trade and the enlargement of the revenue." In October, however, Parliament, having decided to keep westward expansion under its own authority, scotched the plan.

The following spring, Parliament did indeed decree that the colonies could not print legal tender. Then came news that Parliament was considering imposing what would be the first-ever tax on Americans. This information was not in the form of a rumor or a leak. The British leaders wanted to involve the Americans in their thinking. They were acting on Dinwiddie's advice, informing the Americans of the benefits they themselves would enjoy from such a tax. They hoped to show men such as George Washington that their dreams of developing the western wilderness could best be done under British administration.

The news was not received in that spirit. Americans had been fascinated by the John Wilkes affair. What about the "English liberty" that Wilkes was trumpeting? What about the English Bill of Rights? Was it not the law that British subjects could only be taxed by their representatives? Taxation without representation seemed an ominous step away from individual freedom. Washington huddled with the other burgesses to consider a response. They scribbled out a list of actions for Edward Montague, their representative in England, to follow. Montague was to make it known to His Majesty's government that Virginians had "Liberties & Privileges as free born British Subjects," that they could not be taxed "without their personal Consent or the Consent by their representatives." This they took "to be the most vital Principle of the British Constitution."

Parliament did not consider Montague's objections. In March 1765, following the advice of Robert Dinwiddie and the strong urging of George Sackville and with almost no opposition, it voted the Stamp Act into law.

The reaction in the colonies was unlike anything that had happened before. People took to the streets in Boston, New York, Annapolis, Charleston and other cities. Some were outraged over extra fees—German immigrants in Philadelphia feared that the cost of becoming naturalized would now skyrocket—but most saw the advent of Parliament imposing taxes as an announcement that their status as British subjects had been diminished. They were now something more like vassals.

One of the centers of turmoil in the colonies was the eastern wing of the two-story brick building in Williamsburg that served as the capitol of the Virginia colony. In May, George Washington rode hurriedly into town to attend a special session of the House of Burgesses. Here he met a brand-new member of the assembly named Patrick Henry. Henry—who like Washington had failed at tobacco but had afterward gone on to study law—seemed determined to make an independent stand. He did not represent the interests of the aristocratic planter class but rather of the plainspoken, humble folk from his region. His career as a legislator was only nine days old, but on May 29 he submitted a series of resolutions. Though virtually all the assemblymen were opposed to the Stamp Act, Henry's stridency split them into two factions: the gentry, who wanted to move cautiously so as not to upset their British overlords, and everyone else. The former thought the man's speech was so inflammatory in its denunciation of the British government that it could be grounds for treason. Others were moved to passionate support. One of these, a twenty-two-year-old law student by the name of Thomas Jefferson, remarked that Henry's talents as an orator were "such as I have never heard from any other man. He appeared to me to speak as Homer wrote." The resolutions declared it a fact of British law that Parliament had no jurisdiction in Virginia, and that Virginians could only be taxed by their representative body, the House of Burgesses itself. Henry submitted his resolutions strategically, when the more conservative members (he had pegged George Washington as one of these) were out of the room. They passed. Newspapers published the resolutions, and soon news of the Virginia House of Burgesses' defiance carried around the colonies and across the ocean.

Patrick Henry's judgment of George Washington as being among the conservative gentry would have been accurate earlier but not anymore. Washington was as angry at the Stamp Act as his fellow Virginians, and for him it was only the latest affront. The colonies' crisis and his personal crises were becoming one. Britain had scorned him—repeatedly, over a period of years—in his quest for military dues. Britain then had visited him with financial burdens that he felt denied him the freedom to prosper. Then Parliament barred him from developing western lands, thus blocking him from benefiting from the years of hard soldiering he had done. On the heels of all of that came the Stamp Act.

His frustration came to a head in September 1765 in one sustained outburst directed at arguably the most appropriate person to receive it: his British financial agent, Robert Cary. He had just received a letter from Cary asking that Washington pay his debt. Washington erupted. "It cannot reasonably be imagined that I felt any pleasing Sensations upon the receipt of your Letter of the 13th of February," he began. He accused the man of pricing Washington's goods below market value. He threatened to move his business elsewhere. Then brought up the latest source of upset. "The Stamp Act, imposed on the Colonies by the Parliament of Great Britain," he informed Cary, was looked upon by virtually all colonists as an "unconstitutional method of Taxation" and "a direful attack upon their Liberties." The extra burden of the new tax, he warned, meant that Americans such as him would surely be unable to pay off the debts to their English agents.

The length of the letter and its garbled, wandering sentences gave evidence of Washington's unquiet state of mind. To be sure, he had other vexations beyond business. While he certainly couldn't have laid blame for it on the British Parliament, it was a source of deep frustration to realize, as he would have by this time, that he and Martha were unable to have children. She had brought with her into the marriage two children by her first husband, in effect proving her fertility. That left Washington with the inescapable conclusion that this particularly painful "failure" was his own. Economically, politically, socially, and now in the most basic sense, he felt emasculated.

A winter's night, a new year: the second of January 1766, and Abraham Yates was asleep in bed. Suddenly, there was a noise at the door. The agitated men on his stoop demanded that he come with them to Thomas Williams's tavern. They were drunk but full of some strange energy. Yates got dressed and hurried through the cold the few blocks to the inn. Yates was a fussy man, who didn't like disruptions, and he had a lot on his mind as he marched through the frosty night. He was building a house, for one thing, and, as he lamented to a friend, "I am an Intire Stranger to architectory." He and Anna and little Susanna needed more space, plus the couple hoped for more children. So he had sold his house for 550 pounds and bought a well-situated lot right in the busy center of town for 600 pounds, and was now up to his neck in construction details. Besides that, his law practice was all-consuming, with sixteen cases to handle before the Inferior Court and three other circuit court cases. And as a member of the city council he was continuing to build his new sort of political party, one based not on connections to one of the great families of the area but on the economic issues that mattered to common workers.

Inside the inn all was bright, warm and energetic. "I found about 40 or 50 people gathered," he later reported. It was a raucous group, all men aged from twenty-five to forty, in New Year's celebration mode, but with an edge. He knew them all: Cuyler, Ten Broek, Wendell, Roseboom. . . . They had an air of danger about them, something underhanded.

They were calling themselves the Sons of Liberty. They had banded together to protest the Stamp Act. The law had gone into effect two months earlier; a week before that, the specially stamped paper that henceforth had to be purchased for all printed material had arrived in New York Harbor. Each region was to have a new official whose job it would be to distribute the paper. The revelers had gotten names of local men who had applied for the position, gone to their homes, dragged them out of bed and brought them here to swear an oath and sign an affidavit that they would not do the ugly work for the British. They wanted Yates, as a lawyer and city councilor, to make it official.

Yates wasn't one of the Sons of Liberty—he was a stickler for propriety, and the questionable legality of the group's activities conflicted with his position as a city councilman—but he agreed with them. Of the five men dragged to the tavern to swear they wouldn't work to enforce the Stamp Act, four did so immediately. The fifth, Henry van Schaack, was a different story. He was the postmaster, and a stubborn man. While he readily swore that he had not applied for the post and didn't intend to, he would not sign a promise that he would never do so in the future, saying he thought such a demand "unreasonable." The men roughed him up; he countered that their behavior was "illegal, unconstitutional and oppressive." They let him go, but with a warning that they wanted his promise.

Three days later Yates was taking part in a city council meeting when Van Schaack showed up at city hall to protest the way the Sons of Liberty had treated him. As a matter of principle, he did not feel it right to swear that he never would apply for a future position. He was shocked when the council members—Yates included—suggested that it would be better for him to swear it anyway. Virtually the whole of Albany was united against the Stamp Act to the point of militancy.

Van Schaack again refused. The next day Abraham Yates watched a crowd that he estimated at about 400 descend on Van Schaack's house. They broke windows and destroyed furniture. Van Schaack signed the affidavit.

As a member of the city government and a man of fastidious sensibilities, Yates deplored the chaos. But he understood the anger that lay behind it. In violation of the concept of individual liberty that Britain itself had enshrined into law, England, he lamented, was determined "to raise a revenue in America" without the Americans having a voice in the matter. He supposed this was more alarming to New Yorkers than to some others because of their previous experiences dealing with the equally egregious quartering of troops in civilians' homes. The turmoil, he said, all came down to "the mischievious politics of the mother country."

T he king was out of sorts. He forgot things. Sometimes he flopped on the ground and a servant had to sit on him to keep him still. He would start a sentence and find himself unable to finish, as if he feared a full stop would become literal for him. The symptoms went on for months, then they vanished. His counselors hoped the madness would not return.

George III emerged from his illness to find a host of troubles, not the least of which emanated from across the Atlantic. Rioters were rioting, effigies had been burned, the Virginia legislature had been suspended by the royal governor for refusing to accept the stamp tax. A customs collector wrote that "the Americans to a man seem resolved" not to pay it, and went so far as to suggest that "some people are determined to die rather than submit."

More than a few members of Parliament were also against the tax. William Pitt, who had been cast into exile in 1761, was back in government. He believed that the Bill of Rights of 1689 had real political meaning, and that its force and power extended to America. He was in bed with gout when the issue came up again but said in a letter, "If I can crawl or be carried, I will deliver my mind and heart upon the state of America." He had felt all along the precedent of a tax in America imposed by Parliament would meet with disastrous results. "There is an idea in some that the colonies are virtually represented in this house," he declaimed before his colleagues in the House of Commons. "I would fain know by whom an American is represented here. Is he represented by any knight of the shire, in any county in this kingdom?" The Americans were right to assert that the power to tax them rested in their own legislatures, otherwise, he said, they would be "slaves." He pushed the House to repeal the law.

The king was against repealing. So was the prime minister, George Grenville. Many British officers in North America were convinced that protests of the tax were the work of organized gangs; they wanted a tough response from London. Among these was Major Thomas Moncrieffe, the father of young Margaret, who had taken part in the military crackdown on protesters in New York. "Dam'n me, if I will Beleive there was one Spark of Patriotick Virtue in all their Maneuvres," he wrote a friend.

George Sackville was likewise in favor of standing firm. He confessed to a friend, regarding America, that he found "the spirit that rages there is beyond conception." As more and more members of Parliament and ministers in government came out for repealing the law, Sackville's growing rage offered a glimpse into his inner self, suggesting that beneath the urbane exterior of the London statesman there still lived the boy of Knole House, who held close to feudal notions of government based on a beneficent but iron-willed overlord and his obedient vassals. The Bill of Rights of 1689 notwithstanding, a colony, he believed, owed fealty to the home country, and the home country had to punish disobedience. The fuss in America, he insisted, was all "riot and ill-grounded clamour." The Americans were "undutiful children," and "nothing but military power" would do to put them in their place.

Sackville's feudal fulminating went unheeded. The House voted to repeal the Stamp Act. The government was reacting not only to reports of riots in America and constitutional arguments of men like Pitt, but to appeals from British merchants, who were holding large amounts of debt from American farmers and businessmen, which they feared would never be paid with the new law in place.

Americans celebrated. They took the repeal as a sign that the constitutional arguments had won the day, that they could move forward as dutiful and respected subjects of Great Britain. John Wilkes, whose tirade had started it all, was once again hailed as a hero. "Wilkes and Liberty!" was the toast given in taverns around the colonies. Some people even named their children after him. The city of Wilkes-Barre, Pennsylvania, which was founded around this time, chose to honor Wilkes and Isaac Barré, another radical, freedom-proclaiming member of Parliament, in its name.

George Washington dashed off a letter to Robert Cary that was far more genial in tone than his recent ones had been. "The Repeal of the Stamp Act, to whatsoever causes owing, ought much to be rejoiced at. . . ." he wrote. And, as if sensing that the government had been swayed more by the work of men such as Cary than by republican sentiments, he closed with, "All therefore who were Instrumental in procuring the Repeal are entitled to the Thanks of every British Subject & have mine cordially."

With the lifting of the tax, and what it seemed to mean for the future, Washington felt a sense of dawning opportunity, and with it came an explosion of creativity. He began to think outside the traditional system into which he had been born. If he couldn't achieve economic freedom as a tobacco planter, or via westward expansion, he would do it in other ways. He began experimenting with other crops that could bring in money—wheat, oats, rye, hemp—and settled on wheat as his main cash crop. He became an enthusiastic student of modern farming theory, in particular of the English agricultural innovator Jethro Tull. Putting together the Virginia militia more or less from scratch had unleashed a hidden genius for organization. That now came fully to the fore as he transformed Mount Vernon. His slaves learned to work exotic machinery that he fancied, such as a Rotherham plow and a forbidding-looking device—with an operator sitting in a chair above a large spindle bristling with iron barbs—called a spiky roller. He also taught them trades: some became carpenters, brewers, blacksmiths and masons, producing high-quality products. While standing on the banks of the Potomac and marveling at the shouldering schools of sturgeon, shad and other fish, he hit on the idea of developing a fishery. He became a major marketer of fish, selling hundreds of thousands of herring a year. By the late 1760s he had accomplished a kind of internal revolution against his native culture, which equated genteel success with tobacco farming. He stood like a general on the hilltops of Mount Vernon, transforming what had been a sleepy landscape into an efficient, cutting-edge business enterprise. Where the early years of the decade were a time of financial and political strife, in the last years Washington came into his own as a farmer and businessman. His goal was "independence," and he had taken huge strides toward achieving it.

Like others in the colonies, he had reason to hope that the leaders in England had seen the repeal of the Stamp Act not merely as an expedient to quiet the situation but as a balancing of the scales of justice. Justice was much on his mind at this time. In 1768, he ran for, and won, a judgeship on the Fairfax County Court. He had no experience, of course. As he had done as a teenager who was eager to learn etiquette, and again when he assumed command of an army, he purchased a self-help book—*The Justice of the Peace and Parish Officer*—and studied it for guidance.

Justice was on Venture's mind too. In one way or another, justice was probably on the minds of all of the 254 blacks who lived in Stonington, Connecticut (out of a total population of 3,900), the majority of whom were slaves.

The world was changing fast. Stonington was growing, and on every trip into town Venture picked up news. A new highway was laid out from the Road Church, north of town, to the waterfront in neighboring Mystic. Two new businesses—a weaveshop and a tannery—opened up in Captain Richard Wheeler's old house. Jeremiah Browning, from

Block Island, bought up a huge tract of land in the western part of Stonington with the intention to develop it. People took up a subscription to build a schoolhouse on a site between Asa Elliott's house and Nathan Chesebrough's meadow.

While all this was going on, the white people were chattering about freedom: about England, the Stamp Act and its repeal. They demanded justice, and were pleased when they got it.

*Justice.* One day Venture was working in the barn and heard a sudden racket coming from the house. The master was away "a gunning" on Long Island. Fearing the worst, Venture ran to the disturbance. He, Meg and their children apparently lived in the main house, possibly in the attic or in a wing off the kitchen. Besides Venture's family, Thomas Stanton likely had only a few other slaves; while about one out of every three farms on New England's "slave coast" kept slaves, the numbers were usually small, which meant a certain intimacy between them and their owners. It wasn't like in George Washington's Virginia. Slaves with knowledge of conditions in both the North and South definitely preferred the North. James Mars, who was born a slave in Connecticut to a father from New York and a mother from Virginia, had learned the difference from his mother, and he spelled it out succinctly: "The treatment of slaves was different at the North from the South. At the North they were admitted to be a species of the human family." When his owner, a Congregational minister, announced he was planning to move to Virginia, Mars's father took his family into hiding in an effort to avoid southern slavery.

But life in the North came with its own difficulties. The larger groups of slaves on a southern plantation helped to maintain traditions and a sense of community. The close living quarters in the North meant slaves were more strictly controlled: they might be locked in their rooms at night. And living under constant scrutiny exacerbated tensions. As it happened, Meg and the mistress, Sarah Stanton, had a testy relationship. Venture reached one of the rooms and discovered the two women in front of the hearth locked in a vicious fight, with the mistress beating his wife. Venture got between them and was able to determine that the "violent passion" was over a trifle. "I earnestly requested my wife to beg pardon of her mistress for the sake of peace," he said later, "even if she had given no just occasion for offense. But whilst I was thus saying my mistress turned the blows which she was repeating on my wife to me. She took down her horse-whip, and while she was glutting her fury with it, I reached out my great black hand, raised it up and received the blows of the whip on it which were designed for my head. Then I immediately committed the whip to the devouring fire." That ended the confrontation. But it wasn't the end of the affair. Venture had put himself in a position of power over his mistress; he knew there would be repercussions. When Stanton returned from Long Island, his wife recounted the episode for him, apparently with either Venture or Meg present. Stanton said nothing. For the next several days, his silence became progressively more ominous. Then one morning while Venture was bending down to put a log on the fire Thomas Stanton came up behind him, raised a two-foot club and brought it down on Venture's head. The wound was bad, but Venture didn't lose consciousness. He staggered to his feet in time to see Stanton raising the club again. Venture grabbed it in one hand and Stanton in the other and hauled the man outside. Stanton ran off. Venture knew where he was going: to get his brother.

Venture didn't wait. He took the club and made his way to a justice of the peace, where he laid the weapon down before the man as evidence, showed his bleeding wound and told what had transpired. Venture knew that slaves had some rights in Connecticut, including a right not to be mistreated. On the other hand, the overriding concern of the justice system, in all of the colonies, was the maintenance of the economic status quo, which included the institution of slavery. Judges tended to side with owners provided there was not a wider social cost.

Beating a slave in public, for instance, could incite other violence, and therefore might be grounds to punish the owner. But that didn't apply in Venture's case. The judge advised Venture to go back to Stanton and be dutiful and submissive; if the violence was repeated, he said, then Venture would have grounds for a complaint.

Just then Thomas Stanton appeared at the door along with his brother Robert. The judge, Venture said, "improved this convenient opportunity to caution my master. He asked him for what he treated his slave thus hastily and unjustly, and told him what would be the consequence if he continued the same treatment towards me." Then he let them go. They headed back to the Stanton farm with the two brothers on horseback and Venture walking between. "When they had come to a bye place," Venture said, "they both dismounted their respective horses, and fell to beating me with great violence. I became enraged at this and immediately turned them both under me, laid one of them across the other, and stamped both with my feet what I would."

Before Venture could go back to seek justice, justice came to him. Stanton went to a constable to complain of a dangerously violent slave. The constable, with two strong men at his side, took Venture to a blacksmith, who fixed a pair of stout handcuffs onto him. Back at the house there was a gaudy little scene with Stanton and his wife gloating over their victory over the slave who had had the temerity to try to use the justice system against them. When Stanton and Venture arrived, Sarah Stanton brightly inquired whether Venture was indeed handcuffed. At the news that he was, she exclaimed with vengeful delight. Venture's posture of reserve cracked. He presented himself before her, showed her his manacles and, with baleful impudence, thanked her for his "gold rings."

The impudence infuriated Stanton anew. He had another slave wrap a heavy chain around Venture's legs and snap it tight with two padlocks. So he stayed, barely able to move. But the imprisonment within the prison of slavery wasn't enough to appease Stanton. He enacted another little scene for the slave. He went to the chest where Venture kept his belongings and took a piece of paper from it. Venture knew what it was: the promissory note that Stanton's brother had signed, acknowledging that he had accepted 21 pounds in New York currency from Venture—Venture's life savings—and guaranteeing to pay it back. With the chained slave watching, Stanton tore the note to pieces.

The central event of Venture's childhood—watching his father die rather than divulge where his money was hidden—was still alive in him. It had always been there, glowing like an ember. Money was not just a means of exchange. Money was the essence of his life. He had painstakingly earned it, saved it, registering each new gain. It was all toward a secret goal: eventually buying his freedom. Much as it became for George Washington, money for Venture was the means to independence. Money was freedom. Stanton tearing up the note was an act of aggression that—Stanton surely knew—went right to the big African's heart.

After Venture had lain in chains for about three days Stanton came to him again. The man's anger hadn't diminished; he spat contempt at the slave and asked if he'd had enough of the chains and was ready to go to work. But Venture had had long hours to seethe and ponder. They were playing a game, and he wasn't willing to lose. "No," he answered. If Stanton figured he was teaching the slave a lesson, Venture knew that by staying locked up he was depriving Stanton of his labor. He would stay in chains.

"Well then, I will send you to the West Indies or banish you," Stanton replied, "for I am resolved not to keep you." Conditions in a Caribbean plantation meant a virtual death sentence.

Venture was ready for this. "I crossed the waters to come here," he shot back, "and I am willing to cross them to return."

## Chapter 8

# THIRTEEN TOASTS

Around the time that Venture was locked in his psychological standoff with Thomas Stanton, George Washington sat himself down, picked up a pen and, with anger tempered by resolve, began to write:

> RAN away from a Plantation of the Subscriber's, on *Dogue Run* in *Fairfax*, on Sunday the 9th Instant, the following Negroes . . .

As was his custom when angry, he let his sentences roam, loading the advertisement with extraneous detail that served more to vent his feelings than to inform ("they went off without the least Suspicion, Provocation, or Difference with any Body, or the least angry Word or Abuse from their Overseers"). As George Mumford had done when Venture ran off, Washington named and meticulously described each of the four slaves who had fled, down to the clothing they had on. "Whoever apprehends the said Negroes," he wrote in closing, would have "Recompence paid them, by GEORGE WASHINGTON."

Washington prided himself on treating his slaves humanely. He tended to their medical needs, and in selling them he never split up families. But by definition keeping people enslaved could not be a humane activity. People naturally resisted captivity. They ran off; they dragged their feet. To maintain order and establish a thriving business, he fashioned a dictatorial presence. Walking the grounds of Mount Vernon with him, a visitor was stunned at the change that came over the ordinarily genteel Washington when he turned to address his slaves: "he amazed me by the utterance of his words," said the man, who found that in his sudden and violent expression of anger Washington was "quite another man."

Washington's expanding businesses all relied on slave labor, and he was determined to turn a profit. He worked his slaves from dawn to dusk six days a week. And while he did not divide families when he sold slaves, he often found it necessary to split them up in installing workers around his five farms. Since he preferred to have men as house servants, dressed in neat scarlet and white uniforms, a husband might be in the Mansion House during the week while his wife and children were on a distant farm loading dung, tending cattle and picking apples. Those families who lived together did so in conditions that European visitors found appalling. One noted the slave quarters consisted of "wretched wooden shacks" in which adults slept on a "mean pallet" while children huddled on the bare ground around "a very bad fireplace."

When Washington felt that a slave's impudence made him unusable, he resorted to precisely the solution that Thomas Stanton had threatened Venture with. In 1766 he wrote to the captain of a ship bound for the Caribbean that he was sending him a slave named Tom who was "both a Rogue & Runaway." Washington had had enough of Tom; he instructed the captain to sell him "in any of the islands you may go to," where the slave would find life much harsher. Washington thought Tom would sell for a good price "if kept clean & trim'd up a little when offered to Sale," and suggested what he would like in return: rum, molasses, a barrel of limes and, to please Martha and her sons, "mixed sweetmeats." In closing he noted to the captain that he would "very Chearfully allow you the customary Commissions on this affair."

For one or two days after his confrontation with Thomas Stanton, Venture remained locked in chains. Then a man named Hempstead Miner appeared at the house. Like Stanton, Miner hailed from one of the founding families of Stonington. The two men had known each other all their lives but were not on especially friendly terms. Venture surely knew Miner as well. His house was in the center of town. Miner managed to get a private word with the bound slave. He asked if Venture would like it if he bought him. Figuring that life under Stanton's roof would henceforth be unbearable, Venture said yes. Miner then got conspiratorial. He proposed that Venture continue his moodiness toward Stanton a bit longer so as to drive down the price. And he held out an irresistible carrot: if he could get Venture cheap, Miner promised that he would let him buy himself out of slavery.

Wrapped in chains, in the true depths of human bondage, Venture glimpsed a light of promise: nothing less than the future he had longed for from the moment he was captured by the army that invaded his home village of Dukandarra all those years ago. It was uncommon for slaves to purchase their freedom, for a slave owner to enter into such an arrangement, but it happened on occasion. Continuing to act sullen and recalcitrant was the easiest thing in the world for Venture. He did, and eventually Stanton had had enough. He agreed to sell the slave to Miner for 56 pounds, below the going rate for a healthy, skilled man. The moment the two men shook hands, Stanton unlocked the chains, and Venture stepped outside, headed toward Hempstead Miner's house and the prospect of eventual freedom.

Once the transfer of ownership was complete, Miner revealed his actual motive. He didn't need a slave; he had simply heard about

Venture's standoff with Stanton and saw a way to make some money. He would buy him cheap and sell him for a profit. Since everyone in and around Stonington knew the Stantons and knew of their big, self-possessed slave, trying to sell him in the area would be complicated. So he took Venture 60 miles inland to Hartford. There he offered him to a man named William Hooker. But Venture immediately disliked Hooker, and when he heard that Hooker proposed to take him to German Flatts, in central New York, he balked. In agreeing to be sold to Miner he knew he was playing a risky game: he had reasoned that while he would be separated from Meg and their children at least all of them would be in the same town, and he would have a chance to work for his freedom. Now that hope was gone and the situation was getting worse. German Flatts was 250 miles from Stonington. Venture told Hooker he would not go. Hooker liked the look of the big African, saw a lot of use in him, and was ready to tame him. "If you will go by no other measures, I will tie you down in my sleigh," he responded. But while, as with Stanton, Venture knew that most of the advantages in the power struggle they were engaged in were on the other side, he also knew how to leverage his position. "I replied to him," he said later, "that if he carried me in that manner, no person would purchase me, for it would be thought that he had a murderer for sale." Hooker thought some, then backed off. This slave was too ornery, too wily. It wasn't worth it.

Miner, who apparently needed fast money, then struck a provisional deal with a man named Daniel Edwards. He pawned Venture, essentially renting him to Edwards for 10 pounds. Venture didn't resist; he liked Edwards from the start. For a short while he worked as a butler in the man's Hartford residence: getting wine from the cellar, serving at table. When someone was fair with him, Venture responded in kind, so he worked well and efficiently, and Edwards quickly saw him as an asset. The two men found that they could be honest with each other.

Edwards asked why Miner wanted to part with him, and Venture told him it was his surmise that Miner's goal was "to convert me into cash."

But the arrangement was not to last. Venture didn't like being so far from his wife and children, and Miner eventually made it known that he was thinking of selling him to another man in Stonington. Edwards was decent enough to give Venture a horse and let him ride back to Stonington to assess the situation. His first stop was the Stanton farm, where he had a brief reunion with his family. But as soon as Stanton realized he was there, Venture hurried away. He went on to pay a visit to a man named Oliver Smith. Miner had been in discussion with Smith about possibly buying him, and Venture wanted to investigate him. He had achieved what was surely an unusual stature and presence for a slave, such that white men tolerated him interviewing them and giving his opinion on whether one would make a suitable master.

Smith was about ten years younger than Venture. He was originally from nearby Groton. He had connections, and he seemed to have integrity. Venture determined that he could perhaps trust him in the answer he gave to the most important question Venture put to him: "if he would consent to have me purchase my freedom." Smith said that he would, in time, give Venture the opportunity to do so. Venture therefore announced to Smith and Miner that, between the two of them, he would prefer to be owned by Smith. The two white men agreed on terms. Smith and Venture agreed on terms as well: the price for Venture's freedom would be 85 pounds, a substantial sum, equivalent to a year's salary for a skilled laborer, to be paid off gradually as Venture earned it. Venture had a new owner, one of his choosing, and a new chance at freedom.

George Sackville had no intention to let the repeal of the Stamp Act stand as the final word on the British governing of America.

The reports of celebrations taking place from Virginia to New England confirmed his fears that the Americans would see the repeal as a formal acknowledgment of their autonomy on the matter of taxation, and by extension on other matters. He had previously entered negotiations with a group of like-minded parliamentarians. The result was "An Act for the Better Securing the Dependency of His Majesty's Dominions in America Upon the Crown and Parliament of Great Britain," otherwise known as the Declaratory Act, in which Parliament asserted that its legal authority encompassed the American colonists as fully as it did subjects in the British Isles.

Having thus established the question of the legality of taxing the colonists, Parliament then set about doing so once again. Sackville, as spokesman for the group that wanted to bring the Americans to heel, exchanged gossipy letters with Charles Townshend, the Chancellor of the Exchequer, befriending him and pulling him into their circle. Soon they had framed a series of new taxes. The group believed that the essence of American objections to the Stamp Act had been that it was a tax on products bought, sold and used within the colonies; they reasoned that taxes on British goods that America imported would circumvent the objection.

Sackville was pleased with the resulting measures. The taxes were on staples, things the Americans needed, so they could hardly boycott. Who, after all, could do without tea?

It was early April 1769, a chilly, overcast day. George Washington's desk was littered with journals and his head churning with the ideas they conveyed. Taking a break from overseeing his slaves as they carried out their spring chores—threshing wheat and sewing grass seed—he picked up a pen and wrote his neighbor and fellow burgess George Mason: "At a time when our lordly Masters in Great Britain will be satisfied with nothing less than the deprication of American freedom, it seems highly necessary that something shou'd be done to avert the stroke and maintain the liberty which we have derived from our Ancestors. . . ."

The moment the Townshend Duties had been reported, he, like other Americans, had reacted in outrage. Americans hated the new taxes as much as they had hated the Stamp Act. There were boycotts. There was anger in the streets—enough to prompt Britain to send a warship sailing into Boston harbor to keep the peace. But more striking were the hotly worded and intensely reasoned missives and essays that suddenly appeared. A series coyly titled "Letters from a Farmer in Pennsylvania," penned two years earlier by a Philadelphia lawyer named John Dickinson, was reprinted in newspapers around the colonies. Their effect was signaled in the first words of the first letter. "My dear countrymen," it began, and indeed as Dickinson's writings were picked up by newspapers all around the colonies, the notion began to cohere that the letters' readers did not see themselves any longer as first and foremost Virginians or Pennsylvanians or Rhode Islanders but rather as Americans. Where British leaders considered that they were asserting proper governmental authority for the eventual benefit of all, Dickinson saw a betrayal of the British concept of the rights of individuals. Like many other Americans, he still held warm paternal feelings for the king, and he tried to hold George III blameless for the overreach of Parliament ("We have an excellent prince, in whose good dispositions toward us we may confide"). But the repeated assaults on "American liberty" by England had brought him to the point of pondering violence, and he turned the tables on the home country: "If at length it becomes undoubted that an inveterate resolution is formed to annihilate the liberties of the governed, then *English* history affords frequent examples of resistance by force."

Another letter, written by a Boston brewer and politician named

Samuel Adams, was also read all over the colonies, and it too declared that the taxes imposed by Parliament on Americans were "infringements of their natural and constitutional rights."

Washington consumed these sentiments, and found that they reinforced his own. In writing to George Mason, the former soldier went so far as to suggest that matters might come to military conflict, though he took pains to mask the word "arms" so as to avoid a potential charge of treason: ". . . no man shou'd scruple, or hesitate a moment to use a—ms in defence of so valuable a blessing. . . ." The blessing in question, of course, was freedom. He was broadening his idea both of what it was and of what Americans needed to do to secure it.

Before Venture left Thomas Stanton's farm for the last time, he took a shovel out to the main road just above the house and dug at a spot "in the road over which [Stanton] passed daily." In the back of his mind he never fully trusted the Stantons to redeem the note for his life savings, so he had done with a portion of his money just as his father had with his treasure: buried it. And there it was, still safe in the ground.

Where his father's hidden treasure had marked the beginning of Venture's life of slavery, he hoped that his own buried treasure would be the key to freedom. Venture and Oliver Smith quickly recognized one another as men of business, and they set about making a formal arrangement by which Venture would eventually purchase his freedom. It could not be a simple matter of Venture handing money to Smith. Venture understood the law: "as I was the property of my master," he said, "[I] therefore could not safely take his obligation myself." A man who was the property of someone else could not enter directly into a business arrangement with that person. He had to go through an intermediary. Venture knew a free black man in town who agreed to serve as his agent. Venture gave his buried savings to him, paperwork was drawn up, and the agent gave the money to Smith as the first payment toward Venture's freedom.

Oliver Smith wasn't motivated to help Venture strictly out of feelings of altruism. He recognized Venture's value but was also aware of his sense of justice: his ability to defy and confound an owner if he felt demeaned. By helping him to win his freedom, Smith had nothing to lose. The man would literally pay for himself, and by assisting him toward what Venture so openly desired, Smith believed he would create a valuable ally, a multitalented laborer who would likely continue to work for him.

Still, there were legal impediments to the arrangement. Most of the colonies had laws on the books that made it difficult for owners to free slaves. In the past, owners had gotten out of the burden of caring for old or sick slaves by freeing them when they could no longer work. It then fell to the government to care for them. Taxpayers didn't like that, so most of the colonies had forbidden the freeing of "aged or infirm slaves" for the purpose of relieving "the master from the charge of supporting them," as one Massachusetts statute put it. Connecticut law stipulated that if a freed slave became destitute then the cost of caring for him or her must be borne by the former owner. Venture wasn't aged or infirm, however, so Smith was able to work around the law, though he would still be liable to pay for his keep in the event that Venture became infirm. It was for this reason, he told Venture, that he had demanded such a high price for Venture's freedom.

Smith agreed to let Venture spend part of his work week in freelance money-making pursuits. In the predawn darkness, before starting his chores, Venture walked down to Long Point, the outcrop where the town of Stonington stuck a rocky finger into Long Island Sound, and fished. He sold his catch in the town market and turned the proceeds over to his agent, who would then pay the money toward Venture's freedom. There was a fertile patch of land adjoining the Stanton brothers' property that Venture had long had his eye on. He obtained it and began making it profitable: "By cultivating this land with the greatest diligence and economy, at times when my master did not require my labor, in two years I laid up ten pounds." Smith didn't have a lot of work for him in the wintertime, so Venture struck a deal with him. Fishers Island, across the Sound, was where he had spent his formative years, working for the Mumfords. There were new caretakers installed on the island; no one knew the island better than Venture. He proposed that he spend the winter there, chopping wood and doing other off-season jobs. Smith agreed. The arrangement was that one-quarter of his earnings would go to Smith as profit, and the other three-quarters Venture would give to his agent, who would then pay it to Smith toward Venture's freedom.

So it went through the mid-1760s. While George Washington and Abraham Yates fought the Stamp Act, rejoiced in its repeal, then began to contemplate military measures as the likely response to the imposition of the Townshend Duties, Venture chopped, hoed, seeded and harvested. As white Americans simmered over what they increasingly felt was a form of slavery imposed on them from English leaders like George Sackville, and as they circulated lofty quotes from English writers about individual liberty and natural rights, Venture, on his own and with no printed wisdom to guide him, worked exhaustively toward the same end. He kept a careful tally of what he had paid off toward his own liberty: "four pounds sixteen shillings . . . thirteen pounds six shillings . . . fifty-one pounds two shillings." As he approached his goal, he spurred himself harder than any master ever had: fishing for lobsters and eels in the night and early morning hours; working the land by day, harvesting and hauling ten cartloads of watermelons to market; chopping enough firewood to heat a village.

As his goal got closer, Venture put every penny he earned toward it, depriving himself of all but the barest necessities. He had one pair of shoes. He slept on the ground, with only "one coverlet over and another under me."

After one long stint of laboring, he returned to Oliver Smith and personally handed him what he had earned. He knew precisely what remained on the account following this payment: "thirteen pounds eighteen shillings to make up the full sum for my redemption." To his great surprise, Smith released him on the spot, saying that he could pay him the rest at some point in the future, or not.

Bewildered by the suddenness of it, Venture stepped outside Smith's door and into a brash new light. He had a lot to think about at this wondrous juncture, and, as was typical for him, he converted his musing on his life to financial terms: "I had already been sold three different times, made considerable money with seemingly nothing to derive from it, been cheated out of a large sum of money, lost much by misfortune, and paid an enormous sum for my freedom." He was in his early forties, still strong, with an uncertain future—one that, as had never been the case before, was up to him to chart.


On December 16, 1769, Elizabeth Germain, George Sackville's unofficial godmother, who had lived at Knole House during his childhood, died, not at Knole, where she had planted thousands of trees, but at her townhouse in St. James's Square, London. She had survived her children and her husband and, in accordance with her husband's wishes, in her will she left most of her fortune to one of the sons of the Duke of Dorset. Lady Betty having long favored George Sackville, upon her death he received word that her wealth would pass to him, with one proviso. He was to legally assume the family name.

Sackville seems not to have had a moment's hesitation. Swiftly, at the age of fifty-nine, he became someone else. George Sackville ceased to be. He was now Lord George Germain. His enemies quipped that he was even eager for the change, for it distanced him from the stain of his dishonor at Minden: it was Sackville who had disastrously failed to carry out an order in battle, not Germain.

If he thought the memory of his humiliation would go away, he was wrong. In the midst of a speech in Parliament late in 1770, the now Lord George Germain made a passing reference to England's honor. Another member of the House piped up. George Johnstone was a career naval officer with a reputation for bravery and hotheadedness, whose long-standing loathing of Sackville—that is to say, Germain—was only deepened by the Minden affair. He declared in the chamber that he found it wondrously strange that "the noble Lord should interest himself so deeply in the honour of his country, when he had hitherto been so regardless of his own."

It was a public slight of the first order. George Germain had no choice but to challenge the man to a duel. Unfortunately for him, Johnstone was an expert marksman with a history of success in affairs of honor. They met with pistols in Hyde Park, took aim and fired. Both bullets missed. Johnstone's second shot twanged off the barrel of Germain's pistol: enough of a hit to satisfy the demands of honor. Both men walked away unscathed.

Germain hoped his upright conduct in this most gentlemanly of encounters—Johnstone publicly acknowledged afterward Lord George's manly calm when staring down a gun barrel—would finally silence the charge of cowardice that had been flung at him for more than a decade. But for someone with his personality, his penchant for going at opponents with unbridled aggression, the Minden affair would never end: it was simply too fine a weapon for his enemies to ever abandon. They managed to spin the story of the duel in such a way that it underscored Minden rather than erase it. Since it had taken several days after Johnstone's public slight for Germain to challenge the man to a duel, they gossiped that in that time Germain had been trying to squirm out of it, just as he had ducked his duty in the German countryside, and only formally challenged the naval officer when he realized that to do anything else would bring humiliation. George Sackville may have been no more; but Minden lived on.

On May 17, 1769, shortly after noon, the door of the Raleigh Tavern in Williamsburg burst open and in spilled dozens of men, bewigged and bothered, talking raucously and thrumming with nervous energy. Among them were Patrick Henry and Thomas Jefferson. Also among them was George Washington. Echoing in their ears were unprecedented words that they had just heard. The day before, meeting in the House of Burgesses, they had unanimously passed a series of resolutions in opposition to the Townshend Duties, asserting that they, as their colony's elected representatives, had the sole right to tax Virginians. On returning to session the next day, a messenger from the royal governor had charged in and demanded that they appear before him at once. His office was upstairs; they all marched up and crowded into the Council Chamber. The governor—Norborne Berkeley, the Fourth Baron de Botetourt, a member of the House of Lords who had only recently arrived in the colony but had orders to be firm—was brief: "Mr. Speaker, and Gentlemen of the House of Burgesses, I have heard of your resolves, and augur ill of their Effect: You have made it my Duty to dissolve you; and you are dissolved accordingly."

With that, Virginia's legislative body was shut down. The unprecedented act had the effect of spurring the rattled gentry to consider responses that previously most would have shied away from. They promptly formed themselves into a "nonimportation association," which would use the tactic of boycotting British goods as its organizing principle. The tavern would be their new assembly hall. Washington was appointed to a committee to draw up a plan of action. They agreed that they were suffering extreme economic distress, that the cause was "unconstitutional" acts of Parliament, and that they would henceforth do whatever they could to boycott English products. They took pains to specify the target items, including:

> Spirits, Wine, Cyder, Perry, Beer, Ale, Malt, Barley, Pease, Beef, Pork, Fish, Butter, Cheese, Tallow, Candles, Oil, Fruit, Sugar, Pickles, Confectionary, Pewter, Hoes, Axes, Watches, Clocks, Tables, Chairs, Looking Glasses, Carriages, Joiner's and Cabinet Work of all Sorts, Upholstery of all Sorts, Trinkets and Jewellery, Plate and Gold, and Silversmith's Work of all Sorts, Ribbon and Millinery of all Sorts, Lace of all Sorts, *India* Goods of all Sorts, except Spices, Silks of all Sorts, except Sewing Silk, Cambrick, Lawn, Muslin, Gauze . . .

They further vowed that they would resist the temptation to import more slaves "until the said Acts of Parliament are repealed."

Then they drank a toast, to "The King," and a second toast, to "The Queen and Royal Family," for despite all they had suffered, they still held the royals in parental regard. Then, as a precaution, and a reflection of their nervousness over the dangerous step they were taking, someone proposed a toast to the governor who had just abolished their assembly. They drank that. Then they drank a toast to prosperity for Virginia. And then—again hedging their bets—they drank to "a speedy and lasting Union between Great-Britain and her Colonies." Then, as a qualification to the previous toast, they drank to "constitutional British liberty in America." And then to "all true Patriots, and supporters thereof." Then, further reflecting the extent of their nervousness, they drank six more toasts.

So fortified, they pronounced their business over for the present and staggered out into the light of day.

It was October 14, 1772, and Abraham Yates was celebrating. He was having a very good year. Indeed, he had to think that all in all he was enjoying quite an acceptable life. He was forty-eight years old, in excellent health, living in a fine home he had built on Market Street in Albany with a loving wife and, the jewel of his life, their ten-year-old daughter Susanna. He had risen from the humblest of beginnings to become a man of substance. It was years since he had stitched a pair of shoes. As one of the city's busiest lawyers, he had handled more than 900 cases in the past decade, with clients ranging from the wealthy Livingston family to local farmers and carpenters, and cases that ran from disputed inheritances to a woman who had fled her abusive husband.

Meanwhile, like George Washington, he had worked through the 1760s to make himself financially independent by investing in land. He bought city lots and rolling country acreage. He partnered with Philip Schuyler, the powerful scion of one of Albany's old Dutch families, to buy four acres of land along a waterway called the Battenkill, north of his wife's hometown of Schaghticoke. There was a fine waterfall here; Yates had a sawmill built on it and rented out the land and the mill. But most meaningfully, he was a leader of his beloved city, and it was political success that he was now celebrating. The election results that had just come in showed him winning a seat on the city council for the tenth straight year. In that time he had helped the city to grow. Five years earlier he had overseen the construction of three stone docks on the Hudson River, the first permanent docks in the city's history. Three years later, the council found that four more docks were necessary to accommodate the burgeoning traffic. Ships sailed up constantly: barrels of rum and molasses from the West Indies rolled ashore, and wheat and timber from the interior were hauled aboard. The population of the county had surged to more than 42,000. Albany was taking on some aspects of a big city; the year before, Yates and his five fellow councilmen had initiated an experiment in public safety, erecting oil lamps high atop poles at twenty intersections around town, to be lit every evening.

Maybe what he was most proud of was how he had steadily carved a path through the thicket of Albany's unique politics. There were the old Dutch and English families. There were the patricians who owned much of the county's land and who had for more than a century held all power. There were the British soldiers who had settled in the city following the quartering of troops during the French and Indian War, who had married local girls, put down roots and wanted to exert their influence. There were newcomers from New England, and those from Europe and from New York City. Each was an interest group, which spoke its own language, literal or otherwise. Out of this babble Yates had, from the time of his first election as assistant alderman in 1753, steadily built his own coalition of common laborers and skilled craftsmen. He had made them see that their interests were not necessarily tied to those of people who may happen to have come originally from the same country or to those who had traditionally demanded their fealty. Their interests were linked to others in their economic class: people who were hurt by the imposition of British taxes, by sudden restrictions in trade.

And on this very day, the long steady trail of his work had reached something of a climax. A year ago, Yates had succeeded in getting his nephew and political protégé, Robert Yates, elected to the council. Now the returns showed that another nephew and protégé, Peter Yates, had won as well. Together the three men made up half the council. Abraham Yates's new ideology was taking over Albany. People were talking of a "Yates party," one that would serve the interests of ordinary workers.

But all the while he was rising, Yates had also been making enemies.

Much of his legal work over these years was on behalf of newcomers who wanted to settle on land in the county. The old Dutch families still claimed ownership of vast tracts of it, little of which they actually used. Yates questioned their title to that land, arguing that the Dutch West India Company, from whom their forebears had received it in the days of the Dutch colony of New Netherland, had never properly procured it from the natives. While Yates was gaining a reputation as an activist lawyer for the common man, he was thus focusing the entrenched elite in its opposition to him. The rise of his party, in the 1772 election, triggered them into concerted action. As a result, Yates was stunned, in the fall of 1773, to find that he had been voted out of office.

He launched an investigation, and uncovered evidence of bribes and other voting irregularities. He challenged the election, but the results were upheld.

Probably he would have begun preparing to run again the following year, but two months after his loss, electrifying news reached Albany. In response to the boycotts of English products throughout the colonies, Parliament had repealed the Townshend Duties. Members like George Germain, however, insisted that a new law was necessary that would assert Parliament's right to levy taxes on American subjects. In May of 1773 it passed the Tea Act, which was meant both to help the East India Company, which had massive surpluses of tea in its warehouses as a result of the boycotts, and to assert once and for all the right of Britain to tax the colonists. The act set off a new wave of boycotts and protests. The news that reached Albany indicated that the situation was now a crisis. On the night of December 16, enraged locals in Boston had boarded three British ships that were due to deliver tea and dumped their entire cargo—342 chests, weighing a total of 92,000 pounds and valued at nearly 10,000 pounds—into the harbor.

"The Destruction of the Tea," as the incident became known at the time, was not just another protest but an act of wholesale vandalism, a rent in the fabric of Empire, which demanded an unprecedented response. Abraham Yates put aside his thoughts about running for city council. He seemed at once to understand that the landscape of his life had changed.

Frederick North, Fifth Earl of Guilford, the prime minister of England, stood before a packed chamber in the House of Commons. With goggly eyes and a wide fleshy mouth he tended to look, one contemporary said, like "a blind trumpeter." As a politician, he had wisdom, but his ascent to the leadership of the British government was due more to the fact that, as Horace Walpole observed, "he offends nobody." Following the arrival of news of the dumping of shiploads of tea in Boston Harbor, he read out to the assembly a message from the king: "His Majesty, upon information of the unwarrantable practices which have been lately concerted and carried on in North America, and particularly of the violent and outrageous proceedings at the town and port of Boston... with a view to obstructing the commerce of this kingdom . . . hath thought fit to lay the whole matter before his two Houses of Parliament." The king, in other words, wanted the government to act. And Lord North needed guidance.

Among the first to speak was Edmund Burke, an Irish philosopher and Whig politician. The experience of England's dealings with Ireland had colored Burke's perspective on America. The Americans, he was lately given to observing, were not an alien people but cousins of the English; they should not be bludgeoned with principles but treated with common sense. After Parliament had repealed the Stamp Act, he observed, the colonies became quiet and obedient. Giving in on the matter of taxation, therefore, had been prudent, and that was what he now advised his colleagues to do.

Lord George Germain rose to his fleshy height and disagreed weightily, saying that after the repeal of the Stamp Act "the contrary was the case" in America, that the Americans had been "totally displeased" because Parliament still asserted its right to tax them. The problem, he insisted, was Parliament's failure to assert its power and authority.

British leaders grouped themselves around these two poles. In the following weeks Germain elaborated his views before the House. What the colonies needed, he said, was a structural reorganization. He considered it an "absurdity" that the colonial government of Massachusetts was an elected body. It was obvious to him that the colony's representatives should be appointed, which would make them easier to control. As to local government, he would "put an end to their town meetings." The colonies' various assemblies he denounced as "the proceedings of a tumultuous and riotous rabble." He assured his colleagues that "by a manly and steady perseverance, things may be restored from a state of anarchy and confusion, to peace, quietude, and a due obedience to the laws of this country."

Lord North, with his mild character, gravitated to Germain's forcefulness. As soon as Germain finished speaking, he stood up to declare that Germain's ideas "are worthy of a great mind, and such as ought to be adopted."

Several Whig members, Edmund Burke notable among them, vehemently debated the approach Germain had outlined. Ramming the "supreme sovereignty" of British government down the colonists' throats was counterproductive, Burke argued: ". . . you will teach them by these means to call that sovereignty itself in question. When you drive him hard, the boar will surely turn upon the hunters. If that sovereignty and their freedom cannot be reconciled, which will they take? They will cast your sovereignty in your face. Nobody will be argued into slavery."

But North picked up Germain's line and extended it. "The Americans have tarred and feathered your subjects," he declared to the members in April, "plundered your merchants, burnt your ships, denied all obedience to your laws and authority; yet so clement, and so long forbearing has our conduct been, that it is incumbent on us now to take a different course." Shortly afterward, Parliament passed a series of what it called Coercive Acts (which the Americans took to calling the Intolerable Acts), which closed the port of Boston, gave Parliament direct control of Massachusetts's government, provided for the quartering of British troops throughout the colonies and enabled British officials accused of crimes to be tried in England.

Germain was satisfied with the legislation. He believed with all his heart that it would quell the "anarchy and confusion" in the colonies. But he cautioned the government that the follow-through was crucial. The Acts, he said, must be enforced "with a Roman severity."

Around the time the Coercive Acts were being enforced in North America, a Seneca man strode through the gates of the city of Albany and began making inquiries about a certain resident. Cornplanter was in his early to mid-twenties at the time, tall and erect. His appearance would not have been remarkable, for Iroquois were regular visitors. He would have shown up in the city dressed in a combination of European and native clothing: a shirt possibly manufactured right in Albany, made for the native market, wool leggings, leather moccasins decorated with beads. The beadwork would have been stitched by his wife, for he had recently married.

Maybe it was reaching the state of marriage that got him thinking more about his childhood and family. Or it could have been the mounting tension with the whites. For just as his dress was a mix of European and Iroquois, so too was he, and lately his white father's absence in his life had been haunting him. He had been teased about it as a boy: not just that the man was white, but that he played no role in the boy's life.

Family bonds were paramount to the Iroquois. Where was this ghost of a man?

The world of the whites, for all its nearness, was completely alien to Cornplanter. And yet he was part of it, thanks to this stranger.

He knew his father's name: John Abeel. He knew he was a trader. Other Senecas had given him some information about him, for he not only did business with them but preferred their company to that of white people. People in Albany knew John Abeel. He lived in a rough settlement along the Mohawk River called Fort Plain. Cornplanter went there.

Abeel's years of familiarity with the natives had led to his fashioning a split nature of his own. He lived among whites, but otherwise he shunned them. As a result, over the years, the people of the area had come to consider him as something of a madman. His wife had in the past run to the authorities for help in dealing with him, complaining that "Sinneca Indians" had the run of the house, that he had barred from their home all those "that are of white couller" and "only suffers a few Nigros to Stay," and that he "takes Loaded arms Every night Into his Bead." He had gone so far as to kick his wife out of their marriage bed and set up cohabiting there for a time with an Indian woman. If a man from town came calling whom he didn't care to see, he was known to stick a hatchet into his front door as a way of asking him to leave.

Cornplanter found the house and knocked on the door. He knew no English, but Abeel spoke Seneca. He told him who he was, and Abeel invited him in. Cornplanter had no idea what to expect from the encounter: anger, scorn, maybe a loving embrace. What he did not anticipate was indifference. His father gave him something to eat; otherwise he seemed uninterested in him. Maybe the wild old man's mind was too far gone for him to engage in a substantive conversation with his son. Perhaps he was shuttered by shame.

Cornplanter felt particularly rebuffed as he was leaving. He had traveled 200 miles for this. Ordinary decency, among both whites and Indians, called for a host to give his guest food for his journey. As the man's son, Cornplanter expected more than that. He had made it clear to Abeel that he and his wife lived in their village largely in the native manner, without any comforts that European products could provide. Yet, "when I started to return home," he later said, "he gave me no provision to eat on the way. He gave me neither kettle nor gun. . . ." Cornplanter had been hardened by battle, by a life lived close to nature. He was a man in every respect, which, to a Seneca, included having control over his emotions. It seemed to surprise him that he felt wounded by this encounter.

Sometime in 1772, a letter arrived at Miss Beard's, the Dublin boarding school where Margaret Moncrieffe had spent the past seven years. Her father had decided that her formal education was over and was summoning her back to America. She and her brother boarded a ship bound westward across the Atlantic.

Several weeks later they sailed into the bristling, forest-rimmed natural cathedral of New York Harbor. Their immediate concerns were narrow and domestic: for the first time, at the ages of ten and fourteen, they would take up life as a family with their soldier father and his forbidding wife. At the same time, stepping ashore, they couldn't help but be overwhelmed by the wider world into which they had been delivered. New York had the façade of an English colonial city, but it seethed with exotic life. German and Dutch were common languages on the street. Taverns lining the waterfront were packed with sailors from Danzig, Stockholm, Bristol and Nantucket. Prostitutes, dressed like gaudy versions of proper ladies, displayed themselves openly around St. Paul's Chapel. Rich merchants rolled through the streets in private coaches. Slaves—dressed in rags and worked to the bone, to the horror of European visitors, which Margaret for all intents and purposes was—hauled barrels of flour and salted fish through the maze of horse traffic. Around the time the Moncrieffe children arrived, the celebrated Mrs. Ferrari opened a new coffee house on Maiden Lane with a reception at which customers were "genteelly regaled with arack, punch, wine, cold ham, tongue &c." That same night a fire broke out nearby in St. George's Square, destroying most of its houses. That winter was so cold Margaret and her brother Edward could have played games on the East River or walk, as many did, across it to Brooklyn.

For two years, life was peaceful. Edward attended King's College and Margaret was looked after by a governess. Relations with their stepmother did not become especially warm, but when her father was not on maneuvers with General Gage, Margaret was able, as she said, "to bask in the heart-cheering smile of paternal fondness." She also dutifully imbibed her father's less than heart-cheering political views. Regarding the situation in London, where Whig politicians were berating the government's management of America, Major Moncrieffe wrote to a colleague, "If some heads had been lopped off long ago, the King would not be insulted now." As to the colonial upstarts, they were, as far as he was concerned, "raskals."

Then in 1774, Thomas Moncrieffe's second wife died. He did not wait long before getting back into the game. A wife was virtually a necessity for keeping a household running, but besides that he had a great eye for women ("the finest race of Young women I ever saw are at present in New York," he had opined to a friend not long before he became a widower again, and noted of one young lady in particular that "if I was two & twenty, I would not wish for more than her, & six thousand bottles of her father's old wine"). Just six months after his wife's death, he married again. He also had a knack for using marriages for social leverage. His deceased second wife had been a Livingston; his new wife was a member of another of New York's important families, the Jays.

Margaret took to her second stepmother in a way she never had with the first: the young woman was warm, funny and maternal. The girl came to love her and was delighted when she became pregnant. But, just ten months into her marriage to Margaret's father, her second stepmother died, in childbirth.

Her father was in Boston at the time, where General Gage and his army were confronting a rapidly deteriorating situation with the militant locals. Being the daughter of a British officer gave Margaret an awareness of political events, but then again a simple wander through town provided a vivid sense of things. Walls were covered with placards and broadsides. Many contained news from Boston: acts of defiance, skirmishes, bloodshed. There was a reprint of a speech King George had given to Parliament: "Those who have long too successfully laboured to inflame my people in America by gross misrepresentation . . ." Another—shocking to the loyal daughter of a British officer—contained the lyrics to a song attacking General Gage: "such a sot whose conduct is a slander." One was a warning to Britain's disloyal American subjects that they were in danger of annihilation; another promised American patriots that they were on the threshold of a new era of freedom.

The battle of the broadsides reflected the fact that, unlike Boston or Williamsburg, New York was a hotbed of loyalist sensibility. Many of its elite families had close ties to England. That the city was the center of the British Army in North America also gave it a strongly pro-British cast, which Margaret and her brother, with all the upheaval around them, found comforting.

But with her father away in the service of the King, his wife's death suddenly made life complicated. The children, along with their newborn brother, were taken into the household of her stepmother's twenty-eight-year-old brother-in-law, Frederick Jay. Jay had joined an independent militia company that had been hastily formed in anticipation of military action. Margaret felt tossed about by vast and confusing forces. At the same time, she knew exactly what was happening. No formal conflict had been declared, but her teenaged instincts were sharp. "I found myself," she said, "in the midst of republicans in war against the crown of Great-Britain."

## Chapter 9

———❦———

# ASSUMING COMMAND

The welcoming trees—sassafras and locusts, dogwoods and maples and tulip poplars—lazed in their late season fullness. Down below loomed the Potomac: massy, blue, wide enough that it could have been a bay opening toward the ocean. It was August 30, 1774, when two men, Edmund Pendleton and Patrick Henry, having made the trip from their homes further south, rode their horses into the serenity of this landscape. Martha Washington greeted them at the door of the fine house that stretched across the hilltop, surrounded by its crosshatched fields. They found that she had an impressive presence. While Pendleton later condescended in calling her a "dear little woman," they observed that in fact as she moved about the house, settling them, ensuring that their beds and meals were prepared, she engaged them in serious conversation. Her husband, in contrast, was mostly silent, deferring to her and doting on her, calling her "Patsy." Martha Washington not only knew perfectly well what these men were about but all but instructed them on it, telling them that their undertaking would demand all their strength. "I hope you will stand firm," she said. "I know George will." In the morning the three men set out on horseback for Philadelphia.

A month earlier the Virginia Convention—as the members of the dismissed House of Burgesses called themselves—had voted to take part in a Continental Congress, an unprecedented gathering of representatives from all of Britain's American colonies. They had then voted Pendleton, Henry and Washington to be part of Virginia's delegation. The three men clattered into Philadelphia's cobbled streets on September 4, weary from the journey but braced for business.

A volcano of chatter erupted the next morning in the carpenters' guild hall on Chestnut Street, as seemingly all of the fifty-six delegates began speaking at once. Or at least fifty-five of them seemed to do so. Washington, who was never loquacious to begin with, was uneasy being surrounded by so many lawyers and other varieties of professional orator, all of whom were filled with pent-up energy and convictions and perspectives. But he didn't need to engage others; they came to him. They had known that among the delegates chosen by the Virginians was the man whose fame from the days of the war with France still resonated. He met John Adams, the chatty and self-righteous lawyer from Massachusetts, famous for having taken, as a matter of principle, the case, in 1770, of British soldiers who had shot and killed five people during what became known as the Boston Massacre. And he met his cousin Samuel Adams, who had led opposition to the Stamp Act. He met John Jay, the celebrated New York lawyer, who was also the brother of Frederick Jay, who was at this moment the guardian of Margaret Moncrieffe. He met William Livingston, the lawyer who had run the radical Whig journal the *Independent Reflector* and had served as mentor to Abraham Yates.

Many of them later gossiped about their first encounter with Washington. They noted his "easy Soldierlike Air" and his "manly Gait." One observed that he spoke little and had a cool refinement about him, "like a Bishop at his prayers."

It quickly became clear that the delegates were divided into two camps regarding how to proceed, or even what they wanted. One group thought they were in Philadelphia to work out a joint strategy for rec-

onciling with the British government. The other wanted to agree on a
list of rights to submit to England as an ultimatum for their continued
allegiance. Everyone knew that Massachusetts, which had been at the
forefront of activism against British policies, was in the radical camp.
Some were surprised to learn that Virginia's representatives—whose
planter-constituents had felt their economic independence especially
impinged by British politicians—were just as radical in how far they
were willing to press matters. John Adams declared them "the most
spirited" members of the Congress.

Both camps wanted the same thing: "freedom." The question was
whether it was to be had under British rule or not. Though he spoke
little, Washington made his feelings known. He was guided, as he had
written to an associate before setting out for Philadelphia, by "an Innate
Spirit of Freedom." But freedom was not simple; it could be cleaved,
apportioned, shaded. Most of the delegates maintained a stark double
standard, which Washington expressed in the same letter. "The Crisis
is arrived," he said, "when we must assert our Rights, or Submit to
every Imposition that can be heap'd upon us, till custom and use will
make us as tame & abject slaves, as the Blacks we Rule over with such
arbitrary sway." Like many of his fellow slaveholding Virginia radicals—
Thomas Jefferson, Patrick Henry—he was able to positively assert the
"innate spirit of freedom" for Virginians whose ancestors had come
from Europe and at the same time to positively deny it to Virginians
whose ancestors had come from Africa.

The delegates spent two months hashing out their differing views
("tedious beyond expression," Adams called the debates). In the evenings they carried the discussions to taverns; they continued them over
card games (Washington won seven pounds) and between dances at
balls. They were getting to know each other, and in doing so were unit-
ing colonies that had always seemed foreign to one another.

In the end, they agreed on a lengthy list of "resolves" to be sent to the king: statements of their rights as British subjects, and of specific acts of Parliament that violated these. They agreed further to a continentwide boycott of British goods. And they authorized the creation of "committees of safety" throughout the colonies, to carry out the boycotts, and if need be to act as de facto governments.

Washington was back at Mount Vernon at the end of October. Though he had spoken little in Philadelphia, he wholeheartedly backed the resolves. And though he didn't know what was to come, he confessed anxiety to a fellow planter on returning home, saying "the times are ticklish." He then set about doing his part to put the resolves into effect. All the colonies were building up their militias. He put his old militia officer's uniform on and rode out to help drill local companies of recruits.

In the spring of 1775 he was observing the blossoms on his cherry trees when profound news reached him from two quarters. There had been an actual military confrontation, or rather a pair of them, in the Massachusetts towns of Lexington and Concord. British troops had attempted to secure the colonials' military stores. Militiamen had gotten wind of the plot and engaged them in a series of violent battles; first reports were that dozens had been killed on each side. Meanwhile, the British had succeeded in a parallel maneuver in Virginia, taking the militia's gunpowder store in Williamsburg. War had arrived, even as Washington and other leaders were still debating its inevitability. Many Virginians wanted to follow the lead of the Massachusetts militia and attack. Peyton Randolph, the chairman of the Virginia Convention, asked for calm. Washington supported him, advising the Fairfax County militia to stand down. At this news, a twenty-five-year-old up-and-coming political force in Virginia named James Madison—a small, nervous, sickly man, but a passionate proponent of radical Whig philosophy concerning the sanctity of individual freedom (who nevertheless owned more than 100 slaves)—lashed out at what he guessed was timidity in Washington and other planters, whom he accused of backing down because their "property will be exposed in case of a civil war."

There may have been something to that. Washington had, through enormous exertion and considerable ingenuity, built a small empire for himself. Britain's economic policies were attacks on it; but actual war would be a more visceral threat, as he knew better than neophytes like Madison.

And yet, of course, everything he had been about had tended toward this. The steadily building tension between the colonies and the home country—the taxes, the threats, the boycotts, the tea dumped in the harbor, the diplomatic and political maneuvers—all of it had followed from the period of his youth and early manhood, the military disappointments that the British system had visited on him.

He was busy now, preparing to travel. As luck would have it, the Continental Congress had scheduled its second meeting for a week hence. Clearly, news of the violence in Massachusetts would completely rewrite its agenda. A young recruit wrote Washington before he left, saying what all Virginia knew: "It is imagined the first thing that will come on the carpet at the meeting of the Congress will be that of establishing Regular Armies. . . ." The young man wanted to be kept in mind for a commission. Why write to Washington? That too seemed obvious to people: "there is not the least doubt," he wrote, "but you'll have the command of the whole forces in this Colony."

On a hot, still morning in early May, Washington headed back to Philadelphia. This time he chose not to ride on horseback but to take a coach and livery: he wanted to make a particular impression. And this time he packed his uniform.

Ships arriving at London carried grim news. "We were fired on from all sides," an officer wrote of the confrontations at Lexington and

Concord. Massachusetts militiamen had ambushed the British regulars who were sent to seize military stores, shooting from inside houses, from behind hills and trees. Some of them, intent on venting their fury, fell on wounded soldiers and "scalped and cut off the ears." Further, officers reported that British leaders were wrong to think the American militiamen were "Fools and Cowards," for "they take all possible pains to improve themselves in military skill." Perhaps most alarmingly, the officers noted that the Americans expressed outright "abhorrence" for Lord North, the prime minister of England. It was "shocking," one wrote, "to pass the streets and hear what imprecations are thrown out against the King's ministry."

The first, confused reports finally clarified: 73 British soldiers had been killed and 174 wounded at Lexington and Concord. Englishmen in the street were stunned. Members of Parliament assumed that the violence meant the failure of Lord North's policy and that his government would fall.

George Germain took a different view. "The news from America is as bad as possible," he confided to a friend, but the correct response, he insisted, was not to change course but "to adopt real offensive measures." He began a campaign in Parliament, urging his colleagues to move aggressively against the now openly rebellious colonists. Others counseled patience, but Germain was inexorable. His energy became a magnet. Ministers turned to him for guidance. Henry Howard, the Earl of Suffolk, who at thirty-five was the youngest man in government (he was Secretary of State for the Southern Department, which included the American colonies), wrote to Germain asking for his counsel.

Germain responded with a primer on the situation. He already considered the state of affairs "a war." He advised that General Thomas Gage, the highest-ranking officer in America (under whom Margaret Moncrieffe's father served and in whose household she had lived for a time as a young girl), "finds himself in a situation of too great impor-

tance for his talents." He suggested replacing him with General William
Howe. He then outlined a course of action for rapidly defeating the colonials, which involved bringing in forces from Canada and focusing not
only on subduing the boisterous Bostonians but also taking New York
City, the most vital port in the colonies.

The old soldier also analyzed the situation that British troops had
found themselves in at Lexington and Concord. He faulted them for following European-style tactics, saying that British commanders should
have learned from Braddock's debacle that in America troops must
"separate and secure themselves by trees, walls or hedges" rather than
fight in the open.

In all of this, Germain was reflecting on the Seven Years' War, and
not just on the tragic mistake of Braddock. His own disaster at Minden
had never left his thoughts. This time there would be no wavering. He
counseled for "the utmost force of this kingdom to finish this rebellion
in one campaign."

Still, there was resistance in Parliament. Some members had been
swayed by Edmund Burke, who carried out his quarrel with Germain at
the philosophical level, by going on—maddeningly, Germain thought—
about this airy notion of "freedom." Only weeks earlier Burke had laid
out his argument: "First, the people of the colonies are descendants
of Englishmen. England, Sir, is a nation which still I hope, respects,
and formerly adored, her freedom." The Americans "are therefore not
only devoted to liberty, but to liberty according to English ideas and on
English principles." There were times in history, Burke argued, when
abstractions became real and tangible. The American resistance to taxation without representation was not reprehensible but in fact laudably
patriotic, a carrying-forward of the English Bill of Rights. Freedom was
an abstraction, yes, but in America just now it was "fixed and attached
on this specific point of taxing." Freedom was alive in the Americans,
Burke declared: "they felt its pulse."

But the bloodshed at Lexington and Concord swept away Burke's rhetoric. The government committed itself to taking hard steps. And Prime Minister North was convinced that George Germain's grit and experience made him the right man for a crucial job. Undersecretary of State William Eden offered it to him in the most flamboyant language: "There never perhaps was a commission of such importance for any individual in the annals of mankind." The plan the government had concocted was to prepare for war but at the same time to send a commissioner to America who would be authorized to "settle everything." The entire quagmire with the colonials, ranging from economic issues to lofty concerns about freedom and rights, would be in the hands of this commissioner. He would be given the broadest powers to make deals, to avert war. And, Eden told Germain, the prime minister "thinks you the fittest man in the Kingdom."

George Germain was highly susceptible to flattery. He plumped like a peacock when he was being praised. The words and the trust behind them were deeply pleasurable. But he declined the offer. He could see perfectly well that in creating this role of commissioner the government was setting up a scapegoat. Though North and the other leaders made a show of preparing for war, they wanted a magical diplomatic solution; if the commissioner failed in this, the commissioner would be to blame. And putting himself an ocean away from the center of power would in itself be professional suicide; it would give his enemies free rein to pick him apart. As before, he held to the truism that America was not a place to realize ambitions but to have them demolished.

No sooner had he declined, however, than another offer was put in front of him. Britain's irresolute prime minister continued to be captivated by Germain's steadfastness. Since Germain had called his bluff, he now upped the stakes. He asked him to serve as Secretary of State for the American Department.

This brought Germain up short. Truly, he had to think. This was an entirely different role.

In a way, it had to be amusing to him. Unlike many of his colleagues, he had never in his life exhibited a fascination for America. He had never even expressed a desire to travel there. His interests, beyond politics and the military, were chiefly confined to England: its rolling hills and splendidly rocky coasts, its great estates, the broad civilized thoroughfares of London. Beyond England he gave some scant attention to the Continent as a cultural entity: German symphonies and Italian art. And that was it. But America simply would not leave him alone.

He had to admit that he had amassed a great deal of knowledge of the colonies over these years of increasing turmoil, which, combined with his long military experience and the historic nature of the current crisis, put him in a unique position. And American Secretary was a ministry position: it didn't require actually going there. Indeed, he would be at the very center of power. If there was to be all-out war, he, in that capacity, more directly than anyone else in the government, would be the man running it.

Most of all, this was shaping up to be a historic test. The real fight was not against ragtag rebellious outlanders; it was within the halls of the British government. It was a fight for Britain and for empire; it would be a fight to dispel the hopelessly vague notion that the turmoil in the colonies was over gauzy issues of "individual freedom," which he knew in his soul to be window dressing, pablum to appease the masses. Men such as Burke and Wilkes—not to mention the Americans themselves—needed to be taught a lesson. And Britain needed leadership. Conflicts such as this were not about ideas; from the time of Caesar they had been and always would be about power.

Indeed, power was George Germain's meat and wine, and this offer was one of unprecedented power. It was a chance, surely the only one he would ever get, to exorcise the demons that had plagued him since Minden. It was, in the end, too sweet a thing to refuse.

One hundred and fifty miles after Washington's coach left Mount Vernon, and just six miles from its end in Philadelphia, it was met by a disturbance. Looking out the window, Washington and his fellow delegate Richard Henry Lee saw a crowd of 500 or so people. What seemed at first like a gathering riot turned out to be a contingent of militiamen and others from the city who had come out to greet them. A band struck up. And so they were escorted into Philadelphia in style.

The Second Continental Congress, meeting this time in the colony's assembly hall, contained some new delegates. From Massachusetts was John Hancock, a shipper who would serve as president of the Congress. Thomas Jefferson joined the Virginia delegation. Benjamin Franklin, seventy years old and feeling moody, had just that week returned from more than ten years in London, where he had served as representative of the Pennsylvania colony and more recently of the colonies as a whole. (Just before leaving he had met with British leaders—including Edmund Burke—in a failed attempt at conciliation.) He had barely had time to rest from the voyage before hastening the few blocks from his home on Market Street to join the Pennsylvania delegation.

Committees formed. People debated interminably. Slowly, they voted: to borrow money, to procure weapons and ammunition, to recruit companies of soldiers. Washington, with his soldierly striding among the tables, stood out. "Col. Washington appears at Congress in his Uniform," John Adams wrote to his wife, "and, by his great Experience and Abilities in military Matters, is of much service to Us."

Then came the moment Washington knew would come. June 15, a Thursday, at the end of the day, the delegates resolved: "That a general be appointed to command all the continental forces raised or to

be raised for the defence of American liberty." There were several can-
didates for the position, including John Hancock. The next morning
Hancock himself, as president of the assembly, announced the result.
Washington was the unanimous choice.

Washington unfolded himself to his full height. Remaining at his
table rather than step to the front of the room, he took out a paper and
read the response he had carefully prepared: "Mr. President, Tho'
I am truly sensible of the high honor done me in this appointment,
yet I feel great distress from a consciousness that my abilities and
military experience may not be equal to the extensive and important trust. However, as the Congress desire it, I will enter upon the
momentous duty and exert every power I possess in the service and
for the support of the glorious cause. I beg they will accept my most
cordial thanks for this distinguished testimony of their approbation.
But lest some unlucky event should happen unfavourable to my reputation, I beg it may be remembered by every gentleman in the room,
that I this day declare with the utmost sincerity I do not think myself
equal to the command I am honored with." Money was never far from
his thoughts and he ended with what he no doubt felt to be a magnanimous flourish: that he would accept no pay beyond having his
expenses met.

He was surely sincere in his admission that he did not feel equal to
the task. His military career was years in the past, and nothing he had
done then compared with what he was now asked to do. He wrote as
much to his wife, saying that he had "a consciousness of its being a trust
too great for my Capacity."

And yet, this was another instance of a familiar tactic: to feign at the
last minute not to want the very thing he had long desired. The advice
of his old mentor, William Fairfax, to be "Roman," to couple a burning
ambition with a frosty exterior of gentlemanly reserve, was ingrained
in him. Surely, he did want this, had hungered for it even, for it was

the very honor he had longed for decades earlier, but now in a different context and for a wholly different cause.

Something more than two months later. It was fall: the leaves of the maple trees surrounding the Seneca village of Conawaugus were burning red; the houses were ornamented with braids of corn hung up for drying. People were stringing beans, hanging tobacco leaves. One day a runner appeared from the eastward trail. Everyone gathered to hear the news. Cornplanter was among them: he was in his late twenties or early thirties now, and, while not a hereditary chief, he had shown bravery and wisdom and was gaining stature as a leader. The messenger approached the chiefs and handed them the wampum belt he carried, the panel of woven beads that certified his mission. There was a tally stick attached to it, with notches to indicate a date in the future. The date was tied to an event. The message was that the leaders of the American colonies wished to meet with the Six Nations of the Iroquois Confederacy.

The Senecas knew what was afoot. Runners went off eastward, to the other five Iroquois nations, to arrange a council at Conawaugus. In time, delegations arrived from the Cayugas, Onandagas, Oneidas, Mohawks and Tuscaroras. The request from the Americans was that they assemble at Fort Pitt, at the Forks of the Ohio; the Iroquois chose representatives from each nation to go. The Seneca delegation included Cornplanter, a young chief called Red Jacket, and Cornplanter's teenaged nephew, whom the English would come to know as Governor Blacksnake. Blacksnake was young and eager; this was his first notable adventure, and he would remember it vividly all his life. The diplomatic party traveled westward to the shore of Lake Erie, then followed the shoreline southwest for 70 miles. The boy took note of remote cabins of white settlers. At one spot, where the Iroquois stopped to construct bark canoes, an old white man came out of the forest like a ghost and offered them bread; they gave him venison in return.

Several days later the Iroqouis delegation reached the Forks. The morning after their arrival their white hosts fed them breakfast. A man who introduced himself as commissioner of the American Continental Congress arranged places in an open field for the various parties, then he began, reading an address that had been prepared weeks earlier by Washington, Adams, Jefferson and the others of the Congress:

*Brothers, Sachems, and Warriors,*

   *We, the Delegates from the Twelve United Provinces\* . . . now sitting in general Congress at Philadelphia, send this talk to you our brothers. We are sixty-five in number, chosen and appointed by the people throughout all these provinces and colonies, to meet and sit together in one great council, to consult together for the common good of the land, and speak and act for them.*

The delegates in Philadelphia told the Iroquois that, "as we are upon the same island," they wanted to inform them of their impending break with Great Britain. The speech was long, beginning with the first English settlers in America. It told of the goodness of King George—the delegates knew well that the Indians had a fondness for the English king, or at least for the idea of him—but noted that "many of his counsellors are proud and wicked men," and that these men "now tell us they will slip their hand into our pocket without asking, as though it were their own; and at their pleasure they will take from us our charters or written civil constitution, which we love as our lives—also our plantations, our houses and goods." Against all reason, the evil counsellors had persuaded the king "to send an army of soldiers and many ships of war, to rob and destroy us."

---

\* Georgia had not sent representatives to Philadelphia.

The "island" that the commissioner referred to—North America—was the turtle's back that Sky Woman had landed on when she fell from her home in the Sky World. His implication was that the Americans, as fellow inhabitants of the island of Iroquois mythology, knew the world of the Iroquois and could be trusted.

Cornplanter and the others listened throughout the morning; toward noon the commissioner came to the point. Congress, he said, had declared that the war was "between us and Old England. . . . You Indians are not concerned in it. We don't wish you to take up the hatchet against the king's troops. We desire you to remain at home, and not join on either side, but keep the hatchet buried deep."

The American leaders that had met in Philadelphia knew that if all-out war with England was destined they needed at all costs to keep the Iroquois out of it. They tried, in their appeal, to suggest that a British victory would be disastrous for the Iroquois: ". . . for, if the king's troops take away our property, and destroy us who are of the same blood with themselves, what can you, who are Indians, expect from them afterwards?"

The Iroquois had previously agreed that Red Jacket would speak for all. Blacksnake remembered him starting by referencing the Iroquois' God-given right to the land, as "citizens of this island God made us here to inhabit," and going on to note (completely untruthfully) that they had "never" needed to engage in wars to protect their land. He said that while "we acknowledge it is important to hear" what the Philadelphia congress had to say, the Iroquois leaders gathered at the Forks were not authorized to make a promise without consulting their constituents back home. The commissioner expected this. He told them that the American leaders asked them to attend a later council in Albany, to deliver their answer. Then he invited them into the newly rebuilt fort, to inspect its features, to show them how the Americans were preparing for war. After the tour, the commissioner invited them to take food for their journey home. The Iroquois loaded three canoes with provisions. In the morning the canoes slipped into the water, and they paddled toward home.

The moment Cornplanter, Blacksnake and the others returned to Conawaugus, runners went out to all villages in Iroquois country as well as to other Indians, spreading word of what was said at the Forks. The next weeks were a time of confusion. Runners came in from every direction. They brought news that the great Mohawk chief Thayendanegea, whom the Americans called Joseph Brant, who spoke English and took to wearing an English suit, had sailed for London to bargain for backing of Mohawk land claims in exchange for fighting alongside the British. Other runners reported that some Mohawk warriors had joined the British in fighting American soldiers who had launched an invasion of British territory in Canada.

Cornplanter for one did not like this. The six nations of the Iroquois Confederacy had freedom to go their own ways, but he knew that this storm would be larger than others. Unity would be important.

Then came another messenger with the request from the Americans for a second council, at Albany, where they hoped to hear the Iroquois answer to their plea for neutrality. American leadership had by now clearly coalesced around one man, for Blacksnake reported that the request came "from Washington." Once again the Senecas prepared to go. Following custom in important matters, the chiefs made the decision this time not to choose which warriors would accompany them. Everyone was free to join or not. As a result, said Blacksnake, "quite a large number elected to go with the chiefs."

The large party from Conawaugus made its way through the forest to a place where they had arranged to meet with other Senecas. That night, before the fire, all agreed that they would try to "see clear with the naked eyes and open our ears to hear truth" at Albany, that they "did not want to hold their heads down and see nothing." The

Senecas traveled together the next day. The following day they split up into companies.

Five days later they arrived in Albany. They found the city—civilians and soldiers—in an expectant, nervous mood. Rumors and gossip were flying.

The other Iroquois nations, and other Indians, arrived. They held meetings prior to the start of the council with the Americans. Decisions were made. There was a change in leadership. Red Jacket had recently been the first among Seneca chiefs, and Cornplanter's uncle, Guyasuta, had been prominent since the time of Pontiac's War. But when the American commissioner began the council by posing the question "Who is the head man of the Seneca nation?" it was Cornplanter who rose and said, "I am."

———— ⧓ ————

## Chapter 10

# A NATURAL INCLINATION
# TO LIBERTY

Cannon fire lit the icy darkness. The guns' smoking snouts were swiveled toward New England's great port city of Boston. General Washington had given the command to fire. His intended target was not, of course, the inhabitants themselves, but the Bostonians didn't necessarily know that: after each blast the men doing the reloading could hear the screams of women and children huddled in their houses.

Washington directed his men from nine feet in the air, sitting majestically atop his horse, providing the spectacle of leadership that his lifelong reading and training had pointed toward. The bombardment was aimed at British troops holed up in the city, but in reality the fusilades were a distraction. For Washington's first operation against the army he had once longed to be a part of was a dodge, a feint. By the time he had reached Boston from Philadelphia—the journey itself was remarkable, surreal, with people at every town coming into the street to cheer him, to shower him with songs and goodwill, calling him "Excellency"—he was fully aware that he had no true army under his command. Instead, four different groups of American would-be soldiers, most of whom had only ever shot at animals before, each under its own commanding officer, had converged on the city. They had no uniforms and carried whatever weapons they possessed. Somehow Washington had to make them into an army. And he had a secret so terrible he kept it from nearly everyone: the army had only enough gunpowder for each man to fire nine shots.

Maintaining military control of Boston, the seething center of rebellion in the colonies, had been the first order of business for Britain. Its warships patrolled the harbor, and a 9,000-man army—now under the command of William Howe, a forty-seven-year-old veteran who had learned to respect the colonials' abilities in his service during the French and Indian War—occupied the city. The previous June, colonial forces that had encircled the city clashed with the occupiers; the British had won the so-called Battle of Bunker Hill (whose center was actually nearby Breed's Hill), but the experience had emboldened the Americans. Nevertheless, Washington knew that attacking the crack British regulars directly with his untrained and virtually unarmed bands of men would be foolhardy. His strategy was to get his troops on top of Dorchester Heights, a hill to the south of Boston. From that vantage they would have a chance. But how to mount the hill without being cut to pieces?

Deception was Washington's answer. With bales of hay as screens and the mortar and cannon fire to hide the groans of the wagon wheels, 3,000 men started up the hill by moonlight on the night of March 4, hauling with them the heavy guns whose shot, from the heights, could reach the ships in the harbor. They had mounted the summit and set up a rampart before dawn, to the bewilderment of the awakening British soldiers. "When the Enemy first discovered our Works in the morning," Washington wrote to John Hancock with satisfaction, "they seemed to be in great confusion, and from their movements to have Intended an Attack."

He braced for a fight—he had two more contingents ready to attack—but General Howe surprised him by evacuating the city. Washington had no way of knowing what Howe was up to and was stunned by the amount of goods the British had left behind in their rapid retreat. But the sight of the enemy ships' receding sails was enough for him to conclude that, without an actual clash of soldiers, he had won a battle.

Others thought so too. Newspapers crowed about the great victory of General Washington. He became a hero almost literally overnight. When news of the British evacuation of Boston reached Philadelphia, the giddy members of the Continental Congress voted to have a medal struck: Washington's bust on one side and on the other the general on horseback surveying Boston from Dorchester Heights. Among those who wrote fawning letters to the commander in chief of American forces, a Massachusetts businessman called him "the Savior of your Country" and declared that he was to be congratulated by "every Friend to Liberty and the Rights of Mankind. . . ."

Of course, that sentiment had to be qualified. Prior to the battle, at a council of war with his officers, Washington had put up for a vote several matters that might improve the military, including whether to allow the enlistment of "any Negroes in the new Army." Doing so would seemingly make a statement about how far the patriots' belief in liberty might carry. Washington, with his vast experience of slaves and his conviction that they could not be trusted unless closely watched, had already issued orders against enlistment of "any deserter . . . negro, or vagabond." After brief consideration, he and his officers voted "to reject Negroes altogether." Undermanned though they were, the American patriot leaders wanted no help from blacks, not if it involved even the possibility of extending "liberty and the rights of mankind" to them.

One hundred miles south of Boston, Venture was working on his own expansion of freedom. He went about it in his typical fashion: doggedly, systematically. Having bought himself out of slavery, he next determined that he needed a name. For a slave, one name was generally considered to be enough. Often, as in Venture's own case, it was given to you by your owner. But parents were often able to name their own children. African-American slaves in the eighteenth century looked all over for names for their children. Some liked the ring of the classics: Caesar, Virgil, Cato, Minerva, Cleopatra. For their daughter, Hannah, and their first son, Solomon, Venture and his wife Meg had looked to the Old Testament. For their second son, Venture had followed an African tradition of naming a child after the day of the week on which he or she was born; Cuff was a West African name that corresponded with Friday. If slaves had two names, the second was usually to help owners and overseers distinguish them on a large plantation: Crippled Rose, Yellow Sam. There was no need to identify them beyond that.

But freedom changed things. With freedom you wanted a proper surname. It was a marker of your new status, as vivid as a flag. As with first names, people grabbed surnames from different sources. Some went for loftiness: Duke, Prince, King. Others chose a name to signify their change of condition, calling themselves Freeman or Liberty. Others took last names that would serve as an advertisement for their skills: Carpenter, Mason, Weaver, Tailor.

Venture followed the most common practice among freed slaves: he took his last owner's name. What might seem counterintuitive was in fact practical, and Venture was practical to his very bones. Freedom, heady as it was, was moorless, a leap into the void. There were no networks or societies to aid former slaves by teaching them to read or how to negotiate business deals or otherwise become functioning members of society. On the contrary, great swaths of society wanted nothing to do with them; communities passed laws blocking freed blacks from settling. Venture knew he was stepping into a gray zone. He needed to tie himself to whatever was solid, known and reliable. Oliver Smith was a person of substance; everyone in Stonington, and many beyond in southeastern Connecticut, knew him. And the man who had sold Venture his freedom was possessed of one of the sturdiest and most common surnames in America. "Big Venture," "Venture the Giant," became Venture Smith.

Then he got to work. He grew watermelons; by night he fished for eels and lobsters. He stayed on good terms with Oliver Smith, who was in, among other things, the shipping business. Venture took advantage of a chance to go on a whaling voyage on one of his vessels. He had never done such a thing before, and it proved to be a harrowing experience. But it was good money. They sailed back into port seven months later with the ship's hull packed with 400 barrels of whale oil, the profits from which Venture got his cut.

Mostly, though, he cut wood. Over a period of four years he traveled all over the region—sailing back and forth between the mainland and Long Island and to various wooded islands in Long Island Sound—in search of jobs. He worked himself to the limit of his endurance. In one six-month span, he said, "I cut and corded upwards of four hundred cords of wood"—enough to heat twenty houses for a year. In the course of four years he cut several thousand cords. While performing what he called "singular and wonderful labors" with his ax, he saved every penny, living on the barest necessities. "All fine clothes I despised in comparison with my interest. . . . Expensive gatherings of my mates I commonly shunned, and all kinds of luxuries I was perfectly a stranger to." He took particular care to stay away from alcohol. He remained grimly focused, month after sweaty month. He desired only two things: "money and prudence."

After getting paid for a job on Ram Island, he did his usual tally of his savings and realized that he had reached the point he had been working toward: 500 dollars. Without delay, he made his determined way back across the Sound to Stonington, and the Stanton farm. He presented himself to Thomas Stanton, the man who had beaten him savagely and locked him in manacles, whose wife had despised and taunted him. For the Stantons still owned his wife and children. The money in his pocket gave him a rush of power and confidence. He entered into negotiations with Stanton. He wanted to buy his two sons.

Stanton knew Venture, knew what "freedom" meant to him, fanciful though the notion was in a real world that was and would continue to be controlled by white men. That wider world—white America—was itself rocking and swaying over the meaning of the word. Men like Stanton thought slaves were misguided to want freedom, which would only bring hardship and insecurity. But if Venture—or Mr. Venture Smith, as he now called himself—wanted to pay good money, he would take it from him.

They settled on 200 dollars for each boy. It was a high price, but Stanton had him over a barrel. Venture knew the going rate for every commodity—as well for a cord of wood as for two slave boys—but of course he had expected Stanton to bargain hard. He had presumably been ready to pay more, thus the extra 100 dollars in his pocket.

He had previously purchased a piece of land on Long Island and built a rough house on it. That's where he headed now: back across Long Island Sound with his two sons, the sea air fresh in his face and a sense of accomplishment swelling his chest. But he had much yet to do. His wife and daughter were still in bondage. The decision to leave them behind had been the result of a straightforward bit of mathematics. Two strong boys would earn more with their labor than two women. Venture, Cuff and Solomon could raise funds to buy Meg and Hannah more quickly than Venture and the women could to buy the boys.

But his plan—his future—revolved around the womenfolk. They were still in Stonington, and he intended to return there. As an indication of his intent, on one of his trips to visit Meg he met with a man he knew in town named John Denison and offered to buy a 26-acre plot of land from him. It was rocky, and Denison didn't do anything with it. But it was near the Stanton homestead; Venture could point it out to Meg and tell her it would be their future home. He and Denison agreed on a price of 60 pounds. Then, deed in hand, he left: back across the water to Long Island.

And so they went to work, he and his boys. They could do a lot: Cuff was about twelve; Solomon about fourteen. Back and forth across the Sound they traveled, seeking out jobs, and all the while Venture was building up his network of associations. What he was doing was highly unusual. The vast majority of freed blacks chose to live in cities. There they could form communities, support each other at a time when white New Englanders looked at them with confusion and mistrust. But Venture had never been a city type. His childhood in Africa had unfolded on the savanna; he had grown up beneath the broad sky, in a society shaped by animals, sun and rain. He felt at home here on the Sound, among the farmers and small-scale shippers and manufacturers. But he had to build trust, convince whites that he was a man of substance.

Shortly after he bought his sons' freedom Venture met another black man, a slave, who was presumably owned by a white man for whom Venture was doing work. If there was an explosion of energy that came with freedom, then freeing your own children had a doubly energizing effect. He opened up to this man about what he had done, and the man convinced him to buy him out of bondage as well, promising to pay him back out of future earnings. Venture struck a deal with his owner, and bought the man for 60 pounds, becoming a de facto slave owner. As the man went to work, Venture took his earnings, keeping careful tally of what was still owed him. His "slave" had paid him 20 pounds when, one day, he vanished, never to be seen, leaving Venture 40 pounds in the hole. He felt betrayed, muttering about how the man "ran away from me." He had now played the game, and tasted its bitterness, from the other side.

Things got bitterer still. When Solomon was seventeen, Venture hired him out to a Rhode Island man named Charles Church. It was routine—the sort of thing Venture had been doing since he had freed his boys three years earlier. The deal was for a year's work. Church would pay the boy 12 pounds, and Solomon would learn some new skills. Then Venture got word that Church was outfitting a whaling ship and had offered Solomon a place on it. He had enticed the boy with the promise of adventure and a bauble—a pair of silver shoe buckles—in addition to the agreed-upon wages. Venture's own time on a whaler had been hellish, and as a boy he had traveled across the ocean, seen the pitiless power of the sea, watched people die like animals out there. He raced to the dock, determined to stop his son, but "to my great grief, I could only see the vessel my son was in almost out of sight going to sea." Months later came the news he most dreaded: Solomon had died at sea, of scurvy. In his brittle way of reducing life's lessons to monetary terms, Venture noted afterward that "besides the loss of his life, I lost equal to seventy-five pounds."

After Solomon's death he made his way back to the Stanton place and bought Meg. The joy in it was tempered by anguish at their son's death. Venture reckoned their reunion in financial terms as well: he gave Stanton 40 pounds for her and, since she was pregnant, counted himself lucky that in buying her before she gave birth he "prevented having another child to buy." In honor of their dead son they named the baby Solomon II. Then, moving with the inexorability of a wound clock, Smith made his way to the home of a man named Ray Mumford. Mumford, a relative of Robinson Mumford, who had bought and named him aboard the *Charming Susanna* off the coast of Anomabo, had bought Venture's first-born, Hannah, from the Stantons. She was the last of his family whose freedom he was determined to purchase. But now Venture got a surprise. Hannah, who was twenty years old, and who had given him "much trouble" in the past, informed him that she was in love with a "free negro" named Isaac who worked for Mumford, and she didn't want to leave the man.

One child dead, now another pulling away. Venture had worked himself to the limit of human endurance in order to reunite his family in freedom. In the unlikely event that he had seen a production of *King Lear* (which was popular in New York and New England, but Venture had little patience for such diversions), he would have identified with the old king's lament "How sharper than a serpent's tooth it is / To have a thankless child." He was feeling a kind of pain he had never felt before, and formulating a theory about children and ingratitude. Later, he gave someone his own mute echo of *Lear*, saying "a father's lips are closed in silence and in grief!" In the end, he let Hannah have her way. He paid for her freedom and left her behind.

He needed a home for his family, or what was left of it. Conditions in the Long Island community where he had based himself for some years now were becoming unstable. The irony was apparent but not surprising to Venture: as the white people in town talked more and more about needing freedom, they passed a law to bar freed blacks from living there. They made an exception for Venture Smith—because, as he said, of "my industry"—but he wasn't comfortable there anymore, so he sailed back to Connecticut.

Stonington was roiling too, as were other communities along the coast. It was summer 1774. The news from Boston was of chaos: the harbor blockaded, British troops in the streets. Nearly everyone in Stonington crammed into a special town meeting to offer support to Boston. Venture had not bothered himself too much over the fuss the white people had felt recently toward England and its policies. To the extent that those policies affected business, they mattered to him, but the "freedom" talk left him cold. Now, however, it was hard to avoid. Seemingly all the white people Venture knew in Stonington—including Hempstead Miner, who had bought him on pretence of offering him his freedom only to turn around and try to sell him for a profit—were at the meeting, professing alarm at "the many repeated attacks upon the liberties of the English American colonies." Then came word of the battles at Lexington and Concord. The white men of Stonington formed a militia. One day in late summer a 20-gun British frigate appeared off the Point. The army in Boston, which was essentially under siege by American troops surrounding the city, had sent it in search of food for the soldiers there. A loyalist from the area had gotten word to them that a shipment of cattle had arrived in Stonington from Block Island, and the cows were being hidden in a cove north of town and a short distance from the Stanton farm. James Wallace, captain of the frigate *Rose*, swooped in to try to steal some of the small vessels in the harbor. A contingent of local militiamen under the command of Captain Oliver Smith, Venture's former owner, hoisted their antiquated Queen Anne muskets and repelled the invaders. In retaliation, Wallace let loose his ship's cannons on the little town where so much of Venture's life had played out. Nearly every building around the Point was damaged.

Venture Smith, so intent on his own march toward freedom, wanted no part of the larger one. He fled the place: loaded Meg, Cuff and little Solomon into his vessel once more and sailed west. He watched the familiar coastline go by: the harbor of New London, the wide sweep of Niantic Bay. Passing the little village of Lyme, he nosed the craft into the mouth of the Connecticut River, sailing past old John Burrows's Black Horse Tavern and continuing inland. They glided by wooded banks and around serpentine bends, past a place called Potapoug Point where a finger of land formed an inviting natural harbor, which might have suited him, but he kept going.

About 20 miles north of the coast he came to a pair of towns that straddled the river called Haddam and East Haddam. It was quiet here, peaceful, with meadows full of birdsong and insect thrum; the soil was loamy. The unrest seemed far away. He knew some people here who could help him make a start. He did five weeks of work for Timothy Chapman. Then he did a job for a man named Abel Bingham. He got along with Bingham. And he liked the look of Bingham's large stretch of land. It sat near the confluence of the Connecticut and Salmon rivers. He marched up and down it, pondering. It was rugged: hilly and heavily wooded, tumbling steadily downward toward the shore of the Salmon River. There was a cart path along the river, and Bingham had a dry dock for servicing vessels. The river gave easy access to the coast and its market towns, and inland to Hartford. A lot could be done here, and it seemed a safe distance from whatever commotion might be coming. Venture Smith had money in his pocket and an idea in his head.

George Germain disliked effeminacy. He disliked the Irish possibly even more. And here they were, Edmund Burke and his fellow Whig Isaac Barré, two pink-faced and cherubic Irish radicals, lined up against him, waving their hands about and prattling in their brogues against the war, mewling about rights and liberty. They were clearly afraid of manly English aggression. Well, maybe Barré wasn't; he had that nasty scar across his face to remind everyone of his time in action against the French. But their parliamentary speeches were practically treasonous in their defense of the Americans. Barré had gone so far as to call the rebels "Sons of Liberty," a name the Americans took to waving like a flag. The whole radical Whig contingent in the House—the same members who had whined about the Townshend Duties and the Coercive Acts—had been outraged when Germain was chosen to lead the British effort in America. He knew they considered him a hidebound antique, a man whose political sensibility was lodged somewhere in the Middle Ages. They themselves, meanwhile, were very much of like minds with the men gathered in Philadelphia. They believed that individual freedom was a real and tangible thing, that England had been singled out by fate to promote it, but that the country had so far largely failed in that task. The Whigs believed the seed of freedom—after slowly germinating for more than a century in Europe and England—had suddenly burst into leaf and flower in America. For them the colonists were not some rebellious "other"; they represented the very essence of Britain.

Stuff and nonsense. Germain had been tasked with running a war to punish rebellious subordinates, and, by God, that's what he would do. He marched into Parliament—this time not as a member of the House of Commons but as a minister of the king—and defended the government's progress. He outlined the military actions he was overseeing. In beating back the protests, he at one point articulated a fake retreat, echoing the words George Washington had spoken to Congress when they chose him to command the rebel army, reminding the opposition members that "I never sought the office I have now the honor to fill, nor wished for it further than I flattered myself I might be serviceable to my country."

The sniping of the Whigs in Parliament was only one element of a much bigger problem: the British public was ambivalent at best about the war, while the Americans were positively infused with righteous energy. If this was a war of ideas, America had all the ammunition. The ambivalence extended into the halls of government. Indeed, Germain owed his post to the fact that his predecessor had been so uncomfortable with the idea of clashing with Britain's American cousins over their liberties that he had resigned. The squabbling in government grew loud enough that Pierre Beaumarchais, a French spy who was then in England, quipped in his report to Paris that "the war is raging more ferociously in London than in Boston."

The official unrest was due not only to the shaky state of British public opinion but to simple military calculations. The army, the navy, the treasury: none of these had fully recovered from the Seven Years' War. The vaunted British navy was in disrepair. Even if they employed every ship, some felt there still weren't enough to transport all the men and supplies necessary. The army had 48,000 men, but these were spread across the earth in the ongoing effort to maintain an empire; obviously they could not all be shifted to America. Fighting a full-scale war across the vastness of the Atlantic was unimaginably more difficult than conducting a war on the European continent. Officers and soldiers alike were mostly unfamiliar with the terrain. Communicating with generals in the field who were thousands of miles away, involving as it did months of delay, added maddening complexity and uncertainty.

Germain appreciated these facts. He endured the sniping and the fretting. But he was so full of grit, so full of his own brand of righteousness, not to mention his need for personal redemption, that he considered it, all in all, a bracing challenge. The more difficult the task appeared, the greater would be the glory that came from subduing the rebels. One member of Parliament noted in his diary after watching the American Secretary bustle in and out of the place that Germain "seems in very great spirits—is quite persuaded that all this will end after the first campaign." As for the rebels themselves and their character, Germain would have nodded vigorously with the sentiment that the great literary wag Samuel Johnson was penning to an acquaintance at about this same time: "The Americans, sir, are a race of convicts and ought to be thankful for anything we allow them short of hanging."

Besides, the king was with him, and so was the prime minister. And he was precisely where he wanted to be and felt he deserved to be: at the control center of a vast operation for the preservation and maintenance of the British Empire. In his new office in Whitehall, the cluster of buildings that formed the center of government, just around the corner from the prime minister's office at 10 Downing Street and in a precinct that echoed with the voices of England's leaders of old, surrounded by maps depicting the features of a continent he was learning intimately but would never visit, he dictated letters to generals, received coded messages from spies, shifted battalions, organized supply chains. Before

Germain had stepped into the office of American Secretary, General Thomas Gage, after having lost the battles at Lexington and Concord, had taken the decision to make Boston the center of military operations. Germain had known at once that was a mistake. The virus of the rebellion couldn't be excised by attacking the center of the affected limb. The limb had to be severed from the body. He had replaced Gage with William Howe, and sent Howe to Boston with new orders.

Meanwhile, a second front had opened up. The American rebels—following an idea suggested by a brash thirty-five-year-old colonel named Benedict Arnold—had executed a surprise maneuver by launching an invasion of Quebec. The province having until recently been under French control, the Americans hoped to coerce its inhabitants—whose patriotism had perhaps not hardened—to join their cause. Germain found the notion of one subordinate part of the empire invading another to be of vibrant concern: so much so that he determined he needed to field not one but two armies in North America. The government had already put Guy Carleton in charge of defending Canada. Carleton had served in the Seven Years' War and following that had served as governor of Quebec. He knew the province, was intimately familiar with America's wild hinterlands, was a decorated soldier and a capable leader. Unfortunately, Germain hated him. The enmity dated back to Minden; Carleton, then a fellow officer, had been among those who had openly sneered at Sackville's perceived cowardice in the battle. But Germain would have to work with the man. Anyway, both were professionals; surely there were larger issues at stake than personal affronts.

Every day a new raft of problems reached him. He threw himself into each with gusto.

Problem: there were not enough trained troops to fulfill the needs of Howe's and Carleton's armies. Solution: hire mercenaries from the German states. This required negotiating treaties with each of those states, which required first getting Parliament to approve said treaties.

Once again, Whigs protested, as if hiring foreigners were a treasonous act. Germain stood up in the House and showed, with meticulously prepared data, that the British government had used mercenaries in nearly every war it pursued.

Problem: even as British forces were colliding in the field with their American opposites, the king and the prime minister still persisted in pursuing the idea of sending a peace commission to treat with the rebels. They appointed as commissioner Admiral Richard Howe, and decided that his brother, General William Howe, whom Germain had sent to head the army, would support him on the commission—so that the two brothers were to treat for peace while fighting a war. Forced to deal with the peace commission, Germain pushed for the strongest possible terms: the commissioner, he argued, should insist that Britain would negotiate with the rebels only after they recognized "the supreme authority of the Legislature to make laws binding on the colonies in all cases whatsoever." Of course they would never do that, which would mean he could go ahead with the plan to crush them into obedience. Admiral Howe wrote to Germain, saying he could not possibly head a peace commission on those terms. The solicitor-general weighed in on the matter, and the Lord Chief Justice. The prime minister threatened to resign. So did Germain. The king stepped in; Lord North called a series of cabinet meetings. Germain marched in and out of No. 10 to push for the hardest possible line. In the end, Admiral Howe sailed for America without the burden of the condition Germain had wanted, but with other terms so onerous—all congresses and armies to be dissolved, colonial governments reformed by British officials—that the commission was almost certain to fail. Germain, in effect, got his way.

Then came good news. Early in 1776, word reached London that British forces had routed the colonials in Quebec. Germain exulted. He could send Carleton with a smaller-than-planned force to ensure that Canada stayed British, and otherwise could direct his attention to what he had long since determined would be the stroke to break the rebels' will and end the war quickly. It was clear that New England was the center of the rebellion. Military science dictated that dividing an enemy was the best road to vanquishing him. The maps spread out in Germain's office showed that the Hudson River separated New England from the other colonies. Taking possession of this river would maroon the most rebellious region of the colonies. Doing that required, first, an all-out assault on the chief port city in the Americas. Germain therefore directed General Howe to take New York. This would be the explanation for George Washington's surprising first victory, on Dorchester Heights. Even before Washington had reached Boston, Howe had decided on a plan to evacuate the city.

At the same time, Germain and others in Whitehall were working on a larger strategy. Once Canada was secure, the army there could move down the Hudson and join forces, in some as-yet-undetermined way, with Howe's army. This would complete the strangulation of the rebellion.

That step, however, was months in the distance. First, the object of Germain's unceasing effort was supplying 31 battalions, comprising approximately 21,000 men, all to be put under General Howe's direction. Weeks of meetings followed: of shuffling papers and scraping pens, of secretaries with heads bent in transcription, of rounds of coffee giving way to bumpers of brandy, of heated arguments with periwigged colleagues, the end of each day signaled by the whinnying of horses outside in the darkness indicating the coach that would take him home to his devoted Diana.

Somehow in the midst of this organizational and political undertaking, he found the time, and the nerve, to broach a topic that most British officials considered out of bounds. In one of his first letters to General Howe, he noted that "the Indians of the Six Nations" were "a consideration of no small importance." Left at that, the observation simply underscored an unremarkable fact. But Germain was nudging his colleagues toward the unthinkable: attempting to bring in on their side warriors whose tactics most British officials considered "savage" and "barbarous."

In the early months of 1776, ships set sail from ports all around the British Isles with guns, gunpowder and provisions, as well as troops. Their destination was Halifax, where Howe sailed after evacuating Boston. On June 6, 1776, after biding his time for two months, Howe watched a British ship, the *Mercury*, arrive in port. The wild and stupendous harbor—a mile across and four miles long, with "a bold shore"—was already crowded with ships of war; but this was the one he had been waiting for. A Captain Emmerick strode from the vessel with a thick packet in his hands, marched across the breezy and bustling port, and delivered it to Howe. Inside were copies of dispatches— letters Germain had exchanged with the Lords of the Admiralty and others—as well as a letter from Germain to Howe. The packet contained Germain's full update on political and military matters, and the order sending him forth into battle. Howe sat down to reply even as more sails on the horizon signaled the arrival of the last troops he had been expecting: a convoy of Scottish Highlanders. He penned a thankful response to Germain, expressing "my utter amazement at the decisive and masterly strokes for carrying such extensive plans into immediate execution, as have been effected since your Lordship has assumed the conducting of this war." The general knew perfectly well that at the core of Germain's herculean efforts lay a longing for personal redemption. He hoped, he wrote, that "you may finally receive the acknowledgments of a grateful country" and "the lasting glory which such services merit."

Two days later, Howe's fleet set sail, the vessels crowded with veteran soldiers, their hulls packed with all that was needed to rain destruction on an enemy. As grand a sight as they made, they were due to rendez- vous with the rest of the fleet, under his brother, Admiral Howe, making for a combined force of 32,000 men. Their destination was New York.

• • •

Abraham Yates was also preparing to head to New York in June of
1776. He wasn't going there to fight, however. He was fifty-two
and riddled with gout; the trip alone, what with the jostle of waves
and the horse cantering, was sure to be agony. But he had a role to
play, and he was consumed by it, so he said his goodbyes to Anna and
fourteen-year-old Susanna and boarded a sloop for Manhattan.

Besides, he was angry, and the only way to deal with it was to confront the situation that was playing out in Manhattan among his fellow
New York insurgents. In a sense, he had been seething ever since he was
ousted from Albany's city council two and a half years earlier. For ten
years he had worked painstakingly to build a new kind of political party,
one comprised of ordinary workers and tradesmen. In doing so, he had
given a voice to people who had never played an active part in politics.
Then the old guard outsmarted him.

After losing his city council seat, Yates had gone back to his legal
practice. Much of his time, however, he spent at his home on Market
Street, reading. Someone looking in his window and seeing the small
man bent over his books may have assumed he was pursuing a leisurely activity. But with him, reading was an act of engagement. He was
searching for context, trying to understand the unprecedented times he
was living through. The obvious question involved the impingement of
Americans' rights and what recourses history spoke of. But a related
issue tugged at him as well. What, exactly, had come over his fellow
Albanians, his fellow New Yorkers, and the rest of the colonists? Americans were conservative: farmers, churchgoers, people who respected
order, tradition, routine. What had made so many of them into radicals?
Britain's policies over the previous decade had been provocative, but
the reactions to them—parading in the streets, delivering thundering
sermons from church pulpits, dressing up as Indians and committing

acts of vandalism, engaging in battle with trained soldiers—seemed extreme even to him.

In search of answers, he turned to his books. He read Polybius, the ancient historian of the rise of the Roman republic. He read Montesquieu and Locke, Grotius and Goldsmith. He was interested, he said, in "the different principles of a monarchical and republican government," and in how and when the one gave way to the other.

The concept of freedom was ancient, but Yates was able to locate the beginnings of the modern mania for it a century and a half before his time. As Yates's own ancestors were emigrating from England and the Dutch Republic to found American colonies in the early 1600s, European monarchs were gathering power. At the same time, philosophers like René Descartes were reorienting knowledge, declaring that the proper basis for human understanding was not received wisdom from the church or the state but rather human reason. A bold new idea was born out of this divergence of politics and philosophy. If everyone possessed the ability to reason, then one had to conclude that there was something special about the individual human being, which meant that each person, male or female, rich or poor, was equally deserving of education, equally deserving of respect, equally entitled to participate in society. It followed, said the Dutch philosopher Baruch Spinoza, that the best form of government—really, the only legitimate one—was one in which each individual had an equal say. Since monarchies had become so very powerful, some people concluded that the only way out was revolution.

Such thinking had been so radical in the previous century that it was illegal even to own books by Spinoza. But that one central idea—that individual freedom was as necessary as air—continued to expand. Through the 1600s and early 1700s there were attempts to found utopias based on democratic principles and redistribution of wealth. These schemes mostly went nowhere, but as Yates pored through his volumes and watched the parade of history go by, he saw that core idea spreading like a subterranean fire. Whereas, he noted, in the Middle Ages "the lower people were reduced to servitude . . . slaves fixed to the soil," in recent times people both in America and Europe had discovered "a natural inclination to liberty."

*Vrijheid*, it was called in his native Dutch. Freedom. He was particularly interested in how the various Dutch provinces had united into one nation in the Eighty Years' War that ended in 1648. The Spanish king, Philip IV, had imposed harsh taxes on these vassal states, and brought the Inquisition in to enforce his rule. This "violation of the people's rights and liberties," Yates observed, "gave rise to the union of the seven united States and the declaring themselves independent." The result, the Dutch Republic, was a new European nation, led not by a monarch but by a government with a rudimentary form of popular representation. Might that be a precursor to what the Americans were about?

In England, meanwhile, the watershed came in 1688, with the so-called Glorious Revolution, which resulted in one monarch replacing another: not in itself a thoroughgoing transformation, but it left the country with a newly strengthened Parliament and a bill of rights. That era's political advances were captured in the writings of John Locke. Among other things, Locke dismantled the prevailing wisdom about the absolute power of kings, arguing that human beings are born into a "state of liberty," that "all men are by nature equal" and that a just society is governed by "the consent of every individual." In subsequent decades Locke's writings were picked up by Whigs in Parliament, who were frustrated that many of the freedoms promised in the Bill of Rights had not been granted.

Yates too had latched onto this manifesto of freedom. It had first gripped him during his struggles with British military officials in the French and Indian War twenty years before. More and more Americans had in the past decade likewise caught the freedom fever; they had reconfigured and refined it, and focused it on their own matters. The framers of the Virginia resolutions against the Stamp Act had expressed this same thinking. So had the colonial leaders assembled in Philadelphia.

But, remarkably, so too had droves of ordinary people—the sort who formed the membership of the Yates party: people like Isaac Fonda, a carpenter, and Robert Hoaksley, who ran a liquor store, and the farmers and craftsmen of nearby Schenectady, who erected a "liberty pole" in defiance of the British. These were the types who gathered at Richard Cartwright's tavern in December 1774 and unanimously agreed to support the people of Boston in their struggles against "the Arbitrary Measures of a designing Ministry" and agreed further that the sufferings of the New Englanders were part of "the common Cause of America." Yates was there too, watching and marveling.

The same group met the following month, January 1775, now calling themselves the Albany Committee of Correspondence, Safety and Protection, in answer to the call of the Continental Congress in Philadelphia for localities to form shadow governmental authorities to replace those still loyal to Britain. After swearing an oath of secrecy, vowing "on the Holy Evangelists of Almighty God" not to divulge one another's names, they unanimously elected Abraham Yates Jr.—who they all knew as a mighty organizer and who had been pursuing this path since before some of them were born—as their chairman. He was back in politics.

He cast his books aside and got to work. He set up subcommittees in each of Albany County's fifteen districts and began communicating via secret dispatches with all of them, focusing on how to raise funds and troops in the area. At the next meeting of the Committee, Yates and his colleagues learned that the New York Assembly had refused to nominate members to the upcoming session of the Continental Congress. The meaning of this refusal was perfectly clear: most of the official representatives of the colony still backed the British.

This was infuriating—expected, but infuriating. Yates's Committee of Correspondence took it upon itself to put forth names—effectively elbowing the official governing body to the side. He dashed off a letter to county leaders: "take the Sense of your District in respect to the appointment of Delegates"—again, quietly. When the news of the battles of Lexington and Concord reached Albany, secrecy became irrelevant: people brought their outrage into the streets. From that moment, the Committee of Correspondence met openly, at City Hall. Realizing they would henceforth be taking on the duties of governing, and feeling that they did "not conceive themselves fully invested" with a popular mandate, the members put out notices for elections. Yates won his seat, and the chairmanship. He was now the head of local government. Through the extraordinarily roundabout means of taking part in a multicolony revolt against a distant empire, he had come charging back onto the Albany political scene. And he had the exquisite satisfaction of having defeated his old foes.

Except that they hadn't gone anywhere. This was what angered him: the elite, which had kept an utterly undemocratic hold on power for so long, had not acquiesced to the modern reality that was right in front of them but had merely regrouped. Some of them were outright Tories, supporters of George II; but these were on the run now, or soon would be. Others, however, had insinuated themselves into the revolutionary movement, complicating and weakening it. Debates were flaring all up and down the Hudson River from Manhattan to Albany. Some would-be revolutionaries—lawyers, merchants, owners of large estates, people like the Livingstons and Van Rensselaers—believed a break with England was right and necessary, but wanted it done in a cautious and orderly way, with a respect for tradition and property. They wanted, in other words, to be sure that in the new era they would continue to run things. They maneuvered so as to give the English hope for reconciliation. Others—sailors and farmers, masons and tanners, unschooled men who did hard work and felt abused by the old system—wanted to break things, to riot and rebel, and hoped that in the aftermath there would be spoils.

Yates didn't exactly fit into either group. He believed political revolution was just, and after Lexington and Concord he believed it was necessary. While his shoemaker's inclinations were with the lower classes, he didn't like the disorder of the mob. Yet he distrusted the elites with every fiber of his being. He believed the impulse to freedom he had tracked through his reading pointed not just to a break from England but toward something more broad and revolutionary: genuine and just popular rule. A revolution, he was coming to conclude, if it were to be true to the force of history, had to be not only against the British elite but against the American elite as well.

Thus the anger he had felt for two and a half years. This was no time for delay and compromise. Yet the same forces that had ejected him from the city council were undermining the vital work being done in the colony. Some of those who had engineered his ouster were on the same Committee of Correspondence he led. Stephen De Lancey, for one, a member of one of the wealthiest families in the colony, was quietly leading a movement to counter the work Yates was about, buying time, trying to forestall the call for independence. The moderates had likewise taken root in New York City's Committee of Correspondence, where, out of fear of losing their wealth, they were trying to check the radicals' rush to war. As one noted, "Many People of Property dread the Violences of the lower Sort." Another elitist revolutionary, fellow New Yorker Alexander Hamilton, likewise tempered his zeal for independence with a frank distrust of commoners. Hamilton believed that "the multitude . . . have not a sufficient stock of reason and knowledge to guide them, for opposition to tyranny and oppression, very naturally leads them to a contempt and disregard of all authority."

If Yates felt torn between the two revolutionary forces, his mind was made up in January of 1776. Even as he was in the midst of his historical study, a new addition to the rapidly growing library of freedom reached him. Thomas Paine, an Englishman who, like Yates himself, had been apprenticed in a humble craft (corset maker) but pushed on to more intellectually adventurous pursuits, had emigrated to America two years earlier. Through a friendship with Benjamin Franklin he became editor of the *Pennsylvania Magazine* and immersed himself in the political crosscurrents of the colonies. In his writings he came to express a radical and thoroughgoing form of the freedom ideology: equal rights for women, an end to slavery, a belief in reason as the religion of the modern world, and most of all an abhorrence for monarchy and an unyielding commitment to democratic principles. In a pamphlet he wrote partly at Franklin's urging, Paine applied radical Whig notions, fresh from England, directly to the American situation.

The effect was stunning. *Common Sense: Addressed to the Inhabitants of America* was printed in Philadelphia in January 1776 and became the first American publishing sensation, selling 120,000 copies by the year's end. Yates paid two shillings for a copy, a relatively high price for a pamphlet, but he was hardly alone. Wherever he went in Albany—at Cartwright's Inn, on the docks, in the fort, on the streets of his riverside neighborhood—people were waving copies of *Common Sense*. "The cause of America," Paine proclaimed, as though he had read the same histories of the past century that Yates had, "is in a great measure the cause of all mankind." Perhaps as many as one-third of Americans were still loyal to Britain. Paine spoke directly to them, spelling out the flaw in their reasoning: "I have heard it asserted by some, that as America hath flourished under her former connection with Great Britain, that the same connection is necessary towards her future happiness, and will always have the same effect. Nothing can be more fallacious than this kind of argument. We may as well assert, that because a child has thrived upon milk, that it is never to have meat." But was not England their mother country? "Then the more shame upon her conduct," said Paine. "Even brutes do not devour their young." He made a case for radical change, and did it in powerful, plainspoken sentences: "A government of our own is our natural right." And, speaking directly to America as if it were not only already a nation but a sentient being, he gave it a mission: "Freedom hath been hunted round the globe. Asia, and Africa, have long expelled her. Europe regards her like a stranger, and England hath given her warning to depart. O! receive the fugitive, and prepare in time an asylum for mankind."

Yates felt the same energy as Paine: this was not a time for moderation. He was in constant motion in the early months of 1776: out to the hinterlands and in daily meetings of the Committee, dealing with loyalists, raising troops for the militia, appointing officers and, constantly, trying to find money and gunpowder.

Yates and others also met with Iroquois leaders in Albany in hopes of keeping the Indians out of any fighting that would come. But the Continental Congress sent word that they wanted to take over Indian affairs. Yates considered this "very unfortunate," for Albany's residents had more than a century of experience in dealing with the Iroquois. He acquiesced, but with a frostiness that indicated he felt the gentlemen in Philadelphia were making a mistake.

New York had thus far held three provincial congresses to attempt to deal with the rapidly deteriorating situation at a colony-wide level. All had ended in disorder and disagreement, with the conservative faction each time gaining enough leverage to quash votes toward declaring outright war and independence. Delegates to similar gatherings in Virginia and Massachusetts, and at the Continental Congress in Philadelphia, were growing impatient with the vacillation of the New Yorkers. At the end of May the Continental Congress asked each provincial congress to form a functioning government, but New York's, with the conservatives holding sway, declined to do so.

That set up new elections. On June 27, 1776, yet another delegation was elected to yet another provincial congress. Yates was one of twelve men voted to it from the Albany region. Here he was, then, preparing to go to New York City, even as a constant stream of news was flowing upriver to him, from Manhattan and elsewhere. The Continental Congress was meeting again in Philadelphia, and this time might take the long-awaited step of formally breaking with Great Britain—but it still awaited support from New York. Meanwhile, General Howe's fleet was gathering in New York Harbor, preparing to unleash the dogs of war.

Yates was feeling creaky and unwell; even in the best times he was known to be a bit of a curmudgeon. But the long train of history pointed to independence, and he would be damned if New York's waffling elites—or 32,000 British soldiers—were going to stand in the way. He boarded the sloop and sailed south. His objective was clear: push New York into the future; tip the province into open revolt. How to accomplish it was another matter.

Washington went to New York too, at the head of an army. His recruits were a ragged lot, dressed in hunting shirts or whatever else they had, forced to shamble along on foot most of the way through muddy spring roads. But, ever mindful of image, the general, before leaving Boston, had created a personal guard to accompany him, and he was meticulous about its appearance. Each officer in charge of a regiment, he ordered, was to send him four men for his guard, and he specified that they should all be "handsomely and well made . . . neat, and spruce," and should be between five feet eight inches and five feet ten inches tall: that is to say, of relatively uniform size, but none taller than Washington himself. Washington personally chose a design for their uniforms: blue and buff, with rounded hats topped with feathers.

He designed his own uniform as well, with an eye for maximum effect, telling his tailor he wanted "a blue coat with yellow buttons and gold epaulettes (each having three stars)." Even in camp he was careful to strap a splendid sword to his side and to have boots outfitted with shining silver spurs, and he capped the appearance with a plumed hat and a purple sash. His horse was part of the spectacle: a regal beast with its tail nicked so that it bobbed upward with an attention-getting flourish as the army traveled through byways and towns.

It was all to a purpose. His lifelong preoccupation with fashion and spectacle as markers of status was reaching potentially historic significance. He was leading not only an army but a would-be nation into battle. He knew that his countrymen were a humble, pious, plainspoken lot, for whom the supernatural was mixed into the real world. For them a king was a being with one foot in another realm. If they were to lose their king, there was a gap in the foundation of their being. He understood that he needed to fill it.

At the same time, he was a practical man, who had agreed to forgo a salary but intended to have his expenses reimbursed, so he kept his receipts on the journey to New York: "ferry . . . mending carriage . . . 1 dozen of Wine."

He traveled through Connecticut, heading from New London to Saybrook Point—once again coming close to crossing paths with Venture Smith, who was hoping to ride out the coming mayhem in his new home just to the north—then traveled the last leg by ship, reaching New York on April 14.

Washington had made only two short visits to the city before and had little appreciation for its complex geography. Once he arrived, he began studying in earnest how to defend it and quickly saw the difficulties. The city itself—with a population of 25,000—was tidily huddled at the southern tip of Manhattan Island, but the overall landscape comprised islands and coves, bays and deep harbors, exposed beaches and high palisades, stretching for miles in every direction. He had 19,000 men, many of whom were sick or hurt. He would have needed five times as many to adequately defend such an ornate locale.

He had sent Major General Charles Lee ahead to fortify the city. Lee, a British Whig who had emigrated to Virginia only three years earlier and joined the rebel cause, was equally bewildered when he reached Manhattan. Knowing the British had the finest navy in the world, he wrote to Washington, "What to do with the city, I own, puzzles me, it is so encircled with deep, navigable water that whoever commands the Sea must command the Town." He did his best, ordering gun batteries to be installed in the city itself, along the east side of the island, which was flat and thus exposed, as well as on the Long Island shores opposite. He also had redoubts and barricades constructed along the Hudson shoreline.

So far, there was no sight of the British fleet. Washington—who had brought Martha with him—took over an elegant, tree-shrouded mansion two miles north of the city whose owner, the British paymaster of New York, had recently fled. He had brought a featherbed, pillows and other niceties, so they were able to make it into a passably comfortable home. Riding from there down to military headquarters at the foot of Broadway, he found the city a different place from the one he had first encountered twenty years earlier, when he ran up shopping bills in its stores filled with European goods. Many of the residents had fled the city. He had given Major General Israel Putnam the task of preparing the remaining populace for the coming battle, and Putnam had instituted martial law. Sentries were posted at intersections, and residents had to obey a curfew. "We all live here like nuns shut up in a nunnery," a resident complained in a letter.

Washington cherished order and thus detested the chaos his army was bringing to the city. The soldiers tore up fences and cut down trees for barricades; the streets filled with garbage; shopkeepers jacked up their prices. He particularly frowned on sexual waywardness, and so deplored the fact that the army spawned a corresponding army of prostitutes—"bitchfoxy jades," one local called them, complaining about their "unparalleled conduct" in broad daylight.

The news he had been expecting for weeks arrived on June 4. He had posted Benjamin Tupper, a trusted thirty-eight-year-old veteran who had served in the French and Indian War and recently against the British in Boston, as a lookout in the harbor. A messenger thrust a hastily scribbled note from Tupper into Washington's hand: "Eight Sail of Square wrigd Vessels and five small Craft besides the Asia & her small Tender . . ." The first British ships had arrived.

It would take time for Howe to assemble his army. Meanwhile, Washington's problems were compounded by New York's provisional government, which continued to drag its feet. It had gone so far as to try to block General Lee and his men from coming into the city to erect defenses. Fortunately, a new provincial congress had just been elected. Washington could only hope its leadership would show some interest in helping him save their city.

Meanwhile, the city was crawling with loyalists. Many were hiding in plain sight, biding their time, expecting Howe to deliver them. Others maneuvered secretly to undermine the revolutionaries. Rumors flew: that a ring of spies was at work, that money was being offered to American recruits to jump to the British side once the fleet arrived, that the ring included people close to Washington, that the general was in danger of having his food poisoned.

Some rumors turned out to be true. The provincial congress did one good piece of work: it uncovered a network of spies. Washington learned that a member of his personal guard named Thomas Hickey was working for the British. He ordered a court-martial.

Summer heat settled over the island, more British sails appeared, and the whole city followed Hickey's trial. Details of an elaborate plot to undermine the American army emerged, involving the city's mayor and William

Tryon, the British governor of the colony. Hickey confessed his role. Washington knew this was a crossroads, not only for the army but for the American people. They needed a display, a testament to the seriousness of what was transpiring. He ordered the man hanged. On June 28, at eleven in the morning, the whole army as well as nearly the entire population of New York watched Hickey's body twitch at the end of a rope and go limp.

Immediately afterward, Washington issued general orders. He observed that "the unhappy fate of Thomas Hickey" should be "a warning to every soldier," then pivoted toward the gathering fleet in the outer harbor: "Officers are without delay to inspect the state of the Ammunition which the men have and get their Arms in good order for service and strongly to inculcate upon all Sentries especially on night duty the greatest vigilance and attention. . . ."

Washington had to know that defending such an exposed locality against the massing power of a crack army and a peerless navy was hopeless. The geography, the enemy fleet, and the yawning inexperience of his own forces together told a clear and sobering story. It might have been more expedient to pull out, give up the city and retreat to more defensible ground. But, like Germain, Washington believed the war would be brief. It might in fact end here. Then too, the Continental Congress expected him to fight. And to simply hand over the second-largest American city would have been a blow to morale not only in the army but throughout the colonies. He felt he had no choice but to build up the barricades and brace for the attack.

If George Germain set New York as the place to break the colonial rebellion, forcing George Washington (and an army) to defend it, and sending Abraham Yates there in his effort to defy both the British and recalcitrant fellow colonists, the strife also made it a riotously, kaleidoscopically intriguing place for Margaret Moncrieffe to come of age.

For this city of spies, soldiers and streetwalkers, of rotting trash and mounting anxiety, of stench and sweat and signal fires and summer rain, was her home. As General Washington sent aides and messengers paddling across the rivers and galloping up and down the island, setting in motion troop shifts and artillery repositionings, Margaret, aged fourteen, flitted through the streets, eyes darting, soaking it all in. She was precocious, crackling with self-awareness and magnetically connected to her surroundings. It was thrilling.

It was also appalling and maddening and frightening. The intrigue was palpable. Next-door neighbors—revolutionaries and loyalists— plotted against one another. As the naturally combative daughter of a British officer, she was nearly insufferable in her adolescent loyalty to king and country, yet she was forced to live in the household of her late stepmother's revolutionary brother. As far as she was concerned, she was trapped behind enemy lines.

As the city spiraled toward chaos, Frederick Jay, her protector, decided it was becoming too dangerous for children; she found herself ferried across the Hudson River to stay with friends of the Jays in Elizabethtown, New Jersey. The people who took her in, a family called the Bankers, were ardent patriots; dinnertime conversation was all about the evils of the English soldiers. Margaret was barely able to contain her fury; she felt herself "persecuted on every side" and "forced to hear my nearest and dearest relations continually traduced." Then, in late June, she thrilled to see the sails of the British fleet on the horizon. Elizabethtown looked out directly onto Staten Island, where the ships put to anchor and began unloading men and equipment. She knew that one of the soldiers setting up camp there, just a few hundred yards away, was the man who had eluded her for most of her young life and now, through the exigency of war, seemingly continued to taunt her with his absence: her father.

Just as her father came within reach, she was pulled away from him. The Banker family decided the British army was too close, so they, and seemingly half of Elizabethtown, packed what they could and moved inland, in their case to a village 10 miles to the west. Margaret felt desperate. She wanted to send her father a signal, to make him aware of how close she was. If ever there was a time for him to play the hero and rescue her, this surely was it.

On a Sunday, while the others were at church, she acted. She took a horse and simply fled. Not knowing where else to turn or how she might get herself to the British army, she rode back to Elizabethtown and showed up breathless at the door of another family who had known her since she was a baby. Sarah De Hart, the mother, welcomed her, took her in, in spite of the fact that she had several children of her own and was six months pregnant.

She stayed with the family while General Howe's army built to its full complement. At the same time, Washington's recruits were also streaming into the region from all points. One especially hot and humid day, as Margaret was in the garden searching for a breeze, she found herself suddenly surrounded by a company of militiamen. They had marched eastward from Pennsylvania and were trying to figure out how to get themselves across the river to Manhattan. They accosted her with a rowdy mix of militant patriotism and sexual intimidation. When she didn't wilt but rather confronted them, meeting their patriotism with her own and beating back their advances, some were sparked to anger. Suddenly, she was staring at bayonet points. Her heart beat furiously, giving the lie to the brave front she'd exhibited. She wondered if this was to be it, her brief life extinguished in a New Jersey garden. But one of them came to his senses and called the others off.

When the men had swept onward and her heart had calmed, she determined not to stay with the De Hart family any longer but to try to get to the British army by another means. She had learned that another relation of one of her father's dead wives was the head of the New Jersey militia, based here in Elizabethtown. She managed to get to his headquarters, where she hoped he would take pity on her and find a way to ferry her across to the enemy. William Livingston— the same one who had founded the radical journal the *Independent Reflector* and served as Abraham Yates's mentor in the law and who was a lawyer with no previous military experience—was, at the moment she was brought to him, overwhelmed with the task of trying to raise and equip an army on the fly even as the largest naval fleet ever in America was assembling right in front of him. He was in the midst of penning a series of increasingly frantic updates on the situation to Washington— "we are fully Confirmed in the Enemy's having Posts along the whole Staten Island Shore. . . . It is said that last night they brought two pieces of cannon to the nearest work . . ."—and finally breaking out into a naked plea: "Your Excellency must be sensible that as the department I now act in is to me entirely new, I must be desirous of every aid that can possibly be obtained—If you Sir could spare a few experienced Officers to assist me in this important Business."

Looking up distractedly, he found himself staring at a girl who purported to be a distant relation of some sort, who seemed to want him to set aside the business of trying to hold back the British army so as to heed her plight. What was she going on about? *Everyone* had a plight just now. "He behaved to me with harshness," Margaret related, "and even added insult to his reproaches." She was shown the door.

Back at the De Hart home, she cast about for other ideas. She could think of no one else she knew who could help her. People in the household, meanwhile, talked of nothing but soldiers and officers. In the stream of adult chatter one name stuck out: Israel Putnam. He was a prominent player in the American defense of New York—a general, in fact. She knew the name: he had been a friend of her father's. Now they were fighting on opposite sides, but maybe he would help. She had to know he would be at least as harried and busy as William Livingston, but she wrote to him anyway. She had nowhere else to turn.

*Chapter 11*

———— ⌗ ————

# THE CITY OF NEW YORK WILL, IN ALL HUMAN PROBABILITY, VERY SOON BE THE SCENE OF A BLOODY CONFLICT

Abraham Yates hobbled off the sloop from Albany not in New York City, as originally planned, but 30 miles short of the city. Due to the rapidly deteriorating situation on Manhattan, the fourth Provincial Congress had decided to meet in the town of White Plains, in Westchester County. On Tuesday morning, July 9, Yates trundled into the county courthouse building. After some bureaucratic shuffling due to the fact that he and the other delegates from Albany had neglected to bring credentials proving that they were the men duly elected to the new body by their constituencies, the meeting was called to order. The first matter on the agenda was a letter from Philadelphia that contained the text of the declaration the members of the Continental Congress had signed five days earlier. It was no ordinary declaration. The New Yorkers agreed that the entire document should be read aloud. For the next ten minutes or so Yates and his colleagues gazed out into the morning sunlight or down at their own buckled shoes as they listened:

IN CONGRESS, July 4th, 1776,

A Declaration by the Representatives of the United Sates of America, in General Congress assembled.

When in the course of human events it becomes necessary for one people to dissolve the political bands which have connected them with another, and to assume among the powers of the earth the separate and equal station to which the laws of nature and of nature's God entitle them, a decent respect to the opinions of mankind requires that they should declare the causes which impel them to the separation. . . .

*

We, therefore, the representatives of the United States of America, in General Congress assembled, appealing to the Supreme Judge of the world for the rectitude of our intentions, do, in the name and by authority of the good people of these Colonies, solemnly publish and declare, that these United Colonies are, and of right ought to be, free and independent States. . . .

The same document was being read aloud on the same day to the troops assembled on the Commons in lower Manhattan, the large open area that had been turned into a military camp. George Washington, on receiving a copy, had ordered all the soldiers to hear it. Having the words ring in the open air was a small but important part of his strategy for running this war. He and George Germain—his opposite, the man who was running the war for Great Britain, of whom Washington was well aware and whose intellect he surely could feel animating the British maneuvers—had some things in common, including the fact that neither was especially a man of ideas. But there was this one difference: where Germain insisted the central issue in the conflict was power, pure and simple, Washington realized this would be a war about ideas, or rather about one idea. He wanted to make sure that that idea was planted in his men's minds before they went into battle: "that all men are created equal," that governments derive "their just powers from the consent of the governed," that the king "has kept among us, in times of peace, Standing Armies, without the Consent of our Legislatures," that the king "has affected to render the Military independent of, and superior to, the Civil Power," that the king had given his assent "For imposing taxes on us without our consent" and "For taking away our Charters, abolishing our most valuable Laws, and altering fundamentally the Forms of our Governments."

Washington had no need to worry about the soldiers' motivation: they had caught the freedom fever as well. They gave three huzzas when the reading was over, then, together with a mob of residents, charged downtown and tipped over the 4,000-pound statue of George III that had presided over the city and harbor since 1770. Washington was annoyed by the unruliness but pleased at the ardor. As for him, the long-awaited day had arrived. He was ready for whatever the future held.

But he felt by no means certain of victory. He had a secret plan, should he fail and be hunted down for treason: to slip away into the thousands of wild acres he owned in the Ohio Country. In "the worst event," he wrote to his brother-in-law, who was managing those lands for him, they would "serve for an Asylum."

After the echoes of the final words of the declaration had died in the White Plains courthouse, the New York Convention, as the provincial congress now chose to call itself, set up a committee to craft a response to the document. Yates was one of the five men selected for it. In the afternoon session the committee presented its reply:

*Resolved unanimously*, That the reasons assigned by the Continental Congress for declaring the United Colonies free and independent States are cogent and conclusive; and that while we lament the cruel necessity which has rendered that measure unavoidable, we approve the same, and will, at the risk of our lives and fortunes, join with the other Colonies in supporting it.

Yates and his colleagues then voted to have the Declaration, together with the Convention's unanimous resolution, made public "with beat of drum," and ordered 500 copies to be sent to every county in the state.

The recent election had pushed aside a number of the more conservative delegates. In Albany, in addition to Yates, his nephew Robert Yates and a close friend, Matthew Adgate, were part of the delegation. The Yates Party was alive again. The new Convention was able to act with one voice, at least for now, at least for purposes of backing the step taken by their colleagues in Philadelphia. The next day they ordered a change of language: henceforth they were no longer a colony but "the State of New York." They then divided up into committees for the purpose of defending their state.

July 12, half past three in the afternoon. George Washington—along with nearly the entire population of New York—stood watching as two British warships, one of forty guns and the other of twenty, detached themselves from the vast fleet out in the bay and began sailing directly toward the city, "availing themselves of a brisk & favourable breeze with a flowing tide," as Washington put it in a hasty letter to John Hancock in Philadelphia. The ships then turned suddenly and headed up the Hudson, their gun ports opened and their cannons began blasting away as they ran alongside the island's western shore. Cannonballs came thundering into the sides of buildings and skittered down streets, setting men, women and children running and shrieking.

The maneuver was meant to test the American fortifications, and the test, from Washington's perspective, failed miserably. Instead of hurrying to their positions, men who had supposedly been trained to operate the cannons onshore stood and stared at the sleek and seemingly supernaturally efficient ships. He dictated general orders that included a scolding ("such unsoldierly Conduct must grieve every good officer, and give the enemy a *mean* opinion of the Army"), tightened discipline, and concluded, "The General hopes this is the last time he shall have occasion to take notice of any such neglect."

Then he sent a rider northward with a letter to the New York Convention in White Plains explaining that he feared what mischief the two British ships might get into: "Gentlemen, The passage of the Enemy up the North River is an event big with many consequences to the public interest." He wanted the delegates to ensure that the ships would not rendezvous with Tories, and wouldn't take control of any of the high grounds along the river. Yates and his colleagues sent a message back ensuring him that they would see to it. To do so, they borrowed 90 pounds from one of their number, Peter Livingston, to defray "the expenses of transporting a quantity of lead" to various positions.

At almost the same time the two ships had run the gauntlet, another British warship, the two-decked, 64-gun *Eagle*, sailed into view of New York City and put to anchor alongside the fleet. Admiral Howe—General Howe's brother and the head of the peace commission that Whitehall had insisted upon over Germain's opposition—had arrived at last. He set to his task almost at once. A barge appeared on July 14, with a white flag and carrying emissaries of the admiral. Washington and his officers watched it approach. He had given some thought to the matter of how best to deal with this peace commission. Like Germain, he considered it a distraction. But it had to be handled with delicacy, and there was the possibility of getting some use out of it. He chose his three most trusted aides to meet the boat, and instructed them on exactly how to behave and, in particular, to pay precise attention to language. One of the English officers stood up. He was the captain of the *Eagle*. He addressed himself to Colonel Henry Knox, Washington's aide. "I have a letter, sir, from Lord Howe to Mr. Washington."

Knox, following Washington's instruction, replied, "Sir, we have no person in our army with that address."

This seemed to flummox the man. He held up the letter. It was addressed to "George Washington, Esq." Knox informed him that he was unable to take it.

The next day another barge appeared, with a white flag. The officer aboard had another letter, this time addressed to "George Washington, Esq., and etc. etc." Knox again declined to take it.

Washington was a stickler for details, and details were the essence of diplomacy. Independence had been declared; therefore, for a peace commission to have any meaning it had to begin by acknowledging the role of the commanding officer of the other side. There was no ego involved; to correctly acknowledge him was to acknowledge his nation as a sovereign state, with which one might negotiate. Otherwise there was nothing to discuss.

On the third day another vessel appeared, also with a white flag. By this time many people onshore were following the unfolding diplomatic sideshow, including a reporter for Benjamin Franklin's newspaper, the *Pennsylvania Gazette*. Another British officer stood up and brandished another letter. But, to the bewilderment of the reporter as well as, no doubt, that of the American commander, it was not addressed to George Washington at all, but rather to a "Miss Margaret Moncrieffe."

. . .

As it happened, Major Thomas Moncrieffe, Margaret's father, had been looking for her. He had gone to Boston with General Gage and come back with General Howe to a different New York, a place of chaos and confusion. He was living in a tent city on Staten Island, in a world of crisp British military discipline, looking out across the bay toward lower Manhattan, waiting along with everyone else for battle to commence. He apparently sent word to the Jay family that he wanted Margaret with him, and had learned that the Jays had fled to New Jersey and that she had then fled from them. She was a fourteen-year-old girl, on her own in a city about to be engulfed by violence.

Having no other way to find his daughter, he decided to send a letter to the American command. Thus Margaret's small personal affair interrupted the diplomatic dance that, for all anyone knew, might result in a negotiated settlement that would end America's war of independence. Major Moncrieffe knew the American leaders, and they knew him: according to Margaret, her father was well enough acquainted with officials of the rebellious government and military that they had "repeatedly, at the commencement of the war, offered my father a command in the northern army."

Major Moncrieffe's letter reached the American headquarters at about the same time as Margaret's desperate letter to General Putnam asking for help in getting her to her father. (Putnam had also heard about her from William Livingston, who apparently felt bad about the way he had treated the girl.) Shortly thereafter, Margaret, who was still staying with the De Hart family in New Jersey, was surprised and delighted to receive a reply from Putnam saying that he was willing to help her. She had explained in her letter that her father was with the British forces, and she feared that by assisting her the general would feel that he was abetting the enemy. Putnam wrote back with kindness, saying that he had much regard for Major Moncrieffe, and that "any political difference alters him not to me in a private capacity." While noting that "as an officer, he is my enemy," Putnam asserted that as a friend he would "with pleasure, do any kind office in my power for him or any of his connexions."

The next day, a strapping twenty-two-year-old American officer, Colonel Samuel Webb, aide-de-camp to General Putnam, appeared at the door of the De Hart family's home, ready to conduct Margaret to New York. They crossed the river and within a few minutes of landing arrived at 1 Broadway, headquarters of the American army and temporary home of General Putnam. Margaret was thrilled when the general and his wife received her "with the greatest tenderness," and introduced her to Mrs. Putnam's two daughters, who were a few years older than she was.

The general turned out to be a plump, jovial man whose looks and mannerisms seemed more suited to a tavern than an officer's banquet. Over time Margaret came to observe that he was devoted to his troops and that they treated him like a father; his lack of education, which was evident in his every utterance, endeared him to them, and to Margaret. She found it amusing that he said "ginrole" for general and referred to the radical Whigs in Parliament as "twigs."

Margaret was given a room in the house. Apparently, she would be staying for some time, as the small diplomatic issue of transporting her to the enemy was tangled up with the considerably larger one. The irony of her present situation, meanwhile, fairly screamed at her: her new home was the epicenter of the rebellion in New York. American military personnel streamed in and out of the building. Much of it was off-limits to her. Soon after settling in, she made her way to the top floor, where there was a little gallery that wrapped around the cupola. From here she had a spectacular view of the city spread around her: horse traffic, ladies with their hoop skirts and parasols, men in knee-length coats and tricorn hats, the open ground just opposite filled with the tents of soldiers. Beyond was the sweep of the harbor. In the distance lay the British fleet, which had swollen to the point where an American officer described the warships as extending "more than a Mile in Length from East to West, and so thick & close together for the greatest part of the Way, that You cant see through where they are no more than if it was a thick Swamp."

The day after her arrival, General Putnam formally introduced her to his superior. The gentleman before her was uncommonly tall and refined, with thin lips and narrow, intelligent eyes. His face was marred by pockmarks, however. The woman at his side, who was dwarfed by her husband, exuded self-possession but offered her a welcoming smile. Miss Moncrieffe felt ready to burst with her loyalty to the English crown, but she held it in check and told General and Mrs. Washington that she was grateful for the sanctuary. In return, the esteemed couple, Margaret said, "made it their study to show me every mark of regard."

But she found it annoying that she was rarely allowed to be alone—the American leaders were concerned that she might stumble onto information that she could share with the enemy once they shipped her to her father. It annoyed her even more that Mrs. Putnam put her to work. Having spent much of her young life in Ireland, and considering herself on the British side of the conflict, she was able to take a foreigner's view of America when she chose. "Mrs. Putnam employed me and her daughters constantly to spin flax for shirts for the American soldiery," she said, adding sardonically, "indolence in America being totally discouraged."

Shortly after Margaret arrived at 1 Broadway, she would have been able to witness the spectacle of Washington's personal guard in their trim custom uniforms lining the entrance to the building at stiff attention to welcome a visiting British military officer. On the third try, Admiral Howe had acquiesced and addressed a letter to "His Excellency, General Washington," at which Washington, having made his point, agreed to the meeting that was requested in the letter. Lieutenant Colonel James Paterson, representing Admiral Howe, arrived on July 20. The meeting was cordial, but awkward. Paterson placed before the American commander yet another letter from Admiral Howe. This one was addressed to "George Washington &c. &c. &c." Washington refused to receive it. Paterson said he should not be offended, that the "&c. &c. &c." implied "everything that ought to follow." Washington countered that it "also implied any thing." Paterson attempted to push on. He explained that Admiral Howe had been appointed to head a peace commission, and he wished to begin that process. Washington showed his familiarity with the orders that George Germain had given to Admiral Howe. The only tool that the admiral had been given, he said, was the authority to grant pardons. There was thus a fundamental flaw with the peace commission, for "those who had committed no Fault wanted no Pardon." The Americans' position, he said, was that "we were only defending what we deemed our indisputable Rights."

Washington suspected all along that the real purpose of the peace commission was to encourage the moderates among the revolutionaries and thus to hamper their military buildup. With one artful meeting he all but ended it. Paterson communicated the details to Admiral Howe, and Howe wrote to Germain, saying that the meeting "was more polite than interesting" and "it induced me to change my superscription for the attainment of an end so desirable."

The days leading up to the British assault were frantically busy, but, when possible, formal dinners were held at 1 Broadway. Washington was not often in attendance. When he was, they were decorous affairs:

wine served, toasts given, protocol rigidly observed. Formality aside, they were occasions to release the tensions of the day, to distract oneself in candlelight and conversation. At one, the toast was to the Continental Congress. People raised their glasses. But the commander noticed one glass still on the table. His countenance, which even acquaintances said tended to be icy, turned toward the girl in the room. The most powerful man in America was staring directly at Margaret. "Miss Moncrieffe, you don't drink your wine," Washington observed.

Silence. The words were spoken with the clear solemnity of a superior addressing a disobedient child.

Margaret was trying to follow the dictates of her loyalty, but she was embarrassed at being caught out. She didn't know what to say. Finally, her innate spunk rising, she held up her glass and cried, "General Howe is the toast."

The table erupted in indignation. Putnam, who had assumed the role of her protector, came to her aid, suggesting to the commander that "everything said or done by such a child ought rather to amuse than affront you."

Washington was not mollified, but he realized the matter must be brought to an end. A light rejoinder popped into his mind. "Well, Miss," he said, "I will overlook your indiscretion, on condition that you drink my health, or General Putnam's, the first time you dine at Sir William Howe's table, on the other side of the water."

In an instant Margaret went from embarrassment to relief to joy, for not only was the moment of social awkwardness at an end, but this was the first real indication she had been given that the Americans would indeed get her to the British. She promptly assumed the role of obedient girl and promised Washington that she would do as he asked.

Her wishes were not gratified at once. Instead of being taken to Staten Island, she found herself whisked to Kingsbridge, at the northern tip of Manhattan, where the colonials were constructing a fortification.

She considered it some sort of punishment, but it was more likely done to keep her from overhearing military plans. General Thomas Mifflin was in command here, and his wife, Sarah, took charge of Margaret.

So she took up residence in another military household. Officers came and went. Almost at once, she fell powerfully, hypnotically in love with one. He was twenty-one years old, a colonel, with dark hair, an angelic face, and soulful eyes. He had studied theology, then switched to law before leaving to join the army. He'd served valiantly in the effort to take Quebec, which had attracted Putnam's notice, so here he was assisting in the effort to defend New York. His name was Aaron Burr.

Burr was developing a reputation as a lady-killer. He was seven years older, but Margaret was highly sexually aware and both of them had a magnetic affect on the opposite sex. They had very little occasion to be together, but they managed to find some time to be alone, for she admitted later that "to him I plighted my virgin vow," that he "subdued my virgin heart," and that "the immutable, unerring laws of nature" had pointed him out to be her husband. As July gave way to August, a heat wave was engulfing Manhattan Island, and it particularly inundated Margaret Moncrieffe. She was smitten beyond words, but she tried to use them to convey the storm of feelings. Burr was "the Conquerer of my soul." She had no more thoughts about her father and the need to fly to him for protection. Instead, she dreamed of running away from the war with her lover into the wilderness, with "the woods affording us our only shelter, and their fruits our only repast."

In her fiery and spontaneous way, she dashed off a letter to General Putnam, at the other end of the island, informing him that she intended to marry. If she was looking for his approval, she did not get it. Putnam was alarmed and flabbergasted at this turn of events. Assuming the role of a disapproving parent, he pushed ahead plans that were already underway to send her to the British side.

Margaret was filled with a new dismay. What she had longed for—

to be reunited with her father—was now about to happen, and suddenly she didn't want it. Why should she care about him? He had spent most of her life in other places, rejecting her. Now it was her turn to reject him. She wanted to stay on Manhattan, with *him*.

But two military commands that were in the midst of preparing to attack one another in a battle that could dictate the future of the British Empire had managed to come together on this one point. The American high command had arranged to deliver this girl to their British counterparts. There was nothing she could do. August 7 was a blustery day. The boat that rowed her out into the bay tossed violently; she was soaked by the waves. They came within hailing distance of the *Eagle*, Admiral Howe's flagship, and a boat from it headed toward them. As an indication of the seriousness with which the American side viewed the matter of handing over this teenaged girl, the job of doing so was given to Washington's top aide, Colonel Knox. He exchanged shouted formalities over the wind with the British officer who had rowed out to meet them, and Margaret stepped from the American barge to the British.

That evening she found herself at an officers' dinner hosted by General Howe. There were forty or fifty people present, and as she entered the room, she was rattled by their gazes and murmurs: "a sweet girl"; "divinely handsome." She was just noticing, with relief, that she had been seated next to a woman she knew, the very elegant Frances Montresor, wife of a British officer, when she found that, as a matter of politeness to her as the new arrival, and one who had reached them through such dramatic circumstances, she was being asked to offer a toast. After a pause to gather her thoughts, she did as Washington had asked and uttered the name of General Putnam.

The reaction was a mirror image of the last time she had offered a toast: gasps. But where Washington's first impulse had been to censure her, General Howe saw fit to reply with a joke. Apparently, they had heard that the girl had fallen in love while she was with the Americans. Everyone knew that Putnam was a round, rough and elderly man. "If he be the lady's sweetheart, I can have no objection to drink his health," Howe cried, to general laughter.

The next day Margaret boarded a coach and was driven nine miles away, to the other end of Staten Island. Hugh Percy, a thirty-four-year-old nobleman who had the rank of brigadier general, had his quarters in a fine house here. The coach pulled up, and there, standing on the lawn, conferring with Lord Percy on military plans, was her father. It had been more than a year since she had seen him. The last few weeks had felt like ages. She fainted in his arms.

"The Army under my command," General Washington declared to the leader of the Massachusetts provincial congress on August 14, "are in good Spirits." He knew battle was shortly to commence, and he hoped his troops would act like men "fighting for every thing worth living for, in this case with the Smiles of Providence." He had trained them hard in the weeks of waiting, and he was feeling optimistic.

On August 22, a bright morning that followed a wracking nighttime summer storm, the British landed on Long Island. The sails, the precision oarwork of the barges, the disembarkation of 22,000 soldiers on the beach, who then formed themselves into neat lines on the nearby plain made for, declared Admiral Howe's secretary, "one of the finest & most picturesque Scenes that the Imagination can fancy or the Eye behold."

In short order, this vast and efficient fighting machine decimated the American troops in the vicinity. With all the time he had to prepare his defense, Washington had done virtually everything wrong. In defiance of one of the oldest maxims of war, he had divided his army against a superior enemy. Having no idea where Howe would strike, he had put some of his men on Long Island and others across the East River on Manhattan. Further diluting his strength, he had spread out the troops on Long Island thinly across six long miles of shoreline.

Over the next few days Washington was constantly on horseback, moving back and forth from Gravesend to Brooklyn Heights, scope in hand, scanning the horizon, trying to guess Howe's strategy even as it was unfolding. On the night of the twenty-sixth, Howe made his move. He had discovered that Washington had left the Jamaica Pass undefended. He sent 10,000 men through it, while two smaller forces attacked as well. All converged on Brooklyn Heights, which looked directly onto the city of New York. In some places the American soldiers blazed away and slowed the oncoming enemy. But all the columns advanced, murderously. After routing the colonials along the Gowanus Road, the Scottish Highlanders, together with the Hessian forces that George Germain had brought into the conflict, pressed forward in a gory frenzy, slashing at the retreating men with sabers and sticking them through with bayonets.

Washington had a steady stream of messengers riding to him with news of each setback. Hundreds of his men were killed in the first phase of the battle, and two of his generals were captured. The rest of the army that was on Long Island was pinned down, and it looked like Howe would move forward in one final grand assault and utterly destroy him, potentially ending the American rebellion.

But Howe did nothing. Washington was confounded. As it turned out, one general's inexperience was pitted against another's excessive caution. Washington had hoped to win a great victory. Now he was forced to exert every effort to organize a massive retreat. A storm swept in on the night of August 29; taking advantage of the wind, and the thick fog that blanketed the East River at dawn, he did some brilliant scrambling and managed to get his troops across to Manhattan.

His men had been harried for days; they were sick, wet, hollow-eyed from lack of sleep. Washington himself had spent forty-eight straight hours on his horse in his effort to avoid calamity. Reaching Manhattan, however, gave them no relief. They were being hunted.

Now New York City itself became the issue. Its 4,000 or so houses, its little network of streets, the churches and stables, the inns and taverns, and of course the inhabitants: if his army stayed in or near it, the swarms of redcoats and their bayonets would be upon them. The destruction would be appalling. More prudent, in strategic terms, would be to evacuate the city and set fire to it, and flee northward up the river. It was a hard choice to make, but war was about hard choices. That would at least deny the British their prize.

Washington sent a rider up the highway to the little village of Harlem perched at the northern end of Manhattan. Three weeks earlier, the members of the New York Convention, in order to exchange information with Washington more efficiently, had moved themselves here from White Plains. Washington's messenger dismounted in front of the church where they had taken up residence, rushed inside and delivered his letter to the Convention's chairman, Abraham Yates.

Yates took the message and read it aloud to his colleagues. Washington informed the delegates that "the city of New York will, in all human probability, very soon be the scene of a bloody conflict." He asked them to "form, and execute some plan for their removal and relief." The members chose a committee to carry out an evacuation of the city, and Yates scribbled a hastily composed reply to Washington and stuffed it into the messenger's hand:

*Sir*

*I am directed to inform your Excellency that immediately upon the receipt of your favor of this morning respecting the Women,*

*Children and Infirm persons remaining in the City of New York—the Convention appointed a Committee for the purpose of removeing and provideing for such persons—I inclose a Copy of the Resolves for that purpose and hope you will soon be releived from the Anxiety which their continuence in Town has occationed. And I have the Honor to be with verry great Respect Your Most Obedt Hume Servt*

*Abm Yates Junr President*

Yates had until recently been consumed by another task: setting up a government for the new state. To the consternation of some of his colleagues, he had objected to their plan to draft a state constitution. Such a document, in his eyes, concerning itself with defining the powers of the state, would inevitably leach away rights to which individuals were naturally entitled. His close friend Matthew Adgate put forth a resolution that the constitution be accompanied by a bill of rights. The delegates divided into two groups in debating whether this was necessary, with those who had previously counseled moderation in dealing with Britain believing such a statement of individual rights was not necessary, while Yates and his party insisted it was.

This debate was put on hold by the disaster just to the south. Yates and Washington exchanged letters again on August 22 as Washington shared his grim deliberations about New York: "that if the fortune of War should oblige our Troops to abandon that City, it should be immediately burnt by the retreating Soldiery. . . ." The delegates were themselves surrounded by war. They were dealing not only with the situation around Manhattan but also with fears of another British army moving from Canada into the Hudson Valley to the north; with buying muskets; with pleas from imprisoned Loyalists; with efforts to obstruct the Hudson River so as to block Howe's ships; with mustering companies of soldiers; and with money. War was real for them now, and it made them decisive. Yates responded: "The Convention will chearfully submit to the fatal Necessity of destroying that Valuable City whenever your Excellency shall deem it essential to the Safety of this State or the general Interest of America."

But Washington didn't do it—he couldn't bring himself to do it, though reason told him it was right. Besides, the Congress had instructed him not to burn New York.

When word reached the Convention that the British were soon to invade Manhattan, Yates and his colleagues decided that for safety's sake they had to leave Harlem and move north. They packed everything up once again, sailed 65 miles up the river, and relocated themselves at the town of Fishkill.

One of the pressing issues Yates and his colleagues were trying to assist Washington with was his army's lack of cannons. Yates wrote Washington on September 5, to say that the Convention had voted to authorize the army to remove all church bells from New York. They would then be sent across the river to New Jersey to be melted down and turned into cannons. Washington responded three days later: "The measure I highly approve of, & shall accordingly have it carried into execution." As soon as the messenger rode off, he remembered another thing he had wanted to say, and scratched out a second note to Yates: "I wrote you this Morning by your Express, but forgot to mention a Matter of Consequence. It being determined to remove our sick to Orange Town, we shall want four large Albany Sloops for that purpose." He asked the Convention to "send them down with as much Dispatch as possible to this City." Yates wrote back: ". . . we have directed every vessel down the river be impressed." In the midst of chaos, the two men—the general and the local politician—were working well together.

Washington was profoundly exhausted, yet he had no time for rest. He had to consider what Howe was going to do, and what strategy he himself should employ. Having failed in his initial plan to face and defeat

Howe in one grand battle on Long Island, he had partially redeemed himself by executing a clever escape. This gave him the idea that the best general tactic to employ was to "on all occasions avoid a general Action," as he wrote to John Hancock, and rather to stay quick and nimble, to retreat and then make sudden turns to attack. In short, he should use the size and slowness of Howe's army against it. At his order, the army pulled out of the city and headed northward, up the island.

By the logic of his new strategy, the best move would be to leave the island altogether while there was still time, let the British pursue him on the mainland, and look for skirmishes that he could win. But no sooner did Washington formulate this new strategy than he reverted to the previous, failed one. He expected Howe would land his men at Harlem, so he moved his army there and began digging in for a head-on battle. He was in a house on the heights at the northern end of the island, which he had made into his headquarters, when he heard an echoing boom of cannonfire from the south. The British were not landing at Harlem after all, but at Kip's Bay, six miles away, on the east side of the island. He mounted his horse and galloped in that direction. Five British warships were firing simultanously, creating a broadside screen for a full-scale amphibious landing, with dozens of flatboats carrying thousands of men ashore. Washington arrived in time to find the troops he had posted there "flying in every direction and in the greatest confusion." Right in front of him some of his own men, in frantic retreat, dropped their weapons and ran. He was being met by a parade of panic, a rout, an unconscionable wave of dishonor.

His frosty facade fell; he screamed in rage, unsheathed his sword and pulled his pistol, bellowed at the cowards to hold their positions. He threatened to shoot them. But the soldiers ignored him in their wild flight.

He was alone then when the first wave of British soldiers advanced. Fifty of them were heading straight for him. And he froze. His aides ran up, pushed him, shook him; it was like trying to waken a statue.

One later declared his belief that Washington at that moment had chosen an honorable soldier's form of suicide: to face the enemy alone. The line of redcoats advanced, now 80 yards away. Finally, Washington's men dragged him off the battlefield.

Howe had outgeneraled him again. The British took control of New York City. But the prize was not pristine: whether through an unofficial order from Washington or not, arsonists set the city ablaze.

As the invaders pursued Washington's army to the high ground at Harlem, he was able to regather himself and his men. They turned and fought off the pursuers in a two-hour battle, winning a small but heartening victory.

On September 23, Washington sent Yates an account of the battle, seemingly as much in an effort to calm his own mental unrest as to inform the president of New York's governing body. The British maneuvers, he admitted, were at first "various and perplexing" to him, but then suddenly they became "extremely plain and obvious." On reaching Kip's Bay, he told Yates, he found "to my extreme astonishment . . . the troops who were posted on the lines retreating in the greatest disorder." He omitted any reference to his breakdown, but went on to describe the feisty resistance of the colonial army in the woods before the Harlem Heights, and ended on a cheery note: "I am in hopes this little success will be productive of salutary consequences, as our army seems to be greatly inspirited by it."

In fact, Washington was far from inspirited. When he sat down in the mansion in which he had taken up residence to write his cousin, who was taking care of Mount Vernon, he opened up to him in a way he had never done with anyone. He confessed that he felt cornered and hopeless, and that he all but wished for death. "I am bereft of every peaceful moment," he said. "I am wearied to death. . . . In short, such is my situation that if I were to wish the bitterest curse to an enemy on this side of the grave, I should put him in my stead with my feelings."

Abandoning his now famous reserve, he admitted that "I do not know what plan of conduct to pursue. I see the impossibility of serving with reputation, or doing any essential service to the cause by continuing in command, and yet I am told that if I quit the command inevitable ruin will follow from the distraction that will ensue. In confidence I tell you that I never was in such an unhappy, divided state since I was born."

He ended this report from the depths of misery with an almost comically jarring segue into a series of directives about work to be done at Mount Vernon, saying, "With respect to the chimney, I would not have you for the sake of a little work spoil the look of the fireplaces," and "You ought surely to have a window in the gable end of the new cellar."

But there was a certain logic in his switch of topics. He was a creature of honor who now saw no honorable way forward. He had been beaten soundly not only by a superior enemy but by himself. He had little faith in his army. In truth, it wasn't a proper army. (One of his generals, frustrated over the lack of uniforms, had sent his men into battle with tree boughs in their hats as a way to mark them as a unit.) The British now had New York: the city and the port. Loyalists were coming out of hiding and making the city their home again. He had let everyone down, including the gentlemen in Philadelphia, who less than three months ago had ceremoniously proclaimed independence, and who had placed their faith and hope in him. And he and his harried men were still being pursued. It seemed everywhere he looked he saw regiments of redcoats approaching: "like a clover field in full bloom" was how a private in his army described the sight. The scene before him held nothing but misery. But if he closed his eyes, he was back home.

## Chapter 12

⎯⎯◈⎯⎯

# SO CELESTIAL AN ARTICLE

The surface of a lake does not show the lake itself but the sky. This world, the world of humans, is a reflection of the Sky World. Since everything in the Sky World is invested with consciousness—is, in a sense, a person—so too are all the things on earth. A tree is a kind of "person," as is a rock, a lizard, a meteor, a corn beetle, the yarrow root, the sun, a snake. Thunder is a person and ice is a person. You can speak to all of these, whisper hot prayers or encouragements, and they will hear. It is possible, furthermore, for a "person" to change from one form to another, or to have his or her form changed: root to snake, rock to moon, flower to woman, child to mouse, man to tree stump. Certain objects are special; they can transform themselves or work the effect on others. These are *aaskouandy*: charms. A snake bone, a twist of husk or hair, the castor sac of a beaver, a claw, a black stone found glistening in a deer's stomach. What we see before us does not remain as it is, but shifts. This is reality. These things happen here in the world.

Such was the knowledge pool from which Cornplanter, warrior of the Wolf Clan of the Senecas, drew. When he met with Americans or British, sat smoking, drank, laughed, listened to them boast of the greatness of their society, discussed the quality of a musket or the need to share the "island" of North America, his perspective was animated by such knowledge. His sense of the world was ontologically different from that of his counterparts, the American and British leaders. For him everything was alive and conscious. Magic was ordinary truth.

When the Iroquois had met with the agent of George Washington in the fall of 1775, and Cornplanter had declared himself leader of the Senecas, they had agreed to stay out of the conflict. Now, as George Washington led his army in retreat from the British on Manhattan, Cornplanter and the Senecas at Conawaugus were harvesting corn and preparing for the fall hunt. Cornplanter and his wife (whose name has not come down to us) had a two-year-old son. As far as they were concerned, their world was complete. Cornplanter lived with other members of his wife's extended family in one longhouse, with high, sloping ceilings and firepits spaced down the center to delineate the immediate family units. He, his wife and their son would have had, as their own area, one of the low bunks that ran along the sides and, above it, a storage shelf that held their personal belongings: baskets, clothing, jewelry, pipes for smoking, soft hides of bear and fox and deer, maybe a dried elk's bladder used as a canteen, stoppered and fitted with a string for wearing around the neck. As the winds of autumn swept in and nights grew colder, as Cornplanter settled into his bed with his loved ones, the coughs and rustlings and intimate noises of the other relatives in the house signaled not a lack of privacy but the wider bounds of familiarity. In Seneca society, you were close. You knew everyone by sound and smell. You were not alone, not ever.

Though they preferred not to think of the affairs of the whites, agents had, over the previous months, come to the village requesting them to appear at councils. John Butler had come. Cornplanter knew him. He had been brought to Iroquois country as a child by his father, and learned several Iroquois languages as he grew up. He had served in the Seven Years' War and learned firsthand how the Iroquois fought, the value they put on torture, the meaning of the charms that they adorned themselves with, braiding them into their hair, tying them to the pipes they smoked at councils. He knew their world. He came with rum and presents. He was on the British side in the war, and he wanted the Iroquois to join in, to fight alongside the redcoats. He assured them that the Americans were going to lose; if the Iroquois helped the British now, the British would remember it and reward them.

Cornplanter didn't like this. Seneca country was far from the fighting; this war was not their affair. But some Iroquois, who lived to the east, joined the British in the Canadian battles. They fought the Americans at a place called the Cedars, near Montreal; some died there.

After that came another call to council, this time from the American side. The involvement of Iroquois at the Cedars had gotten their attention. They wanted to talk, and they were suddenly very insistent. The council took place in Mohawk country, a 160-mile walk due east, at a place the Americans called German Flatts. Many Senecas from Conawaugus made the journey. In all, 1,700 Iroquois—men, women and children—gathered at the behest of General Philip Schuyler.

This was inauspicious ground for a peace council: two decades earlier German Flatts had been the location of a bloody attack by Iroquois and Frenchmen; they had killed some of the German settlers there and taken others prisoner. Now the Senecas arrived to find the Americans building a fort, with the slender and imperious figure of General Schuyler in command. At age forty-three, Schuyler was an almost exact contemporary of Washington, and, like Washington, he had a frosty, aristocratic mien. But where Washington's sense of entitlement had come from the Anglo planters of Virginia, Schuyler was a native of Albany who traced his ancestry to the Dutch period. As a member of the Albany elite, he had a long and mostly contentious relationship with Abraham Yates. He had been named by Congress to head the Northern Army, and reported to Washington. While Washington was at this moment preparing for the British invasion of New York, Schuyler was tasked with keeping the Iroquois out of the war.

The Iroquois found Schuyler in a foul mood, for he had been waiting for them for more than three weeks. His disregard for them ("haughty princes of the wilderness," he called them) was plain.

Despite their tardiness, the Iroquois insisted on being properly feted before getting down to business. Schuyler was further annoyed: "The Consumption of provision and Rum is incredible," he reported.

Eventually—it was August 6, 1776—the council fire was lit. The Iroquois began with a ritual request for condolence for the recent death of two of their chiefs. This was standard protocol, but for Schuyler it was too much to bear. These warriors had been killed in action against Americans: in violation of a solemn agreement, the violation being the very reason for this present council. He would not take part in the condolence ceremony. The Iroquois considered, and decided they would not press the matter. Whereupon General Schuyler must have held aloft the first of many strings of wampum and, trying to calm himself, intoned, "With this String we open your ears that you may plainly hear what the independent States of America have to say to their Brethren of the Six Nations." He reiterated the facts that led the Americans to break with England, and reminded the Iroquois that in the council the previous year they had agreed—and he quoted them—"not to take any part" in the war, as it was "a family quarrel."

Then he brought up the machinations of John Butler, how he had stirred some Iroquois to fight for the king, and listed several instances in which Iroquois warriors had fought against Americans in Canada. He closed by affirming that if they would keep their promise to stay out of the fighting, then the "independent States of America" would vow to live in friendship not only with the Iroquois but with all Indians.

Cornplanter was a man of depth, who had an appreciation of subtlety, of reality's layers and changeability. He may have seen both the

Americans and the British as rather childlike in their seeming clarity. There were many occasions, like this one, when he and other Iroquois leaders—the Oneida chief Good Peter and sachem Jimmy Tayaheure, Sagwarithra of the Tuscaroras, the Cayuga Fish Carrier, his own half-brother Handsome Lake—might have tried to enlighten an American or British interlocutor on the power structure of the Six Nations, which had built into it the autonomy not just of its six major divisions but of every single Iroquois. If a small group of them wished to join in a fight, there was little the confederacy could do about it. The Americans, who were at war over their freedom, had difficulty comprehending that among the Iroquois each individual, with his or her unique consciousness, had freedom, and each cherished it. Freedom, in other words, was basic to the Iroquois.

But the Iroquois leaders did not make this point at German Flatts. Neither the Americans nor the British would truly understand, just as they could not fathom the use of an *aaskouandy* for altering reality. To them the Iroquois concept of freedom came across as shiftlessness, irresponsibility.

The point was made in a different way by the hundreds upon hundreds of Iroquois present at the council (their consumption of food and drink, General Schuyler complained, "equals that of an army of three thousand men"), whose numbers spoke to the diffusion of power among them. At any event, the leaders mollified the general by reaffirming their intention to remain neutral. They promised to be deaf to John Butler's repeated and insistent attempts at persuasion. They accepted the wampum belts, ate and drank some more, then went home.

John Butler's backwoods cajoling of the Iroquois to join the British had its origins in London. It had its origins, to be precise, with George Germain. When he sent Guy Carleton to Canada, Germain included instructions to "employ" Indians in "making a Diversion and exciting an alarm" among the colonists. While he considered himself to be respectful of codes of military conduct, Germain also believed it was appropriate to use every available means to do the job he had been assigned. Carleton—who had longtime knowledge of American Indian nations and believed that their methods violated principles of proper conduct in war—chose not to follow Germain's order.

If Germain wanted assistance in his effort, it showed up in timely fashion. In what must have seemed like an apparition, a genuine Mohawk warrior appeared before him one day in March of 1776. Thayendanegea, known to the Americans as Joseph Brant, was handsome, intelligent, dressed in European clothing and spoke good English. He was a perfect foil to the notion prevalent among the British that the American natives were creatures outside the boundaries of civilization. Even better, Thayendanegea had come expressly to forge an alliance between the Iroquois and Great Britain. He had been groomed from childhood by William Johnson, the Irish-born powerbroker who lorded over the Albany region from his estate in Mohawk country. Johnson, a devout loyalist, had died recently, but he had given Brant not only a taste for all things British but a conviction that England, with its mighty army and navy, was certain to win the war. Brant had traveled to England with Johnson's nephew, Guy Johnson, a colonel in the British army, and everything he saw as he walked the streets of London reinforced his awe at the power and grandeur of Britain. The English, meanwhile, were intent on wooing him. They arranged for him to have his portrait painted. He received visitors at the inn where he was staying, the Swan with Two Necks. He had an audience with the king. And he met with Germain. The American Secretary was happy to overlook the fact that the Mohawk leader addressed him as "Brother Gorah," for Brant quickly got to the point:

We have crossed the great Lake and come to this kingdom, with our superintendent Col. Johnson from our Confederacy the Six Nations and their Allies, that we might see our Father the Great King, and joyn in informing him, his Councillors and wise men, of the good intentions of the Indians our bretheren, and of their attachment to His Majesty and his Government.

Brant, as he moved through London society, was the very picture of sophistication, and he provided the support Germain needed in his quest to get the Iroquois on the British side. The Secretary began exploring ways to work around the reluctance of General Carleton to employ Indian fighters. In the spring of 1776 he sent another general, John Burgoyne, to Canada. Burgoyne would technically serve under Carleton, but Germain planned to give him command of the army that would move south, down the Hudson River, cutting the New England colonies off from the others. Before Burgoyne left, Germain told him pointedly that "the assistance of the Indians" was "highly necessary." At the same time, he wrote to General Howe in New York, saying that "the securing of the affection and assistance of our old friends and allies, the Indians of the Six Nations, is a consideration of no small importance."

Most of the British generals resisted this push, but Germain kept at it, determined to see to it that, as he said, "proper persons are employed to negotiate" with the Iroquois. So began the campaign of councils, conducted by Indian agents loyal to Britain, to work on the Iroquois. The agents knew this would not be easy work. They had some awareness of the Iroquois method of decision-making: that it required patience, time and effort for the various villages and tribes to come to a consensus, and that even then it would not be universal. This kind of outreach also required money, so even before Congress had declared America's independence, Germain devoted 5,000 pounds to buying presents to help sway the Iroquois.

Initially, the agents reported no progress, but Germain was insistent. Once Burgoyne was installed with Carleton's forces, he wrote him again, saying, "I hope every precaution has been taken to secure the Indians to our interest. The Congress is exerting all their influence to debauch them from you." He knew that Burgoyne recoiled at the Indians' brutal tactics, but, he said, those tactics were precisely the point: "The dread the people of New England &c. have of a war with the savages proves the expediency of our holding that scourge over them."

Meanwhile, news reached the offices of Whitehall in the fall of 1776 that must have caused the American Secretary to expel a stupendous sigh of relief: Howe had taken New York. Hugh Percy—the same friend of Major Thomas Moncrieffe to whose quarters on Staten Island Margaret Moncrieffe was taken for her reunion with her father—was also a confidant of Germain. Lord Percy had been part of the campaign as Howe's men chased Washington from Long Island to Manhattan and took control of New York City. He wrote Germain from America: the battle "was ably planned and nobly executed. The behavior of both officers and men on that occasion did honour to the country they came from and to the cause in which they are engaged. The rebels have severely felt the blow, and I think I may venture to foretell that this business is pretty near over."

Germain was exultant. The peace commission, which he had been against from the start, had failed. "Roman severity" was succeeding. *He* was succeeding. The larger strategy—an army from Canada would move south, while Howe's would move north from New York, using the Hudson River as a conduit for splitting the rebellion in two—was still in motion, but it might not be necessary. For all he knew the next packet of letters might bring news that Washington and his misfit army had been vanquished.

. . .

Once more, as he had at Kip's Bay before an oncoming line of British soldiers, Washington froze. Summer—the summer in which his colleagues in Philadelphia had declared American independence from Britain—was over. The wind off the river was cold now, and leaves were turning. His fellow officers believed the army had to get off Manhattan, which had been lost, and find another place to make a stand. Yet day after day he stayed holed up on the Harlem Heights, paralyzed with indecision. He was trying to second-guess Howe. What would the British general do? Would he charge up the Hudson, en route to a rendezvous with the oncoming army from Canada? Would he lead his troops across the Hudson and into New Jersey, and storm Philadelphia?

Then Howe made his move. Word came that the British had maneuvered their ships through a thick fog and landed 4,000 men on Throg's Neck, a spit of land at the place where the East River spilled out into Long Island Sound. Howe was coming directly for Washington.

Washington acted. He marched his men 18 miles north, to White Plains. (Yates and the rest of the New York Convention had previously abandoned the town, as had many of its residents.) Howe pursued; there was a hard, close fight as the Americans tried to hold a hilltop. They failed, and lost 175 men in the process. Howe then surprised Washington by spinning back to the south. His target this time was the last place on the island where Washington had troops: the fortification that guarded the northern end of Manhattan. There was a psychological as well as a strategic reason to take the post. The rebels had named it Fort Washington.

Washington couldn't decide whether to abandon the fort or not. In fact, there was no sense in trying to hold it, but his subordinate, General Nathanael Greene, decided the matter for him: they would defend. Thousands of British and Hessian troops clawed their way up the steep ridge and engaged the men crammed into the fort. After a bloody fight the Americans realized they were trapped. The American commander, Robert Magaw, offered his sword. More than 2,800 hungry and sorry-looking soldiers marched out of the fort and surrendered. They were taken to prison ships, where many, if not most, eventually died. The British renamed Fort Washington as Fort Knyphausen, after the Hessian leader of the attack.

Washington, meanwhile, escaped across the Hudson with the main body of his army and retreated into New Jersey. Howe's much larger army followed. At Newark, Washington paused to scribble an update to John Hancock and the Congress: "The situation of our Affairs is truly critical & such as requires uncommon exertions on our part. From the movements of the Enemy & the information we have received, they certainly will make a push to possess themselves of this part of the Jersey." Four days later, with icy rain pelting his men, he reported that "the enemy . . . are advancing this way." In fact, they were upon them; he ordered a swift evacuation of Newark; the men in the rear got glimpses of the advance guard of the British entering the town as they fled. On November 30 he stopped again, at Brunswick; his scouts spotted British divisions advancing toward them along two different routes.

The next day, with enemy troops again within sight, he wrote to Hancock that as it was "impossible to oppose them with our present force, we shall retreat to the West side of the Delaware," and so into Pennsylvania. To make a desperate situation worse, he lost almost 2,000 of his men in one go. In its fear of military rule, Congress had refused to authorize a standing army. These New Jersey troops were under enlistment contracts that ran out on this date, December 1, and so they simply left the army and headed for their homes. Washington now had only 3,400 men, and was being chased by an army of 12,000.

He was riding into a dead zone: gray hills, bare trees, a landscape hunkering into winter. His mind was in a fog brought on by exhaustion. He was bitterly aware that rather than defending his country he was running for his life, buying time, scrambling. And he was losing the confidence of his staff. Several of his fellow officers were openly griping about his leadership. General Lee, who had erected the fortifications on Manhattan in advance of him, wrote to General Horatio Gates, in a letter thick with sarcasm, that the "ingenious maneuver of Fort Washington has completely unhinged the goodly fabrick we had been building," and, with bald reference to Washington, declared his belief that "a certain great man is most damnably deficient."

Washington pushed his remaining troops onward—they were now, he admitted, "broken and disspirited," wearing rags, with old blankets to shield them from the elements instead of coats, their bodies covered in sores. To Princeton they marched. The weather got colder. On December 2 they arrived at Trenton—a hundred-odd houses clustered near the riverbank, all of them now deserted—and looked out across the slate-colored surface of the Delaware to the tangle of barren trees on the other bank. What with the nervous whinnying of horses and the trudging efforts of weakened men hauling heavy artillery, it took five days to cross the river.

They made it to the western shore just as Howe's army arrived in Trenton. Over the next few days, Washington sent letters in which he tried to arrange for the defense of Philadelphia while keeping an eye on Howe's army, which was busy rounding up boats for a crossing. And he was agonizing over something else: the contracts of another contingent of his army were to expire on January 1. "The Enemy," he wrote, "are most assuredly waiting for that Crisis."

Then, with options dwindling, his mind, instead of shutting down, hatched an idea. The enemy hadn't advanced across the river toward them; in fact, the main body was gone. It appeared Howe would end the campaign for now, and was pulling back to winter quarters within the comfortable confines of New York City. He had left about 1,000 men, mostly Hessians, in Trenton, holding Washington's army at bay on the Pennsylvania side.

Washington had to do something before his army dwindled. The last thing Howe would expect from a weakened enemy in the midst of a wintertime retreat would be a counterstrike.

On Christmas night, he gambled everything. He rushed his men back across the Delaware. He chose a spot north of the town, so that the crossing would not be detected. What had taken five days before he insisted they do in a matter of hours, under cover of darkness. A storm moved in as the night deepened; ice formed on the river and the long canoe-like boats had to cut through it. A thick mix of rain and snow fell, obscuring vision and slowing progress. Washington became anxious, as his gambit depended on darkness and surprise, and with the delay they would get there hours later than planned. But there was no turning back. Dawn arrived; a weak light illuminated the bent heads of his bedraggled men as they trudged along two roads toward the town center. At eight in the morning the division Washington was in encountered the Hessian guards posted on the outskirts. Three minutes later the sound of gunfire to the south told him the other division had likewise met the guards on that road. Both divisions pushed into the town, forcing the Hessians to run backward and return fire as they retreated.

In the center of Trenton, Washington saw the main body of the enemy, hundreds of them, staggering into formation. He read the chaos in their movements. Some tried to rush up the Princeton Road to get out of town, but Washington sent men running across it to block them. Then came a stuttering moment of silent suspension: gray skies, bayonet points, breath visible in the cold air, eyes sweeping the scene of stone houses and snow-tipped trees. The Hessians saw the situation plainly, saw that they were surrounded. With a gentle clatter, they laid down their arms. Washington took 886 soldiers and 23 officers prisoner.

It was a small victory, but for the commander of the Continental Army it changed everything. He had known from the beginning—in fact, ever since his days with Braddock—that creative, asymmetrical tactics were his only hope. Only now, having been forced into such a strategy after so many failed attempts at classical warfare, did he take it to heart.

As Washington's spirits rose, Abraham Yates suffered a setback. At the very moment the Hessians were giving themselves up in Trenton, Yates, in Fishkill with the other members of the New York Convention, the state's de facto governing body, was struck by a fever. His gout had worsened as well, and his condition became so severe that he was forced to leave his colleagues and hobble aboard a sloop for Albany so that Anna could take care of him.

It was an unfortunate moment to go down. The members of the Convention were working seven days a week, involved in seemingly every part of the war effort. They were sending out orders to the counties to enscript more men for military service, buying clothing for soldiers, ordering artillery to be moved into position to defend cities, debating a general pardon for "all persons who have joined the enemy, and shall return within a limited time," processing a stream of communiqués from Washington and other generals in the field, and, perhaps of most immediate importance, ordering that a fellow named Uriah Mitchell be paid 47 pounds 8 shillings for his work. Mr. Mitchell was the Convention's express rider, without whom they would have no news of distant events.

On January 3, in the midst of winter and the turmoil of war, the post rider brought them a copy of the first number of Thomas Paine's latest publication. Paine had observed firsthand Washington's army as it trudged through defeat and freezing temperatures in New Jersey, and the experience led to him writing *The American Crisis*. The Convention members ordered the pamphlet read aloud in session. Its first words heartened the harried politicians, just as they had the troops in New Jersey when Washington had it read to them:

> These are the times that try men's souls. The summer soldier and the sunshine patriot will, in this crisis, shrink from the service of their country; but he that stands by it now, deserves the love and thanks of man and woman. Tyranny, like hell, is not easily conquered; yet we have this consolation with us, that the harder the conflict, the more glorious the triumph. What we obtain too cheap, we esteem too lightly: it is dearness only that gives every thing its value. Heaven knows how to put a proper price upon its goods; and it would be strange indeed if so celestial an article as FREEDOM should not be highly rated.

The members of the Convention ordered 1,000 copies of Paine's pamphlet to be printed and distributed.

Somehow, in the midst of bullets flying, with enemy armies ranged to the north, west and south, and with all the pressing matters of running a war, the Convention also managed to follow the request of the Continental Congress and had begun some weeks earlier setting up the foundations of a state government (though one of them quipped that first "it would be well to secure a state to govern"). Yates had gotten himself assigned to the committee to write a constitution, and had thrown himself into the work, for he saw it as nothing less than a chance to cement into the foundations not only of his city but of the entire state of New York the principles for which he had been fighting for years. He wanted true popular representation. He wanted state offices to be elective. He wanted to ensure that the widest number of people were entitled to vote. He pushed for voting to take place via secret ballot. And he wanted individual liberties to be specified in the constitution.

The wrangling began at once, with delegates split along familiar lines: the radicals, like Yates, versus the conservative faction—the large land-owners, members of wealthy families, men like Gouverneur Morris, Robert R. Livingston and John Jay—who wanted to keep the political structures of the new state as close as possible to what they had been under the English.

Jay led the crafting of the document. He was a small, ferret-like man, careful in his habits and with piercing powers of observation. He had had a highly successful law practice in New York City before the war and was related to several of New York's great families; with so much to lose, he had held out for reconciliation with England until the last possible moment. He was thus, in many ways, Yates's opposite. Yet both men possessed politicians' souls; both understood compromise, and Yates worked with Jay, giving in on several items for the sake of unity, before being felled by the fever.

Yates stayed home recuperating from December of 1776 to April of 1777. When he returned—the Convention had moved yet again to flee the British, to Kingston, on the west bank of the Hudson—the constitution was nearly finished. He shuffled into the hall on a Tuesday morning after the session had started. While his colleagues were debating a motion regarding the makeup of the state's court, he struggled to get himself up to date. Overall, he discovered, the constitution was much as it had been before he left, and it was a remarkable piece of work. Having nothing to guide them but English precedents, their own convictions and the Declaration of Independence (which they included in its entirety), the delegates had crafted a document that was intended to provide "such government as shall, in the opinion of the representatives of the people, best conduce to the happiness and safety of their constituents in particular, and America in general." It provided a structure of representation: a governor, a senate, an assembly and other officials. It provided for elections.

But to Yates it was clear that the conservatives had won the day. In their fear of mob rule, they wanted to ensure that only the wealthiest and most educated citizens would have a voice in government. Therefore, with John Jay leading, they limited voting privileges to adult white male freeholders (i.e., those who owned or rented substantial amounts of property). They put further checks on the vagaries of the masses by decreeing that several state offices would be filled not by elections but by appointment by high officials, and that the governor and other state officers could at any time "revise all bills about to be passed into laws." Seeing, upon his return, that there was no stipulation that voting be conducted by secret ballot, Yates tried to get his colleagues to agree to that provision, but he failed. The most glaring omission was the failure to include a bill of individual rights and liberties that would be guaranteed to all citizens of the state. Yates didn't push it. Maybe he was too weak. Maybe he was satisfied, for the time being, with the fact that the document guaranteed freedom of religion, trial by jury, and separation of church and state. Later he would complain about those conservative colleagues on the constitution committee who worried, as he put it, "that too much would be taken out of the aristocratical reservoir." But he voted in favor of the document.

Then too, the delegates had reason to hurry. The British victories, and the swift capture of New York City, had emboldened loyalists in the state and sent others streaming in from elsewhere. Yates and his colleagues were suddenly dealing with insurrections in every city and town, as people they had known all their lives—friends, neighbors, family members—transmitted troop movements to the enemy, stole guns, burned houses and signed up with British regiments. As Yates would later say, "the alarming situation . . . facilitated the completion of the Constitution of New York."

. . .

On February 28, 1777, while Abraham Yates was convalescing at his home in Albany and George Washington was in winter quarters in Morristown, New Jersey, Margaret Moncrieffe stood before the altar at Trinity Church in lower Manhattan, resplendently dressed but red-faced with fury, surrounded by British military officers in formal attire, listening to the Reverend Samuel Auchmuty perform her marriage ceremony. She was not yet fifteen years old.

It was six months since she had fainted in her father's arms at Lord Percy's quarters on Staten Island following her ordeal of being caught between the American and British armies. For a happy few weeks she stayed there, enjoying her father's attention when he was not otherwise engaged. She took part in the ceremony at which he was promoted to Major of Brigade, then said goodbye as he went off as part of General Howe's invasion of Long Island. She stayed well behind the front lines, awaiting news of the battle like everyone else. She heard of the retreat of General Washington's forces from Long Island, received word that her father had been taken prisoner by Washington's men, then learned that the unit that had captured him had shortly thereafter itself been forced to surrender to a party of Hessians. So eventually she was reunited with him again.

With the taking of New York, the British army and its attendants—Margaret included—moved into the city, and she found herself once again living in her own home. The house may have been more or less the same, but the city had changed utterly. New York was now under martial law. Its patriot residents had fled or were hurrying out, while loyalists flooded in from all over the region. The streets crawled with refugees, the homeless, children orphaned by war. Street hawkers sold most everything—pigs, rum, boots, toys—but at wildly inflated prices. A third of the city was a smoking ruin. The barricades Washington's men had thrown up at the end of every street blocked traffic and contributed to the chaos. The ditches they had dug to slow the enemy's advance were now filled with stagnant water. An Englishman noted in his diary that the sudden inrush of loyalists resulted in "people being crowded together in so small a compass almost like herrings in a barrel." Disease, he noted, was rampant—"the Itch, Pox, Fever, or Flux"—and the city comprised "a complication of stinks."

Yet this place of filth and disease was not the city Margaret experienced, at least not most of the time. The British officers quickly set up a separate zone for themselves: a surreal world of scarlet jackets and powdered wigs and fancy-dress balls, of billiards at the King's Head Tavern, of shops selling French furniture and gilt clocks. *This* New York—the capital of British-occupied America—was meant to be simultaneously a reminder of the grandeur of England, a place for aristocratic officers to rest from the ravages of war, and a celebration of the coming victory over the rebels. At its head was General William Howe. When Washington was peering across the Delaware River in December of 1776, trying to fathom why Howe's army was abandoning its pursuit of him, he could not have guessed that this was the answer. For Howe viewed war as a job, and, dedicated though he was to it, he liked to keep regular hours, and was equally devoted to his off-time.

All armies adhered, more or less, to the concept of "winter quarters," but Howe, who was known by his colleagues to be fond of the good life, took it especially to heart. *"Toujours de la gaieté!"* he supposedly cried on arriving in the city. With Washington on the run and the defeat of the colonial forces a near certainty, Howe made himself a regular presence at the balls and gaming tables of occupied New York that winter. He spent lavishly and showed himself to one and all as the epitome of a bold and smart commanding officer.

Margaret, however, who took part in many social activities, would have found the general less interesting than the woman who was nearly always at his side. Elizabeth Loring became the center of gossip in town not merely because she was the general's mistress but because of the brazenness of the triangular relationship that had been arranged. Betsey, as Howe called her, was the wife of Joshua Loring, an American officer who had sided with the British. Howe and Mrs. Loring having established that they fancied one another, the general made a proposition to Loring: in exchange for the "use" of his wife, he would make Loring commissary of prisoners. It was a good job: not in the sense that it was pleasant, but it was easily exploitable. Loring took the deal, looked the other way as Betsey and the general made the New York scene, and got rich, in part by limiting rations for the unfortunate members of George Washington's army who became his prisoners and diverting the funds into his own account.

The image that Mrs. Loring offered to a willful girl like Margaret was almost extraterrestrial. Women *always* acted with propriety and within the bounds of their prescribed roles. If they did not, society knew how to punish them: they were treated as objects of shame and derision. But here was the general's mistress defiantly transgressing social codes yet exhibiting herself with confidence and wit. She was nothing if not a model of freedom, a woman defiantly crafting her own path through the chaos of the times.

As extraordinary a figure as Mrs. Loring was, however, there were other models of behavior for Margaret to take note of as well in the odd little netherworld of New York under British rule. They provided clues to how a young woman of conviction might move forward in life.

Part of General Howe's strategy in establishing a zone of pleasure in New York had been to lay out a stark contrast with the rebels. The English thought of Americans as dour Puritans; the fact that the Continental Congress had banned public performances in 1774 fed into the idea. If the rebellion co-opted English ideas about liberty, then Howe wanted to offer Americans a counter-narrative: that England represented culture, sophistication, wealth. Mightn't the Americans want to reconsider their revolt and keep themselves aligned with the country that could advance their backward culture?

To this end, one of Howe's first commands on arriving in New York was to reopen the city's single playhouse. The John Street Theatre, which was renamed the Theatre Royal, came back to life in January 1777, and it commenced an explosion of entertainment such as the city had never seen, putting on eighteen plays that year.

Margaret soaked up the culture, and the theater was a focal point during these months. Its plays were staged by British officers, with proceeds going to war widows. Perhaps at her urging, her father signed on as one of the theater's managers. One play that might have especially struck her was called *Polly Honeycombe: A Dramatick Novel of One Act*. It revolved around a smart, headstrong girl and her search for love. The eponymous heroine is addicted to reading novels and chooses to believe that life follows literary conventions. She wants to marry her beloved, but her father chooses someone else for her. She rebels, confident that, as in the stories she reads, after many travails love will conquer. The not especially life-like twist at the end of the plot is that, in fact, love does conquer: Polly squelches her father's plans, and she and her beau live happily ever after.

"Polly" was not a unique figure. The character in the play was part of a swirl of change taking place at the street level in the revolutionary era in which Margaret was coming of age. Individual identity itself was in flux; everyone, in a sense, was trying to figure out who they were. The war was part of the change, but it was also a cause of it. In Britain, an individual had always been defined in relation to the Crown. What were you? Why, a *subject*, of course. Being a British subject meant you had certain rights, but the emphasis was on your subservience to your monarch. Suddenly, the Americans were tearing up that social contract. An individual, in their new reckoning, had obligations to society and to the government, yes; but first and foremost an individual had rights. The individual came first, and the state served him or her.

But what about women? In Britain and America, they were considered not truly individuals but dependents. They were classed together with children and slaves. And yet even for them plays such as *Polly Honeycombe* and flesh-and-blood examples like Elizabeth Loring showed that the rules were changing, or at least that they were being challenged.

Margaret would surely have read herself into the lead role of *Polly Honeycombe* and cast Aaron Burr, whom she refused to forget, as the love she was destined to have. Surely, eventually, somehow, he would come for her. But not long after her return to New York, real life mimicked one of the play's twists. At a social event she met a soldier named John Coghlan. She didn't give him a moment's thought, but later her father informed her the man had asked him for her hand in marriage and he had agreed. The match made sense to Major Moncrieffe. Coghlan's family had money and pedigree: his grandfather had been a member of Parliament, his father had made his fortune in the slave trade. Coghlan himself had previously served in the navy before joining the army. He was twenty-two years old and he presented himself well, as a young man of breeding. The major himself, meanwhile, was uncertain where his own military service would take him next. His son, Margaret's brother, was now installed in a military career. Margaret was very young, but of age to marry, and war often called for irregularities. All in all, this seemed a wise path, and Major Moncrieffe fixed himself to it. Margaret would move out of his care and begin assuming the duties of a wife.

Margaret had a passionate nature, one side of which, her temper, she kept in check around her father. But, like Polly Honeycombe, she refused to accept this fate. She met with John Coghlan and explained to him, delicately, that she had no affection for him. She suggested that "as a man of honor and humanity" he should rescind his offer of marriage. His response was chilling. "He valued not any refusal on my part, so long as he had the Major's consent," she said. "Indeed, my refusal signified nothing." Going back to her father to plead her case, she came to realize that the two men had had lengthy discussions on the matter, in the course of which Coghlan had convinced the major of the rightness of the match. Whereupon Margaret finally unleashed her fury. Her father responded by confining her to her room. When she didn't relent, he took the step of refusing to see her.

Major Moncrieffe's line of reasoning followed standard, respectable and responsible channels. Children submitted to parents just as surely as wives submitted to husbands. A father decided what was best. In this case, he was providing for his daughter's future. He was outraged by Margaret's reaction.

The wall between them was in part generational. Margaret could see it reflected in, for example, family portraits. Her father was in his mid-fifties. In his day a family was always painted with the mother and children seated while the father stood. The man was different, on another plane. Nowadays the fashion was for the whole family to be on the same level.

Margaret's rejection of the idea of forced marriage was likewise a feature of her era, part of the impulse to social change that was rooted in the makeup of the 1770s generation. It was, in fact, related to the way the colonies had rejected the mother country. The force that had impelled men like Washington and Yates to break from England sprang from deep within the individual. Yes, it was based on reason, but Enlightenment thinkers all knew that reason was something that lay within every human being, so that employing reason involved a personal examination. By the 1770s, listening to the inner voice was part of the zeitgeist. Thomas Paine told the readers of *Common Sense* to "examine the passions and feelings," which would reveal the path forward, and to reject whatever felt "forced and unnatural." He was talking about politics, but the same advice was being applied in life. Novels, plays, even newspapers, were alive with stories of people following their inner voices, listening to their feelings, believing they knew which way personal happiness and fulfillment lay, and believing they had a right to those things.

The *Pennsylvania Magazine* had recently published a series of articles about marriage; according to these, in the modern world, a world based on individual reason and individual feeling, men and women should only marry if both felt the proper degree of love and conviction. *Polly Honeycombe* had the same theme, and its message of self-determination was pointed at the very dilemma Margaret now faced. "You may depend on my constancy and affection," Polly tells her lover at the end of the play. "I never read of any Lady's giving up her lover, to submit to the absurd election of her parents. . . ."

The standoff with her father built toward a climax. Margaret stayed locked in her room, holding out as long as she could, feeling "wretched in mind, smarting under the sad reverse, I who had only known the heart-cheering smiles of parental fondness, to become the object of parental anger. . . ." Eventually, her brother returned home for a time and she asked his advice. He told her she had no choice but to submit to her father's wishes.

Finally, she did. She married John Coghlan, against her every wish, convinced she was denying her nature, casting aside the lover who had been meant for her. She felt the man she was marrying was not just wrong for her but fatally so. "My union with Mr. Coghlan," she wrote, "I never considered in any other light, than an honourable prostitution, as I really *hated* the man whom they had compelled me to marry."

"They" were three men: her father, brother, and Coghlan himself. She was caught between two historic forces. There was a new wind blowing, a wind of freedom, and it compelled her to follow her inner voice. Yet social convention, which was ruled by men, was unyielding.

Nature itself seemed caught up in the tension. The wedding bore out her forboding. She had previously known the Reverend Auchmuty, who performed the marriage, and found him a "truly amiable man." During the wedding banquet the Reverend complained of "indisposition." Three days later, in what Margaret felt to be a black premonition, the man was dead.

## Chapter 13

## CANNONS MUSKETS DRUMS

With a few weak signals of incipient New England spring evident outside the window, Venture Smith stood in the cramped, low-ceilinged parlor of Jabez Chapman, justice of the peace of the town of East Haddam, Connecticut. In his hand was one of the few tools he did not feel comfortable wielding: a quill pen. It was March 14, 1777. Margaret Moncrieffe had recently become Margaret Coghlan. George Washington was camped at Morristown, New Jersey, pondering how to attack General Howe's army when it moved out of winter quarters. As far as Smith was concerned, America's war for independence was a distant and inchoate thing. More consequential were the two legal documents before him, which would, he hoped, bring the freedom and security for which he had longed ever since he had been forced from his homeland nearly four decades earlier.

It was more than two years since he had moved here. His new home was a small, rural community, or rather two communities. Haddam sat on the west side of the Connecticut River, East Haddam on the east side. The main thing that had attracted him to this area, besides its being away from the coast and the trouble of the war, was that not one but two rich rivers dominated the landscape: the Connecticut, and the

Salmon River, which flowed into it. All rivers were highways; these two, in addition, were particularly fecund sources of life and income, wriggling with salmon and shad.

Venture Smith had found that the two men he began working for on arrival—Timothy Chapman and Abel Bingham—were both people he could deal with. Chapman, who was born and raised in East Haddam, owned a sawmill, and he came to realize that Smith was an expert at felling trees and handling lumber. Bingham, meanwhile, who had only recently moved to Haddam, owned a large triangular-shaped tract of land right smack between the two rivers, at a place called Haddam Neck, and this was what Smith found himself pondering in those first months. It was wild, thickly timbered and hilly, with a fine fertile meadow. Shortly after his arrival he struck a deal with Bingham to buy some of it.

It was an odd bit of real estate to possess: a thin, rambling strip, too narrow, long and steep to have much agricultural use. But it cost him only 25 pounds, and it was a foothold. A "free Negro," he well knew, had no standing at all in Connecticut. He would have to forge a local identity, and the only path to that, he concluded, was through real estate. The population hereabouts was small, close-knit, conservative, and overwhelmingly white. Yet soon after his arrival he decided he wanted to make the place his home. For the next two years, as he went about his work, Venture hiked his strip of land, as well as Bingham's adjacent larger parcel, studying it. It was darkened by ancient trees whose canopies closed out the sky. Yet as he tramped it, he realized he knew this land. He knew its seasons: bud and shoot, leaf and thistle, wing and hoof. He knew that when autumn came mushrooms, meaty and loamy, would encrust the hillsides and cluster along dead logs. He knew the insects that would bite his flesh, the plant called goldenrod that would shoot up four feet high in late summer, topped with sweet-smelling yellow flowers that made a good tea. He knew the nuts that would plummet down through the leaves. He knew how soft the land would be in summer after a day's sweaty heaving work, and how hard to death it would be most other times.

Most of all he knew the trees, their trunks vaster around than three men could reach, piling themselves hundreds of feet into the air. These he could cut, saw, bite into with his blades. He could send them rocketing groundward, make the earth shudder as if it had feelings. He could strip and hack these trunks, use oxen to haul them downhill to the river, turning the steepness of the land to advantage. The trees were money. They were his future.

For two years, then, he harvested trees from his narrow strip of property and sold his wood, floating it down the Salmon River to Bezaleel Brainerd's sawmill near the East Haddam Landing. He got to know everyone in the area, became financially tangled with them. There was no other way, for in a rural community goods weren't bought and sold for ready money. All transactions were on account. People even settled their taxes in goods, using an official ledger to calculate their payment in grain, wood or meat. When he needed staples, Venture went himself, or sent Meg or his young son Solomon, to Ezra Brainerd's, to pick up leather, candles, beef, cider. Brainerd recorded each purchase, and at the end of the year he agreed with Smith on a means of repayment: so many cords of wood, so many days of labor scything hay. In the same way, he made neighborly connections with Amos White, the cooper, and with James Green, a blacksmith and musket maker. Venture Smith was transactional by nature; he reckoned all his relationships, even with family members, in dollars or pounds. In doing business with local people, calculating the fruits of his labor against theirs, he stitched himself into the community. People began to talk about him, saying that he was as sturdy in his character as in his physical self.

On this day, then, he was ready to make a complex deal, which involved a considerable understanding of the law and the frank goodwill of these two white neighbors. Abel Bingham didn't use the 70 acres that bordered Smith's property, and in fact he was getting ready to leave the area, having signed on as a sergeant in a regiment gathering to join General Horatio Gates's army in its assault on Burgoyne's forces. He was willing to sell the land for 140 pounds. Venture Smith didn't quite have that much money saved. But Timothy Chapman stood ready to assist. Before justice of the peace Jabez Chapman they executed a pair of agreements. In the first, Bingham agreed to sell to "Venture a free negro of Haddam" his plot of land for 140 pounds. In the second, Venture Smith agreed to sell half of this same parcel to Chapman, for 55 pounds. Chapman wasn't actually buying the land. It was a mortgage, a back-country loan, arranged without banks or intermediaries. Chapman's 55 pounds—which Smith would repay later—made it possible for Smith to buy the land that would give him his security.

As they were filling out the papers, they noted a problem. The line for the date on the preprinted form said:

In the _____ Year of the Reign of our Sovereign Lord G E O R G E the Third, of Great Britain.

They crossed out the line and wrote:

In the first year of Independency of American States.

Then Smith, who had never learned to read and write, put an X beside his name. He now owned 80 acres of Connecticut real estate. He was part of the community.

Also in March of 1777, George Germain sat down at his desk in Whitehall and penned a letter to Sir Guy Carleton, the general in charge of British forces in the northern theater. He tried to put to one side his long-standing enmity toward Sir Guy, the fact that his fellow nobleman had questioned his honor in the aftermath of the Battle of Minden. He tried to be delicate. But then delicacy was not really part of his nature.

"With a view of quelling the rebellion as soon as possible," he wrote, "it is become highly necessary that the most speedy junction of the two armies should be effected." It was time to set in motion the master plan: to bring the northern army down the Hudson and the southern army up, strangling the rebellion. However, Germain told Carleton, "the security and good government of Canada absolutely require your presence there." Germain was informing the leading general of the northern army that he would not be part of that army's major action in the war. He was instead being ordered to stay behind and guard the back door. Meanwhile, two other generals would sweep south. Germain instructed Carleton to send them into action. John Burgoyne, with the greater part of Carleton's army, was "to force his way to Albany" and meet up with General Howe's army, while Barry St. Leger, with a smaller force, was "to make a diversion on the Mohawk River." Germain went into detail regarding which companies and detachments would accompany which commander.

Further, he stated that "As this plan cannot advantageously be executed without the assistance of Canadians and Indians, his Majesty strongly recommends it to your care to furnish both expeditions with good and sufficient bodies of those men." Germain was no longer willing to put up with the failure of his generals to engage the Iroquois. He now made it not only his wish but the king's, and he wanted Carleton to see to it. He added a further push for Carleton to get the Indians on board, an attempt at flattery that was almost oily, telling the general, who had often boasted of his deep knowledge of North America and its native peoples, that "your influence amongst them is so great that there can be no room to apprehend you will find it difficult to fulfil his Majesty's expectations."

Carleton was livid when he received the letter. He scratched out a heated reply, declaring to Germain that "from your first entrance into office, you began to prepare the minds of all men" toward his eventual emasculation. He accused Germain of running the war as a means of exercising old grievances, of acting out of "private enmity" toward him. He demanded to be recalled to England, where he could begin to clear his name.

But, good soldier that he was, in the meantime Carleton did everything he was ordered to do for the coming action, including, finally, compelling the Iroquois to join the British cause.

Several weeks later, a messenger arrived at Conawaugus. Cornplanter greeted him and asked his business. The message was that the British government wanted to meet in council with the Senecas and other nations of the Iroquois confederation. The meeting place was to be Oswego, on the banks of Lake Ontario. The villagers discussed the matter and decided they would go. The British were particularly eager for the Senecas to attend, as, traditionally, this westernmost nation, which during the French and Indian War had been closest to the French, geographically and otherwise, was the least inclined of all the Iroquois to side with the British.

It was a long trek—about 100 miles—but a great many Senecas went, including many women, who understood that something important was in the offing and wanted to have their say. Even before they reached the site, they knew the British had chosen an atmospheric location. The name in Iroquois meant "flowing out"; it referred to the spot where the Oswego River emptied into Lake Ontario. Here, atop high bluffs, the British had constructed a fort. They would deliberate while looking out across the endless water of the great lake, beyond which, Cornplanter knew, lay the expanses of forest that were home to the Algonquin and Huron peoples, against whom, generations earlier, Iroquois warriors had fought brutal territorial wars.

The women in particular had been worried that the British might have lured them into a trap of some kind, so there was some fear when British officers in their red uniforms appeared. They seemed friendly, however. And they offered rum. Indeed, there was "a flood of rum," as it seemed to Cornplanter's sixteen-year-old nephew. The British rolled out barrels of it, more than anyone had ever seen. Then came cows, and barrels of flour, and other presents. People were impressed. Was Britain, they wondered, really so great that it could bestow such a plenitude of gifts? For three days the Iroquois relaxed and talked and celebrated with those from distant villages.

On the fourth day, after breakfast, the council began with the British commissioner asking whether all six nations were represented by chiefs. Red Jacket, of the Senecas, answered that all were present but that the Onondagas had not sent a chief. "But we are ready to hear your proceeding," he said.

The commissioner—whose name was not recorded—wove his remarks around the theme of fathers and children. He had been sent, he said, by "the father . . . the King of England" with a subject of "the greatest importance to be communicated to the red bretheren." The Americans, he said, were "children" of England, and they had become disobedient, and needed to be punished. The father, he said, "wants you all, the Six Nations and other Indian nations, to turn out and join with him and give the Americans a dressing and punishment for their disobedience and for violating his laws." The commissioner promised to provide "all the necessary war utensils, guns and powder and lead and tomahawks and sharp edges and provisions and rations." Referring to King George as having a familial authority over the Iroquois, he declared, "Your father offers you to take his axe and tomahawk and hold it against the Americans." Then, apparently holding a blade aloft for drama, he added: "Here is the butcher knife that you will also use to take American locks and scalps. Our father will pay for each scalp."

The council adjourned, and the Iroquois gathered to deliberate. First to speak was the Mohawk Thayendanegea, aka Joseph Brant, who had recently returned from meeting with George Germain and others in London. Brant was about Cornplanter's age and, like him, was not a hereditary chief but had risen to prominence through his leadership in battle. A rivalry of sorts had been developing between the two Iroquois leaders. Just as the Senecas historically had the most distant relationship with the British, the Mohawks, the easternmost nation, had had the closest dealings, first with the Dutch and then with the English. Brant's time in England had convinced him of the country's overwhelming superiority. Philadelphia, the great American city, was a mere village compared to the incomprehensibly vast metropolis of London. The British, he felt certain, would conquer the Americans in this war, and the Iroquois needed to align themselves with the victors. "The king of Great Britain is the father," he proclaimed. If the Iroquois were to do nothing, to appear to be "sleeping" during the fighting, "then woe for all of us because there will be no peace for us." He urged the Iroquois to "take up the offer by the red coat man." After the war, he believed, the British would treat the Iroquois well.

As the emerging leader of the easternmost nation of the confederacy finished, his opposite, Cornplanter of the Senecas, rose. He knew his people well. He knew that young men such as Thayendanegea were eager to prove their manhood. He knew that decisions made out of bravado often led to years of pain and suffering. By now Cornplanter had developed dual reputations, as a fighter and a sage. The people listened carefully to him. "Warriors," he said, "you must all mark and listen.

War is war. Death is death. A fight is a hard business." He reminded everyone of the meeting with the Americans at German Flatts, where General Schuyler had asked them to remain neutral, and they had agreed. He said the affairs between the Americans and British were filled with complications that "we, the Indian nations of several different parts of this continent," simply did not understand, and concluded, "We are liable to make a mistake." He asked that they hear more from the British commissioner. He warned them that they were "very apt to be deceived."

He hadn't even finished before Brant was on his feet again. "Nephew!" he cried at Cornplanter. It might have been an ordinary form of address if they had been of different generations, but since they were close to the same age, it rang as an insult. "Stop speaking! You are a very cowardly man. It is hardly worth taking notice of what you have said. You have shown your cowardice."

There were hundreds of Iroquois at the gathering, and after Cornplanter and Joseph Brant had stated their positions, they quickly fell into two camps, arguing their positions all through the next day.

When the British commissioner reconvened the council, it was with a dramatic flourish: "Brothers, our father in old England loves you as well as the white people, because he believes we are one." He let that sink in, then reiterated: the king's American children were disobedient and he was in the process of disciplining them; he wanted the Iroquois to assist. Then came the kind of coaxing that George Germain had been pushing for. "Come, go along with the father, and he will give you all you want," he said. "Your children and women shall not suffer." The Americans "are poor, and the father is very rich." He exhorted them: "Take up the hatchet and sharp edge and paint against the enemy." He promised to fulfill all their needs: "Eat and drink and ware and money."

Still, after the second session the Iroquois remained divided, and continued to discuss for another day and a half. Then a ship arrived, and it swayed the deliberation. The British soldiers commenced to offload and distribute a procession of gifts. The money that George Germain had earmarked for wooing the Indians had been carefully spent. Each one of the hundreds of Iroquois present received, as one participant recalled, "a suit of clothes, a brass kettle, a gun and tomahawk, a scalping knife, a quantity of powder and lead [and] a piece of gold." There were many other interesting items, such as "jingling bells" and ostritch feathers, which delighted the women and girls. The Iroquois people, Cornplanter's nephew said, "never did see" such quantities of fine goods. Finally, the commissioner produced two ancient belts of wampum, one of twenty rows, which he said represented the old covenant between the Iroquois Confederacy and Great Britain.

The Iroquois regathered. Once again, Cornplanter voiced his opposition to entering the war on either side.

By now, however, Governor Blacksnake believed that the women had been swayed to the British side. They liked the baubles, but they were entranced by the household goods. A brass kettle, they knew, could enrich life for a whole longhouse, an entire extended family, and be passed down to the children and grandchildren. More to the point, however, was the covenant chain, the alliance the Iroquois had made with the British long before. The Iroquois agreed to fight with the British.

Cornplanter rose to speak. He did not believe in the wisdom of entering the fight, but, his people having decided on it, he made plain his intention not only to follow the general will but to lead in this war. He understood that it would be different from all other wars they had engaged in, with greater consequences. This was not about America or Britain. It was about Iroquois freedom, his people and their way of life. Now that they had committed themselves, the Iroquois would have to put everything into the fight. "Every brave man must show himself now," he declared. "Hereafter, we will find many dangerous times.

During the actions of the war we will see many a brave man among the American soldiers we meet. Therefore I say you must stand like a good warrior against your white brother, because as soon as he finds out that you are against him he will show no mercy. I say, therefore, stand your post."

Joseph Brant was pleased. "I suppose our minds are all settled," he said. When they met for the last time with the British commissioner, Brant informed him the Iroquois would "turn out and fight for the king." Then he asked what would be the first objective.

The commissioner thanked the Iroquois and proposed that "we will firstly go to dinner and drink rum and sugar." There followed a night of happy excess. The next day, the commissioner announced the battle plan. First they would attack Fort Stanwix, to the east. After that, they would swing south and wreak terror on rebel strongholds in Pennsylvania's Wyoming Valley. The Iroquois were to be part of the campaign of Barry St. Leger, which George Germain had set in motion as a diversion from the main British force under Burgoyne in the Hudson Valley. But to the Iroquois the commissioner presented the campaign they would participate in as the central fight, a potentially fatal blow. They would rain down lethality and ruin on the American outposts. British soldiers and Iroquois fighters, side by side, would bring blood and suffering. "When we do these things," he said warmly, "the Americans may reconsider and surrender all at once."

Ten o'clock in the morning, June 25, 1777: two men and a dog slipped out of Fort Stanwix for a morning's bird hunt. It wasn't much of a fort. Actually, it wasn't even called Stanwix anymore. The American forces manning it had renamed it Fort Schuyler, after the general in charge of the north. Like Fort Pitt at the Forks of the Ohio, it had been built during the French and Indian War to take advantage of a strategic intersection of waterways. When an advance party of Seneca fighters reached it, what they saw was essentially a ruin. The pickets had rotted away; supporting timbers lay akimbo; a relic of a drawbridge stood devoid of purpose, as the moat that had once existed was no more. There were 550 American militiamen inside, trying to figure out how to make it a defensive structure once again.

The Indians, hidden among the trees, watched the two men head out, saw their rifles, and surmised their task. They let them walk a mile or so from the fort. Then two of them followed.

That afternoon, the search party sent out to look for the men—which was led to the scene by the dog—found both shot, scalped and, for good measure, chunked in the head with tomahawks. Remarkably, one, Captain Gregg, was still alive. The officer in charge of the fort, militia colonel Peter Gansevoort, who was not yet used to war, let alone Iroquois fright tactics, scribbled a frantic note to General Schuyler to let him know that the Iroquois had sided with the British and were massing. Of the man lying before him, caked in gore, he added, "Gregg is perfectly in his senses, and speaks strong and hearty, notwithstanding that his recovery is doubtful."

Colonel Gansevoort was right in thinking the enemy was approaching. As he wrote, 2,000 men, under Barry St. Leger, were marching toward him. About half were Iroquois; the rest included American loyalists, Canadians, and a contingent of German mercenaries. Cornplanter, Joseph Brant and the other Iroquois who had been at Oswego led, walking in five widely spaced columns through woods and meadows. Iroquois fighters also wrapped around to flank the main body of soldiers.

The army arrived at the fort and commenced a siege. Weeks went by; the trapped militiamen ran low on food. They sent out parties to cut down trees to build up the walls of the fort, but even though the parties were accompanied by armed guards, they were attacked by

Iroquois raiders. On August 3, St. Leger sent a messenger into the fort with terms of surrender. They were rejected. Some reinforcements had arrived, emboldening the Americans. With the reinforcements had come news. Eight weeks earlier, the Congress had authorized a flag for the new country. The militiamen tore strips of red, white and blue fabric, stitched them together and raised the hodgepodge on a pole, in what would apparently be the first time the young country's flag would fly in battle.

The initial response to the defiance within the fort came from the Iroquois. Evening fell, and as the light faded from the sky, one officer recorded the sensation of fear that gripped his men: "the Indians, who were at least one thousand in number, spread themselves through the woods, completely encircling the fort, and commenced a terrible yelling, which was continued at intervals the greater part of the night."

Meanwhile, people throughout the county had observed the advance of St. Leger's army toward the fort. At Fort Dayton, 25 miles to the east, a militia leader named Nicholas Herkimer rustled up 800 men to march to its rescue. Ten miles from the destination, near an Oneida village called Oriska, the path through the forest narrowed and crossed a ravine. A group of 400 Iroquois, with Brant in the lead, formed a semicircle around the ravine. They were primed for battle, faces painted, many of them stark naked. Once Herkimer's men had clambered down the banks, the Iroquois closed the circle and let out their warbling cries. Rifle cracks sounded, and the men in the front and rear fell. Herkimer's horse was shot, and as it fell it crushed his leg. Musket balls and arrows whirred. Iroquois fighters charged forward to tomahawk fallen men. Herkimer's soldiers propped him against a tree and from here, despite a wound from which he would later die, he shouted orders. The Americans pulled themselves into a circle and returned fire. But the Iroquois were relentless. Knowing that after a man fired it took at least twenty seconds to reload, they would rush a soldier whose musket had discharged and hack him to death. The ravine was filling with gore. But before the end came, the Americans were saved by a sudden, savage summer storm. For the next hour the rain fell so hard it forced all sides to stop. When the storm ended, the Americans had regrouped, and the fighting began again, now at close quarters. Men lunged at one another with bayonets and spears and the butts of their muskets. Now that they were so close, many of the loyalists and revolutionaries, who were all from the same region, recognized each other—cousins, neighbors, former friends—and the killing and mauling became personal. A scout who returned to the scene several days after the battle found the bodies of "the Indians and white men were mingled with one another, just as they had been left when death had first completed his work." What would later be referred to as one of the bloodiest battles of the American Revolution, both for its savagery and the percentage of casualties, ended inconclusively. The Americans held the fort, which blocked St. Leger from continuing down the Mohawk Valley and meeting up with General Burgoyne. But the Iroquois lost only about 50 men, while a participant at the battle reported that upwards of 500 of the 800 Americans had died.

Eventually, Cornplanter and his Senecas, bodies streaked with blood, made their way back to their camp, carrying the injured. There, they received possibly the biggest shock of the day. While they were ambushing Herkimer's party of reinforcements, men had slipped out of Fort Schuyler, found their camp, and taken everything. The Indians were left with nothing to eat, nothing to sleep on and, since they had stripped for battle, nothing even to cover themselves with. They normally traveled with medicine packs, which, after the hard fight, they had been desperate to get to. These included such things as a concoction of dried and powdered herbs, tree parts and animal hearts, which their healers combined with spittle and applied to gunshot wounds. These were taken; the survivors would have to go without. Maybe most

forboding of all, their charms, the mystic connectors to the supernatural arena, were gone as well. It was surely a foul omen.


Two weeks after the battle, George Washington, huddled in the temporary refuge of a stone farmhouse in Pennsylvania, opened a letter
from Philip Schuyler. The general in command of the north gave him a
lengthy (and largely inaccurate) report about what had transpired near
the fort that had been named after him. He concluded with a seemingly
offhand observation: "General Burgoyne is advanced to Saratoga, seventeen miles from hence."

Washington had been keenly following news of Burgoyne. Mostly,
however, he was obsessing over the thrusts, parries and feints of the
enemy general closer to hand, William Howe. Howe had established
a base in New Brunswick, New Jersey, so Washington had made his
camp in Middlebrook, 10 miles to the east. In late June, Howe abruptly
moved several thousand troops westward, causing Washington to
believe he was marching on Philadelphia, so he alerted the militia in
the area and began to muster his forces. But then Howe's army doubled back and settled in at Amboy. Several days later, the British lines
suddenly pushed forward again, so quickly that this time Washington
thought they were making a charge directly at his camp. But the British
looped back to the same base once again. Washington confessed that
he was "much at a loss to account for these strange Maneuvers," which
were meant to confound him, and did. He spent much of the summer
marching his own army around New Jersey and southeastern Pennsylvania on a series of fruitless pursuits.

Then came yet another surprise: he received word that Howe's entire
army had marched back to Staten Island and from there loaded itself
into ships. Washington was thrown into a different kind of quandary.
Where would his nemesis sail to? He could be making for an invasion

of Philadelphia. But he might also be heading north, to rendezvous with Burgoyne's army. "I am yet perplexed to find out the real intentions of the Enemy," Washington wrote on July 4, the first anniversary of the Declaration of Independence. He tried to cover both eventualities, sending one division northward and keeping the rest of his army, with himself at their head, in the south.

Finally, four weeks later, the British ships were spotted in the Delaware River; Howe, Washington now knew, would move to take Philadelphia. At the same time, with an exercise of great intuitive insight, Washington dismissed the notion that Burgoyne's presence in the north was a mere distraction: "One Reason operates strongly against this, in my opinion, and that is, that a Man of General Burgoyne's Spirit & Enterprize would never have returned from England, merely to execute a plan, from which no great Credit or Honor was to be derived."

Washington was now, in the middle of the hot and complex summer of 1777, faced with a puzzle that stretched the length of the eastern seabord of the new nation. The British had divided themselves into two armies, which necessitated the Americans doing the same. Howe, with the main army, was advancing on Philadelphia, and Washington would have to deal with him in some manner. But what exactly would be Burgoyne's move in the north? And how should the Americans prepare for that threat?

Whatever plans Washington was developing on the matter were thrown into confusion when he learned that Congress had decided to remove General Schuyler as commander in the north and replace him with Horatio Gates. Schuyler had been taking steps against what he expected would be a major push southward by Burgoyne. But he had enemies in Congress. The feelings there were partly related to his being an aristocratic New Yorker of Dutch background: all characteristics that alienated him to the New Englanders. When, without so much as a fight, Burgoyne's army took Fort Ticonderoga, 100 miles north of Albany, blame fell on Schuyler.

Washington had had a comfortable rapport with Schuyler. The Virginian and the Dutch New Yorker were alike in their sensibilities, their belief in the nobless oblige of the gentry, their sense that members of their class were the natural leaders of the rebellion. They spoke the same language. Washington had an entirely different relationship with the blustery and bawdy Gates. They had known each other for more than twenty years. Their careers had followed parallel trajectories, but Gates's had been the path that was denied to Washington. Gates, an Englishman by birth, had risen as a commissioned officer in the British army. He had served alongside Washington on Braddock's march to the Forks of the Ohio, and had fought with him against the French on that fateful day in 1755. Eventually, he had left the British army, bought a large tract of land in the Shenandoah Valley and moved there in 1772. When the war broke out—he had actually been a guest of Washington's at Mount Vernon when news of the clashes at Lexington and Concord reached there—he joined the American cause.

For all the familiarity he had with Washington, Gates didn't think the Virginian was up to the job he had been given. Washington's vacillations and missteps on the battlefield seemed to bear out what Gates feared, and fueled the campaign he undertook to be named as Washington's replacement. Tensions between the two men had first come to the surface in May. Gates was at the time serving under Schuyler in the Northern Army. He complained to the commander in chief that, in denying a shipment of tents for the troops in the north, Washington had favored his own army in the south. Gates accused him of "saying This Army has not the same Necessities, or does not require the same Comforts, as the Southern Armies. . . ." Gates's very bluntness expressed, at the level of manners, the differences between the two men. Washington was appalled at the tone of the man's letter. He wrote back stiffly, "I cannot help taking notice of some expressions in your letter," and assured Gates that the northern army was "as much the object of my Care and Attention as the one immediately under my command."

In June, Washington got a letter from John Hancock about routine matters the Congress was dealing with. It was the postscript that must have unnerved him: "Genl Gates is here; I hope he will soon be establish'd in a Command equal to his Merit." Gates, it seemed, was in Philadelphia, personally and nakedly promoting his ambition.

By the time Gates got the commission to replace Schuyler, in early August, Burgoyne's plans were set: he would march southward, using the Hudson River as a means to cleave the colonies in two. But so too was the elaborate defense that Schuyler had prepared. Gates, in effect, inherited the plan, and was poised to accept praise if things went well for the Americans and to deflect blame onto Schuyler if they did not.

The situation in the north bedeviled Washington. While he now had to concentrate all his attention on Howe, Gates, with his ambition to replace him, was ever-present in his mind.

Howe, meanwhile, had undertaken an exotic maneuver with his vast floating army, landing his troops well south of Philadelphia and marching overland to invade the city. In doing so, he seemed to be trying to lure Washington into a classical battle, to be fought in matched columns. And, despite having recognized repeatedly that his chances were better in nontraditional combat, Washington took the bait. Gates may have been part of his calculation. In his worry about being removed from command, yet again he succumbed to the idea that greater honor came from traditional battle, from executing "one bold stroke."

So he fought. On September 11, with the air still heavy with late-summer heat, Washington lined up his army—14,000 strong—against Howe's 15,000 better-equipped men, at a place called Brandywine Creek. He intended to use the natural barrier of what was less a creek than a river to help block the British advance to Philadelphia. He compounded the error of submitting to a straight-ahead battle by committing an even less forgivable one: not fully familiarizing himself with his own terrain. He was unaware that a simple ford of the river existed to the north. Howe's scouts found it, and it allowed Howe to stage a trap. He sent 5,000 men headlong at the American center, with enough murderous drive to convince Washington that it was the main force, while the actual main body of troops swung around to the north. All morning and well into the afternoon the Americans fought, with Washington visible high atop his horse, encouraging his men toward what he hoped would be a smashing victory. Then, at four in the afternoon, he realized how thoroughly he had been fooled. A thunder of artillery fire signaled the entrance onto the battlefield of the main part of the British army. The Americans were stunned as they pivoted and met the onslaught. The firing of the British muskets was so thick that branches and twigs snapped in the trees overhead; to one soldier the falling leaves made it seem like autumn. As the British lines plunged forward, they crashed fully into the Americans, and a melee of hacking and stabbing ensued. An American private recorded the gory death match with semiliterate impressionism in his diary: "Cannons Roaring muskets Cracking Drums Beating Bumbs Flying all Round, men a dying wounneds Horred Grones which would Greave the Heardiest of Hearts to See Such a manner as this."

Late that evening, an exhausted Washington dictated a letter to John Hancock. "Sir," he began, "I am sorry to inform you that in this day's engagement we have been obliged to leave the enemy masters of the field." Mindful that Gates might upstage him in the northern theater, he tried as best he could to spin the terrific loss to his advantage. Rather than accept responsibility for failing to reconnoiter the area, he blamed his error on "intelligence."

Nevertheless, members of Congress and the press began to openly question Washington's leadership. Many would have agreed with a young colonel who fought under Washington at Brandywine, who said that prior to entering his service "I had an exalted opinion of General Washington's military talents," but that after the battle "my opinion was exceedingly lowered."

Howe's troops marched into Philadelphia on September 26. Congress had fled so rapidly that members hurriedly packed up what things they could and rushed out into the night, eventually reconvening 100 miles west, in the village of York. Meanwhile, on learning that Howe had divided his army in two, with one part camped in the city of Philadelphia and the other on the outskirts at Germantown, Washington, truly desperate for a victory, decided to make a surprise lunge at the forces in Germantown. He had his men swarm the village at dawn from four directions. The British were indeed surprised that the Americans would launch an attack so soon after their defeat. But Howe had picked the location for its defensibility, and Washington hadn't accounted for the dense early morning fog that lay over wheat fields and cobbled streets, confusing his men as they tried to execute his overly intricate plan of battle. The fight was short but intense; the result was not what he had hoped. "Upon the whole, it may be said the day was rather unfortunate, than injurious," he reported to John Hancock. Still, 150 more of his men had given up their lives in trying to get him a victory. He was now doubly conscious of the need to protect his reputation, and he stressed to the president of the Congress that the decision to attack was not his alone but rather involved "my Genl Officers, who were unanimously of Opinion, that a favourable Opportunity offered to make an Attack. . . ."

While Washington's army was recuperating from its back-to-back losses, stupendous news came from the north. Gates had defeated Burgoyne's army on the banks of the Hudson. Burgoyne had begun his advance down the Hudson River valley. On taking over, Gates found that Schuyler's troops had nicely prepared the landscape, felling trees and blowing up bridges, to make it more difficult for an army to move through. Meanwhile, throughout the summer, as Burgoyne had waited for reinforcements, more and more militiamen had streamed into the American headquarters, swelling the rebel force to more than 9,000 men. Gates had at his disposal a brilliant Polish military engineer named Tadeusz Kosciuszko, who chose the place from which the Americans would make their stand. About 30 miles north of Albany the land rose into a bluff known as Bemis Heights. From here, cannons could reach both the river and the road that ran along it, so that whichever way the British tried to advance they would be at the mercy of the American guns. Burgoyne tried to outmaneuver by splitting his army into three columns. But by using the terrain to his advantage, as Washington had not, Gates trounced the British general. At Saratoga, on October 17, Burgoyne surrendered his army to Gates. One by one, as gawping rows of American troops looked on, 5,895 soldiers laid their muskets on stacks and gave themselves up.

As Washington knew would happen, Gates was lauded as the hero of the battle: indeed, the hero of the American army. Rather than be magnanimous, Gates expressed his animosity toward Washington by sending word of his victory to Congress and to two other generals but not to the general who was his commander in chief. In his general orders to his own troops, Washington took the proper step of formally lauding the success, but he did not highlight Gates's role, choosing instead to congratulate "the army, on the success of the American Arms, at the northward." He also ordered, in celebration, a gill of rum for each of his men and a 13-gun salute.

Gates crowed. He was convinced the victory at Saratoga was all his and that it was decisive. "Burgoyne and his whole army have laid down their arms, and surrendered themselves to me and my Yankees," he trumpeted to his wife, and went on to add, "If Old England is not by this lesson taught humility, then she is an obstinate old Slut, bent upon her ruin." Certain men in Congress and in the army now actively plotted for Washington to be sacked and Gates installed in his place. "Look at the characters of both!" Benjamin Rush declared to John Adams, referring to Gates and Washington. "The one on the pinnacle of military glory—exulting in the success of schemes planned with wisdom, & executed with vigor and bravery. . . . See the other outgenerald and twice beated . . . forced to give up a city the capital of a state and After all outwitted by the same Army in a retreat."

Rush was one of the members of a cabal—which seemed to be led by Thomas Conway, a general on Washington's staff—intent on removing the commander in chief from power. Washington's friends warned him of the plot. He was at the moment dealing with funding problems, with trying to find winter quarters for his army and weapons and supplies for recently arrived recruits, and perhaps most of all with the state of his men's feet: "Our distress for want of Shoes & stockings is amazingly great," he lamented, so much so that many soldiers were unable to walk, let alone fight. The fact that some leaders were plotting to unseat him shouldn't have been surprising, but it exasperated him, apparently to the point of considering resigning. "I have been a slave to the service," he complained to Richard Henry Lee, a fellow Virginian. "I have undergone more than most men are aware of, to harmonize so many discordant parts but it will be impossible for me to be of any further survice if such insuperable difficulties are thrown in my way."

He decided to confront the apparent conspirators directly. He wrote a letter to Conway that consisted only of a quoted sentence from one of Conway's letters to Gates, referring to Washington as—and the phrase must have echoed in his brain—"a weak general." The letter's terseness, its utter lack of commentary, made it a particularly icy way of informing a man who was currently in his service that he was aware of his machinations. He signed off with a curt, "I am Sir Yr Hble Servt." He also wrote to Gates.

He hoped to have thus quelled the plot. However, in November,

Congress named Gates to a new position, president of the Board of War, which technically put him above Washington. And Gates's resounding victory at Saratoga continued to resonate in the increasingly chilly autumn air. It was being sung about, recounted around blazing hearths in taverns. It thrilled Americans with hope, even as it caused George Washington the gravest concern.


Perhaps the most talked-about event in London during the summer of 1777 was the case of William Dodd, a popular clergyman whose taste for the good life led him to spend beyond his means. Desperate to get out of debt, he committed forgery and got caught. When a wildly excessive sentence of death was pronounced, the case catapulted to the level of an outright sensation. Samuel Johnson himself took up the parson's cause, penning an essay under Dodd's name that appeared while the clergyman languished on death row. When pressed to confess his authorship, with the claim that Dodd did not have the literary powers to write it, Johnson remarked (in a turn of phrase that would become an enduring part of the language), "Depend upon it, Sir, when a man knows he is to be hanged in a fortnight, it concentrates his mind wonderfully." The essay was to no avail, and Dodd's public hanging shocked the nation.

There was, of course, much else to occupy Londoners that summer. The carpenter John Harrison, who had recently died, was being memorialized for his invention of a device for determining longitude at sea, which would save mariners from being lost. There were new books published about the wonders of electricity and about "diseases peculiar to women."

And there was the ongoing saga of the American war. The news had been mostly favorable of late, with accounts of Howe, the wily old general, outwitting Washington on his own turf. But the government's finances were dire, and many continued to question the wisdom of it. One commentator gloomily compared the state of affairs in England with that in other European nations: "In France, the minister is reducing taxes. . . . In Holland, the Dutch are augmenting their navies, increasing their trade. . . . In Russia, the empress leaves no stone unturned to promote manufactures and trade . . ." while "In poor Old England, the minister is intent to find out articles that will bear fresh taxation, to support a war against her once best friends, at a time when she is least able to support it." There was the sense that one note of sour news from America would swing the pendulum of public opinion sharply to the negative.

For much of the summer Lord George Germain had reason to bustle about Whitehall with a cheery disposition. His generals were doing their job. Soon, surely, would come news that the armies of the north and south had converged to execute his grand strategy. Roman severity was being brought to bear on the Americans.

Then, in September, came a confusing sequence of reports. General Howe had packed his men into ships and seemingly vanished. They had not sailed north. "The Howes are gone the Lord knows wither," Horace Walpole wrote. Germain was among the most perplexed, for he had given Howe orders to move northward. In fact, it was Howe's own idea to divert from the master plan and move on Philadelphia, and to do it by sea. He was banking on intelligence that Pennsylvania seethed with loyalists who were eager to join the conquering army, as well as on the notion that taking the capital would demoralize the rebels.

Germain updated King George, putting a positive shine on things: "The progress of General Burgoyne is as rapid as could be expected, and the difficulties he has surmounted do him great honor." Germain also told the king, however, that he had received a letter from Burgoyne in which "he complain'd of not hearing from Sir. W. Howe, or of not knowing anything of his operations. He had dispatched Ten Messengers to New Yorke, and not one of them had returned." A few days later, Germain, who was beginning to fear for the strategy he had devised, insisted to a colleague that if Howe did not head north to complete the strangulation of the colonies it would be "the more honour to Burgoyne if he does the business without any assistance from New York." Privately, though, Germain was worried that Howe had gone off mission.

Finally, in October, a dispatch from Howe arrived. Germain tore it open and learned that his general had altered his plans and "intended for the recovery of the province of Pensilvania," with the thought that after doing so he would head north to meet Burgoyne. But where Howe had hoped for a friendly reception, he had been "greatly impeded by the prevailing disposition of the inhabitants, strongly in enmity against us; many having taken up arms, and by far the greater number deserted their dwellings, driving off at the same time their stock of cattle and horses." He was forced to acknowledge that he would not be able to meet the northern army.

This was a blow. It may have felt like a premonition, for there was worse to come. At the beginning of December, Germain received a letter that had been written on October 20, at the Albany mansion of Philip Schuyler, where General John Burgoyne had been invited to stay after relinquishing his army. Rumors had trickled into London over the past few days, but now Germain absorbed the letter's contents with growing incredulity: Indians had proven unfaithful allies. Many American loyalists had deserted the army. There was the heat, the trudging across difficult forest countryside. The letter was a catalogue of explanations for Burgoyne's failure, for his having—surrendered his entire army. *Surrendered his entire army.* The general took pains to note that he had won favorable terms: his men would not be imprisoned but shipped back to England, once they swore never again to take up arms in America.

Germain's workday came to a halt. His world came to a halt. Outside the window, London was in its usual bustle of church bells and horse-clop. But, something like two months earlier, somewhere in the wilds of North America, an entire British army had surrendered. Had such a thing ever happened before in all of English history? So much blood and treasure wasted. The strategy that he had engineered for subduing Britain's rebellious colonies was undone.

On December 3, Germain dressed himself with his usual grim dignity, gathered his sheafs of documents, and, together with the prime minister, Lord North, marched into the chilly, echoing chamber of the Houses of Parliament. There was a regularly scheduled debate on military matters, involving questions and answers concerning the numbers of soldiers in various places. He waited until he was pointedly asked whether there was any news of Burgoyne. He rose. He said that, indeed, he had received news. He spoke plainly: a bloodless recital of facts. ". . . General Burgoyne and his army were surrounded by a force greatly superior—cut off from fresh supplies of provisions, and unable to pierce through the numbers of the enemy, so situated, he had been forced to capitulate, and had surrendered himself and his army prisoners, on condition that they should engage not to serve during the war in America. . . ." The loss of Burgoyne's army, he told the chamber, "was a most unfortunate affair." But, he said, he hoped the House would "not be over anxious in condemnation," and he hoped the members would "suspend their judgments both on the conduct of the general and of the minister."

An uncharacteristic silence seems to have fallen over the chamber at the conclusion of his statement, expressed in such calmness and coming in response to a routine question. Then Colonel Isaac Barré, one of Germain's steadiest foes, rose. He declared himself "shocked at the easy manner" in which Germain related the fate of "the brave Burgoyne." And he was even more shocked that Germain would attempt to deflect blame for the sorry affair away from himself by insinuating that the House might point the finger at the general. It was clear that "the man who planned the expedition was to blame. The minister alone who concerted the scheme, was obnoxious to reprehension for its failure. It was an inconsistent scheme, an impracticable one, unworthy of a British minister, and rather too absurd for an Indian chief."

Then Barré felt the need to back up to earlier debates, when Germain had first presented his strategy to the House. He asked his colleagues to "remember how frequently, how earnestly, how sincerely, I have warned the minister of the effects of this plan." And to Germain he fairly spat: "I foresaw the consequences. I foretold the event." Letting his emotions unfurl as the information Germain had imparted sunk in, Barré went on: "Does the noble lord know the extent of his criminality? Does he know the resentments of this House? I believe he knows neither."

Another Whig member, James Luttrell, rose, and used the occasion to question the very notion of waging war against the Americans. "The Americans, it is evident, will not give up their liberties, they will die first," he proclaimed. General Howe, the overall commander of British forces in North America, he went on, with his great army, his ships and supplies, had all he needed to defeat the Americans, except for one thing: "I mean a just cause." The Americans, he declared, had right on their side. He reached back to the thirteenth century, the time when Englishmen had won a list of individual rights from King John: "our Magna Charta was obtained by men so resolved; and the Americans have not proved themselves less deserving of their liberties, than those Britons. An American Magna Charta is what they wisely contend for; not a Magna Charta to be taxed by strangers, a thousand leagues distant."

All the Whigs were lining up to speak now. Edmund Burke took the floor. He thanked his colleagues who had spoken first, which gave him "some time to calm the tumult and perturbation" in his breast. Then he pondered aloud: "A whole army compelled to lay down their arms, and receive laws from their enemies," he said, was "a matter so new" that he could not think of another such instance in the whole of English history. And yet, he had to reflect on the manner in which this surrender was handled. The Americans, he said, had repeatedly been characterized by the ministry as cowards, as backwards, as morally inferior to Englishmen. But consider the conduct of the Americans who defeated Burgoyne. "Our army was totally at their mercy. We had employed the savages to butcher them, their wives, their aged parents, and their children. And yet, generous to the last degree, they gave our men leave to depart on their parole, never more to bear arms against North America."

Charles James Fox spoke next, and he took aim directly at Germain. "An army of 10,000 men destroyed through the obstinate, wilful ignorance, and incapacity of the noble lord," he cried, "called loudly for vengeance." He demanded an inquiry.

On and on it went, with one opposition member after another denouncing both Germain and the war. Germain listened. He had no choice. He stood like a colossus, seemingly fancying himself, as he weathered the attacks, as the last pillar holding up the edifice of the British Empire, defender of the notion that colonies were dependents, which had obligations to the home country. He was motivated, he said, by "the supreme authority of Parliament over the colonies."

Eventually, Lord North was called on. "As to the noble lord in the American Department," the prime minister said, he believed that he had "acted on the soundest principles of candour and deliberation." But his backing of Germain was not quite wholehearted. He had been in favor of going to war over the matter of taxation, but, he said, he had been "dragged" into what had been his own government's policy "against his will." He didn't explicitly say who had dragged him, but there weren't many candidates.

The staggering news of the Battle of Saratoga became public. The stock market plummeted. The criticism expanded and became more personal. It was Minden all over again. George Germain, his enemies claimed, who had nearly been executed for treason at the infamous battle during the now long-ago Seven Years' War, had used the American rebellion as a means of achieving personal redemption. He had manipulated generals, whole armies, as if they were pieces on a game board. He had been ruthless in his zeal, Charles Fox asserted, employing "the most violent, scalping, tomahawk measures" against the Americans. And now: disaster. Lord George Germain, Fox declared, was "solely responsible in the first degree."

As December wore on, more bad news came. Howe wrote from Pennsylvania, asking permission to resign his command. Burgoyne was gathering documents and preparing a defense of his behavior, in which he would certainly point blame at the American Secretary.

Then, on January 15, Diana, Germain's wife of twenty-three years, died after an attack of measles. She had stood by him in his early days, through the universal public disgrace of the Minden trial, when it had appeared that his career was over before it had even begun. Her last days had been robbed of solace by this new disgrace. Her death was a primal loss to him, and also a bracket. It gave definition to his life. It put everything in context: his childhood at Knole, his loping years as a proud warrior on the Continent, the tenacious period of rebuilding his public persona, culminating with the commission to save Britain's greatest prize, her American colonies. Diana's death very neatly set all of it in a category: "the past."

Nine days after her death, Germain turned sixty-two years of age. He believed he had truly done his best in his capacity as American Secretary, acting not out of personal motivations but with regard to his notion of the law and of Britain herself. He had tried with all his might to be a good steward of empire.

He picked up a pen and wrote his colleague, William Knox, that he was ready to leave office, saying that "if my being permitted to retire answers any publick end, I shall rejoice in having proposed it. A man at my time of life, depress'd by misfortune, will make a bad figure in an office that requires vigor of mind, activity and diligence."

The king, on hearing that his American Secretary would offer his resignation, was elated, calling it "a most favourable event," for, as he noted, Germain "has so many enemies." His Majesty had been trying to figure out how to remove him without causing too much of a stir. "Now," the king remarked, "he will save us all the trouble."

———⧜———

## Chapter 14

# WHITE FREEDOM

J ohn Coghlan left his wife shortly after he had all but forced her to marry him. He was a soldier, after all, and his regiment was sent off to New Jersey, to take part in a series of raids meant to harass George Washington's army.

Just like that, then, Margaret Moncrieffe—who was now Margaret Coghlan—was free again. She settled into life more or less as it had been: with her father and other families of the regiment, which was now stationed on Long Island. The year 1777 wore on and news came in. They learned of the battle near the Oneida village of Oriska, at which, in alliance with the British, Cornplanter led Senecas in one of the bloodiest assaults of the war. Margaret was surely pleased to hear that George Washington, who had been so condescending to her, had been outwitted at Brandywine Creek by General Howe.

Then, as she was sitting one evening with her father, the door opened and in walked her husband. She had not gotten a single letter from him in all the months he had been gone, so she had allowed herself to believe he might not return. She froze. Her father, however, welcomed his son-in-law and got ready to hear of his exploits. But while Coghlan did indeed have news, he didn't want to talk about the war. In fact, he was done with it. He announced that he had sold his officer's commission and planned to sail at once for England. His wife would come with him.

Things happened terribly fast now. A military convoy would leave in a month, and they would sail with it. Where to? To what kind of new life? Margaret got little information, only that her husband was done with the military and looking forward to getting home. In the meantime, Coghlan took temporary lodgings in New York and Margaret went with him. Now that the two of them were alone together, Coghlan began revealing more of himself, and she liked him even less. He took her to nightclubs that soldiers frequented. He introduced her to prostitutes, with whom he was clearly on familiar terms. When she asked how his father—a respected merchant—felt about his decision to leave the army, he freely admitted that the old man disapproved. To be a commissioned officer in the army was to possess a certain status in the empire. Selling one's commission, as if it were a mere commodity, while legal, was tawdry, and his leaving the service in the midst of war was not a step that would reflect well on Coghlan Senior.

But John Coghlan had had enough of the military life. His career had begun, against his will, in 1772, when his father had gotten him a commission in the British navy and arranged to have him serve as midshipman to his friend, Captain James Cook. His first assignment was aboard the *Resolution*, taking part in Cook's second attempt to circumnavigate the globe. It was a grand and historic mission, and serving under the great commander might have been an honor for most sailors, but though Coghlan was still a teenager he showed himself to be unruly. Twice at sea he was punished for fighting; once, as they were nearing the Cape of Good Hope, he pulled a knife on the cook. A shipmate described him as "wild & drinking." After the ship's return to England in the summer of 1775, his father, still committed to taming the boy, bought him his commission into the army and shipped him off to America. He had thus spent his early adulthood battling first Antarctic ice and then American rebels, neither of which he gave a damn about. Now he had gotten free. He was twenty-three years old, and he was determined to start enjoying himself.

On February 8, 1778, Margaret said farewell to her father, and to America, and boarded a ship in New York Harbor that was bound for Cork. She was leaving all that she knew, and the only person she had for company was the man she considered her captor. The weather was icy as the ship set sail, but she was suffering less from cold than from fear. And the war she was leaving behind, a historic conflict that had comprehensively upended her life, was the least of her worries.

On the day Margaret Coghlan's ship was sailing out of New York Harbor, George Washington was making disciplinary decisions. A Lieutenant Grey, who had sneaked out of camp and committed theft— "behavior unbecoming the character of an officer and gentleman," in Washington's estimation—was sentenced to "have his sword broke over his head." Thomas Butler, a civilian found guilty of attempting to carry flour into Philadephia to sell to the enemy army, was to receive 250 lashes. Another civilian who was caught hauling "eight quarters of mutton and a bull beef" to the enemy was fined 50 pounds and locked up.

Washington was staying in the stone farmhouse of a miller named Isaac Potts, along the Schuylkill River in southeastern Pennsylvania. There was an iron forge nearby, so the place was called Valley Forge. Stepping outside, he could see the rows of wooden huts that housed his army. It all looked rather orderly now, but it had been a hellish winter. With Howe's army in Philadelphia, Washington had had to find a place outside the city to sustain his men. He marched them up to this plateau, which he figured would be a good vantage point. Just getting here was hard work, given the pitiable state of the army. One-third of the men were shoeless; the sight of bloody footprints in the snow filled him with anger at the way Congress had mismanaged military procurement. A sleety winter set in. His men slept on the frozen ground until they got the huts built. Supplies dwindled and they were reduced to eating "fire cakes" made of flour and water. Yet they submitted to his drilling, and as they took on more and more the aspect of a professional fighting force, they complained less and less, and he found himself overcome with emotion, thrilling in his heart at the feeling that he was becoming one with them.

As he worked the army, he developed a professional staff, and, as with the army as a whole, he found his heart opening up to some of the officers who served him so fervently. He had become skilled at spotting talent and binding smart young men to him. Five months earlier, as the army was preparing to attack Howe at Brandywine Creek, an outrageously foppish twenty-year-old French aristocrat named Gilbert du Motier rode improbably into their midst, requesting a commission. Like many other ardent young Frenchmen of his generation, he had become intoxicated by Enlightenment ideas of individual freedom. Unlike most, he was fabulously wealthy, and had purchased a ship in order to sail to America to participate in its war of independence. Washington liked him. The Marquis de Lafayette, as he was titled, had substance in his character to go with his enthusiasm. He had had some military training in Europe, and showed himself ready to learn. He wasn't in the least put off by the dismal state of the Continental Army. Washington assigned him to a division, and he got shot in the leg in the loss at Brandywine Creek, but the injury only bound him all the more to the cause. Washington for his part was disarmed by the combination of the young man's aristocratic bearing and his utter personal devotion to him. Lafayette's father had died when he was only two; not long after entering Washington's army, he was likening himself to the general's son. And Washington, who had never had a son of his own, seemed surprised by the feelings that opened up inside him toward the young Frenchman, the heat of war having melted some of the aristocratic reserve in his nature. Despite his precious upbringing, Lafayette rode headlong into the muddy countryside, and proved capable at recoinnoitering the enemy and gathering intelligence. By now, February 1778, he was a fixture.

Washington had also recently brought onto his staff a short, slender, fox-like young officer named Alexander Hamilton. Hamilton was about the same age as Lafayette, and equally as smart and resourceful. Washington was communicating daily with the Congress, with generals scattered all over the country, with members of the various state legislatures and a long train of miscellaneous others; he desperately needed someone to help him deal with correspondence. Hamilton, who had performed valiantly in battles in New York, took the job of aide-de-camp, and quickly became the general's right arm. Like Lafayette, he was tireless in his will to learn and serve, but where the French aristocrat was able to give Washington his heart and soul, Hamilton, who had been born illegitimately on the island of Nevis in the Caribbean and was determined to pull himself up from his hard early life, had too much pride to fawn over the commander in chief. Washington didn't care. "Hamilton has informed me . . ."; "I have sent Colo. Hamilton . . ."; "Colo. Hamilton, one of my Aids, is up the North River doing all he can . . .": Washington had found an aide whose meticulousness, intelligence and zeal made him indispensable.

As Washington waited out the winter at Valley Forge, several men from Haddam, Connecticut, where Venture Smith had settled, were heading off to join the cause, to serve under him or General Gates. Despite Washington's own misgivings, free Africans had been serving in the Continental Army in one capacity or another since 1775, but Smith had never seen that as his path. He had other things on his mind. He was rooting himself. He had bought land. Now he needed to build a house.

He chose a location on the eastern edge of his tract, just up the bank from the languorous Salmon River Cove. The house would look out on the one flat piece of his otherwise steeply sloping land, which would be his farm. And so he began. He was a big man and he wanted his house to be nice and roomy, so he measured it out amply: 36 feet by 20. He dug a foundation, built a central chimney out of stone. He erected the walls with his own wood. After thinking deeply about the exact location of the house, he had made an idiosyncratic decision, to build it into a hillside, which gave protection from winter winds. The finished home had three levels: a main floor, an attic and a cellar. Because he had tucked the house against the hillside, the upper room, which he called his office, had its own door that opened onto a path at the top of the hill, while the door from the main room opened at a lower level, facing his farmland. He didn't build stairs: you reached the upper floor and the cellar via ladders. When the house was finished, he began work on other structures: a barn, a forge for blacksmithing and a wharf on the cove.

In some ways, the home of Venture and Meg Smith was like that of white inhabitants of Haddam. But there were differences. There were no crucifixes, Bibles or other indications of affiliation to a Christian church: unlike virtually all whites, the Smiths were not part of a congregation. And after Venture Smith finished his house, he buried rock crystals near the doorways and windows, apparently holding in his memory a similar practice from his African childhood, based on a belief that it would ward off evil and lead to good fortune. Other Africans in the area became regular visitors. Smith began referring to them as "my countrymen." In all his years as a slave, and then as a free man working to buy his family's freedom, he had been focused on matters at hand. Now that he was living on his own land, in a place he had chosen, he had freedom to begin rebuilding his African identity.

As soon as he had bought his parcel from Abel Bingham, Smith turned his attention to the property on the other side of him. The owner was willing to sell. Smith had put all his savings into the parcel he had just purchased, and in doing so had put himself in debt to Timothy Chapman, but he wanted this additional land, and he wanted it now. He turned to another white friend. Stephen Knowlton was about the same age, born in East Haddam, and had recently done a stint of service in the local militia. He and Smith formed enough of a bond that Knowlton agreed to buy the 48-acre lot jointly with Smith. He put up the 250 pounds, in what was in effect a loan; Smith later bought him out.

Venture Smith now owned 128 acres: more land than most well-to-do white Connecticut farmers possessed. He was building boats, harvesting trees, planting crops. And, having established himself as a presence in the small black community, he began forging a settlement. One of his friends, a thirty-year-old man named Whacket, was slave to a local man, Daniel Brainerd. Brainerd died, and freed Whacket in his will. But if Whacket showed up at Smith's house one day to celebrate, he also had something to bemoan, for his girlfrend, Base, who was also slave to Brainerd, had not been freed in the will but remained the property of Brainerd's widow. Meanwhile, another "free Negro of Haddam" named Peter Freeman, who was about twenty, wanted to marry a girl named Peg, but had no house or property on which to begin a life with her.

Venture Smith solved the puzzle for these young people. Whacket bought Base out of slavery, then Whacket and Base and Peter Freeman and Peg got married at a double wedding in East Haddam. Two months later, in July 1777, Venture Smith offered 12 acres of his land to the two couples. They purchased it for 66 pounds, which they would pay in labor, built homes and moved in. As an indication of Smith's role in this intricate affair, and of the esteem he had built up, the deed was witnessed by Dyar Throop, East Haddam's most prominent attorney and its representative to the State Assembly, as well as Throop's wife.

Smith became a source of stability to Africans in the area.

In December of the same year, a man named Sawney Anderson asked him to buy his freedom. Smith obliged. He bought him for 40 pounds, plus 10 bushels of corn and 10 bushels of rye, whereupon Anderson and his wife, Susannah (who was a free woman), and their four children seem to have taken up residence as well on Smith's property. For the next ten months, until Anderson had worked off the purchase price, he was technically Smith's slave. When both men were satisfied that the terms of their financial arrangement had been met, Smith formally freed him. Dyar Throop, the assemblyman, witnessed the manumission.

The black population of East Haddam in the 1770s totaled only 65 individuals. By the spring of 1778, 14 of them lived on or next to Venture Smith's property. He was a man of means and standing. Physically too he was a presence: people nowadays described him as six feet tall and six feet around; they liked to tell stories of his feats of strength. Some noted that when he paid a visit he had to turn sideways to fit through the narrow doorways of village homes. And for all his seriousness, his inexorable work ethic, he had a playful side. On visiting an acquaintance, he was known to get down on his knees and chase the children around the house.

In a sense, Venture Smith, as he turned fifty, had achieved the New England equivalent of George Washington's ambition of becoming a gentleman planter. Like Washington at Mount Vernon, he was a provider and protector. A visitor to either man's estate would have seen a well-ordered property, with black folks working the land. But the blacks on Smith's property were free.

Abraham Yates was feeling lost. He was temporarily residing in Kingston, where the New York State Assembly was meeting. His wife, Anna, had come with him, but he had brought only a few possessions. He missed his books. Most of all, he missed his maps. News of the war flowed in from every direction, including field reports from Washington's aide-de-camp, Alexander Hamilton. He was a self-taught shoemaker whose life had been confined to a small area of upstate New York and the surrounding region. How was he to make sense of what was happening in distant places without his maps?

To his great good fortune, he had engaged a capital assistant, who remained behind at Albany taking care of all his needs. Matthew Visscher was twenty-six years old, a lawyer who, like Yates, had grown up in a Dutch-speaking household. He was eager and capable, and burned with revolutionary fire. He loaded two barrels of Yates's books and papers onto a sloop, and sent with them, as he wrote Yates, "your Maps and Globes." Visscher was also looking after the shop: "I have sold the Hogshead of Wine to Dr. Potts at 60/ p Gallon, he has forty Gallons of it, and there is about seven left: which he will fetch to day." All of this gave Yates some pleasure, but he was upset by Visscher's description of the chaos in Albany: "You cannot conceive the distresses I daily am obliged to be a Spectator of—Boats loaded with Women & Children, hardly bedding with them, and no provisions or Money to buy it—large droves of Cattle Sheep &ca going thro the Town."

Meanwhile, the state constitution Yates had worked so hard to complete now had to be heeded. It called for the election of statewide officials. Setting up the mechanism for elections—jurisdictions, ballot places, election overseers, the fielding of candidates and disseminating of their policy positions—was enormously complex in the midst of war, especially with much of the state under British occupation. But the election went off. For the office of governor Yates threw his support behind George Clinton, a son of Irish immigrants from Ulster County, who had fought in the French and Indian War and then became an early opponent of British policies in North America. Two factions had quickly developed in the nascent state politics, and they were the same ones that had emerged in the crafting of a constitution. Clinton was the leader of the radicals, who were angling to keep power concentrated at the local level. The conservatives chose Philip Schuyler to go up against Clinton in the election. Clinton won, and became the state's first governor. Yates himself won a seat in the State Senate. No less than four other Yateses, all relatives, won elective offices, and Yates's clerk, Matthew Visscher, became a member of the State Assembly. The radicals had taken the state in a rout.

But there was no time for celebrating. Not long after the new state government met, the British invaded Kingston and burned the city. Yates and the other legislators fled for their lives. They moved to a series of temporary capitals, trying to conduct business in between periods of packing up, saddling up, hurrying out. At the same time, Yates began maneuvering for the 1778 election, at which he believed he had a chance to become lieutenant governor.

In the free-for-all of the young state's politics, Yates was also running for State Senate again, and in this race his opponent was Philip Schuyler. Schuyler, who had been dismissed from his position as general of the Northern Army and then lost his bid for governor, had in the past repeatedly run into Yates's stubborn insistence on the rights of the common man. The Albany patrician was filled with indignation and scorn when he learned that Yates was now in contention to be the second-most-powerful man in the state. He led a smear campaign against him, accusing Yates of electoral fraud and of being a commoner. Schuyler trumpeted the fact that Yates had once been a shoemaker as if it were an obvious disqualification for political office, pointing out to his fellow New Yorkers the outlandish notion that "Ab. Yates . . . late Cobler of Laws and Old Shoes, is to be put in Nomination for Lieut. Governor."

Yates was spoiling for a fight, and being scoffed at by the blue-blooded Schuyler only whetted his appetite. But fellow radicals approached him with concerns. While he had a sizable upstate following, and had become a leader in the Senate, his very popularity was a problem. One official voiced the fear that "elevating Yates will forward a Severance between the Popular and the Landed Interest and they will mutually pull each other down." Yates pondered the possibility of New York's state government, riven by factional strife, descending into chaos in the midst of the Revolution. He removed his name from consideration as lieutenant governor.

But he won his other race, for senator, and he took particular delight in beating Schuyler.

The Atlantic crossing was hell on earth. Winter winds strafed the decks of the British military convoy that carried Margaret Coghlan to her fate. Belowdecks, meanwhile, she was locked in deadly combat with her abusive husband. Freed from the constraints imposed by her father, she violently protested Coghlan's taking her away against her will as if she were a slave. Her stubborn heart had never let go of Aaron Burr. The soldier who had won her love was at this moment with Washington's army at Valley Forge, which might as well have been China. What was happening to her life? This was not the way the plot of *Polly Honeycombe* played out. Against the inexorability of reality, against the pounding of the waves and the tossing of the ship, she somehow held on to the conviction that the age of forced marriages was a thing of the past, that she had a right to freedom.

Her defiance inflamed Coghlan's propensity to drunken brutishness. A man, society had taught him, was supposed to be master of his wife. Coghlan's ample insecurity—he had yet to achieve anything in his life, had in fact left behind him a series of failures and abortive efforts—heightened his need to dominate. Together, they made a spectacle: he young, roguishly attractive and roaring with profanity, she a black-haired, alabaster-skinned teenaged beauty who deflected his violent outbursts with sarcasm and sneers. The fact that virtually every passenger on the ship except the two of them was a soldier being redeployed, and that every one of them knew that Coghlan had left the service of his country and was in the process of returning home, presumably to a life of leisure, added shame to Coghlan's stew of mental distress. And the shame was intensified by the humiliating way his child-wife treated him, her refusal to subordinate herself to him. Finally, the captain was forced to intervene, telling Coghlan he would throw him in the brig if he did not act as a gentleman.

Three weeks after leaving New York Harbor the fleet sighted land, but rough winds forced them off course and they made an unscheduled landing at Crookhaven at the southernmost tip of Ireland. As soon as they did, Coghlan had his horse put ashore, pulled himself into the saddle and rode off, "leaving me," Margaret wrote, "young and unprotected, in the midst of six or seven hundred men, for the space of fourteen days, without a single individual of my own sex in the whole fleet." Coghlan eventually returned, but in the meantime she had to deal with an onslaught of loitering soldiers "practicing their arts of seduction against me."

Finally, they made it to Cork, and there Coghlan informed her of a decision he had made. He had rented an old mansion in Wales, and he proposed to take her there and lock her up in it; "his design," she declared, "was to break my spirit."

She protested. But this extraordinary step, this act of violent possession, he had apparently determined, was necessary for the sake of his masculinity and his honor. He was hell-bent. It was as though all of his life's wandering debauchery and dereliction of duty could be rectified by imprisoning his wife.

They traveled to Dublin, where the city was alive with news that France, ancient enemy of England, would come into the American war on the side of the revolutionaries. People on the streets of Dublin had

mixed feelings about the goings-on in America. They too had long suffered under English oppression, but the home country was much nearer
to them, the ties were tighter, and most Irish radicals viewed the American war more with fascination than a desire to follow suit.

Coghlan, however, was presumably not interested in engaging the
locals in conversation about the war. He had left that behind. As soon as
he could, he got himself and his wife onto a ship, and they sailed across
the Irish Sea from Dublin to the medieval-walled Welsh city of Conwy.
There, in the shadow of its thirteenth-century castle, he wrestled her
into a room at an inn where they would rest before continuing on to the
place where he would confine her. Coghlan left her alone briefly while
he attended to a few things.

Margaret had been thinking furiously ever since they had left
America. Somewhere along the way she began to see the war, which
she had once unquestioningly viewed through the eyes of a loyal British subject, in a different light. What were the Americans doing but
breaking away from an unjust captivity, asserting their God-given rights
to freedom? In sailing back to Europe—or no, before that, when she
allowed herself to be ferried from the American army on Manhattan to
the British on Staten Island—what had she done? When she wrote it down
later, it was in capital letters: ". . . turned MY BACK ON LIBERTY!"

Her freedom and American freedom: were they, somehow, twin
struggles? In the course of her primal battle first against her father and
then her husband, and through the transformative act of being shipped
to another continent, she had reached a new stage of awareness, a matu-
rity. She was still herself: brash, passionate. She was one of those people
who was born into the world with a personality seemingly fully formed;
she would never change. But she was no longer a girl. She had run off
once before: hopped onto a horse and fled the New Jersey family with
whom she had been staying in a desperate attempt to find her father.
But what was rash in the past, the thoughtless impulse of a girl, could

become something other if it involved mature consideration. She was a woman now, ready to act and responsible for her actions. She knew what she was doing.

She opened the door of the inn and marched off, through the town and into the wasteland of the Welsh mountainside. Live or die, she would have freedom.

On March 13, 1778, Emmanuel Marie Louis de Noailles, France's ambassador to Great Britain, presented Lord North, the British prime minister, with a formal notification that France had, the month before, signed a treaty with the "Thirteen United States of America" indicating that it would join the Americans in their fight for independence. France had been eager to get back at England ever since the Seven Years' War, in which it had lost Canada and much else. An American delegation, led by Benjamin Franklin, had been in Paris since the end of 1776, impressing on French officials that the American revolution was a manifestation of Enlightenment values that the French themselves espoused. French leaders had been waiting for a sign that the Americans were strong enough to warrant their backing them. The victory at Saratoga was the sign. Lord North presented the French document to King George, who declared that it "must entirely overturn" British plans.

Among the things the French entry into the war overturned was any thought of the government's accepting the resignation of George Germain as American Secretary. What had been a civil war, in which the parent country was attempting to discipline a rebellious child, was now, suddenly, an international conflict involving Britain's greatest rival. It was no longer a matter of using the Hudson River to divide the colonies, or of taking New York or Philadelphia or Boston. The game board now extended, potentially, to British possessions in the Caribbean, to the European continent, to Asia. With his deep military and diplomatic experience and his intricate involvement in the American situation, Germain was necessary. His aggression, his unyielding determination not just to avert loss but to extend empire, to carry forward the progress of England's ancient rulers in extending her dominions, which until now was seen by his enemies as pure folly, was suddenly an asset. The king in particular, who was committed to punishing the colonists and keeping America British, had to admit that Germain, for all his flaws, was a bedrock of imperial strength. He now asked him to run what was in effect a whole new war.

Germain, of course, accepted. Like a phoenix risen from its ashes, he stood again, a tower of spleen and sinew, terrible in his imperial dynamism, before Parliament in May of 1778. The occasion was a show-down, for General Burgoyne had returned from his humiliating loss at Saratoga and was defending his actions in the House of Commons. He had been a popular figure in Britain, and, despite his having surren-dered an army, he still was. He used that popularity in his defense, and, knowing that Germain was largely loathed, put blame for the failure on the American Secretary. "I expected cooperation," he told the House, meaning that he had expected Germain to send him reinforcements and make certain that General Howe's army would join his at Albany. Germain counterargued, saying that Burgoyne chose his route of travel poorly and weighed down his army with unnecessary baggage for the comfort of the officers, creating the conditions for the defeat. Burgoyne scoffed, and referred to Germain and other leaders "who were obliged to cover their ignorance and inability." Back and forth they went before the assembly. An observer remarked that the opponents "scolded like two oysterwomen." Temple Luttrell, one of Burgoyne's defenders, then rose to remind everyone that Germain had received "the most decisive censure of a court martial" in the past; he denounced Germain as "a minister whose loss of a nation's confidence and his own character is a matter of public record," and declared snidely that had Burgoyne "disobeyed the commands of his superiors and hid himself from danger," such conduct would have entitled him to "the honours and emoluments of the American Secretaryship."

As always, Germain's enemies could count on Minden to raise his ire. Germain leaped to his feet, grabbed the pommel of his sword and challenged the younger man to a duel. There was a scuffle as Luttrell marched out of the chamber to give Germain satisfaction, only to be hustled back by his colleagues. For two hours the House was in an uproar.

Invective, outrage, threats of violence: George Germain was back. He had survived Minden, and now, apparently, he had survived Saratoga. Both were failures, dramas of humiliation that had played out before the whole nation, but still he stood, like a tree battered by hurricane winds that could not be uprooted.

He got down to business. He was now, in effect if not in name, promoted to secretary of war. His enemies howled at the outrageous irony that the very failure of Germain's leadership would result in his being assigned an even grander role, but such was the nature of politics. He marched back to Whitehall to refashion the British strategy. Even before Burgoyne had returned to defend himself, General Howe had offered his resignation, making a similar charge that he had not been adequately supported in London. Germain accepted the resignation with pleasure, and installed Henry Clinton as his successor.

The matter of a general in charge of ground forces was important, of course, but the focus of action now lay elsewhere. The French were sending a fleet. The next stage of the war would be conducted at sea.

The British leaders knew that a French fleet had left the port of Toulon in April. There was some disagreement about where it was headed and what its intentions were, but Germain felt certain both of its goal and of the stakes. The French vessels were bearing down on "our Fleet and Army and our possessions in North America," he declared, and he pressed his colleagues to appreciate that not just the colonies but the "fate of the country" hung in the balance. He convinced other members of the government, and they drafted their new strategy for winning the American war. They would send a comparable British fleet across the Atlantic: thirteen ships of the line. They would raid ports in the American north, crippling the economy and the shipbuilding capabilities there. When that was accomplished, General Clinton's army would invade the southern colonies and take control of them. With the northern ports destroyed and the south in British hands, the northern colonies would have no choice but to give up the fight.

Germain wrote to General Clinton, in Philadelphia, apprising him of the new plans. He informed the general, who after all had only recently taken command, that "the generality of the people" in America wanted only "their rights and liberties under the British constitution. Part of the reason for shifting toward the southern colonies was his conviction that most of the inhabitants there were loyalists, who could be relied on to aid the army.

But Germain was acutely aware of the situation that had led to the loss at Saratoga. He knew now how impossible it was for orders to be followed to the letter from across the ocean. So he told his new general that what he was giving him were guidelines, that he wanted him to "use your own discretion in planning as well as executing all operations. . . ." Indeed, he noted that his own preference was that all of his guidance be rendered unnecessary by an altogether different move on Clinton's part as the spring fighting got underway: "to bring Mr. Washington to a general and decisive action early in the campaign."

Washington got the news of the French alliance while he was in the midst of drilling his men in the spring sunshine of Valley Forge. He had been pondering which way to attack the British, and had been giving serious thought to marching right into Philadelphia. Now everything changed. He told his officers the wondrous news. Lafayette, who always seemed oblivious of the perimeter of frosty reserve that Washington kept about his person, grabbed his commanding officer and kissed him on both cheeks. Washington ordered a general assembly and addressed his army with a rare burst of spirituality:

> It having pleased the Almighty ruler of the Universe propitiously to defend the Cause of the United American-States and finally by raising us up a powerful Friend among the Princes of the Earth to establish our liberty and Independence upon lasting foundations, it becomes us to set apart a day for gratefully acknowledging the divine Goodness & celebrating the important Event which we owe to his benign Interposition.

Then, with his customary fastidiousness for detail, he announced the precise manner in which the army would celebrate the alliance with France, right down to dictating how the men would cheer:

> Upon a signal given, the whole Army will *Huzza!* "Long Live the King of France"—The Artillery then begins again and fires thirteen rounds, this will be succeded by a second general discharge of the Musquetry in a running fire—*Huzza!*—"And long live the friendly European Powers"—Then the last discharge of thirteen Pieces of Artillery will be given, followed by a General runing fire and Huzza! "To the American States."

The army was now fired up, and so was Washington. Not long after, General Sir Henry Clinton, having decided against Germain's suggestion of a direct attack at Washington's army, prepared to evacuate Philadelphia and head for Sandy Hook, where ships would be waiting for his troops. Washington got word of his intentions and sounded out his officers on what to do. Should they attack? Most were against it. But Washington had endured a string of losses and a long, grueling winter, and he was deeply impressed by the work done in a few short months by a Prussian officer named Friedrich Wilhelm Ludolf Gerhard Augustin von Steuben, who had arrived in camp in late February, powerful astride his horse (one soldier remarked that he looked like "the ancient fabled God of War"), and established a revised mode of military discipline, which included new drills and training the men in the proper use of the bayonet.

So Washington wanted to go at Clinton. Though Charles Lee, his senior-most officer, opposed it, his young bucks, Hamilton and Lafayette, sided with the chief. Clinton's army left Philadelphia and headed northeast, following the Delaware River. Washington proposed to send an advance guard to harass the British troops and keep them occupied until he could bring the rest of the army up. Lee at first dodged the assignment to lead the advance, then, when Washington gave the command to Lafayette, Lee decided he would do it after all. Such vacillation was strange behavior in a seasoned officer, but Washington reassigned Lee the task. Lee rode off at the head of 5,000 men.

June 28 was a blisteringly hot and humid day. An aide rode up to Washington after dawn to report that the British lines were on the move. Washington got his men up and marching. They stripped off their shirts in the heat. On and on they marched; some of the men fainted; those who couldn't continue were left by the side of the road. Finally, Washington heard the sound he had been waiting for: cannon fire. Lee was doing his job.

A short while later they passed a farmer. Washington rode his white charger up and asked what news he had. At first he assumed the man didn't know what he was talking about, for the farmer reported that the Americans were in retreat. But it turned out to be true. Clinton had left a small force behind at a place called Monmouth Court House, and Lee had attacked it, but then another force, under Charles Cornwallis, had doubled back and surprised the Americans. In the confusion Lee had pulled back.

Washington spurred his horse; when he found Lee, he was in a fury. He had chosen this moment, this place, because the British were hemmed in by a marsh and a steep defile. Such opportunities couldn't be wasted. And here was Lee with 5,000 men, not pressing the advantage but in full retreat. He thundered up to Lee's side. "What is the meaning of this?" he roared. "What is all this confusion for, and retreat?" Lee looked bewildered, wounded, as if he felt he were being criticized unjustly for taking the proper action. "Sir?" he asked. "Sir?"

Everything was undone. But the action was underway. Washington looked around, saw the land sloping down toward the British troops; he had this advantage, at least. Hamilton, at his side, noted the general's "coolness and firmness" as he took stock. Anthony Wayne, one of his generals, appeared, at the head of a column, ready for action. Wayne had been eager for this fight, had, in pressing for it, coined a verb: "Burgoyning Clinton" was what he'd advocated. They could yet do this.

Wayne's men charged ahead. Washington ordered Nathanael Greene to his right and Brigadier-General Lord Stirling to his left. A line of British cavalry came charging at them; the American rifles opened fire and men and horses slammed to the earth. Then in a steady roll came the British infantry. His officers, Washington later remarked, "seemed to vie with each other in manifesting their zeal and bravery," and the behavior of the troops "was such as could not be surpassed." The battle wore on through the long hot day. Washington's horse collapsed under him and died. Night fell, and the fighting ceased. Washington spied the British campfires in the distance and plotted a dawn raid. But when morning came they saw the fires had been a ruse: the enemy was gone. Each side lost hundreds of men. Washington chose to call the battle at

Monmouth Court House a victory. But the British army had escaped, and continued on its way to Sandy Hook. There, the soldiers boarded ships that would redeploy them, as General Clinton began executing the new strategy that George Germain had dictated.

Three days later and 150 miles away, Cornplanter and his fellow Seneca war captain Old Smoke were leading more than 400 Iroquois fighters, armed with muskets and tomahawks and stripped and painted for violence, in surrounding a fort called Wintermute in the Wyoming Valley of eastern Pennsylvania. With them was Major John Butler and 110 of his Rangers, who included loyalists and runaway slaves. Burgoyne's surrender at Saratoga had changed the nature of the war in the north. In place of a classic offensive, the British were now relying on raids, and on their Iroquois allies. The Indians were armed with muskets and ammunition supplied by the British.

The serene setting—broad meadows astride a wide lazy stretch of the Susquehanna River—contrasted strikingly with the business of death. This was farm country; the objective was both to plunder and to stop supplies from going to the American army. Inside the fort, militiamen huddled with their wives and children. The attack would be easy work, and the Indians prepared to do it quickly. But Butler wanted to see if they could accomplish the task without violence. He asked the men inside the fort to surrender; if they did, he said, their lives would be spared. Somewhat to his surprise, they agreed. The same thing happened at the next fort. But when they reached the third, a place called Forty Fort, which had been named after the number of men who had built it, the terms were rejected.

Cornplanter had an idea. The fort sat right on the riverbank; a hill rose above it. He took ten of his men and crept to the top. From here they were able not only to see inside, but actually to count the militiamen and observe their preparations. When, at two o'clock in the afternoon on July 3, 1778, the gate creaked open and the 400 militiamen inside rushed out, weapons raised, intending to surprise the attackers, Cornplanter's men were ready. Iroquois and Rangers alike were belly-down on the ground, several hundred yards distant, undetectable. They waited until the militiamen had advanced a distance from the fort and had shot three rounds. Then the Senecas and their British allies opened fire as the Indians moved to outflank the enemy. The battle was short and horrifically one-sided. Three hundred Americans were killed. The Senecas lost five men.

Americans in the region quickly put out the news that the "savages" had conducted a "massacre." In fact, what Cornplanter led was a crisp, decisive military action against armed combatants. While the disinformation was meant to excite Congress into sending troops their way, more immediately it served to alarm other settlers, enough that four more forts in the Wyoming Valley surrendered the next day. Cornplanter had an understanding of the agreements the white men valued. The Senecas freed the militiamen in the forts on the condition that they not engage in future military action against Indians.

But the men of the Wyoming Valley were in a stew of rage and hurt following the deaths of so many of their brothers and neighbors. Several weeks later, Thomas Hartley, a thirty-year-old lawyer who had served under Washington at Brandywine Creek, organized a raiding party that would make a counterstrike against the Indians, which he declared was meant to stop "the Barbarians from Deluging our Country with the Blood of Helpless Mothers & Infants." That the strike was against Delaware Indians who lived in the region, and not the Senecas who had attacked Forty Fort, did not matter. His 200 men burned down a string of Indian villages and killed a number of inhabitants, including killing and scalping "a very important Indian Chief."

Cornplanter was back in his home village of Conawaugus when Delaware messengers arrived with news of the raids and requests to help. It was October, the time for drying beans and harvesting corn rather than making war, but many Senecas were angry that they had been accused of committing a massacre under circumstances that, had they involved a white army, would have been considered normal warfare. Cornplanter knew perfectly well that while in formal councils the Americans referred to the Iroquois as a noble civilization, outside the council fire they considered them little more than beasts. In using the term "massacre" to whip up support against them, they were playing on an existing image. The Senecas had no choice but to act. Cornplanter's son was now four years old. As a father, he had to protect the boy. As a leader, he had to protect the Seneca people. Once, he had held out for neutrality. Now he wanted to fight.

He led more than 300 Senecas eastward. They met up with Mohawks under Joseph Brant, and a contingent of John Butler's Rangers led by his son, Walter Butler. The place of attack, the settlement of Cherry Valley, was another area of farmland that Washington's army relied on for supplies.

The fort here was strong, and well defended, but the leader was stupid. Despite warnings of the enemy's advance, Colonel Ichabod Alden stayed in town rather than in the fort, together with his officers, in the comfortable home of a man named Robert Wells. Butler and Cornplanter, leading the advance party, captured four people on their way into the town, and learned from them where the leaders were staying. Cornplanter sent a party of Indians led by the Seneca Little Beard to surround the Wells house. They waited through an all-night rainstorm, and attacked at dawn. Alden came charging out, dodging arrows and musketballs in a desperate run for the safety of the fort. Just before he got there someone threw a tomahawk; the blow to the head killed the man. The Indians swarmed into the house and killed everyone inside, soldiers and family members alike.

The main party of attackers had been trying to gain entry to the fort. When it was clear they could not, groups of Senecas broke away into the town, where they avenged the attacks on the Delaware villages, and, as if feeling it necessary to show the Americans what a real Indian massacre was, set about marauding. Besides American soldiers, the Indians and their allies murdered 32 civilians. Cornplanter and Brant tried to stop the attacks on unarmed villagers. Quite apart from morality, they knew that wanton ugliness would eventually reflect on them.

And the wantonness could not have been more ugly. The wife of one of the Indians later dispassionately declared that "they plundered and burnt every thing that came in their way, and killed a number of persons, among whom were several infants, whom Hiokatoo butchered or dashed upon the stones with his own hands." Hiokatoo was her husband.

The news from Cherry Valley reached George Washington as he was grappling with two other issues. Suddenly, he had three decisions to make that, together, brought him to a historic crossroads. The outcome of the war, and of much else in America's project for freedom, was at stake.

The war had gone on now for three years and seven months. As it progressed, he found that two sources of worry were in some ways deeper and more insidious than the threat from the British. He was increasingly worried about slaves. And now his fears of what the Indians might do had been realized.

The next phase of George Germain's strategy was unfolding, as news reached Washington that British ships had landed in Georgia and a force of 3,000 men had taken the city of Savannah. The English were changing their focus to the southern states; Washington would need soldiers there.

At the same time, one of Washington's aides, John Laurens, a twenty-four-year-old lieutenant colonel, offered up a plan that, he stressed, could simultaneously add the needed soldiers in the South and end the scourge of slavery. Washington knew that Laurens, like Lafayette and Hamilton, wanted the war to result in both independence from Britain and a new American society in which all inhabitants were free. Laurens hailed from a family of South Carolina slaveholders, but he had been educated in England. When he returned to America, the naked reality of the institution was like a slap in the face, and he became obsessed with trying to "reconcile our spirited Assertions of the Rights of Mankind" with "the galling abject Slavery of our negroes." He proposed that the army offer 3,000 southern slaves their freedom in exchange for military service.

Washington could not help but be fond of Laurens. After the young man had overheard the continuously troublesome General Charles Lee speaking of Washington "in the grossest and most opprobrious terms of personal abuse," he challenged the general to a duel. The two men squared off in a wooded area near the army's camp; Laurens's pistol shot wounded the older man slightly, ending the matter. The affair left Washington even firmer both in his dislike for Lee and in his affection for Laurens. Laurens then pressed his plan for turning slaves into soldiers on Washington, as well as on his father, Henry Laurens, who was a member of the Continental Congress and had recently taken over from John Hancock as its president.

But Washington could not accept the idea. "The policy of our arming Slaves is in my opinion a moot point," he wrote, and declared his reasoning to be that if the American army brought in a great number of slaves then the British would do likewise, and "the upshot then must be who can Arm fastest."

This was nonsense, and Washington knew it. The British had already been arming slaves. They had first begun doing so in his native

Virginia at the start of the war. Thousands—including a number of Washington's own slaves from Mount Vernon—had escaped the plantations of patriots and taken up the offer of freedom in exchange for serving in the British army. Indeed, in rejecting Laurens's plan, Washington had his own situation in mind. At the time Laurens presented his idea, Washington was corresponding with his cousin, who was managing Mount Vernon, and in the exchange he made clear his economic reliance on slaves. Once again he was pondering the possibility of losing the war. This time, he wondered whether it would be a smart investment for him to sell all his slaves and buy loan office certificates, which would help fund the war. If Britain were victorious, he reasoned, "it would be a matter of very little consequence to me, whether my property is in Negroes, or loan office Certificates." But assuming the Americans won, then, he said, "the only points" that mattered to him were "whether it would be most to my interest . . . to have negroes, and the Crops they will make; or the sum they will now fetch and the interest of the money."

Washington admired the verve of the officers on his staff who railed against slavery. But Lafayette, Hamilton and Laurens were all young men. The tentacles of American society—its economic realities—hadn't woven around them. Lafayette was French, Hamilton grew up poor in the Caribbean, and Laurens had been raised in England. None had families. In conversation, Washington agreed that slavery was an immoral institution. And he could point to steps he had taken, such as having recently given tacit approval to a request for Rhode Island to arm a regiment of slaves, as evidence of broad-mindedness.

But the South, to a Virginia planter, was an altogether different matter. Slaves there were so numerous, their conditions were so harsh, that practically from birth Washington had thought of them as a latent threat, a potential enemy. Southern slave owners like him followed closely events on plantation islands in the Caribbean. At the outset of the war they had gotten a proper scare when news reached them that hundreds of slaves in Jamaica had attempted an uprising. Even more troubling, the Jamaican slaves had apparently been inspired by the very ideals of freedom that Washington and his fellow rebels proclaimed. The Jamaica rebellion had been crushed, its leaders executed and either burned alive or had their bodies displayed as a public warning. For a man like Washington, the affair underscored the dangerous double-edged nature of the ideology the Americans espoused. Uprisings were a nightmare that all southern slaveholding families lived with. To give weapons to the people they had been systematically abusing for generations was beyond his comprehension. Freedom was what Washington was fighting for. But not for them. Not now. It was an irony, an incongruity, a flaw in the American project of bringing true individual liberty into being: he did not deny that. But he couldn't solve it. He was not a philosopher.

Washington longed to clarify the war by reducing it to two sets of players: the Americans and the British. But the African slaves were an inescapable complication. And so were the natives: "the savage tribes," as he called them. All his life they had manifested themselves as beyond the bounds, problematic, in the way. He had grown up around them as well, as a young man relying on them as guides in the wilderness, eating with them, laughing with them. But always there was an anthropological distance. He could in some way comprehend that they were fighting for a form of freedom. But whether they allied with the Americans or with the British or tried to stay out of the war altogether, their conception of freedom was alien to him. His was built around crisp notions like property rights and written contracts. Theirs was something entirely other. In comparison, even slaves had a more graspably transactional definition of what it meant to be free. A deed of sale or of manumission, a contract, was a piece of paper whose firm import both sides comprehended. Indian notions of freedom were like the water in a stream.

Their freedom was too free. It shaded to waywardness. It led him to distrust even the small number of Iroquois who had pledged to support the Americans. Could the two freedoms—the Enlightenment freedom that grounded his fellow revolutionary leaders and the Iroquois freedom that was rooted in their traditions—be reconciled? Probably not. He was not a philosopher.

Brigadier General Edward Hand, an Irish physician turned patriot soldier who had taken part in Washington's recrossing of the Delaware maneuver, was the one who sent him the grim news of what "the savage tribes" had done at Cherry Valley: "Destroyed the Settlement, & Murdering many Women & Children . . ." Up to this point the Indians had not been a major factor in the war. But now they had forced his hand. The frontier was aflame with fear. Washington was now, he said, "perfectly convinced, that the only certain way of preventing Indian ravages is to carry the war vigorously into their own country." He selected John Sullivan, a thirty-nine-year-old bulldog of a man who was raised in New Hampshire by Irish parents, to lead a mission against the Iroquois. Washington wanted to be as clear as possible in his orders:

> *The expedition you are appointed to command is to be directed against the hostile tribes of the six nations of Indians, with their associates and adherents. The immediate objects are the total destruction and devastation of their settlements and the capture of as many prisoners of every age and sex as possible. It will be essential to ruin their crops now in the ground and prevent their planting more.*

Few white settlers forayed into Iroquois territory, which straddled the boundaries of Pennsylvania and New York. It was as yet a world apart, alien, forbidding in its geography, a place parents told scary stories about to their children. Sullivan was to lead a massive force there:

4,000 men, fully one-quarter of Washington's entire army, with cannons, howitzers, attendant ammunition and supplies, through an intricacy of mountains and rivers, of gorges and forests, "into the heart of the Indian settlements." Washington would feel vulnerable with so many of his men sent away, but he realized the stakes. He needed to pivot and fight the British in the South; he could not afford to have, behind him, a conflagration of terror spreading outward from Iroquois country. Sullivan's job was not to do battle but to destroy a civilization.

Although they did not have the resounding clarity of a battlefield action, the pair of decisions Washington made regarding slaves and Indians formed a focal point. He reduced and clarified the task at hand. American freedom would mean white freedom.

*Chapter 15*

———❦———

# I AM YOUR SON!
# I AM A WARRIOR!

Cornplanter could see them through the trees. He could see that they could not see him, that they saw nothing. The American soldiers, the white men, were obsessed with the darkness all around them. To him this forest was home, its murmuring rhythms matched his own. To them it was a primeval hell.

Earlier they had been secretive and moon-eyed, the men led by Sullivan, careful not to discharge weapons, running around like loons as they tried to catch turkeys with their bare hands, stopping to marvel at vast open meadows of grass surrounded by distant mountains, at stands of white oak interlaced with pea vine, at herds of deer.

As the army climbed, the woods got thicker, rain fell, and the men found themselves swallowed by fog. They forded deep streams, the horses struggling and snorting to keep their nostrils above the water. The men lumbered and sweated like dogs in the heat, maneuvering the carts carrying the six-pound cannons and the howitzers: "thunder trees," Cornplanter's people called the big guns. On July 4 they paused to celebrate. They offered a toast to "General Washington and the army," and another to the sentiment "Civilization or death to all savages."

They reached a vast swamp. The branches of the trees overhead were so thick it seemed nighttime at noon. Rain fell incessantly. They found human skulls, then heaps of skeletons: evidence of the Iroquois attacks on settlers the previous summer. They called the place the Shades of Death. The evidence of what they took to be wanton massacres steeled their spines.

Cornplanter, Brant and Butler had brought their men back together to meet this threat: 400 Iroquois fighters and 300 loyalists. They had heard of Sullivan's army long before it set out; they had watched its noisy approach. They were ready to meet the Americans in battle. It puzzled Cornplanter at first that as Sullivan's force got deeper into their territory they became louder. Not only were they no longer trying to conceal their presence, they were trumpeting it: at intervals a cannon blast echoed through the wooded slopes. But for all their noise, the Americans didn't seem interested in doing battle. Instead, one by one, they sniffed out Iroquois villages, which had been abandoned as the people fled in advance of the army, and torched them. They set fire to acre after acre of corn, and stood there, feeling the heat compounding the summer's intensity, watching the smoke blacken the summer sky.

Cornplanter and Butler decided to make a stand. At a place called Newtown they put their men to the task of felling trees. They forged a defensive works, with a brook on one side, a river on another and a large hill behind. When the two armies finally squared off, on August 29, 1779, Cornplanter began to understand that the enemy's strategy was to overwhelm. The cannons blasted away from the flanks, wreaking terror, sending many of his men fleeing. The battle raged for three hours before Cornplanter, Brant and Butler organized a retreat.

The big guns didn't stop there; they rolled onward, through the jungly woods, across streams, crawling up gray rock faces. The

Iroquois sent word northward to abandon villages in the heartland of their territory. Up the long finger of Seneca Lake, Sullivan's army continued, fending off minor attacks, leveling villages while first stopping to admire the neat log construction of the houses, the glass panes in the windows, the woven baskets, the domesticity of it all. They marveled at the expertness and scope of the native agriculture, the fields of "Corn, Beans, peas, Squashes, Potatoes, Inions, turnips, Cabage, Cowcumbers, watermilions, Carrots, parsnips &c," as one soldier recorded in his diary. Then they burned it all to nothing.

The American army overwhelmed the small groups of Indians it encountered. Some of these they scalped, in imitation of their enemy. Some they burned alive in their houses. They skinned two dead Indians and made pairs of leggings for officers out of them, leaving the horror of the remains behind. They were intent on making a statement, one the Iroquois would understand.

As he raced back to his village of Conawaugus to alert everyone, and herded people toward the protection of the British fort at Niagara, Cornplanter did indeed come to understand what the Americans' intention was. And, as the American army rolled forward like a force of nature, as village after village—Cayuga, Onondaga, Seneca—was obliterated, he knew who was behind it all. He had never met George Washington, but all the Iroquois knew of him. And the name they had called the man from Virginia, which had originally applied to his grandfather, came back to Cornplanter with rueful and prophetic force. Town Destroyer.

In April 1779, while George Washington was giving orders for the assembly of the army under Major General John Sullivan that was intended to crush the Iroquois, Abraham Yates rode a sloop back up the Hudson River to Albany. From there, he and his wife Anna took a sentimental journey to the little Dutch church in the village of Schaghticoke, 20 miles to the north, where, thirty-two years earlier, they had married. Now it was the turn of their seventeen-year-old daughter Susanna. The bridegroom, Abraham Lansing, was a stout, thick-faced son of an Albany gunsmith. Apart from a bit of awkwardness owing to the fact that Lansing had previously committed to marrying another local girl, Yates seemed to be delighted with his son-in-law. Lansing was a working-class Albany Dutchman who was known to be, as one of his friends said, "rough and somewhat abrupt in his manner, but upright, frank, and fearless in conduct and in character." The newly-weds moved in with Abraham and Anna, which was just what the older couple wanted; Yates had built his house in downtown Albany large enough to accommodate an extended family. In addition to his love for Susanna, Lansing was bonded to the family by his ardent admiration for her father, who had risen from the working class just as he hoped to do. He supported Yates's radical politics, and, when he was not on militia duty, hoped to work alongside him in some civic capacity. On the domestic front, Abraham Yates had to be well pleased.

The wider world was another matter. Everyone in New York was alarmed by the Iroquois attacks to the west, state politics was a nest of vipers, and both the state and the national governments were bankrupt. The Articles of Confederation, which the Continental Congress had adopted in late 1777, had set up an awkward means of raising revenue to fund the war. Each state was to obtain loans from wealthy citizens. The men charged with obtaining the money were called continental loan officers. Yates asked Governor Clinton to appoint him to one of the posts, and the governor obliged.

It was an odd and impossible job, but Yates had an ideological reason—he would say a patriotic reason—for wanting it. He had been watching with alarm as "aristocrats" in the Congress, as he termed them, maneuvered toward giving the national government the power to raise taxes. To Yates it would be an outrageous betrayal of the people for the national leaders to impose their will upon them in such a way—and at the very time they were fighting and dying for individual freedom, and over the matter of unjust taxation, no less. He took careful note when, shortly after the signing of the treaty with France, the delegates to the Congress agreed to form a committee of commerce whose very name—the Secret Committee—showed it to be, he believed, a conspiracy to usurp individual rights. The fact that the committee stipulated that its first report be restricted to a small circle and that "the printer be under an Oath not to devulge any part of the said Report," raised Yates's suspicions to the highest level. He monitored the subsequent journals of the Congress and determined that they "reveal the progress of the conspiracy."

He had concluded that the best way to stay abreast of the growing threat of economic usurpation was through being a part of the system. The job of continental loan officer, which he performed alongside his Senate duties, required him to be available every morning from nine to twelve and every afternoon from two to five so that anyone who wanted to make a loan to the government could do so. He hired as his assistant Abraham Lansing, his new son-in-law. After he collected money, he had to send it on to Congress and issue bills of credit to the lenders. The problems were endless. There weren't enough lenders to fund the war, and those that did come forward discovered that it was a losing proposition. The bills of credit they received didn't allow for interest, and the inflation that raged during the war quickly made them nearly worthless. After two years, the system had amassed, nationwide, $241 million in bills of credit, but they were worth a mere $4.8 million. As the papers Yates had given them dwindled in value, lenders became more and more irate.

Thankless as it was, Yates clung to the job. He wasn't raising his quota, but he was still helping to fund the war effort. And he was keeping an eye on the man who had become head of the American financial system, Robert Morris. Morris, a congressman from Pennsylvania, was fantastically wealthy, having made money on overseas trade, including slaves, as well as in banking. He was a wizard at accounting, and set about reorganizing the national government's wobbly financial system. At the same time, he used his firm, Willing & Morris, to do much of the country's trading with European nations for war supplies. Critics, led by Thomas Paine, accused him of war profiteering. Yates believed Morris was pulling the country toward a system of national taxation.

Throughout 1779, then—as Spain joined the alliance with France and America, as a combination of American and French forces failed to retake the city of Savannah, Georgia, as American merchant raider John Paul Jones tangled with British frigates off the coast of England—Yates performed his various political jobs and kept a close watch on Robert Morris. He complained when Congress established a Board of Treasury, which he felt certain would become a bureaucratic mechanism for fiscal tyranny. Then came an even clearer indication of the direction Congress was taking. In January 1780 it voted that the journals of its activities would henceforth be published without indication of who had voted for or against a given item. Secrecy, Yates believed, was the soil in which tyranny grew. He was now openly worried that the Revolution, even as it progressed, was veering off course, that Congress—"the Center of Intrigue and cabal," he took to calling it—was working to enlarge its own powers "at the expense of the Liberties of the People."

At the same time came other, brighter news. Precisely nine months after his daughter's marriage to Abraham Lansing, Susanna gave birth to a baby girl. The couple gave her a sturdy Dutch name: Jannetje. For years Yates had been working toward a new American future. Suddenly, here it was. The big brick house in Albany rang with his granddaughter's cries.

. . .

George Germain's fight wasn't confined to America anymore. A British fleet clashed with French ships off the coast of Brittany. The encounter caused a political storm in London, which, exacerbated by popular anger over high taxes and rising debt, spilled into the streets. Why was England funneling its resources into a costly and dangerous war simultaneously with France and with its American colonies while people at home were suffering? In February 1779, mobs formed. One of the places they targeted was the townhouse of the American Secretary, who personified the war and was widely detested as an aristocrat and a bully. The crowd smashed windows, broke inside and began tossing furniture out into the street while Germain's daughters shuddered in their beds.

In June, the crisis expanded on yet another front. Spain declared war on England, and Spanish troops joined the French in besieging Gibraltar, the possession of which gave England control of access to the Mediterranean Sea.

People seethed at the situation their government had gotten them into. Whigs in Parliament responded to the ugly mood by issuing demands for reforms of the monarchy and the aristocracy. Edmund Burke called for abolishing sinecures for noblemen, meaningless positions that cost the taxpayers money, such as "the several keepers of buck-hounds, stag-hounds, fox-hounds, and harriers." To laughter, he insisted that "It is not proper that great noblemen should be keepers of dogs. . . ." He railed against corruption and bureaucracy in government, and demanded that the king's power be curtailed. Given the prevailing mood, his bill seemed sure to pass. But King George pushed back by audaciously wrapping himself in the very Constitution he was accused of diminishing. He had his men in Parliament fight the measures on the grounds that any attack on the monarchy was an attack on "the present Constitution of the country in its pristine lustre." The reforms were defeated.

Popular outrage over the defeat blended with a sudden outburst of anti-Catholic sentiment, and the result was an even larger wave of rioting. Soldiers marched into the streets, but the angry crowds insisted on making a statement. Three buildings in particular were targeted: Newgate Prison, the home of the chief justice, and, once again, the Pall Mall house of the American Secretary. Germain was at home with friends. Together they barricaded the doors and windows.

Meanwhile, Germain was again unhappy with the leader of British forces in America. Sir Henry Clinton wrote to him complaining about everything from the rugged terrain of America to French ships off the coast to the lack of funds. "To say truth, my Lord," he whined, "my spirits are worn out by struggling against the consequences of so many adverse incidents." A fellow officer wrote to Germain from New York with his own worries about Clinton: "I am convinced nature has not given him an enterprizing and active spirit . . . his affection for New York (in which island he has four different houses), induces him to retire to that place, where without any settled plan he idles his time . . . and suffers himself to be cooped up by Washington with an inferior army."

Yet again, Germain had a general who was overly fond of the comforts of New York. This was especially vexing because Germain had become convinced that, as the French had not yet exerted themselves in force in America, with a strong commander the war could be won fairly swiftly. But he agreed with Admiral Sir George Rodney, an advisor he trusted, who, after spending time in New York, wrote him about what it would take:

> Believe me, my dear Lord, you must not expect an end of the American war till you can find a general of active spirit, and who hates the Americans from principle. Such a man with the sword of war

*and justice on his side will do wonders, for in this war I am con-*
*vinced the sword should cut deep. Nothing but making the Ameri-*
*cans feel every calamity their perfidy deserves can bring them to*
*their senses.*

Rodney further advised that the British concentrate on the South, in particular on the James River in Virginia: "Be assured, my Lord, if Lord Cornwallis and his army were to act up that river and in the Chesapeak the rebels would be undone."

For some time, Germain had been pushing Clinton to move in that direction, but Clinton had resisted. When Germain sent Charles Cornwallis to America as Clinton's number two, he gave Cornwallis a "dormant commission": i.e., the power to take the command away from Clinton, upon Germain's order. Cornwallis was a seasoned aristocrat who like Germain had fought in the Seven Years' War. Germain believed he could count on him to pursue his policy of aggression. If Clinton wanted to stay snug in his New York residences, Germain would have the option of transferring authority to Cornwallis.

At the end of 1779, Clinton finally moved. He, Cornwallis, 13,500 soldiers and thousands of horses boarded ships in New York Harbor and headed south. They laid siege to Charleston, South Carolina. Washington had been unable to divert forces southward, and the city fell on May 11, 1780. In a stroke, the British had won the most vital harbor in the southern states. Hundreds of South Carolinians suddenly announced themselves to be loyal British subjects. Germain exulted.

And he dared ponder one other notion that his advisor had opined. Rodney had learned that the American commander in chief had a weakness. From his earliest days he had longed for one thing in life above all others: a commission in the British army. "Washington," he wrote Germain, "is certainly to be bought—honours will do it."

. . .

The information that Germain received concerning the American commander was years out of date. Holed up in his winter quarters in Morristown, New Jersey, Washington had a hundred things on his mind, none of which involved British honors. He had struggled to keep his soldiers alive through the coldest winter in living memory, in which the vast Hudson River completely froze over and snowfalls of five feet were charted. He became obsessed with recording the weather, and through March and April eagerly observed every anemic sign that the season was changing: "the Trees and Earth being glazed looked beautiful . . . Morning lowering & raw . . . Raining moderately all the forenoon with a little thunder—thick and misty afterwards . . ."

Uppermost in his mind was the failure of Congress to put the tottering country on any kind of financial footing. Relying on income to be raised by continental loan officers in each state (Abraham Yates among them) had proved to be a total failure. As a result, the currency that Congress issued shriveled in value, and, compounding the frigid conditions, Washington could not feed his army. One of his generals lamented that in "a country overflowing with plenty" the men protecting it were about to "perish for lack of food."

Then, in May 1780, with the late breaking of the weather came the stupendously bad news of the fall of Charleston. It was infuriating in its own right, but doubly so because Washington had been constrained from acting due to the fact that Congress, in its fear of military tyranny, had not given him authority over the South. Even with 2,500 American soldiers now in enemy hands and the British general Cornwallis in command of the port of Charleston, Congress did not expand Washington's power but instead turned to his continual nemesis, the man who had tried repeatedly to wrest authority from him. Horatio Gates was put in charge in the South.

Washington, meanwhile, had to stay where he was, for Clinton was headed back to New York with much of the British army. So he drilled his men. He studied his maps. And he had learned to appreciate small pleasures, such as taking breaks from pondering strategy by tossing a ball with his young officers.

Then came word from further north. After Sullivan's fine job of decimating Iroquois villages, Washington had hoped the Indians would have learned their lesson, so that he could focus his attention henceforth on the British. Washington had instructed Philip Schuyler to offer the defeated Iroquois peace in exchange for laying down their arms. But the reply surprised him, darkened his mood and compounded his difficulties. The Iroquois had rejected his offer.

After Sullivan's army had left, the Iroquois had surveyed their homeland and began trying to comprehend the devastation. "[W]hat were our feelings," one asked, "when we found that there was not a mouthful of any kind of sustenance left, not even enough to keep a child one day from perishing with hunger." They made the long march eastward to the British base at Fort Niagara, and set up in and around it as refugees. By late fall 1779 their makeshift villages held 5,000 men, women and children and stretched for eight miles along the Niagara River. Then came the same severe winter that Washington's men suffered through, with snow five feet deep and temperatures so bitingly cold that people froze to death. Many died of hunger. The people they sent back to the sites of their destroyed villages to scavenge for food in the snow returned with handfuls of burnt corn. "When the snow melted in the spring," one Seneca said, "deer were found dead upon the ground in vast numbers; and other animals, of every description, perished from the cold also, and were found dead, in multitudes," so that food was scarce for the subsequent year as well.

Cornplanter had not gone to Niagara. His village was one of the few left untouched by Sullivan, so he spent the winter there. He wasn't on hand, therefore, when four men appeared from out of the white mist of the winter landscape in February 1780 and rode into the Iroquois camps around the fort. The four were themselves Iroquois leaders, but from villages that had chosen to side with the Americans. They were the messengers Washington had sent, via General Schuyler. They offered wampum belts signifying peace.

Although he wasn't at the council, and although he had in the past rejected calls to join in the war between the white nations, Cornplanter was fully in agreement with the Iroquois leaders who declined to receive the belts. They castigated the messengers as "inconsiderable people" for having broken with the Six Nations and sided with the Americans, and for now presuming to instruct them how to proceed. "We have no reason to be ashamed of what we have done," the Mohawk leader known as Aaron Hill told the messengers.

Cornplanter felt the same. Town Destroyer had burned their home-lands but had only sharpened their will. He sent word to the Iroquois leaders at Niagara that he was ready to renew the fight. Guy Johnson, the British Indian officer at Fort Niagara, updated George Germain in London: "four disaffected Indians" had tried "to draw off the Six Nations," but the Iroquois were more eager than ever to fight. He esti-mated that they had 1,200 warriors in readiness.

In the spring of 1780 the Iroquois fanned out once again. They swept into American villages in the most agriculturally rich area of New York, burning crops, killing and scalping. By summertime they were targeting Oneida and Tuscarora villages, punishing those Iroquois who had sided with the Americans. This was a historic change of behavior. The Six Nations of the Iroquois Confederacy had been united in the remote past by the mythic figures Deganawidah and Hiawatha, who had bound them together through a sacred promise to abide by the

Great Law of Peace. Now, in the effort to preserve themselves amid the conflict among the English-speaking whites, Cornplanter was leading war parties against other Iroquois. They burned their villages to the ground, and made a special point of torching Christian churches that had sprouted up in them.

In early August, Cornplanter was leading a large Iroquois army along the Mohawk River in search of American settlements. When they reached the town of Canajoharie, they found it deserted, as word of their approach had come before and people had run off. They set about methodically torching every structure. Three miles north they came to Fort Plain, a simple settlement comprised of a fort and a handful of houses clustered around it, and set everything afire. Some Americans here had not gotten word of their approach; Cornplanter's people captured these and took them with them as they retreated into the forest.

Many of Cornplanter's relatives were part of this war party, including his highly perceptive half-brother, Handsome Lake, so some may have noticed him growing increasingly agitated as they left Fort Plain. Finally, 10 miles from the settlement, Cornplanter stopped, overflowing with emotion, and turned to face one of the prisoners they had captured.

A Seneca warrior in Cornplanter's army had as his wife a white woman who had been captured as a girl and adopted by a Seneca family. Her original name was Mary Jemison, but the Iroquois called her Dehgewanus; like other Seneca women, she often traveled with war parties. She recounted in English the words Cornplanter spoke to this white prisoner.

It had been eight or ten years since Cornplanter had traveled to Albany in hopes of establishing a relationship with his Dutch-American father. John Abeel had been impassive at that time, offering him a meal but little else: no accounting for his absence in his son's life, or even any interest in it. Now, in the midst of the raid at Fort Plain, Cornplanter had recognized him through the smoke, and had pulled him out of his burning home. The old man had changed for the worse. Apparently, he didn't know who the Seneca leader was, even when the man stood before him, covered in sweat and warpaint and bristling with emotion. "I am your son!" Cornplanter cried, unable to contain himself any longer. "You are my father!"

Here in the forest, in the midst of doing the work of war in the service of his people and their freedom, Cornplanter saw that fate had given him an opportunity, a last chance to connect to his father, to make him see his son as a man. With her knowledge of both languages and cultures, Mary Jemison translated his words in a way a white audience of her time could digest, and also in such a way that the young man's feelings, his pent-up pain and frustration and anger, and as well his longing for connection and even for parental approval, came through:

> You are now my prisoner, and subject to the customs of Indian warfare: but you shall not be harmed; you need not fear. I am a warrior! Many are the scalps which I have taken! Many prisoners I have tortured to death! I am your son! I am a warrior! I was anxious to see you, and to greet you in friendship. I went to your cabin and took you by force! But your life shall be spared. Indians love their friends and their kindred, and treat them with kindness.

The naturally contemplative Seneca fighter—who was in some way at war with his own identity in the midst of a wider war—had a chance to confront the father who had abandoned him. Cornplanter wanted to squeeze something out of it. Meaning. Healing, perhaps. He must have been mulling what he would do with the old man ever since he had pulled him out of his burning cabin 10 miles down the trail. Now an idea came to him: an idea of compassion, of reaching out in love. It was a way, perhaps, to make peace not only with his father but the world of the white men. "If now you choose to follow the fortune of your yellow son, and to live with our people," Mary Jemison recorded Cornplanter as saying, "I will cherish your old age with plenty of venison, and you shall live easy. But if it is your choice to return to your fields and live with your white children, I will send a party of my trusty young men to conduct you back in safety. I respect you, my father. You have been friendly to Indians, and they are your friends."

But, no. John Abeel said he did not want to live with his son and his people, did not want Cornplanter's venison and his offer of an easy life, even though he had spent much of his life trading among the Senecas. Whatever affinity the old man had had for the Iroquois earlier in his life, he wanted nothing to do with them now.

Later, when the Iroquois held a council, Cornplanter asked his fellow leaders to free his father as well as the others they had taken at Fort Plain. The leaders agreed, "as a compliment to Cornplanter," said his nephew, Governor Blacksnake. The Iroquois army moved on, and left John Abeel behind.

## Chapter 16

# NUMBERLESS METEORS GLEAMING THROUGH THE ATMOSPHERE

Margaret Coghlan had been waiting for a chance to escape from her husband. She took it when he left her alone in the Welsh inn. But she had no plan beyond that. She simply ran out the door, and down the lane, and into the craggy, exposed, baleful wastes of the Welsh countryside. She knew he would be minutes behind her, so she did her best to conceal herself in the hillside that immediately confronted her. Rain fell, the winds whipped, there was no cover. She kept walking; walking turned into hiking. Eventually she found an inn. The innkeeper suspected that she had run away from her parents. She told him the truth; he took pity and gave her a room. The next day she set out again. "I fled from my tormentor, and fought my way across the mountains, destitute of money, and without a hut to afford me shelter from the inclemency of the weather," she wrote, "but supported by the native innocence of my own heart, I escaped from the great regardless of all lesser evils." She crossed paths with assorted characters. Men wondered what she was doing on her own, offered their services as her escort. She declined.

Eventually—after a journey of 60 miles—she came out of the mountains and into the town of Nantwich, England. Here she wrote a letter to Lord Thomas Clinton, a friend of friends and a man of stature, whose relative, General Sir Henry Clinton, was now running the British army in America. She outlined her situation and begged for his help. By return of post came a letter with 20 pounds and a promise that the powerful man would protect her.

Not long after, John Coghlan, who had somehow learned of Clinton's offer of aid, burst into Clinton's country home to the west of London in a murderous rage, declaring that he knew for a fact that Clinton was having an affair with his wife and demanding to search the house. Clinton assured Coghlan that the woman was not his lover and was not in his house. Coghlan eventually left, but not before "denouncing vengeance" on Clinton if he discovered the man had been lying to him.

Clinton set Margaret up in a townhouse in London, and provided a woman to look after her. Then he paid her a visit. "I am sorry to remark," Coghlan later wrote, "to the utter disgrace of Lord Clinton, that his behaviour to me, when I fell within his power, was such as reflects dishonour on both his *head* and his *heart*." She was trapped again: trapped by a man who used his power, the power that society gave men over women, for sexual advantage. Worse, after having his way with her for a short while, Clinton proposed to give her as a kind of prize to one of his friends. She resisted, which angered him. In desperation, she wrote to a friend, Margaret Kemble Gage, the wife of General Thomas Gage, with whom she had lived on Manhattan when General Gage was in charge of British forces. She spilled out her sad story to the woman.

Somehow her letter got into the hands of General Gage himself, who was close with her father. Shortly after, Margaret was shocked to find General Gage in person—sixty years old, flowing gray hair and a face of steely propriety—on the doorstep of her Lower Seymour Street residence. He had contacted both her father and her husband's father. On behalf of the male keepers of society's order, they had formed a little committee. Young married ladies could not be running about the countryside, taking up with gentlemen. It was unseemly and reflected badly on the men and their reputations. They concluded that she had become sullied. They decided the best thing was to get her to a nunnery: a convent in France, for a term of three years, which, they hoped, would rehabilitate her and allow time for the scandal she had caused to blow over.

So off she went, across the English Channel to Calais, partly convinced that she had sinned and was in need of reform. But the convent scared the hell out of her. She recoiled at the "melancholy habits of its superstitious inhabitants." Her disgust turned to terror on All Saints Day, when she was forced to attend a midnight mass at which the bones and skulls of the dead were piled up to be venerated.

When, out of the blue, Thomas Clinton showed up one day, she all but fell into his arms. He bribed the abbess to let her go and took her back to England. Once again he set her up in London. Yet again General Gage found her. This time he used a different tactic: he informed her that her father had fallen into a state of "misery" and despondence over her waywardness. This hit her hard. As had been the case since she was a child, her feelings for her father comprised a mix of slavish devotion and something close to hatred. But the devotion, the longing to appease and delight him, had always won out, and it did once again. She pronounced herself "unable to endure the thought of afflicting the tenderest of parents, whom I most affectionately loved." She had grown up in a world in which calls for freedom rang out in the air, inspiring whole armies. She had been foolish enough to think that some portion of this freedom might apply to her. She was wrong. She was a stupid girl who had shamed her father. She gave up, decided to "forego those visionary and fatal schemes of happiness, which my imagination had formed."

Gage set her up in the home of a respectable family near Grosvenor Square in London, where she lived quietly for a time. The attacks by General Washington's northern army under Sullivan on the Iroquois homelands made news in England during this time. So did a vote of the Irish parliament to imitate the Americans in embargoing British-made goods, setting off British fears that the Irish might eventually rebel too. People in England were feeling closed in, vulnerable. The king gave a speech to Parliament in which he called on Whigs to rally around the government as it faced an "unjust and unprovoked war" against not only America but France and Spain and was "contending with one of the most dangerous confederacies that ever was formed against the Crown and people of Great Britain."

Then one day Margaret received a letter from Mrs. Gage. It contained news more shattering than anything the king of England could deliver. After long consideration, Margaret's father had decided that she had brought such shame and dishonor on herself that he was no longer willing to claim her as his daughter. He had decided to disown her. She would not be receiving money from him; she would not be in his will. He advised her to learn a trade, to take up "mantua making": to become a sewer of ladies' robes.

Her first reaction was indignation. Then, through yet another intermediary, she pleaded with him. She was frightened at the thought of being financially on her own, but even more at the prospect of permanently losing his affection. Her father, however, had made up his mind. The finality settled in, and led her to a conclusion: "the actual dishonour of a beloved daughter pleads sufficient excuse for any harshness which I may have experienced from him." Translation: it was all her fault.

But self-blame gave her no solace. Instead, her father's desertion of her made her "almost frantic." She ran back to Thomas Clinton, who took her in again. Clinton was at this moment campaigning for the House of Commons seat for the city of Westminster. His opponent was the renowned Whig Charles James Fox. Margaret Coghlan chanced to meet Mr. Fox at an event, and she thrilled at the man's wit and rhetoric. He was short, dark and plump, certainly not to be compared with Aaron Burr, but something in him captivated her. It was also true that she was still reeling from the shock of her father's abandonment of her. She needed to find a way forward. Virtually on the spot, she dropped her protector, Lord Clinton, for his archenemy—who also vanquished Clinton in the political contest—and she and Charles Fox became lovers.

In a short time she had gone from wandering alone and desperate in the Welsh mountains to permanently losing her father's affection to being a fixture of London society. The freedom she had insisted on when she had first rejected John Coghlan had been a vague thing in her mind. For a man its features were clear: power, career, the ability to travel the world at will. But for a woman, what was freedom exactly? She had a few guides and models. There had been Mrs. Loring in New York, the mistress of General Howe, who had presided over the occupied city like a queen in some fanciful universe, one in which women did not need marriage to win respect. But even then Elizabeth Loring had needed a powerful man. That, Margaret understood, was the only logical course. Here in London, the mistresses to aristocrats and members of Parliament projected elegance and confidence. Some were also celebrated actresses, which seemed only appropriate—were they not also acting in real life? Margaret believed she could play that role.

Besides, she was genuinely intrigued. She had never before encountered such a person as Charles James Fox. He had a somewhat piggish face but a hypnotic zeal. Fox was famed for his orotund denunciations of the American Secretary, Lord George Germain, whom he decried for "willful ignorance" and "incapacity" in exercising his office, and famed for his impassioned support of the Americans' quest for liberty. She had also never before appreciated the cause of America in philosophical terms. She learned from Fox something of the historic roots of the American cause. He also reinforced what she had intuited in New York, how freedom was not a cold abstraction but a hot and human desire.

"The war of the Americans is a war of passion," Fox had told Parliament not long before he took up with Margaret. "It is of such a nature as to be supported by the most powerful virtues, love of liberty and of country . . ." and for this reason, he warned his colleagues, "such a war is without end" for it "inspires a spirit that is unconquerable."

Fox didn't stop there in his championing of liberty. He denounced as well the barbaric American practice of human slavery, and called for religious toleration in England. There was, he understood, a great, historical transformation in human values underway. America—in its rebellion, if not in its practice of slavery—was on the right side of it, and England was not.

In Fox's company Coghlan began to feel a bit of lightness opening up inside her. She was only seventeen: she had a life ahead of her. Fox mentioned that he knew the great playwright Richard Sheridan. The plays she had seen in New York had captivated her, the bright lights of the stage contrasting so vividly with the darkness of the city under military occupation. She blurted out that she felt "a natural inclination for the stage," and Fox promptly introduced her to Sheridan. She began making plans. The following season, she would, with any luck, make her debut as an actress at the Drury Lane Theater, which Sheridan owned.

Moving through London with Fox, attending events at his side, Margaret Coghlan was moderately alarmed by his fondness for gambling and drink, but delighted in the constant stream of political discourse. At around this time Fox took part in a debate in the House about suspicions that George Germain had profited from his post of American Secretary. Fox gleefully resurrected the Battle of Minden, declaring to Germain's face that he was "a coward, and always had been." That sort of boldness was part of what thrilled her about him.

She thrilled him as well, but only for a time. It hurt when he pushed her aside and moved on, but she so admired him that she worked out a calculus of his rejection of her that made sense to her. "The giddiness of extreme youth, and remarkable levity of my disposition," she decided, were "not calculated to secure the attachment of this illustrious character." Besides, she had kept herself mindful of the fact that she had been playing a role, that eventually the play would end.

Yet again, then, she was on her own. And there was one other thing now. She was pregnant.

Affection didn't come naturally to George Washington. It took war to bring it out in him. Now, in the full throes of conflict, with his young country finding itself surrounded by blood and pain, as he was suffering alongside his soldiers in the cold and heat, he was feeling and expressing personal fondness as never before. He had forged warm relationships with his men and the officers on his staff. And in the wider world—in America and beyond its shores—an affectionate image of him had formed. In September 1780 he met the leader of the French forces that had been sent to aid him—Jean-Baptiste Donatien de Vimeur, Comte de Rochambeau—at Hartford, Connecticut, in order to plan what he hoped would be a joint offensive against the British. Washington's fame had grown throughout Europe, and Rochambeau's officers found that the American general lived up to their expectations. He was dignified but without the stuffiness of the Old World; they saw that his men clearly adored him. So did the people of a local village; one French officer marveled at how they "pressed so closely around us that they hindered us from proceeding" and addressed Washington as "father."

Washington didn't get what he had wanted from Rochambeau. The aristocrat seemed to suggest that a French fleet would not be in a position to mount a full attack until the following year, which almost certainly meant the war would drag on. This was frustrating because Washington knew that across the ocean pressures were mounting on his inexorable antagonist, George Germain, so that a decisive blow might end things. But he needed the French to help deliver it.

Washington's next stop after his meeting with Rochambeau was an inspection of the military fortress at West Point on the Hudson River. The most pleasing part of this excursion would be the small get-together that had been set with another of the younger officers for whom he had developed an emotional attachment. Benedict Arnold had endured a great deal in the war. He had fought bravely and brilliantly at Saratoga, had been unjustly denied a promotion by Congress and had been crippled by a battle injury. Washington felt for the man, and looked forward to spending time with him and his wife, Peggy, at the mansion on the east bank of the Hudson where they were staying. But when he got there for a scheduled breakfast meeting, they weren't in. He changed his plans and returned to meet them for dinner, but, again, the couple didn't show.

Washington was puzzled. He was resting in his own room in the mansion a short while later when Alexander Hamilton burst in and thrust a packet of letters at him. Lafayette appeared as well, breathless to see what was up. A British spy named John André had been caught nearby; these papers were found hidden in his boot. Washington read with an enveloping sense of dread. "Arnold has betrayed us!" he gasped at length. He looked at his two closest aides and asked, "Whom can we trust now?"

As his disgruntlement over being denied promotion grew and festered, Arnold had come to wonder whether the British might value him more. He contacted Sir Henry Clinton; eventually he wrote directly to George Germain, suggesting, as had others, that Washington himself might be willing to switch sides if offered "a title." What Washington held in his hand was an account, copied out by Arnold, of Washington's own directions to the army, and of the fortification of West Point. Arnold was assisting the enemy in an attempted takeover of the American headquarters on the Hudson.

What amazed him was not that an officer of his had turned traitor. Such things happened in war. But Arnold was one of those he most trusted. The revelation shook his confidence in his intuition. He told Hamilton to find Arnold.

The revelation didn't seem to dampen Washington's feelings for those in his immediate circle. He had become dependent in particular on the long talks he had with Hamilton: about military strategy, about the French and whether they would ever truly come to their aid, about the unworkability of the Articles of Confederation, which Congress was voting on and which was already proving a cumbersome foundation for a national government. Washington marveled at Hamilton. The man had had far fewer advantages than he, but he had made excellent use of his brilliant mind. He was still in his early twenties and was on his way to becoming an outright expert on military science, on government, and especially on finance. Washington found himself swayed by Hamilton's argument that Congress needed to have the power to tax, that a national tax was the only firm basis for a stable government and thus the only means to ensure individual liberty.

But Washington's very reliance on Hamilton had blinded him to the younger man's growing unhappiness. Hamilton longed to distinguish himself in battle; he had soaring ambitions beyond the war. He took one step in advancing his career by marrying Elizabeth Schuyler, the daughter of Philip Schuyler, who remained a force in New York politics. But because he was so valuable to Washington, Hamilton had been overlooked for promotions and reassignments. As he stayed confined to a job that he considered to be beneath his abilities, he became bitter, and the more openly Washington expressed warmth toward him, the more closed he became toward the general. He wrote to his father-in-law about Washington, declaring, with a young man's grim fervor, that "for three years past I have felt no friendship for him and professed none."

Washington remained oblivious to his aide's distress until it burst forth in one childish incident. Washington had ordered Hamilton to attend him; Hamilton kept him waiting for ten minutes. The general, who was not used to having to wait for his subordinates, upbraided him: "I must tell you, sir, you treat me with disrespect." Hamilton shot back: "I am not conscious of it, sir, but since you thought it necessary to tell me so, we part!" Washington was unprepared for his secretary to quit his service over a trifle. He took the unusual step of reaching out to the junior officer to try to make amends. But Hamilton would not reconsider. Washington eventually reassigned him. Once again, he was flummoxed by the vagaries of human affection.

At almost the same time, he was blindsided by yet another personal blow. Benjamin Harrison, the head of the Virginia House of Burgesses, sent him a letter saying that he had received a petition for financial assistance from Washington's mother. With the onset of the war Washington had let his testy and painful relationship with his mother go dormant. He didn't write her a single letter. Nor did she contact her son. He had bought her a house in Fredericksburg and arranged that a cousin would oversee her needs. But dating back to his boyhood, his mother had exerted a dark, downward pull on him; he had too many demands on his attention to allow himself to be dragged into the kind of battle that she favored. But she found a way to get at him. Her letter to the burgesses, declaring that she was destitute and in need of assistance, seemed calculated to embarrass him. It did. He wrote a fumbling, awkward reply to Harrison, detailing all the care he had devoted to establishing his mother's comfort, and concluded: "I request, in pointed terms if the matter is now in agitation in your assembly, that all proceedings on it may be stopped." It must have begun to seem to him that, in comparison with the complexity of human relations, war was a rather simple business.

. . .

It had been clear to Washington for some time that George Germain planned to make the South his primary target. The British were now using Charleston, South Carolina, as a base. After the taking of that city, Sir Henry Clinton had shifted back to New York, leaving General Cornwallis in command in the South. Then, in August, Cornwallis had annihilated Horatio Gates's army at Camden, South Carolina, forcing Congress to admit its mistake in choosing Gates for the position. After the loss, Congress finally enlarged Washington's powers, giving him authority over the South. Washington picked Nathanael Greene to command there. Greene had a much smaller force to work with than did Cornwallis, but he set about a series of deft maneuvers, splitting up his forces and launching surprise attacks, and so began chipping away at the British advantage.

Still, the numbers were against the Americans. To compound the problem of lack of soldiers, in the first week of January 1781, unable to endure their horrendous living conditions, 2,000 Pennsylvania soldiers mutinied. Washington desperately needed to raise troops. Calls went out to the states for new recruits.

Among the towns that answered the call was Haddam, Connecticut. On January 29, a gangly group of local men mustered under their new commanding officer, Captain Caleb Baldwin, who had until recently been a schoolmaster and town clerk. Of the 330 men in the second Connecticut regiment, about 10 were black. One of these was Cuff Smith, Venture Smith's twenty-two-year old son, who had enlisted for service a month before. Venture and Meg Smith and their six-year-old son Solomon said their goodbyes, and Cuff marched off with the town's other new recruits into the landscape of a New England winter. Like his father, Cuff was tall and uncommonly strong, and he was in excellent physical condition from hauling timber on his father's estate and from the work he sometimes did at the local stone quarry. But Venture and Meg had to feel the sting of the parting. They had already lost two children in difficult circumstances; they knew they might never see him again.

Cuff Smith and his fellow enlistees marched 100 miles west, made camp at a desolate spot east of the Hudson River, and spent the rest of the winter there. They built huts and drilled, but otherwise didn't do much of anything. Within weeks of joining the Continental Army, they found themselves hungry and threadbare, waiting interminably through freezing days and nights for something to happen.

Then, as spring broke, orders from General Washington arrived. They were to march south, following the Hudson. Washington had two possible courses of action. Either he would attack Clinton's forces in New York, and try to retake Manhattan, or he would pull the army south toward Virginia and mount an all-out assault on Cornwallis. As he seemed to favor the attack on Manhattan, they camped near Dobbs Ferry, just 10 miles from the northern tip of Manhattan. Here Cuff Smith got an experience he had been waiting for: not battle, but a sighting of their leader. The soldiers gazed at General Washington—erect in the saddle and with his uncommon bearing, eyes slitted as he surveyed them, lips tightly compressed—as an almost superhuman being. An officer who arrived in camp at this time noted that Washington appeared somehow on a different plane from everyone else: "calm . . . calculated . . . admirable . . . the leader of his army."

Washington had waited for months for the French allies to commit to aiding him. Finally, the French were acting. French ships disembarked soldiers in Providence, Rhode Island, and they marched south and joined the Americans. On July 8, Cuff Smith, who had little experience of the world outside the wooded hamlets of Haddam, East Haddam and Haddam Neck, watched with the other men of the Connecticut Line as the French forces—5,300 men—conducted a formal parade that was unlike anything any of them had ever seen. Their uniforms were white, and they weren't soiled in the least but, amazingly, were truly as pure as snow, with flashes of crimson, pink and azure to signify their regiments. They executed their formal maneuvers with an exactness that had the Americans gawping. The French were equally thunderstruck by the American troops but for different reasons: "soldiers composed of men of every age, even children of fifteen, of whites and blacks, almost naked, unpaid, and rather poorly fed," an officer described them. But he was equally struck that such a ragtag army could "march so well and withstand fire so steadfastly," and this he attributed to their commander.

At eight o'clock in the morning of July 21, Washington organized his army to move on New York. They aligned in four columns; Cuff Smith was in the far right. The French were all the way to the left. Field pieces, twelve-pounders, howitzers: the engines of war were maneuvered into position. They advanced southward. As a private, Venture Smith's son wasn't told anything beyond the fact that they would make a reconnaissance of the British defenses around Manhattan. For all he knew, if General Washington thought conditions were right, they would then launch the attack on New York that would spell the end of British control of America.

In Haddam, meanwhile, once Cuff had marched off along with so many other local boys, life was even quieter than usual. Venture Smith rode his two-wheeled, horse-drawn cart on his rounds: to the ferry, to Bezaleel Brainerd's sawmill, to a store in East Haddam where people tended to congregate and where, if pressed, he would perform feats of strength, such as carrying a tierce of salt—a 42-gallon cask—across the room. When he had to travel down to the coast at Stonington, he would stop in to see Rebecca Mumford, the youngest sister of his first owner, who, despite their difference in status, had been a playmate in his youth, and they would reminisce about their childhood on Fishers Island.

Trips to Stonington and New London were routine. Sailing vessels came up and down the Connecticut River, for the men of Haddam, looking to make money from the war, were heavily involved in privateering and shipping. Venture Smith, in addition, kept up his land speculation. In February 1781, in the days after he had seen Cuff off, he did a bit of business with two of the town's most respectable men. James Green was a wealthy blacksmith; Amos White was a cooper who also managed the business of Humphrey Lyon, a local shipowner and merchant. Smith sold 28 acres of his land to White and Green, for 174 pounds. It wasn't a true sale. Venture needed capital just now, and without banks, you made deals like this with friends and neighbors. He would pay "rent" until such time as he could repay the loan. The arrangement spoke to the position of trust he had in town.

More noteworthy, however, was a tiny detail on the deed. In all previous transactions he had been identified as "Venture, a Free Negro." The custom of slaves being referred to by only one name was long-standing, and it tended to linger even for those who had won their freedom and chosen a surname. This time, however, whether consciously or not, the town clerk had taken a modest step toward healing a transcendent wound. "To all People to whom these Presents shall Come, Greeting," the deed of transfer began, and then the clerk picked up his pen and wrote: "Know Ye that I, Venture Smith . . ."

The decision to focus Britain's full military might on the South was George Germain's. Henry Clinton, his commander in the field, did not agree with it, but Germain went behind his back and gave Cornwallis instructions to proceed. Clinton had wanted to bring forces northward again, but Germain sent him an order that not a single one of

Cornwallis's soldiers was to be shifted from the Chesapeake, that rather he should send troops southward to aid Cornwallis, that the final conquest of America was to be mounted from there.

Cornwallis then conspired with the American Secretary against his superior officer. He and his army would make for the coast: Clinton was to send ships and men to meet them. He wrote to both Clinton and Germain ensuring them that his position was strong. But then things changed, swiftly. Cornwallis was supposed to be aided by the droves of loyalists in the South, but there didn't seem to be as many as Germain had thought. Washington had sent Lafayette south with an army of 4,500 men; soon after they arrived, they began small-scale attacks that harassed Cornwallis's larger force as it traveled eastward. And as the summer wore on, his men—marching through the humid Virginia countryside, from Charlottesville to Richmond to Portsmouth—were stricken with malaria. He dashed off a note to a fellow officer, admitting, "My situation here is very distressing."

His goal was Yorktown. Here the ships that Clinton was to send from New York would provide reinforcements. It was a risky plan because Yorktown was on a peninsula; if the American army arrived in force, he would be trapped. But even if that happened, he reasoned, the ships coming from New York would allow the possibility of escape by sea.

In London, George Germain agonized as he waited the interminable time for reports from his two American armies to make their leisurely way across the ocean to him. He seemed to sense that things were coming to a head, and he knew there was cause for concern. He had few close friends; with his wife gone, he was mostly alone with his anxiety. He attended his oldest daughter Elizabeth's wedding but was too preoccupied to fully enjoy the occasion. His youngest daughter, Caroline, was sometimes able to distract him with a game of chess. Then would come a letter, which he pounced on. In September, his nephew, George Damer, who was serving in Cornwallis's army, wrote him from the precarious peninsula, noting a "considerable part of our force cut off and besieged" and declaring, "I do not believe the most sanguine admirer of my Lord Cornwallis or of his army could expect him to hold out longer than from two months to ten weeks." If Clinton's ships arrived, the army would be saved, and the great offensive begun. But where were Clinton's ships? And, meanwhile, where on earth was the main American force? Had Washington remained on the outskirts of New York, or was he moving south? It was now the desperate goal of the British at Yorktown, Damer informed his uncle, "to discover Mr. Washington's true design."

"I begin, at this Epoch, a concise Journal of Military transactions &ca. I lament not having attempted it from the commencement of the War."

After six years of fighting, it was dawning on George Washington that a decisive "Epoch" had at last arrived, prompting him, belatedly, to start recording events as they unfolded.

In July, he marched 5,000 of his soldiers, among them Venture Smith's son, from their camp near Dobbs Ferry to Kingsbridge, just opposite the northern tip of Manhattan Island. Manhattan was the center of British power in America. Washington remained convinced that taking it would end the war. After doing extensive reconnaissance of the British positions, however, he pulled his men back to camp. He was bitterly disappointed with the state governments, which had sent him far fewer recruits than he had requested. This put him all the more at the mercy of promised French ships. He could not act until and unless he knew they were making for New York Harbor.

The joy that came with the first news of a French alliance had long since worn off. France had its own affairs to manage, only one small component of which involved assisting the Americans against England. The main French fleet was in the West Indies. Washington was informed that a detachment would sail north to aid him. But he didn't know when, or how big it would be, or what kind of assistance to expect. What caused him the most anxiety was having no idea where this detachment would even sail to. As conflicting reports reached him, he concocted plans for a grand attack on New York, then switched to pondering a joint assault against Cornwallis's army in the Chesapeake, then switched back to New York, then back to the South.

Meanwhile, he had Rochambeau, and a French army, here in camp with him. They too were awaiting word. Wanting to impress the French officers and keep them primed to assist, he went out of his way to stage lavish dinners for them. The French were indeed impressed, but less by the meals—they noted with displeasure that salads had vinegar but no oil, and they were not given clean plates for each course—than by Washington himself, who presided with "unaffected cheerfulness."

On August 14 he got a dispatch from the Comte de Barras, the French admiral who was then in Newport, Rhode Island. With a mixture of excitement and anxiety, Washington read that de Barras's colleague, the Comte de Grasse, was leaving the Caribbean imminently. Amazingly, wondrously, he would have with him between 25 and 29 ships of the line and 3,200 troops. Aided by such a force, Washington knew he could wreck the British. But, he read further, the French assistance came with a catch. De Grasse considered his main duties to be in the Caribbean. He would have to sail back there on October 15. Thus, he was not heading for New York, which was too far away. He would sail for the Chesapeake.

Washington had to let the French plans dictate his prosecution of the war. He would not attack New York. Instead, he had to get his entire army more than 400 miles to the south. And the clock was ticking: he had to do it with all possible speed in order to take advantage of the French timetable. If he was angry, however, it was less at the French, who had no emotional stake in the fight, than at his country's own leaders. In his diary he noted that his fighting force was limited by "the feeble compliance of the States to my requisitions for Men."

The next day he sent word to Lafayette, who was doing a fine job of pestering Cornwallis's army, telling him to "prevent if possible the retreat of Cornwallis toward Carolina." Everything now depended on the element of surprise. If they could fool the British into thinking New York was their objective, perhaps Clinton would keep his main force there and Cornwallis could be trapped.

He gave the orders to march. He was so concerned with keeping his plans secret that his own men didn't know where they were headed. They had to begin by marching north in order to cross the Hudson River without alerting the British. On the evening of August 21, after a long and satisfying day, Washington wrote in his diary, "In the course of this day the whole of the American Troop, all their baggage, artillery & Stores, crossed the river." It was a huge undertaking, and getting it done so rapidly pleased him. But that turned to exasperation when the French army took an unconscionably leisurely four days to make the same crossing.

At the end of the month he rode ahead of the army into Philadelphia. He was hoping to arrange for ships to take men and supplies as much of the way as possible, but those he was able to locate he found "inadequate to the purpose of transporting both Troops & Stores," which meant his men would have to continue trudging on foot all the way to the northern tip of the Chesapeake Bay.

He rode on southward. Couriers pounded up to him giving him progress reports. On September 5 he learned that his army, marching behind him, had passed through Philadelphia and the French army had just entered the city. Another courier, this one from the south, reached him. He tore open the letter and read words that were perhaps sweeter than any he had ever read in his life. The Comte de Grasse had arrived in the Chesapeake: "with 28 Sail of the line & four frigates," he wrote in his diary, and "with 3000 land Troops which were to be immediately debarked at James town & form a junction with the American Army under the command of the Marqs. de la Fayette."

Standing, shortly after, on the shore at the town of Chester, Pennsylvania, he spied a small boat approaching. In it were General Rochambeau and other French officers. Their arrival meant that his army would be there soon, and he now knew the French fleet was already in place. This confluence of forces, which he had worked for not just for days but for years, sent him into an uncharacteristic state of giddiness. The Frenchmen in their boat saw a figure dancing and hopping on the bank, waving his hat at them. They could not believe it was the famously reserved commander of the American forces. One of them reported, "I have never seen a man more overcome with great and sincere joy than was General Washington."

Washington greeted them with the news that de Grasse was in the bay. All the forces were aligning. He just had to get his own army another 270 miles south.

When he reached the Maryland town called Head of Elk (because it was located at the mouth of the Elk River, where it enters the Chesapeake), he was disgusted to find "a great deficiency of Transports." He had hoped to sail his men and supplies the length of the bay, and he thought he had made arrangements for this. He commenced a furious round of letter-writing, calling on "Gentn. of Influence on the Eastern shore" to assist him in getting boats. His actions betrayed his anxiety and exasperation, as he sensed how much was at stake and seemingly wondered that others in the country, who were supposedly ardent fellow patriots, were going blithely about their lives without urgency.

He decided it was better that he ride onward to meet personally with de Grasse than wait for the army to catch up to him. The route southward carried, as he well knew, right past his front door. He had not been to Mount Vernon in six years. He rode over the familiar rolling hilltops, and finally the main building came into view. The house was still incomplete when he had left; work had been done since; he was seeing now for the first time his home as he had envisioned it. Its mix of grandeur and simplicity suited him. Here a man could feel at peace. The architectural pedigree was as frankly European as were the Enlightenment principles he had been in the service of these many years.

Martha was here, as were his stepchildren and their own children, some of whom had been born in his absence. The slaves formed dutiful lines to greet him. He had repeatedly in the past year longed to get back home. But now that he was here he could not rest. The next day Rochambeau and other officers arrived. The foreign officers had been curious to see what a great American's estate was like. They were somewhat disappointed. Instead of opulence, there was simplicity and a sense of austerity about the place, which they supposed reflected America's puritan tendencies. One of them described the general's wife as "small and fat."

After three days, Washington was back on his horse, hurrying southward. Early on September 18, off Cape Henry, at the southernmost point of the bay, he saw what he had long dreamed of: 32 French vessels, elegant machines of war, their sails and guns catching the orange light of the morning sun. He was rowed out to the *Ville de Paris*, de Grasse's flagship, and had his first meeting with the admiral, in which he "settled most points with him to my satisfaction." De Grasse had deep experience with siege warfare, and he informed the American general that the French would run the siege. It was not, they told him, a matter of cleverness but of method; it was, as Washington reiterated, "reducible to calculation."

For weeks now, Washington had been hoping that Cornwallis would stay on the long finger of land that protruded out into the bay, where he could be trapped. And, inexplicably, he had. Cornwallis had taken over the little village of Yorktown, which sat at the edge of the peninsula on the banks of the York River, as well as the village of Gloucester across the river.

Over the next two weeks, the French and American armies dug trenches, built walls and hauled cannons into position. Washington was amazed that Cornwallis, once he became aware of their presence, did not lunge forth in attack. He figured the British general had at most 6,000 men. The combined American and French armies totaled more than 18,000. Cornwallis was clearly waiting, but for what? Did he expect Clinton to rescue him?

On October 9, at three o'clock in the afternoon, the first French guns, way to Washington's left, began blasting. After two hours of unrelenting noise, the American battery to his right opened fire. The attack on the enemy positions, which continued through the next day, was so successful the British had to pull back the cannons with which they had been returning fire. In the night, the French cannons took aim at enemy ships at anchor. They had loaded with "red hot shot"—balls heated until they glowed—and sent them with expert precision at their wooden targets. Washington watched in awe as four British ships, including one frigate, caught fire and sent roaring columns of flame into the night sky. By morning they were gone.

The deafening blasts continued over the following days. From time to time the British mounted a strong counteroffensive, which then subsided. Steadily, the trench building continued, edging the allied armies and their artillery closer to the walls the British had built.

For all his supreme exertions over the years of the war, here at Yorktown Washington had a curiously reduced role. He was the chief commanding officer, but diggers and artillerymen controlled the action, along with the French engineers who had planned it all out with mathematical calculations. From runaways he learned that Cornwallis was living underground somewhere behind the walls, in a cave his men had built him, directing the defense and, apparently, waiting for a British fleet.

Then on the morning of October 17, after eight days of unrelenting, shuddering onslaught, a courier handed Washington a message from the enemy:

> *Sir, I propose a cessation of hostilities for twenty-four hours, and that two officers may be appointed by each side to meet at Mr. Moore's house to settle terms for the surrender of the posts of York and Gloucester. I have the honor to be, &c., Cornwallis*

Washington could not believe it had come so quickly. But he sensed a possible trap. Maybe Cornwallis had gotten word that reinforcements were en route, and was stalling for time. While he had "an ardent desire to spare the further effusion of blood," he wrote in reply, he would agree to a ceasefire not of twenty-four hours but of "two hours from the delivery of this letter" so that Cornwallis could deliver his terms for surrendering. Cornwallis sent his terms. Washington found them agreeable. The cannons fell silent. The silence rose up and filled the skies above the heads of the thousands of hot, sweat-soaked, blood-and-mud-spattered men on both sides. The sun set, and the cold autumn sky filled up: with "ten thousand stars," one soldier declared, and "numberless meteors gleaming through the atmosphere."

It was a big, wide, confusing world, as it had been since the dawn of time. General Sir Henry Clinton was still holed up in the fortress he had made of Manhattan Island. There were men in far-off places still locked in combat. A British fleet was out there somewhere, intent on menace. Washington knew it wasn't over yet. But he also knew, or sensed at least, that it was.

# PART THREE

*Chapter 17*

THE CAUSE OF HUMANITY

Late November 1781, and people on the streets of London, huddled against an icy wind coming off the Thames, were talking of only one thing. Customs officials had seized a huge shipment of illegal brandy and had been transporting it to a warehouse when "a daring and outrageous Gang of Smugglers, on Horseback" swept in, armed with "Blunderbusses, Musquets, Pistols and other offensive Weapons," attacked the officers and made away with the goods. The alert published in the *London Gazette* promised a smacking reward of 100 pounds for anyone with information of the crime.

The very next day, other news arrived that shouldered aside gossip about brandy and reward money. The information from America had made its way first to France. The packet boat from Calais had no sooner tied up to the dock at Dover than copies of a French journal were unloaded. The journal, said Horace Walpole, contained an astonishing account, "of Lord Cornwallis and his whole army having been made prisoners at York Town by General Washington."

When George Germain brought the news to his prime minister, he was appalled to observe the normally reserved Lord North receive the information "like a ball in the breast." Stern old soldier that he was,

Germain was even more disgusted when North gasped weakly, "Oh God, it is all over!"

In public houses and gentlemen's clubs the reaction was much the same. Not that people felt, as North did, that their careers were ruined, but they felt that England, in its quest for global empire, was suddenly on a downward trajectory, which would affect their lives mightily. On the heels of the news from America came reports of French victories in the Caribbean and coastal South America, which took away valuable British possessions. James Lowther stood up in the House of Commons to declare that the American war had been "obstinately, fatally pursued" and that "the country was drained, exhausted, dejected."

The same members of the House who had long opposed Germain—Edmund Burke, Isaac Barré, Margaret Coghlan's recent lover Charles James Fox—now renewed their attacks on the whole war effort, and in particular on the man who had led it. Their colleague Edward Gibbon, a member of the House of Commons, had published the first volume of his *History of the Decline and Fall of the Roman Empire* with unintentional irony in the year 1776; the Whigs now referred to it, likening the British situation to what Gibbon described as Rome began its collapse. One of them stood up to quote Gibbon on the signs of Rome's decay, citing that the empire "ceased to be formidable abroad, and became odious and oppressive at home: that taxes increased with the poverty of the state; and that the emperors wasted the resources of the empire, in carrying on wars against rebels that they themselves had made."

Lord North, once he had recovered from the news of Yorktown, tried to fashion a new strategy, in which Britain would offer the Americans peace without outright independence but with a status as adjuncts to empire. "Peace with America seems necessary," he told the king, "even if it can be obtained on no better terms than some Federal Alliance."

A problem with his strategy was that, while seemingly everyone in the country was ready for peace, one man who was not was George

III. He vowed that he would abdicate before giving up. Instead, he called for a new general to lead the fight, and for new, more forceful military plans.

The prime minister had suggested to the king that, in light of everything, Lord George Germain had to be replaced as American Secretary. The king was willing to consider this, but, he said, "above all I must be certain that a new Secretary is not of the yielding kind." This put North in a quandary, for arguably the only man in government who was still not of the yielding kind on America was Germain himself.

Indeed, Germain remained vigorously active. He wrote a lengthy memo to the king, warning him against heeding those who called for peace: "If you consider the consequences of totally abandoning the colonies, you must not confine yourself only to the dismembring the Empire, and to the losing the commerce you now enjoy, but you must reflect upon the additional weight and strength which France will derive from it." He predicted that if His Majesty let go of America then Canada would "immediately fall, and your fisheries at Newfoundland and all your possessions in the W. Indies." In short, relinquishing the American colonies would bring about the collapse of the British Empire.

Completely in the face of most others in government, Germain pushed the king to fight on: to continue to hold New York in a vise-like grip while redirecting the fleet (which had put to sea too late to reinforce Cornwallis in Yorktown and then returned to New York) to launch attacks on ports along the American coast. He sketched out troop numbers and movements, and he reiterated the belief that there were thousands upon thousands of loyalists in America who could be relied upon.

This was the sort of thing George III wanted from his ministers. He was inclined to support the plan, to support Germain. But men in Parliament were holding meetings. Peace was necessary, and it seemed to most of them that this would require granting America sovereignty. One by one, members of Parliament informed the prime minister that they would not support a continuation of the war. In particular, they would not support Germain.

Germain got wind of this. He went to his country estate to ponder. When he returned to London, he tried to meet with the king, but now the king shunned him. Germain understood what was happening, but was never one for subtlety. He stood gruffly outside the Privy Council chamber, waiting for a meeting to end, and accosted His Majesty as he left. "Am I out?" he asked. The king ducked the question.

Finally, in January 1782, Germain saw the inevitable and abruptly changed tactics. He wrote the prime minister, saying that he knew the government had to take firm actions, and asked Lord North "to dispose of me in that manner which may best answer your Lordship's views for his Majesty's service and the public good." To an outsider Germain may have seemed to be offering to resign unconditionally, but North apprehended what he wanted. Honor was the primary coin of the realm, the true language that one such as George Germain communicated in, and if he were to go, it would be with honor.

Germain received a formal audience with the king. "Is there anything I can do," the king asked, "which would be agreeable to you?" "Sir," Germain replied, "if your Majesty is pleased to raise me to the dignity of the Peerage, it will form at once the best reward to which I can aspire, and the best proof of Your approbation of my past exertions in Your affairs." This had all been worked out in advance; the king gave his formal assent, and further agreed not just to make him a baron but to elevate him one step up, to the rank of viscount.

On February 7, then, the now-retired Viscount Sackville, as he would henceforth be known, exhibited himself before his peers in the House of Lords. A larger than usual number of them were present for the occasion: 128 marquises, earls and dukes, a formidable panoply of powdered wigs and silk breeches and waistcoats. Unfortunately for him, however, they had not taken pains to be on hand in order to honor the new viscount. Rather, they were closing ranks.

The Marquess of Carmarthen began by voicing his displeasure that "a person who had in his military character been publicly degraded" had been elevated to the peerage, and remarked that he considered this "a disgrace." He charged that "Lord George Sackville is guilty of having disobeyed the orders of Prince Ferdinand of Brunswick." The Battle of Minden was rearing its head yet again, twenty-three years after the fact. The peers of the realm had not forgotten, and they would never forget. The Earl of Abingdon went further, declaring that the new peer was "the greatest criminal this country ever knew," who had acted disgracefully as a military officer and "had been infinitely more guilty in his civil situation."

On and on the Lords went, their sonorous and censorious sentences echoing about the chamber, venting at Sackville, responding belatedly to years of his having so stridently pushed himself and his views on the government, all but accusing him of using the American war as a way of exorcizing his own personal demons, and releasing their pent-up outrage over the loss of America, over "the capture of York Town, the whole criminality of which might be brought home to the noble lord," and denouncing the man as "the author of all the calamities of the war."

Germain—Sackville—sat silently through it all. At last he rose. In a strong voice but one tremored with anger, he recounted his career, revived the defense of his conduct at Minden, and added to it a defense of his management of the American war. The British public, he asserted with feeling, never had "a servant who shewed more unremitting assiduity, more close attention to the duties of his situation, or more zeal for promoting the interests of his country."

The whole thing was a demonstration unlike any the House of Lords had ever known. At last the display of aristocratic condemnation came to an end, and Viscount Sackville, shaken but unrepentant and unbowed, went home to his retirement.

The room was dark and stifling. The patient lay on the bed, dying. Unexpectedly, George Washington found himself plunged from the exuberance of battlefield victory into a scene of intimate grief.

He had ridden from Yorktown 40 miles north to the home of his wife's brother-in-law in the little town of Eltham, where he planned to spend the night before continuing on to Mount Vernon. He was surprised to find Martha here, her face wracked by sorrow. Her son, Washington's stepson, Jacky Custis, had served under him in the army at Yorktown. During the siege Jacky had caught "camp fever." He had been brought here to his relative's house to recover. He did not. He died shortly after Washington arrived.

Washington stayed for six days, to assist and to grieve. The event turned his mood from celebratory to contemplative. Indeed, there would be much to contemplate in the coming months. The war existed still, but it went static. Meanwhile, Congress was in chaos. Soldiers had not been paid in years, and, now that they were idle, were turning ugly. American leaders seemed to have no strategy for dealing with the peace that now seemed in the offing. Many were gravitating toward the only governmental organizing principle that any of them had ever known; Gouverneur Morris of New York expressed himself openly on the subject to General Nathanael Greene: "I have no hope that our union can subsist except in the form of an absolute monarchy."

Alexander Hamilton wrote to Washington, trying to convince him that, in the event peace arrived, it was important that the army should remain, for without it anarchy would sweep in. Besides that, Hamilton argued, gingerly, that Washington should be the one to "guide the torrent." Further, perhaps the greatest problem of the moment was the lack of public finances. Hamilton advised that a system of taxation was urgently needed. Men in Congress had no power to convince the state governments of this; but "in this the influence of the army, properly directed, may cooperate."

Many others were making variations of Hamilton's argument: Washington should continue to lead the army and establish himself as the head of a new American government. Washington read his former aide's words with alarm. His answer was direct. Such a situation, with the army and a general running the country, would he said, "end in blood."

It was a disorienting period. Washington was flooded with letters. He found himself being implored for advice from state leaders. He had reached exactly the position he had longed for as a young man: he was honored, revered, respected beyond measure. But in February of 1782, as his fiftieth birthday came, he was able to ponder one of the lessons of experience: that dreams, when achieved, inevitably differ from youthful imaginings.

Washington was tired, and longed to step aside—as he said, to "pass the remainder of life in a state of undisturbed repose"—to let others organize the postwar order. But in the spring of 1782—as Benjamin Franklin, Thomas Jefferson and John Jay sat down with British negotiators in Paris to begin talks toward a treaty to end the war—one of Washington's junior officers, who like many others was pondering these deep waters, wrote him a letter whose bracing vividness clarified things for him. Colonel Lewis Nicola, speaking on behalf of many in the army, stressed that war itself had "shewn to all, but to military men in particular the weakness of republicks." Americans had inherited their traditions from Europe; they would accept a monarch. Washington, Nicola suggested politely but boldly, should become king.

The letter seemed to wake Washington; he replied with eloquence and force: "Sir, With a mixture of great surprise and astonishment, I have read with attention the Sentiments you have submitted to my perusal. Be assured Sir, no occurrence in the course of the War has given me more painful sensations than your information of there being such ideas existing in the Army as you have expressed, and which I must view with abhorrence and reprehend with severity." Colonel Nicola's notion, he went on, "seems big with the greatest mischiefs that can befall my Country." He concluded: "Let me conjure you, then, if you have any regard for your Country, concern for yourself or posterity, or respect for me, to banish these thoughts from your Mind, & never communicate, as from your self, or anyone else, a sentiment of the like Nature."

He understood now that he did not have the luxury to retire to Mount Vernon, at least not yet. In bringing America to the edge of victory, he had gathered a degree of weight, of political capital, that no one else had. It had to be expended. And he now knew toward what end.

In November, American and English representatives signed a preliminary peace agreement. Over the next several months he was occupied with the details of the disbanding of the Continental army. Still there was no sign of an accord among the leadership of the states and of Congress regarding the way forward for the country. In June, Washington wrote a circular letter "to the army," but really to the leadership of the state governments. He had spent the entire war enraged at Congress's mismanagement of finances and the underfunding of the army. There had been a power vacuum in the American government throughout the war; now it threatened to open into a chasm. In the letter, he expressed his happy astonishment that what they had fought for had actually been achieved: that Americans were now "possessed of absolute freedom and Independency." But he stressed that the structure for maintaining that freedom was lacking. Taking his cues from Madison and Hamilton, he suggested that what was needed was "An indissoluble Union of the States under one Federal Head." This required that the individual states "suffer Congress" to exercise authority. Without this, "every thing must very rapidly tend to Anarchy and confusion."

His circular letter was long and eloquent, and it was widely read. It was big news that the commander of the army advocated the creation of a strong federal government. And Washington ended the letter with what was probably regarded as even bigger news. Having expressed his views on the formation of a government, the general ended: "I bid a last farewell to the cares of Office, and all the imployments of public life."

Word of his intention to retire rather than accept the leadership of the newly independent nation—itself a momentous break from the long tradition of military victors becoming dictators—swept through the nation and beyond. In November, he traveled to New York. There, as the last British troops sailed off, he said farewell to a small group of his officers, who had gathered for a celebratory dinner in an upstairs room at Samuel Fraunces's tavern. It was a moment when the reality of what they had done, of what he had been through, struck him with unusual force. He had, he told them, "a heart full of love and gratitude." They believed it, for several of them were struck by the fact that, as their leader poured wine for a toast, his hand was shaking.

From New York, he traveled south to Annapolis, which was the last of the string of temporary homes the Congress had chosen as it fled the British army. Two days before Christmas, following an evening of dining and dancing, he took part in a formal noontime ceremony with the leaders of the new United States, at which he formally relinquished his command. The room was packed, the wives of the congressional delegates filling the upstairs gallery. He ended his short speech with yet another indication of his weariness, saying, "I here offer my commission, and take my leave of all the employments of public life." Then he mounted his horse. His once vast retinue was now reduced to just two aides, who accompanied him on the forty-mile ride to Mount Vernon. Now, surely, he had done everything he possibly could for America and its cause of liberty. He was going home.

. . .

At the end of a war, Cornplanter knew, came a period of confusion. He and his people had suffered through that time of pain and uncertainty. But it was now October 1784: more than a year since the Americans and the British had signed their peace treaty. He wanted clarity. And he hoped to get it from the man who stood before him here at Fort Stanwix: George Washington's trusted aide, the Marquis de Lafayette.

Thanks largely to the devastation of their homelands by Sullivan's army, the Iroquois, since the end of the war, had been caught up in a confused and mournful migration; they were dealing with loss, seeking homes. The more eastern nations had moved west into Seneca territory. Cornplanter had lost his wife in the war, perhaps during the depredations of Sullivan's army. He and his eight-year-old son had taken up residence for a time in the village of Tonawanda, just below the falls at Niagara. It may have been there that he met the woman who became his second wife. Her name was Ke-koi-no-us.

Ke-koi-no-us was from the village of Jenuchshadego, also called Burnt House, along the Allegheny River in northeastern Pennsylvania. Cornplanter and his son moved yet again to her village; with him came his half-brother, Handsome Lake, and his nephew, Governor Blacksnake, and their families. Through the grayness and the suffering came glints of hope. Cornplanter's wife became pregnant. And despite all they had endured, the Iroquois who had sided with the British could pride themselves on the fact that they themselves had not been vanquished. Unlike George Washington, Cornplanter had won many more battles than he had lost. He and his Seneca brothers had done their part to beat the Americans. The British officials in North America knew this. Despite the loss of the war, the Iroquois who had fought alongside the British expected their loyalty to the powerful empire to be rewarded.

It was only slowly, in the course of 1783, that a devastating truth was revealed to Cornplanter. The British officers he had known and had fought alongside took their time in conveying it, but finally he learned the details of the treaty between the British and the Americans. The British affirmed the sovereignty of the American nation. The British agreed that their dominion would extend from a line that cut through the Great Lakes. Territory north of this line—Canada—would be British. All territory south of it would be open to exploitation by the new United States of America.

It took the Iroquois some time to fathom the betrayal. When they had urged the Iroquois to join them in the fight, the British had pointed to the ancient covenant between Britain and the Iroquois and promised to stand by their allies. In the treaty, however, they had not only abandoned them. They had given the Americans access to what was not theirs and had never been theirs. They had all but handed the Americans the land of the Iroquois.

This had not happened by accident or oversight. There had been debate in London. As the treaty was being negotiated, a member of the House of Lords had decried his government's abandonment of its allies, calling it "shameful and unpardonable," and demanding that the government rework the language of the treaty so that it allowed its faithful allies to have "peaceable possession of their native lands." There was a new prime minister now in England: William Petty, the Earl of Shelburne. He led the treaty formulation, which was positively grotesque in its logic. The Iroquois "were not abandoned to their enemies," he had countered; rather, "they were remitted to the care of neighbours, whose interest it was as much as ours to cultivate friendship with them, and who were certainly the best qualified for softening and humanizing their hearts."

As they became aware of all of this, the Iroquois reacted first with outrage and calls for a new war. Messengers went out along the old westward trails. In September 1783 a gathering of disparate tribes of the kind not seen since the time of Pontiac's Rebellion took place, at Sandusky, Ohio. Not just Iroquois but Cherokee, Mingo, Shawnee, Ojibwa and Creek peoples met to discuss their options.

The American Congress knew something had to be done. Its members understood they could not put off dealing with the Indians, who could unleash terror on the frontier. A council was called, to be held at Fort Stanwix, west of Albany. Cornplanter was one of the leaders who made the journey on behalf of the Iroquois.

So here he stood, opposite the Marquis de Lafayette, who was part of the congressional delegation. Cornplanter opened the discussion with a confession that he found the situation confusing. There were representatives from both New York State and from the American Congress. They had been told different things by each regarding their lands. The Iroquois, he said, didn't understand which authority they were to deal with. They did not know where they stood. What kind of future could they expect? Where would they live? What of their lands? He knew, he said, that "ill winds blow from every quarter," but he vowed to close his ears to "evil words" and only listen to and speak honest ones.

Lafayette replied. His words were brisk and direct. He did not dwell on ancient covenants but instead reminded the Iroquois that they had been warned not to take up arms against the Americans. "The American cause is just," he proclaimed; "it is the cause of humanity." He told them that "the great chief Warrior Washington" had prevailed in battle against the Iroquois. They were in no position to bargain. Nevertheless, "the great Council of the United States is, in their goodness, disposed to treat with you." In encouraging the Iroquois to look to the future, the Frenchman stressed the French connection: in winning the war, he reminded them, the Americans had relied on "the intimate friends of your fathers, the French." The Iroquois would have much to gain in the future through trade with both the French and the new American nation. Therefore, he ended, "let the American chiefs, and yours united around the fire, settle on reasonable terms."

There was a great deal of grumbling among the Iroquois leaders. They pointed to the treaty of 1768, by which Americans had agreed to permanent boundaries with the Iroquois. This had now been violated. To this, one of the commissioners replied simply that the Iroquois were now "a subdued people."

Cornplanter, the philosopher, understood power. The Iroquois were not naïve regarding war and its results. Their whole history was one of tension and conflict between competing nations, of war and retribution. Winners of contests exercised power over losers. Lafayette and his fellow commissioners were simply restating the old theme. He advised his fellow Iroquois leaders to accept the situation.

The Iroquois began their deliberations. No sooner had they done so than a messenger arrived with news that halted the council. The messenger had come from Cornplanter's village, Burnt House, with news that his infant child, a daughter, had died. Surely this was not a good omen. The Iroquois paused to perform the ritual of mourning, to give their leader time to grieve.

When they reconvened, Cornplanter's thinking won the day. There was, he reckoned, no other way for the Iroquois to proceed than to accept American might. Agreeing to give up land gave them a chance at a future. Refusing to do so meant the return of the white army and its thunder trees, and even greater devastation. The Iroqouis representatives put their marks on a document in which they ceded land in exchange for promises of protection and trade.

In January 1784 word reached Haddam, Connecticut, that the Continental Congress had ratified the Treaty of Paris. Since negotiators had signed the document four months earlier, Congress's approval was a formality, but the very formality made it resonate among the farmers and tradesmen of the area. Americans had fought for eight years, and they won their freedom. "We hold these truths to be self-evident, that all men are created equal." Those words could now be realized.

A bit later, more news reached Venture Smith's farm. The people in his family and those who had gathered around him as laborers or tenants were all free blacks, but they, and certainly the slaves of the area, had waited for indications that the conviction of America's leaders, that "all men are created equal," might finally be realized. And here it came. The State of Connecticut had just passed a law: "Whereas sound Policy requires that the Abolition of Slavery should be effected . . ."

Some people may have jumped up and whooped. Venture Smith surely knew better. From long experience he had learned to wait for the other shoe to drop. And it did. Connecticut's new law went on to stipulate that the state would abolish slavery "as soon as may be, consistent with the Rights of Individuals and the public Safety and Welfare." What exactly did that mean? The framers of the law stipulated not that all slaves in the state would henceforth be free—for that would have been too great a blow to the property rights of current slave owners—but instead that children born to slaves after March 1, 1784, would be free.

Well, that at least was cause for celebration. There was reason to whoop and holler after all, for these as-yet-unborn children.

But as the blacks of Haddam and other towns in the state slowly learned, the law did not actually free these infants. In fact, it freed no one. What it did was decree that anyone born in Connecticut to an enslaved mother after March 1, 1784, would be emancipated when he or she became twenty-five years of age. In other words, no one would be freed by the law for another twenty-five years. The members of the Assembly were fussed about individual rights, yes, but mostly the rights of white citizens who owned slaves, and those of poor whites who would have to compete for work with former slaves. They prided themselves

on their commitment to the Enlightenment principle of individual freedom and believed they were pushing their state toward abolition, yet
they hedged and hemmed the matter so severely that their new law had
exactly no effect on the black population of the state.

Or rather, it did, but a negative one. For women who gave birth after the
prescribed date found that they and their children, who were now tainted
by the stain of future freedom, were suddenly valued by slave owners less
than other slaves. Owners began breaking up families in order to ship
these slaves to states where there were no gradual emancipation laws.

None of this affected Venture Smith directly. He was one of the very
few Africans to buy not only himself but also his wife and children
out of slavery. As a result, Cuff's children would be free. And when
ten-year-old Solomon had children, they would be free. But Venture
identified with his enslaved "countrymen." He still played in his mind
the scenes of being torn from his family and homeland as a child. He
believed in freedom as surely as the men who had written the Declaration of Independence. But he had also lived for forty-six years now in a
land ruled by white men, and he was not in the least surprised to learn
that a law intended to bring freedom to blacks actually brought them
only more suffering.

Despite his own relative security, he began to grow bitter following
the Revolution. He took to grumbling about being cheated in business. A Long Island man from whom he had bought a shipment of
clams stole his boat after it was loaded up. He chased the man down
and recovered his boat, but the clams, for which he had already paid,
were gone. The affair cost him nine crowns; "I never could obtain any
compensation," he complained.

Shortly after the gradual emancipation law went into effect,
Smith paid a local carpenter named Amos Ranney four pounds
to build a scow boat for him. Months went by and Ranney didn't
deliver. Through his real estate dealings Smith had become com-

fortable using the law. On November 8 he marched into the home of
Ezra Brainerd, justice of the peace of the town of Haddam, and filed
suit against Ranney for return of his money plus damages. Ranney
denied that he owed Smith anything; the evidence suggested otherwise. Smith won his suit.

But Amos Ranney couldn't let the matter rest. There was simmering
anger among whites in Connecticut in the wake of the emancipation
law, which may have added an extra complexion to his feelings at being
bested by a black man. Three months later, Smith was alone, working
on his own property one evening when three men jumped him. They
tried to disguise themselves, but he knew perfectly well who they were.
One was Ranney. The other two were Elisha Day and Jonathan Bowers.
They were all white men from Haddam, all in their thirties. Smith was
still a powerful man, but there were three of them, they were younger
and they had surprised him. They beat him senseless. He appeared in
Ezra Brainerd's doorway looking like he had been run over by stam-
peding horses, and filed suit. The suit charged that the three men
"assaulted, beat, wounded, maimed and greatly terrified and put his
life in danger." He had spent forty shillings getting his injuries tended
to by a doctor; he asked for "the sum of forty shillings lawful money" in
damages. The justice of the peace held a trial and summoned the three
men to appear. They pleaded not guilty. Brainerd examined witnesses
and gave his ruling. The court, he wrote, "is of the opinion that the said
Amos, Elisha and Jonathan are guilty." He ordered them each to pay
Smith nine shillings in damages and to pay a further five shillings apiece
to the town of Haddam.

The three white men each paid Venture Smith. He had played the
game and won, twice over. But as far as he was concerned, life was as
riddled with ugliness as it ever had been. You didn't wait for justice
in the new America. You had to go out and get it. And the taste was
often bitter.

• • •

While George Washington moved from victory at Yorktown toward what he hoped would be his retirement at Mount Vernon, and while the members of the Continental Congress fussed and railed over how actually to govern a nation, Margaret Coghlan was doing the Grand Tour of Europe. Pale Greek ruins, Roman columns standing proud in orange sunlight, the brooding mystery of Vesuvius, the languor of Venice's canals, the gardens of the Villa Pamphili on the outskirts of Rome: she moved through a landscape that was probably as far from the America in which she had been born as was possible for her to imagine.

She was still seeking freedom, of course. Was this it? Had she achieved it at last? If not, it was very close. Surely that was what she smelled through the carriage window, in the olive and lemon orchards and lavender fields she passed, heavy and sweet in the humid Mediterranean air.

Practically the moment that her Whig lover, Charles James Fox, had let her go, she had attached herself to a man whom she quickly characterized as being Fox's opposite in nearly every way. Fox was one of the leading intellectual politicians of his day; Samuel Fazakerley, the wealthy young scion of a family that owned a large swath of the Lancashire countryside, was a bit of a dunce. Fox was a lively chatterbox and an expansive personality; Fazakerley, she observed, was "morose and capricious."

Yet for all his flaws, Fazakerley was wealthy, generous and unmarried, and when she warned him, shortly after they had taken up with one another, that she was four months pregnant, he gallantly waved the matter away as a minor difficulty. The dismissive wave was like a benediction. Fazakerley lived in a world in which the starchy proprieties of marriage and illegitimacy did not hold. His money and his class were like wings that carried him above convention, and they could carry her as well. She felt free in this upper realm. And when Margaret gave birth, not only did he accept her daughter as part of the package, he refused to let her write to Charles Fox, the father of the child, for support. He happily brought mother and child both into his orbit, and promised Margaret he would show her the world.

And so they set out for the Continent. Though they did not marry, Coghlan presented herself as Margaret Fazakerley in hotels and inns and among the Italian and French nobles they met in society. They followed in the wake of so many other wealthy British and American travelers, spending long periods in each place, soaking in art and antiquity and culture. This, then, was the completion of Margaret's education, and she reveled in it, and considered that, by the end of four long and languorous years of travel, during which people in the United States were processing the reality of their independence, she had reached the point where she could see herself in relation to the wider world; she had, she pronounced with satisfaction, "certainly acquired graces and accomplishments."

Her very sense of satisfaction and accomplishment led to the end of her relationship with Fazakerley. It was her doing as much as his. Amenable though he was to many things, Fazakerley never even pretended to pay the slightest attention to her thoughts and ideas. Over time, she came to insist on being taken seriously. Tensions arose, and in the end they parted. Once again, she was on her own. But she didn't mind. The relationship had run its course. She had gotten a great deal from her latest lover. She had tasted that free, refined air. She liked the view from up here. She would surely find a way to stay aloft.

An enormous tree shaded the back entrance to Viscount Sackville's country estate. He had been out riding with Richard Cumberland, his former aide, who, unlike almost everyone else in his professional life, was still devoted to him. They had been discussing resolutions concerning the trade with Ireland, which would be up for consideration in the House of Lords, and what position Sackville would take on them. They stopped beneath the tree and dismounted. Suddenly, Sackville's face took on such a haggard look that he could read the younger man's alarm in his eyes. He had been suffering from kidney stones for several years, and other ailments had mounted.

They sat on a bench under the tree. It was May 1785, a lovely, pastoral day in the English countryside. Sackville recovered from his moment of agony. "I know as well as you can tell me, what you think of me just now," he said, "and that you are convinced if I go to town upon this Irish business, I go to my death." He asked the younger man not to voice that warning, for he intended on going, and he worried that if Cumberland advised him not to go and he did in fact die Cumberland would "repent of it."

Later, after dinner, the two men sat outside again on chairs on the lawn, gazing meditatively toward the line of the forest in the distance. Of all things, Sackville brought up the subject of Minden. He recounted the events of the battle—which despite the loss of America he still saw as the great shattering tragedy of his life—in an even, relaxed tone. "He appeared to me throughout his whole discourse like a man who had perfectly dismissed his passions," Cumberland later wrote.

Sackville was dying, and he knew it. In the three years since his retirement from government, he had appeared regularly in the House of Lords, as much to defy his enemies there as to hold forth on policy. Otherwise he enjoyed corresponding with his children and making occasional visits to their families. He was disappointed that neither of his two sons had pursued careers in politics; it didn't seem to occur to him that the tempestuous example he had set might have been the reason.

He followed with growing dismay the fallout from the peace treaty that Britain had signed simultaneously with America, France and

Spain. Hemmed in by so many adversaries, the English negotiators had given up some possessions in the Caribbean, in Africa and in India. Meanwhile, the American negotiators, led by Benjamin Franklin, had pushed for and won England's relinquishment of claim to land on the continent as far west as the Mississippi River. That ensured the new nation a boundless vista of future promise, and on the other hand the concessions made the British public feel that they had been bested both by their former colonies and their age-old European enemies. Sackville, to his very last, believed that his way had been right, and that the only thing lacking was the conviction to see it through.

He spent most of his time these days at his country estate. He threw himself into religion, insisting that the entire household, down to the lowest scullery maid, accompany him to Sunday service. When it was time for the sermon, he would stand and turn to face the congregation with a censorious countenance, making sure everyone was paying attention. The old aggression that had punctuated debates in the House of Commons would manifest itself when he became caught up in a particularly fine sermon. "Well done, Harry!" he was known to bray at the reverend in the midst of his remarks.

He had never been a reader in his life and had no hobbies. He wasn't moved to write his memoirs. He had few real friends, though he did dutifully host social events, and could make the odd show of humor: he got a charge out of pointing out to people that his baker's surname was Butcher and his butcher was a Baker.

Very occasionally, he folded himself into a carriage and rode off to Knole, the magnificent estate where he had spent his boyhood and whose feudal architecture had become his own. It had probably been the happiest period of his life, but he didn't like visiting the place now. The house had passed into the family of his brother Charles, who, thanks to his debts, had let it decay. Most depressing to Sackville, Charles, who had suffered from a mental condition and had died some years before, had, on a whim, had the entire forest of beech trees that Lady Betty Germain had planted in George's youth hacked down.

Sackville made good on his vow to Richard Cumberland and went to London for the debate on Ireland. When he returned, as he had predicted, he was near death. Cumberland came to be with him; the priest was called in. It was August 26, 1785. In his last hours Sackville was craving light and air: he wanted the heavy curtains around his bed and over the windows thrown open. Cumberland dutifully took down his last words: "I have done with this world, and what I have done in it, I have done for the best; I hope and trust I am prepared for the next." It was a sturdy and unrepentant final utterance, perfectly in keeping with the life it summarized, suggesting that George Sackville may well have composed it in advance.

## Chapter 18

⎯⎯⎯⎯⎯❧❧❧⎯⎯⎯⎯⎯

# ROUGH HEWER

The day after Viscount Sackville expired, Abraham Yates sat down at his home in Albany to compose a letter. He was angry, as he often was these days. "I am reather Suspitious," he wrote, of "the advocates for augmenting the powers of Congress . . . I think this quarter Should be <u>Watched</u>." His correspondent—David Howell, a member of the Continental Congress from Rhode Island—was likewise alarmed at the rapidly growing movement among many in Congress to amass power. Yates outlined for Howell the faults that these advocates of federal authority found with the existing system. The federalists, he said, argue that "Congress have not Sufficient powers," that "We are in Danger from foreign Trade and Commerce" and from "the increasing of the public debts, and from banks & paper Credit." And in his estimation the federalists believed that both a free press and "the liberty of voting by ballot" were threats to the American system, which had to be curtailed.

Yates considered these federalist fears to be in themselves threats to American liberty. And in his job as continental loan officer he experienced the pressure to restructure the financial system very directly: it was personally bankrupting him. He was supposed to raise funds by obtaining loans, and his salary came in the form of a percentage of what he raised. But Robert Morris, who as Superintendent of Finance was leading the effort to change the system of financing the government, had sidestepped Yates's unyielding criticisms by keeping him in his position but creating a new one—receiver of taxes—that superceded it. Morris chose Alexander Hamilton for this new position. Yates had long since identified Hamilton, his fellow New Yorker, as one of the chief threats to American liberty. And Hamilton had nothing but contempt for Yates. He warned Morris about him, calling Yates "a man whose ignorance and perverseness are only surpassed by his pertinacity and conceit." Hamilton and Yates had both risen from humble beginnings, but where Yates was proud of the fact, Hamilton shunned his past and hungered for advancement in America's class system. His pretenses, coupled with Yates's sneering disregard for elites, increased his scorn. Yates, Hamilton informed Morris, "hates all high-flyers, which is the appellation he gives to men of genius." He warned Morris that Yates was proud to be one of the common people, that he considered himself "a preacher to their taste." He also misrepresented Yates's opposition to federal taxation, claiming that Yates saw it as his mission to assure common people that "they are too poor to pay taxes."

Yates was furious at being outmaneuvered by Morris and Hamilton. He had been borrowing money from friends to live on in these uncertain times. Now Hamilton had been appointed to, as he said, "an office as it were taken out of my office with a generous and Immediate Salary (it is Said between three and five hundred Pounds) when I Am Dayly Obliged to Shift for the necessarys of life." This, he complained, was "such a hardship that Nothing but the times Will oblidge me to Submit to Without Remonstrating."

While he technically maintained the post of continental loan officer, his chief task in that role had shifted from collecting funds to arguing with Robert Morris about the limits of Congress's power. He was also still a state senator. But these positions did not give him sufficient outlet to express his alarm over the way things were developing among the country's leaders. The people had to be warned. So he began writing. It was common to publish under a pseudonym; he had recently admired essays under the pen name Jonathan of the Valley. He decided to call himself Rough Hewer. It had a nice ring to it, and it suggested a healthy separation from the powdered elites he opposed. Even before the Treaty of Paris was officially ratified Rough Hewer's essays began to appear in the *New-York Packet*, published in New York City, and in the *New-York Gazetteer*, which was based in Albany. From Virginia to Massachusetts, others were speaking out against the federal threat. Rough Hewer stood out as one of the strongest and clearest voices in defense of the principle of liberty that the Revolution had been fought over.

By 1785 the battle lines were being drawn over a move to amend the Articles of Confederation to give Congress the power to raise customs duties: a so-called federal impost. Yates decided the occasion warranted a twenty-page pamphlet. As he nearly always did, he kept his focus on his state and region. He pushed for New York to reject the federal impost amendment. If it did, then, since the Articles of Confederation could only be amended by unanimous support of the states, it would kill the measure.

Despite the use of a pseudonym, Rough Hewer felt he needed, at the beginning of his essay, to make his readers understand who he was, or at least where he was coming from: "I look to the rulers of my country with respect but not servility; as I have to ask no favors, I fear no man's frown. I profess to be loyal yet free, obedient yet independent." Then, with his customary vitriol, he charged ahead, outlining the case against the federal impost in apocalyptic language. It was not, he wrote, "an innocent program to raise federal funds but a nefarious plot to destroy American liberties by joining the power of the purse and the power of the sword in a mighty continental legislature." If Congress was granted the authority to raise taxes directly in the states, superceding state governments, it would, he warned, "swallow up" the state legislatures.

New York rejected the impost, which killed this particular effort by the national government to raise taxes over the authority of the states. But Yates knew the federalists were only just beginning. This failure made it clear to them that what was needed was a complete overhaul of the Articles of Confederation. They believed that the kind of rabid defense of liberty that Yates espoused was naïve, that without a strong central government, able to fund itself, the new nation would collapse. In his insistence that they were undermining the long years of battle that George Washington and the Continental Army had endured, Yates, they decided, had become the enemy. John Jay, with whom Yates had collaborated on the creation of New York's constitution, now considered him an enemy. So did Gouverneur Morris. Alexander Hamilton saw Yates's movement to bring politics down to the level of the common man as an outright danger to the American project. He warned his fellow federalists in New York State that "the Yates' and their Associates" were out to destroy the very concept of private property, and that it was imperative that he and his fellow elitists "put men in the Legislature whose principles are not of the *levelling kind*."

The machinations of the federalists were not only about money, but went deeper, into the class system that America had inherited from England along with so much else. Federalists targeted Yates in particular in popular essays and even poems, belittling him in language that equated his commoner status with barbarity and that mocked his self-taught literary style:

*The blunt* Rough Hewer, *from his savage den,*
*With learned dullness loads his lab'ring pen . . .*

Meanwhile, evidence of the class conflict underlying the struggle for power in the new country was right in front of Yates, in Albany. Even before the war had ended, Alexander Hamilton had married

Elizabeth Schuyler, the daughter of Philip Schuyler. Schuyler was not only Yates's longtime nemesis but one of the most self-exalting of New York's would-be aristocrats. The marriage of the ardent young federalist into the Albany elite—in the parlor of the grand Schuyler mansion on Catherine Street, just a few blocks south of Yates's house—must have registered darkly in Yates's mind. Yates prided himself on being "a Suspitious Man," and he had reason to be. The elites were plotting. A new American aristocracy was in the offing.

Cornplanter's decision to put his X on a treaty with the Americans, giving up Iroquois lands in exchange for peace and trade, was not popular among his people. He and his nephew, Governor Blacksnake, returned to their village of Burnt House and everyone gathered for a grand council to hear what had transpired at Fort Stanwix. Cornplanter presented a skin on which the treaty was written, and proceeded to explain it. No one understood. For two days they sat, arguing and going over points again and again. A main source of confusion concerned Britain's treaty with the Americans. How, even according to the strange logic of the white men, was it possible that the British had ceded Iroquois lands to the Americans when they had never claimed those lands to begin with? Cornplanter himself failed to comprehend that the Treaty of Paris concerned itself with European law. Under it, Britain had given up claims to the territory in question, which included much of the North American continent and all of the Iroquois territory. In relinquishing its interest in this land, Britain did not claim that it was granting it to the new American nation, but the United States chose, in its negotiations with the Iroquois, to act as though it was already U.S. soil.

Cornplanter tried to make people understand that, while the Fort Stanwix Treaty was unsatisfactory, the alternatives for the Iroquois were worse. They refused to accept this. At the end, they made a determination—to reject the treaty. As Governor Blacksnake later said through an interpreter, "The offer that was made by General Washington, they will not take it." Rather than abide by it, they would "continue war—for they are not willing to give up their Rights of the Soil."

The prevailing sentiment among the Iroquois was outrage at Cornplanter for relinquishing their lands. He understood, and, like politicians before and since, he allowed himself to be pulled back in their direction. He agreed to make another trip. He would visit General Washington and the Congress to explain the unhappiness of the Iroquois, and to bargain, even though he had little to work with. With five young Seneca men he set out along the shore of Lake Erie, then headed south. After about 30 miles they came to a settlement of friendly white families. They spent the winter here, making birch bark canoes and hunting. In the spring they set off again, by canoe as far as Pittsburgh, then turned eastward and headed toward Philadelphia on foot. They kept mostly to forest trails. This part of Pennsylvania was now well-established white settlement; it had been years since Indians roamed here freely. Isolated families they came upon thus started at the sight of them and ran, fearing they would be murdered. The Seneca party tried to stop some, saying they were on a peaceful mission, asking if they could buy bread. At one cabin, Governor Blacksnake extended his hand to the man and woman. The Senecas were invited in; the family gave them bread and meat and did not charge them for it.

They made their way to Carlisle, Pennsylvania, where, Cornplanter knew, Richard Butler, one of the Indian commissioners with whom he had dealt at Fort Stanwix, lived. Their ultimate goal was New York, where the Congress sat, but Cornplanter thought that on the way he might as well present the Senecas' grievances to Butler. He requested a meeting in front of the town courthouse. Many of the local citizens turned out to see the spectacle. The Indians were interesting in their own right; on top of that, now that the war was over and they had their own country, Americans were deeply concerned over how relations with the natives would evolve. In addition to all of that, Cornplanter himself had built up a reputation. He was known for having been a ruthless military captain against Americans. Then he had turned that warlike persona toward peace, negotiating with sensitivity to the realities his people were facing. All of that made him something of a sympathetic figure. In addition, the story of his white father had become known. Americans lived with Indians as a reality in their lives, but for the most part the Indian presence was ghostly, evanescent. Cornplanter represented a bridge between the two worlds. Somehow his father's Dutch surname, Abeel, had become attached to him; Americans began referring to him by it, but with an oddly Irish-sounding twist on the name, along with a nod to his role as a leader of war parties: "Captain O'Bail" people called him. That was how Benjamin Franklin's *Pennsylvania Gazette* referred to him in reporting on his impromptu meeting in Carlisle.

The Seneca party—Cornplanter and the five young Seneca men—stood with strings of wampum at the ready in the square outside the courthouse. Cornplanter spoke through an intepreter. "The ground upon which we now stand formerly belonged to my people," he said to Butler. "Hearken to my words, brother, for I am now about to divulge to you the cause of my distress." He spoke at great length, as was the Iroquois way in council, weaving repeatedly back to his point, adding information with each pass, and punctuating his utterances with strings of wampum. He wanted to see the treaty the British and the French had signed following the Seven Years' War, and the treaty between the British and the Americans. He and his people had difficulty understanding the differing land claims. He complained that the English were now settling in Canada. He suggested that the king of England had deceived the Iroquois; in that case, the Iroquois would fight the British. He proposed that the Americans join them. He had no cards to play, but he tried to maneuver Butler into some kind of agreement along these lines, stressing cooperation: "Let us unite our strength. . . . Let us live in friendship, that we may be able to prevent all people from doing us an injury."

Butler—a sturdy forty-three-year-old Dublin-born former gunsmith who had fought under Lafayette at Yorktown—knew how to decorate his talk with the diplomatic flourishes the Indians liked, but he did not forget that his work on behalf of the thirteen states of the new union—the "Thirteen Fires," as the Indians called them—was to get the Indians' lands. He exhibited the treaties Cornplanter had requested to see, offered to explain them again, as he had at Fort Stanwix, and promised to maintain "a friendly intercourse between your nations and the Thirteen Fires." But he could not authorize a new fight with the British. "I approve of your going on to Congress," he told Cornplanter, "as I think the measure argues the goodness of your intentions." But he assured Cornplanter that Congress would not renege on the treaty Cornplanter had signed.

About 30 miles from Philadelphia, Cornplanter and his men encountered some more wary but friendly Americans. These people suggested the Senecas stay in their village awhile and have European clothes made there. When the Senecas asked why, they politely noted that in their mostly native garb the Senecas made an intimidating impression, which would likely hamper their cause when they came to the big city. Cornplanter thought that made sense, so he and his young colleagues got themselves measured by a tailor, and within a few days each was sporting a coat, pants and shirts, in colors they chose according to their individual taste.

It must have been utterly bewildering, then, that when the Senecas reached Philadelphia dressed as white men they found a contingent of white men ready to receive them with their faces painted Indian-fashion and sporting fanciful feathers and bucktails. The locals marched them in parade down to the banks of the Schuylkill River, where cannons and maypoles were set up, and a crowd of 2,000 people had gathered. Very slowly, through an interpreter, Cornplanter was made to understand some version of what was going on. Decades earlier an annual springtime celebration had started in Philadelphia, which revolved around a seventeenth-century Delaware Indian chief named Tamenend, who had befriended William Penn, the originator of the Pennsylvania colony. Tamenend had impressed people in his time for his wisdom and humor, so that the festival that evolved was a celebration of good fellowship between whites and Indians, in which the colonists donned fanciful Indian clothing. Over time the now-legendary Chief Tamenend had become known, somewhat bizarrely, as Saint Tammany. During the period of the Revolution, patriotic overtones were added to the feast of Saint Tammany. As luck would have it, Cornplanter and his men had arrived in town as the celebration was getting underway. The local members of the Society of Saint Tammany considered it fortuitous, and insisted that the renowned Seneca leader take part.

The festival involved a great deal of drinking and merrymaking. The Philadelphians were eager to sing their fake "Indian language" songs for Cornplanter, and they demonstrated their "war dances." They begged the Senecas to show them theirs, and the Indians obliged. At some point, Cornplanter, who must have figured that the sheer size of the crowd made this an opportune moment to appeal yet again to Americans on behalf of his people, asked to speak. The seriousness of his message may not have been in keeping with the festival, but it was received respectfully enough that the *Daily Advertiser* took it down verbatim.

"Brothers," he began, "hearken to what I tell you. This great gathering of our brothers is to commemorate the memory of our great grandfather." He must have gestured toward a flag bearing the likeness of Chief Tamenend. The forebears of the Indians and the whites, he went on, had "loved each other, and strongly recommended to their children to live in union and friendship." (Like any diplomat, he was not afraid to employ overstatement for political effect.) Therefore, he implored the crowd, "Let us keep fast the chain of friendship." He enriched his appeal with spirituality: "I heard it said our great grandfathers are dead—they are not dead. They now look down upon us, and what we are doing. Much more God looks upon us, he sees what we are doing." By now the Philadelphians assembled for merriment on the riverbank would have realized something of the depth of suffering that was being expressed by this Iroquois from a distant place. "I think God Almighty at this time is sorry for the poor Indians," Cornplanter said. "He is grieved at the afflictions now come upon them." Cornplanter had become a very good public speaker by this time. He knew how to build an argument, how to pause for effect, to scan the crowd. "I hope you have observed that I have always tears in my eyes," he declared. Referencing the fact that his people had sided with the British, he added, "I am sorry that we have been led astray. I hope you will do everything to put me right. Then God will look upon you and us, and help us. He will have pity on us both if we do right."

A stunned silence seemed to follow his words. The Saint Tammany festival was a lighthearted affair, but everyone knew that at its center was an Indian leader of the past who personified wisdom. It must have seemed as though he had been reincarnated—except that this latter-day wise Indian was dressed in European clothes while the white men were made up as Indians. Life was strange.

Then the crowd roared—gave, in fact, three cheers. Thirteen cannons, one for each state of the new union, blasted away in salute. The Tammany leaders made a circle for Cornplanter and his companions to sit in. A pipe was proffered. Everyone smoked. Cornplanter took a glass of wine that was offered to him and poured it onto the soil as a libation. There was goodwill all around. Maybe everything would work out—maybe everything would be just fine.

The goodwill extended: Cornplanter and his followers were put up in fine style—at the Indian Queen Hotel, no less—and the citizens of Philadelphia offered them a coach and driver for their trip to New York. On the way, the good fortune ended. The carriage tipped over and several of the passengers were hurt, Cornplanter worst of all, with a deep gash in his forehead above his eye, which permanently disfigured him.

The accident may have been disorienting, but so was the crossing of the river and the entry into New York. If Cornplanter had previously fashioned a sense of the power of the new American nation, of how vast and mighty was this force the Iroquois were dealing with, that sense was now magnified. New York was feverishly throwing off the vestiges of its long years of military occupation. Bricks were stacked everywhere as buildings were being repaired. The population had doubled from what it was just a few years before. Tailors, butchers, ropemakers, cobblers, chandlers and saddlers plied their wares, and people lined up to buy. Lawyers hustled along the streets, the sheafs of papers under their arms denoting land deals, marriages, inheritances. Enormous wooden vessels sat at anchor in the harbor. Wagons and carriages roared by—the danger of these was uppermost in the Senecas' minds now—carrying everything from logs to hogs. Shop windows displayed frying pans hanging from hooks, boxes of tea and salt and tobacco; there were advertisements for "QUEENS-WARE quart MUGS," paint brushes, toys, tureens, sets of claret glasses, "Jamaica spirits," cognac, molasses, Russia duck, codfish in barrels and "pickled sturgeon, cured in the Holland mode."

After having run this gauntlet, the Senecas found themselves, on Tuesday, May 2, 1786, at City Hall, which was serving as the latest home of the Congress of the Confederation (as the nation's governing body was now known). Cornplanter was disappointed that George Washington was not on hand. Washington was the great victor in battle over England; he assumed he would now sit at the head of the government. But he was hundreds of miles away, in Virginia. Richard Butler, who had negotiated the treaty at Fort Stanwix and met with them in Carlisle, introduced Cornplanter to the delegates. Cornplanter spoke as he had in Carlisle and Philadelphia. He said that he represented Indians who felt that they had been cheated by the combined effect of the treaties of Paris and Fort Stanwix. The chairman of the Congress, David Ramsay of South Carolina, asked him to return in three days to receive the official American response. Cornplanter did so, and Ramsay began by outlining the details of the treaty between the United States and England concerning North American territory. He held the document and actually pointed to the place where King George had signed it, and told Cornplanter he wanted him to assure all the Indians that "the King of England" had "given up, to them the lands of the Indians." The Americans had then negotiated with the Iroquois at Fort Stanwix, and signed a treaty, which ascribed certain lands to them. "The United States," he said, "will take care that none of their Citizens shall intrude upon the Indians within the bounds which in the late Treaties were allotted for them to hunt and live upon." The Congress, he said, "will do what is right and proper for the Indians."

The Senecas were overwhelmed—presumably as much by New York itself as by the definitive declaration that the Americans had officially and permanently taken possession of much of the Iroquois' traditional homeland. Once again, Cornplanter was made to understand what the Iroquois were up against. Then too, if the Congress did indeed live up to the promise David Ramsay made him, that would, perhaps, be something to hang on to. His back was against the wall; it was not within him to issue a call to war that would bring the American army down on his people. "Brothers, what you have said is good," he replied. "My mind had been disposed to war, but you wisely recommend peace, and I thank you for your advice, and for the good things you have said, and pray that the Great Spirit above may take care of you."

Cornplanter and his men stayed for six weeks in New York. In the midst of whatever touristic missions they undertook, Cornplanter made repeated visits to a studio, where he sat before an artist named Frederick Bartoli who was visiting from Europe. Someone—perhaps Butler, on behalf of the Congress—had commissioned a portrait of the Seneca leader. The Congress had also earmarked 400 dollars to be spent on presents for the Seneca delegation; among those that Cornplanter received were a silver medal, silver armbands, and a red blanket. He decided to be painted adorned with these, as well as a collection of other items, both native and European. The artist chose not to show the ugly wound above the eye that he had suffered in the carriage accident. But he seems to have done justice to the man's expression, which, in the course of the sittings, showed many things: pride, pain, suffering, hope tempered by sad wisdom, endurance.

George Washington, in retirement, was the celebrated squire of Mount Vernon. If he was gratified to have thrown off a king, and happy not to have become a dictator, then he reveled in emulating a hero of his: Lucius Quinctius Cincinnatus, who, after serving as all-powerful ruler of Rome, threw off the mantel of power and took up the plow and tools of a simple farmer.

Washington farmed his estate with renewed vigor. He felt at ease and at peace, and outlined his situation in a letter to Lafayette: "At length my Dear Marquis I am become a private citizen on the banks of the Potomac, & under the shadow of my own Vine & my own Fig tree, free from the bustle of a camp & the busy scenes of public life." He made clear that he wanted nothing but more of the same for himself in the future: "I am not only retired from all public employments, but I am retireing within myself; & shall be able to view the solitary walk, & tread the paths of private life with heartfelt satisfaction. . . . I will move gently down the stream of life, until I sleep with my Fathers."

But retirement was not so simple. The most celebrated man in America, the universally recognized hero of the new nation, could not hide from the public. People came to Mount Vernon by twos and tens, in official delegations and as unannounced drop-ins. He and Martha were forced to play hosts on a daily basis. He came to understand that this was inevitable. He personified something: the public needed to make human contact with the fact of their country's new status. And so the Washingtons readied beds, offered dinners; he poured wine and dutifully recounted stories of battle. Some of the visitors were French aristocrats. Others were Virginia dignitaries who wanted his blessing or support for their schemes. Accolades rolled in steadily. The city of Fredericksburg—"Our Sincere Congratulations on your safe return from the Noisy Clashing of Arms"—wanted to host a ball in his honor. He acquiesced, and decided that, as his mother lived in the city, he would bring her along. True to her nature, when the city delegation showed up at her door to invite her to accompany "His Excellency," Mary Washington shot back: "His Excellency? What nonsense!" She was perhaps the one person whose acknowledgment of his success he would have welcomed, but she denied him that satisfaction. She did, however, attend the ball.

Just as exhausting as the visits from strangers was the unending stream of letters: about plans for the expansion of the country, about Indian relations, about business. A visiting Italian nobleman wanted to pay a visit. Noah Webster wrote asking for his support for "my grammatical publications." (He replied with best wishes "in the prosecution of your design of refining the language . . . so as to reduce it to perfect regularity.") He plunged into correspondence about the possibilities of extending navigation on the Potomac River. He paid great attention to the compiling and amassing of his wartime correspondence, anxious as he was to preserve it so that his biography and the history of the Revolution could be written.

One topic that he no doubt wished would go away but which came up again and again was slavery. Lafayette was now positively indignant with Washington and other American leaders, insisting that abolition be among the first steps the new government took. "I would never have drawn my sword in the cause of America if I could have conceived that thereby I was founding a land of slavery," he said. He wrote to Washington in his retirement suggesting that the two of them "unite in purchasing a small estate where we may try the experiment to free the Negroes and use them only as tenants."

Along with other slave owners, Washington ducked these attempts. In conversation with abolitionists he expressed his moral condemnation of the institution, but he took no public steps to end it. In fact, on more than one occasion he peculiarly reversed logic and suggested that it was slave owners like himself who were the victims, presumably out of a feeling that he was caught in a moral-economic vice. In a letter to Robert Morris he declared that "there is not a man living who wishes more sincerely than I do, to see a plan adopted for the abolition of it," but also insisted that "when slaves who are happy & content to remain with their present masters, are tampered with & seduced to leave them; when masters are taken at unawares by these practices . . . it introduces more evils than it can cure."

Many of the letters he received at Mount Vernon were from the gentlemen of the Congress. His fellow Virginian James Madison in particular took to schooling him on what was transpiring among the delegates: the growing number of ideas for reforming the government, for starting a paper currency, for fomenting a "federal spirit." He told Madison he considered "the foederal governmnt" to be "the great, & most important of all objects." From his pastoral distance, he urged the delegates to take a long view of things. "Let prejudices, unreasonable jealousies, and local interest yield to reason and liberality," he wrote. "Let us look to our National character, and to things beyond the present period. No Morn ever dawned more favourable than ours."

He offered such lofty sentiments in hopes that they would suffice, that the others would figure it out themselves. But Madison was cultivating Washington with a purpose in mind: to get him involved, when the time was right. Finally, he judged that it was. A new convention was to be held, in Philadelphia, to reform the government. Virginia would send its delegation. And Virginia wanted Washington to lead it.

Washington didn't give a firm answer. But other events were calling out to him. In Massachusetts, farmers clashed violently with state tax assessors, and then with a private militia that the state was forced to raise in the absence of a national army. News of Shays's Rebellion, as it was called, after its leader, swept through the states. In Virginia, Washington saw it as further evidence that something had to be done immediately. The looseness of the confederation of states, which was meant to ensure individual liberty, was threatening to devolve into chaos.

Madison wrote him again in the spring of 1787, saying that he had developed "some outlines of a new system" and "I take the liberty of submitting them without apology, to your eye." Madison considered that it was now clear that the idea that each state would have complete independence was "utterly irreconcileable with their aggregate sovereignty," and that therefore "a consolidation of the whole into one simple republic" was a necessity. He proposed, therefore, that the national government have clearly stipulated powers. He suggested that the "Legislative department might be divided into two branches," and that a "national Executive must also be provided."

Washington was as aware as anyone else of the fulminations of men like Abraham Yates, who feared the rise of a new, homegrown tyranny. He understood such concerns. But he also saw that the system was collapsing. In April he sat down with pen and paper and summarized for himself the suggestions that Madison, John Jay and Henry Knox had sent him for the proposed restructuring. Despite the call of the land, despite his former determination to "tread the paths of private life . . . until I sleep with my Fathers," he was getting involved. He sent word that he would attend the convention. On May 9, he said good-bye to Martha and swung himself up into his saddle. He felt conflicted enough—over the state of the nation and his own anxiety at being pulled back into the vortex—that he was overcome by physical nausea as he set off. But he had made his decision. He was going to Philadelphia.

Abraham Yates stepped from the chilly deck of a sloop onto the shore of Manhattan Island. Nagged by his gout, he made his laborious way to the house of William Bedlow, a onetime ship's captain whom he had known since the Revolution. Yates hauled his personal belongings to a room in the home of Bedlow and his wife Catharine: he would be boarding here. In January 1787, after a tempestuous campaign, he had been elected as one of the state of New York's delegates to Congress.

Yates was sixty-two years old and feeling moody. His long battle with Robert Morris over his position as loan officer had come to an end with him finally losing the job. He had gotten nothing out of the fight but misery: his political opponents in Albany had taken advantage of it to accuse him of mismanaging funds. And he was now more than ever "suspitious" of what the gentlemen in the Congress were up to, which was why he had worked so hard to be elected to that body.

Shortly after he arrived in the governmental chamber in lower Manhattan, a resolution came before them. Five states had earlier sent representatives to a meeting at Annapolis to look at ways to "remedy defects of the federal government." Their resolution, now before Congress, proposed a general convention to be held in May in Philadelphia.

The resolution did not include the frank details that James Madison had spelled out for Washington: there was no mention of a plan to scrap the Articles of Confederation and start over, to develop a new constitution for governing the nation. To do so would have incited the wrath of the many who, like Yates, wanted to keep power in the states.

Even with its mild language, the resolution infuriated Yates. He objected to the proposed convention, which he already suspected would lead to a vastly more powerful government sitting above the states. But others overruled the objections; each state chose representatives to go to Philadelphia. Yates maneuvered to ensure that New York's delegation tilted toward states' rights. He got his way. The three men chosen included his nephew, Robert Yates, and John Lansing, who was his son-in-law's brother; both men followed Yates in their opposition to the massing of power at the national level. The third member chosen for the delegation was Alexander Hamilton, one of the most forceful advocates of centralized power.

Yates conferred with Robert Yates and John Lansing on strategy. They decided that the two antifederalist delegates would travel to Philadelphia with Hamilton, distribute copies of one of Abraham Yates's essays opposing the federalist agenda, then lead a coalition in blocking any attempt to create a new government. If circumstances warranted, at a propitious moment they would leave the convention in protest. Yates knew there was substantial opposition to the Philadelphia convention. Patrick Henry had refused to be part of it. Richard Henry Lee considered the effort "an elective despotism." In New York, the governor, George Clinton, was against it as well. And the entire leadership of the state of Rhode Island had declared it would boycott the convention. So Yates had reason for hoping that this gambit would send the whole thing crashing down.

Meanwhile, he bided his time in Manhattan, attending to other matters before the Congress, scribbling essays against the growing sentiment for national power, and getting news from home. He had much to be happy about. He and Anna now had four grandchildren, all under the age of six, living, along with their parents, in their Albany house. His son-in-law, Abraham Lansing, sent regular updates on the goings-on in the family and the town, and even added some literal sweetness: in one letter, Lansing told Yates he had sent him "a small Cake of Maple Sugar about 5 or 6 lb."

Then things turned sour. Yates had worried that the seemingly indomitable Alexander Hamilton would exert his will over his two antifederalist colleagues in Philadelphia. In the beginning of June he received a letter from his nephew, Robert Yates. He was bound by an oath of secrecy not to reveal details of the convention, but "my forbodings," he indicated darkly, "are too much realized."


There was a spring rain falling outside the windows. By twos and threes, officious-looking men in waistcoats, breeches and stockings entered the red brick State House in downtown Philadelphia shaking off the weather, voices echoing in the vestibule as they greeted one another. It had been a long while since most had seen each other. There were twenty-nine of them: a quorum. They could begin.

Robert Morris stood before the wood-paneled walls and indicated that, on behalf of the Pennsylvania delegation, he wished to propose that George Washington, late commander in chief of the Continental Army, be named president of the convention. All knew that Morris was a stand-in for this ceremonial function. Benjamin Franklin, the only other American to rival Washington in stature, was supposed to enter Washington's name, but Franklin was too unwell to travel the few blocks from his home. John Rutledge of South Carolina seconded the motion. The delegates voted unanimously to approve the selection. Washington was conducted to the chair at the front of the room by

Morris and Rutledge. James Madison was taking notes; he recorded that Washington "thanked the Convention for the honor they had conferred on him, reminded them of the novelty of the scene of business in which he was to act, lamented his want of better qualifications, and claimed the indulgence of the house towards the involuntary errors which his inexperience might occasion." Despite all he had achieved, the presence of such an array of educated men seemed to stir Washington's old feeling of inferiority regarding his own lack of formal education.

It was a Friday; they did little more that day. The following Monday they began in earnest. Franklin was well enough to be carried to the State House in a litter and took his seat among them. There was a presentation and discussion of the rules that would govern the convention. Among the rules was one for secrecy, which prohibited delegates from advertising the debates until their business was concluded. Their worry was that antifederalists such as Abraham Yates, if they got wind of the actual intent of the convention, would cause an uproar that would shut it down.

The next day Edmund Randolph of Virginia outlined the main business of the convention, detailed the defects in the Articles of Confederation and—in an indication of how organized the federalists were—suggested a new structure for the government, including a bicameral legislature, a "national executive" and a national judiciary. Charles Pinckney of South Carolina then presented his own "Plan of a Federal Constitution," which declared the manner in which the new nation should be formally styled: "The United States of America."

They were underway. They had cast off the pretension of revising the Articles of Confederation, under which they had gathered. In secrecy, they were creating a new government.

Throughout, Washington said little. He knew that his mere presence at the head of the gathering was more resonant than any amendments or revisions he might offer. The small group of men had little in the way of authority for what they were doing. To one such as Abraham Yates—who was desperate to know what they were about even as he all but intuited it—they were in fact stealing the Revolution, taking it away from the states and the people who had fought it, assuming command like so many dictators. Eventually, they would present their results to the states, to the people. But in the meantime they needed weight, ballast, foundation. Washington, who had first risen to renown in the colonies back in the days of Braddock's march, when American militia-men fought alongside British regulars against the French; who had in fact helped bring about that war with his youthful blunders and then overcame disaster through his dogged commitment to decency and decorum, his painstaking efforts to teach himself the rules of military engagement and apply them in the raw real world; who had become convinced, as had they, that an idea that had been building for a cen-tury and more, in which individual human beings were seen as funda-mentally and necessarily important and thus to be empowered; who had then, on the strength of that conviction, led a loose and wayward soldiery through the uncharted thicket of an eight-year war against the parent nation; who had suffered more defeats than victories and who had battled his own insecurities and foibles as much as he had enemy generals; and who had come to the realization that even final military victory did not ensure the underlying commitment to individual human freedom that had underlain their efforts: he was the only man who could provide that ballast and foundation.

The delegates were not all of like mind. The deliberations soon descended toward chaos. The split was most evident in the New York delegation. John Lansing and Robert Yates were opposed to the move-ment to craft a new system that would give the national government clear power over the states. Alexander Hamilton, the other member of the delegation, believed just as strongly that the plan put forth by Virginia delegates did not go far enough. In one long, hot June afternoon, Hamilton lectured his colleagues for six straight hours, arguing that central strength was the paramount need, that they should create a system in which the states gave up power to the federal government, and that the government should be led by an elected official who would rule for life.

The other delegates were mostly appalled by Hamilton's speech, which they saw as all but demanding an American monarchy. Lansing and Yates took this opportunity to enact the emergency plan they had worked out with Abraham Yates: they left the convention in protest over its direction. Hamilton—whose impetuousness had dissipated only slightly since he had huffily quit Washington's military staff—also announced that he was suddenly needed back home in New York, and left. Meanwhile, the delegates were deeply divided on slavery, and on how the chambers of the legislature would be apportioned. Small states were afraid of being engulfed; larger states wanted to be sure their populations were represented.

There was an adjournment. Washington dined with Robert Morris and his wife. He took tea at the Indian Queen, the same hotel where Cornplanter had been put up the year before. He went fishing. He and Gouverneur Morris rode out to Valley Forge; he recalled there was a fine trout stream in the area. They cast their lines and enjoyed the summer peace, then he rode alone among the remains of the American encampment, pondering the terrible winter of 1777–78 that he and his army had endured here. It gave him time to ruminate on what they had done then and what they were attempting to do now: that the two tasks were of a piece.

Hamilton wrote him from New York. He had seemingly regretted the fit of pique that caused him to leave so abruptly. He wanted Washington to know that Americans were aware of what the delegates were about in their secret gathering. Riding through New Jersey, he had heard from ordinary people that they believed a stronger government was necessary, that the leaders must not give up their effort to fashion one. "I am more and more convinced that this is the critical opportunity for establishing the prosperity of this country on a solid foundation," he told Washington. Washington wrote back, saying he fully agreed with the sentiment, and went so far as to add, "The Men who oppose a strong & energetic government are, in my opinion, narrow minded politicians." Then, stirred maybe by the wartime affection he had felt for the younger man, he added, "I am sorry you went away—I wish you were back."

A breakthrough came. Few antifederalists were as strident and unyielding as Abraham Yates. Those in Philadelphia compromised, as did the federalists. They reached agreement on the manner in which the Senate and the House of Representatives would be apportioned.

Another breakthrough, of sorts, came on the matter of slavery. They chose not to end it, not to curtail it. They agreed, for purposes of determining the population of each state, to count each slave as three-fifths of a person, thus giving slave states even more control over the country's future. As to the slaves themselves—roughly 500,000 people, 20 percent of the country's population—the delegates, nearly half of whom were themselves slave owners, voted that the federal government would not have the authority to decide the legality of their status. For all the complex array of powers they were giving themselves with the new Constitution, and in the wake of their historic revolution, which they had boldly declared to be in the service of human liberty itself, America's leaders extravagantly failed their own challenge. Liberty was an inalienable right for all people. But economic considerations crimped the leaders' moral beings. When they finally read out in the chamber their laboriously crafted and finely wrought words, which were intended to "secure the Blessings of Liberty to ourselves and our Posterity," they had a distinctly hollow ring.

By September, the delegates had their consensus: they had a constitution. On the evening of the seventeenth, Washington sat down with pen and candle and noted the day's momentous event with laconic brevity: "Met in Convention & Signed the proceedings—all except Govr. Randolph, Colo. Mason & Mr. Gerry. Dined all together at the City Tavern & returned to my lodgings."

*Chapter 19*

———— ❦ ————

# GLOWING WITH ZEAL FOR
# THE GENERAL HAPPINESS AND
# IMPROVEMENT OF MANKIND

A man might come as Nobody. Or a Cherokee chief. Or—
a carrot. A society matron might be dressed as a Greek slave,
or a harlot. A harlot might appear as a society matron. The
mansion would glitter from the light of thousands of candles; musicians
would be placed throughout the building. Tables groaned with food
and drink. Sometimes, in darkened corners, the revelers paired off.

Circa 1785, Margaret Coghlan was a regular at these London mas-
querades, the masked balls that were vital social outlets, in which a rigidly formal society could let its hair down. And there were many other
affairs to attend: teas and soirees and society dinners. It was seven years
since she had been wrenched away from America by the man she had
been forced to marry, whom she had then escaped, and she was now a
fixture in London society. In that time, Americans had won their freedom. Perhaps she had not quite attained her own, but she had proven
herself to be a survivor.

Of course, she owed her acceptance at society functions to the fact
that she arrived on the arm of an important man. She had broken off

her relationship with Samuel Fazakerley after returning to London from their long and languorous Grand Tour of Europe. At around the same time, a charming, gracious, good-souled aristocrat named John Augustus Hervey had also arrived in the city, back from his service as a captain in the British navy in Quebec. He was married, but by now Coghlan understood that a woman who dared to be independent would have to situate herself in a certain niche of society. Among the upper classes it was proper—or at least expected, or at the very least tolerated—for a nobleman to have a mistress. And such a mistress, if she knew how to comport herself—what to say and wear, where to be seen and with whom to be seen—could be a figure of some regard, maybe even of some respect. Most important, of course, was the quality of gentleman to whom one attached oneself. Captain Hervey, aka Lord Hervey, was of the very highest quality. He knew everyone. He was young and stylish and serious, with a career in the diplomatic service ahead of him.

With him, Margaret found her way in London. He set her and her daughter up in style, with a fine home in a fashionable neighborhood. Margaret was twenty-three: a very young woman by most standards, but with the life she had led she could only consider herself a veteran. As she aged, she came to value education and perspective. Her own formal education had been spotty, thanks to the war, but she was a keen student of society; she did everything she could these days to learn from those around her. Women in England were certainly not treated as the equals of men, but she had discovered that they had more involvement in public affairs than did American women. The Houses of Parliament were stuffy and cramped quarters for airing ideas; men in government preferred to conduct much of their political discussion in other settings. There were clubs and taverns for all-male conversation, but England's leaders also valued the role that women could play. The wives of government ministers and members of Parliament hosted dinners at which public policy was aired and debated. Women were conduits of information and could also influence policy.

Despite the fact that the American war was over, many of the issues that had animated it still dominated these gatherings. English leaders were fiercely divided on the topics of republicanism, the monarchy, religious freedom and individual rights. Coghlan's former lover, Charles James Fox, and other Whigs, including Edmund Burke, were still active; Burke had moved from decrying British injustice against America to recently declaring that the exploitative practices of the British East India Company in India were devastating that country; meanwhile, theologians like Richard Price and Joseph Priestley, who had also supported the American cause, were championing the separation of church and state in England and trying to reconcile Christian beliefs with science.

There was much in these ideas to attract Coghlan. As the teenaged daughter of a British officer caught in the middle of the Revolutionary War, she had stridently supported the British cause, but these days she openly professed her attachment to, as she wrote, "my native country (America)," and she declared herself to be "by no means a friend to arbitrary principles." Even as she settled herself into English society, she identified with the new American nation and with the "natural rights" on which it was founded. Her public persona was not merely that of a mistress but a proud expatriate American.

She had also become deft at managing her feelings. She knew where she stood with Hervey; she understood her role, accepted it, played it adroitly. With him she enjoyed, as she said, "all the comforts and delights of domestic life"—or at least all that could be expected considering that he had a wife and daughter at home. She knew that their relationship would end eventually. It lasted until sometime in 1786, when Hervey received the news that he had been appointed by the king to be minister to the Grand Duchy of Tuscany. He was sweet and gracious in parting, and generous—he left her money.

That was just as well, for he also left her another child. The baby, a girl again, was born several months following his departure, but she died soon after. Coghlan spent some months in mourning. Then she found herself another position, as it were. The new lover—whom she chose not to name when she later wrote about him—was also a renowned captain, this time in the British army. He was a sweet man; he doted on her. With him, however, she made a fatal mistake: she allowed herself to succumb to, as she said, his "tenderest affection." She fell in love. She knew better, but suddenly she desperately wanted to be wanted, both for the transcendent joy of it and for the security. She hoped that some lasting bond was forming between them. When she became pregnant, and gave birth to a son, she allowed herself to feel that that was happening. Then the next year she bore him a second son. Surely they were becoming a family.

Maybe she dared let herself hope that he would offer to marry her. If so, it was doubly cutting when he informed her, as gently as he could, that he was engaged to be married. His fiancée, he reported, expecting that Margaret would understand, was a lady, an aristocrat, a fixture in polite society. She would make an appropriate wife. And she would make a fine mother. For, he also quietly added, he was taking their two sons, to be raised by him and his new wife. Since Margaret loved the boys and cared about them, he was sure she would agree that this would offer them the best future.

It was a man's world: she had no say in the matter. She tried as hard as she could to put a good face on the situation. The woman, she told herself, repeating what he had told her, possessed "every virtue and every necessary accomplishment to secure his happiness."

But the psychological blows were enormous. In a short span, death had taken one child and fate—society—had taken two others as well as the man she loved. She staggered, felt desperately alone. She needed help. To comfort herself, she indulged in what had already become something of an addiction. When she was still with her beloved captain and all was well, she had allowed her taste for luxury to flare dangerously. She had spent freely, and put everything on account. Her lover had paid off some of the debts, but, she acknowledged once he was gone, "his fortune could not keep pace."

After he left her, she lost all restraint. London's population was pushing toward 1 million; with such a consumer base, all the world's finest and most delicate items were on display in its shops. Surely she wasn't compelled by addiction alone. Just as, before the war, George Washington, the gentleman farmer, was driven to continue spending by his straitened finances so as to project an image of success, Coghlan understood that a mistress to the highest class of gentlemen needed to be seen at the right balls, at the theaters and soirees in Soho and Covent Garden. She needed not just a horse-drawn hackney carriage but one of the latest model, with a driver properly outfitted. She needed to spend lavishly on her hair. She needed the most fashionable gowns, the subtlest perfume, petticoats and riding habits, parasols and corsets and combs and scarves. Because there were occasions for entertaining at home, her rooms in Cavendish Street had to be exceedingly well appointed. One needed elegant chairs and fashionable candelabra, a card table, a finely wrought tea board and service, sculptures and paintings to suggest ease of living and cultural richness. And a lady's bedroom had to fairly ripple with silky folds.

She found another man, again a kind and generous lover—she had a knack for attracting men of gentle disposition—by the name of Thomas Giffard. He came from one of England's most ancient families; he also had the advantage of being intimately connected at the royal palace, for one of his closest friends was the twenty-three-year-old Prince of Wales. She felt herself steadying, even as she let herself be caught up in the excitement and pageantry and possibilities. "While with Mr. Giffard, my humble roof was often visited by princes of the Blood Royal," she wrote breathlessly, "and by Nobles of the highest distinction."

But in one sense she and Thomas Giffard made a disastrous pair: while Coghlan pursued her own addiction to shopping and luxury, her new lover, who had an open and trusting nature, was unlucky enough to be drawn to the gaming tables. On his arm at tableside, she gasped at the way hucksters took advantage of him, watched as elegantly dressed con men pursued "schemes of plunder and robbery against him." His gullibility was particularly worrisome given that he had promised to pay down her debts. Instead, he had to divert his funds to satisfy the "nefarious gamblers and intriguers of every description" who preyed on him.

Everything came crashing down at once. Giffard sold his carriage and one of his homes, raising 1,000 pounds, which he gave in payment of those debts of hers for which he had personally signed. But she owed nearly 3,000 in total, and her creditors were no longer willing to be put off. Paying such an amount—for reference, a housemaid could expect to earn eight pounds for an entire year's wages—was simply impossible. Giffard left her.

She reeled. Under English law, those unable to pay their creditors faced being thrown into debtors' prison. The phrase itself was a horror. So many dire associations came with it: misery, disease, disgrace. As the likelihood of it moved toward certainty, she fell into fits of panic. She dreaded the squalor, not only for herself but for her daughter. But worse than that would be the shame. It would be the end of her career, the end of her. What friends she had, or thought she had, had abandoned her.

People were known to go to extraordinary lengths to avoid Marshalsea, King's Bench, Coldbath Fields and other debtors' prisons. Margaret Coghlan, the actress playing the role of mistress, was no stranger to the dramatic exit. She had fled from protectors in New Jersey and from her husband in Wales. In the depths of her despair she dreamed up her grandest exit yet.

On June 4, 1787, a Mr. Thomas Vaughan of Suffolk Street must have been struck on turning the pages of the *Daily Universal Register* to find a terse, abbreviated obituary:

> In Cavendish-street, Portland-squ. Mrs. Margaret Coghlan, lady of John C. esq; and dau. of Col. Moncrieff.

She had died, the newspaper said, "after two days illness." Mr. Vaughan was considerably shaken to read this news, for Thomas Giffard had chosen him to deal with Margaret Coghlan's creditors. How was he to tell them that the woman who had racked up such a stupendous mountain of debt had shaken free of their clutches in the most decisive and permanent manner?

Summer was coming on. Across the ocean, in Philadelphia, George Washington, the great general with whom a defiant Margaret had dined as a teenager, was presiding over a convention to determine a constitution that would govern the land of her early years. Truly, that heralded a new beginning and would provide a seedbed for the nurturing of individual liberty. But for Margaret Coghlan, née Margaret Moncrieffe, who had longed all her young life for just such freedom, who had believed the declarations of journalists and playwrights and society doyennes that freedom was in the air, ready for the taking by modern young women, and who had acted on that belief by striking out on her own in defiance of father and husband, it was not to be. History had failed her; society had defeated her.

That, anyway, was what she wanted her creditors to think. Sometime later, in Paris, a woman with her features—the same beguiling eyes and milky complexion, the same poutiness of expression undergirded by a ferocious and uncanny will to survive—checked into the Hôtel de l'Université. America wasn't the only place where the forces of change were making themselves felt. There were rumblings on the European continent. Another revolution in the offing, and with it came, perhaps, another chance for an inordinately clever and resourceful woman to clutch at a life that would be truly her own.

I t was apparently a season for false death notices. In late January 1788 Abraham Yates was in Poughkeepsie, where the state assembly was in session, when he learned of his own supposed demise. Melancton Smith, a fellow New York antifederalist, wrote him from Manhattan to say there was a rumor going around the Confederation Congress "that you was defunct, and that your funeral had been solemnized with great pomp & your pall supported by a number of illustrious Characters." The rumor had apparently been started by federalists who were so sick of Yates's unrelenting opposition that they tried to will him out of existence. "I am happy to hear, however, that you are in the land of the living," Smith added, and he went on to speculate on the possibility that Yates had indeed died but had "been restored to this mortal life" by a righteous deity "in order to oppose the new system of government."

For the battle against the Constitution was not over. The Philadelphia convention had passed it, but it required ratification by nine states before it could become the foundational document of the nation. After five states ratified in late 1787 and early 1788, the antifederalists pressed harder than ever, trying to stop others from following suit.

Massachusetts was to vote next. Yates's sources told him that most officials there were opposed to ratification, but, Melancton Smith noted darkly, "the <u>better sort</u> have means of <u>convincing</u> those who differ from them." In February came news that the federalist pressures, whatever they were, had worked: Massachusetts had voted in favor. All the more reason to stand firm. Yates knew his fellow New Yorkers viewed the document with distrust. But most newspapers were on the federalist side. He joined with like-minded men in the state to promote antifederalist printers. His son-in-law wrote him in March that he had signed the family up for six subscriptions to a new antifederalist paper, and at the same time he informed him that Susanna, who was expecting another child, was "still well tho restless and uneasy." Yates knew his daughter was having a hard pregnancy; he suspected that Lansing was keeping details from him. He pushed politics aside as he nervously waited for the stage coaches from Albany that would bring the next letter. Finally, ten days later the coach driver handed him good news. "Dear Sir," Abraham Lansing wrote, "I have the satisfaction to inform you that on Monday last between the hours of 10 & 11 Susan was safely delivered of a—fine Boy—and herself and the Child have been in very good health."

Yates had little time to rejoice. As spring weather came on, the pressure mounted anew on the political front. Since he was both a member of the State Assembly and a New York delegate to the Confederation Congress, he was traveling up and down the Hudson between Poughkeepsie and Manhattan. He entered the "Congress Room" of Federal Hall in lower Manhattan on May 27 to find delegates in excited conversation. South Carolina had become the eighth state to ratify. Only one more was needed. Would New York capitulate? All eyes in the chamber turned to him. He was treated "With Civility" by his fellow delegates, he reported to his son-in-law, and he returned the favor, but he felt the pressure. When he went to his rooms at William Bedlow's house that evening he found that Alexander Hamilton had stopped by; there was a note inviting him to a one-on-one dinner meeting. Yates had little patience for Hamilton. Besides his conviction that Hamilton was practically a monarchist, he knew that Hamilton had stolen his job as continental loan officer. But politics was politics: he would of course meet. Before doing so, Yates did some checking and came up with an estimate that the New York convention would probably vote to reject the Constitution by a good margin: 40 votes to 25. He knew Hamilton would try to play him, but he didn't know in what way.

When they met the next day, Hamilton, speaking with seeming off-handedness, told Yates it was his guess that "the Antis" would eventually come around and adopt the Constitution, provided it was fitted out with "amendments." This was the first Yates had heard of any amendments, but he dismissed the notion as "An Absurdity."

The two men were a study in contrasts—Hamilton thin, young and beakishly handsome, Yates old, gray-haired and fusty and creaky—but they were equally hardheaded. Hamilton stayed focused. Yates had power among the antifederalists; he had to try to win him over. He told Yates that if nine states did not adopt he feared the new nation would divide before it even started its life. Yates said he would be sorry of that but that he would risk it. Hamilton then said something lofty about the Constitution being the will of "Providence." Yates practically erupted. He knew perfectly well that Hamilton was lowborn like him, but that instead of being true to the common people he had lusted for status his whole life. He had led the way in twining social privilege and political power. He had pressed for an all-powerful national government to be headed by a leader-for-life. And now he had the gall to talk about Providence. A government that suited the will of Providence, Yates roared at the young man, would certainly have "for its pillars righteousness and truth." Regarding the Philadelphia convention, he declared, "I could hardly think that Providence had a hand in a government were it required to wade through such a scene of corruption, falsehood and misrepresentation."

Yates believed in the antifederalist cause as surely as he had in the American cause during the Revolution and in his stance against the British army in the days of the French and Indian War. He believed in the steadfastness of his allies as well. George Clinton, New York's governor and his friend, saw the constitutional debate in Poughkeepsie as a battle between "the friends of the rights of mankind" and "the advocates of despotism." But Yates's passion seemed to blind him to a softening in the antifederalist ranks. As more states adopted the Constitution, men like Clinton and Melancton Smith felt they had to move, as Hamilton had suggested, toward accepting the document provided it was fitted with amendments that addressed their concerns.

Summer wore on. In June, New Hampshire adopted the Constitution. Enough states now approved of it for it to take force. Four days later, Virginia did likewise.

Attention then turned to New York. Its ratification, strictly speaking, was not needed, but it would give the Constitution added force in its early stages. The federalists applied more pressure, and at the same time put forth a slate of amendments in an effort to bring antifederalists to their side.

It worked. The state voted in favor of the Constitution in late July. Yates was away at the time. Even his son-in-law, a staunch "anti," was happy with the result: "our Friends are much better pleased with it than we had reason to expect," he told Yates, and he gave the reason for the happiness, which he hoped his father-in-law would share. "The Bill of Rights which is interwoven with the Adoption is considered by the Majority of those whom I have shewn it as a security against the Encroachments of the Genl. Government."

Yates had been blindsided by this Bill of Rights. Besides the fact that the Constitution laid out vast powers for the federal government, he had vigorously objected to the fact that it did not stipulate rights guaranteed to American citizens. He had been certain the federalists would never agree to such a thing. He was so stubborn in his distrust of their intentions, so convinced that they were in the process of crafting a two-tiered system, in which a wealthy landed elite would exist on a different plane and abide by different rules from everyone else, that he could not imagine his enemies putting forth, on their own, a list of guaranteed freedoms. But here they were, crafted mostly by the small, pale, rather sickly but unstoppable Virginia federalist James Madison. Free exercise of religion. Freedom of speech and assembly. Freedom of the press. The right to petition the government for redress of grievances. Perhaps best of all, in Yates's eyes, was an amendment stipulating that the list of stated rights "shall not be construed to deny or disparage others retained by the people." In other words, the federal government's powers were to be limited to what the Constitution enumerated, while individual rights were not so limited.

Yates remained suspicious. Lansing went on to say that the City of Albany had set aside the following Friday as a public holiday to celebrate the passage of the Constitution. He and other Albany antifederalists had decided they should keep a low profile and "remain quiet at Home on the rejoicing day." But Lansing could barely hide his glee as he described the parade that was planned: a boat fixed on a carriage would hold, as representatives of Albany's history, an Indian and a trader, and it would be festooned with flags honoring the city's different occupations. There would be a whole roasted ox, and "several scores of barrels of beer" for a proper celebration.

Yates must have read the buoyant description with mounting confusion. He had fought against the encroachment of government most particularly in order to uphold the empowerment of the citizens of his beloved city. Others had joined him in that fight. Now, however, those same citizens seemed practically to celebrate their loss of power. Yes, the new system of governmental authority contained assurances of rights, but he remained convinced that government, any government, was a thing to be mistrusted, that once it got a portion of power, it would never relinquish it but would rather push for more, and keep growing and expanding, always at the expense of individuals. During the years of the Revolution he had been in his element, fully connected to the currents of the day. Now he was suddenly out of touch with the world around him.

Truly adding insult to the injury of the Constitution's adoption and the celebration of it in his home town, Yates learned that Philip Schuyler—his old antagonist who was, to boot, Hamilton's father-in-law—would lead the parade holding aloft a copy of the Constitution, while Schuyler's insufferable son, also called Philip, would drive the carriage. Unconsciously reinforcing Yates's conviction that what was being celebrated was an elitist victory, Lansing cheerily referred to the younger Schuyler as "the Lord of the Manor."

Five days later, in an altogether moody frame of mind, feeling squeezed like a melon, Yates sat down with Alexander Hamilton and the two other members of New York's delegation to the Confederation Congress, Ezra L'Hommedieu and Egbert Benson, and asked them to attest an affidavit he had written. With the states having approved the Constitution, it now fell to the Congress to certify it. Yates had planned to vote against certification, on principle. But Benson and L'Hommedieu would likely be out of town for the vote. As it happened, the Iroquois, in their anger at Cornplanter for having given away their lands, were raiding upstate settlements, and the two politicians had to head north to negotiate with them. That left only Yates and Hamilton to represent the state in Congress. Should New York's delegation not vote a clear yes on the pro forma certification, other states would not support it in what was already shaping up to be a brisk confrontation: the bid to become the seat of the new federal government.

Yates had sweated and strained to block the Constitution. From its very first words—"We the people . . ."—it indicated an arrogant presumption on the part of a federal government to represent all. But now it was inevitable. And he wasn't even to be given the dignity of voting his conscience. At the very least, he wanted it attested why he was not able to do so. With the same twisty energy that he used to pen his Rough Hewer essays, he put in writing in the affidavit the negative conditions that compelled him to vote for something he believed was wrong. He began with gale force: "Being Confident that the Constitution for the general government in its present form Will be destructive to the liberties of the People And as Such by every means to be avoided as one of the Greatest of all Evils . . ." He went on to state his concern that without a positive vote from the New York delegation the Congress might move out of the state, and added, further, his fear that without the full support of the New York delegates the Bill of Rights might not be attached to the final document. He said he considered that the Bill of Rights was "indispensably necessary for the Security of the Liberty and freedom of the People." Therefore, with deepest reservations, he wrote, "I Shall Join in the vote to Compleat the Ordinance."

Hamilton, his enemy, sitting across from him, all but gloated. He had won his great victory, assuring a strong federal government. And he had won this small victory, over the quarrelsome, nettlesome, squinty old man from Albany. It was quite possibly the most painful moment of Yates's life.

"The executive Power shall be vested in a President of the United States of America." The Constitution was now in force, and it called for a chief executive.

George Washington stood in a Virginia field, staring darkly at stubby cabbage heads. He had planted his cabbages between his corn rows. The crop had failed, and he didn't know why. Buckwheat was also a disappointment, huge, white-headed stands of hogweed having crowded it out. He blamed it on the wet spring.

It was September. Well before news of the official certification of the Constitution, he had started to see in newspapers calls for him to serve as the first executive. Some appeals were spiritual, declaring it divinely ordained. Others waxed psychological, noting that, as he had no children of his own, Washington would be the father of all Americans—and, as a bonus, the nation would have no fear of a hereditary rule being established.

Then the letters started arriving. He tried to stay quiet on the matter of what he would do. Deep within him was a longing for peace. Part of him hoped that the electors "by giving their votes in favor of some other person, would save me from the dreaded Dilemma of being forced to accept or refuse." Then too, ever since he had been coached as a boy by William Fairfax to adopt a "Roman" facade, he had followed the strategy, when he was close to achieving something, of holding back, waiting for it to be thrust at him. Maybe he didn't know himself, this time, whether he wanted this thing or not. Maybe he wanted events to decide the matter for him. But his actions said that he was tired, spent from a lifetime of hard service.

Then came a blunt appeal from a trusted quarter. Hamilton wrote him with disarming frankness: "on your acceptance of the office of President the success of the new government in its commencement may materially depend." No one, Hamilton said, had Washington's stature, either at home or abroad. On the off chance that Washington feared for his legacy, Hamilton thought it worthwhile to add that if the new system "should miscarry," the blame wouldn't be assigned to Washington but to the men, such as Hamilton himself, who had constructed it.

As if the two beloved younger officers of his staff were acting in concert, Lafayette wrote as well, with his customary verve: "in the Name of America, of Mankind at large, and Your Own fame, I Beseech you, my dear General, Not to deny your Acceptance of the office of president." Lafayette knew him as well as Hamilton did, understood his quiet vanity, and like Hamilton he added a note concerning Washington's regard for his reputation, declaring his belief that the presidency "will furnish An Admirable Chapter in your History."

In the end, Washington allowed his name to be put forth. Things happened very quickly. In February 1789, a letter arrived from New York. It was from Henry Knox, his old comrade-in-arms, who was following events. The electors had cast their ballots, he solemnly informed Washington, and "your Excellency has every vote for President, and Mr John Adams 28 for Vice President exclusively of New Jersey and Delaware whose votes for Vice are not Known."

Martha was not pleased. His health had deteriorated; she considered him too old to begin a large public responsibility. And while she enjoyed entertaining guests at Mount Vernon, she had no taste for official pomp. He left in April; she said she would come later. He began his journey with "a mind oppressed." He seems to have thought he could slip quietly through the countryside, accompanied by his two aides. In fact, he was waylaid with parades and celebrations in Alexandria, Wilmington, Philadelphia, Trenton.

At the riverside in New Jersey a "presidential barge" was waiting for him, with musicians and white-clad oarsmen, ready to row him across the Hudson. A band of dignitaries greeted the barge as it pulled up to the dock on the Manhattan side. There were speeches. As Washington moved forward into the city, the crowd—soldiers, children, women in their spring hats—thronged him. Being a man of breeding, he bowed politely, over and over, to each well-wisher. They may have been a bit surprised at the sight. He was famous, after all, as a military man, but here he was dressed in a sober brown suit and white stockings. He did, however, have a sword at his side. He was older than they expected, too, having himself become aware of rapid, premature aging in the past few years: "descending the hill," as he put it.

The Constitution stipulated a simple oath that would render a newly elected leader president. He stood on the balcony of Federal Hall next to Robert Livingston, the chancellor of New York, and repeated the words: "I do solemnly swear that I will faithfully execute the Office of President of the United States, and will to the best of my Ability, preserve, protect and defend the Constitution of the United States."

The crowd cheered. Then he and the other members of the government entered the Senate chamber. He had thought it fitting to give an
inaugural address. He had given thought, in fact, to the many ways in
which what he now did would, as he said, "serve to establish a Precedent." He chose in his speech to paint in broad strokes, bringing the
theme of the Revolution into the Republic, beseeching the legislators,
who were likewise setting a precedent as the first Congress under the
Constitution, to govern with "a reverence for the characteristic rights
of freemen." It was a short speech. Some members of Congress were
struck by the weakness in his voice, and by the fact that he seemed to
tremble as he spoke.

Eventually, he was able to be alone with his thoughts. Congress had
rented a house at the corner of Cherry Street, a few blocks away, as the
president's mansion. There were oriental rugs and lots of mahogany
furniture. It was tasteful. But of course it was not home. Outside the
windows, the trees were in blossom. The whole city seemed overflowing with hope and affection for him. But he was alone. And Martha
wouldn't arrive for weeks.

To occupy himself constructively, he wrote a letter to his vice president, John Adams of Massachusetts. "The President of the United
States wishes to avail himself of your sentiments on the following
points," he began. Basically, he was wondering what to do with himself. He was not a king, and did not wish to act like one; but he was by
nature reserved, and, especially in his current mood, craved privacy.
Did Adams think it would be suitable if he set aside just one day per
week for receiving "visits of Compliment"? Would it be enough if he
offered "about four great Entertainments in a Year"? And would there
be "any impropriety in the President's making informal visits—that is
to say, in his calling upon his acquaintances"? He had only just entered
the office of president, and already he seemed to be looking for ways
out of it.

. . .

I f you were fleeing London, and were a person of some ambition, there was really only one place to go. From a hill on the outskirts of Paris, Margaret Coghlan, runaway debtor, looked down, in the summer of 1787, into a shimmering whitewashed maze of architecture, punctuated by the grandest of steeples and spires, signifying nothing less than the epitome of human civilization. London was larger, but Paris was the home of luxury, refinement, art, science, fashion, theater and philosophy. It was the city of salons whose walls were studded with magnificent art and through whose exquisitely appointed spaces drifted the world's most interesting people. It was the city of the future, which at this very moment was completing work on a novel project to affix a number to each building, so that every single resident could be scientifically accounted for. Yes, it was also a place that in many parts smelled like a sewer, with streets that crawled with disease and crime and cat-sized rats. But someone in Margaret's situation had to focus on the positive. Paris was the city of silk and perfume and cognac and wine. It was the city of love. Paris, she felt, putting the best possible face on her circumstances, was her natural home.

Margaret Coghlan was not alone in fleeing her past. The practice of imprisoning people for inability to pay their bills forced many to such extremes. For her, starting over was an act of defiance, an assertion of the will to live.

She knew the city well enough to know where she wanted to be. And despite having to leave London in a hurry, she had done it in style, bringing her maid with her and as much furniture as she could manage. She settled in at her hotel, a fashionable place for foreigners in exile, and promptly found herself a companion. William Dalrymple was a Scot who had served in the American war as a major general and had recently been elected to Parliament. They had shared experiences over which to break the ice, he having served for two years in Halifax, the city where she was born. On the arm of an illustrious military man, she was back in her element. Dalrymple, she gushed, "made me acquainted with all the beauties of that superb and magnificent city; he introduced me into all the gay and brilliant circles, of which he himself shone the splendid ornament." She was being kind regarding his splendor: Dalrymple was in his fifties, with a great round belly. Elsewhere she called him her "cicisbeo," an Italian term for a gentleman who escorted a married woman in society, suggesting, perhaps, that she did not consider him an actual lover. Meanwhile, feeling secure enough to once again be excited by life, she allowed herself to become smitten by a younger relative of Dalrymple's, and the two of them began a tryst behind the general's back. Dalrymple suspected them, hid himself in her room and surprised them at what she referred to as the act "that lovers dedicate to the deity of their adoration." Her association with both men ended at once.

After that she thought it best to change to another accommodation catering to foreigners. Her new headquarters was a fashionable hotel run by a Madame Lafar, a woman whom Margaret was assured respected her guests' privacy, "never asking impertinent questions."

Meanwhile, she could not escape noticing that the cobbled streets through which her coach rattled were thrumming with nervous energy. The city was on edge. King Louis XVI, facing bankruptcy, had asked Parlement to issue new taxes, including a stamp duty similar to the one Americans had rebelled against, and Parlement had refused to do so. For a time, the atmosphere of impending strife made the gaiety of society that much gayer. Every evening Margaret was surrounded by "the greatest splendour," tables "continually crowded by persons of the highest rank." A wealthy gentleman named Mr. Beckett "flattered me by his addresses, at a time when all the Parisian beauties were emulous with each other for his affections." She succumbed, and for four months she whirled through the city at his side, rubbing shoulders with the Duc d'Orléans, with Prince Louis d'Arenberg of Belgium. She even made the acquaintance of the Comte d'Artois, the handsome, thirty-year-old brother of the king.

Then the troubles descended. Riots broke out in the streets. The king ordered the members of the Paris Parlement out of the city for their insolence, and set his brothers the task of enforcing the new taxes. But at the Palais de Justice, the Comte d'Artois, Margaret's royal acquaintance, encountered a furious crowd numbering in the thousands. He tried to advance, aided by mounted Swiss and French guards; the crowd rushed him. He fled the scene, pale and shaken at the unprecedented act of violence against a royal person.

Alongside British Whigs, French intellectuals—most notably Voltaire and Jean-Jacques Rousseau—had given voice in the previous decade to notions of individual liberty and a society based on natural rights, and some had pointed to America as proof that a such a society could actually exist in the real world. People at the salons Margaret attended began whispering about a shocking notion being voiced: that Louis XVI, their absolute ruler, would be advised to allow some measure of popular rule. With even more anxiety, the powdered and bewigged crowd gossiped about Louis' answer, which was transmitted through his Keeper of the Seals, Chrétien-François de Lamoignon. It was "universally acknowledged," he declared with finality, that "the King alone must possess the sovereign power in his kingdom." As to popular rule, de Lamoignon added, "the legislative power resides in the person of the King independent of and unshared with all other powers."

Margaret meanwhile had her own personal turmoil—a familiar one. She had once again been living beyond her means. Her landlady insisted she pay her outstanding bill, which amounted to 500 pounds. She announced that she couldn't pay, at least not right away. Later, at a party, she found herself accosted by the police. Her friends went to the

English ambassador to ask him to intercede, but he was away. At two o'clock in the morning she was taken to the Hôtel de la Force, the debtors' prison: the "mansion of slavery," she called it. She was shown to her cell: empty except for a bed of straw on the floor and a blanket. In her arms was her two-year-old son. She was also seven months pregnant. She spent the night with her maid, who insisted on accompanying her, wailing at her fate, aghast that she had fallen so far. In the morning, she sent out appeals to friends, asking them, in her desperation, to contact the Comte d'Artois. Miraculously, they reached the king's brother and he interceded in her behalf. She was released into his custody.

From rags back to riches: she spent the next six months as a guest of the prince. Soon, however, she learned that all of her belongings had been seized by her creditors. Margaret had spent lavishly in Paris, including purchasing not one but two expensive vehicles, a post-chaise and a chariot. Everything was now gone.

Summer came on in full force. It was July 1789. Enormous angry crowds massed in the streets. The king—absolute, untouchable monarch that he was—was being openly reviled. The air was heavy with the threat of violent change. Like many other foreigners, Margaret decided she had better leave the country.


George Washington was not settling contentedly into his role as first president of the American republic. Martha eventually joined him in New York, but she didn't much like it either. Despite his long early years of studying the mannerisms of the Virginia gentry, he and his wife both felt like bumpkins in their new social circle, studded as it was with foreign dignitaries and members of what was for all intents and purposes an American aristocracy. At state dinners, Washington adopted a frozen smile. One participant remarked that in his boredom Washington "played on the dinner table with a fork or knife, like a drumstick."

One reason for his wandering attention may have been a growing deafness: the president simply couldn't hear much that went on around him.

Yet he did work hard at setting up an executive administration. And he took careful note of events in the wider world. He was keenly aware that the fever for individual freedom that had occupied the whole of his adult life and led him to this position was at work elsewhere. When news reached New York that massive public demonstrations in Paris had climaxed with the storming of the Bastille, the medieval prison that stood as a symbol of French tyranny and injustice, and that an all-out revolution was taking place in Europe's most deeply monarchic nation, Washington was stunned at the power and sweep of historical forces. His friend Lafayette was back in France; Washington had not heard from him since he had assumed the presidency. He picked up a pen: "The revolution, which has taken place with you, is of such magnitude, and of so momentous a nature that we hardly yet dare to form a conjecture about it. We however trust, and fervently pray that its consequences may prove happy." Lafayette wrote back expressing his amazement that "Every thing that was is No More," and his hope that "a New Building is Erecting, Not perfect By far, But Sufficient to Ensure freedom." As events in France grew more menacing, however, Washington found himself fearing the worst. Where America's revolt had been against the state, in the form of a distant empire, the French had taken up arms against both their king and the Catholic Church. The Enlightenment commitment to reason as a new organizing principle for society called in both countries for a radical change of government, and the installation of a rule by the people. But where American society was young and flexible, in France the political structure was ancient and deeply woven into the social fabric. And the ardent commitment by the revolutionaries to follow the dictates of reason in throwing off the "superstition" of the Church brought their fight onto an entirely different level, one that promised unprecedented violence and turmoil.

Washington confided to Gouverneur Morris his fear that in France "the revolution is of too great magnitude."

If part of Washington's discomfort with the presidency had to do with New York, that situation at least changed in the summer of 1790, when he boarded a boat and sailed across the river to New Jersey, en route to a new, albeit temporary, national capital. Abraham Yates's agreement to support the Constitution in hopes of keeping the capital in lower Manhattan had been for naught. James Madison and Thomas Jefferson had lobbied for the construction of a new capital on the banks of the Potomac River. Washington, their fellow Virginian, had liked the idea as well. Northerners, including Alexander Hamilton, were bitterly opposed. Meanwhile, the Congress became caught up in debating Hamilton's proposal that the federal government should assume all the debts of the states, as part of a general reorganization of federal finances. In one quietly momentous dinner meeting, Hamilton, Madison and Jefferson reached a compromise. Hamilton agreed to move the capital to the Potomac, and in exchange the Virginians accepted the debt assumption. In order to win Pennsylvanians to the plan, they offered to make Philadelphia the interim capital for a period of ten years, until the new city was built. Thus, Washington made his stately way south to Philadelphia in August of 1790, met en route by parades and cheering crowds. Along with the rest of the government, he would have a new home.

As he settled in—he had been given a four-story mansion that was a much more comfortable home than he had had in New York—he was flooded with reports from the frontier. Following the war, the government had planned for future expansion by organizing a region officially known as the Territory Northwest of the River Ohio, which extended from the Pennsylvania border to the Mississippi River and as far north as Canada. Agents had negotiated treaties with Indians in this vast region similar to the one Cornplanter had agreed to at Fort Stanwix.

Then the fighting began. Shawnees, Kickapoos, Wyandots, Ottawas, Miamis and other tribes were outraged by the terms of the treaties and by the groups of white settlers who began felling trees and building homes in their lands. And the Iroquois, with whom the Americans had the longest and closest association, had also racheted up their outrage, as Americans, exulting in their own freedom, set about constricting the Indians' freedom.

Washington sent out an army to deal with the western tribes. The Iroquois, however, were closer to home; their concerns had to be heard. He agreed to take an active part in discussions. He had long known of the Seneca leader Cornplanter, who had been one of the fiercest enemies of America in the war but had since become one of the most pragmatic and diplomatic of Iroquois leaders. Now they would meet.

On the first day of December, Cornplanter, having returned to Philadelphia four years after his appearance at the Saint Tammany spectacle, stood outside the door of the presidential mansion along with two other Seneca leaders, Half-Town and Big Tree. Cornplanter had known of George Washington practically all his life. Back in 1753, his uncle Guyasuta had guided a twenty-one-year-old Washington to the French headquarters at Fort Le Boeuf. When Cornplanter was still a child, he learned of the white Virginian from his uncle, and knew to apply the name Town Destroyer to him. With the devastation of Sullivan's army, the prophecy in the name had been realized.

Despite, or in part because of, that devastation of Iroquois lands, Cornplanter held Washington in some regard. He knew how the Americans felt about him. He knew that they considered their victory over the British and their forming of their own nation to be a momentous thing, and that they gave Washington much credit for their success. Such things held value too for Cornplanter, even though they had happened at the expense of his people. As a child in the longhouse, Cornplanter would have heard tales of a strange creature called Tadadaho. Tadadaho was a kind of wizard, with a twisted body, who lived in a swamp and controlled people by sowing fear. As part of the coming-together of the Iroquois Confederacy, the figure known as the Peacemaker was able to work magic on Tadadaho, converting his evil into good, so that his natural leadership abilities could be put to positive use. As a result, Tadadaho became the grand chief of the Confederacy. The story of Tadadaho fit the history of George Washington, and Cornplanter seemed to believe that, like the Peacemaker, his task as spokesman for the Iroquois was to try to convert Town Destroyer into a leader who would help rather than harm his people.

The Indians were shown into Washington's office, where they found him flanked by three soldiers. Coming face to face at last, the two leaders must have seen evidence of one another's stature and experience. But where Washington had become stooped with ailments, his face rutted and his lips pursed, Cornplanter was still vital. His eyes expressed almost shocking force. He began by acknowledging their respective roles, referring to himself as "the voice of the Seneca nation" and to Washington as "the great Councillor, in whose heart the wise men of the thirteen fires have placed their wisdom." Then he offered an acknowledgement of Washington's greater power: "When your army entered the Country of the Six Nations, we called you the Town-destroyer and to this day, when that name is heard, our women look behind them and turn pale, and our children cling close to the neck of their mothers."

He spoke at length. He could not know whether he would ever get another meeting with the leader of all Americans, so he wanted to set the situation in perspective. He had no notes, and as Washington's interpreter took it all down, it became clear that the Seneca held a prodigious amount of historical information in his head. He went back to the time before the Iroquois had formed their Confederacy, remarking on how the various Indian nations had fought with one another. Then the Confederacy brought peace. He talked about the arrival of the French and the English. In coming to the period of the Revolution, he recounted how the Americans themselves had warned the Iroquois that the king of England was a fearsome leader whom they must obey, suggesting, ever so slyly, that the blame for their entering the war on the British side might reasonably be laid at the Americans' feet. He discussed the Treaty of Fort Stanwix, and how he now understood that a trick had been played on them, the Iroquois being alternately told they were dealing with British law, then with various state governments, then with the American government. Further, the treaty had contained a promise that once they gave up certain lands, "we should be secured in the peaceable possession of the lands which we inhabited." But that promise had been violated almost at once. He went into details of discussions with the State of Pennsylvania, and how that state's negotiators had insisted even in the midst of the discussions that it was all moot because the land "was already ceded to them by the great King."

Cornplanter made Washington understand that he was no fool, that, as far as he was concerned, the Americans, with their seemingly inexorable civilization, were toying with the native inhabitants of the continent. He concluded with a bold demand: "You have said we were in your hand, and that by closing it, you could crush us to nothing. Are you determined to crush us? If you are, tell us so." Many Iroquois, he said, wanted to know plainly if the Americans were going to obliterate them, in which case they preferred to do the work themselves: "eat the faral root," and sleep with their fathers in peace.

But rather than leave the president with the taunt to finish them off and be done with it, he added a caveat: "Before you determine on a measure so unjust, look up to the God who made us, as well as you."

It was a stunning address, one that summarized a civilization, its claims to its land, its very claim to existence. Washington could not give an answer on the spot. He promised to reply after he had had time to consider the remarks. When they next met, he was ready, and spoke in the clear, frank terms of one who holds power and knows it. He informed Cornplanter that the Fort Stanwix treaty was not up for renegotiation. They would have to live with a territory that was much smaller than what they had before the war. But he also promised that the existing boundaries would be upheld. The American government, he vowed, would "never consent to your being defrauded, but it will protect you in all your just rights."

Washington was aware that the Iroquois needed to restructure their society in the face of a rapidly growing American nation, and he seemed to accept that helping them to do so was part of his responsibility. The president of the United States went so far in a subsequent meeting as to personally walk the Senecas down the street from his mansion to do some shopping for their settlement. (Cornplanter's nephew was struck enough by the novelty of this that he recalled the order in which they strolled: "Red Jacket was next to Washington as we went along on the sidewalk; I was far behind.") Meanwhile, the State of Pennsylvania made Cornplanter a grant of 1,500 acres of land for the formation of a new Seneca town. It also gave him and his party 65 pounds in cash; the Senecas used the money to buy equipment for the new settlement.

Having seen a great deal of the scope and spread of American civilization, and having thought much about how to ensure the long-term survival of his people, Cornplanter, in his meeting with the president, expressed his desire to have Iroquois children learn English and some of the ways of the Americans. Washington liked this. He agreed to provide teachers for the new town, as well as experts who could demonstrate some of the latest agricultural methods.

Cornplanter left Philadelphia without getting the commitment to return native lands that his people were hoping for. He knew that many would refuse to accept this, and that there would be more bloodshed.

But Washington had treated him with respect and had promised—had solemnly promised, and surely that was something—to uphold the new boundaries. The American government, he had said, "will protect you." So Cornplanter had to think that there were some grounds for hope: that he had successfully played the role of Peacemaker, and that the evil in the white Tadadaho had been transformed to good.

On the way out of the city, the relatively hopeful mood was violently broken. The Senecas were attacked by a party of American militiamen who had been lying in wait for them. They robbed them of all the items they had purchased for their new village.

Margaret Coghlan's English creditors were not stupid. She may have thought that with the passage of time she would be able to slip back into London unnoticed, but shortly after her return, they pounced. She was arrested and taken to a "sponging house," a private house that served as a temporary prison for debtors. Seven weeks she languished there, until her case came up at the King's Bench court. Her creditors—drapers, perfumiers, hairdressers, furniture makers—paraded before the judge. She was found guilty. Unable to pay, she was sentenced to two years in prison.

This time it was real: iron bars, rats, lunatic screams, watery gruel for meals. And, again, she was pregnant. As the time of her delivery approached, she became reflective on her long, mad quest for happiness, for freedom: "I ever have grasped at a shadow—the substance I could never attain." She rued having given herself over to the promises of men. "Beware, then, ye lovely victims of their crocodile caresses!" she wrote, addressing any young women who might heed her warning. She had known perfectly well that for a woman to get ahead by using men she had to be very calculating; but she had stumbled in her calculations, and she offered advice to others: "make the false dissemblers, while they pay homage to your beauty, provide also for your interest: lay up stores against a rainy day." She gave birth in squalor, assisted by a young prison doctor who had no experience. So vile were the conditions that, after her son was born and her bloodied clothes removed, she and the baby lay naked for two days before they received any attention.

Shortly after she was released from prison, in late 1791, she learned that her father had died in New York. He had been buried in Trinity Church, where her ghastly marriage had taken place. The news shook her terribly—she declared that she had had a premonition of it—but, worse, it brought a new round of creditors after her. There were still many people to whom she owed money, and they now assumed she would have received an inheritance. She had not. But the lawsuits resulted in her once again being hauled to prison. Her father's death, though, had one happy result: it brought her in contact with her long lost brother. He sent her money: not a lot, but, she said, enough "to raise my drooping head, and to sooth the miseries of the King's Bench prison."

When she stepped outside after another two years, the pale sun showed a ghostly pallor to her skin. The arresting beauty that had clung to her her whole life, as much a curse as a gift, was gone. Searching for some peace and security, she made her way 70 miles south to Portsmouth, where she tracked down two aunts. They invited her into their cozy home, fed her, sat her by the fire. She unwound her long, sad and exhilarating story for them, and for once she felt a bit of relief.

It didn't last. Back in London, another bailiff appeared at her door. Other creditors demanded that she pay. "Arrest after arrest pursues me," she wrote weakly. Her body was breaking down, but her will remained firm. She wracked her brains over this new round of debts. "I am certain that Four Hundred Pounds would discharge them," she thought. "But to raise that sum, where is my hope?"

And then she had a new idea. Not a man, for once. A book.

Everyone in England was riveted by the French Revolution. Would its ideas spread across the Channel? People were devouring the works of French writers. An Englishwoman named Mary Wollstonecraft had noted a glaring hole in the reasoning of these fine thinkers. Rousseau, one of the inspirations of the revolution, in the midst of arguing for the elevation of reason over superstition, added a caveat that women did not have the same capacity for reason as men and therefore were not entitled to the same kind of education. Educating women in the ways of the world would only encourage them to challenge men, which was unnatural. "If woman is made to please and to be subjugated to man," he wrote, "she ought to make herself pleasing to him rather than to provoke him."

What particularly stirred Mary Wollstonecraft to action were similar remarks by one of France's revolutionary figures, Charles-Maurice de Talleyrand, who declared that the enlightened French Republic would be a nation in which women would stay out of worldly affairs and instead "accustom themselves to a calm and secluded life." The book Wollstonecraft wrote in response, *A Vindication of the Rights of Woman,* argued that all people, regardless of sex, had the same God-given natural rights. Society treated women like "slaves," she said; education would free them: an "enlightened nation" should conduct an experiment, allowing women "to share the advantages of education and government with man," and "see whether they will become better, as they grow wiser and become free. They cannot be injured by the experiment; for it is not in the power of man to render them more insignificant than they are at present."

Wollstonecraft's book was being read as Coghlan got out of prison. One passage in particular seemed to reach right into her core: "Consider . . . whether, when men contend for their freedom, and to be allowed to judge for themselves, respecting their own happiness, it be not inconsistent and unjust to subjugate women . . . ? Who made man the exclusive judge, if woman partake with him the gift of reason?"

Coghlan's very life had in a sense been a search for the freedom that both recent historic revolutions promised. Why had she failed so miserably? Obviously, because she was a woman. The men who led the Enlightenment movement toward freedom had excepted half of the species from their grand program. She had not fully understood this before; she had instead charged ahead in pursuit of her own freedom. She had had no choice, really; she had needed to do what she did; she would have lost her mind living in servitude to the abusive beast she had been forced to marry. Yes, she had gotten sidetracked: she had forgotten that she was only playing a role; she had let herself be lured by silk and champagne and the possibility of love. But her life had been animated by the same forces that were driving these world-historic movements. It deserved to be put into a book; there would be lessons in it for young women. When she had told her aunts of her mad adventures, she hadn't spared them any of the lurid details. Why not do that in print?

She met a man named Pigott. He was an oily little fellow, but he knew the business of printers and books and such. As a political radical, he was consumed by the goings-on in France, which had now reached the level of what seemed like mass insanity. While she was in prison, first the king had been executed, then his wife, Marie-Antoinette; then the revolutionary leaders began turning on one another. There were riots in the streets of Paris. Charles Pigott had once been a newspaperman. The revolutions in America and France had given him a new career: publishing books on the louche sex lives of English aristocrats as a way to highlight their decadance. It was sleazy, but he had a political motive that he thought of as legitimate: to undermine the upper class and help bring revolution to England's shores.

When Margaret mentioned her idea to Pigott, he made it happen. He encouraged her to be herself, to pour out her story in whatever manner came most naturally to her. And she did. She named names. She described high passion and low squalor. She showed herself the

proud and defiant mistress of a duke, a general, a captain, a businessman: she reveled in tolling the succession of lovers. She described the
travails of trying to live as a free and independent woman. It wasn't, in
the main, a philosophical piece of writing, but she had learned a great
deal and was suddenly conscious of her whirlwind of a life having taken
place at a fulcrum of history. She had been shaped by the collision of the
old—British feudalism and the French old regime—with the insurgency
of values that comprised the American and French revolutions. She had
lived through, she said, "an aera replete with events still in the womb of
time to produce," an era that "threatens destruction to long established
systems—to long established orders."

She filled sheet after sheet with her clean, strong handwriting, and
while the work was focused on her own affairs, as she neared the end,
she saw how the larger story of the times had given her her identity.
"Born in America, and resident many years in England," she concluded,
"I feel no partialities, no prepossessions or disgusts—my country is the
world!" She begged the reader to excuse her political digressions, but
didn't really excuse them herself, declaring them to be "the spontaneous emanations of a soul fraught with sensibility, and glowing with
zeal for the general happiness and improvement of mankind."

She brought her personal story right to the present moment:
December 1793, with the threat of jail hanging once again over her head
for want of 400 pounds. The pen scratched its way to the end. At the
last moment she thought of a dedication. She had come to identify with
the republican spirit of her native land, but America and its revolution
were far away. Her own life had played out mostly in England, the book
was being published in England, and her underlying motivation in publishing it was to win the pity of English readers, who might relieve her
of her suffering. She scribbled the dedication: "To the British Nation."

And what to call it? She had taken particular, dark pleasure in detailing the abuses her husband had subjected her to. If there was a prime

mover to the tragedy that was her life it was surely John Coghlan. But the conventions surrounding the institution of marriage, which violated a woman's freedom just as she was setting out in life, were also to blame. She chose a title that pointed at both her odious husband and marriage itself. She called it the *Memoirs of Mrs. Coghlan*.

The cane tapped purposefully along the street. Abraham Yates had appointments to hurry to, but then too the tapping was itself part of his work.

The struggle over the United States Constitution had left Yates a creature of the past in many ways, but here in his hometown he still had another act to live out. Albany had always been his focus and his passion, and in 1790, following the federalist victory, Governor George Clinton, his old comrade, appointed him mayor of the city.

Yates hadn't seen it coming, but the appointment ushered in the happiest and most rewarding period of his life. He took to the task with as much zeal as he had ever shown for anything. He had served the city in so many capacities through the years, now that he was given a chance to run it, he was keen to do everything in his power to make it flourish. He began with a new effort at paving the streets. It was an enormous job— Market Street alone, where his own house was, required thousands of cartloads of stone—hence the tapping to test the work. He set up an additional ferry crossing the Hudson River, and a new system of lamps to light the streets. Under his administration, local residents established a bank, which they sensibly named the Bank of Albany. The place was growing: the city itself had only 3,500 residents, but Albany County's population swelled to 75,000, surpassing even New York City.

The year 1793 was a hard one. In August, his dear friend and one-time protégé, Matthew Visscher, died, at the age of forty-two. Outbreaks of smallpox and yellow fever to the west and south required Yates to institute a quarantine on travelers from certain regions. In September, he got word that a high government official was being held across the river, and he was furious at being denied entry into the city. The official was the secretary of the United States Treasury, Alexander Hamilton, who was traveling with his wife to visit her parents, the Schuylers. Since yellow fever was raging in Philadelphia, where they had come from, they were being detained. Yates sent a physician to examine his old enemy and Mrs. Hamilton; the report came that they seemed in good health; he cleared them to enter, perhaps grudgingly.

Hamilton's appearance in Albany under threat of infectious disease must have seemed metaphorically apt to Yates. For the federalist threat, led still by Hamilton, had not abated, and Yates was still doing everything he could to resist it. The French Revolution had indirectly brought his fears of tyranny—along with those of many other Americans—back to the fore. Relations with Britain had remained poor since the end of the war. In the fallout from France's revolutionary turmoil, England and France were now at war. The American government had to pick a side. Antifederalists strongly supported France, whose populist ideals, they felt, closely matched those that had sparked the American Revolution. Federalists sided with England. Hamilton urged President Washington to turn his back on the nation that had given crucial support to the Americans and instead ally with their former enemy. Fearing another war with the British, Washington went along with Hamilton's advice. He sent John Jay to negotiate a treaty with England that was intended to ensure peace and settle grievances left over from the Revolution.

Jay's treaty, which the Senate quickly voted on, incensed the American public. People had suffered financially from an ongoing trade imbalance since the end of the war, which the treaty was supposed to rectify, but it ignored the issue. Jay had given much, and gotten very little in return. The outcry reached the level of outright fury—angry crowds surrounded Washington's mansion, people threw rocks at Alexander

Hamilton in public—not just because of the terms of the treaty but also because it had been ratified by the president and the Senate without any popular input.

Yates went back into essay mode. The danger that the treaty's swift passage pointed up, he said, was of a future president becoming an out-and-out tyrant. All a president needed was enough power to control the Senate. With that, he could force through Supreme Court justices that were to his liking. Then he could proceed to dismantle press freedoms and other checks on power. Yates's fear was that the Constitution, in its very construction, allowed for America's hallowed fight for freedom to be subverted into dictatorship.

Because he kept hounding them, the federalists continued to attack Yates. Several times they tried to oust him from the mayor's office. He fought them off with gusto. Meanwhile, in his spare hours, he began writing, as a postmortem on the American experiment, should it become necessary, a history of the state of New York. It was a lopsided history: he devoted most of it to the Dutch period, and to the background of the Dutch in Europe, describing in page after page the steady development among them of the concept of "the people's rights and liberties."

Between the mayor's day job and his history project, he worked doggedly, despite his seventy-one years and wobbly health. Then, quite suddenly, Antje, his wife of forty-eight years, died. He tried to soldier on despite his sorrow. In the months following her funeral the big house on Market Street remained as boisterous as ever. As if to make up for the sole child Abraham and Antje had had, that daughter, Susanna, and her husband, Abraham Lansing, had thirteen children all told; the entire extended family continued to live together, for Yates relished being surrounded by his grandchildren. But Antje had been as vital to him as his work had been, and he declined rapidly after her death. For a short time he continued overseeing the weekly meetings of the city council. Then in the early summer of 1795 he suddenly stopped attending them.

A year later, still clinging onto the office of mayor, he managed to get himself to one last municipal meeting. Nine days later he died. Much of Albany turned out to see him laid to rest next to Antje.

Never one to spare words, Yates, just before he died, wrote his own epitaph, which he intended to be inscribed on his tombstone. In typical fashion, it was long: fifty-nine turgid and overwrought words. Not surprisingly, it was never carved. But the *Albany Register* published it. It highlighted the two things he wished to be remembered for. "Beneath lies Abraham Yates Jun.," he had written, "who uniformly opposed the tyranny of Britain, and the corrupt perfidious Establishment of the funding system." To the very end of his life, and even in a sense beyond it, he cried out to Americans to heed his warning: that the federal system of the United States government would, in the end, "prove most injurious to the equal rights of man."

———⟨≫⟩———

## Chapter 20

# WHICH NOTHING ELSE
# CAN EQUAL

G eorge Washington was toothless. Or virtually so: by the time he had reached the age of sixty, he had exactly one of his own teeth in his mouth. Steady dental rot had been a nagging, debilitating affliction throughout his life. And if, during his presidency, his deafness made him an ineffective listener, the dentures that he wore, made of human teeth held together with ivory and gold, rendered him an awkward speaker as well. Plus, he had the devil of a time chewing food.

As his political career wound down, he came to feel metaphorically toothless as well. He was determined at the outset of his presidency to do what he could to ensure that the new nation did not divide itself into political parties, which he felt would lead to its ruin, yet that was precisely what happened in the split between Federalists and Anti-Federalists, or Democratic-Republicans, as the latter came to be known. Washington himself had fueled the divide by installing leaders of the two parties—Alexander Hamilton and Thomas Jefferson—in his cabinet, giving each a power base from which to nurture a constituency.

The treaty that Washington had sent John Jay to negotiate may have staved off another war with England but it exacerbated the political rift in the country. And the Jay Treaty became the means for politicians to do what had been unthinkable a few years before: attack Washington himself. As word leaked out that Washington and the Senate had kept the treaty's terms secret until it was signed, thus seeming to act in violation of the prime principle of a democratic government, newspapers unleashed waves of invective. Writers fed on the growing public anger, and in a remarkably short time everything Washington had done in his life was turned on its head. In his early military days in the French and Indian war, one writer declared, Washington had been "ignorant of war both in theory and useful practice." During the Revolution, he had waged a "stupid policy" that dragged out the war. A writer went so far as to suggest that General Washington had taken bribes from the British. As president, newspapers charged, he had been monarchical, antidemocratic and pompous.

Anti-Federalist leaders joined in the attacks. James Monroe wrote a highly critical book on Washington's conduct of foreign affairs. Freed by the sudden change of mood, Thomas Paine felt at liberty to air long-standing grievances, and to get deeply personal, declaring that while he had an acquaintance with Washington that went back decades there had never been friendship between them, for Washington "has no friendships" and "is incapable of forming any." The president, he charged, had no principles; he could "serve or desert a man, or a cause, with constitutional indifference." Whipping himself to the kind of rhetorical lather he had once devoted to supporting the American cause, Paine charged that Washington had duped everyone into thinking he possessed "prudence, moderation, and impartiality," when in reality he simply had no human warmth, only a "cold hermaphrodite faculty."

At times Washington no doubt wished he had not given in to the figures on both sides of the political divide who had urged him to stand for reelection to a second term. He did have achievements in his second term. Three new states—Vermont, Tennessee and Kentucky—

entered the union. He worked out a treaty with Spain that was much more happily received than the one with England. Spain controlled virtually all territory west of the Mississippi River; with the treaty, it acknowledged the river as the United States' boundary, vastly extending the nation's exploitable territory. The treaty also granted American vessels the right to use the Spanish port of New Orleans.

But the political storms kept coming. Abolitionists accused him of being the ultimate hypocrite, for purporting to be, as one wrote, "the great champion of American Freedom" while holding on his estate "FIVE HUNDRED of the HUMAN SPECIES IN SLAVERY" twenty years after the founding of the republic. It was true that his position on slavery was as fraught as ever. He truly hated the institution: for how it destroyed the lives of the enslaved, for how it led white owners into moral reprehensibility, and for the way it undermined the ideology of freedom that the country was founded on. He had not freed his own slaves (nor had any of his fellow leaders in government) in part because he was still caught in the economic trap of a planter, but probably also because it would have been political suicide. The southern slave owners were a powerful bloc.

In the fall of 1796 he decided he would definitely retire at the end of his second term as president, and, eager for the end, he prepared a farewell address. He didn't actually deliver it in public, but rather arranged to have it appear in a newspaper, thus letting the world know of his intention to leave public life without having to face the reaction. He took pains in the address to advise "friends and citizens" of one thing in particular as they looked to the future: "the danger of Parties in the State." After all he had witnessed in his years of military and public service, he seemed most shaken by the damage that the split into two factions had caused the nation, and he implored America's leaders to find a way to dispense with political parties. "They serve," he said, "to Organize faction, to give it an artificial and extraordinary force—to put in the place of the delegated will of the Nation, the will of a party." He seemed truly to fear what could happen if the federal system that he himself had helped champion were subverted by parties. "The alternate domination of one faction over another," he said, is "itself a frightful despotism" which could lead to "a more formal and permanent despotism." Just months after Abraham Yates's death, Washington seemed belatedly to agree with Yates's fears for the system he had helped create, almost to wish to reverse his own support of a strong central government, in light of the tendency of his fellow citizens to form factions. Sounding much like Yates, Washington said he now saw that periods of turbulence would "gradually incline the minds of men to seek security & repose in the absolute power of an Individual: and sooner or later the chief of some prevailing faction more able or more fortunate than his competitors, turns this disposition to the purposes of his own elevation, on the ruins of Public Liberty."

There were five churches nowadays in the Connecticut towns of Haddam and East Haddam, and black residents, slaves and free, were joining the congregations. This was somewhat new. From the time the first slaves had been dragged to America, many owners had preferred to keep them separated from the Christian faith, reasoning either that they were too brutish for it or that it would encourage them to push for freedom. But in the 1790s a mass revival movement swept through the country; people gathered by the thousands in vast tents or in the open air to sing and pray and dedicated themselves to Jesus Christ. In the egalitarian spirit of the Revolution, blacks were now being welcomed. The preachers wove together in their sermons the themes of religious freedom, political freedom and the joy of the spirit taking flight, the combination of which moved them toward calling with new energy for the abolition of slavery.

Venture Smith did not join a church. But he was thinking about mortality, and he began preparing for his own end with customary practicality. He was over seventy years old now and described himself as "bowed down with age and hardship." He maintained his girth but was weaker: "it is with fatigue that I can walk a couple of miles, stooping over my staff." His eyesight had faded; he now used one of his grandchildren as a guide when he went about in town.

Two of his four children were dead. Of the two remaining, Cuff, after serving in George Washington's army, had come back to Haddam, married, begun having children and lived on his father's land. He was a "large, tall, bony man" a local woman said, and in addition to working for his father he hauled stone in the local quarry and loaded vessels on the Connecticut River. But he had his problems, and in time his father pulled away from him. He developed a reputation as a drinker and a thief. Venture did not drink and didn't like it, but theft was for him an altogether other issue, and when in December 1794 Cuff was convicted for stealing two cords of wood, his father was mortified. Ezra Brainerd, the justice of the peace, who had known Venture Smith a long time and knew his sense of propriety, tried to save him some embarrassment by leaving out his last name in his verdict, referring to the guilty party only as "Cuff Negro." But the sentence—"to be whipped ten stripes on his naked body and pay a fine of forty shillings"—must have stung Venture anyway. It echoed almost verbatim the language in the state's dreaded Slave Code, which stipulated conduct and punishment for slaves. To be associated with the Slave Code at all, this many years after Smith had bought his freedom, was a source of immense shame. He all but ruled Cuff out of his life.

That left Solomon, the baby of the family, the second child he and Meg had given that name to. He was now twenty-four years old, the only one of Venture's children to receive an education. He lived on the family land with his parents. Venture wanted to arrange things so that when he died his property would pass to Solomon, and the boy would have care of Meg.

But the situation wasn't straightforward. He had his property: rich, alternately wooded and under cultivation, running downhill to the peaceful cove. It was a piece of paradise, really. But the world was changing in ways that were difficult to fathom. Before the war, land meant security. Now banks were popping up everywhere; a young man needed money. He could potentially sell a portion of his land, converting it to cash, and then will his estate to Solomon. But he seems not to have trusted in wills. What he understood, what had worked for him up until now, was real estate.

He began to see a way forward when, in 1798, he learned that Oliver Smith, his former owner down in Stonington, from whom he had bought his freedom and taken his last name, was in court for bankruptcy. Venture had kept in contact with the Smith family, was in some way still tied to them. He hatched a plan and laid it before Edward Smith, Oliver's son, who was struggling to deal with his father's business failure. For 200 pounds, Venture offered to mortgage his 100-plus acres of land to Smith, except for one choice three-and-a-half-acre parcel, which he transferred to Solomon. Edward accepted. He signed an agreement with Solomon Smith, the result of which was a cash payment to Solomon and a portion of his father's former land. Venture Smith used his former owner's misfortune as a vehicle for transferring his property into his son's name and providing him an inheritance as well. Solomon would take care of the land and his two aged parents. Surely now Venture Smith could live out his remaining days in peace.

It was a big, sturdy log house. Cornplanter stepped out of it and onto his porch. The town he looked out onto, which he had organized—Cornplanter Town, it was called—was not composed of traditional longhouses, the kind of communal dwellings from which his people had taken their name, but the buildings were strong and secure and surrounded by rich farmland. His house was connected, by the shared porch, to that of his half-brother, Handsome Lake. With Cornplanter lived his wife, five daughters and one son. The boy suffered from mental retardation, and Cornplanter liked to keep him close. Handsome Lake had his own children and grandchildren living in his half of the compound. Around them were forty similar, newly built houses. The Senecas' farmland was fenced in now, in the manner of the Americans. The house of Cornplanter, the head of the community, faced the central square of the town, in which stood a wooden statue of Sky Holder, grandson of Sky Woman, a central figure of Haudenosaunee myth.

There were 400 people living in the village. Many of them gathered on this day in the fall of the year and joined Cornplanter for a journey. They traveled west to the village of Canandaigua. Days later, there was a stir among the people there when the Seneca party arrived, for Cornplanter's presence was considered essential for what was to come. In all, 1,500 Iroquois gathered for a new council with the Americans. The year was 1794; in the three years since Cornplanter had met with President Washington, the American leader had had endless trouble with Indians in the Ohio Country. He desperately wanted to settle those western lands. That coupled with growing irritation from the Iroquois, who were insisting they had claim to some of those lands, had finally convinced Washington that it was necessary to renegotiate the Treaty of Fort Stanwix.

The man he sent, Timothy Pickering, who had been a general during the war, faced Cornplanter and other Iroquois leaders on November 11. Cornplanter had learned from his past mistakes. Rather than plead for mercy for his people, he put on a stoic face and held his ground, threatening to break up the negotiation if Pickering did not accede to his demands. In the end, the United States agreed to give back much of the land from the Fort Stanwix Treaty; in exchange, the Iroquois gave up claims to Ohio Country territory. The Iroquois celebrated. The Treaty of Canandaigua was a victory. It showed that they could stand up to the Americans.

That situation lasted until 1797, when a consortium of government agencies and commercial companies put new pressure on the Senecas to sell land. Some were interested in selling because white settlement near the lands in question had made them less fertile for hunting. Cornplanter tried to take a broad view. He had spent a good deal of time learning the Americans' ways. He was interested, in particular, in the concept of banks. He was informed that, should they agree to sell, rather than be given goods that would be used up, they could receive money that would be held in an account in the Bank of the United States. This money would earn interest, and the interest would be paid out, year after year, thus providing an assurance for his people's well-being long into the future. This was appealing, but it was a difficult concept to understand.

Before meeting with negotiators, therefore, Cornplanter traveled once again, in February 1797, to Philadelphia to see George Washington one last time before the end of his presidency. He hoped to speak with him directly.

Washington had that very day completed one of his last acts as president, vetoing a bill that would have reduced the size of the army. There were many other things to attend to. But he agreed to see the Seneca leader. It had been six years since their first meeting. Both men had aged, both had become sadder. "Father," Cornplanter began, using the term of respect, "I thank the Great Spirit for protecting us through the various paths which we have trod since I was last at this place. As I am told you are about to retire from public business, I have come to pay my last address to you." Cornplanter was capable of expressing a disarming frankness, and he did so now. He informed Washington that his hope was "to provide for the rising generation," which he knew would face a different world from the one that he had grown up in. The forefathers of the Iroquois, he said, "thought that their posterity would pursue their tracks, and support themselves by their hunts. . . . But the great revolution among the white people in this country has extended its influence to the people of my color. Turn our faces which way we will, we find the white people cultivating the ground which our forefathers hunted over. . . . If a few years have made such a change, what will be the situation of our children . . . ?"

What he wanted from Washington, Cornplanter went on, was "to have your candid and friendly advice" on "how we can best provide for posterity." He had studied the Americans as they went about their business here in Philadelphia. "Your people have a different mode of living from ours," he said; "they have trades and they have education, which enables them to take different pursuits, by which means they maintain themselves." Then he got to the point, and in doing so he showed that he was completely putting himself in Washington's hands. "I am also told that your people have a strong place for their money," he said, "where it is not only safe, but that it produces them each and every year an increase without lessening the stock. If we should dispose of part of our country, and put our money with yours in that strong place, will it be safe? Will it yield to our children the same advantages after our heads are laid down, as it will at present produce to us? Will it be out of the reach of our foolish young men, so that they cannot drink it up to the prejudice of our children?"

Washington's reply was not recorded by the interpreter who took down Cornplanter's words, but it must have reassured him, for he left Philadelphia intent on taking the next step. Before he did, he gave a heartfelt farewell to this man who had vanquished his people but for whom he held a confusion of feelings that included warm regard. "I congratulate you on your intended repose from the fatigues and anxiety of mind, which are constant attendants on high public stations," Cornplanter said, "and hope that the same Good Spirit which has so long guided your steps as a father to a great nation, will still continue to protect you." Cornplanter likewise won Washington's admiration, as a token of which the president gave him his sword.

Six months later, in high summer, Cornplanter was one of 1,200 Iroquois gathered at the village of Geneseo, also known as Big Tree, in the center of the traditional Seneca homeland. He and other Iroquois conducted a lengthy series of negotations with American officials, at the end of which they agreed to sell large swaths of their lands for cash and United States government bonds. The Treaty of Big Tree fixed boundaries around the remaining Iroquois territories, which would forever be reserved for their use and hence would be called reservations. There, they were assured, they would have total sovereignty.

Margaret Coghlan's book came out in London in December 1794. People bought it, and gossiped. It was thrilling for its frank coverage of what one reader called "the licentiousness of elevated life." It gave private insights into personalities as diverse as George Washington, General Cornwallis and Charles James Fox. It read like a drawing-room accompaniment to the history of the previous decades. Among the many liaisons Coghlan detailed in the book was a brief one she had had with the Prince of Wales, which was what *The Times* focused on in the brittle little notice it gave it: "The publication of Mrs. Coghlan's Memoirs just on the eve of a Royal Duke's return, will not prove very acceptable to him; the anecdotes there are of a singular nature; nor should we wonder if on that account they were to be suppressed."

The book was not, however, suppressed. And many readers saw the underlying point to her sad story. One reviewer noted that the author, "who has long been known in the circles of gallantry, but who is now a prisoner for debt, imputes the cause of her misfortunes and her deviation from the paths of virtue, to a marriage against her wishes," and lamented that forced marriages were the cause of misery for many British women.

The memoir aroused enough interest that a second edition appeared the following year in New York. The publisher there, who saw her tale as a tragedy, and Coghlan as a woman sacrificed on the altar of freedom, explained in a preface that the social value in bringing her story to America was to highlight "the absurd practice" of forced marriage.

But while the book caused a bit of a stir, it did not bring the financial relief that Margaret had hoped for. No pitying benefactor, no champion of the rights of women, stepped forward to assist. In 1797, she was once more before the King's Bench, and then again in debtors' prison.


On March 9, 1797, Washington stepped into a carriage and rode out of Philadelphia, and out of public life. He was sixty-five years old, looked a decade older, and felt that at long last he had earned a true and final retirement. And for a time it seemed he would get it. He rose at dawn, spent the early part of his day riding the farms at Mount Vernon, studying peas, wheat, pumpkins, flax, soils and manures, sun slant and rainfall. He wore a wide-brimmed hat, and he frowned a lot. Yet again the buildings of the estate were dilapidated, the farms less productive than he had hoped. His finances were a disaster.

He became wistful. He rode past Belvoir, the estate of the Fairfax family, and saw that it had fallen into ruins. Had it not been for that family taking him to their bosom, he might have remained tied to his mother, and had the career of a Virginia planter. His path in life had in a sense begun in this mansion. He felt prompted to write Sally Fairfax, with whom he had fallen in love as a young man but who had married his friend George William Fairfax. That had been half a century ago. She and her husband had moved to England before the war; George William had died in 1787, but she lived there still. Washington began his letter by glancingly referencing the catalogue of his achievements since their youth, then said something utterly remarkable: "None of which events, however, nor all of them together, have been able to eradicate from my mind, the recollection of those happy moments—the happiest of my life—which I have enjoyed in your company." *The happiest of my life.* The military hero, the father of his country, was feeling the passage of time as an ache, was overcome with melancholy for the road not taken.

He felt his cares leaving him as he wrote to this woman from his past, and he opened up further to her. He confessed himself "Worn out in a manner by the toils of my past labour," and said that he wished "to spend the remainder of my days (which cannot be many) in rural amusements."

He went on to describe for her one of his pet projects. "A Century hence, if this Country keep united (and it is surely its policy and Interest to do so) will produce a City—though not as large as London—yet of a magnitude inferior to few others in Europe, on the Banks of the Potomack; where one is now establishing for the permanent Seat of the Government of the United States." The Federal City, as it was being called, was to be completed in two years' time, so that John Adams, Washington's successor, would be the first to preside over it. Washington believed its very existence could help heal divisions in the country, since it would not be part of any existing state and was situated on the line between the north and the south. He had gone so far in promoting it as to purchase land there, around the site of the Capitol Building.

Washington's retirement was interrupted. Tensions between the two political parties heightened as the French, incensed at America's signing a treaty with England, seemed on the verge of declaring war. The Anti-Federalists were pro-France, the Federalists favored an English alliance. Once again, Washington was asked to bring his political clout to bear. Hamilton exhorted him to take a stand. And Washington found that he did have strong feelings on the matter. There was evidence that the postrevolutionary French government was plotting to undermine the United States. President Adams was preparing for a possible war. Adams wrote him for advice. Washington wrote back to say that if the country were attacked he himself would be willing to serve again. Whether he meant this or not, Adams took him at face value and named him commander in chief of American forces. He did so without even bothering to alert Washington, who learned of his appointment from the newspaper.

Washington left Mount Vernon for Philadelphia, his head swirling with considerations of how he would once again lead troops in battle. As he situated himself amid the political players who were now active, however, he began to feel out of his element. He disliked the way Adams ran things, disapproved of some of the military officers chosen, and began to realize that Adams, despite his having appointed him to a major post, harbored a toxic jealousy toward him. The rumors of war faded, and Washington returned home.

The fall of 1799 turned toward winter. On December 12, Washington sat down to write Alexander Hamilton. Hamilton had sent him some observations about establishing a military academy. Washington wrote to say that he approved, that he had long thought such a thing was vital to the country. He spent the rest of the day riding out on his farms. He wanted in particular to inspect a new kind of cattle pen that his farm manager, James Anderson, had installed. It was raw weather—rain, hail, snow, wind—and the next day he was overcome with congestion and a sore throat. He wrote a note to Anderson saying he didn't think the cattle pen would work: "Such a Pen . . . would, if the Cattle were kept in it one Week, destroy the whole of them." He sat up that evening with Martha and his secretary, Tobias Lear, reading through his mail. He went to bed in a cheerful mood, though still with the cold symptoms.

At two in the morning Martha woke up to the sounds of struggle. Her husband was having trouble breathing. She called for Lear, who sent for the doctor. They bled him twice, and the doctor had him inhale steam from a pot of vinegar and hot water. He began to suffocate. They bled him a third time. Eventually, he held out his hand to Lear and said, "I feel myself going." He asked the doctor to let him be, and after a while he became calm. At about ten o'clock in the evening, the doctor put his hand over Washington's eyes. "Is he gone?" Martha asked, and Tobias Lear indicated that he was.

Venture Smith was not quite finished with hatching clever ideas. Or perhaps someone suggested it to him. A black man who had freed himself and his family from slavery and become a landowner and person of substance in rural Connecticut was a highly unusual figure. He was, in fact, a local celebrity. The idea for Smith to dictate his memoirs may have occurred first to Charles Holt. Holt was from New London, a place Venture regularly visited. He was twenty-five, about the same age as Solomon, and he had set himself up as a newspaper publisher, with a goal to, as he said in the first issue, "circulate political intelligence." He was a man of action. He called his paper the *Bee*, and he wanted it to buzz; he wanted it to sting.

Venture had his vanity: all his life he loved showing off his strength, and he was proud of what he had accomplished. He had always stayed clear of politics, but in agreeing to dictate his story for the editor of the *Bee* he was inadvertently wading into the center of what was threatening to become an American civil war. As the Federalists grew in power, they came to believe that they, by definition, represented the American viewpoint, and that those who argued that rights should be maintained principally in the states and in individuals were a danger to national stability. The ongoing turmoil in Europe fed their fear that the American government could collapse at any time. They became all the more suspicious of Thomas Jefferson's Democratic-Republican Party, whose supporters tended to be tradesmen and farmers as well as non-English immigrants. As fear of a French invasion of America built up again, and with it rumors of foreign spies, President Adams and the Federalist majority in Congress passed a series of laws that undermined the Bill of Rights and weakened Jefferson's opposition party. The Alien Acts made it harder for immigrants to become American citizens and gave the government power to imprison foreigners. The Sedition Act made it a crime to criticize the federal government.

Charles Holt was one of many young idealists around the country who started newspapers as an act of defiance against the government's smothering of individual rights; he was, in essence, continuing the work of Abraham Yates. One of the forces that drove him was the anti-immigrant tone of the Federalists. Another was slavery: it was an embarrassing and shameful violation of the principle of freedom on which the country was founded, Holt argued, and the federal government, in its very Constitution, had perpetuated it, ensuring that it would remain a part of American life far into the future. Holt set up his presses and published his first issue in June of 1797. At the same time, he published books that he offered for sale in his New London office on topics that highlighted the moral shortcomings of the federal government.

Everyone in the area knew that Venture Smith had stories from his childhood in Africa, stories of the passage to America, stories of pain and suffering in slavery. And his life after he had bought his freedom, with all the humiliation and cheating he had endured, through which he had nevertheless prospered, cast the promise of America in a sober light. Holt wanted that story.

Venture Smith couldn't write, but he could talk. And he remembered. Once he agreed on the project, he relaxed into it, let his mind drift back. The old man sitting in the chill of a Connecticut autumn returned to the African savanna. He remembered Broteer Furro: the boy he was. Scenes flickered. Skinny cows in blinding sunlight, the green wall of vegetation after a heavy rain. Names came back. His siblings: Cundazo and Soozaduka. Saungm Furro, his father. His father's example, his toughness, the frank way he valued money. The scene of his father being beaten, being "cut and pounded on his body with great inhumanity," tortured so that he would tell where his treasure lay buried. But, with the boy watching, the father had "despised all the tortures . . . until the continued exercise and increase of torment, obliged him to sink and expire." He let himself relive the horror of that moment, of watching his father's death. Then the forced march with the invading army. Being held in the black dungeon of the Anomabo fortress, being rowed out to a slave ship off the coast. The young man Robinson Mumford taking him for his own, buying him for "four gallons of rum, and a piece of Calico," and then owning him, naming him. Venture. Broteer became Venture, and then sailed off on the grim and occasionally soaring adventure that was to be his life.

Elisha Niles was the local schoolteacher. He was an abolitionist, possibly a friend of Charles Holt. He probably was the one who listened to Venture and took down his words. If he added any words of embellishment, they were few, which suggests that Venture Smith demanded to have it read back to him and to make corrections. It was his story, he would tell it, and it would go out into the world as he wanted it. Like Margaret Coghlan, he brought his story right up to the present: the autumn of 1798, leaves coming down and winter starting to make itself felt. He was feeling mournful. "My strength which was once equal if not superior to any man whom I have ever seen, is now enfeebled so

that life is a burden." He expressed the bitterness he felt toward his
children. He lingered over the cheating he had endured both as a slave
and a free man.

The bitterness worked for Charles Holt. He could use it. He made
typographic adjustments to highlight the racial injustice of Venture's
story, such as the time he was cheated by a Captain Elisha Hart of
Saybrook. "Captain Hart was a *white gentleman*, and I a *poor African*,
therefore it was *all right*, and *good enough for the black dog.*" It was supposed to get attention.

Holt knew that a black man's story needed to have a white seal of
approval, so he got five respected white men from Stonington to attest
to it, including Edward Smith, to whom Venture Smith had recently
linked himself financially in order to transfer his property to Solomon.
The men certified at the back of the book that they had known Smith
for years, that he was "a temperate, honest and industrious man," that
after years of being "ever intent on obtaining his freedom" he had done
so, and become a respectable member of the community.

Holt printed the book, and put it up for sale in his shop on November
3, 1798. The day after Christmas, he ran an ad in his paper:

*Just published, and for sale at this office*
Price 1S.
A NARRATIVE
*of the*
LIFE AND ADVENTURES
*of*
VENTURE,
*A native of Africa, but above sixty years an inhabitant*
*of the United States of America.*
*Related by himself, and attested by respectable witnesses.*

Holt added a little verse of his own construction to underscore the dark truth that for many people the promise of American freedom was more in the nature of a trick or a mirage, noting the irony of American freedom, that Venture Smith was

*Descended from a royal race,*
*Benevolent and brave;*
*On Afric's savage plains a PRINCE*
*In this free land a SLAVE.*

The book sold. It contributed to Holt's reputation as a fiery opponent of the Federalist Party—which, in the eyes of the Federalists, meant the American government. As his publications got fiercer, Federalists accused him of anti-American agitation. He set his lead type as fast as his fingers would work and fired back: "The editor of this paper is an AMERICAN—his principles are AMERICAN—and his paper is supported by AMERICANS." After the Sedition Act passed, he went right at it, charging that in muzzling the press the act was "directly contravening one of the most essential articles in the code of freedom, and as clearly defined as any other clause in the bill of rights, namely *liberty of speech, printing and writing*." For his pains—specifically, for publishing an account of the raising of an army under Alexander Hamilton to fight the French in the event of war—he was imprisoned, under the very act he had attacked.

Venture Smith's autobiography did not change many minds on the question of slavery. In 1801, Congress extended the slave codes of Virginia and Maryland into the new capital city of the United States, officially working slavery into the nation's political heart and, simultaneously, into the future metropolis that was now named for George Washington.

Nor did the book change Venture Smith's life much. He became, if anything, sadder in his last days. Solomon, the son whom he had set up with money and to whom he had entrusted his precious land, began selling off parcels of it literally out from under him, setting off a new wave of sadness and anger in the old man. In the summer of 1804, after an argument, despite his blindness and difficulty walking, Venture had enough and simply went off. Solomon ran an ad in the newspaper that was more legal notice than missing person report; it showed that the fight had been about money, and it revealed him to be truly his father's son:

> Whereas Venture Smith, my father, has departed from my house, and refuses to return and receive a comfortable support, which I am willing to provide for him. All persons are forbidden to harbour or trust him on my account, as I shall not pay any expence or contract of his making.

Eventually, the old man came back and grumbled and complained through the last months of his life. The following year, in September of 1805, Venture Smith died. Meg died four years after him. Both were buried in the cemetery of the First Congregational Church. Despite his numerous complaints, his last years were not entirely filled with bitterness. He acknowledged that "amidst all my griefs and pains, I have many consolations." Two things in particular stood out as sources of pleasure at the end of his life. One was Meg: "the wife of my youth, whom I married for love." And despite being systematically cheated by fate and his fellow human beings, despite "all the losses I have suffered by fire, by the injustice of knaves, by the cruelty and oppression of false hearted friends," one other thing shone out like a torch to light his last days. "My freedom," he said, "is a privilege which nothing else can equal."

• • •

It was 1803. Margaret Coghlan had emerged from her most recent stay at King's Bench Prison further weakened, only to face more financial woes. The former friends from her days of high living had abandoned her. She cast about for others who might help and began contemplating her more distant connections, those from her time in America.

America was suddenly much on the minds of people in London. Thomas Jefferson, who was now the third U.S. president, had sent Robert R. Livingston—the man who had given the oath of office to George Washington—to Paris to negotiate the purchase of New Orleans, which the French had recently acquired from Spain along with much of the interior of North America. Instead, Livingston wound up dealing with something else entirely. Napoleon Bonaparte, the French leader, no longer had an interest in North America. As a result, Livingston found himself negotiating for the purchase of an enormous stretch of the continent's interior, from the Mississippi River west to the Rocky Mountains, and from the Gulf of Mexico to Canada. Rarely in human history had a nation obtained such a vast swath of geography at the stroke of a pen. The Louisiana Purchase stunned Americans and Europeans alike.

Margaret Coghlan, meanwhile, in pondering how to extricate herself from debt, heard that Livingston's private secretary and son-in-law, Robert L. Livingston, was in London on his way back to the United States following the completion of the purchase. She knew that he was a member of the same Livingston family her father had married into when he wedded her first stepmother. Margaret hadn't liked Mary Livingston, but she considered it a stroke of luck that an American official with wealth and a connection to her was nearby. She dashed off a letter to him in her flowing, assertive hand, providing a rapid summary of her life and misfortunes:

*Sir*

*With the greatest submission to your goodness, I take the Liberty to address you and rely solely on your politeness to plead in my behalf —*

*Permit me therefore Sir to inform you, that I am the only daughter of the late Major Moncrieffe, who married at New York, Miss Mary Livingston. . . . I had the misfortune Sir to lose my Mother when I was only eleven years of Age—and in 1791 death deprived me of my father who is buried at New York. I was married during the American War in obedience to the Commands of my father ere I had seen fifteen years, to a Captain in the Army, whose barbarous ill usage and abandonment has plunged me into an Abbeyss of Woe. . . .*

Eventually, she got around to the point: she was destitute and "deplorably situated." She indicated the depth of her misery by referencing the small amount of money needed to keep her from being hauled back to prison: "Should you deign Sir to stretch forth your kind hand to my relief whatever you please to afford will be safely delivered to me by the bearer and be ever most gratefully remembered for I am liable to be confined in a horrid prison, for want of Three pounds which I am unable to obtain."

Whether Livingston responded or not, whether or not he handed her messenger a few pounds, her situation was not much improved in the next months. She did have occasion to ponder the path her life had taken, thanks to more news from America. Her lunge for freedom, her refusal to marry the man her father had chosen for her, had come about at least in part thanks to her having fallen in love with another. She must have been thrilled, three years earlier, to learn that that other man, Aaron Burr, had run for president of the United States, lost by the narrowest of margins, and ended up as vice president. He was one of the most powerful men in her native country, a leader in the self-proclaimed "land of freedom." He had stolen her heart when she was still a child, and then he was gone, swept away from her by the winds of war. Had she been able to find her way back to him, how different everything might have been for her. But now came news of a twist of fate that must have seemed like something out of a fable. Aaron Burr and Alexander Hamilton had become bitter political enemies; Burr, feeling that Hamilton had besmirched his honor, had challenged him to a duel. Hamilton, whose impetuousness went back to his hasty decision to leave George Washington's service during the war, accepted. Standing on the bluffs overlooking the Hudson River and Manhattan, Burr had shot and killed Hamilton. Now the founder of the Federalist Party and the American banking system was dead, and the vice president was charged with murder.

Margaret Coghlan must have thought of herself and Burr on a parallel with Shakespeare's doomed, star-crossed lovers, hurtling toward tragedy, for while he was on the run, she was once again facing prison. This time, straining to find a savior, she shot her final bolt. On January 11, 1805, she sat herself down and, in a hand resolutely firm and composed, wrote:

> *To The Kings Most Excellent Majesty,*
> *The Humble Memorial*
> *of Margaret Coghlan*
> *Daughter of the late*
> *Major Thomas Moncrieffe*
> *Major of Brigade on the Staff*
> *Of Your Majesty's Forces*
> *In North America*

Her plea to the king of England outlined the loyal military service of her father and brother during the American Revolution, and indicated that after the war her father's property had been "taken from him by the Rulers in that Country." She touched on her own straitened circumstances only vaguely, and ended abjectly: "Humbly I pray your Majesty's Pity that you would be graciously pleased to take my fathers tried Loyalty under Your Royal Consideration and be pleased by Your Royal Clemency to relieve my Distress."

It didn't work. Soon she was back in prison, spiraling downward. And then . . .

Nothing. Margaret Coghlan disappeared. Earlier she had succeeded in faking her death and transporting herself to another country to evade creditors, so perhaps she did it again. Maybe this time, on her release from custody, she changed her name and left England for good, went to Paris or Rome or the Mogul Empire, where she led a wholly new life of luxury and exoticism. But it seems unlikely. Her health had been failing and her beauty, on which she had long banked, was gone. It had been years since she had attracted a wealthy protector. It's more likely that she continued on her steep downward trajectory and died, in squalor and pain sometime after the failure of her final and most desperate petition for aid, without leaving even a record of her death.

Two years later, John Coghlan, the man who had forced her to marry him, died, "in the most abject state of poverty and distress," according to an obituary, without even a single friend to sit by him in his suffering or to claim his body. If she was evilly conjoined with him in life, Margaret Moncrieffe Coghlan probably also matched her estranged husband in the doleful circumstances of her leaving it.

I t was the din of industry: a clatter that you had to shout to be heard over, an insistent, driving noise that seemingly would never stop. That indeed was what set it apart from any sound that had come before: the absolute regularity of its racket.

For Cornplanter it was a good sound, a hopeful one. He was in his fifties now, a very busy man, and this was his latest project. He had bought the parts, hauled them to this spot on the river, hired white men to assemble the whole crazy structure of it, with its big wooden wheel, the buckets of which filled with river water and set it in motion, set the cogs and pistons and crossbeams moving, all of which pulled the blade of the saw up and down, incessantly. He had built the first sawmill in Warren County, Pennsylvania. His Senecas worked it. They chose the trees the white people found most desirable as building material: chestnut, black walnut and, most of all, white pine. They chopped them down, hauled them on sleds, rafted them to the mill, cut them into smooth boards. He hired a white man named George Hildebrandt to manage the mill and maintain its complex functioning. His men shipped the finished boards to Pittsburgh, where they helped build the endlessly growing city. Cornplanter had never learned to read or write but he had an Americanized form of his name put at the bottom of each contract—CAPT. O.BEAL.—and he made his X beside it.

For a while following his farewell meeting with George Washington, Cornplanter enjoyed a golden period. He founded a gristmill in addition to his sawmill. He was a businessman, a farmer, a husband and father, and the de facto mayor of the town. And as a representative of the Iroquois Confederacy, he was repeatedly called to councils at reservations.

Cornplanter Town—guarded by cliffs and surrounded by thick forest—was difficult to reach, on purpose, for Cornplanter was trying to have it both ways. He wanted his people to participate in white society and yet to be apart from it. His Senecas still hunted, still foraged for medicinal herbs in the forest. In March and April there was the age-old ritual of gathering sap from maple trees and boiling it into sugar. In June, as in his childhood, everyone took part in the strawberry festival. At the same time, he had made contact with Quaker missionaries following his first meeting with Washington, when he had told the president he would like his people to learn the English language and modern farming principles. In 1798, five Quakers arrived with a goal to set up a model farm. As it turned out, the men were not themselves farmers, and they hadn't brought the equipment they needed. Comically enough, the Senecas—who after all had their own highly developed agricultural methods—helped them by setting up the model farm themselves and showing the white men how to operate it. Somewhat more successfully, the Quakers built a school in the town and began teaching the children English.

The cultures, however, clashed. The Quakers were horrified to learn that it was customary, when a dignitary came to visit, for a woman from the village to spend the night with him, as a comfort and a courtesy. The Senecas didn't like the fact that the Quakers wanted them to stop their traditional dances, believing them to be the work of the devil.

In the main, though, Cornplanter approved of the assistance the newcomers provided, especially in combating alcoholism, which was rampant. His men who delivered wood to Pittsburgh would come back with jugs of spirits; people killed one another in drunken fights, or were found frozen to death in the snow. He was especially disappointed in his son, Henry, whom he had sent to Philadelphia to learn American ways; since he had returned, he was drunk much of the time. Henry believed he knew best how to deal with whites, and thought his father naïve and backward. They argued often.

Among those who had succumbed to alcohol was Cornplanter's half-brother, Handsome Lake, whose condition became so severe that he spent most of his time in bed. Even when Handsome Lake's son died from a drunken accident, it wasn't enough to stir him. Then in 1799, Handsome Lake fell into a stupor and was feared dead. Miraculously, when he woke, he was a changed man and began preaching about the evils of alcohol and the importance of family and traditional values.

Cornplanter assisted him in spreading his message. It caught fire among all six Iroquois nations, where lives and traditions had been systematically upended. In a remarkable short time the teaching, which became known as the Code of Handsome Lake, sparked a renewal of the traditional Iroquois religion.

The stunning reversal in Handsome Lake's fortunes continued. In 1801, just two years after his miraculous awakening, he was named Supreme Leader of the Six Nations. The next year he led a delegation to Washington, D.C., to meet with President Thomas Jefferson. Cornplanter accepted the transformation in his brother, and the lessening of his own status. He was pleased at the sudden turn toward tradition and family among his people. But he remained firm in his conviction that the Iroquois needed to make accommodations to the future, which meant adapting to the ways of the United States of America.

He tried meanwhile to focus on his own issues. Though he was now in his sixties, he was still plagued by remorse at having been shunned by his white father. He knew the man had died some years before, but in 1810 he decided to undertake the difficult 300-mile journey to Fort Plain, New York, where John Abeel had lived. He had no notion what to expect, or even why he was going. But when he got there, he found himself welcomed by Abeel's family members who still lived in the area. He and the Senecas who had come with him were treated to a feast that lasted for days. It was a celebration of a long-lost relative returned, and an acknowledgment too of Cornplanter's fame. It was a moment of healing.

Then came successive waves of troubles. In 1812, the Americans and the British went to war again, and the Iroquois became caught up in it. Cornplanter wanted to stay neutral, but many Senecas fought on the American side, including his son Henry, who served as a major in the U.S. Army. The war furthered divisions within the Iroquois Confederacy and hastened another round of pressure from new commercial enterprises that had designs on Iroquois land. The policy of the American government now was to relocate as many tribes as possible west of the Mississippi River. Cornplanter resisted, as did other chiefs. As one said, if they were to move "towards the setting sun," they would be looked upon "as foreigners and strangers, and be despised by the red as well as the white men."

Cornplanter argued against further land sales. He complained that money promised to the Senecas in previous agreements had not been fully paid. In some cases they had received only half of what was owed. In other cases, the annuities they had been promised had failed, and they were left with nothing. But by 1826—with the Erie Canal completed and cities in the region growing exponentially—speculators had the means to apply overwhelming force. A former New York congressman named David Ogden created the Ogden Land Company, which used bribes to play chiefs against one another. As a result, all the Seneca reservations along the Genesee River—Cornplanter's ancestral homeland, where he had been born and raised—were sold, as were many others.

Cornplanter, who was around eighty years old at the time, did not play a central role in these events. His health was failing, he was blind in one eye. But he offered what resistance he could. He appeared in court. He joined with other chiefs in denouncing the sales that had taken place and vowing never to sell more land. Meanwhile, there was an influx of Christian missionaries in Seneca villages. Cornplanter had long accommodated Christian teaching; like many Iroquois, he believed it could be compatible with traditional ways. But now the missionaries were demanding an end to many ancient practices.

At some point, the two rapidly swelling negative forces—the loss of land and the erasure of beliefs—merged in his mind, seemed to squeeze his mind. He had a dream, a vision. He had never been one for spiritual flights, but his brother, the mystic of the family, was dead now, and it was as though Cornplanter felt the need to take on this role too. The dream seared him, annihilated him with its clarity. The Creator came to him in his dream and spoke to him at great length. He started at the beginning, reminding Cornplanter of how Sky Woman had fallen from the Sky World into the sea and the animals had built the turtle's back into a home for his people, the Haudenosaunee.

The first part of the Creator's message to Cornplanter was about transgressions. The whites had transgressed in coming to the land of the Iroquois, which had been theirs from the time of the creation. The Iroquois had transgressed in following the ways of the whites, which were unnatural for them. The Christian religion was not for them. They had no business with rifles or whisky, nor with sawmills. Even cow's milk was not for them: the fact that so many Indians got sick from it was proof of this. All of these alien things had bound them like chains. If they were to live, they needed to be free. Cornplanter himself had been the main transgressor, for he had led the Iroquois toward the Americans. The Creator instructed him to rid himself of everything alien. Cornplanter made a fire and burned items he had been given over the years, things he had cherished. There was a French flag, some ceremonial papers with markings from the Americans, a hat that was a gift from the governor of Pennsylvania, and the sword that George Washington had presented to him. He destroyed them all.

The other side of the Creator's message to Cornplanter was hopeful. It was about the clarity and rightness of living a good life. Inhabiting the land that was created for him and his people. Hunting and fighting, each as necessary. Loving fully. Dying well. This was freedom. Cornplanter knew he would not be the one to lead people forward toward what had been. But he also knew that dreams had truth in them. And the dream said freedom.

safely delivered to me by the bearer and be ever most gratefully remembered for I am liable to be confined in a [blot] prison, for want of Three pounds which I am unable to obtain — let me implore Sir your pity and assistance

I have the honor to be

Respectfully, Sir

Your Most Obedient
Humble Servant
M Coghlan

Dec 28 — 1803

4 Charles Court
Charles Street
St James's Sqre

# EPILOGUE

The past is not as far away as we think. In many ways it's right here with us.

The six people whose stories I have told in this book, each of whom represents some part of the struggle for freedom at America's founding, all had descendants, biological or metaphorical or both, who have carried their legacies forward through time and into the present.

Abraham Yates's passion for grassroots politics spread through his extended family. The history of New York State includes a host of feisty Yateses and Lansings (his only daughter having married a Lansing) serving as aldermen, assemblymen, judges and mayors. More to the point, Yates's dogged devotion to the common man and his alertness to the dangers of the accumulation of power have had many echoes through the centuries, from both the left and the right sides of the political spectrum. In the 1890s, the leftist Populist Party, fueled by farmers and laborers, rose to prominence by warning that elites had taken over American society. In our day, the anger that fueled both Donald Trump's rise to the presidency and impassioned opposition to Trump would be recognizable to Yates. Indeed, it seems that today, more than perhaps at any other time in American history, Yates's fears are ours.

*A page from one of Margaret Coghlan's pleas for financial assistance.*

Margaret Coghlan felt the pull of freedom that was in the air in the eighteenth century, but she realized, too late, that it did not then apply to half the human race. History does not record what became of Coghlan's children, the poor waifs she dragged around with her as her tragic life wound down, but her ideological descendants span the history of the women's movement, from Elizabeth Cady Stanton to Gloria Steinem, and for that matter include people like Amelia Earhart, Ellen DeGeneres and every woman who broke a gender barrier.

George Washington had no descendants of any kind. He was childless, and even in symbolic terms he had no parallels or descendants in American history. There is only one George Washington. Then again, the United States itself might be thought of as his descendant. You could argue that the nation inherited his bravery in defying historical convention, his belief in the ideal of individual freedom, his willingness to fight and die for it and to lead the cause of it, and also his failure to live up to that ideal.

Washington's British opposite in the war, George Sackville, was a true product of empire, and his quasi-feudal vision lived on throughout the nineteenth century and into the twentieth as the British Empire expanded and then waned. He was also the scion of an aristocratic family, and Sackvilles remained connected to that history down through the centuries. To this day, Knole, the grand house where he spent his boyhood and which is now run by Britain's National Trust and open to the public, is still in the care of the Sackville family.

At the time of Cornplanter's death in 1836, he was living in a town largely comprised of his own progeny: children, grandchildren, greatgrandchildren, spouses and various others. They lived not on a reservation but on land that the State of Pennsylvania had given him, which was known as the Cornplanter Grant. His descendants continued to inhabit the Grant well into the twentieth century. When Congress authorized construction of the Kinzua Dam on the Allegheny

River in the late 1950s, which eventually inundated most of the Grant and forced those living there to move, it constituted the first breach of the 1794 Treaty of Canandaigua, which Cornplanter had taken part in negotiating. His descendants still gather for a summertime "Cornplanter Descendants Picnic" at the Cornplanter Gazebo in Salamanca, New York.

As to the Iroquois people as a whole, their reservations in New York State are scattered across the geographic region that was the nations' traditional homeland. While I was visiting the Tonowanda reservation in 2016, a Seneca woman named Go-wa-yah-doni Jimerson offered to show me around the tribal-run museum. I had noted a variety of Christian churches on the reservation, which prompted me to ask about her faith. She stunned me by saying, "I follow the Code of Handsome Lake." I felt that visceral rush that a writer of history gets only rarely, of the past flooding into the present. Cornplanter's brother's vision of renewal, I discovered, lives on, as, of course, do the Iroquois.

Many of Venture and Meg Smith's descendants stayed in Connecticut, and quite a few lived in the towns of Haddam and East Haddam. Their granddaughter Eliza, Solomon's daughter, dutifully took care of their graves in the cemetery of the Congregational Church. In her old age she arranged to put her own tombstone right next to theirs and beside her father's, and there they all are today. Venture's great-grandson, Nelson, lived in Haddam in the mid-nineteenth century, working as a laborer and stonecutter. Nelson's son George enlisted there in the 29th Connecticut "Colored" Regiment of the Union Army in December 1863, and died nine months later at the Siege of Petersburg.

Venture Smith's story became part of the birthright of each generation of his family. In the twentieth century, a descendant named Mandred Henry, who worked as a health care sales rep in Hartford, took it particularly to heart. In the 1960s, the era of Malcolm X and Martin Luther King Jr., he became the president of the local chapter of the National Association for the Advancement of Colored People, told the story of Venture to his children and dreamed of making a pilgrimage to Africa.

Mandred Henry died in 2007, never having fulfilled his dream. But in late 2014 three of his children, along with one granddaughter and a great-grandson, traveled to Ghana to see the place their father had longed to visit, the place where Broteer Furro's saga had begun. I learned about their plan while I was organizing my own research trip to Africa for this book, and so was fortunate enough to join them.

Angi Perron, Corinne Henry Brady, Floyd Henry, Gina Ryan and Gina's son Jasir all live in New England, not so far from where Venture Smith settled. Most had never been out of the United States before. Together we shopped for souvenirs in Accra, toured the national museum of Ghana and ate fried fish at a seaside restaurant. But the focal point of our visit was their ancestor. At the former slave port of Anomabo an American preservationist named Chandler Saint had installed an exhibit of Venture Smith's life, and to launch the exhibit he arranged a ceremony at which local dignitaries would welcome the descendants. The event, at the town hall, was a mixture of grandeur (lavish costumes and fine speeches) and some comedy (a tribal chief's cell phone went off at one solemn moment, its ringtone a few bars of "We Wish You a Merry Christmas"). Then, together with much of the town, we processed down to the sea.

The whitewashed hulk of the British-built fortress on the shore was in ruins, but the slave pens were still pitch-dark and horrid, there were still a few manacles on the walls, and along the ramparts lay rusted cannons bearing the insignia of King George III. We stood there a long while, high above the sea, the wind in our faces, silently watching the merciless waves.

The next day Angi, Corinne and Floyd, the three children of Mandred Henry, went back down to the beach together. Corinne pulled an Advil bottle out of her purse and flung its contents into the wind. In it she had mixed soil from Venture Smith's grave in Haddam together with some of her father's ashes. Then the siblings said a quick prayer at the foot of the fort where their ancestor had been held in captivity before sailing off to play his part in America's founding.

# ACKNOWLEDGMENTS

Thank you to the friends and experts who read this book in manuscript. Your suggestions were invaluable in helping me to tame and shape it, and your corrections saved me from embarrassment. Each of you devoted many hours to it, and I am deeply grateful for your time, care, knowledge and creativity. Robert Cwiklik, my old friend, who also happens to be a crack editor, devoted himself particularly to helping me hone the prologue, and thus to helping me figure out what the book was about. Tim Paulson, another longtime friend who is a skilled editor, provided thoughtful line edits and wide-ranging commentary. Barnet Schecter, who has written revolutionary history with such clarity and insight, not only critiqued the history in the manuscript but offered excellent suggestions for reshaping it. Michael Martin brought a poet's eye to the task and assisted me in particular in understanding the forces at work in Margaret Moncrieffe Coghlan's life. Dennis Maika helped me to appreciate the complexities of that fraught word, "freedom," both in the revolutionary era and in later interpretations of it. Sarah Knott likewise brilliantly and thoughtfully parsed and recast my concept of freedom in the revolutionary era, and provided helpful observations about women's freedom and female sexuality in the era. Charles Gehring brought his unparalleled understanding of early America to bear on the manuscript, tweaking and correcting everything from tribal nomenclature to the geography of Albany and the surrounding region.

Karl Stofko gave me the benefit of his deep knowledge of Venture Smith and his world, flagging errors in the manuscript, offering up his own research, guiding me through the land records of the town of Haddam, and helping me broaden my sense of Smith and what he accomplished. Stefan Bielinski, who knows more about Abraham Yates Jr. than anyone alive, pointed me to Yates in the first place, gave me access to his remarkable Yates archive and deepened my understanding of Yates and his Albany. Michael Galban of the Seneca Art and Culture Center gave me the benefit of his profound knowledge of the Senecas in the eighteenth century, and delighted me with insights on Iroquois ways of seeing the world.

I want especially to thank my editor at Norton, Maria Guarnaschelli, who believed in this idea when it was nothing more than a rambling monologue and shepherded it along with grace and intelligence. Thanks too to Nathaniel Dennett for working hard and well on so many aspects of this project, and for the encouraging words. Thanks also to John Glusman, Rachel Salzman, Meredith McGinnis, Eleen Cheung, Ingsu Liu and Beth Steidle. Fred Wiemer copyedited the manuscript with a light and thoughtful touch.

Thanks as always to my agent and friend Anne Edelstein; Anne, you outdid yourself on this one.

Thank you to my wife, Pamela Twigg, for every little thing.

My thanks to Laurel Daen for fact-checking the manuscript with uncommon care and diligence.

The New Netherland Institute was extremely supportive of this work, naming me its Senior Scholar and thus enabling me to use the wonderful facilities of the New York State Library and New York State

Archives as a base for my research. Thanks especially to Marilyn Douglas for her steadfast support of my work.

A special thank you to Angi Perron, Corinne Henry Brady, Floyd Henry, Gina Ryan and Jasir Ryan-Lee, descendants of Venture Smith, for letting me accompany you on your family history adventure in Ghana.

Like any writer of history, I owe a debt of gratitude to the geniuses behind the Internet Archive, who have revolutionized the work of historical research. Thanks also to the Fred W. Smith National Library for the Study of George Washington at Mount Vernon, for making the papers of George Washington available online.

In no particular order, my thanks to all of these wonderful people who guided me with advice, assistance, inspiration and information: Carol Morrison; Len Tantillo; Peter Rose; Elizabeth Covart; Mayor Kathy Sheehan of Albany, New York; Fred Bassett, New York State Library; Lucianne Lavin, Institute for American Indian Studies; Thomas Lannon, New York Public Library; Lisa Malloy, Haddam Historical Society; Elizabeth Sell and Stacy Winters, Washington Street Library, Cumberland, Maryland; Go-wa-yah-doni Jimerson, Seneca-Iroquois National Museum; Dennis Northcott, Missouri History Museum; John Levin, University of Sussex; Cameron Blevins, Northeastern University; Nancy Steenburg, University of Connecticut; Steve McErleane, New Netherland Institute; Pierce Rafferty, Henry L. Ferguson Museum, Fishers Island, New York; Geoff Benton, Crailo State Historic Site; Peter R. Henriques; Tricia Barbagallo, University at Albany; William Starna; Jaap Jacobs; Benjamin Carp, Brooklyn College; Louise Mirrer, Michael Ryan and Edward O'Reilly, New-York Historical Society; Stephan Wolf; Rabbi Meir Soloveichik, Congregation Shearith Israel; Robert Bantz; Joseph Weaver; Paul Lovejoy, York University; Stanley Welch, Loretta McCray and Marguerite Burke; Chandler Saint; Lindsay Turley, Museum of the City of New York;

Emmanuel Saboro; Kwadwo Opoku-Agyemang, University of Cape Coast; Rebecca Shumway; Mariano Pavanello, Sapienza University of Rome; Chris Kelly, historian, town of Schaghticoke, New York; Kathie Ludwig, David Library of the American Revolution; Kurt Jordan, Cornell University; Jim Folts, First Church in Albany, New York; Paul Otto, George Fox University; Thomas Abler; Jayne Ptolemy, Clements Library, University of Michigan; Al Saguto, master shoemaker, Colonial Williamsburg.

# NOTES

## Prologue

2 Its meaning in the Seneca language: Abler, *Cornplanter*, 2.

2 **On this night:** Hazard, *Pennsylvania Archives* 7:589–594; Godcharles, *History of Fort Freeland*, 28.

2 **had organized a formal council:** Abler, *Chainbreaker*, 71–80.

3 **"War is war":** Abler, *Chainbreaker*, 75.

3 **"stop speaking":** Abler, *Chainbreaker*, 75.

3 **"rather womanly":** Brown, *American Secretary*, 38.

4 **"decisive, direct, and firm":** Force, *American Archives*, 6:184.

## Chapter 1: Sons of Fathers

13 **In the summer of 1716 . . . newborn baby:** Germain was born at his father's house in Haymarket, London. I am assuming the trip was taken by carriage on the turnpike, which by 1710 had been completed through Sevenoaks to Woodsgate and Tunbridge Wells, and have relied on Johnston, *Abstract of Turnpike Acts Relating to Sussex.*

13 **The house was called Knole:** Sources on Knole include Robert Sackville-West, *Inheritance,* and V. Sackville-West, *Knole and the Sackvilles.*

13 **a succession of luminaries:** Valentine, *Lord George Germain*, 3.

14 **"splendidly sombre":** V. Sackville-West, 10.

14 **forty-two for the interior alone:** Valentine, *Lord George Germain*, 5.

15 **"I have not genius":** Brown, 39.

16 **"the boundaries of Empire":** Govier, "Royal Society," 203.

16 **"set to sea ships":** Govier, 206.

17 **Broteer Furro opened his eyes:** I am following Africa historian Paul Lovejoy

in his assertion that Broteer was probably born between 1727 and 1728. Lovejoy, "The African Background of Venture Smith," in Stewart, *Venture Smith,* 39–40.

17 **the blue sky:** Stewart, 39–40.

17 **His father, Saungm Furro:** Smith, *Narrative,* 5. (Unless otherwise indicated, all references are to the 1798 edition.)

17 **Broteer's people may have been Fulani:** I am following Paul Lovejoy in his presumption that Broteer was Fulani. Lovejoy bases his belief on a number of clues in Venture Smith's memoir. However, as Lovejoy himself notes, Broteer could have belonged to any of a number of herder tribes.

17 **Their basic communal unit:** On cattle culture in Africa, my sources include Adebayo, "Of Man and Cattle," and Jeffreys, "Mythical Origin of Cattle in Africa."

18 **In one variation:** Adebayo, "Of Man and Cattle," 7.

18 **At dry times:** Oppong-Anane, "Ghana: Country Pasture/Forage Resource Profile."

18 **one of the earliest African peoples:** Paul Lovejoy, in email correspondence.

18 **One day when Broteer was about ten:** Smith, *Narrative,* 5–7.

20 **"raise up and place":** Quoted in Wieneck, *Imperfect God,* 31.

22 **"I was more afraid than of my own":** Conkling, *Memoirs,* 17.

23 **"If they happen to hear":** Ehrenpreis, *Swift,* 3:627.

23 **"I must here":** Great Britain, Royal Commission on Historical Manuscripts, *Report on the Manuscripts of Mrs. Stopford-Sackville,* I:160 (hereafter, *Stopford-Sackville*). Note that "onely" is in the original.

25 **Dutifully following suit . . . American colonies:** Moore, "Devouring Posterity," 680–681.

25 **Whereas in Elizabethan times . . . four or five:** Wittkowsky, "Swift's Modest Proposal," 79–84.

26 **"good breeding":** Fitzmaurice, *Life of William,* 1:341.

27 **"I cannot but think":** Swift, *Works,* 2:762.

27 **"He studied no choice phrases":** Brown, 39.

27 **"My Lord Lieutenant's speech":** *Stopford-Sackville,* 1:166–167.

27 **a man on horseback:** Smith, *Narrative,* 8.

28 **By the 1480s:** Elbl, "The Volume of the Early Atlantic Slave Trade," 35.

28 **The practice of capturing:** Lovejoy, "Indigenous African Slavery," 19.

28 **Prior to European contact . . . slave labor:** Sparks, *Where Negroes Are Masters,* 15–17.

29 "have for the last month": Lovejoy, in Stewart, 45.

29 had been invaded: Smith, *Narrative*, 8.

31 "Allah, for the sake": Aziz Sow and Angell, "Fulani Poetic Genres," 63.

31 "He thus died": Smith, *Narrative*, 11.

32 "the trees and the richness": Fitzpatrick, *Writings of Washington*, vol. 1, *Journey over the Mountains,* 1748.

33 He got his hands on: http://gwpapers.virginia.edu/documents/the-rules-of-civility/.

33 110 "rules of civility": http://gwpapers.virginia.edu/documents_gw/civility/civil_01.html. Note that I have cleaned spelling and punctuation slightly in order to improve readability.

34 The rector of St. George's Church: Lorenz, "'To Do Justice to His Majesty,'" 352.

35 "roape dancings": Isaac, *The Transformation of Virginia,*101.

35 "Phyllis, lay aside": D'Urfey, *Wit and Mirth: Or Pills to Purge Melancholy* 6: 107. The songbook was popular both in England and in the colonies, especially Virginia. See Darling and Wiggins, "A Constant Tuting," *Music Educators Journal* 61, no. 3 (November 1974): 58.

35 "There is a Thing": D'Urfey, 6:106.

36 "The Britains Through": D'Urfey, 6:5.

36 Virginia planter society: Longmore, *Invention of George Washington,* 3–4.

## Chapter 2: A Tide in the Affairs of Men

37 It was June 1743 . . . in Bavaria: Townshend, *The Military Life of Field Marshal George First Marquess of Townshend,* 13–14.

38 Georg Friedrich Handel: Trench, George II, 217–223.

41 In the new "dining room": Wenger, "The Dining Room in Early Virginia," 149–159. William Hugh Grove, Gregory A. Stiverson and Patrick H. Butler III, "Virginia in 1732: The Travel Journal of William Huge Grove," *Virginia Magazine of History and Biography* 85, no. 1 (January 1977):18–44.

42 "baggage prepared": Flexner, *George Washington: The Forge of Experience,* 30.

42 "planter's pace": Longmore, 10.

43 "Memorandum to have my Coat made": Memorandum, 1749–1750. *The Papers of George Washington Digital Edition,* ed. Theodore J. Crackel et al. (Char-

lottesville: University of Virginia, 2007–), http://rotunda.upress.virginia.edu/
founders/default.xqy?keys=GEWN-search-1-1&expandNote=on#match1.
Punctuation added. (Throughout, all Washington letters can be found at the
source given in this note; the general URL is http://rotunda.upress.virginia.
edu/founders/GEWN.)

43  a little over 21 pounds: http://www.kenmore.org/genealogy/washington/
probate.html.

44  "They clear a large Circle": "A Journal of My Journey Over the Mountains," *The Papers of George Washington Digital Edition*, ed. Theodore
J. Crackel et al. (Charlottesville: University of Virginia, 2007–), http://
rotunda.upress.virginia.edu/founders/default.xqy?keys=GEWN-print-01-
01-02-0001-0002. (One must be logged-in to access.) I have added punctuation and modernized some of the text to improve readability.

45  more than 2,000 acres: Chernow, *Washington*, 23.

45  "enraptured": Washington, "Voyage to Barbados", 1751.

45  But overcome as he was: Flexner, *George Washington: The Forge of
Experience*, 52.

46  He asked William Fauntleroy: "From George Washington to William
Fauntleroy, 20 May 1752," Founders Online, National Archives, http://
founders.archives.gov/documents/Washington/02-01-02-0020. Source:
*The Papers of George Washington*, Colonial Series, vol. 1, *7 July 1748–14
August 1755*, ed. W. W. Abbot. (Charlottesville: University Press of Vir-
ginia, 1983), 49–50.

46  coat of arms: Fauntleroy, "The Fauntleroy Family," 210.

47  man named Baukurre: Smith, *Narrative*, 11.

47  "man-stealing": Atkins, *Voyage to Guinea, Brasil, and the West Indies*, 53.

48  The people of Anomabo: Lovejoy, "The African Background of Venture
Smith," 42.

48  Anomabo was a center of the slaving industry: Getz, "Mechanisms of Slave
Exposition," 83.

48  Anomabo had specialized workers: Berlin, "From Creole to African," 260.

49  "boat trade": Shumway, *Fante and the Transatlantic Slave Trade*, 92.

50  "Royal African": T. Thompson, *Account of Two Missionary Voyages*, 47–50;
Shumway, "The Fante Shrine of Nananom Mpow and the Atlantic Slave
Trade in Southern Ghana," 33–34; *The Royal African; or, Memoirs of the
Young Prince of Annamaboe*, 25–29; Shumway, *The Fante and the Transat-
lantic Slave Trade*, 75–81.

50 "black Portuguese": Berlin, 258. Shumway, *The Fante and the Transatlantic Slave Trade*, 35.

50 Selling slaves . . . cutlasses and firearms: Atkins, 160–162; Alpern, "What Africans Got for Their Slaves."

51 "many considerable Articles": Atkins, 162.

51 87 slaves: Trans-Atlantic Slave Trade database (slavevoyages.org), record number 36067.

51 *Charming Susanna*: The ship is listed in the records compiled by the Trans-Atlantic Slave Trade database (slavevoyages.org); it is record number 36067. One researcher, Haddam town historian Karl Stofko, believes Broteer was more likely transported two years earlier, on a ship not listed in the database.

51 had struck a deal: Smith, *Narrative*, 13.

52 "There is a tide": *Julius Caesar*, IV.iii.216–222.1.


### Chapter 3: The Turtle's Back


53 Before there was the world . . . where flowers glowed: The version I give here follows William Fenton, "This Island, the World on the Turtle's Back," with emendations from Michael Galban, Ganondagan Seneca Art and Culture Center.

54 "this beautiful valley": Beauchamp, *Aboriginal Place Names*, 102–103.

54 A boy was born here: The timing of Cornplanter's birth is the subject of much speculation. Early historians placed it around 1740 or earlier. Thomas Abler, the most recent scholar to write extensively on Cornplanter, puts it at 1752 or 1753. I think it would have likely been several years earlier, based in large part on the report of Philip Tome, who met Cornplanter in 1816, when he was an old man, and asked him his first experience of battle. Tome says Cornplanter told him it was at Braddock's defeat, in 1755. There seems no reason for Tome to have invented the detail, and while Cornplanter could have been a boy at the battle, he would not have been an infant.

55 stinking water: Beauchamp, 31.

55 "lineage matron": Abler, *Cornplanter*, 19–20.

55 Iroquois names: Abler, *Cornplanter*, 2.

55 "took notice of my skin": Abler, *Cornplanter*, 16.

56 "that incorrigible villian": Johnson, *Papers of Sir William Johnson*, 9:397–398.

56 "constantly carried great quantitys": Johnson, 2:388.

56 **Generations before:** Jordan, *Seneca Restoration*, 292–293.

57 **"extended 3 or 4 English miles":** Peter, "A Description of the Wild Pigeons," 56.

57 **The pigeons roosted . . . whole family:** Swatzler, *A Friend Among the Senecas*, 152.

58 **Seneca children also learned:** As indeed they still do. Many of these activities continue among the Iroquois.

58 **Besides the tale of creation:** Sources include Starna, "Retrospecting the Origins of the League of the Iroquois"; Kuhn and Sempowski, "A New Approach to Dating the League of the Iroquois"; Fenton, *The Great Law and the Longhouse*, chap. 6.

58 **a mystical "white stone" canoe:** Michael Galban, in correspondence.

59 **But the Senecas, at the far western edge:** Here I am following the argument of, among others, archaeologist Kurt Jordan, especially in *The Seneca Restoration*.

59 **The overall population was small:** Jordan, *Seneca Restoration*, 55.

59 **Senecas had the upper hand:** Jordan, "Not Just 'One Site,'" 105.

59 **party of blacksmiths:** Jordan, *Seneca Restoration*, 101–104.

59 **100 miles a day on foot:** Morgan, *League of the Ho-dé-no-sau-nee*, 105.

59 **The Iroquois . . . in the world:** Jordan, *The Seneca Restoration*, 50–51, 84–86.

60 **As in European civilization:** Richter, "War and Culture," passim.

61 **Near his home:** Grant, *Memoirs of an American Lady*, 32–33.

61 **It was also in a sense an Iroquois town:** Bielinski, "A Middling Sort," 276–277.

61 **They served butter chicken:** Food historian Peter Rose, in correspondence.

61 **Abraham couldn't even take up:** Bielinski, "A Middling Sort," 282.

62 **"Een paar schoenen":** Yates, Account Book, 17, in Yates Papers, NYPL; Bielinski File, NYSL.

62 **When he walked through the doors:** Munsell, *Collections on the History of Albany*, 1:57–80a.

63 **ran for the same office:** Bielinski, *Abraham Yates*, 4.

63 **De Ridder offered as dowry:** Wolf, "Abraham Yates, Jr.," 28.

64 **he began selling:** Yates, Account Book, 14, in Yates Papers, NYPL; Bielinski File, NYSL.

64 **In September 1753 . . . one of their own:** Wolf, 30.

65 **"middle sort":** Quoted in Staughton Lynd, "Abraham Yates's History of the Movement for the United States Constitution," 224.

65 **He won:** Munsell, *Collections on the History of Albany*, 1:85–86.

65 **For the sick . . . the waves:** Mustakeem, "'I Never Have Such a Sickly Ship Before,'" 480–482.

65 **"An ordinary passage":** Smith, *Narrative*, 13.

65 **If Captain Collingwood followed the procedure:** Smallwood, "African Guardians," 685.

65 **Of the 87 slaves:** Slavevoyages.org., ship number 36067.

66 **An experienced officer:** Lovejoy, "The African Background of Venture Smith," 38; Smallwood, passim.

66 **"in the cool of the evening":** Washington, *Diaries*, November 4 and 5, 1751.

66 **40,66 slaves:** Levy, "Slavery and the Emancipation Movement," 5.

66 **molasses:** Ostrander, "Colonial Molasses Trade," 82.

66 **The industry was as lucrative:** Thomas and McCloskey, *Economic History of Britain*, 1:91.

67 **Of the 74 slaves:** Slavevoyages.org, ship number 36067, and Smith, *Narrative*, 13.

67 **his sister Mercy:** Smith, *Narrative*, 14; Stofko, "Reading Between the lines," 1.

67 **Newport outfitted:** Elaine Crane, A *Dependent People*, 17–18; "Newport," in *History of World Trade Since 1450*, encyclopedia.com.

67 **calling for the abolition of slavery:** For example: William Johnston, *Slavery in Rhode Island, 1755-1776*, 39–42.

67 **Venture took in the cityscape:** Hodge, "Widow Pratt's World of Goods," passim; www.newporthistory.org/about/brief-history-of-newport/.

68 **put in at Narragansett:** Smith, *Narrative*, 14.

69 **"he had been in his native place":** Smith, *Narrative*, 15.

69 **he made one friend:** Stofko, unpublished genealogy of the George Mumford family; Stofko, "Reading Between the Lines: Venture and Rebecca."

69 **13 percent of the inhabitants:** Fitts, "The Landscapes of Northern Bondage," 55.

70 **Robinson Mumford had died . . . the weather:** Saint and Krimsky, *Making Freedom*, 33.

71 **"to serve two masters":** Smith, *Narrative*, 15.

71 **One day . . . hauled him down:** Smith, *Narrative*, 15–16.

71 **"for love":** Smith, *Narrative*, 31.

71 **"broke out into a great rage":** Smith, *Narrative*, 15–16.

## Chapter 4: The Charming Sound of Bullets

76 "all the territories": Galbreath, *Expedition of Celeron to the Ohio Country*, 18.

77 "require of them" . . . "force of arms": "Commission from Robert Dinwiddie, 30 October 1753," *Founders Online*, National Archives.

77 Also, he had the idea: Chernow, 32.

77 "excessive Rains": Washington, *Journal of Major George Washington*, 3.

78 "the Land in the Fork": Washington, *Journal of Major George Washington*, 4.

78 "extremely well situated": Washington, *The Journal of Major George Washington*, 5.

78 He found his way: Washington, "Journey to the French Commandant: Narrative," *Founders Online*, National Archives.

78 He also astonished Washington: Humphreys, *Life of General Washington*, 10.

79 cooked and eaten: Misencik, *George Washington and the Half-King*, 51.

79 "houses upon our land": Washington, *Journal of Major George Washington*, 7.

79 "the great Being above": Washington, *Journal of Major George Washington*, 7.

80 "through many mires and swamps": In present-day northwestern Pennsylvania, near the shore of Lake Erie.

80 "incontestable rights of the King": Washington, *Journal of Major George Washington*, 26–27.

80 "As to the summons": Washington, *Journal of Major George Washington*, 27.

81 an ungainly group: *New York Gazette*, April 1, 1754.

83 Half of all British shipping: Kenneth Morgan, "Robert Dinwiddie's Reports on the British American Colonies," 341–342. The figures include the Caribbean as well as the North American colonies. See also Edwin Burrows and Mike Wallace, *Gotham: A History of New York City to 1898*, 170.

84 the Duke praised him for his "gallantry": *Stopford-Sackville*, I:290.

84 But this time: Walpole, *Memoirs of the Reign of King George II*, I:279.

85 "If I had a peerage": Walpole, *Memoirs of the Reign of King George II*, I:282.

85 "I despise it": Walpole, *Memoirs of the Reign of King George II*, I:282.

86 "Nobody stands higher": Quoted in Alan Valentine, *Lord George Germain*, 29.

87 **"Run Away from George Mumford"**: *New York Gazette*, April 1,1754.

88 **Some newspaper accounts . . . his friends would benefit**: Flexner, *George Washington: The Forge of Experience*, 80; *Pennsylvania Gazette*, February 5, 1754, March 12, 1754; *New York Gazette*, March 25, 1754; *South Carolina Gazette*, March 26, 1754.

89 **"I was employed"**: George Washington to Augustine Washington, August 2, 1755.

89 **"to act on the Difensive"**: Robert Dinwiddie to George Washington, January 1754.

90 **"Tu n'es pas encore"**: Chaussegros de Léry, *Journal,* 19.

91 **"I heard the Bullets"**: George Washington to John Augustine Washington, May 31, 1754.

91 **Tanacharison . . . said so**: Hazard, *Pennsylvania Colonial Records*, VI:151–152.

## Chapter 5: World on Fire

92 **"deceived by our interpreter"**: Washington, *Papers of George Washington*, I:169–170.

93 **"were the most infamous"**: Quoted in Longmore, *Invention of George Washington*, 23.

93 **"Washington and many such"**: Flexner, *George Washington: The Forge of Experience*, 108.

93 **Among the most vigorous**: Bradley, *Fight with France*, 68.

93 **"the Protection of Our Possessions in America"**: George II, "His Majesty's Most Gracious Speech to Both Houses of Parliament" (1755).

94 **In eight years**: Albany Dutch Church Burials, 1722–1757, http://www.rootsweb.ancestry.com/~nycoloni/chbur.html; Wolf, *Abaham Yates Jr.,* chap. 1, p. 19.

95 **As winter settled in . . . checkered cloth**: Yates, Account Book, in Yates Papers, NYPL; Bielinski File, NYSL.

95 **requesting that they come together**: Brodhead, *Documents Relative* 6:802, 828.

96 **"a Turky. . . . killed for our diners"**: Benjamin Franklin to Peter Collinson, April 29, 1749.

96 **"Republics and limited monarchies"**: Benjamin Franklin, "Advice to a Young Tradesman," http://founders.archives.gov/documents/Franklin/01-03-02-0130; "On Freedom of Speech and the Press," *Pennsylvania Gazette,* November 17, 1737.

98 **"up the hill"**: Quoted in McAnear, "Personal Accounts of the Albany Congress of 1754," 733.

98 **As tribal chiefs . . . of the speech**: McAnear, "Personal Accounts of the Albany Congress of 1754," 741.

100 **"the Wel being"**: Yates, The Journal and Copybook of Abraham Yates Jr., 2–4, in Yates Papers, NYPL; Bielinski File.

101 **"two johannes, three old Spanish dollars"**: Smith, *Narrative,* 18.

102 **"You must entertain"**: George Washington to William Fitzhugh, November 15, 1754, in *Papers of George Washington.*

102 **And so he "retired" . . . "Negroe slaves"**: Lease of Mount Vernon, December 17, 1754, in *Papers of George Washingon.*

103 **"will be very glad of your Company"**: Robert Orme to George Washington, March 2, 1755.

104 **His mother arrived . . . so dangerous a mission**: George Washington to Robert Orme, April 2, 1755, in *Papers of George Washington.*

105 **took out advertisements**: Bell, "Franklin and the 'Wagon Affair,'" 551–558.

105 **When he heard . . . into the future**: Flexner, *George Washington: The Forge of Experience,* 122.

106 **"Honourd Madam"**: George Washington to Mary Ball Washington, June 7, 1755, in *Papers of George Washington.*

108 **Indeed . . . their own men**: George Washington to Robert Dinwiddie, July 18, 1755, in *Papers of George Washington.*

108 **"engage the enemy"**: Washington, Remarks 1787–1788, in Fitzpatrick, *Writings of George Washington,* 23:43.

109 **They came staggering . . . needing refuge**: Yates, Journal and Copybook, 1, Yates Papers, NYPL; Bielinski File, NYSL.

109 **The immediate problem . . . to replace him**: Johnson, 5:419, http://www.nysm.nysed.gov/albany/bios/vd/jovdh5697.html; Wolf, 39.

110 **"A victory"**: Yates, Journal and Copybook, 27, in Yates Papers, NYPL; Bielinski File, NYSL.

111 **"next to impossible"**: Yates, Journal and Copybook, 39. Note that I have cleaned up Yates's spelling of place names, except for "Nistigeione," which is closer to what it was called at the time than the name of the same place today: Niskayuna.

111 "like Brutes in Human Shape": Yates, Journal and Copybook, 54.

112 "let the City Burn": Yates, Journal and Copybook, 70.

112 "to impress an idea": Untitled history document, Abraham Yates, Jr., Papers, New York Public Library, Box 3, typescript, p. 32; Bielinski File, NYSL.

112 "Let him now": Yates, Untitled history document, Yates Papers, NYPL, Box 3, typescript, p. 32; Bielinski File, NYSL.

113 Yates wrote to Governor James De Lancey . . . the army's rule prevailed: Yates, Untitled history document, Yates Papers, NYPL, Box 3, typescript, p. 34; Bielinski File, NYSL.

114 "lay in the same bed": Yates, Journal and Copybook, 96.

115 "the bewitching Charms": Quoted in John Mulder, "William Livingston: Propagandist Against Episcopacy," 91.

115 "the Vanity of Birth and Titles": Quoted in John Mulder, "William Livingston: Propagandist Against Episcopacy," 83.

115 "monopolizer of power": Quoted in Mary Lou Lustig, *Privilege and Prerogative*, 100.

116 "The pretended power": Yates, Journal and Copybook, 112. Note that for the sake of clarity I have cleaned up punctuation and capitalization of the original.

116 "the most iniquitous": Yates, Journal and Copybook, 163–164.

117 "the product of force and violence": Yates, Journal and Copybook, 105.

117 "Abm: Yates Jun Esq": Yates, Journal and Copybook, 130.

117 "repeated complaints": Yates, Journal and Copybook, 134.

118 "but I don't think": Yates, Journal and Copybook, 134–136.

Chapter 6: This Land I Have Made for You and Not for Others

120 By the time Venture intersected: Stanton, *A Record, Genealogical, Biological, Statistical, of Thomas Stanton*, 9–11, 35–40.

120 That January, of 1755: Hempstead, *Diary*, 644.

120 A man-of-war left the harbor: Hempstead, 643.

120 He commented with satisfaction: Hempstead, 655. Spelling has been modernized.

121 about 370 pounds: Figured at 11.74 pounds per gallon, and 31.5 gallons per barrel.

121 **Venture too took pleasure:** Smith, *Narrative,* 18.

121 **two sloops from Boston:** Hempstead, 668.

121 **In June of 1757:** Hempstead, 690.

122 **"he hath been to advise":** Hempstead, 665.

122 **hired from a man named Powers:** Hempstead, 665.

122 **Then, in June:** Hempstead, 665–670.

123 **"I have quit":** George Washington to Richard Washington, May 7, 1759.

124 **"Your safe Return":** William Fairfax to Washington, July 26, 1755.

124 **"Mr. Washington had two Horses":** Quoted in Samuel Hazard, *Minutes of the Provincial Council of Pennsylvania,* VI:488.

124 **"the merit of Washington":** Quoted in Paul Longmore, *Invention of George Washington,* 29.

124 **"it would reflect eternal dishonor":** George Washington to Mary Ball Washington, August 14, 1755.

125 **"How the Officers":** Humphrey Bland, *A Treatise of Military Discipline* (London, 1743), passim.

126 **"conveyed much more terror":** George Washington to Robert Dinwiddie, August 3, 1757.

126 **It was Washington's first trip:** Details on the trip come from W. C. Ford, *The Writings of George Washington,* 1:231–233.

127 **"Split me, madam!":** Singleton, *Social New York Under the Georges,* 374.

127 **"Microcosm or the World":** Washington, *Writings,* 298.

128 **"a gentleman who has deservedly a high reputation":** *Boston Gazette,* March 1, 1756.

128 **"If bleeding, dying!":** George Washington to Robert Dinwiddie, April 22, 1756.

129 **letter to Loudoun:** George Washington to John Campbell, Earl of Loudoun, January 10, 1757.

129 **Washington dashed off a letter:** George Washington to Thomas Gage, April 12, 1758.

130 **Diseases swept through the army . . . two horses:** Flexner, *George Washington: The Forge of Experience,* 213.

130 **"The enemy, after letting us":** George Washington to Francis Fauquier, November 28, 1758.

131 **a shift of allegiance:** Johnson, 2:812–830, 3:1–10.

132 **"the heroick spirit":** George Washington to Horatio Sharpe, April 24, 1754.

132 "more happiness in retirement": George Washington to Richard Washington, September 20, 1759.

133 he had ducked yet again: Valentine, *Lord George Germain*, 33.

133 "the conduct of this old King": Watson, *Reign of George III*, 4.

134 In aligning himself: Brown, 2–3; Valentine, *Lord George Germain*, 32–33.

136 "Voilà cet homme": Walpole, *Memoirs of George II*, 2:367.

137 "kindled up such a blaze": David Hume and Tobias Smollett, *History of England*, XIII:225.

137 "a damned chicken-hearted soldier": Valentine, *Lord George Germain*, 58.

137 "I gave you the opportunity": *Stopford-Sackville*, I:312–313.

138 "I find myself": *Stopford-Sackville*, I:315.

138 "Lord Sackville seemed not to understand them": *The Proceedings of a General Court-Martial, Held at the Horse Guards on Friday the 7th, and Continued by Several Adjournments to Monday the 24th of March, 1760: And of a General Court-Martial Held at the Horse Guards on Tuesday the 25th of March, and Continued by Several Adjournments to Saturday the 5th of April 1760, upon the Trial of Lord George Sackville* (Edinburgh, 1760), 16.

138 "guilty of having disobeyed": *Proceedings of a General Court-Martial*, 224.

139 Not only . . . saving his son's life: Valentine, *Lord George Germain*, 67.

139 "are Subject to Censures": Valentine, *Lord George Germain*, 68.

140 "So finishes a career": Valentine, *Lord George Germain*, 72.

142 Under the terms of this agreement . . . their subordinate role: Grimes, "We 'Now Have Taken up the Hatchet Against Them,'" 228–232; Jay Miller, "The Delaware as Women."

143 Presque Isle: Misencik, 53–56.

144 At the same time: Parmenter, "After the Morning Wars," 63–64.

144 "handsomely entertained": *Minutes of the Provincial Council of Pennsylvania*, VI:124.

145 "We expect to be killed": *Minutes of the Provincial Council of Pennsylvania*, VI:37.

145 "savage fury": George Washington to Robert Dinwiddie, April 22, 1756.

145 Amherst had served as page: Valentine, *Lord George Germain*, 455–456.

146 Within a short time: Dowd, *War Under Heaven*, 64.

146 "expect nothing but that the general": Johnson, X:317. Spelling corrected.

147 In 1761. . . . stand down: Thomas Abler, "Kayahsota," in *Dictionary of Canadian Biography*.

147 "This land where ye dwell": Cave, "The Delaware Prophet Neolin," 272.

147 **The language of the treaty:** "The Definitive Treaty of Peace and Friendship Between His Britannick Majesty, the Most Christian King, and the King of Spain," 1763, Article VII.

148 **"the Indians by means of Blanketts":** Bouquet, *Papers*, Series 21634, 161.

149 **"two Blankets and an Handkerchief":** Bouquet, *Papers of Col. Henry Bouquet*, Series 21655, 210; Fenn, "Biological Warfare in Eighteenth-Century North America," 1554.

150 **To an Iroquois, the whorl:** Michael Galban, Ganondagan Seneca Art and Culture Center, in personal correspondence.

150 **That you and your enemy:** Pouchot, *Memoir from the Late War in North America*, II:246–247.

## Chapter 7: The Spirit That Rages

151 **his roan mare:** Washington, *Diaries,* June 8, 1762.

151 **they named Susanna:** Wolf, *Abraham Yates Jr.,* chap 1, p. 19; Robert Livingston to Abraham Yates, September 13, 1762, in Yates Papers, NYPL; Bielinski File, NYSL.

152 **daughter of an officer:** Coghlan, *Memoirs,* 15–16. (All citations of the Coghlan *Memoirs* refer to pages of the New York edition.)

152 **named her older brother:** Coghlan, *Memoirs,* 119.

153 **"I did not like my new mother":** Coghlan, *Memoirs,* 21.

153 **On October 25, 1760, George II:** Walpole, *Memoirs of the Last Ten Years,* 2:454.

154 **He kept a leisurely . . . for sixpence:** Flanders, *Memoirs of Richard Cumberland,* 325.

155 **"I pretend now to some knowledge of midwifery":** George Sackville to John Irwin, July 6, 1762, and July 10, 1762, in *Stopford-Sackville.*

155 **"offices might be open to him":** *Stopford-Sackville,* 1:58.

156 **"the cause of freedom":** Pauline Maier, "John Wilkes and American Disillusionment with Britain," 387.

156 **Wilkes was bringing his attacks:** Valentine, *Lord North,* 1:116.

157 **"of all the middling and inferior class of people":** Russel, *A New and Authentic History of England,* 797.

158 **"the Juries of London":** *Stopford-Sackville,* 92.

158 **Robert Dinwiddie, the former royal governor:** Ritcheson, 546–547.

159 "a strange doctrine": *Stopford-Sackville*, 105–106.

160 "nervous compactness": Valentine, *Lord George Germain*, 87.

161 "there is no relying": James Wood to George Washington, July 7, 1758.

161 The goal . . . from London merchants: Breen, *Tobacco Culture*, 58.

161 "strips off his coat": Chernow, 119.

161 He bought coaches, linens, lace: Invoices, George Washington to Robert Cary, September 20, 1759; George Washington to Robert Cary, September 28, 1760.

162 "swallowed up": George Washington to Robert Stewart, April 27, 1763.

163 As he became . . . "a free mind": George Washington to Robert Cary, August 10, 1764.

163 "be condemned forever": Breen, 134.

163 Under the pressure: Breen, 132f.

163 "servant": Chernow, 110.

164 "set the whole Country in Flames": George Washington to Robert Stewart, May 2, 1763.

164 "increase of the people": Mississippi Land Company Memorial to the King, September 9, 1763, http://founders.archives.gov/documents/Washington/02-07-02-0150.

165 "Liberties & Privileges": E. J. Miller, "The Virginia Legislature and the Stamp Act," 234–237.

165 The reaction in the colonies. . . . like vassals: Henry Young, "Agrarian Reactions to the Stamp Act Crisis in Pennsylvania," 25–30.

166 "such as I have never heard": *National Quarterly Review*, no. 27 (1873): 152.

167 "It cannot reasonably": George Washington to Robert Cary, September 20, 1765.

167 A winter's night: Yates correspondence, January 3, 1766, in Yates Papers, NYPL; Bielinski File, NYSL.

168 "I am an Intire Stranger": Yates correspondence, January 3, 1766.

169 "illegal, unconstitutional and oppressive": McAnear, "The Albany Stamp Act Riots," 492.

170 "the mischevious politics": Yates, untitled history manuscript, in Yates Papers, NYPL, Box 3; Bielinski File, NYSL.

170 "the Americans to a man seem resolved": Valentine, *Lord North*, I:124.

170 "If I can crawl": Taylor, *Correspondence of William Pitt*, 2:362.

170 "There is an idea in some": Knight, *Popular History of England,* 5:91.

171 The king was against repealing: Valentine, *Lord North,* I:129.

171 "Dam'n me": Johnson, 12:4.

172 "The Repeal of the Stamp Act": George Washington to Robert Cary, July 21, 1766.

173 In 1768, he ran for . . . for guidance: Longmore, 87.

173 the 254 blacks: Haynes, *Stonington Chronology,* 39.

173 Stonington was growing . . . Nathan Chesebrough's meadow: Haynes, 39.

174 "a gunning": Smith, *Narrative,* 18.

174 "The treatment of slaves: Mars, *Life of James Mars,* 4.

175 "I earnestly requested": Smith, *Narrative,* 18–19.

175 raised a two-foot club: Smith, *Narrative,* 19.

175 slaves had some rights in Connecticut. . . . punish the owner: Wahl, "Legal Constraints on Slave Masters," 6–7.

176 "improved this convenient": Smith, *Narrative,* 20.

176 "gold rings": Smith, *Narrative,* 20.

177 "Well then, I will send you": Smith, *Narrative,* 20.

177 "I crossed the waters": Smith, *Narrative,* 20.

## Chapter 8: Thirteen Toasts

178 "RAN away": *Maryland Gazette,* August 20, 1761.

179 "he amazed me": Hirschfeld, *George Washington and Slavery,* 58.

179 Washington's expanding businesses . . . picking apples: Mary Thompson, *Lives of Enslaved Workers,* 3.

179 "wretched wooden shacks": Mary Thompson, 6.

179 "both a Rogue & Runaway": George Washington to Joseph Thompson, July 2, 1766.

181 "If you will go by no other measures": Smith, *A Narrative,* 21.

183 exchanged gossipy letters: *Stopford-Sackville,* 62–67.

183 "At a time when our lordly Masters in Great Britain": Washington, *Diaries,* April 4, 1769.

184 "If at length it becomes undoubted": John Dickinson, "Letters from an American Farmer," Letter 3, http://oll.libertyfund.org/titles/690.

185 "infringements of their natural and constitutional rights": Massachu-

setts Circular Letter, February 11, 1768, http://avalon.law.yale.edu/18th_
century/mass_circ_let_1768.asp.

185 **"no man shou'd scruple":** George Washington to George Mason, April 5,
1769.

186 **one Massachusetts statute:** Sumner Eliot Matison, "Manumission by Purchase," 147.

186 **Connecticut law:** George Williams, *History of the Negro Race in America,
from 1619 to 1880*, 257.

189 **"the noble Lord":** Jaques, *The History of Junius*, 267.

190 **"Mr. Speaker":** West, *Source Book in American History to 1787*, 383.

191 **"Spirits, Wine, Cyder":** http://founders.archives.gov/documents/
Jefferson/01-01-02-0019.

192 **It was October 14, 1772:** Reynolds, *Albany Chronicles*, 270.

192 **more than 900 cases:** Wolf, chap. 3.

192 **He bought city lots . . . and the mill:** Yates, Account Book, 95, in Yates
Papers, NYPL; Bielinski File, NYSL.

192 **The election results . . . to be lit every evening:** Reynolds, 263–271.

193 **A year ago . . . ordinary workers:** Bielinski, *Abraham Yates, Jr., and the
New Political Order*, 12.

195 **"he offends nobody":** Valentine, *Lord North*, I:192.

195 **"His Majesty":** *Parliamentary History of England*, 17:1159.

196 **"totally displeased":** *Parliamentary History of England*, 17:1162.

196 **"put an end to their town meetings":** *Parliamentary History of England*,
17:1195–1196.

196 **"you will teach them by these means":** Moffatt, *Burke's Speech on American
Taxation*, 63.

196 **"The Americans have tarred and feathered":** *Parliamentary History of
England*, 17:1280.

197 **"anarchy and confusion":** *Stopford-Sackville*, I:315.

198 **"takes Loaded arms":** Johnson, 13:321–322.

199 **"when I started to return":** Stone, *Life and Times of Red Jacket*, 452.

199 **gaudy versions of proper ladies:** Kenneth Jackson and David Dunbar, eds.,
*Empire City*, 84.

200 **"genteelly regaled with arack":** Bayles, *Old Taverns of New York*, 255.

200 **a fire broke out:** *New York Gazette and Weekly Mercury*, May 4, 1772.

200 **That winter was so cold:** Burrows and Wallace, *Gotham*, 213.

200 **"to bask in the heart-cheering smile":** Coghlan, 68.

200  "If some heads had been lopped off": Johnson, 7:650.

200  "raskals": Johnson, 12:4.

200  "the finest race of Young women": Johnson, 12:1144.

201  "Those who have too successfully labored": Stokes, *The Iconography of Manhattan Island*, I:35.

201  "such a sot": James Mooney, *Loyalist Imprints*, 144.

202  "I found myself": Coghlan, 22.


## Chapter 9: Assuming Command

203  "I hope you will stand firm": Brady, *Martha Washington*, 92.

204  He met John Jay: Coghlan, 22.

204  "easy Soldierlike Air": Longmore, 138.

205  "the most spirited": Adams, Diary, September 2, 1774, in Charles Francis Adams, *The Works of John Adams*, 2:362.

205  "The Crisis is arrived": George Washington to Bryan Fairfax, August 24, 1774.

205  "tedious beyond expression": John Adams to Abigail Adams, October 9, 1774. Founders Online, National Archives, http://founders.archives.gov/ documents/Adams/04-01-02-0111.

205  In the evenings they carried the discussions to taverns: *Washington Papers*, Card Playing Expenses 1772–1774.

206  "the times are ticklish": George Washington to John Tayloe, October 31, 1774.

207  "property will be exposed": James Madison Papers, I:144. *Founders Online*, National Archives, http://founders.archives.gov/documents/ Madison/01-01-02-0044.

207  "It is imagined the first thing": Alexander Spotswood to George Washington, April 30, 1775.

207  "We were fired on from all sides": Hibbert, *Redcoats and Rebels*, 34–36.

208  "The news from America": *Stopford-Sackville*, I:135.

208  Germain responded with a primer: *Stopford-Sackville*, II:2–3.

209  "the utmost force of this kingdom": *Stopford-Sackville*, I:137.

209  "First, the people of the colonies": William Crane, ed., *Edmund Burke's Speech on Conciliation with the Colonies*, 72.

210 "There never perhaps was a commission of such importance": *Stopford-Sackville,* II:10–12.

210 "thinks you the fittest man": *Stopford-Sackville,* II:10–12.

212 The second Continental Congress. . . . the Pennsylvania delegation: Isaacson, 288.

212 "Col. Washington appears at Congress": John Adams to Abigail Adams, May 29, 1775.

212 "That a general be appointed": *Journals of the Continental Congress,* June 15, 1775.

213 "Mr. President, Tho' I am truly sensible": *Journals of the Continental Congress,* II:92.

213 "a consciousness of its being a trust too great": George Washington to Martha Washington, June 18, 1775.

214 The Seneca delegation. . . . all his life: Abler, *Chainbreaker,* 43–51.

215 Brothers, Sachems, and Warriors: *Journals of the Continental Congress,* Speech to the Six Nations, July 13, 1775.

216 The "island" that the commissioner referred to: Abler, *Chainbreaker,* 39.

217 "from Washington": Abler, *Chainbreaker,* 51.

217 "see clear with the naked eyes": Abler, *Chainbreaker,* 52.


Chapter 10: A Natural Inclination to Liberty

220 the army had only enough gunpowder: Ramsay, *Life of George Washington,* 29.

220 "When the Enemy first discovered": George Washington to John Hancock, March 7–9, 1776.

220 Washington had no way of knowing: George Washington to Joseph Reed, March 19, 1776.

221 "the Savior of your Country": Josiah Quincy to George Washington, March 21, 1776.

221 "any deserter": Wiencek, 200.

221 "to reject Negroes altogether": *Washington Papers,* October 8, 1775.

222 African-American slaves in the eighteenth century: Inscoe, "Carolina Slave Names," 541–542.

222 Cuff was a West African name: Inscoe, 533.

223  eels and lobsters: Smith, *Narrative*, 25.

223  "I cut and corded": Smith, *Narrative*, 25. The calculation is based on an estimate in Howard Russell, *A Long, Deep Furrow: Three Centuries of Farming in New England*, 175.

223  "All fine clothes": Smith, *Narrative*, 23.

224  They settled on: Smith, *Narrative*, 24.

225  He and Denison agreed on a price of 60 pounds: Cameron Blevins, "'Owned by Negro Venture': Land and Liberty in the Life of Venture Smith," 32; Stonington Town Land Records, 9:110.

225  "ran away from me": Smith, *Narrative*, 26.

225  Charles Church: Smith, *Narrative*, 24.

226  "to my great grief": Smith, *Narrative*, 26.

227  "How sharper": Act 1, Scene 4.

227  they passed a law: Smith, *Narrative*, 27.

227  a special town meeting: Richard Anson Wheeler, *History of the Town of Stonington*, 36–37.

227  "the many repeated attacks": Wheeler, *History of the Town of Stonington*, 36.

228  a 20-gun British frigate appeared: Wheeler, *History of the Town of Stonington*, 38–39.

228  A contingent of local militiamen: Wheeler, *History of the Town of Stonington*, 36.

228  Passing the little village of Lyme: National Park Service, Inventory Nomination Form, "Black Horse Tavern."

230  "I never sought the office": Brown, 54.

230  "the war is raging more ferociously": Valentine, *Lord George Germain*, 118.

231  The army had 48,000 men: Valentine, *Lord George Germain*, 124.

231  "seems in very great spirits": Valentine, *Lord George Germain*, 136.

231  "The Americans, sir": Middleton, *British Historians and the American Revolution*, 43.

233  "the supreme authority of the Legislature": Brown, 65.

233  Admiral Howe wrote: Stopford-Sackville, 2:29.

234  31 battalions: Brown, 55.

234  "the Indians of the Six Nations": Force, *American Archives*, Fourth Series, 5:527.

235  "you may finally receive": Force, 6:766.

236 **preparing to head to New York:** Yates, correspondence, June 17, 1776, and July 26, 1776, in Yates Papers, NYPL; Bielinski File, NYSL.

237 **"the different principles":** Yates, Rough Hewer and Political Essays, in Yates Papers, NYPL, Reel 2, p. 36; Bielinski File, NYSL.

238 **"the lower people":** Yates, Rough Hewer and Political Essays, Reel 2, p. 12.

238 **"violation of the people's rights and liberties":** Yates, untitled history manuscript, in Yates Papers, NYPL, Box 3, p. 2; Bielinski File, NYSL.

238 **"state of liberty":** Locke, *Two Treatises of Government,* 107.

238 **"the consent of every individual":** Locke, 146.

239 **"the Arbitrary Measures":** Yates, Yates Papers, NYPL, Reel 1, 126; Bielinski File, NYSL.

239 **"on the Holy Evangelists":** Albany Committee, Minutes, 1775–1778, 1:1.

240 **"take the Sense of your District":** Bielinski, *Abraham Yates Jr. and the New Political Order,* 17.

240 **"not conceive themselves fully invested":** *Minutes of the Albany Committee of Correspondence,* I:15.

241 **"Many People of Property":** Schecter, *Battle for New York,* 51.

241 **"the multitude":** Alexander Hamilton to John Jay, November 26, 1775. "From Alexander Hamilton to John Jay, 26 November 1775," *Founders Online,* National Archives, last modified March 30, 2017, http://founders .archives.gov/documents/Hamilton/01-01-02-0060.

242 **In a pamphlet he wrote:** Craig Nelson, "Thomas Paine and the Making of *Common Sense,*" 236.

242 **"The cause of America":** Paine, *Common Sense,* Introduction.

242 **"I have heard it asserted":** Paine, *Common Sense,* 32.

243 **"Even brutes":** Paine, *Common Sense,* 34.

243 **"A government of our own":** Paine, *Common Sense,* 58.

243 **"Freedom hath been":** Paine, *Common Sense,* 60.

243 **"very unfortunate":** Yates, untitled history manuscript, in Yates Papers, NYPL, Box 3, p. 38; Bielinski File, NYSL.

243 **He acquiesced:** Abraham Yates to Philip Schuyler, August 4, 1775, in Yates Papers, NYPL; Bielinski File, NYSL.

244 **"handsomely and well made":** Washington, General Orders, March 11, 1776.

245 **"a blue coat with yellow buttons":** Chernow, 190.

245 **a plumed hat and a purple sash:** Longmore, 182.

245 **"ferry . . . mending carriage":** George Washington, Expenses of Journey to New York, April 4–13, 1776.

246  "What to do with the city": Charles Lee to George Washington, February 19, 1776.

246  He also had redoubts and barricades: Schecter, *Battle for New York*, 77–78.

246  a passably comfortable home: Flexner, *George Washington in the American Revolution*, 87.

246  "We all live here": Irving, *Life of George Washington*, 2:59.

247  "bitchfoxy jades": Gallagher, *Battle of Brooklyn, 1776*, 69.

247  "Eight Sail of Square wrigd Vessels": Benjamin Tupper to George Washington, June 4, 1776.

247  New York's provisional government, which continued to drag its feed: Force, 4:1095–1096.

247  He ordered a court-martial: Washington, Council of War, June 27, 1776.

248  "the unhappy fate of Thomas Hickey": George Washington, General Orders, June 28, 1776.

249  "persecuted on every side": Coghlan, 22.

250  On a Sunday. . . . six months pregnant: McGuire, *Stop the Revolution*, 80.

251  "we are fully Confirmed": William Livingston to George Washington, July 4, 1776.

251  "Your Excellency must be sensible": William Livingston to George Washington, July 4, 1776.


## Chapter 11: The City of New York Will, in All Human Probability, Very Soon Be the Scene of a Bloody Conflict

253  IN CONGRESS, July 4th, 1776: New York, *Journals of the Provincial Congress*, 516.

253  We, therefore, the representatives: New York, *Journals of the Provincial Congress*, 517.

254  "the worst event": George Washington to Burwell Bassett, February 28, 1776.

255  *Resolved unanimously*: New York, *Journals of the Provincial Congress*, 518.

255  "with beat of drum": New York, *Journals of the Provincial Congress*, 517.

255  "availing themselves of a brisk & favourable breeze": Washington to John Hancock, July 12, 1776.

256  "such unsoldierly Conduct": Washington, General Orders, July 13, 1776.

256 "Gentlemen, The passage": New York, *Journals of the Provincial Congress*, 523.

256 "the expenses of transporting a quantity of lead": New York, *Journals of the Provincial Congress*, 524.

257 "I have a letter": Brooks, *Henry Knox*, 58.

257 "Miss Margaret Moncrieffe": *Pennsylvania Gazette*, July 24, 1776.

258 "repeatedly, at the commencement of the war": Coghlan, 23.

258 Putnam had also heard: Israel Putnam to "Miss Montcriffe," July 26, 1776, Aaron Burr Papers, Missouri History Museum.

259 "any political difference alters him not": Israel Putnam to "Miss Montcriffe," July 26, 1776, Aaron Burr Papers, Missouri History Museum; Force, *American Archives: Fifth Series*, 1:471.

259 "ginrole": Coghlan, *Memoirs*, 35.

260 "more than a Mile in Length": Schecter, *The Battle for New York*, 111.

260 "Mrs. Putnam employed me": Coghlan, *Memoirs*, 27.

261 "those who had committed no Fault": *Washington Papers*. Memorandum of an Interview with Lieutenant Colonel James Paterson, July 20, 1776.

261 "was more polite than interesting": Davies, 12:177–179.

262 "Miss Moncrieffe, you don't drink your wine": Coghlan, *Memoirs*, 27.

263 "to him I plighted my virgin vow": Coghlan, *Memoirs*, 29–30.

263 "the woods affording": Coghlan, *Memoirs*, 31.

264 "a sweet girl": Coghlan, *Memoirs*, 34.

265 "The Army under my command": Washington to James Bowdoin, August 14, 1776.

265 "one of the finest": Schecter, *Battle for New York*, 127.

266 Hundreds of his men were killed: Ferling, *Ascent of George Washington*, 110.

267 "the city of New York": New York, *Journals of the Provincial Congress*, 578.

269 "The Convention will chearfully": To George Washington from Abraham Yates Jr., August 22, 1776, Founders Online.

270 "on all occasions avoid a general Action": George Washington to John Hancock, September 8, 1776.

270 Five British warships: Schecter, *Battle for New York*, 184.

270 "flying in every direction": George Washington to John Hancock, September 16, 1776.

271 One later declared his belief: George Greene, *The Life of Nathanael Greene*, 2:428–429.

271 **"various and perplexing"**: George Washington to Abraham Yates Jr., September 23, 1776.

271 **"I am bereft"**: George Washington to Lund Washington, September 30, 1776.

272 **One of his generals**: Schecter, *Battle for New York*, 130.

272 **"like a clover field"**: Schecter, *Battle for New York*, 183.

### Chapter 12: So Celestial an Article

273 **The surface of a lake . . . in the world**: Blanchard, "Who or What's a Witch?"; Druke, "The Concept of Personhood in Seventeenth and Eighteenth Century Iroquois Ethnopersonality"; Curtin, *Seneca Indian Myths*; Michael Galban, interview.

275 **In all, 1,700 Iroquois**: Philip Schuyler to George Washington, August 6, 1776.

276 **"haughty princes of the wilderness"**: Lossing, *Life and Times of Philip Schuyler*, 106.

276 **"The Consumption of provision"**: Abler, *Chainbreaker*, 40.

276 **"With this String"**: Lossing, 107–112.

276 **Cornplanter was . . . the Iroquois**: Michael Galban, interview.

278 **"employ" Indians in "making a Diversion"**: Valentine, *Lord George Germain*, 183–184.

278 **If Germain . . . Swan with Two Necks**: Stone, *Life of Joseph Brant*, 150–151.

279 **"We have crossed"**: Brodhead et al., 8:670–671.

279 **"the assistance of the Indians"**: Valentine, *Lord George Germain*, 187.

279 **"the securing of the affection"**: Brown, 60.

279 **"proper persons are employed to negotiate"**: Brown, 60.

280 **"I hope every precaution"**: *Stopford-Sackville*, II:40.

280 **"was ably planned"**: *Stopford-Sackville*, II:40.

282 **"The situation of our Affairs"**: George Washington to John Hancock, November 23, 1776.

282 **3,400 men**: Flexner, *George Washington in the American Revolution*, 160.

283 **"ingenious maneuver of Fort Washington"**: Charles Lee to Horatio Gates, December 13, 1776.

283 **"The Enemy"**: George Washington to Pennsylvania Council of Safety, December 22, 1776.

285  47 pounds 8 shillings: New York, *Journals of the Provincial Congress*,
      I:753–756. (Hereafter, *Journals of the Provincial Congress*.)

286  read aloud in session: *Journals of the Provincial Congress*, I:756.

286  "These are the times": Paine, *American Crisis*, No. 1, in Rhodehamel,
      *American Revolution*, 238.

286  ordered 1,000 copies: *Journals of the Provincial Congress*, I:756.

286  "it would be well": Bielinski, *Abraham Yates, Jr., and the New Political
      Order*, 28.

287  "such government as shall": Cumming, *Constitution of the State of New
      York*, 43.

288  "that too much would be taken": Yates, Rough Hewer, February 23, 1789,
      in Yates Papers, NYPL; Bielinski File, NYSL.

288  "the alarming situation": Yates, Rough Hewer, February 23, 1789.

290  "people being crowded": Cresswell, *Journal of Nicholas Cresswell*, 244.

290  "*Toujours de la gaieté!*": Burrows and Wallace, 247.

291  Elizabeth Loring . . . into his own account: Thomas Jones, *History of New
      York During the Revolutionary War*, I:1351.

292  one of Howe's first commands . . . eighteen plays that year: Oscar Barck,
      *New York City During the War for Independence*, 170–177.

292  her father signed on: Barck, 171.

292  In Britain . . . that social contract: Gundersen, "Independence, Citizen-
      ship, and the American Revolution," 60–63.

293  Coghlan's family . . . the slave trade: http://www.captaincooksociety.com/
      home/detail/john-coghlan-1754-1807.

294  family portraits: Fliegelman, *Prodigals and Pilgrims*, 10.

295  The *Pennsylvania Magazine*: Blakemore, *Literature, Intertextuality, and
      the American Revolution*, 15–16.

295  "You may depend": Colman, *Polly Honeycombe*, 32.

295  "wretched in mind": Coghlan, *Memoirs*, 40.

295  "My union with Mr. Coghlan": Coghlan, *Memoirs*, 41.


## Chapter 13: Cannons Muskets Drums


296  More consequential: Haddam Town Land Records, 10:148, 10:275.

298  For two years . . . grain, wood or meat: Haddam Town Land Records,
      2:126.

298 When he needed staples . . . scything hay: Blevins, 46.

298 he was ready: Haddam Town Land Records, 10:148, 10:275.

300 "With a view of quelling": *Stopford-Sackville*, II:60.

300 "to force his way to Albany": *Stopford-Sackville*, 2:60.

300 "your influence amongst them": *Stopford-Sackville*, 2:61.

301 "from your first entrance": Valentine, *Lord George Germain*, 191.

301 Several weeks later: Abler, *Chainbreaker*, 70–80.

302 The father, he said, "wants you all": The account of the Oswego council comes from Cornplanter's nephew, Governor Blacksnake. A Seneca named Benjamin Williams wrote it down in pidgin English. For clarity, I have, here and elsewhere, corrected syntax and spelling.

305 "a suit of clothes": Seaver, *Narrative of the Life of Mrs. Mary Jemison*, 66.

306 Ten o'clock in the morning: Stone, *Life of Joseph Brant*, 226–227.

307 When an advance party: We know they were Seneca because the Seneca chief Old Smoke led them. Abler, *Cornplanter*, 43.

307 "Gregg is perfectly in his senses": Stone, *Life of Joseph Brant*, 226.

307 2,000 men . . . the main body of soldiers: Stone, *Life of Joseph Brant*, 219.

307 The army arrived . . . fly in battle: https://www.nps.gov/fost/learn/history culture/flag-of-ftstanwix.htm#CP_JUMP_3680052.

308 "the Indians, who were at least one thousand": Stone, *Life of Joseph Brant*, 231.

308 At Fort Dayton . . . stark naked: Brodhead et al., *Documents Relating to the Colonial History of the State of New York*, 8:721.

308 Once Herkimer's men . . . became personal: Stone, *Life of Joseph Brant*, 238.

309 "the Indians and white men": Stone, *Life of Joseph Brant*, 243.

309 What would later be: Abler, *Cornplanter*, 44.

309 But the Iroquois lost: Brodhead et al., 8, 721; Abler, *Cornplanter*, 44.

309 While they were ambushing Herkimer's party: Brodhead et al., 8:721.

309 They normally traveled . . . gunshot wounds: Fenton, *Little Water Medicine Society of the Senecas*, 22.

310 "General Burgoyne is advanced": Philip Schuyler to George Washington, August 17, 1777.

310 "much at a loss": George Washington to Philip Schuyler, July 2, 1777.

311 "I am yet perplexed to find out": George Washington to John Armstrong, July 4, 1777.

311 "One Reason": George Washington to Philip Schuyler, July 2, 1777.

312 Washington had had . . . the American cause: Brandow, "Horatio Gates," 10.

312 "saying This Army": Horatio Gates to George Washington, May 13, 1777.

312 "I cannot help": George Washington to Horatio Gates, May 19, 1777.

313 "Genl Gates is here": John Hancock to George Washington, June 20, 1777.

313 "one bold stroke": George Washington, General Orders, September 5, 1777.

314 "Cannons Roaring muskets Cracking": Ferling, *Almost a Miracle*, 249.

314 "Sir, I am sorry to inform you": George Washington to John Hancock, September 11, 1777.

314 "I had an exalted opinion": Pickering, *Life of Thomas Pickering*, 2:84.

315 "Upon the whole": George Washington to John Hancock, October 5, 1777.

316 "the army, on the success": George Washington, General Orders, September 28, 1777.

316 "Burgoyne and his whole army": *Historical Magazine* IV:9.

317 "Look at the characters": Benjamin Rush to John Adams, October 21, 1777, *Papers of John Adams*, V.

317 "Our distress for want of Shoes": George Washington to John Hancock, October 10–11, 1777.

317 "I have been a slave": George Washington to Richard Henry Lee, October 16, 1777.

317 "I am Sir Yr Hble Servt.": George Washington to Horatio Gates, January 4, 1777.

319 "In France": *London Magazine, or, Gentleman's Monthly Intelligencer* 46 (September 1777): 471–472.

319 "The Howes are gone": Valentine, *Lord George Germain*, 238.

319 "The progress of General Burgoyne": Valentine, *Lord George Germain*, 239.

320 "intended for the recovery": Valentine, *Lord George Germain*, 214.

320 At the beginning of December . . . arms in America: Stopford-Sackville, II:78.

321 "General Burgoyne and his army": *Parliamentary History of England*, 19:533.

321 "was a most unfortunate affair": *Parliamentary History of England*, 19:534.

321 "shocked at the easy manner": *Parliamentary History of England*, 19:534–535.

322 "The Americans, it is evident": *Parliamentary History of England*, 19:535.

322 **"some time to calm"**: *Parliamentary History of England*, 19:538.

323 **"An army of 10,000 men"**: *Parliamentary History of England*, 19:540.

323 **"the supreme authority"**: *London Magazine, or, Gentleman's Monthly Intelligencer* 46 (September 1777): 593.

323 **"As to the noble lord"**: *Parliamentary History of England*, 19, 541.

324 **As December wore on . . . the American Secretary**: Brown, 140.

325 **"if my being permitted"**: Brown, 141.

325 **"a most favourable event"**: Brown, 146.

## Chapter 14: White Freedom

326 **John Coghlan left his wife**: Groves et al., *Historical Records of the 7th or Royal Regiment of Fusiliers*, 80.

327 **His career had begun**: *Morning Chronicle* (New York), May 4, 1807, 2.

327 **"wild & drinking"**: http://www.captaincooksociety.com/home/detail/john-coghlan-1754-1807.

328 **"behavior unbecoming"**: Washington, General Orders, February 8, 1778.

328 **"eight quarters of mutton"**: Washington, General Orders, February 8, 1778.

328 **Washington was staying . . . military procurement**: George Washington to John Banister, April 21, 1778.

329 **Five months earlier . . . general's son**: Lafayette to George Washington, October 14, 1777.

330 **Despite his precious upbringing**: Lafayette to George Washington, November 26, 1777.

331 **He chose a location . . . 36 feet by 20**: Per email correspondence with Lucianne Lavin, and based on Lucianne Lavin and Marc Banks. "Final Report Phase 1 and Phase 2 Archaeological Investigations of the Connecticut Yankee Atomic Power Company Property in Haddam Neck The 2005-2006 Field Seasons and an Overview of the Entire 7-Year Archaeological Study, volumes 1–3." Haddam Neck, August 2007.

331 **There were no crucifixes . . . good fortune**: Lucianne Lavin, "Venture Smith Homestead," 20.

331 **As soon as he had bought . . . bought him out**: Haddam Town Land Records, 10:191; Blevins, 48; Karl Stofko, unpublished "Notes on Knowlton Family of East Haddam and East Hampton."

332  Whacket bought Base: Karl Stofko, "Whacket Freeman" and "Peter Freeman," unpublished talks presented on Venture Smith Day, East Haddam, Connecticut, September 2, 2004.

332  Two months later . . . moved in: Haddam Town Land Records, 10:201.

332  As an indication of Smith's role: Dexter, *Biographical Sketches of the Graduates of Yale College,* 2:619.

333  In December of the same year . . . Smith's property: Blevins, 53; Stofko, Karl, "Sawney Anderson."

333  The black population: Blevins, 54.

333  Physically too he was a presence: Venture Smith, *A Narrative of the Life and Adventures of Venture,* Revised and Republished with Traditions, by H. M. Selden, 32.

333  he had to turn sideways: Smith, *Narrative,* Revised, 34.

333  On visiting an acquaintance: Smith, *Narrative,* Revised, 35.

333  Abraham Yates was feeling lost . . . Alexander Hamilton: Abraham Yates to ———, Yates Correspondence, September 7, 1777, in Yates Papers, NYPL; Bielinski File, NYSL.

334  "your Maps and Globes": Matthew Visscher to Abraham Yates, Yates Correspondence, August 15, 1777.

335  "Ab. Yates . . . late Cobler of Laws": Philip Schuyler to Gouverneur Morris, February 3, 1778, Gouverneur Morris Papers.

336  "elevating Yates will forward": Bielinski, "Abraham Yates Jr. and the New Political Order," 38.

336  The Atlantic crossing . . . her fate: Coghlan, *Memoirs,* 44.

337  forced to intervene: Coghlan, *Memoirs,* 44.

337  "leaving me": Coghlan, *Memoirs,* 45.

337  "his design": Coghlan, *Memoirs,* 46.

338  "turned MY BACK ON LIBERTY!": Coghlan, *Memoirs,* 33.

339  "must entirely overturn": Wharton, *The Revolutionary Diplomatic Correspondence of the U.S.,* I:347.

340  "I expected cooperation": Valentine, *Lord George Germain,* 295–297.

340  "who were obliged": Valentine, *Lord George Germain,* 329.

340  "scolded like two oysterwomen": Toynbee, *The Letters of Horace Walpole,* X, 254.

340  "the most decisive censure": *Parliamentary History of England,* XIX:1200.

341  "the honours and emoluments": Adolphus, *History of England,* 2:560.

341  "our Fleet and Army": Brown, 163.

342　He convinced . . . give up the fight: *Stopford-Sackville*, II:94–99.

342　"the generality of the people": *Stopford-Sackville*, II:95.

342　"use your own discretion": *Stopford-Sackville*, II:99.

342　"to bring Mr. Washington": *Stopford-Sackville*, II:96.

343　"It having pleased": *Washington Papers*, General Orders, May 5, 1778.

343　"Upon a signal given": *Washington Papers*, General Orders, May 5, 1778.

344　"the ancient fabled God of War": Kapp, *Life of Frederick William Von Steuben*, 637.

345　Washington spurred . . . steep defile: George Washington to Henry Laurens, June 28, 1778.

345　"What is the meaning of this": Flexner, *George Washington in the American Revolution*, 305.

345　"Burgoyning Clinton": Anthony Wayne to George Washington, June 18, 1778.

345　"seemed to vie with each other": George Washington to Henry Laurens, July 1, 1778.

346　Three days later . . . eastern Pennsylvania: Richard Cartwright, *The Life and Letters of the Late Hon. Richard Cartwright*, 29–31.

346　Cornplanter had an idea . . . their preparations: Betts, *The Hatchet and the Plow*, 69.

347　Americans in the region. . . . armed combatants: Abler, *Cornplanter*, 46.

347　"the Barbarians from Deluging": *Pennsylvania Archives*, VII: 3.

347　"a very important Indian Chief": *Pennsylvania Archives*, VII: 5.

348　He led more than 300 Senecas . . . for supplies: Abler, *Chainbreaker*, 103–105; Betts, 77–80.

349　"they plundered": Seaver, 131.

350　"reconcile our spirited Assertions": David Wallace, *The Life of Henry Laurens*, 475.

350　"The policy of our arming Slaves": George Washington to Henry Laurens, March 20, 1779.

351　"it would be a matter": George Washington to Lund Washington, February 24–26, 1779.

351　Slaves there were so numerous . . . attempted an uprising: O'Shaughnessy, *An Empire Divided*, 151–154.

352　the Jamaican slaves: Sheridan, "The Jamaican Slave Insurrection Scare," 290–308.

353　"Destroyed the Settlement": Edward Hand to George Washington, November 18, 1778.

353 "**perfectly convinced**": George Washington to Henry Laurens, November 16, 1778.

353 "**The expedition you are appointed to command**": George Washington to John Sullivan, May 31, 1779.

354 "**into the heart of the Indian settlements**": George Washington to John Sullivan, May 31, 1779.


**Chapter 15: I Am Your Son! I Am a Warrior!**


355 **Earlier they had been secretive . . . herds of deer**: Cook, *Journals of the Military Expedition of Major General John Sullivan*, 5–7.

357 "**Corn, Beans, peas**": Cook, 90.

357 **The American army overwhelmed . . . in their houses**: Cook, 13.

357 **They skinned**: Cook, 244.

358 "**rough and somewhat abrupt**": Worth, *Random Recollections of Albany*, 23.

359 "**the printer be under an Oath**": Lynd, "Abraham Yates's History of the Movement for the United States Constitution." 234.

359 **He had concluded . . . a mere $4.8 million**: Schoderbek, "Robert Morris and Reporting for the Treasury," 3.

360 **In January 1780**: Lynd, 234–235.

360 "**the Center of Intrigue**": Lynd, 241.

361 **In February 1779, mobs formed . . . in their beds**: Valentine, *Lord George Germain*, 401.

361 "**the several keepers of buck-hounds**": Burke, *Plan for the Better Security of the Independence of Parliament*, 69.

362 "**the present Consitution**": Knight, 227.

362 **Soldiers marched . . . doors and windows**: Knight, 231; Valentine, *Lord George Germain*, 399.

362 "**To say Truth**": Valentine, *Lord George Germain*, 364.

362 "**I am convinced**": *Stopford-Sackville*, II:192.

362 "**Believe me, my dear Lord**": *Stopford-Sackville*, II:192.

363 "**Be assured, my Lord**": *Stopford-Sackville*, II:193.

363 "**Washington,**" **he wrote Germain**: *Stopford-Sackville*, II:194.

364 "**the Trees and Earth**": Washington, weather diary, March–May 1780.

364 "**a country overflowing**": Flexner, *George Washington in the American Revolution*, 355.

365 Washington, meanwhile . . . young officers: Chernow, 364.

365 "[W]hat were our feelings": Seaver, 74.

365 "When the snow": Seaver, 75.

366 "inconsiderable people": Graymont, 227.

366 "four disaffected Indians": O'Callaghan, VIII:797.

367 They burned their villages: Graymont, *The Iroquois in the American Revolution*, 235.

368 "You are now my prisoner": Graymont, 235.

369 "If now you choose": Seaver, 78.

369 "as a compliment": Abler, *Cornplanter*, 54.

## Chapter 16: Numberless Meteors Gleaming Through the Atmosphere

370 "I fled from my tormentor": Coghlan, *Memoirs*, 47.

372 "melancholy habits": Coghlan, *Memoirs*, 54.

373 "unjust and unprovoked": Hume and Smollett, 6:186.

373 "the actual dishonour": Coghlan, *Memoirs*, 57.

375 "The war of the Americans": Fox, *Speeches of the Right Honourable Charles James Fox*, 31.

375 "a coward": Toynbee, 11:309.

376 "The giddiness of extreme youth": Coghlan, *Memoirs*, 59.

376 "pressed so closely": Chernow, 378.

377 "Arnold has betrayed us!": Flexner, *George Washington in the American Revolution*, 386.

377 "a title": Brookhiser, *Founding Father*, 37.

378 "for three years past": Alexander Hamilton to Philip Schuyler, February 18, 1781. "From Alexander Hamilton to Philip Schuyler, 18 February 1781," *Founders Online*, National Archives, last modified March 30, 2017, http://founders.archives.gov/documents/Hamilton/01-02-02-1089.

379 "I must tell you, sir": Alexander Hamilton to Philip Schuyler, February 18, 1781. "From Alexander Hamilton to Philip Schuyler, 18 February 1781," *Founders Online*, National Archives, last modified March 30, 2017, http://founders.archives.gov/documents/Hamilton/01-02-02-1089.

379 "I request, in pointed terms": George Washington to Benjamin Harrison Sr., March 21, 1781.

380 On January 29: Johnston, *Record of Connecticut Men in the Military and*

*Naval Service During the War of Revolution*, 363, http://historicbuildingsct
.com/?p=8282.

380 Of the 330 men: Barnes, 44.

381 Cuff Smith . . . something to happen: Johnston, *Record of Connecticut Men*,
302.

381 "calm . . . calculated . . . admirable": Flexner, *George Washington in the
American Revolution*, 435.

382 "soldiers composed of men": Flexner, *George Washington in the American
Revolution*, 434–435.

382 In Haddam, meanwhile. . . . on Fishers Island: Grace Denison Wheeler,
*Homes of Our Ancestors in Stonington, Conn.*, 67.

383 he did a bit of business: Haddam Town Land Records, X:297, 334.

383 "To all People": Haddam Town Land Records, X:297, 334.

383 The decision to focus. . . . mounted from there: Valentine, *Lord George
Germain*, 418.

384 "My situation here is very distressing": Valentine, *Lord George Germain*, 417.

385 "considerable part of our force": *Stopford-Sackville*, 212.

385 "to discover Mr. Washington's true design": *Stopford-Sackville*, 212.

385 "I begin, at this Epoch": Washington, *Diaries*, May 1781.

386 "unaffected cheerfulness": Flexner, *George Washington and the American
Revolution*, 435.

386 On August 14 . . . for the Chesapeake: Washington, *Diaries*, August 14,
1781.

387 "the feeble compliance": Washington, *Diaries*, August 14, 1781.

387 "with 28 Sail": Washington, *Diaries*, September 5, 1781.

388 "I have never seen": Flexner, *George Washington in the American Revolution*, 443.

389 "small and fat": Chernow, 410.

389 "settled most points": Flexner, *George Washington in the American Revolution*, 452.

389 "reducible to calculation": George Washington to Francois-Joseph de
Grasse, September 25, 1781.

391 Sir, I propose a cessation: Cornwallis, *Correspondence of Charles, First
Marquis of Cornwallis*, 1:523.

391 "an ardent desire": Cornwallis, 1:524.

391 "ten thousand stars": Scheer and Rankin, 491.

## Chapter 17: The Cause of Humanity

395 "a daring and outrageous": *London Gazette*, November 24, 1781.

395 "of Lord Cornwallis": Walpole, *Last Journals*, 2:378.

395 "like a ball": Valentine, *Lord George Germain*, 439; Lecky, *A History of England in the Eighteenth Century*, 5:122.

396 "obstinately, fatally pursued": *Parliamentary History of England*, 22:802.

396 "ceased to be formidable": *Parliamentary History of England*, 22:804.

396 "Peace with America": Valentine, *Lord George Germain*, 447.

397 "above all I must": Valentine, *Lord George Germain*, 445.

397 "If you consider": *Stopford-Sackville*, 2:216–220.

398 "Am I out?": Valentine, *Lord George Germain*, 452.

398 "to dispose of me": Valentine, *Lord George Germain*, 454.

399 "a person who in his military character": *Parliamentary History of England*, 22:999–1006.

399 "the capture of York Town": *Parliamentary History of England*, 22:1020.

399 "the author of all": *Parliamentary History of England*, 22:1001.

399 "a servant who shewed": *Parliamentary History of England*, 22:1013.

400 "I have no hope": Anderson, *Forgotten Patriot*, 339.

400 "guide the torrent": Hamilton, *Papers of Alexander Hamilton*, 254–255. "To George Washington from Alexander Hamilton, 13 February 1783," *Founders Online*, National Archives, last modified March 30, 2017, http://founders.archives.gov/documents/Washington/99-01-02-10638.

401 "end in blood": Hamilton, *Papers of Alexander Hamilton*, 278. "To Alexander Hamilton from George Washington, 4 March 1783," *Founders Online*, National Archives, last modified March 30, 2017, http://founders.archives.gov/documents/Hamilton/01-03-02-0171.

401 "pass the remainder": George Washington, Circular Letter of Farewell to the Army, June 8, 1783.

401 "shewn to all, but to military": Lewis Nicola to George Washington, May 22, 1782.

401 "Sir, With a mixture": George Washington to Colonel Lewis Nicola, May 22, 1782.

402 "to the army": Washington, Circular to the States, June 3, 1783.

403 "a heart full of love": Flexner, *George Washington in the American Revolution*, 524.

404 Ke-koi-no-us: Abler, *Cornplanter*, 202.

404 **Burnt House:** Abler, *Cornplanter*, 57.

404 **moved yet again:** Abler, *Chainbreaker*, 203.

405 **"shameful and unpardonable":** Graymont, 261.

405 **"were not abandoned":** *Parliamentary History of England*, 23:410.

406 **In September 1783 . . . their options:** Abler, *Cornplanter*, 61.

406 **"ill winds blow":** Abler, *Cornplanter*, 64.

406 **"The American cause":** Neville Craig, ed., *Olden Time*, 2:428–429.

407 **his infant child:** Abler, *Cornplanter*, 65–66.

408 **"all men are created equal":** Menschel, "Abolition Without Deliverance," 189.

409 **"I never could":** Smith, *Narrative*, 30.

409 **Shortly after:** Brainerd, Court Papers of Ezra Brainerd, 1784 to 1798, Thankful Arnold House, Haddam, Connecticut.

410 **"assaulted, beat, wounded":** Brainerd, Court Papers of Ezra Brainerd, 1784 to 1798.

412 **And so they set out . . . in society:** Elizabeth Gooch, *Life of Mrs. Gooch*, 136.

413 **"I know as well":** Flanders, H., ed. *Memoirs of Richard Cumberland*, 276.

414 **"Well done, Harry!":** Flanders, *Memoirs of Richard Cumberland*, 274.

414 **his baker's surname:** Flanders, *Memoirs of Richard Cumberland*, 323.

414 **Very occasionally . . . hacked down:** Toynbee, VII:250.

415 **"I have done":** Cumberland, *Memoirs*, 279.

## Chapter 18: Rough Hewer

416 **"I am reather Suspitious":** Abraham Yates to David Howell, August 29, 1785, in Yates Papers, NYPL, Reel 1, Piece 168; Bielinski File, NYSL.

417 **"a man whose ignorance":** Alexander Hamilton to Robert Morris, August 13, 1782. "From Alexander Hamilton to Robert Morris, 13 August 1782," *Founders Online*, National Archives, last modified March 30, 2017, http://founders.archives.gov/documents/Hamilton/01-03-02-0057-0001.

417 **"an office as it were":** Abraham Yates to James Duane, September 7, 1782, in Yates Papers, NYPL; Bielinski File, NYSL.

419 **"the Yates' and their Associates":** Alexander Hamilton to Robert Livingston, April 25, 1785. "From Alexander Hamilton to Robert Livingston, [25 April 1785]," *Founders Online*, National Archives, last modified March 30, 2017, http://founders.archives.gov/documents/Hamilton/01-03-02-0428.

419 "The blunt *Rough Hewer*": Gilje and Pencak, *New York in the Age of the Constitution*, 154.

420 "a Suspitious Man": Abraham Yates to Jeremiah van Rensselaer and Henry Acthandt, August 29, 1787, in Yates Papers, NYPL; Bielinski File, NYSL.

420 presented a skin: Abler, *Chainbreaker*, 169–170.

421 "The offer that was made": Abler, *Chainbreaker*, 170.

421 along the shore of Lake Erie: Abler, Thomas, *Chainbreaker*, 170–171.

421 in front of the town courthouse: *Pennsylvania Gazette*, April 12, 1786.

422 "Captain O'Bail": *Pennsylvania Gazette*, April 12, 1786.

423 About 30 miles: Abler, *Chainbreaker*, 173–174.

423 It must have been utterly bewildering: Walsh, 83–84.

424 "Brothers," he began: *New York Daily Advertiser*, April 25, 1786.

426 The goodwill extended: Merle Deardorff, "The Cornplanter Grant," 9.

426 "QUEENS-WARE quart MUGS": *New York Daily Advertiser*, April 27, 1786, 1.

427 "the King of England": *Journals of the Continental Congress*, May 5, 1786.

428 Cornplanter and his men: Overton, "Commentary on Deardorff's Notes Concerning Bartoli's Portrait of Cornplanter."

428 "At length my Dear Marquis": George Washington to Lafayette, February 1, 1784.

429 "Our sincere Congratulations": The Citizens of Fredericksburg to George Washington, February 14, 1784.

429 "my grammatical publications": Noah Webster to George Washington, July 18, 1785.

429 "in the prosecution": George Washington to Noah Webster, April 17, 1786.

430 "I would never have drawn my sword": Lafayette to George Washington, July 14, 1785.

430 "there is not a man living": George Washington to Robert Morris, April 12, 1786.

430 "a federal spirit": James Madison to George Washington, November 1, 1786.

431 "some outlines": James Madison to George Washington, April 16, 1787.

432 Abraham Yates stepped . . . boarding here: Abraham G. Lansing to Abraham Yates Jr., April 8 1787. Yates Papers, NYPL, Reel 1, Piece 183; Bielinski File, New York State Library (hereafter, NYSL).

432 "remedy defects of the federal government": George Washington to James Madison, November 5, 1786.

433 **"an elective despotism":** Richard Henry Lee to John Lamb, June 27, 1788, John Lamb Papers, New-York Historical Society.

434 **He and Anna now had:** Baptismal Records, Reformed Dutch Church of Albany.

434 **"a small Cake":** Abraham G. Lansing to Abraham Yates Jr., April 8 1787, in Yates Papers, NYPL, Reel 1, Piece 183; Bielinski File, NYSL.

434 **"my forbodings":** Robert Yates to Abraham Yates Jr., June 1, 1787, in Yates Papers, NYPL, Reel 1, Piece 184; Bielinski File, NYSL.

435 **"thanked the Convention":** James Madison, *Debates in the Several State Conventions*, 5:124.

435 **"The United States of America":** Madison, *Debates*, 5:126–129.

437 **Washington dined:** Washington, *Diaries*, July 2, 1787.

437 **He went fishing:** Washington, *Diaries*, July 1787.

438 **"I am more and more convinced":** Alexander Hamilton to George Washington, July 3, 1787, *Washington Papers*.

438 **"The Men who oppose":** George Washington to Alexander Hamilton, July 10, 1787, *Washington Papers*.

439 **"Met in Convention":** Washington, *Diaries*, September 17, 1787.


### Chapter 19: Glowing with Zeal for the General Happiness and Improvement of Mankind

440 **A man might come . . . paired off:** *Gentleman's Magazine*, February 1770, 98.

441 **Women in England. . . . influence policy:** Chalus, "Elite Women, Social Politics, and the Political World of Late Eighteenth-Century Women," 680.

442 **"my native country":** Coghlan, *Memoirs*, 62.

442 **"all the comforts and delights":** Coghlan, *Memoirs*, 62.

443 **"every virtue":** Coghlan, *Memoirs*, 64.

444 **"While with Mr. Giffard":** Coghlan, *Memoirs*, 66.

445 **a housemaid could expect:** https://www.oldbaileyonline.org/static/Coinage.jsp#costofliving.

446 **"In Cavendish-street":** *Daily Universal Register*, June 4, 1787.

446 **Mr. Vaughan was considerably shaken:** Coghlan, *Memoirs*, 67–68.

446 **That, anyway, was what:** The few historians who have charted Margaret Coghlan's life all assumed that the obituaries of June 1787 were correct, and

that the portion of her life after that period that is documented in her autobiography was manufactured by someone else. My determination that she
faked her death to escape her creditors is based on the letters of hers I have
found that date after this period, on the passage in her memoir in which she
details her flight to Paris, and on the simple fact that her life continues, and
continues to be documented by multiple sources, well beyond 1787.

447 **"that you was defunct"**: Melancton Smith to Abraham Yates, January 23,
1788, in Yates Papers, NYPL, Reel 1, Piece 192; Bielinski File, NYSL.

447 **"the better sort"**: Melancton Smith to Abraham Yates, January 28, 1788, in
Yates Papers, NYPL, Reel 1, Piece 193; Bielinski File, NYSL.

448 **"still well"**: Melancton Smith to Abraham Yates, March 2, 1788, Yates
Papers, NYPL, Reel 1, Piece 197; Bielinski File, NYSL.

448 **"I have the satisfaction to inform you"**: Melancton Smith to Abraham
Yates, March 12, 1788, in Yates Papers, NYPL, Reel 1, Piece 198; Bielinski
File, NYSL.

448 **"With Civility"**: Abraham Yates to Abraham Lansing, May 28, 1788, in
Yates Papers, NYPL, Reel 1, Piece 202; Bielinski File, NYSL.

449 **"An Absurdity"**: Abraham Yates to Abraham Lansing, May 28, 1788, in
Yates Papers, NYPL, Reel 1, Piece 202; Bielinski File, NYSL.

449 **"the friends of the rights"**: Narrett, "A Zeal for Liberty," 296.

450 **"our Friends"**: Abraham Lansing to Abraham Yates, August 3, 1788, in
Yates Papers, NYPL, Reel 1, Piece 223; Bielinski File, NYSL.

451 **"remain quiet at Home"**: Abraham Lansing to Abraham Yates, August 3,
1788, in Yates Papers, NYPL, Reel 1, Piece 223; Bielinski File, NYSL.

452 **"the Lord of the Manor"**: Abraham Lansing to Abraham Yates, August 3,
1788, in Yates Papers, NYPL, Reel 1, Piece 223; Bielinski File, NYSL.

452 **Five days later. . . . had written**: Yates Papers, NYPL, Reel 1, Piece 224;
Bielinski File, NYSL; Hamilton, *Papers,* Certificate by Ezra L'Homme-
dieu, Egbert Benson, and Alexander Hamilton of a Statement by Abraham
Yates, Junior, Respecting His Vote on the Constitution of the United States,
August 8, 1788.

452 **"Being Confident"**: Yates Papers, NYPL, Reel 1, Piece 224; Bielinski
File, NYSL.

453 **George Washington stood**: George Washington to Richard Peters, September 7, 1788.

454 **"by giving their votes"**: George Washington to Alexander Hamilton, October 3, 1788, *Washington Papers.*

454 "on your acceptance": Alexander Hamilton to George Washington, September 1788. *Washington Papers.*

454 "in the Name of America": Lafayette to George Washington, January 1, 1788.

455 "your Excellency has every vote": Henry Knox to George Washington, February 16, 1789.

455 "a mind oppressed": Washington, *Diaries*, April 16, 1789.

455 "descending the hill": George Washington to Lafayette, December 8, 1784.

456 "serve to establish a Precedent": George Washington to James Madison, May 5, 1789.

456 "The President of the United States": George Washington to John Adams, May 10, 1789.

457 London was larger ... accounted for: Garrioch, *The Making of Revolutionary Paris*, 237–238.

457 She knew the city ... to Parliament: Coghlan, 70; Young, *Revolutionary Ladies*, 165.

458 "made me acquainted": Coghlan, *Memoirs*, 70.

458 "the greatest splendour": Coghlan, *Memoirs*, 73.

459 The king ordered ... royal person: Luckett, "Hunting for Spies and Whores," 122–124.

460 "played on the dinner table": Chernow, 581.

461 "The revolution": George Washington to Lafayette, October 14, 1789.

461 "Every thing that was": Lafayette to George Washington, January 12, 1790.

462 "the revolution is of too great magnitude": George Washington to Gouverneur Morris, October 13, 1789.

463 stood outside the door: Most historians seem to have assumed that Cornplanter and Washington did not meet face to face in 1790 but merely exchanged written declarations. But Cornplanter's nephew, late in life, recounted details of the series of meetings (Abler, *Chainbreaker*, 176–80). The fact that he is mistaken in some details, such as dates, is no reason to discount his assertion of the events he took part in.

464 Tadadaho: I am indebted to Michael Galban of Ganondagan State Historic Site for this insight.

464 flanked by three soldiers: Abler, *Chainbreaker*, 176.

464 "the voice of the Seneca nation": To George Washington from the Seneca Chiefs, December 1, 1790.

466 He promised to reply: Abler, *Chainbreaker*, 177.

466  "never consent": From George Washington to the Seneca Chiefs, December 29, 1790.

466  to personally walk the Senecas: Abler, *Chainbreaker*, 192.

466  "Red Jacket was next to Washington": Abler, *Chainbreaker*, 192.

466  Meanwhile, the State of Pennsylvania . . . new settlement: Abler, *Cornplanter*, 83.

467  Senecas were attacked: Abler, *Cornplanter*, 83–84.

467  "I ever have grasped": Coghlan, *Memoirs*, 122.

467  "Beware, then, ye lovely victims": Coghlan, *Memoirs*, 100.

469  "If woman is made to please": Rousseau, *Émile*, 358.

469  an "enlightened nation": Wollstonecraft, *A Vindication of the Rights of Woman*, 250.

470  a man named Pigott: Sarah Knott, "Female Liberty," 5.

470  had given him a new career: Knott, 12–14.

471  "an aera replete": Coghlan, *Memoirs*, 84–85.

472  He took to the task . . . paving the streets: Street paving and other details, Munsell, *Annals of Albany*, III:147–157.

472  In August: Munsell, *Annals of Albany*, III:158.

473  he was furious: Alexander Hamilton to Abraham Yates Jr., September 26, 1793, "From Alexander Hamilton to Abraham Yates, Junior, 26 September 1793," *Founders Online*, National Archives, last modified March 30, 2017, http://founders.archives.gov/documents/Hamilton/01-15-02-0268.

473  people threw rocks: Chernow, 731.

474  The danger: "Sidney," December 18, 1795, Yates Papers, NYPL (Bielinski File, NYSL); Wolf, chap. 7, 41.

474  he began writing: Yates, untitled history document, Yates Papers, NYPL, Box 3, typescript, p. 32; Bielinski File, NYSL.

475  "Beneath lies Abraham Yates Jun.": *Albany Gazette*, July 8, 1796.

## Chapter 20: Which Nothing Else Can Equal

477  "ignorant of war": Tagg, "Benjamin Franklin Bache's Attack on George Washington," 226.

477  highly critical book: James Monroe, *A View of the Conduct of the Executive in the Foreign Affairs of the United States*.

477  "has no friendships": Thomas Paine, *Political Writings*, 2:10.

478  "the great champion": Riley, *Slavery and the Democratic Conscience,* 55.

478  "the danger of Parties" . . . "ruins of Public Liberty": Washington, Farewell Address, 1796.

479  There were five churches: David Field, *A History of the Towns of Haddam and East-Haddam*, 25–38.

479  many owners had preferred: Witzig, "Beyond Expectation," 288.

480  had come back to Haddam: Barnes, "Venture Smith's Family," 48.

480  Cuff was convicted: Brainerd, Court Papers, January 9, 1795.

480  "Cuff Negro": Karl Stofko, "A Story About Cuff," September 26, 2009.

480  "to be whipped": Brainerd, Court Papers, January 9, 1795.

480  Slave Code: Menschel, 213.

481  in 1798, he learned: Blevins, 74–80.

481  For 200 pounds: Haddam Town Land Records, 13:48.

481  He signed an agreement: Haddam Town Land Records, 13:252, 13:246.

481  sturdy log house: Abler, *Cornplanter*, 135–136.

482  a new council with the Americans: Campisi and Starna, "On the Road to Canandaigua," 480.

482  The man he sent . . . his demands: Campisi and Starna, "On the Road to Canandaigua," 483.

483  Washington had that very day: Washington, Veto Message, February 28, 1797.

483  "Father," Cornplanter began: J. H. Newton, *History of Venango County*, 89–90.

485  gave him his sword: Abler, *Cornplanter*, 181.

485  "the licentiousness of elevated life": *British Critic*, 1794, 346.

485  "The publication of Mrs. Coghlan's Memoirs": *The Times*, February 10, 1794.

486  "who has long been known": *British Critic*, 1794, 346.

486  "the absurd practice": Coghlan, *Memoirs*, Preface.

487  "None of which events": George Washington to Sally Fairfax, May 16, 1798.

488  "Such a Pen": George Washington to James Anderson, December 13, 1799.

489  At two in the morning: Tobias Lear, "14 December 1799." Founders Online, National Archives.

489  "I feel myself going": Lear, "14 December 1799."

489  "circulate political intelligence": *New London Bee*, June 14, 1797.

490  At the same time: "Books for Sale at C. Holt's Printing-Office," *New London Bee*, August 23, 1797.

491  took down his words: Lovejoy, Paul, "The African Background of Venture Smith," in *Venture Smith and the Business of Slavery and Freedom*, 39.

492	"Captain Hart was a *white gentleman*": Smith, *Narrative*, 30.

492	"a temperate, honest and industrious man": Smith, *Narrative*, 32.

492	"Just published, and for sale": *New London Bee*, December 26, 1798.

493	"The editor of this paper": *New London Bee*, June 6, 1798.

493	"directly contravening": Pasley, *Tyranny of Printers*, 136.

493	he was imprisoned: Pasley, 140.

494	"Whereas Venture Smith": Blevins, 80.

494	Meg died: Blevins, 81.

494	"the wife of my youth": Smith, *Narrative*, 31.

496	"Sir // With the greatest submission": Margaret Moncrieffe Coghlan to Robert L. Livingston, December 28, 1803, New-York Historical Society.

497	"To the Kings": Coghlan, "Petition of Margaret Coghlan, Daughter of Major Thomas Moncrieffe," January 11, 1805.

498	"in the most abject state": *Universal Magazine* 7 (January–June 1807): 275.

499	the first sawmill: Rothenberg, "Friends Like These," 154.

499	boards to Pittsburgh: Sipe, *Indian Chiefs of Pennsylvania*, 467.

500	hadn't brought the equipment: Rothenberg, "Friends Like These," 163.

500	The cultures, however: Swatzler, 160–161.

500	was feared dead: Abler, *Cornplanter*, 142–143.

501	journey to Fort Plain: Whittemore, *The Abeel and Allied Families*, 9.

501	served as a major: Abler, *Cornplanter*, 168.

502	"towards the setting sun": Abler, *Cornplanter*, 174.

502	A former New York congressman: Hauptman, *Conspiracy of Interests*, 187–189.

502	a dream, a vision: There are several accounts of Cornplanter's dream and its aftermath, all of them second- or thirdhand. I have relied on Timothy Alden, *An Account of Sundry Missions*, 142–144; Morgan, *League of the Ho-de-no-sau-nee*, 205–206; and Betts, *The Hatchet and the Plow*, 335–343.

503	how Sky Woman had fallen: Timothy Alden, *An Account of Sundry Missions*, 143.

## Epilogue

507	Venture's great-grandson: Barnes, "Venture Smith's Family," 62.

507	Nelson's son George: Barnes, 70.

# BIBLIOGRAPHY

## Cornplanter

Abler, Thomas S. "Beavers and Muskets: Iroquois Military Fortunes in the Face of European Colonization." In *War in the Tribal Zone: Expanding States and Indigenous Warfare*. Santa Fe, NM: School of American Research, 2000.

———. *Chainbreaker: The Revolutionary War Memoirs of Governor Blacksnake*. Lincoln: University of Nebraska, 1989.

———. *Cornplanter: Chief Warrior of the Allegany Senecas*. Syracuse, NY: Syracuse University Press, 2007.

———. "Governor Blacksnake as a Young Man? Speculation on the Identity of Trumbull's 'The Young Sachem.'" *Ethnohistory* 34, no. 4 (Autumn 1987): 329–351.

Beauchamp, William. "Aboriginal Place Names of New York." New York State Museum, Bulletin 108. Albany, 1907.

Betts, William, Jr. *The Hatchet and the Plow: The Life and Times of Chief Cornplanter*. Bloomington, IN: iUniverse, 2010.

Blanchard, David, "Who or What's a Witch? Iroquois Persons of Power," *American Indian Quarterly* 6, no. 3/4 (Autumn–Winter 1982): 218–237.

Bouquet, Henry. *The Papers of Col. Henry Bouquet*. Series 21655. Harrisburg: Pennsylvania Department of Public Instruction, 1943.

Campisi, Jack, and William Starna. "On the Road to Canandaigua: The Treaty of 1794." *American Indian Quarterly* 19, no. 4 (Autumn 1995): 467–490.

Cave, Alfred. "The Delaware Prophet Neolin: A Reappraisal." *Ethnohistory* 46, no. 2 (Spring 1999): 265–290.

Cook, Frederick, et al. *Journals of the Military Expedition of Major General John Sullivan Against the Six Nations of Indians in 1779; with Records of Centennial Celebrations; Prepared Pursuant to Chapter 361, Laws of the State of New York, of 1885*. New York, 1887.

Craig, Neville. *The Olden Time.* 2 vols. Cincinnati, 1876.

Curtin, Jeremiah. *Seneca Indian Myths.* New York: Dutton, 1922.

Densmore, Christopher. *Red Jacket: Iroquois Diplomat and Orator.* Syracuse, NY: Syracuse University Press, 1999.

Dowd, Gregory. *War Under Heaven: Pontiac, the Indian Nations, and the British Empire.* Baltimore: Johns Hopkins University Press, 2002.

Druke, Mary. "The Concept of Personhood in Seventeenth and Eighteenth Century Iroquois Ethnopersonality." In Nancy Bonvillain, ed., *Studies in Iroquoian Culture.* Rindge, NH: Franklin Pierce College, 1980.

Engelbrecht, William. "Factors Maintaining Low Population Density Among the Prehistoric New York Iroquois." *American Antiquity* 52, no. 1 (January 1987): 13–27.

Fenn, Elizabeth. "Biological Warfare in Eighteenth-Century North America: Beyond Jeffery Amherst." *Journal of American History* 86, no. 4 (March 2000): 1552–1580.

Fenton, William. *The Great Law and the Longhouse: A Political History of the Iroquois Confederacy.* Norman: University of Oklahoma Press, 1998.

———. *The Little Water Medicine Society of the Senecas.* Norman: University of Oklahoma Press, 2002.

———. "This Island, the World on the Turtle's Back." *Journal of American Folklore* 75, no. 298 (October–December 1962): 283–300.

Follett, H. C. "Indian Villages of the Genesee Valley, New York." *Archaeological Bulletin* 4, no. 1 (January–February 1913): 11–13.

Godcharles, Frederic. *History of Fort Freeland.* Williamsport, PA: Lycoming Historical Society, 1922.

Graymont, Barbara. *The Iroquois in the American Revolution.* Syracuse, NY: Syracuse University Press, 1972.

Grimes, Richard. "We 'Now Have Taken up the Hatchet Against Them': Braddock's Defeat and the Martial Liberation of the Western Delawares." *Pennsylvania Magazine of History and Biography* 137, no. 3 (July 2013): 227–259.

Hauptman, Laurence. *Conspiracy of Interests: Iroquois Dispossession and the Rise of New York State.* Syracuse, NY: Syracuse University Press, 1999.

———. "On and Off State Time: William N. Fenton and the Seneca Nation of Indians in Crisis, 1954–1968." *New York History* 93, no. 2 (Spring 2012): 182–232.

———. *The Tonawanda Senecas' Heroic Battle Against Removal.* Albany: State University of New York Press, 2011.

Hazard, Samuel. *Pennsylvania Archives*, vol. 7. Philadelphia, 1853.

Jennings, Francis, ed. *Iroquois Indians, A Documentary History of the Diplomacy of the Six Nations and Their League*. Guide to the Microfilm Collection. Woodbridge, CT: Research Publications, 1985.

Johnson, William. *The Papers of Sir William Johnson*. 14 vols. Albany: University of the State of New York, 1921–1965.

Jordan, Kurt. "An Eighteenth Century Seneca Iroquois Short Longhouse from the Townley-Read Site, c. A.D. 1715–1754." *The Bulletin: Journal of the New York State Archaeological Association* 119 (2003): 49–63.

———. "Not Just 'One Site Against the World'—Seneca Iroquois Intercommunity Connections and Autonomy, 1550–1779." In Laura Scheiber and Mark Mitchell, eds. *Across a Great Divide: Continuity and Change in Native North American Societies, 1400–1900*. Tucson: University of Arizona Press, 2010.

———. "Seneca Iroquois Settlement Pattern, Community Structure, and Housing, 1677–1779." *Northeast Anthropology* 67 (2004): 23–60.

———. *The Seneca Restoration: 1715–1754*. Gainesville: University Press of Florida, 2008.

———. "Smiths and Senecas: Iron Tool Production and Use at the Townley-Read Site, ca. A.D. 1715–1754." Report submitted to the Early American Industries Association in fulfillment of 1999 John S. Watson Grant, March 27, 2001.

Kalm, Pehr. "A Description of the Wild Pigeons Which Visit the Southern English Colonies in North America, During Certain Years, in Incredible Multitudes." *The Auk* 28 (1911): 53–66.

Kuhn, Robert, and Martha Sempowski. "A New Approach to Dating the League of the Iroquois." *American Antiquity* 66, no. 2 (April 2001): 301–314.

Lossing, Benson. *The Life and Times of Philip Schuyler*. New York: 1872–1873.

Miller, Jay. "The Delaware as Women: A Symbolic Solution." *American Ethnologist* 1, no. 3 (August 1974): 507–514.

Morgan, Lewis Henry. *League of the Ho-dé-no-sau-nee, or Iroquois*. New York: Dodd, Mead, 1922.

Newton, J. H. *A History of Venango County, Pennsylvania, and Incidentally of Petroleum*. Columbus, OH: J. A. Caldwell, 1879.

Overton, Albert. "Commentary on Deardorff's Notes Concerning Bartoli's Portrait of Cornplanter," September 4, 1979. File on Cornplanter Portrait, New-York Historical Society.

Parkman, Francis. *The Conspiracy of Pontiac, and the Indian War After the Conquest of Canada*. 2 vols. Lincoln: University of Nebraska, 1994 (reprint).

Parmenter, Jon. "After the Mourning Wars: The Iroquois as Allies in Colonial North American Campaigns, 1676–1760." *William and Mary Quarterly*, Third Series, vol. 64, no. 1 (January 2007): 39–76.

Peckham, Howard. *Pontiac and the Indian Uprising.* New York: Russell & Russell, 1947.

*The Pennsylvania Gazette*, various, 1786–1794.

Pouchot, M. *Memoir from the Late War in North America Between the French and the English, 1755–1760.* Roxbury, MA, 1866.

Richter, Daniel. "War and Culture: The Iroquois Experience." *William and Mary Quarterly*, Third Series, vol. 40, no. 4 (October 1983): 528–559.

Rothenberg, Diane. "Friends Like These: An Ethnohistorical Analysis of the Interaction Between Allegany Senecas and Quakers, 1798–1823." Doctoral dissertation, City University of New York, 1976.

Seaver, James, ed. *A Narrative of the Life of Mrs. Mary Jemison.* Norman: University of Oklahoma Press, 2015.

Sipe, C. *The Indian Chiefs of Pennsylvania, or a Story of the Part Played by the American Indian in the History of Pennsylvania.* Butler, PA, 1926.

Starna, William. "Retrospecting the Origins of the League of the Iroquois." *Proceedings of the American Philosophical Society* 152, no. 3 (September 2008): 279–321.

Starna, William, and Christopher Vecsey. *Iroquois Land Claims.* Syracuse, NY: Syracuse University Press, 1988.

Stone, William Leete. *Life and Times of Red-Jacket, Or Sa-go-ye-wat-ha: Being the Sequel to the History of the Six Nations.* New York, 1841.

Swatzler, David. *A Friend Among the Senecas: The Quaker Mission to Cornplanter's People.* Mechanicsburg, PA: Stackpole, 2000.

Taylor, Alan. *The Divided Ground: Indians, Settlers, and the Northern Borderland of the American Revolution.* New York: Vintage, 2007.

Thwaites, Reuben Gold, and Louise Phelps Kellogg. *The Revolution on the Upper Ohio, 1775–1777.* Madison: Wisconsin Historical Society, 1908.

Tome, Philip. *Pioneer Life: Thirty Years a Hunter.* Buffalo, NY, 1854.

Venema, Janny. *Beverwijck: A Dutch Village on the American Frontier, 1652–1664.* Hilversum, The Netherlands: Verloren, 2003.

Walsh, Martin. "May Games and Noble Savages: The Native American in Early Celebrations of the Tammany Society." *Folklore* 108 (1997): 83–91.

Whittemore, Henry. *The Abeel and Allied Families.* New York, 1899.

## George Germain

Brown, Gerald Saxon. *The American Secretary: The Colonial Policy of Lord George Germain, 1775–1778.* Ann Arbor: University of Michigan Press, 1963.

Burke, Edmund. *A Plan for the Better Security of the Independence of Parliament, and the Oeconomical Reformation of the Civil and Other Establishments.* London, 1780.

Cartwright, Richard. *The Life and Letters of the Late Hon. Richard Cartwright.* Toronto, 1876.

Cavendish, Sir Henry, ed., *The Debates of the House of Commons During the Thirteenth Parliament of Great Britain, Commonly Called the Unreported Parliament.* London, 1841.

Clinton, Henry. Sir Henry Clinton Collection. William L. Clements Library, University of Michigan, Ann Arbor, Michigan.

Coventry, George. *A Critical Enquiry Regarding the Real Author of the Letters of Junius.* London, 1825.

Ehrenpreis, Irvin. *Swift: The Man, His Works and the Age.* Vol. 3. Cambridge: Harvard University Press, 1983.

Elliott, Charles Winslow. "The Men that Fought at Minden." *Journal of the American Military Institute* 3, no. 2 (Summer 1939): 80–103.

Fitzmaurice, Edmond. *Life of William, Earl of Shelburne.* London: Macmillan, 1912.

Flanders, H., ed. *Memoirs of Richard Cumberland.* Philadelphia, 1856.

Force, Peter, ed. *American Archives, Fourth Series, Containing a Documentary History of the English Colonies in North America, from the King's Message to Parliament of March 7, 1774, to the Declaration of Independence, by the United States.* Vol. 6. Washington, DC, 1846.

George II, "His Majesty's Most Gracious Speech to Both Houses of Parliament, on Thursday the Thirteenth Day of November, 1755." London, 1755.

Germain, George. George Germain Papers. William L. Clements Library, University of Michigan, Ann Arbor, Michigan.

Govier, Mark. "The Royal Society, Slavery and the Island of Jamaica: 1660–1700." *Notes and Records of the Royal Society of London* 53, no. 2 (May 1999): 203–217.

Great Britain, Royal Commission on Historical Manuscripts. *Report on the Man-*

*uscripts of Mrs. Stopford-Sackville, of Drayton House, Northamptonshire.* 2 vols. London: Mackie & Co., 1904.

Guttridge, George. "Lord George Germain in Office, 1775-1782." *American Historical Review* 33, no. 1 (October 1927): 23-43.

Hibbert, Christopher. *Redcoats and Rebels: The American Revolution Through British Eyes.* New York: W. W. Norton, 2000.

Jaques, John. *The History of Junius and His Works.* London, 1843.

Johnston, G. D. "Abstract of Turnpike Acts Relating to Sussex." Typescript, Sussex Archaeological Society Library, 1947.

Knight, Charles. *The Popular History of England.* Vols. 5 and 6. London: 1880.

Knox, William. William Knox Papers. William L. Clements Library, University of Michigan, Ann Arbor, Michigan.

Lecky, William. *A History of England in the Eighteenth Century.* Vols. 4 and 5. London, 1918.

Mackesy, Piers. *The Coward of Minden: The Affair of Lord George Sackville.* New York: St. Martin's Press, 1979.

Maier, Pauline. "John Wilkes and American Disillusionment with Britain." *William and Mary Quarterly,* Third Series, vol. 20, no. 3 (July 1963): 373-395.

Middleton, Richard, "British Historians and the American Revolution," *Journal of American Studies* 5, no. 1 (April 1971): 43-58.

Moffatt, James. *Burke's Speech on American Taxation.* Boston, 1905.

Moore, Sean. "Devouring Posterity: 'A Modest Proposal', Empire, and Ireland's 'Debt of the Nation.'" *PMLA* 122, no. 3 (May 2007): 679-695.

Oats, Lynn, and Pauline Sadler. "Accounting for the Stamp Act Crisis." *Accounting Historians Journal* 35, no. 2 (December 2008): 101-143.

O'Shaughnessy, Andrew Jackson. *The Men Who Lost America: British Leadership, the American Revolution, and the Fate of the Empire.* New Haven: Yale University Press, 2013.

*The Parliamentary History of England.* Vol. 17. London, 1813.

*The Proceedings of a General Court-Martial, Held at the Horse Guards on Friday the 7th, and Continued by Several Adjournments to Monday the 24th of March, 1760: And of a General Court-Martial Held at the Horse Guards on Tuesday the 25th of March, and Continued by Several Adjournments to Saturday the 5th of April 1760, upon the Trial of Lord George Sackville.* Edinburgh, 1760.

Ritcheson, Charles. "The Preparation of the Stamp Act." *William and Mary Quarterly,* Third Series, vol. 10, no. 4 (1953): 543-559.

Russel, William Augustus. *A New and Authentic History of England: From the Most Remote Period of Genuine Historical Evidence, to the Present Important Crisis: Containing an Accurate Chronological Account of Remarkable Events; an Entertaining Recital of Singular Occurrences.* London: J. Cooke, 1777–1779.

Sackville-West, Robert. *Inheritance: The Story of Knole and the Sackvilles.* New York: Walker & Co., 2010.

Sackville-West, V. *Knole and the Sackvilles.* New York: Doran, 1922.

Stedman, Charles. *The History of the Origin, Progress and Termination of the American War.* London, 1794.

Swift, Jonathan. *The Works of Jonathan Swift.* Vol 2. London, 1843.

Taylor, William. *Correspondence of William Pitt, Earl of Chatham.* 2 vols. London, 1838.

Townshend, C. V. F., *The Military Life of Field Marshal George First Marquess of Townshend.* London, 1901.

Toynbee, Paget. *The Letters of Horace Walpole, Fourth Earl of Oxford.* Vol. X. Oxford: At the Clarendon Press, 1904.

Trench, Charles Chenevix. *George II.* London: Allen Lane, 1973.

Valentine, Alan. *Lord George Germain.* Oxford: At the Clarendon Press, 1962.

———. *Lord North.* 2 vols. Norman: University of Oklahoma Press, 1967.

Walpole, Horace. *Journal of the Reign of George III, 1771–1783.* London, 1859.

———. *The Last Journals of Horace Walpole, During the Reign of George III, From 1771 to 1783.* 2 vols. London, 1910.

———. *Memoirs of the Reign of King George II.* 2 vols. London, 1846.

Watson, J. Steven. *The Reign of George III: 1760–1815.* Oxford: Oxford University Press, 1960.

Wharton, Francis, ed.. *The Revolutionary Diplomatic Correspondence of the U.S.* Vol. 1. Washington, DC, 1889.

Wittkowsky, George. "Swift's Modest Proposal: The Biography of an Early Georgian Pamphlet." *Journal of the History of Ideas* 4, no. 1 (January 1943): 75–104.

## Margaret Moncrieffe Coghlan

Alden, John. *General Gage in America: Being Principally a History of His Role in the American Revolution.* Baton Rouge: Louisiana State University Press, 1948.

Barck, Oscar. *New York City During the War for Independence*. New York: Columbia University Press, 1931.

Barker-Benfield, G. J. "Mary Wollstonecraft: Eighteenth-Century Commonwealth-woman." *Journal of the History of Ideas* 50, no. 1 (January–March 1989): 95–115.

Bayles, William. *Old Taverns of New York*. New York, 1915.

Blakemore, Steven. *Literature, Intertextuality, and the American Revolution: From Common Sense to Rip Van Winkle*. Madison, NJ: Fairleigh Dickinson University Press, 2012.

*The British Critic*, 1794.

Chalus, Elaine. "Elite Women, Social Politics, and the Political World of Late Eighteenth-Century England." *Historical Journal* 43, no. 3 (September 2000): 669–697.

Coghlan, Margaret. *Memoirs of Mrs. Coghlan, Daughter of the Late Major Moncrieffe, Written by Herself and Dedicated to the British Nation*. London, 1794.

———. *Memoirs of Mrs. Coghlan, Daughter of the Late Major Moncrieffe, Written by Herself, with Introduction and Notes*. New York, 1864.

———. Petition of Margaret Coghlan, Daughter of Major Thomas Moncrieffe. January 11, 1805. Pratt Manuscripts, Kent History and Library Centre, Maidstone, England.

Coghlan, Margaret Moncrieffe, to Robert Livingston, December 28, 1803. New-York Historical Society Library.

Colman, George. *Polly Honeycombe, A Dramatick Novel of One Act*. Third Edition. London, 1762.

Conway, Stephen. "British Army Officers and the American War for Independence." *William and Mary Quarterly*, Third Series, vol. 41, no. 2 (April 1984): 265–276.

Coviello, Peter. "Agonizing Affection: Affect and Nation in Early America," in *Early American Literature* 37, no. 3 (2002): 439–468.

Cresswell, Nicholas. *The Journal of Nicholas Cresswell, 1774–1777*. New York: Dial Press, 1924.

Davis, Matthew L. *Memoirs of Aaron Burr*. New York, 1837.

Ellet, Elizabeth. *The Women of the American Revolution*. 3 vols. New York, 1850.

Fliegelman, Jay. *Prodigals and Pilgrims: The American Revolution Against Patriarchal Authority, 1750–1800*. Cambridge: Cambridge University Press, 1982.

Fox, Charles James. *The Speeches of the Right Honourable Charles James Fox in the House of Commons*. London, 1853.

Garrioch, David. *The Making of Revolutionary Paris.* Berkeley: University of California Press, 2002.

*The Gentleman's Magazine,* April 1807.

*The Gentleman's Quarterly,* 1787.

Gooch, Elizabeth. *The Life of Mrs. Gooch.* London, 1792.

Groves, John Percy, et al. *Historical Records of the 7th or Royal Regiment of Fusiliers.* Guernsey, UK: F. B. Guerin, 1903.

Gundersen, Joan. "Independence, Citizenship, and the American Revolution." *Signs* 13, no. 1, Women and the Political Process in the United States (Autumn 1987): 59–77.

Harvey, Charles, Edmund Green and Penelope Corfield. "Continuity, Change, and Specialization within Metropolitan London: The Economy of Westminster, 1750–1820." *Economic History Review,* New Series, vol. 52, no. 3 (August 1999): 469–493.

Jackson, Kenneth, and David Dunbar. *Empire City: New York Through the Centuries.* New York: Columbia University Press, 2002.

Jones, Thomas. *History of New York During the Revolutionary War.* 2 vols. New York: 1879.

Kemble, Stephen. The Kemble Papers. Vol. 16. Collections of the New-York Historical Society for the Year 1883.

Knott, Sarah. "Female Liberty: Sentiment and Scandal in the Age of Revolutions." Paper presented to the Ohio Seminar in Early American History and Culture, October 14, 2013.

Livingston, Robert. Robert Livingston Papers. New-York Historical Society.

Livingston, William. *Israel Putnam: Pioneer, Ranger, and Major-General, 1718–1790.* New York, 1901.

Luckett, Thomas. "Hunting for Spies and Whores: A Parisian Riot on the Eve of the French Revolution." *Past & Present* 156 (August 1997): 116–143.

McGuire, Thomas J. *Stop the Revolution: America in the Summer of Independence and the Conference for Peace.* Mechanicsburg, PA: Stackpole, 2011.

Mee, Jonathan. "Libertines and Radicals in the 1790s: The Strange Case of Charles Pigott." In Peter Cryle and Lisa O'Connell, eds., *Libertine Enlightenment: Sex, Liberty and License in the Eighteenth Century.* Basingstoke. UK: Palgrave Macmillan, 2004.

Mooney, James. *Loyalist Imprints Printed in America, 1774-1785.* New York: American Antiquarian Society, 1974.

Pigott, Charles. *The Female Jockey Club, or a Sketch of the Manners of the Age.* London, 1794.

Putnam, Israel, to "Miss Montcriffe," July 26, 1776. Aaron Burr Papers, Missouri History Museum.

Records of the King's Bench Prison and the Queen's Prison. National Archives, Kew, Richmond, Surrey, England.

Rousseau, Jean-Jacques. *Emile, or On Education.* New York: Basic Books, 1979.

Sabine, Lorenzo. *The American Loyalists.* Boston, 1847.

Stokes, I. N. Phelps. *The Iconography of Manhattan Island, 1498–1909.* Vol. 1. New York: 1915.

*The Universal Magazine* 7 (January–June 1807).

Wollstonecraft, Mary. *A Vindication of the Rights of Woman.* New York, 1890.

Young, Philip. Philip Young Papers, 1930–2000. Pennsylvania State University Library, State College, Pennsylvania.

———. *Revolutionary Ladies.* New York: Knopf, 1977.

## Venture Smith

Adebayo, A. G. "Of Man and Cattle: A Reconsideration of the Traditions of Origin of Pastoral Fulani of Nigeria." *History in Africa* 18 (1991): 1–21.

Alpern, Stanley. "What Africans Got for Their Slaves: A Master List of European Trade Goods." *History in Africa* 22 (1995): 5–43.

Atkins, John. *A Voyage to Guinea, Brasil and the West Indies; in His Majesties Ships, the Swallow and Weymouth.* London, 1735.

Barnes, Barbara. "Venture Smith's Family." Thesis, Wesleyan University, March 1996.

Bartlett, John Russell, ed., *Records of the Colony of Rhode Island and Providence Plantations*, Vol. IV, 1707–1740. Providence, 1859.

Berlin, Ira. "From Creole to African: Atlantic Creoles and the Origins of African-American Society in Mainland North America." *William and Mary Quarterly*, Third Series, vol. 53, no. 2 (April 1996): 251–288.

Blevins, Conrad. "'Owned by Negro Venture': Land and Liberty in the Life of Venture Smith." Thesis, Pomona College, April 18, 2008.

Brainerd, Ezra. Court Papers of Ezra Brainerd, 1784 to 1798. Thankful Arnold House, Haddam, Connecticut.

Carretta, Vincent. *Equiano, the African: Biography of a Self-Made Man.* New York: Penguin, 2005.

Collins, James. "Whaleboat Warfare on Long Island Sound." *New York History* 25, no. 2 (April 1944): 195–201.

Crane, Elaine. *A Dependent People: Newport, Rhode Island, in the Revolutionary Era.* New York: Fordham University Press, 1992.

Desrochers, Robert E. "'Not Fade Away': The Narrative of Venture Smith, an African American in the Early Republic." *Journal of American History* 84, no. 1 (June 1997): 40–66.

Dexter, Franklin Bowditch. *Biographical Sketches of the Graduates of Yale College.* New York: Holt, 1896.

Egerton, Douglas. *Death or Liberty: African Americans and Revolutionary America.* New York: Oxford University Press, 2009.

Elbl, Ivana. "The Volume of the Early Atlantic Slave Trade, 1450–1521." *Journal of African History* 38 (1997): 31–75.

Field, David. *A History of the Towns of Haddam and East Haddam.* Middletown, CT, 1814.

Fitts, Robert. "The Landscapes of Northern Bondage." *Historical Archaeology* 30, no. 2 (1996): 54–73.

Fynn, J. K. "Asante and Akyem Relations, 1700–1831." *Institute of African Studies Research Review* 9, no. 1 (1972): 58–82.

Garman, James. "'Resistant Accommodation': Toward an Archaeology of African-American Lives in Southern New England, 1638–1800." *International Journal of Historical Archaeology* 2, no. 2 (June 1998): 133–160.

Getz, Trevor. "Mechanisms of Slave Acquisition and Exchange in Late Eighteenth Century Anomabu: Reconsidering a Cross-Section of the Atlantic Slave Trade." *African Economic History* 31 (2003): 75–89.

Gilbert, Alan. *Black Patriots and Loyalists: Fighting for Emancipation in the War for Independence.* Chicago: University of Chicago Press, 2012.

Gordon-Reed, Annette. *The Hemingses of Monticello: An American Family.* New York: W. W. Norton, 2008.

Greene, Lorenzo. "The New England Negro as Seen in Advertisements for Runaway Slaves." *Journal of Negro History* 29, no. 2 (April 1944): 125–146.

Handler, Jerome, and Frederick Lange. "Plantation Slavery on Barbados, West Indies." *Archaeology* 32, no. 4 (July–August 1979): 45–52.

Haynes, Williams. *Stonington Chronology, 1649–1949; Being a Year-by-Year Record of the American Way of Life in a Connecticut Town.* Stonington, CT: Pequot Press, 1949.

Hempstead, Joshua. *Diary of Joshua Hempstead of New London, Connecticut.* New London, 1901.

Hernaes, Per. "A Symbol of Power: Christiansborg Castle in Ghanian History." *Transactions of the Historical Society of Ghana.* New Series, no. 9 (2005): 141–156.

Hodge, Christina. "Widow Pratt's World of Goods: Implications of Consumer Choice in Colonial Newport, Rhode Island." *Early American Studies* 8, no. 2 (Spring 2010): 217–234.

Hyland, A. D. C. "The Architectural History of Cape Coast." *Transactions of the Historical Society of Ghana.* New Series, no. 1 (vol. 16, no. 2) (January 1995): 163–184.

Inscoe, John. "Carolina Slave Names: An Index to Acculturation." *Journal of Southern History* 49, no. 4 (November 1983): 527–554.

Jeffreys, M. D. W. "Mythical Origin of Cattle in Africa." *Man* 46 (November–December 1946): 140–141.

Johnston, William. *Slavery in Rhode Island, 1755–1776.* Providence, 1894.

Klein, Norman. "Slavery and Akan Origins?" *Ethnohistory* 41, no. 4 (Autumn 1994): 627–656.

Lavin, Lucianne, and Marc Banks. "Final Report Phase 1 and Phase 2 Archaeological Investigations of the Connecticut Yankee Atomic Power Company Property in Haddam Neck. The 2005–2006 Field Seasons and an Overview of the Entire 7-year Archaeological Study, vols. 1–3." Haddam Neck, CT, August 2007.

———. "The Venture Smith Homestead." Torrington: American Cultural Specialists, 2010.

Levy, Claude. "Slavery and the Emancipation Movement in Barbados, 1650–1833." *Journal of Negro History* 55, no. 1 (January 1970): 1–14.

Lovejoy, Paul. "Indigenous African Slavery." *Historical Reflections / Réflexions Historiques* 6, no. 1, Roots and Branches: Current Directions in Slave Studies (Summer/Eté 1979): 19–83.

Mars, James. *The Life of James Mars, A Slave Born and Sold in Connecticut. Written by Himself.* Hartford, 1868.

Matison, Sumner Eliot. "Manumission by Purchase." *Journal of Negro History* 33 (April 1948): 154–167.

Menschel, David. "Abolition Without Deliverance: The Law of Connecticut Slavery, 1784–1848." *Yale Law Journal* 111, no. 1 (October 2001): 183–222.

Mumford, James. *Mumford Memoirs, Being the Story of the New England Mumfords from the Year 1655 to the Present Time*. Boston, 1900.

Mustakeem, Sowande. "'I Never Have Such a Sickly Ship Before': Diet, Disease, and Mortality in 18th-Century Atlantic Slaving Voyages." *Journal of African American History* 93, no. 4 (Fall 2008): 474–496.

Nash, Gary B. *The Forgotten Fifth: African Americans in the Age of Revolution*. Cambridge: Harvard University Press, 2006.

Oppong-Anane, Kwame. *Ghana: Country Pasture/Forage Resource Profile*. Ministry of Food and Agriculture, Accra, Ghana. http://www.fao.org/ag/agp/AGPC/doc/Counprof/ghana/Ghana.htm.

Ostrander, Gilman. "The Colonial Molasses Trade." *Agricultural History* 30, no. 2 (1956): 77–84.

Pasley, Jeffrey. *The Tyranny of Printers: Newspaper Politics in the Early American Republic*. Charlottesville: University Press of Virginia, 2001.

Priestley, M. A. "A Note on Fort William, Anomabu." *Transactions of the Gold Coast & Togoland Historical Society* 2, no. 1 (1956): 46–48.

Rawley, James. *The Transatlantic Slave Trade: A History, Revised Edition*. Lincoln: University of Nebraska, 2005.

*The Royal African; or, Memoirs of the Young Prince of Annamaboe*. London, 1750.

Russell, Howard. *A Long, Deep Furrow: Three Centuries of Farming in New England*. Hanover, NH: University Press of New England, 1976.

Saint, Chandler, and George Krimsky. *Making Freedom: The Extraordinary Life of Venture Smith*. Middletown, CT: Wesleyan University Press, 2009.

Shaw, Nathaniel, and Thomas Shaw. Nathaniel and Thomas Shaw Papers, Yale University Library.

Shumway, Rebecca. *The Fante and the Translatlantic Slave Trade*. Rochester, NY: University of Rochester Press, 2011.

———. "The Fante Shrine of Nanom Mpow and the Atlantic Slave Trade in Southern Ghana." *International Journal of African Historical Studies* 44, no. 1 (2011): 27–44.

Sow, Abdoul Aziz, and John Angell. "Fulani Poetic Genres." *Research in African Literatures* 24, no. 2 (Summer 1993): 61–77.

Smallwood, Stephanie. "African Guardians, European Slave Ships, and the Changing Dynamics of Power in the Early Modern Atlantic." *William and Mary Quarterly*, Third Series, vol. 64, no. 4 (October 2007): 679–716.

Smith, Venture. *A Narrative of the Life and Adventures of Venture, a Native of*

*Africa: But Resident Above Sixty Years in the United States of America. Related by Himself.* New London, CT: C. Holt, 1798.

——. *A Narrative of the Life and Adventures of Venture, a Native of Africa: But Resident Above Sixty Years in the United States of America. Related by Himself.* Revised and republished with Traditions, by H. M. Selden. Middletown, CT: J. S. Stewart, 1897.

Sparks, Randy. *Where Negroes Are Masters: An African Port in the Era of the Slave Trade.* Cambridge: Harvard University Press, 2014.

Stanton, William. *A Record, Genealogical, Biological, Statistical, of Thomas Stanton, of Connecticut, and his Descendants: 1635–1891.* Albany, NY: J. Munsell's Sons, 1891.

Steenburg, Nancy, and Elizabeth Kading. "The Venture Adventure." *Wrack Lines* 6, no. 1 (Spring–Summer 2006): 7–10.

Stewart, James Brewer, ed. *Venture Smith and the Business of Slavery and Freedom.* Amherst: University of Massachusetts Press, 2010.

Stofko, Karl. Unpublished talks presented on Venture Smith Day, East Haddam, Connecticut, 2004–2014, and unpublished genealogical notes: "The Story of Sawney Anderson"; "Whacket Freeman"; "Notes on the Knowlton Family of East Haddam and East Hampton"; "Abel Bingham Family of East Haddam, Conn."; "Timothy Chapman of East Haddam, Conn."; "Records of Deacon Ezra Brainerd, Justice of the Peace, Haddam Neck, Connecticut"; "'Reading Between the Lines': Small Claims Court Case: Jonathan Kilborn Versus Venter Smith, 1790"; "Financial Dealings Between Amos White and Venture Smith"; "Robinson-Bingham-Green-Brainerd-Smith Land on Haddam Neck"; "The Amos White Family of East Haddam, Connecticut"; "Venture Smith Court Cases"; "'Reading Between the Lines': What Can Be Learned About Venture from the Estate of His Son, Solomon Smith"; "'Reading Between the Lines': Venture and Rebecca"; "Genealogy of the Descendants of George Mumford."

Stonington Town Land Records, Stonington, Connecticut.

Thomas, R. P., and D. N. McCloskey. "Overseas Trade and Empire, 1700–1860," in R. Floud and D. N. McCloskey, *Economic History of Britain.* Vol. 1. Cambridge: Cambridge University Press, 1981.

Thompson, Thomas. *An Account of Two Missionary Voyages . . . for the Propagation of the Gospel in Foreign Parts.* London, 1758.

Trigg, Heather, and David Landon. "Labor and Agricultural Production at Sylvester Manor Plantation, Shelter Island, New York." *Historical Archaeology* 44, no. 3 (2010): 36–53.

United States Department of the Interior, National Park Service. National Register of Historic Places. Inventory Nomination Form, "Black Horse Tavern," October 2, 1978.

Wahl, Jenny Bourne. "Legal Constraints on Slave Masters: The Problem of Social Cost." *American Journal of Legal History* 41, no. 1 (January 1997): 1–24.

Wheeler, Grace Denison. *The Homes of Our Ancestors in Stonington, Conn.* Salem, MA, 1903.

Wheeler, Richard Anson. *A History of the Town of Stonington, County of New London, Connecticut.* Stonington, CT: Press of the Day, 1900.

Williams, George. *History of the Negro Race in America, from 1619 to 1880.* New York: 1885.

Witzig, Fred. "Beyond Expectation: How Charles Town's 'Pious and Well-Disposed Christians' Changed Their Minds About Slave Education During the Great Awakening." *South Carolina Historical Magazine* 114, no. 4 (October 2013): 286–315.

## George Washington

Adams, Charles Francis. *The Works of John Adams.* Vol. 2. Boston: 1850.

Baker, Norman. *Braddock's Road: Mapping the British Expedition from Alexandria to the Monongahela.* Charleston, SC: History Press, 2013.

Bell, Whitfield, Jr., and Leonard Labaree. "Franklin and the 'Wagon Affair,' 1755." *Proceedings of the American Philosophical Society* 101, no. 6 (December 19, 1957): 551–558.

Bradley, A. G. *The Fight with France for North America.* New York, 1900.

Brady, Patricia. *Martha Washington: An American Life.* New York: Penguin, 2006.

Brandow, John. "Horatio Gates," *Proceedings of the New York State Historical Association*, Vol. 3 (1903): 9–19.

Breen, T. H. *Tobacco Culture: The Mentality of the Great Tidewater Planters on the Eve of Revolution.* Princeton: Princeton University Press, 1985.

Brookhiser, Richard. *Founding Father.* New York: Simon & Schuster, 1997.

Brooks, Noah. *Henry Knox, A Soldier of the Revolution.* New York, 1900.

Chaussegros de Léry, Joseph Gaspard. *Journal of Chaussegros de Léry.* Harrisburg: Pennsylvania Historical Commission, 1940.

Chernow, Ron. *Washington: A Life.* New York: Penguin, 2010.

"Commission from Robert Dinwiddie, 30 October 1753." *Founders Online,* National Archives, last modified February 21, 2017, http://founders.archives .gov/documents/Washington/02-01-02-0028.

Conkling, Margaret. *Memoirs of the Mother and Wife of Washington.* Auburn, NY, 1850.

Cornwallis, Charles. *Correspondence of Charles, First Marquis of Cornwallis.* Vol. 1. London, 1859.

Crocker, Thomas E. *Braddock's March: How the Man Sent to Seize a Continent Changed American History.* Yardley, PA: Westholme, 2009.

Darling, James, and Maureen Wiggins. "A Constant Tuting." *Music Educators Journal* 61, no. 3 (November 1974): 56–61.

Davies, K.G., ed. *Documents of the American Revolution, 1770-1783.* 21 vols. Shannon and Dublin: 1972–1981.

Duhamel, James. "Belvoir." *Records of the Columbia Historical Society, Washington, D.C.,* Vol. 35/36 (1935): 146–153.

D'Urfey, Thomas. *Wit and Mirth, or Pills to Purge Melancholy.* London, 1720.

Fauntleroy, Mary Ellen. "The Fauntleroy Family." *Indiana Magazine of History* 35, no. 2 (June 1939: 210–217.

Ferling, John. *Almost a Miracle: The American Victory in the War of Independence.* New York: Oxford University Press, 2007.

———. *The Ascent of George Washington.* New York: Bloomsbury, 2009.

Flexner, James Thomas. *George Washington.* 4 vols.: *The Forge of Experience (1732-1775); George Washington in the American Revolution (1776-1783); George Washington and the New Nation (1783-1793); Anguish and Farewell (1793-1799).* Boston: Little, Brown, 1965–1972.

Fitzpatrick, John C., ed. *The Writings of Washington from the Original Manuscript Sources, 1745-1799.* 39 vols. Washington, DC: Government Printing Office, 1931–1944; reprint, New York: Greenwood Press, 1970.

Ford, W. C. *The Writings of George Washington.* Vol. 1. New York: 1889.

Freeman, Douglas Southall. *George Washington: A Biography.* 7 vols. New York: Scribner, 1948–1957.

Galbreath, C. B. *Expedition of Celeron to the Ohio Country in 1749.* Columbus, OH: F. J. Heer, 1921.

Hamilton, Alexander. *The Papers of Alexander Hamilton*. New York: Columbia University Press, 1962.

Hazard, Samuel. *The Pennsylvania Colonial Records, Vol. VI, Minutes of the Provincial Council of Pennsylvania*. Harrisburg, 1851.

Henriques, Peter. *Realistic Visionary: A Portrait of George Washington*. Charlottesville: University of Virginia Press, 2006.

Hirschfeld, Fritz. *George Washington and Slavery: A Documentary Portrayal*. Columbia: University of Missouri Press, 1997.

*The Historical Magazine, and Notes and Queries Concerning the Antiquities, History and Biography of America*. Vol. IV. New York, 1860.

Huske, John. *The Present State of North America*. Dublin, 1755.

Irving, Washington. *The Life of George Washington*. 2 vols. New York: Cosimo, 2005.

Isaac, Rhys. *The Transformation of Virginia, 1740–1790*. Chapel Hill: University of North Carolina Press, 1982.

Kapp, Friedrich. *The Life of Frederick William Von Steuben, Major General in the Revolutionary Army*. New York, 1859.

Kierner, Cynthia. "Genteel Balls and Republican Parades: Gender and Early Southern Civic Rituals, 1677–1826." *Virginia Magazine of History and Biography* 104, no. 2 (Spring 1996): 185–210.

Lear, Tobias. "14 December 1799." Founders Online, National Archives. http://founders.archives.gov/documents/Washington/06-04-02-0406-0002.

Longmore, Paul. *The Invention of George Washington*. Berkeley: University of California Press, 1988.

Lorenz, Stacy. "'To Do Justice to His Majesty, the Merchant and the Planter': Governor William Gooch and the Virginia Tobacco Inspection Act of 1730." *Virginia Magazine of History and Biography* 108, no. 4 (2000): 345–392.

Miller, E. J. "The Virginia Legislature and the Stamp Act." *William and Mary Quarterly* 21, no. 4 (April 1913): 233–248.

Misencik, Paul. *George Washington and the Half-King Tanacharison*. Jefferson, NC: McFarland, 2014.

Monroe, James. *A View of the Conduct of the Executive in the Foreign Affairs of the United States*. Philadelphia, 1797.

Morgan, Kenneth. "Robert Dinwiddie's Reports on the British American Colonies." *William and Mary Quarterly* 65, no. 2 (April 2008): 305–346.

O'Shaughnessy, Andrew. *An Empire Divided: The American Revolution and the British Caribbean*. Philadelphia: University of Pennsylvania Press, 2000.

Paine, Thomas. *The Political Writings of Thomas Paine.* 2 vols. Boston, 1859.

Pickering, Octavius. *The Life of Timothy Pickering.* 2 vols. Boston: Little, Brown, 1867.

Ramsay, David. *The Life of George Washington.* London, 1807.

Riley, Padraig. *Slavery and the Democratic Conscience: Political Life in Jeffersonian America.* University of Pennsylvania Press, 2016.

Schecter, Barnet. *George Washington's America: A Biography Through His Maps.* New York: Walker & Co., 2010.

Scheer, George, and Hugh Rankin. *Redcoats and Rebels: The American Revolution Through the Eyes of Those Who Fought and Lived It.* New York: Da Capo, 1987.

Schnabel, Isabel, and Hyun Song Shin. "Liquidity and Contagion: The Crisis of 1763." *Journal of the European Economic Association* 2, no. 6 (December 2004): 929–968.

Sheridan, Richard. "The Jamaican Slave Insurrection Scare of 1776 and the American Revolution." *Journal of Negro History* 61, no. 3 (July 1976): 290–308.

Singleton, Esther. *Social Life in New York Under the Georges, 1714-1776.* New York: 1902.

Tagg, James. "Benjamin Franklin Bache's Attack on George Washington." *Pennsylvania Magazine of History and Biography* 100, no. 2 (April 1976): 191–230.

Thompson, Mary. "The Lives of Enslaved Workers on George Washington's Outlying Farms." A Talk for the Neighborhood Friends of Mount Vernon, June 16, 1999.

Wahll, Andrew. *Braddock Road Chronicles, 1755.* Westminster, Maryland: Heritage Books, 2006.

Wallace, David. *The Life of Henry Laurens.* New York: 1915.

Washington, George. *The Journal of Major George Washington, Sent by The Hon. Robert Dinwiddie, Esq.; His Majesty's Lieutenant-Governor, and Commander in Chief of Virginia; to the Commandant of the French Forces on Ohio; to Which Are Added, The Governor's Letter: And a Translation of the French Officer's Answer.* London, 1754.

——. "A Journal of My Journey over the Mountains Began Fryday the 11th. of March 1747/8." *Founders Online*, National Archives.

——. *The Papers of George Washington.* W. W. Abbot et al., eds. Charlottesville: University of Virginia Press, 1987–2007.

——. *The Papers of George Washington, Diaries.* Donald Jackson et al., eds. Charlottesville: University Press of Virginia, 1976–1979.

———. *The Writings of George Washington from the Original Manuscript Sources, 1745–1799.* Washington, DC: Government Printing Office, 1921.

Wenger, Mark. "The Dining Room in Early Virginia," *Perspectives in Vernacular Architecture.* Vol. 3 (1989): 149–159.

West, Willis Mason. *A Source Book in American History to 1787.* Boston: Allyn & Bacon, 1913.

Young, Henry. "Agrarian Reactions to the Stamp Act Crisis in Pennsylvania." *Pennsylvania History* 34, no. 1 (January 1967): 25–30.


## Abraham Yates


Bielinski, Stefan. *Abraham Yates, Jr., and the New Political Order in Revolutionary New York.* Albany: New York State American Revolution Bicentennial Commission, 1975.

———. "A Middling Sort: Artisans and Tradesmen in Colonial Albany." *New York History* 73, no. 3 (July 1992): 261–290.

Brodhead, John, et al., eds. *Documents Relating to the Colonial History of the State of New York.* 15 vols. Albany: Reed, Parsons & Co., Printers, 1853–1887.

Cumming, Robert, ed. *The Constitution of the State of New York, with Notes, References and Annotations.* Albany, 1894.

*The Dongan Charter and Present Charter, Together with Laws of the State of New York, Applicable to the City of Albany, and the City Laws and Ordinances of the City of Albany.* Albany: Argus Co., 1896.

Friedman, Bernard. "The Shaping of the Radical Consciousness in Provincial New York." *Journal of American History* 56, no. 4 (March 1970): 781–801.

Gannon, Fred. *A Short History of American Shoemaking.* Salem, MA: Newcomb & Gauss, 1912.

Gilje, Paul, and William Pencak, eds. *New York in the Age of the Constitution, 1775–1800.* Rutherford, NJ: Fairleigh Dickinson University Press, 1992.

Grant, Anne McVickar. *Memoirs of an American Lady, with Sketches of Manners and Scenery in America, as They Existed Previous to the Revolution.* New York: Appleton, 1846.

Hackett, David G. *The Rude Hand of Innovation: Religion and Social Order in Albany, New York, 1652–1836.* New York: Oxford University Press, 1991.

Handlin, Oscar. "The Eastern Frontier of New York." *New York History* 18, no. 1 (January 1937): 50–75.

Kenney, Alice P. *The Gansevoorts of Albany: Dutch Patricians in the Upper Hudson Valley.* Syracuse, NY: Syracuse University Press, 1969.

———. *Stubborn for Liberty: The Dutch in New York.* Syracuse, NY: Syracuse University Press, 1965.

Kenney, Alice P. "Dutch Patricians in Colonial Albany." *New York History* 49, no. 3 (July 1968): 249–283.

Klein, Morton. "The Rise of the New York Bar: The Legal Career of William Livingston." *William and Mary Quarterly* 15, no. 3 (July 1958): 334–358.

Kossmann, E. H., and A. F. Mellink, eds. *Texts Concerning the Revolt of the Netherlands.* London: Cambridge University Press, 1974.

Lustig, Mary Lou. *Privilege and Prerogative: New York's Provincial Elite, 1710–1776.* Cranbury, NJ: Associated University Presses, 1995.

Lynd, Staughton. "Abraham Yates's History of the Movement for the United States Constitution." *William and Mary Quarterly* 20, no. 2 (April 1963): 223–245.

Mark, Irving. "Agrarian Revolt in Colonial New York, 1766." *American Journal of Economics and Sociology* 1, no. 2 (January 1942): 111–142.

McAnear, Beverly. "The Albany Stamp Act Riots." *William and Mary Quarterly* 4, no. 4 (October 1947): 486–498.

———. "Personal Accounts of the Albany Congress of 1754." *Mississippi Valley Historical Review* 39, no. 4 (March 1953): 727–746.

*Minutes of the Albany Committee of Correspondence, 1775–1778.* 2 vols. Albany: University of the State of New York, 1923–1925.

Morris, Gouverneur. Gouverneur Morris Papers, 1768–1816. Butler Library, Columbia University.

Mulder, John. "William Livingston: Propagandist Against Episcopacy." *Journal of Presbyterian History (1962–1985)*, vol. 54, no. 1 (Spring 1976): 83–104.

Munsell, J. *Collections on the History of Albany, from Its Discovery to the Present Time.* vols. 1–10. Albany, NY: J. Munsell, 1865–1871.

Narrett, David. "A Zeal for Liberty: The Antifederalist Case Against the Constitution in New York." *New York History* 69, no. 3 (July 1988): 284–317.

O'Callaghan, Edmund, et al., eds. *Documents Relative to the Colonial History of the State of New York.* 15 vols. Albany, NY: 1853–1887.

O'Toole, Fintan. *White Savage: William Johnson and the Invention of America.* New York: Farrar, Straus & Giroux, 2005.

Pearson, Jonathan. *Early Records of the City and County of Albany and Colony of Rensselaerswyck, 1656–1675.* Albany, NY, 1869.

Peña, Elizabeth. "The Role of Wampum Production at the Albany Almshouse." *International Journal of Historical Archaeology* 5, no. 2 (June 2001): 155–174.

Priest, Claire. "Colonial Courts and Secured Credit: Early American Commercial Litigation and Shays' Rebellion." Yale Law School Faculty Scholarship Repository. Faculty Scholarship Series, Paper 1304, 1999.

Reynolds, Cuyler. *Albany Chronicles: A History of the City Arranged Chronologically*. Albany, NY, 1906.

Schoderbek, Michael. "Robert Morris and Reporting for the Treasury Under the U.S. Continental Congress." *Accounting Historians Journal* 26, no. 2 (December 1999): 1–34.

Shannon, Timothy. *Indians and Colonists at the Crossroads of Empire: The Albany Congress of 1754*. Ithaca: Cornell University Press, 2000.

Sullivan, James, ed. *Minutes of the Albany Committee of Correspondence, 1775–1778*. Albany: University of the State of New York, 1923.

Wolf, Stephan. "Abraham Yates, Jr.: Vergessener Gründervater der amerikanischen Republik" (Abraham Yates, Jr.: Forgotten Founding Father of the American Republic). Doctoral dissertation, University of Münster, 1997.

Worth, Gorham. *Random Recollections of Albany*. Albany, NY, 1850.

Yates, Abraham, Jr. Abraham Yates, Jr., Papers, New York Public Library. [Note that the author worked from a photocopied collection of these papers compiled by Stefan Bielinski in the 1970s and housed in the New York State Library in Albany.]

## General Research

Anderson, Fred. *The Crucible of War: The Seven Years' War and the Fate of Empire in British North America, 1754–1766*. New York: Vintage, 2001.

Burrows, Edwin, and Mike Wallace. *Gotham: A History of New York City to 1898*. New York: Oxford University Press, 1999.

Carp, Benjamin. "Did Dutch Smugglers Provoke the Boston Tea Party?" *Early American Studies* 10, no. 2 (Spring 2012): 335–359.

Ferling, John. *A Leap in the Dark: The Struggle to Create the American Republic*. Oxford: Oxford University Press, 2003.

Flexner, James. *Mohawk Baronet: Sir William Johnson of New York*. New York: Harper & Brothers, 1959.

Foner, Eric. *The Story of American Freedom*. New York: W. W. Norton, 1998.

Fortin, Jeffrey A., and Mark Meuwese, eds. *Atlantic Biographies: Individuals and Peoples in the Atlantic World*. Leiden, The Netherlands: Brill, 2014.

Franklin, Benjamin. The Papers of Benjamin Franklin. National Archives. http:// founders.archives.gov/documents/Franklin/01-03-02-0130.

Gallagher, John. *The Battle of Brooklyn 1776*. New York: Da Capo, 1999.

Hume, David, and Tobias Smollett. *The History of England*. 13 vols. London, 1790–1794.

Isaacson, Walter. *Benjamin Franklin: An American Life*. New York: Simon & Schuster, 2003.

Ketchum, Richard. *Saratoga: Turning Point of America's Revolutionary War*. New York: Holt, 1997.

Locke, John. *Two Treatises of Government*. From *The Works of John Locke: A New Edition, Corrected*. Vol. V. London, 1823.

Nash, Gary B. *The Unknown American Revolution: The Unruly Birth of Democracy and the Struggle to Create America*. New York: Viking, 2005.

Nelson, Craig. "Thomas Paine and the Making of 'Common Sense.'" *New England Review (1990– )*, vol. 27, no. 3 (2006): 228–250.

Paine, Thomas. *Common Sense; Addressed to the Inhabitants of America*. Second Edition. Philadelphia, 1776.

Rhodehamel, John, ed. *The American Revolution: Writings from the War of Independence*. New York: Library of America, 2001.

Schecter, Barnet. *The Battle for New York: The City at the Heart of the American Revolution*. New York: Walker & Co., 2002.

Smith, Paul H., et al., eds. *Letters of Delegates to Congress, 1774–1789*. 26 volumes. Washington, DC: Library of Congress, 1976–2000.

Taylor, Alan. *American Revolutions: A Continental History, 1750–1804*. New York: W. W. Norton, 2016.

———. *The Internal Enemy: Slavery and War in Virginia, 1772–1832*. New York: W. W. Norton, 2013.

Wood, Gordon. *Creation of the American Republic, 1776–1787*. Chapel Hill: University of North Carolina Press, 1998.

———. *The Purpose of the Past: Reflections on the Uses of History*. New York: Penguin, 2008.

———. *The Radicalism of the American Revolution*. New York: Vintage, 1993.

# INDEX

Page numbers in *italics* refer to illustrations.

# ABOUT THE AUTHOR

Russell Shorto was born in Johnstown, Pennsylvania. He is the author of five previous books, including *Amsterdam: A History of the World's Most Liberal City* and the national bestseller *The Island at the Center of the World*. His books have been translated into fourteen languages. He is the recipient of the New York City Book Award, the Washington Irving Prize, the City of Amsterdam's Frans Banninck Cocq Medal and the Dutch equivalent of a knighthood. He is a contributing writer at the *New York Times Magazine*, a Fellow of the New York Academy of History and Senior Scholar at the New Netherland Institute. From 2008 to 2013 he was director of the John Adams Institute in Amsterdam. He has three children and three stepchildren, and lives in Cumberland, Maryland.